Controlling
Interest Rate Risk

WILEY PROFESSIONAL BANKING AND FINANCE SERIES
EDWARD I. ALTMAN, Editor

THE STOCK MARKET, 4TH EDITION
Richard J. Teweles and Edward S. Bradley

TAX SHELTERED FINANCING THROUGH THE R&D LIMITED
PARTNERSHIP
James K. La Fleur

CORPORATE FINANCIAL DISTRESS: A COMPLETE GUIDE TO
PREDICTING, AVOIDING, AND DEALING WITH BANKRUPTCY
Edward I. Altman

CREDIT ANALYSIS: A COMPLETE GUIDE
Roger H. Hale

CURRENT ASSET MANAGEMENT: CASH, CREDIT,
AND INVENTORY
Jarl G. Kallberg and Kenneth Parkinson

HANDBOOK FOR BANKING STRATEGY
Richard C. Aspinwall and Robert A. Eisenbeis

THE BANKING JUNGLE: HOW TO SURVIVE AND PROSPER
IN A BUSINESS TURNED TOPSY TURVY
Paul S. Nadler and Richard B. Miller

ELECTRONIC BANKING
Allen H. Lipis, Thomas R. Marschall, and Jan H. Linker

BUSINESS OPPORTUNITIES FROM CORPORATE
BANKRUPTCIES
Rees Morrison

DEREGULATING WALL STREET: COMMERCIAL BANK
PENETRATION OF THE CORPORATE SECURITIES MARKET
Ingo Walter

CONTROLLING INTEREST RATE RISK: NEW TECHNIQUES
AND APPLICATIONS FOR MONEY MANAGEMENT
Robert B. Platt

Controlling
Interest Rate Risk

New Techniques
and Applications
for Money Management

ROBERT B. PLATT

JOHN WILEY & SONS

New York · Chichester · Brisbane · Toronto · Singapore

Library of Congress Cataloging-in-Publication Data:

Main entry under title:

Controlling interest rate risk.

    (Wiley professional banking and finance series,
ISSN 0733-8945)
    Includes index.
    1. Interest rates—Addresses, essays, lectures.
2. Investments—Addresses, essays, lectures. 3. Risk—
Addresses, essays, lectures. I. Platt, Robert B.,
1936–   II. Series.

HG1621.C6   1986   332.8'2   85-22504
ISBN 0-471-82354-6

Printed in the United States of America

10 9 8 7 6 5 4 3

CONTRIBUTORS

ROBERT B. PLATT
Managing Director
Director, Fixed Income Research
Morgan Stanley & Co., Inc.
New York, New York

RICHARD BOOKSTABER
Vice President
Morgan Stanley & Co., Inc.
New York, New York

WILLIAM C. HANEY
Research Manager
Morgan Stanley & Co., Inc.
New York, New York

DAVID P. JACOB
Research Manager
Morgan Stanley & Co., Inc.
New York, New York

GARY D. LATAINER
Vice President
Morgan Stanley & Co., Inc.
New York, New York

SCOTT M. PINKUS
Vice President
Morgan Stanley & Co., Inc.
New York, New York

JAMES A. TILLEY
Principal
Morgan Stanley & Co., Inc.
New York, New York

ALDEN L. TOEVS
Vice President
Morgan Stanley & Co., Inc.
New York, New York

SERIES PREFACE

The worlds of banking and finance have changed dramatically during the past few years, and no doubt this turbulence will continue through the 1980s. We have established the Wiley Professional Banking and Finance Series to aid in characterizing this dynamic environment and to further the understanding of the emerging structures, issues, and content for the professional financial community.

We envision three types of book in this series. First, we are commissioning distinguished experts in a broad range of fields to assemble a number of authorities to write specific primers on related topics. For example, some of the early handbook-type volumes in the series concentrate on the Stock Market, Investment Banking, and Financial Depository Institutions. A second type of book attempts to combine text material with appropriate empirical and case studies written by practitioners in relevant fields. Finally, we are encouraging definitive, authoritative works on specialized subjects for practitioners and theorists.

It is a distinct pleasure and honor for me to assist John Wiley & Sons, Inc. in this important endeavor. In addition to banking and financial practitioners, we think business students and faculty will benefit from this series. Most of all, though, we hope this series will become a primary source in the 1980s for the members of the professional financial community to refer to theories and data and to integrate important aspects of the central changes in our financial world.

EDWARD I. ALTMAN

Professor of Finance
New York University,
Schools of Business

PREFACE

The pace of development in new fixed-income investment technology has been truly extraordinary in recent years: computer-based portfolio optimization routines, duration and bond immunization, financial futures, options, and specialized investment instruments. These and more have become common tools to help portfolio strategists and managers shape the risk/return profile of portfolio returns.

A number of books and articles have been written dealing with these topics. Most often they are either very specialized in nature, covering the more arcane mathematical features, or more general, emphasizing the institutional aspects with intuitive explanations of the instruments or procedures. Little has been written, however, on how this technology can actually be employed in helping professional investors structure their decisions.

This book is intended to be a comprehensive treatment of the modern techniques of today's interest rate risk control using extensive examples of the applications of this technology in various institutional settings and portfolio situations. While it is intended to be fairly rigorous in presentation, the mathematical content is kept to a minimum.

The extensive use of examples and the presentation of specialized industry applications is meant to make the book a useful reference volume for investment professionals managing or supervising the management of fixed-income portfolios. Particular attention has been paid to applications of risk control technology in conjunction with some of the largest pools of investment capital: insurance companies, commercial banks, savings and loans, corporations, and corporate pension funds. It is in these institutional settings that many of the investment technology developments, from purely academic exercises to practical decision tools, have emerged over recent years to meet the critical needs for more sophisticated and flexible tools of asset/liability management.

This book is aimed primarily at investment professionals, but it is hoped that its level of rigor will also make it suitable for use in graduate and upper-level undergraduate courses in modern finance theory and portfolio management which emphasize fixed-income investments. These courses have become more common elements of the ''B'' school curriculum as the needs to control risk in fixed-income portfolios have become more pronounced.

The authors of the book are all senior members of the analytical portfolio research group at Morgan Stanley & Co. They have all contributed to the development of state-of-the-art interest rate risk control procedures and all have had extensive experience in applying this technology in actual portfolio situations. The existence of a group of expert practitioners in interest rate risk control methodology at Morgan Stanley, and similar groups in other institutions, is probably the most eloquent testimony to how integral these procedures have become to modern fixed-income portfolio activities.

We would like to thank the management of Morgan Stanley for their encouragement and support of this project. Also, we would like to recognize the long list of experts who have contributed to the development of the tools and techniques we liberally use throughout the volume. Many, but not all, of these are to be found throughout the book in the footnotes and bibliographies of the various chapters. A special word of gratitude is in order for Amy Levy, Dawn Bendetti, and Frances Mayer. They worked long hours in carefully typing, editing, and preparing the manuscript for publication.

ROBERT B. PLATT

New York, New York
February 1986

CONTENTS

Controlling
Interest Rate Risk

1 Introduction

1 Controlling Interest Rate Risk

ROBERT B. PLATT

INTRODUCTION

Managing fixed-income assets has become more interesting and challenging in recent years. In the past it was not uncommon for money managers and institutions to view these securities as their "riskless" investment, that is, an investment that would provide a steady stream of predictable coupon income with a low volatility of return performance. Changes in the financial and economic environment beginning in the late 1960s and reaching an especially excited state of activity in the period 1979–1982 have altered dramatically the conventional views of the role of fixed-income investments and their riskiness.

The forces at work during this period were driven largely by fundamental changes in the exposure of the American economy to the risk of inflation and to changes in social and political values which have altered the regulatory environment in which many financial institutions operate. All money managers to some extent have been faced with the need to adapt to these forces, but the effects have been most dramatic on some of the largest pools of investable resources: insurance companies, banks, and thrifts. Indeed in these organizations the management and control of their exposure to interest rate risk have become almost integral to managing the financial soundness and viability of the firm.

Corporations as well have been affected by this new investment environment. Most noticeably this has occurred in the management of pension assets where many corporations have been rethinking the role of fixed-income assets in their portfolios. A manifestation of this which has attracted much attention in recent years has been the closer integration of the pension fund asset decision with the overall corporate finance needs of the organization. An example of this has been the large increase in dedicated and immunized bond portfolios. By some estimates these portfolios now account for as much as 10% of all pension fund assets under management. In addition, the traditional treasurer function of managing corporate cash positions has become more complex as firms have found themselves managing larger pools of assets in an environment of heightened risk and increased opportunities for returns.

SECTION I   AN OVERVIEW OF RISK CONTROL TECHNOLOGY

As risk, as a dimension of fixed-income investment, has become more pronounced, there has been a growing disenchantment with the performance of "active" management which relies heavily on interest rate anticipation for return performance. All too often such approaches have led to higher risk without the commensurate increase in returns that theory leads us to expect. The need to manage risk has led to the creation of complex and innovative instruments: options, futures, mortgage-backed securities, floating rate instruments, interest rate swaps, zero coupon securities, and securities with special put features. These need to be understood by money managers, financial institutions, and corporations if they are to be used to their full advantage.

In addition to the creation of new investment instruments, the forces of change in the financial environment have led to the development of a whole range of risk control methodology with which financial institutions and corporations can manage their exposure to interest rate risk. The first salvo in this battle was the resurrection of the concept of bond duration and its use in immunization strategies from the more arcane actuarial journals, and its development into a highly sophisticated and flexible tool for managing the interest sensitivity of assets and liabilities. Similar developments are occuring in the use of complex hedging strategies employing financial futures.

To some extent these developments can be viewed as a knee-jerk reaction to the heightened awareness of risk in fixed income investments, and to the disappointing performance of active fixed-income management. Many bond managers, financial institutions, and corporations faced with these developments have opted for the safest of paths: to seek out the riskless strategy which immunizes completely their exposure to interest rate risk, without adequately reflecting on the costs of such strategies. The riskless investment strategy, while providing the maximum of downside protection, is also the costliest form of portfolio insurance protection since it also truncates most, if not all, of the upside return protection that comes from good investment management.

SECTION II   MOLDING THE RETURN DISTRIBUTION
OF FIXED-INCOME PORTFOLIOS

Considering the truncation of the interest rate risk exposure of a portfolio of assets or liabilities as an insurance policy is a useful analogy. It helps us focus on both the degree of protection we are seeking as well as its costs, since most people think in these terms when they purchase an insurance policy. The same considerations should be used in structuring a portfolio strategy utilizing interest rate risk control methodology. You should never buy more insurance protection than you really need. In this context the riskless strategies employing duration or financial futures hedging may be too costly for many portfolio applications. More flexible forms of risk control are required in such cases—approaches which allow some trade off of different degrees of downside protection for different degrees of upside return opportunities. More and more the attention of practicioners in risk-control technology is turned toward these possibilities.

Immunization (or fully hedged portfolios) and actively managed portfolios can be viewed as the two polar cases along a continuous spectrum of risk. It is possible to construct portfolios with the risk characteristics anywhere along this entire risk spectrum using the techniques and methodology of options. This characteristic of options makes them unique and especially advantageous instruments for controlling interest rate risk.

The utilization of option technology in interest rate risk control is still novel. It necessitates more demands on the flexibility and creativity of the portfolio managers as well perhaps on their mathematical competence. It also requires changes in the way we measure the performance of investment results since we must begin to view our investment activities more in the light of how well we achieve clearly defined investment objectives rather than concentrating myopically on our decile rankings of returns relative to our investment peers.

Despite the added complexity of option methodology, the fundamental attractions of the approach are too strong to be denied. The new wave of bond management is likely to be the molding of returns to meet specific investment objectives. The tool to accomplish this is likely to be option strategies.

As the specialized investment vehicles and tools of interest rate risk control methodology have increased in number and complexity a growing need has emerged for a rigorous and comprehensive treatment of these topics from the point of view of technical practitioners and investment managers. This is the purpose of this book. It is concerned with describing some of the instruments and methodology of interest rate risk control from the viewpoint of the user. Particular emphasis is placed on the uses of these tools in life insurance companies, banks, thrifts, and corporations. The rigorous and comprehensive treatment of the topics, however, also make sections of the book useful in graduate finance courses specializing in fixed income investments.

SECTION III   AN OVERVIEW OF THE BOOK

The book is divided into four parts. Part 1 introduces the chapters. Part 2 provides an introduction to the principal tools of interest rate risk control. Included in this section are a survey of the basic concepts of yield curve analysis (Chapter 2), an extensive treatment of duration as used in the control of interest rate risk (Chapter 3), a discussion of the theoretical and practical considerations in hedging with financial futures (Chapter 4), and a description of the use of options in devising more flexible approaches to structuring portfolio returns (Chapter 5). Each of these chapters represents a stand-alone analysis of these important approaches to interest rate risk control. As a unit they comprise an updated treatment of the full range of risk-control procedures currently available to managers of fixed income assets.

The goal of the book is not only to treat these topics in a rigorous and comprehensive fashion, but to emphasize their practical portfolio applications rather than their mathematical complexities. While mathematics cannot be avoided entirely, we have tried to keep its use to a minimum.

Part 3 of the book introduces some specialized topics of interest rate risk control. One of the most remarkable events of recent years in the fixed-income markets has been the extraordinary growth in mortgage-backed securities and their widespread use in a variety of contexts to achieve specialized portfolio objectives. There is still considerable confusion in the marketplace as to what these instruments represent, how to value them, and how they can be used. Chapter 6 deals comprehensively with some of the special definitional considerations associated with these securities, and provides an analytical framework for valuing mortgage-backed instruments.

A strong impediment to an even wider application of mortgage-backed securities in asset portfolios is the uncertainties regarding prepayments. This problem is not unique to mortgage-backed securities. Increasingly fixed-income securities are appearing with specialized call and put option features which have strained the market's ability to value these assets adequately, and has necessitated the development of hedging techniques designed to control the risks arising out of their uncertain lives. Compounding these problems has been the significant increase in interest rate volatility which has made prepayment rights, call, and put options a more valuable component of fixed-income securities. Ways of hedging the risk of uncertain lives in fixed-income securities is treated in Chapter 7.

All too often in the fixed-income literature, credit risks and interest rate risks are treated as separate and distinct topics. This shows up also in the organization of many fixed-income research departments which make a clear and distinct organizational separation between their credit and analytical research functions. Default risk, however, is only one dimension of risk faced by a fixed-income investor, and the analysis of this risk can often be treated in an analytical framework similar to the approaches taken to other aspects of interest rate risk. The framework for doing this which appears most promising is the use of option methodology within the framework of viewing corporate securities (both bonds and stocks) as contingent claims on the underlying value of the firm. In Chapter 8 we show in detail how this approach can be utilized in the case of developing hedging strategies for high-yield (''junk'') bonds. These instruments play a particularly important role in many specialized portfolio applications, and handling their special default characteristics has become a topic of concern to many portfolio managers.

Part 4 of the book is in some ways the most important and useful of all. Knowledge of the tools and specialized instruments of interest rate risk control, of course, is a precondition for successful applications. However, each type of institution has specialized investment needs and is exposed and sensitive to particular aspects of interest rate risk. This arises out of the special products (liabilities) that they offer, their regulatory environment, their institutional and decision-making structure, and their often unique accounting and tax situations. These considerations make it important to tailor the investment instruments and interest rate risk control methodology to these specialized institutional needs.

In this book we have focused on some of the special interest rate risk control needs of some of the largest institutional pools of investable funds in order to demonstrate a series of practical applications of this technology. Chapter 9 discusses risk control techniques applied to life insurance companies. Chapter 10 discusses applications to banks and thrifts. Chapters 11 and 12 deal with applications for corporations. In Chapter 11 we are concerned with applications of this technology in the management of corporate cash pools. Chapter 12 deals with the development of specialized option technology which leads to more flexible asset allocation approaches which are adaptable to pension fund management. Chapter 13 deals with the application of specialized option methodology in helping ''active'' managers of pension assets structure their maturity decisions in a disciplined fashion. These chapters, particularly those dealing with life insurance companies, banks, and thrifts, are meant to be fairly comprehensive treatments of the application of modern risk control technology in particular institutional settings. As such these chapters can be treated as stand-alone analyses of these important uses, as well as a natural extension of the earlier topics treated in this book.

2 General Analytical Techniques

2 The Term Structure of Interest Rates

GARY D. LATAINER

INTRODUCTION

The term structure of interest rates is one of the most frequently discussed concepts in financial theory and an appropriate place to begin a book on risk control techniques for fixed-income investors. To understand the risk of fixed-income securities, it is necessary to understand the factors determining their yields or prices. While maturity, coupon, credit, refunding provisions, and tax considerations may each interact to determine yields, yields are most usefully analyzed along a single dimension, holding the other factors constant. When this dimension is time to maturity, we are referring to the term structure of interest rates.

This chapter is intended to provide an overview of term structure analysis and its applications. The chapter is divided into four sections and a conclusion. Section I introduces key term structure concepts. The relationship among spot rates, forward rates, and yield to maturity is discussed in this section. The term structure can be represented by each of these rates, and the discussion provides background material for the remainder of this chapter. Section II examines alternative theories of the term structure. These theories attempt to explain the differing shapes of the yield curve and to extract information from these shapes that will be useful to investors. Section III discusses the estimation of the term structure, comparing approaches that have been suggested for this purpose, and Section IV focuses on term structure applications. Among these are the absolute and relative valuation of fixed-income securities, risk/return analysis, financial futures and debt option pricing, and bond immunization.

SECTION I   ALTERNATIVE REPRESENTATIONS OF THE TERM STRUCTURE

The term structure represents the relationship between interest rates and time to maturity. Since the interest rates can be either spot rates, forward rates, or yields to maturity, it is important to have clear definitions of these terms and an understanding of the relationships among them.

To most investors, the term structure and the yield curve are synonymous; that is, the term structure is most frequently thought of as the yield curve for government securities. Yield to maturity is perhaps the most quoted number in the bond market. By definition the yield to maturity of a bond is the single discount rate equating the price of the bond with the cash flows to be received from the bond. It is the rate, y, that solves the familiar bond pricing equation[1]:

$$P = \sum_{t=1}^{N} \frac{C_t}{(1+y)^t} + \frac{F}{(1+y)^N} \tag{1}$$

where P = the bond's price
  N = the number of periods of maturity
  C = the coupon payment on the bond
  F = the face value of the bond

Thus a bond's yield to maturity is its internal rate of return.

While yield to maturity facilitates comparison among investments of different maturities, bond market participants recognize that, as an internal rate of return, there are certain problems associated with the number. Most important, the yield to maturity assumes that the bond will be held to maturity and that intermediate cash flows can be reinvested at that rate. The realized return on any bond will almost certainly differ from its yield to maturity as these assumptions are unlikely to hold. Yield to maturity is a useful starting point in comparing different bonds, but it is generally insufficient for fully expressing a bond's return characteristics.

In a term structure context, yield to maturity has a somewhat different problem. For any given maturity, there will not be a unique yield to maturity. This is true even for a relatively homogeneous class of bonds such as U.S. Treasury issues, because bonds of the same maturity but carrying different coupons will generally have different yields to maturity.[2]

For this reason, the term structure can be more accurately represented by the set of spot interest rates. The spot rate of interest for a given maturity is defined as the yield on a pure discount bond of that maturity, and the set of spot rates across different maturities defines the spot rate term structure. Spot rates are the discount rates

---

[1]In this case, we assume an annual coupon payment for the bond.
[2]Taxes have a significant impact on yields across the different coupons, but even in the absence of taxes, bonds with the same maturity but different coupons will carry different yields.

used to determine the present value of any future cash payment. By using spot rates, the price of a bond can be determined as

$$P = \sum_{t=1}^{N} \frac{C_t}{(1+R_t)^t} + \frac{F}{(1+R_N)^N} \tag{2}$$

In this case Rt is the discount rate applied by the market to a payment to be received in period t. Note that unlike the yield to maturity calculation, a different spot rate is used to discount each cash payment. However, for any maturity, there is always a single spot rate (assuming a default-free investment).

Still a third way of expressing the term structure is as a set of forward rates. A forward rate is the interest rate on money to be loaned in the future with the contract made today. By definition, forward rates and spot rates are related according to the following formula:

$$(1+R_t)^t = (1+R_{t-j})^{t-j}(1+f_{j,t-j})^j \tag{3}$$

where $f_{j,t-j}$ is the j period forward rate for money to be loaned t-j periods from now. If this relationship did not hold, arbitrage opportunities would be present.

To see this consider an investor seeking to lend funds for a 2-year period and faced with the following two alternatives:

1. Lend for two years at 11% per year, or
2. Lend for one year at 10% and enter a forward contract to lend for one year, beginning a year from today, at x%

By arbitrage arguments, x must equal 12%. If it were greater than 12%, 2-year investors would enter into the second arrangement because they would be assured of earning more than the 11% 2-year spot rate.[3] This would lower the supply of 2-year spot money and raise the supply of 1-year spot and forward money. Arbitrage would continue until the returns on the two alternatives were equal. On the other hand, if x were less than 12%, investors could borrow for one year, write a 1-year forward contract, and then invest for 2 years at the 2-year spot rate. This would increase the supply of 2-year spot money, and increase the demand for 1-year spot and forward money. Rates would again change until returns on the two alternatives were equal.

Extending the arbitrage arguments to all time periods, it becomes clear that the term structure of spot rates contains an implicit set of forward rates. The relationship between the term structure of spot rates and the set of implied forward rates is that of average and marginal quantities. Spot rates are a geometric average of forward

[3]For example, if x were 13%, investors could earn a rate of $(1.10 \times 1.13)^{.5} - 1 = 11.49\%$ per year over the 2-year period.

rates, while forward rates represent the marginal cost of borrowing or lending over a future period of time. Thus we can express equation (3) as

$$(1+R_t)^t = (1+R_1)(1+f_{1,1})(1+f_{1,2}) \ldots (1+f_{1,t-1}) \tag{4}$$

It is important to distinguish the implied forward rate from the spot rate expected to prevail in the future. A forward rate applies to contracts made for a period forward in time. Although the actual transaction will occur later, its terms are certain today. The relationship is definitional, and no statement is made regarding investor expectations.[4]

A bond's yield to maturity is mathematically related to both spot and forward rates. Given a set of spot rates or forward rates, one can compute the yield to maturity on a bond in a straightforward manner. Table 2-1 shows this computation for two 4-year bonds, one with a 10% coupon and the other with a 15% coupon.

Two key points are evident from the table. First, the yield to maturity is not a simple average of spot rates. Second, each maturity does not have a unique yield to maturity associated with it. The 10% coupon bond yields nine basis points more than the 15% coupon bond, yet both bonds are fairly priced given the current spot rate structure. When the term structure is rising, low coupon bonds should yield more than high coupon bonds.[5] The reverse is true when the term structure is falling.

Because spot rates (and implied forward rates) are uniquely determined, they are preferable to yield to maturity in a number of financial applications. Any financial concept for which "the interest rate" over a period of time is important, is best approached using spot rates. In the next section we examine various theories explaining the term structure of spot rates.

Table 2-1. Comparative Pricing of Coupon Bonds

Year	Spot Rate	Cash Flow from 10% Coupon Bond		Cash Flow from 15% Coupon Bond	
		Actual	Present Value	Actual	Present Value
1	10%	$ 10	$ 9.09	$ 15	$ 13.64
2	11%	10	8.12	15	12.17
3	12%	10	7.12	15	10.68
4	13%	110	67.47	115	70.53
			$91.80		$107.02

Yield to maturity of 10% coupon bond = 12.75%
Yield to maturity of 15% coupon bond = 12.66%

[4]Only under the pure expectations theory, which is discussed in the next section, is the implied forward rate equal to the expected future spot rate.
[5]We again ignore the impact of taxes.

SECTION II   EXPLAINING THE TERM STRUCTURE OF INTEREST RATES

Figures 2-1*a* to 2-1*c* show three yield curves for U.S. Treasury securities taken from the Treasury Bulletin. In the curve from December 31, 1980 short-term yields are high, but yields decline as term to maturity increases. In the curve for December 30, 1983 the reverse holds true—short-term yields are low and yields rise with term to maturity. In the curve for March 31, 1982 yields are relatively flat across all maturities. Term structure theories attempt to provide a unified framework for explaining such different yield curve shapes, for identifying systematic relationships among yields, and for extracting information from the curves that will be relevant to investors.

Three theories have attracted the widest attention. They are:

1. The pure expectations theory
2. The liquidity preference theory
3. The preferred habitat theory

The Expectations Theory

In a world of perfect certainty, investors seeking to maximize returns across their holding periods would have perfect foresight regarding future spot rates and therefore shift among maturities to that combination of investments providing the highest returns over their holding periods. If any bond could be substituted for any other bond, all possible default-free investment strategies would provide the same return over any holding period. This is so because of the arbitrage arguments of the prior section.

Under these conditions, we can accurately predict future spot rates from the current term structure. A rising term structure tells us that future interest rates will be higher (otherwise no investors would hold short-term bonds), a falling term structure tells us that future interest rates will be lower (otherwise all investors would hold short-term bonds), and a flat term structure tells us that interest rates are not expected to change over time. Thus the forward rates implied by the spot rate curve would exactly equal future spot rates.

Of course, the future direction of interest rates cannot be predicted with perfect certainty. The expectations theory brings the arbitrage arguments of the world of certainty into a behavioral realm. It postulates that the shape of the term structure is determined by market participants' expectations of future interest rates. If market participants expect rates to rise in the future, the yield curve will slope upward. This is because investors, having the possibility of lending short-term until rates rise and then lending at the higher expected rate, will demand higher rates to lend long-term. When rates are expected to fall, investors will require higher yields to hold short-term bonds, and the term structure will be declining. While actual future spot rates may not equal the expected future spot rates, the implied forward rates are unbiased

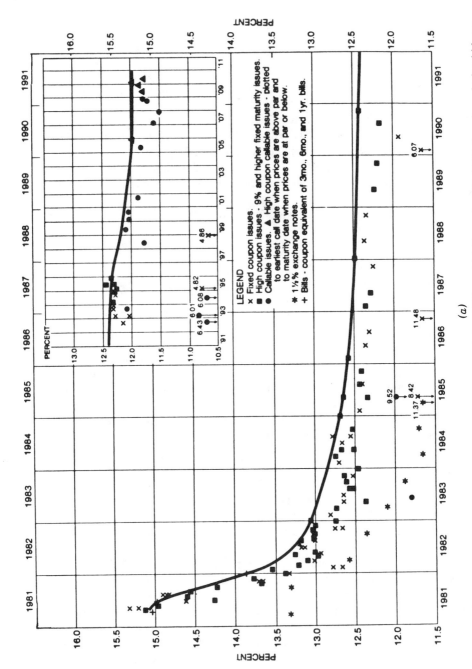

Figure 2-1. Yield curves for (*a*) December 31, 1980, (*b*) March 31, 1982, and (*c*) December 30, 1983, based on closing bid quotations. Note that the curve is fitted by eye and based only on the most actively traded issues. Market yields on coupon issues due in less than three months are excluded.

16

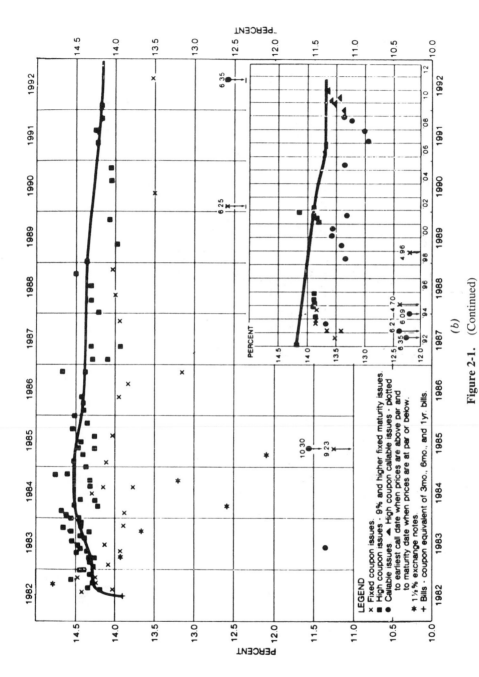

Figure 2-1. (Continued)

17

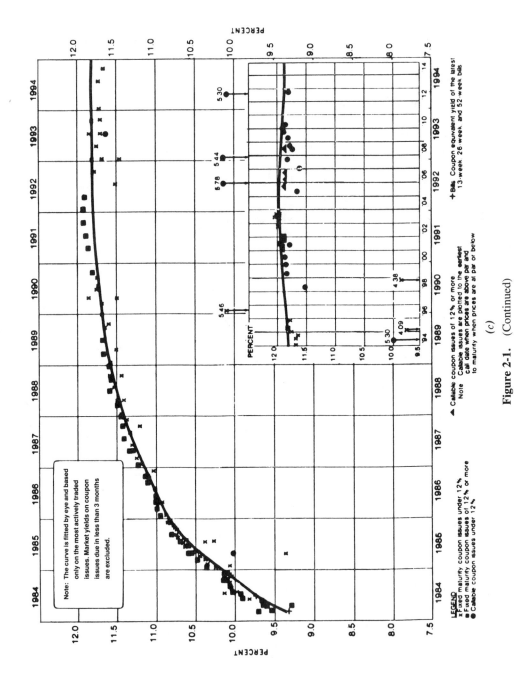

Figure 2-1. (Continued)

18

estimators of future spot rates. Under the expectations theory, the expected holding period yield over any period will be the same for all bond investment strategies.

Besides helping to explain the shape of the yield curve, the expectations theory also helps to explain the relative stability of the yields on long-term bonds relative to those on short-term bonds.[6] Since long rates are averages of current short-term rates and expected future short-term rates, changes in long rates will be an average of changes in current short rates and changes in expected future short rates. This averaging process results in smaller changes in long rates relative to changes in short rates.

Critics of the expectations theory point to two main weaknesses. First, the assumption that all bonds are perfect substitutes to all investors does not appear consistent with real-world investor behavior. Second, the theory assumes that investors are risk neutral. Under uncertainty, however, the longer the maturity of a bond, the greater the risk of fluctuation in value of its principal to the investor. The liquidity preference theory addresses these criticisms.

Liquidity Preference Theory

The liquidity preference theory presumes that, other things being equal, risk averse investors prefer to hold short maturity bonds. In order to attract investors long-term bonds, therefore, must carry a yield premium over shorter-term bonds. The longer the maturity of the bond, the greater this liquidity premium must be.

Recall that in the expectations theory, long-term spot rates were an average of current short-term spot rates and a sequence of expected forward rates. Under the liquidity preference theory, the relationship between spot and forward rates is somewhat different; it is

$$(1+R_t)^t = (1 + R_{t-j})^{t-j}[1 + E(R_{j,t-j}) + L]^j \qquad (5)$$

where L is the premium received for holding a t maturity asset over a t-j holding period. Comparing equation (5) to equation (3), we see that forward rates are greater than expected future spot rates, and that the expected holding period return on a long bond over a short holding period exceeds the short spot rate.

A major implication of the liquidity preference theory is that even if investors expect future short-term rates to remain constant, the yield curve will be upward sloping due to the liquidity premiums. When the market anticipates increases in rates, liquidity premiums will accentuate the upward slope of the yield curve. When the expectations are for lower rates, liquidity premiums will dampen the downward slope of the yield curve.

The effect of the liquidity premium can be seen graphically in Figure 2-2, which displays a spot rate term structure along with the set of 1-period spot rates expected to prevail in the future under both the expectations theory and the liquidity preference

---

[6]The greater volatility of short-term rates has been observed empirically. It is not dependent on any theory of term structure.

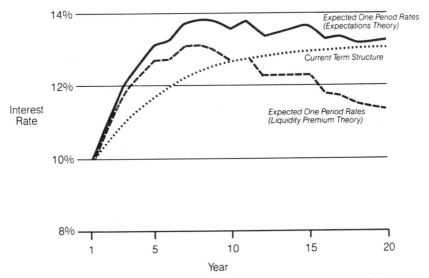

Figure 2-2.   Comparison of expectations and liquidity premium theories.

theory. The forward rates predicted by the expectations theory are always above the current spot rate curve because spot rates are continuously rising. (The forward rates do not rise continuously because the spot rate curve is rising at a decreasing rate.) On the other hand, the forward rates predicted by the liquidity premium theory are above the spot rate curve in early years, but below the spot rate curve in later years. The two theories thus lead to very different conclusions about the market's expectations for future interest rates.

Supporters of the liquidity preference theory point out that it is more consistent with observed yield curve behavior than the expectations theory. Under the expectations theory we should observe negatively sloped yield curves as often as positively sloped yield curves. (Market participants cannot always be expecting rising rates.) Upward sloping yield curves, however, are much more prevalent. This is consistent with a liquidity premium for longer maturities.

The primary criticism of the liquidity preference theory is that it considers risk strictly in terms of price volatility. Consider, however, an insurance company or pension plan with an obligation due in the distant future. To such an investor, a short maturity asset is much riskier than a long maturity asset because it leaves the investor much more open to reinvestment risk. The preferred habitat theory recognizes that both principal and reinvestment risk are of concern to investors.

Preferred Habitat Theory

The preferred habitat theory presumes that institutional investors, because of the nature of their liabilities, have a predetermined demand for particular maturities; that is, investors attempt to hedge both principal and reinvestment risks by matching maturities or durations of their bonds to their liabilities.[7] (For this reason the theory is sometimes called the market segmentation theory or the hedging pressure theory.) The yield on each maturity of bond is determined solely by the supply and demand in each "habitat." In contrast to the prior two theories, the term structure will be independent of investors' expectations about future interest rates.

The preferred habitat theory is often relaxed to assume that investor demands are not strictly fixed in a particular habitat; they may shift slightly depending on the relative yields in nearby habitats. In this case yields in "close" habitats will be directly linked, and those in "distant" habitats indirectly linked.

Practitioners often find the preferred habitat theory intuitively appealing. Traditionally life insurance companies with longer liabilities primarily bought long-term bonds while commercial banks, having predominantly short-term liabilities, purchased short-term securities. In later chapters of this book, we will see that these investment patterns may be changing both as a result of a changing liability structure in these institutions and the possibility of altering effective maturities through such instruments as financial futures.

SECTION III   ESTIMATING THE TERM STRUCTURE

Investors cannot directly observe the spot rate term structure, nor, strictly speaking, can investors observe the yield curve. In general investors can only observe actual bond yields. When investors speak of the yield curve, therefore, they are generally referring to the curve of current coupon Treasury bonds. From the yield curve, the term structure of spot rates must be implied. The elaborate statistical techniques that have been suggested for doing this go beyond the scope of this chapter.[8] However, we offer some relatively simple approaches that can be used to estimate the term structure.

As we saw earlier a coupon bond can be considered as a portfolio of pure discount bonds corresponding to the coupon payments and final maturity. Thus the price of the coupon bond is the sum of the prices of the component discount bonds. As long as a full range of maturities is quoted, we can calculate the term structure of spot rates directly from the coupon bond prices available in the marketplace. The procedure is as follows:

1.   The 1-period spot rate is equal to the yield on a 1-period bond.
2.   Using the 1-period spot rate, discount the first coupon on a 2-period bond. Subtracting this from the bond's price provides the present value of the second coupon and the principal payment. Given this present value, compute the discount

---

[7]This point is a central part of the applications chapters of this book, such as those chapters related to insurance companies and banks and thrifts.
[8]See for example, Vasicek and Fong (1982) and Houglet (1980).

factor equating the present value with the actual cash payment. This is the 2-period spot rate.

3. Continuing in the same fashion, determine the remaining spot rates.

Table 2-2A and 2-2B show a comparison of the current coupon yield curves and the spot rate curves derived in the manner described above for upward and downward sloping yield curves respectively. Notice that the spot rates lie above the yield curve in the former case and below the yield curve in the latter. This point is extremely important to investors who must quote target interest rates for specified time period, such as writers of guaranteed interest contracts or immunized portfolio managers.

While the technique described above can provide a term structure estimate in a relatively easy manner, investors actually have a readily available term structure estimate from the zero coupon Treasury market. Since these securities are default-free, single payment investments, their yield curve should be identical to the spot rate curve.

In practice, however, the Treasury zero curve will usually differ from a spot rate

Table 2-2A. Derived Spot Rates—Upward Sloping Yield Curve

Years	Current Coupon YTM	Spots
.5	10.82	10.82
1.0	11.20	11.21
1.5	11.36	11.38
2.0	11.53	11.56
2.5	11.64	11.68
3.0	11.75	11.80
3.5	11.97	12.06
4.0	12.19	12.32
4.5	12.31	12.46
5.0	12.43	12.61
5.5	12.49	12.68
6.0	12.55	12.75
6.5	12.61	12.83
7.0	12.68	12.92
7.5	12.72	12.97
8.0	12.76	13.02
8.5	12.79	13.06
9.0	12.82	13.10
9.5	12.86	13.16
10.0	12.90	13.23

curve derived in another manner. There are a variety of reasons for this, primarily related to liquidity and supply and demand considerations. The zero coupon Treasury market is not homogeneous, as it consists of stripped treasuries and various types of trust certificates. Each of these will have a different degree of liquidity. Even two strips with the same maturity date, but which have been stripped off different bonds, may carry different yields because a dealer may be able to locate holders of one issue but not the other. In addition, some zeros have been "locked away" in portfolios, thereby creating a supply shortage in certain maturities. Despite these limitations, the ready availability of the information and the ability of investors to actually attain these promised rates with certainty makes the zero coupon curve an often used substitute for the spot rate curve.

A comparison of the theoretical spot rate curve and the zero coupon bond curve can be extremely useful. Table 2-3 presents such a comparison. In some maturities, the zeros are cheap relative to their theoretical levels, while in other cases (particularly the long maturities) they are rich. The comparison therefore enables investors to identify those zeros that represent good value and those that represent poor value.

**Table 2-2B.   Derived Spot Rates—
Downward Sloping Yield Curve**

Years	Current Coupon YTM	Spots
.5	14.20	14.20
1.0	13.50	13.48
1.5	13.15	13.11
2.0	12.80	12.74
2.5	12.57	12.50
3.0	12.35	12.25
3.5	12.20	12.08
4.0	12.05	11.91
4.5	11.96	11.82
5.0	11.88	11.73
5.5	11.81	11.65
6.0	11.75	11.58
6.5	11.71	11.54
7.0	11.68	11.50
7.5	11.65	11.47
8.0	11.62	11.44
8.5	11.59	11.40
9.0	11.56	11.36
9.5	11.53	11.32
10.0	11.50	11.28

Table 2-3. Zero Coupon Curve versus Theoretical Spot Rate Curve

Maturity	Current Coupon Bond	Theoretical Spot Rate	Zero Coupon Bond
6 Month	9.54	9.54	9.54
1 Year	9.99	9.99	9.99
2 Year	10.87	10.93	11.15
3 Year	11.13	11.20	11.50
4 Year	11.29	11.38	11.75
5 Year	11.47	11.59	11.85
6 Year	11.57	11.71	11.88
7 Year	11.67	11.84	11.90
8 Year	11.70	11.86	11.90
9 Year	11.73	11.89	11.90
10 Year	11.75	11.92	11.90
11 Year	11.74	11.88	11.89
12 Year	11.72	11.83	11.88
13 Year	11.71	11.79	11.87
14 Year	11.69	11.74	11.86
15 Year	11.67	11.70	11.85
16 Year	11.71	11.79	11.79
17 Year	11.74	11.88	11.73
18 Year	11.77	11.98	11.67
19 Year	11.80	12.08	11.61
20 Year	11.84	12.20	11.55
21 Year	11.83	12.15	11.53
22 Year	11.82	12.10	11.51
23 Year	11.81	12.05	11.49
24 Year	11.81	12.00	11.47
25 Year	11.80	11.95	11.45

SECTION IV   APPLICATIONS OF THE TERM STRUCTURE

How can investors apply an understanding of the term structure to investment decision-making? While the range of applications that has been suggested is quite wide, we can consolidate most of these under four key headings:

1. Bond valuation
2. Risk/Return analysis
3. Pricing financial futures and options
4. Bond immunization

Bond Valuation

Both absolute and relative bond valuation is influenced by the term structure. Any bond's value can be broken down into a number of subcomponents. The first of these is the value of the bond's cash flows treated as if they were default free. Added to this are the default risk of the cash flows, option features attached to the cash flows (calls, puts, sinking funds), tax considerations, and so on. The term structure, of course, determines the first component, the valuation of default-free cash flows.

By pricing a bond's cash flows under the term structure, investors can analyze whether a bond is fairly priced, and determine which bonds are most mispriced relative to other bonds. Within their portfolio duration constraints, investors should seek to purchase securities for their portfolios that are underpriced according to the term structure, and to sell securities from their portfolios that are overpriced according to the term structure. Analyzing the spot rate structure allows an investor to judge whether bonds are fairly priced in a way that the coupon yield curve cannot. Suppose an investor is considering the two 4-year bonds from Table 2-1 and suppose, further, that the 10% coupon bond yields five basis points more than the 15% coupon bond. While the low coupon bond may appear cheap, Table 2-1 shows us that the bond is actually four basis points too rich. This type of analysis is particularly useful in the government market, where securities are relatively, if not completely, homogeneous.

Risk/Return Analysis

In many portfolio situations, comparison of current bond values represents only a first step in the investment decision process. A more complete analysis requires translating bond values into expected return and risk measures. While there are a number of approaches for doing this, the most complete one involves simulating portfolio returns under a variety of future interest rate scenarios.[9]

A bond's return over any holding period is equal to the sum of its price change, coupon income, and interest earned on coupon income, divided by its initial price. The price change is largely uncertain and it can have a major impact on the bond's return. By simulating a bond's or a portfolio's performance over a range of potential term structures for future time periods, an investor can identify the particular types of term structure movements that positively or negatively affect the bond's or portfolio's return. If an investor can assign probabilities to these term structures, he or she can compute expected returns over a holding period, as well as a variance of expected returns. Even if the investor does not assign probabilities to the term structures, this type of sensitivity analysis is valuable in helping the investor locate securities with desirable or undesirable performance characteristics.

---

[9]Chapter 3 discusses the duration approach to measuring risk and return.

Pricing Financial Futures and Options

While it is not necessary to consider term structure when discussing uses of financial futures and options, term structure is very important to the pricing of these instruments. Financial futures are priced according to arbitrage arguments similar to those used in explaining the term structure;[10] that is, the shape of the term structure determines the relationship of cash and futures market prices in the same manner as it determines the relationship between spot and forward rates. When the yield curve is positively sloped, financial futures will be priced below the cash market. The reverse is true when the yield curve is negatively sloped. These arbitrage arguments also tell us that it is not possible to "lock in" any rate other than that available from the term structure in a hedging transaction.

The shape of the term structure also plays a role in the pricing of interest rate options. When the yield curve is positively sloped, call options will be cheap relative to put options.[11] The reverse is true when the yield curve is negatively sloped.

Bond Immunization

By using the concept of duration, investors have been able to construct immunized portfolios that provide assured returns over a target holding period. Immunization is accomplished by matching the duration of a bond portfolio to a target holding period (or a liability schedule). As Chapter 3 discusses, duration formulas have an implicit assumption about the shapes of, and movements in, the term structure. In most cases, practitioners use a duration formula that assumes the yield curve is flat and that only parallel movements in the yield curve occur. Yield curves generally do not move in such a manner, and other types of term structure movements can cause a portfolio to over or under-perform relative to its target. Techniques therefore have been developed to minimize the exposure of immunized portfolios to more realistic term structure shifts.[12]

Another key issue in immunization concerns the rate that is locked in for the holding period. When a zero coupon bond is used to immunize, this rate is unambiguous—it is the bond's yield to maturity. The rate is less clear, however, when a portfolio of coupon bonds is used. While the yield to maturity on the immunized portfolio is often stated as the yield target, term structure theory tells us that it is the spot rate applicable to the holding period that can be assured. The failure of some

---

[10]Futures prices will not equal implied forward prices exactly for a variety of reasons. These include the uncertainty of the financing costs associated with a futures position and the uncertainty of the exact delivery date for a futures contract.

[11]Arbitrage arguments are again responsible for this. As discussed more fully in Chapter 5, options are priced based on holding positions in the cash markets that "replicate" the option's value. The replicating position for a call option involves holding a long position in the bond, financed by borrowing. For a put, it involves holding a short position in the bond, combined with lending. Thus, in a positive yield curve environment, there will be a positive carry earned on the call replication and a negative carry earned on the put replication.

[12]See Fong and Vasicek (1983).

immunized portfolios to meet their target returns can sometimes be attributed to the initial misstatement of the target returns. The concept of immunization is more fully developed in Chapter 3.

SECTION V   CONCLUSION

The term structure lays the foundation for many other topics in the area of interest rate risk control. In particular, the concept of duration, which is widely used by bond managers to both control and measure interest rate risk, is closely linked to the term structure. Banks and thrifts, insurance companies, pension funds, and corporations can analyze the sensitivity of their assets and liabilities to term structure movements in terms of duration. Money managers utilize duration to structure portfolios with targeted levels of interest rate sensitivity. Chapter 3 focuses on the many uses of duration.

BIBLIOGRAPHY

Carleton, W., and Cooper, A. "Estimation and Uses of the Term Structure of Interest Rates." *Journal of Finance* 31 (1976): 1067–1083.

Chambers, D., Carelton, W., and Waldman, D. "A New Approach to Estimation of the Term Structure of Interest Rates." *Journal of Financial and Quantitative Analysis* 19 (1984): 233–252.

Cox, J., Ingersoll, J. and Ross, S. "A Reexamination of Traditional Hypotheses About the Term Structure of Interest Rates." *Journal of Finance* 36 (1981): 769–793.

Dobson, S., Sutch, R., and Vanderford, D. "An Evaluation of Alternative Empirical Models of the Term Structure of Interest Rates." *Journal of Finance* 31 (1976): 1035–1065.

Fama, E. "Forward Rates as Predictors of Future Spot Rates." *Journal of Financial Economics* (1976): 361–377.

Fong, H.G., and Vasicek, O. "The Hedging Between Return and Risk in Immunized Portfolios." *Financial Analysts Journal* (1983).

Houglet, M. "Estimating the Term Structure of Interest Rates for Non-Homogeneous Bonds." Ph.D. Diss., Graduate School of Business, University of California, Berkeley, 1980.

Langetieg, T. "A Multivariate Model of the Term Structure of Interest Rates." *Journal of Finance* (1980): 71–97.

Malkiel, B. *The Term Structure of Interest Rates.* Princeton, NJ: Princeton University Press, 1966.

McCulloch, J.H. "Measuring the Term Structure of Interest Rates." *Journal of Business* 44 (1971): 19–31.

McCulloch, J.H. "An Estimate of the Liquidity Premium." *Journal of Political Economy* 83 (1975): 95–119.

Modigliani, F., and Shiller, R. "Inflation, Rational Expectations and the Term Structure of Interest Rates." *Economica* 40 (1973): 12–43.

Vasicek, O. "An Equilibrium Characterization of the Term Structure." *Journal of Financial Economics* 5 (1977): 177–188.

Vasicek, O. and Fong, H.G. "Term Structure Modelling Using Exponential Splines." *Journal of Finance* 37 (1982): 339–348.

3 Uses of Duration Analysis for the Control of Interest Rate Risk

ALDEN L. TOEVS

INTRODUCTION

Portfolio managers use duration more frequently than any other group of fixed-income professionals. Particularly well informed are insurance and pension fund managers who, most often, employ duration to ''immunize'' (protect) assets from changes in interest rates so as to fund with certainty actuarially determined future obligations. Recent increases in corporate cash pools to amounts in excess of short-term cash requirements have also induced corporate treasurers to explore applications of duration in interest rate risk control.

The simplest immunization technique invests in assets that throw off cash in exactly the right amounts at the due dates of the liabilities. This ''dedication'' of cash inflows is relatively inflexible and therefore cannot always be accomplished for acceptable costs. A more general immunization approach positions the asset cash flows to occur *on average* on the outflow dates. Such a ''duration-matching'' technique provides more freedom in asset allocation than does portfolio dedication. This should increase asset returns (lower asset funding requirements), and as we will see, do so without increasing interest rate risk.

A particularly troubling problem in funding liabilities with immunized assets (dedicated or duration matched) occurs when liability dates and amounts are uncertain. Some liability dates are interest rate dependent, for example, fixed-rate mortgage prepayment opportunities for the borrower. Others are independent of future interest rates, such as a corporate cash pool that is drawn down unexpectedly early to acquire another firm. Uncertain timing of cash needs has not been adequately addressed in the duration literature. The implications of this oversight are explored briefly in Section VI of this chapter and in Chapter 11 in more detail.

Duration analysis can provide the core of integrated asset/liability management for any financial institution. Firms profit from the spreads in interest rates that exist between assets and liabilities. Interest rate spreads help to determine net interest income and equity value. Variations in interest rates affect both income and equity values. The extent of the resulting uncertainties can be measured and monitored using a duration approach.

Duration analysis may be used in pursuits other than the determination of interest rate risk minimizing positions. Many managers strive for enhanced returns by undertaking interest rate risk. Such active management requires an analysis of the available interest rate risk versus return tradeoffs. These risk-return tradeoffs are easily determined using only rudimentary duration analysis. Furthermore, an immunized portfolio can be employed as a component of an option-like strategy designed to adopt interest rate risk, yet structure the risk to limit downside risk exposure.

The remainder of the chapter is outlined as follows: Section I more completely defines duration and illustrates its uses in measuring the price sensitivity of cash instruments. Section II discusses the immunization of asset returns. Section III describes the role duration analysis plays in asset/liability management. This discussion is expanded upon in Chapter 10. Among other topics, the gap management models frequently used by banks and thrifts are compared to a duration-based asset/liability model of interest rate risk. Section IV presents methods of constructing risk-return tradeoffs using duration. This section briefly reviews the role duration plays in the synthetic construction of a fixed-income portfolio having the return profile of a protective put option strategy. Section V considers the problems introduced by uncertain liability dates. Section VI discusses some of the concerns one can have with the use of duration in risk management. Section VII discusses techniques designed to reduce the limitations of duration as a measure of interest rate risk. These limitations arise largely because duration is a linear approximation to the curvilinear relationship that exists between the price of a bond and interest rate levels. Finally, Section VIII summarizes and concludes the chapter.

SECTION I   DURATION AND ZERO COUPON BOND EQUIVALENCY

Frederick Macaulay developed the duration concept in his search for a correct measure of the life of a bond. (Throughout this chapter the term ''bond'' should be taken to mean any fixed-income security.) Term to maturity is an unambiguous measure of the life of a zero coupon (pure discount) bond. But because term to maturity ignores the amount and timing of all cash flows save the final payment, it incompletely measures the life of a coupon bond. Macaulay decided to standardize coupon bond life in terms equivalent to the term to maturity of a comparably risky zero coupon bond. This reasoning is compelling both because the term to maturity of a zero coupon bond unambiguously measures the bond's life and because any coupon bond might best be viewed as nothing more than a bundle of zero coupon bonds.

The problem Macaulay faced was how to average the maturities of zero coupon bond bundles. For example, a $100 coupon bond currently at par that pays $10 in interest annually for five years may be regarded as a portfolio of five zero coupon bonds: $10 face value zeros maturing in one, two, three, and four years, and a $110 face value zero maturing in five years. One summary measure of these five maturity dates is three years, which is the simple average of the dates. This approach, however, fails to recognize the different dollar values of the constituent zero coupon bonds.

Weighted Averages of Cash Flow Dates

More reasonable summary measures of a coupon bond's life compute average term to maturity using dollar weights. Two possible dollar weighting schemes come immediately to mind. First, the dollar weights could be computed by dividing each cash inflow by total cash to be received. For our 5-year coupon bond, this dollar weighted average term to maturity (WAT) would be:

$$WAT = \frac{10}{150} \times 1\,year + \frac{10}{150} \times 2\,years + \frac{10}{150} \times 3\,years$$

$$+ \frac{10}{150} \times 4\,years + \frac{110}{150} \times 5\,years = 4.33\,years$$

Second, the dollar weights could be computed using present values of future cash flows. Because the present value of any single cash flow is the price of a zero coupon bond with a face value equal to this cash flow, these dollar weights are zero coupon bond price weights. For our example bond, this price weighted average would be:

$$D = \left[\frac{10/1.10}{P}\right] 1\,year + \left[\frac{10/1.10^2}{P}\right] 2\,years + \left[\frac{10/1.10^3}{P}\right] 3\,years$$

$$+ \left[\frac{10/1.10^4}{P}\right] 4\,years + \left[\frac{110/1.10^5}{P}\right] 5\,years = 4.16\,years$$

It was this formulation Macaulay derived and called duration. The weights in this average are given in brackets. The numerator of each weight is the price of the zero coupon bond (its present or discounted value). The denominator is the *total* present value of all five zeros, which is the price of the coupon bond P. Given that our coupon bond was previously assumed to be trading at par, price is $100.

The price-weighted average term to maturity or duration is a superior measure to the WAT. Duration is an average that uses dollar weights computed relative to today's date (present values) and time to receipt of cash computed from today's date.

On the other hand, the WAT is internally inconsistent. It computes the time to cash receipt from today's date but the dollar weights do not depend upon today's date. The importance of this internal inconsistency will become clear as the applications of duration are revealed, not one of which is shared by WAT.

The duration of any series of cash flows ending at date t_N years can be represented in general terms as:

$$D = w_1 \times t_1 + w_2 \times t_2 + w_3 \times t_3 + \ldots + w_N \times t_N \qquad (1)$$

where w_i is the price of the zero coupon bond maturing at date t_i relative to the total price of the bundle of N zero coupon bonds hypothetically comprising the coupon bond. For illustrative purposes Table 3-1 computes the duration of another bond. Again "bond" should be taken to mean any series of cash flows, mortgages, annuities, and so forth.

As a price weighted average term to maturity, duration is measured in years. The duration of a zero coupon bond is its maturity date. (In equation (1), all weights for a zero coupon bond maturing in t_N years are zero except w_N which equals 1.0.) Any series of cash flows with a terminal flow at t_N will have a duration less than t_N. The smaller are the dollar flows occurring before t_N, the smaller are these cash flow weights and the closer the duration comes to t_N years. The relationships among the coupon rate (size of intermediate cash flows), yield to maturity, maturity date, and duration are depicted in Figure 3-1.

The Additivity of Duration

The duration of a portfolio of coupon bonds can be computed using equation (1) considering all cash flows generated by the portfolio. Often an easier approach is to first compute the duration of each coupon bond in the portfolio separately and then make use of the "additivity" characteristic of duration to find the duration of the entire portfolio. Additivity means that the duration of a portfolio is the price weighted average of the coupon bond durations. For example, a portfolio of $1000 invested

Table 3-1. Duration of a $100 Face Value Bond Paying a 7% Coupon

Cash Inflow Date	Cash Inflow Amount	Cash Inflows Discounted at 10%	Price Weights	Price Weighted Maturities
0.5 years	$ 3.50	$ 3.34 [a]	.036 [c]	.018 years [d]
1.0	3.50	3.18	.034	.034
1.5	3.50	3.03	.033	.050
2.0	3.50	2.89	.031	.062
2.5	3.50	2.76	.030	.075
3.0	103.50	77.76	.836	2.508
		$92.96 [b] (Current Price)	1.000	2.747 years [e] (Duration)

[a] $3.50/(1.10)^5

[b] Current price sums all cash inflows discounted by the yield to maturity (10%).

[c] $3.34/$92.96

[d] .036 x 0.5 years

[e] Duration is the sum of all price weighted maturities.

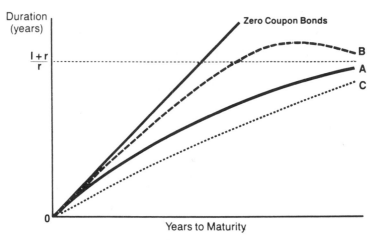

- Duration is related to years to maturity linearly for zero coupon bonds
- OA gives the duration versus maturity relationship for <u>current coupon</u> bonds (bonds priced at par)
- OB gives the duration versus maturity relationship for <u>discounted coupon</u> bonds
- OC gives the duration versus maturity relationship for premium coupon bonds

All coupon bonds have an upper limit to their duration as the maturity date becomes very distant. This upper limit is the number resulting from computing $(1+r)/r$.

Figure 3-1. Duration versus length of time to maturity.

in 3-year duration coupon bonds and \$2000 in 4-year duration coupon bonds has a portfolio duration of D_p = (\$1000/\$3000) $\times$ 3 years + (\$2000/\$3000) $\times$ 4 years = 3.67 years. In general the duration of a portfolio is given by

$$D_p = \frac{(P_1 \times D_1) + (P_2 \times D_2) + (P_3 \times D_3) + \ldots + (P_n \times D_n)}{W} \qquad (2)$$

Here the prices, durations, and total portfolio value are represented by P, D, and W respectively.

Duration as an Index of Price Sensitivity

The notion of cash flow standardization into zero coupon bond equivalence is of paramount importance in fixed-income analysis. Equivalency means an investor in coupon bonds creates synthetically (mimics) the traits of either existing or nonexisting zero coupon bonds. Now we shall see that zero coupon bonds have easily understood pricing and holding period return characteristics. The equivalency argument of duration implies that coupon bonds or portfolios of them, both of which appear to have complex pricing and holding period returns, really exhibit the more obvious pricing and holding period returns of their duration-associated zero coupon bonds.

Recently zero coupon bonds have been issued by corporations in maturities as long as 20 years. U.S. Treasury zero coupon bonds in maturities from 1 to 30 years have also been indirectly marketed by investment banks using coupon stripping techniques. Here investors buy claims to specific individual cash flows from a U.S. Treasury coupon bond that is held in escrow for investor protection. These capital market innovations do not diminish the importance of duration analysis. Investors find duration to be valuable because it helps them simplify the interest rate risk characteristics of complex cash flow patterns. Indeed, now that investors have direct experience with zero coupon bonds, duration analysis is more meaningful than ever.

The pricing characteristics of zero coupon bonds are easily understood. The price of a zero coupon bond maturing in N years (P_N, is the present value of its face amount. If the annualized market rate of interest for N years were to change unexpectedly today, there would be an immediate change in P_N. A useful approximation of this instantaneous change in market value is

$$\Delta P_N = -\frac{N \times P_N}{1 + r} \times \Delta r \qquad (3)$$

ΔP_N represents the dollar change in price today caused by an unexpected change in the N year interest rate (Δr). The approximate *proportional* change in price is given by a simple rearrangement of equation (3):

$$\frac{\Delta P_N}{P_N} = -\frac{N \times \Delta r}{1 + r} \qquad (4)$$

These formulas indicate that price sensitivity, measured in dollars or in proportional terms, depends greatly on the term to maturity. For a given dollar investment, longer maturity zeros are more price sensitive to a given change in interest rates than are shorter term zeros.

Since any cash flow series behaves like its duration matched zero coupon bond, equations (3) and (4) also hold for any cash flow series once the *duration* of the series is substituted for term to maturity (N) in these two equations. For example equation (3) indicates that a $100 investment in a 12% coupon bond with a 4-year duration and a yield to maturity of 12% will have a $3.57 price increase when the yield to maturity falls by one percentage point ($3.57 = -4 \times \$100 \times (-.01)/1.12$). The proportional price change computed with equation (4) is .0357 or 3.6%

It is easy to show that the duration of any coupon bond falls (rises) when either its coupon rate or its yield to maturity rises (falls); that is, duration is inversely related to both the coupon rate and the yield to maturity. For all but substantially discounted coupon bonds, durations rise with term to maturity.[1]

---

[1]The anomaly of deep discount bonds mentioned here and depicted in Figure 1 can best be explained by observing that any perpetual coupon bond has a duration of $(1 + r)/r$. Thus as the term to maturity of any coupon bond rises, duration must converge to this fixed number.

These observations will momentarily lead to a useful summary of the following three traditional bond price rules of thumb. The smaller the bond price sensitivity.

1. The higher the coupon rate
2. The higher the yield to maturity
3. The shorter the term to maturity.

While useful in some respects, the three individual rules for bond price sensitivity provide little information about the price sensitivity of, among other combinations, high-coupon long-maturity bonds relative to low-coupon short-maturity bonds. For example, a 12% current coupon 10-year Treasury bond is less price sensitive than a discounted 5% coupon 8-year Treasury bond, but not a discounted 5% coupon 7-year Treasury bond. It has also been recognized that the third rule does not always hold; the anomaly in deep discount bonds graphed in Figure 3–1 is the cause. The more accurate and general statement about price sensitivity, which encompasses all three rules *and* the exception to rule three, is: **For a given change in interest rates, high duration bonds are more price sensitive than low duration bonds.**

Duration as a Linear Approximation

Equations (3) and (4) approximate price changes, and do so in a manner whereby the error increases with the size of the interest rate change. Consider, for example, a 5-year zero coupon bond with a face value of $100.[2] If r equals .10 initially, then this bond has a price of $62.09. Equation (3) indicates that the value of this bond will increase by $2.82 if r falls to .09.[3] Thus the new price is approximately $64.91. Similarly, should rates rise from .10 to .12, equation (3) predicts the price loss would be $5.64, which gives a new price of approximately $56.45. In the former case, the actual new price is $64.99 not $64.91; in the latter case, it is $56.74 not $56.45.[4]

Figure 3-2 indicates why these price discrepancies arise for zero coupon bonds and coupon bonds. The true relationship between a dollar price change (ΔP) and a change in interest rates (Δr) is nonlinear. This is depicted by the curved line in Figure 3-2. When graphed, the approximate price change relationship of equation (3) is a straight line tangent. This straight line approximation creates errors that grow with the magnitude of the interest rate change. One interpretation of this phenomenon is that as interest rates change, the duration of a coupon bond "drifts" away from its original value. This is but one form of duration drift; another is the tendency for durations to drift with the passage of time, a topic to be discussed in a moment.

The approximation errors just mentioned do not discredit duration analysis, at least not for option-free bonds. (The presence of call or put options increases the

[2]For ease in illustration the approximation errors for zero coupon bonds rather than coupon bonds are given. Approximation errors for coupon bonds of 5-year duration are virtually identical to those of the 5-year zero coupon bond.
[3]$\Delta P_N = -5 \times 62.09 \times (-.01)/1.10 = +\$2.82$.
[4]$\$64.99 = \$100/(1.09)^5$ and $\$56.74 = \$100/(1.12)^5$.

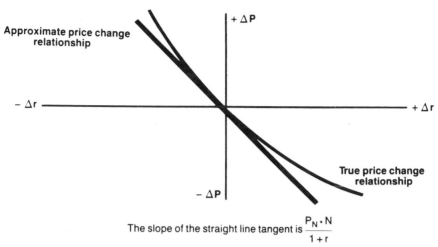

The slope of the straight line tangent is $\dfrac{P_N \cdot N}{1+r}$

Figure 3-2.   Illustration of the approximation error inherent in equation (2).

price curvature of a bond. This topic is discussed in Chapter 7.) First, these errors are quite small for moderate interest rate changes. Second, despite these errors duration accurately *indexes* or ranks the price sensitivities of any bond. All bonds with durations of N years have comparable price sensitivities. While we may not be able to quantify the exact price sensitivities from equations (3) and (4), we do unambiguously know that bonds with longer durations have more price sensitivity, and bonds with shorter durations have less.

SECTION II   HOLDING PERIOD IMMUNIZATION

Coupon bonds or series of cash flows appear to have complex holding period returns while zero coupon bonds do not. Since duration analysis characterizes any cash flow series by the term to maturity of an equivalent zero coupon bond, the holding period implications of a cash flow series is easily determined using the duration concept. This application of duration provides more powerful insights into fixed-income management than those discussed in the previous section. To set the stage we begin by analyzing holding period returns for zero coupon bonds.

The rate of return over a holding period is certain whenever the original investment is placed in zero coupon bonds maturing at the end of the holding period. The discount in the bond's price relative to its face value at the date of purchase will be exactly earned over the holding period, and this yields an annualized return determined by market conditions on the purchase date; that is, the original market interest rate has been immunized (protected) against interest rate risk. If the holding period ends before the purchased zero coupon bond matures, then holding period return becomes subject to price risk. The market price on the sale date may be insufficient to earn the return market conditions originally suggested for this holding period. If a zero coupon bond is held beyond its maturity through rolling over the maturing bond, then the realized holding period return becomes subject to reinvestment risk.[5]

Holding Period Returns for Coupon Bonds

The analysis of holding period returns for zero coupon bonds provides an intuitively appealing method for understanding the holding period returns of any security or group of securities. For simplicity in illustration assume that the yield curve is flat at 10% and that the investor has a 4-year holding period. Consider two par coupon bonds. Bond A has a maturity of four years and a duration of 3.4 years. Bond B has a maturity of 12 years and a duration of 7.2 years. Provided rates do not change, either bond will return 10% per annum over the holding period. But what are the consequences of rate changes?

Bond A does not immunize. Coupon flows received before maturity are subject to reinvestment risk, but no price risk is incurred at the end of the holding period. Thus rising (falling) rates unambiguously increase (decrease) the holding period return associated with Bond A. This is shown in Table 3-2 for both a + 100 basis point change in rates and a − 100 basis point change in rates. Bond B generates as much reinvestable income as Bond A prior to year four, and therefore it has the same reinvestment consequences as Bond A. Bond B, however, has a long term maturity and a long remaining duration at the end of year four. Its price at that point is sensitive to the then prevailing interest rate environment. This end of the holding period price effect will always have a sign opposite that of the reinvestment effect. Rising rates improve reinvestment income but lower the end of holding period price. Falling rates do just the opposite. Note that for Bond B the price effect always dominates the reinvestment effect. For example, when rates rise to 11%, price drops by $5.23 ($100 − $94.77), and reinvestment income increases a mere $.86

As the maturity of a 10% coupon bond is shortened from 12-years, the price effect noted for Bond B falls in magnitude. See Bonds C, D, and E in Table 3-2. Bond E, one with a 5-year maturity, has a price effect that just cancels the reinvestment effect whether interest rates rise or fall. Note that this bond has a duration of four years. Also, consider the price and reinvestment effects of a blend of 84% of Bond A and 16% of Bond B. The result, reported in the final column of Table 3-2, is no net interest rate risk. Interestingly, this portfolio has a duration of four years.[6]

The demonstration of the immunization characteristic of duration given in Table 3-2 has been proven by a number of authors. However, the high level of mathematical sophistication employed does little more than confirm the appealing idea that coupon bonds and portfolios of bonds behave like their zero coupon bond equivalency.

---

[5]Actually, price risk may exist as well. All dollars received from the maturing zero have reinvestment risk. If these dollars are reinvested in securities that mature beyond the terminal date of the holding period, price risk is also present.

[6]Remember that the duration of a bond portfolio is the price weighted average of their durations. Thus for a $100 total portfolio, D_p = ($84 × 3.4 years + $16 × 7.2 years)/$100 = 4 years.

Table 3-2.   Illustration of the Duration Immunization Result

	Bond A	Bond B	Bond C	Bond D	Bond E	Mix of Bonds A&B
	Characteristics for 10% Flat Yield Curve					
Maturity (Years)	4.0	12.0	10.0	7.0	5.0	84% of 4 + 16% of 12
Duration (Years)	3.4	7.2	6.5	5.2	4.0	4.0
Beginning Bond Price	$100	$100	$100	$100	$100	$100
Initial Amount	$100	$100	$100	$100	$100	$100
Promised Annual Return	10%	10%	10%	10%	10%	10%
	No Change in Interest Rate					
Bond Price After 4 Years	$100.00	$100.00	$100.00	$100.00	$100.00	$100.00
Coupon Income	$ 40.00	$ 40.00	$ 40.00	$ 40.00	$ 40.00	$ 40.00
Reinvestment Income	$ 7.75	$ 7.75	$ 7.75	$ 7.75	$ 7.75	$ 7.75
Total Value of Investment	$147.75	$147.75	$147.75	$147.75	$147.75	$147.75
Realized Annual Return	10%	10%	10%	10%	10%	10%
	Flat Yield Curve = 11%					
Bond Price After 4 Years	$100.00	$ 94.77	$ 95.69	$ 97.50	$ 99.16	$ 99.16
Coupon Income	$ 40.00	$ 40.00	$ 40.00	$ 40.00	$ 40.00	$ 40.00
Reinvestment Income	$ 8.61	$ 8.61	$ 8.61	$ 8.61	$ 8.61	$ 8.61
Total Value of Investment	$148.61	$143.38	$144.30	$146.11	$147.77	$147.77
Realized Annual Return	10.15%	9.21%	9.38%	9.71%	10.00%	10.00%
	Flat Yield Curve = 9%					
Bond Price After 4 Years	$100.00	$105.62	$104.56	$102.58	$100.90	$100.90
Coupon Income	$ 40.00	$ 40.00	$ 40.00	$ 40.00	$ 40.00	$ 40.00
Reinvestment Income	$ 6.90	$ 6.90	$ 6.90	$ 6.90	$ 6.90	$ 6.90
Total Value of Investment	$146.90	$152.52	$151.46	$149.48	$147.80	$147.80
Realized Annual Return	9.85%	10.84%	10.65%	10.31%	10.01%	10.01%

Duration Drift

The passage of time creates some difficulties for coupon bond portfolio immunization. Whether interest rates change or not, the durations of coupon bonds do not age like zero coupon bonds. This effect is shown in Figure 3-1. As time passes one moves from right to left along the horizontal time line in Figure 3-1. Zero coupon bond durations shorten year for year, as indicated by the straight diagonal line. Coupon bond durations age more slowly. This phenomenon is referred to as "duration drift" due to the passage of time.

As time passes an originally immunized coupon bond portfolio becomes more and more exposed to rate changes. The nature of the time drift causes the portfolio to be increasingly too long in the duration sense. (Price effects increasingly dominate reinvestment effects.) Thus, continuous protection of the original holding period return requires portfolio restructuring designed to shorten portfolio duration. Portfolio rebalancing need not take place continuously. In a strict sense rebalancing should be done every time cash is received but acceptable results normally accompany less frequent rebalancing.

Table 3-3. Duration Drift and Portfolio Rebalancing Under Various Interest Rate Scenarios (Examples 1, 2, and 3)

Example 1
(No Change in Interest Rate)

Portfolio Structure	Beginning of First Year		Beginning of Second Year		Beginning of Third Year		Beginning of Fourth Year	
(Par Amounts)	Duration (Years)	Allocation (Dollars)	Duration (Years)	Allocation (Dollars)	Duration (Years)	Allocation (Dollars)	Duration (Years)	Allocation (Dollars)
Original 6 Year Bond	4.65	$ 298.06	4.05	$ 276.26	3.39	$ 202.69	2.66	$ 11.96
Original 5 Year Bond	4.05	$ 350.00	3.39	$ 350.00	2.66	$ 350.00	1.86	$ 350.00
Original 4 Year Bond	3.39	$ 351.94	2.66	$ 351.94	1.86	$ 351.94	.98	$ 351.94
New 6 Month Bonds	.50	—	.50	$ 124.30	.50	$ 310.88	.50	$ 626.20
Portfolio Duration at Year Start	4.00	—	3.00	—	2.00	—	1.00	—
Portfolio Duration at Year End	3.07	—	2.18	—	1.31	—	—	—
Total Market Value	—	$1,000.00	—	$1,102.50	—	$1,215.51	—	$1,340.10
Annualized Market Value Return	—	N.A.	—	10%	—	10%	—	10%

Final Portfolio Value at End of 4th Year = $1,477.46
Annualized Market Value Return at End of 4th Year = 10.0%

Example 2
(+ 200 Basis Point Change in Rates)

Portfolio Structure	Beginning of First Year		Beginning of Second Year		Beginning of Third Year		Beginning of Fourth Year	
(Par Amounts)	Duration (Years)	Allocation (Dollars)	Duration (Years)	Allocation (Dollars)	Duration (Years)	Allocation (Dollars)	Duration (Years)	Allocation (Dollars)
Original 6 Year Bond	4.65	$ 298.06	4.01	$ 289.53	3.37	$ 214.51	2.65	$ 16.96
Original 5 Year Bond	4.05	$ 350.00	3.37	$ 350.00	2.65	$ 350.00	1.86	$ 350.00
Original 4 Year Bond	3.39	$ 351.94	2.65	$ 351.94	1.86	$ 351.94	.98	$ 351.94
New 6 Month Bonds	.50	—	.50	$ 110.90	.50	$ 297.09	.50	$ 616.30
Portfolio Duration at Year Start	4.00	—	3.00	—	2.00	—	1.00	—
Portfolio Duration at Year End	3.03	—	2.18	—	1.31	—	—	—
Total Market Value	—	$1,000.00	—	$1,042.02	—	$1,170.81	—	$1,315.52
Annualized Market Value Return	—	N.A.	—	4.2%	—	8.0%	—	9.4%

Final Portfolio Value at End of 4th Year = $1,478.11
Annualized Market Value Return at End of 4th Year = 10.0%

Table 3-3 reports three examples that illustrate the effects of portfolio rebalancing to counter the duration drift due to the passage of time. In each case a 4-year holding period is immunized with an original investment in 4-, 5-, and 6-year current coupon bonds. The yield curve is assumed to be flat at 10% as these experiments begin and unexpected rate changes are assumed to preserve the flat shape of the original curve.

Table 3-3.   (Continued)

Example 3
(Multiple Interest Rate Changes)

Portfolio Structure	Beginning of First Year		Beginning of Second Year		Beginning of Third Year		Beginning of Fourth Year	
(Par Amounts)	Duration (Years)	Allocation (Dollars)	Duration (Years)	Allocation (Dollars)	Duration (Years)	Allocation (Dollars)	Duration (Years)	Allocation (Dollars)
Original 6 Year Bond	4.65	$ 298.06	4.01	$ 289.53	3.36	$ 219.99	2.66	$ 14.32
Original 5 Year Bond	4.05	$ 350.00	3.37	$ 350.00	2.65	$ 350.00	1.86	$ 350.00
Original 4 Year Bond	3.39	$ 351.94	2.65	$ 351.94	1.86	$ 351.94	.98	$ 351.94
New 6 Month Bonds	.50	—	.50	$ 110.90	.50	$ 290.18	.50	$ 621.30
Portfolio Duration at Year Start	4.00	—	3.00	—	2.00	—	1.00	—
Portfolio Duration at Year End	3.03	—	2.18	—	1.31	—	—	—
Total Market Value	—	$1,000.00	—	$1,042.02	—	$1,148.79	—	$1,337.56
Annualized Market Value Return	—	N.A.	—	4.2%	—	7.1%	—	9.9%

Final Portfolio Value at End of 4th Year = $1,478.01
Annualized Market Value Return at End of 4th Year = 10.0%

A persistent myth is that duration analysis *requires* this unrealistic assumption about yield curve shape and movements. This frequent misconception occurs because some of the earliest work on duration made this assumption for mathematical tractability, and because introductory examples of duration analysis, such as the ones in this chapter, use this assumption for illustrative purposes. More realistic yield curve assumptions will be considered shortly.

Table 3-3 reports how portfolio structures change as time passes in order to establish the correct duration at the beginning of each year. In Example 1 immunization protection is not needed as rates are assumed to remain constant at 10%. This example provides a benchmark portfolio turnover rate for comparative purposes. Throughout the three examples in Table 3-3, coupon income and maturing investments are placed in 6-month securities to shorten portfolio duration without unduly large liquidations of longer duration securities. Notice that rebalancing does not cause substantial investment turnover and that the originally promised 10% return is realized. The strategy of investing cash receipts in short-term securities, however, to minimize liquidations of longer duration securities has some undesirable characteristics that will be discussed in the upcoming material on aberrations in yield curve changes.

Example 2 gives a comparable rebalancing analysis when a single interest rate change of +200 basis points occurs just after the original portfolio is purchased. Notice that the needed rebalancing does not depart substantially from the benchmark established in Example 1. Again, at the end of the four years, the portfolio has generated a 10% annual return.

Multiple changes in interest rates are more likely than a single one. Example 3 illustrates the structure and performance of an immunized portfolio, rebalanced once per year, when interest rates change in the following fashion:

Beginning of year 1 rates change from	10% to 12%
Beginning of year 2 rates change from	12% to 13%
Beginning of year 3 rates change from	13% to 11%
Beginning of year 4 rates change from	11% to 9%
End of year 4 rates change from	9% to 7%

Once again portfolio rebalancing occurs primarily through coupons and maturing bond reinvestments. Despite all the interest rate changes, including a large change near the end of the holding period, the realized return is 10%.

Aberrations in Yield Curve Changes

The duration formula given in equation (1) is referred to as Macaulay's duration. The mathematical form of this duration measure, which was the first invented and remains the simplest to compute, implicitly relies on two assumptions: the yield curve is flat and random events cause this yield curve to shift upward or downward in a parallel fashion. Rarely in history has either assumption held. The offsetting advantage of Macaulay's duration is the relative ease of computation.

Applications of Macaulay's duration in instances where yield curves are not flat or are flat but shift in a nonparallel fashion cause the duration calculations to be mis-estimated. The magnitude of the error depends on the extent of the violations of the assumptions. Yet in instances where each cash inflow matches a cash outflow, the duration of the assets is misestimated by exactly as much as the duration of the liabilities. *No net error* arises from the use of an inappropriate duration formula. Hence the measurement error also increases for duration-matched situations with the size of the divergence from exact cash flow matching. For example, a portfolio with $50 in 1-year and $50 in 7-year zero coupon bonds that fund a $100 4-year zero coupon loan has more potential for risk mismeasurement than a 4-year bond that funds a 5-year coupon bond with a 4-year duration. Both asset/liability mixes have matched 4-year durations but the first case has less closely matched cash flows.

Many institutions with matched or closely matched durations have assets and liabilities with reasonably closely matched cash flows. For these institutions the issue of which duration formula most closely associates in its assumptions with economic reality has relatively minor importance. Instances can occur, however, when duration-matched institutions find themselves substantially cash flow mismatched. Sandford Rose in his column in the *American Banker* of October 9, 1983 suggests making fixed-rate mortgages funded by duration-matched 5-year zero coupon Certificates of Deposit (CDs). These substantially cash flow mismatched securities introduce the potential for sizable misestimation of risk exposures using Macaulay's duration.

Much more realistic duration measures must be employed when taking on these contrasting security types.[7]

When neither durations nor cash flows match, the measurement errors from the
use of inappropriate duration formulas become more of a problem. But in such instances these errors may be of relatively small concern to some risk managers. The
misestimated duration gaps still reflect the direction of the rate sensitivity and
roughly quantify the exposure; that is, in these circumstances any duration measure
will signal this exposure, and interest rate hedges based on these numbers will reduce
interest rate risk. The remaining mismatches will now be smaller, and therefore, less
subject to *net* measurement errors.

The use of inappropriate duration formulas has the most serious consequences for
aggressive risk managers. These managers forecast rates and adopt nontrivial interest
rate exposures based on these forecasts. Misestimated durations lead these managers
to believe they are at one position in a risk-return tradeoff when they may be at quite
different positions, presumably less desirable ones given their revealed preferences.
They may even find the entire set of risk-return tradeoffs to be much different than
they supposed.

Value can be added by employing more realistic duration formulas than Macaulay's duration. The alternatives distinguish themselves by making more realistic assumptions about the shape of the current yield curve and about how random events
influence it. Second generation duration formulas use the term structure of interest
rates, which can be thought of as the yield curve for zero coupon bonds, to discount
individual cash flows rather than the yield to maturity used to discount all cash flows
in Macaulay's formula. The assumed random processes of these duration measures
remain relatively simplistic. Some formulas assume that random events shift the term
structure, which can take on any shape—as can the associated yield curve, in ways
that preserve its current shape. Others assume short-term rates are more volatile than
long-term rates when the term structure is inverted, but less volatile otherwise. Still
others require short-term rate volatility to be some fixed multiple of long-term rate
volatility.[8] Third generation duration measures use term structures rather than yield
curves and assume the historically average volatilities of the term structure rates hold
with certainty in the future. Fourth generation measures of interest rate sensitivity
allow short-term rates to be influenced by different random events than longer-term
rates. Fourth generation measures are the only ones that have a chance of providing

---

[7]These two securities also have substantially different rates of duration drift which complicates risk control by requiring extensive rebalancing transactions to keep asset and liability durations, however measured, in line with one another as time passes.

[8]The details of second generation duration formulas are given in G.O. Bierwag, G.G. Kaufman, and
A.L. Toevs, "Duration: Its Uses in Bond Portfolio Management," *Financial Analysts Journal* (July/
August 1983). Second generation duration formulas differ from Macaulay's formula first by the use of
the term structure for cash flow discounting. They also weight the discounted cash flows by a function
of the time to receipt of this cash rather than just the length of time to the receipt of cash, as used in
Macaulay's formula.

full protection against changes in interest rates that cause short-term rates to move in the opposite direction of long-term rates.

Practitioners should use at least second generation duration formulas, preferably third generation ones. The academic work on fourth generation measures of interest rate sensitivity (multifactor duration measures) has yet to establish their superiority in practice. Successful multifactor risk models may be derived, but for now the relevant risk factors remain to be discovered. Remember, though, the value of making duration formulas more esoteric diminishes quickly for institutions that desire to minimize their interest rate risk.

Portfolio Optimization

A logical question to ask at this point is, why not buy zero coupon bonds if immunized returns are the goal? This strategy eliminates rebalancing problems and the risk associated with using the wrong duration formula.

Four factors limit the use of zero coupon bonds. First, the proper zero coupon bond may not exist or may not exist in sufficient quantities to offer the same yield as a coupon bond portfolio of similar duration. Second, many longer term zeros are privately placed or otherwise have limited secondary markets. The illiquidity of these instruments may constrain an early sale of the portfolio should such an unexpected need arise. Third, tax preference zero coupon bonds exist but this market is illiquid and most issues are housing bonds, which limit the diversification of sector risks. Fourth, appropriate credit quality and diversification of default risk may be unavailable in zero coupon bonds subject to default. Nevertheless sufficient advantages remain so that zero coupon bonds should always be considered for inclusion in an immunized portfolio.

The issues raised in the last several pages were structured to leave the reader with an impression that immunized portfolio construction must be executed carefully. This was done because there are many portfolio managers who offer naively conceived immunization services. One area where this naivety becomes most apparent is in the stated promised return from an immunized strategy. Financial theory suggests that only one rate is promised: the rate of return available on a default-free zero coupon bond with a maturity equal to the holding period. In general, this rate is not the yield to maturity of a 5-year coupon bond nor is it, strictly speaking, the yield to maturity of a 5-year duration coupon bond. Furthermore, the promised rate does not come from a "rolling down the yield curve" assumption. Any rate in excess of the promised rate as defined above, which can be easily *derived* from a current coupon Treasury yield curve, simply cannot be guaranteed.

An often encountered promised return is derived from portfolios of bonds subject to default risk. This inflates the "available" return. Implicit in the claim that this return is available is a belief that bonds used in the portfolio will not be downgraded by changes in market assessment of default probabilities. If confidence in this claim on default risk management exists, then such is the promised return. But the promise is a dichotomous one involving both interest rate risk and default risk minimization.

The promised rate of return as stated above ignores several real world constraints that must be addressed in properly constructed immunization routines. These can cause the effective promised return to lie below the hypothetical zero coupon bond rate. Without explicit and sophisticated treatment of these constraints, one purchases ill-specified portfolio strategy advice. Remember that an immunized portfolio synthetically constructs zero coupon bonds. In this construction, however, coupon reinvestment and duration drift corrections generate transaction costs. The risk of a misused duration formula is also present, as are tax effects, market illiquidity, and market gapping. Against these effects, which can reduce the actual returns from an immunized portfolio, is the possibility that the manager can occasionally discover overpriced securities to swap for underpriced ones. Thus the promised rate of return as stated in prior paragraphs is a static concept, but in reality it is a dynamic one. The effective immunized rate of return depends upon market events and the sophistication with which the portfolio is optimized. This reasoning leads in only one direction. The selection of immunization managers should be based not on their claims for the level of promised returns but on their track records in credit analysis and portfolio optimization techniques as practiced in a dynamic rate risk minimization setting.

Empirical Results

How well does duration analysis work in bond portfolio immunization? A number of authors have studied the ability of coupon bonds to replicate the holding period returns of hypothetical "bogey" zero coupon bonds.[9] These tests rely on two sources of historical bond price data: Durand's series for prime corporate bonds and the Center for Research in Security Prices (CRSP) series on U.S. Treasury securities. It should be noted that returns in excess of those reported below are systematically available when proper portfolio optimization techniques are employed.

Briefly there are four important findings in empirical tests of duration analysis. (1) Portfolios that maintain a match between duration and time remaining in the holding period have less holding period risks than simpler hedging strategies, such as continuously rolling over short-term securities or exclusive purchase of bonds maturing at the end of the holding period (maturity matched strategy). (2) Because aberrations in yield curves occur with regularity, duration-matched strategies do not immunize returns perfectly. But if care is taken in portfolio selection and rebalancing, then stochastic process risk exerts a relatively small influence on returns. Since 1954, for example, rates of return in duration-matched portfolios fall within five basis points of the true immunized return at least 80% of the time for 10-year holding periods and 95% of the time for 5-year holding periods. (3) The duration measure given in equation (1) performs almost as well as the more complicated duration measures that are consistent with more realistic assumptions about yield curves and their movements. (4) The three prior conclusions hold over a number of experiments using different sets of data and several empirical techniques employed to derive bond yield

[9]See papers by Brennan and Schwartz; Nelson and Schaeffer; Bierwag, Kaufman, and Toevs; and Babbel in *Innovations in Bond Portfolio Management* (Greenwich, CT: JAI Press, 1983).

curves.[10] Thus portfolios constructed using duration-matched strategies appear to immunize portfolio returns with a large measure of certainty.

Multiple Holding Periods

The prior immunization examples presume that the investor has a single terminal investment date. This date may coincide with the maturity date of a liability or it may be that a corporate cash pool manager decided to lock up today's 4-year yield rather than the yield for some other period of time.

All or even most investors do not have single holding periods. Corporate cash pools may be held to fund a series of payments for the acquisition of a company, the funding of repetitive capital investments, and provision of future working capital at different stages in a forecasted business cycle, and so on. Financial institutions also face a series of dates on which they have to discharge liabilities.

Portfolio managers concerned with multiple outflows can fund and immunize each one separately. The most obvious strategy matches the cash flows generated by an asset portfolio with the cash flows required by the liabilities. Even if feasible, such a dedicated cash flow strategy is complex and restrictive. A more flexible alternative funds the liabilities and matches the duration of the assets with the duration of the liabilities. Here cash inflows may not occur on the liability dates, but the average inflow date matches the average outflow date. Issues of portfolio optimization arise in this context to an even greater extent than in the single holding period case. Chapter 10 discusses the issues that arise in this context in detail. To provide some of the flavor of the use of duration in financial institutions, Section III presents some of the basics.

SECTION III   IMMUNIZATION IN FINANCIAL INSTITUTIONS

Financial institutions might best be viewed as "net bonds." Equity claimants own the net cash flow pattern generated by existing assets and liabilities. Understanding the interest rate risk of the market value of these net cash flows is of singular importance in managing any financial institution. This rate risk constitutes most of the stock price risk of these institutions. Also, the market value of equity serves as a leading indicator of future income flows and future book values: Equity rate risk exposure signals the possibility of variations in future income and book value.

The net cash flows constituting equity claims have a duration. Through diligent asset/liability management, this duration can be made to take on any value. Consider, for example, a financial institution with an equity duration equal to zero. This duration indicates no price sensitivity. (See equations (3) and (4).) Thus the market value of equity cannot fall below its current level as interest rates change. Equity

---

[10]A paper by J.E. Ingersoll in *Innovations in Bond Portfolio Management* provides one exception to these findings. He uses an unusual yield curve model, which may be the cause of his slightly less favorable results.

behaves like overnight money; interest rate changes do not affect principal value, but earnings on equity are highly rate sensitive. Alternatively, suppose the duration of assets and equity are equal. Equation (4) indicates that asset and equity market values will move in equal proportions when rates change. Thus this duration match creates a constant market value of assets to equity ratio. Another possibility structures the duration of equity to establish a fixed dividend payout rate for a given period (duration) of time.

The possible duration strategies discussed in the last paragraph illustrate an important but overlooked fact. There exists no single defensible hedge for financial institutions. Institutions having an equity duration matched with that of the assets, and institutions having a zero equity duration can both be promoted as interest rate risk free. This fact may well become a nail in the coffin of recent proposals to require that banks and thrifts pay interest rate risk adjusted deposit insurance premiums.

The characteristics of the various possible equity hedges given above do differ. A decided advantage of an asset/liability management technique based on duration is that this approach reveals these differences. In turn, this analysis provokes healthy discussions on risk preferences and hedging characteristics that must be antecedent, whatever the asset/liability approach, to asset and liability allocation.

SECTION IV FINANCIAL FUTURES CONTRACTS

Bond portfolios or financial institution balance sheets may be influenced by the presence of contracts for future delivery of financial securities. These "derivative" securities have much to recommend them, so much so that they are treated at length in Chapters 4 and 8. We provide here a brief summary of the issues related to duration.

Futures contracts involve a commitment to purchase or sell a security (the deliverable) at a stated price on some future date. The price established in the contract is the price of the deliverable expected to prevail on the delivery date. On the origination date, the futures contract does not alter the current cash value of the portfolio.[11] As time passes, however, interest rates may change unexpectedly. This changes the price of the deliverable security that is expected to prevail on the delivery date. The difference between the prior expected delivery price and the new one results in a profit or loss on the day it is first noted, not on the delivery date. (Accounting conventions may delay the public revelation of this profit or loss, but they do not change the economic import of this fact.) This daily marking-to-market increases or decreases the total value of the portfolio. We shall see that the extent of the profit or loss depends in part upon the duration characteristics of the deliverable security.

Figure 3-3a illustrates how a purchased (long) futures contract alters the interest rate sensitivity of a cash portfolio. For simplicity assume the yield curve is flat at

[11]The form of the cash portfolio may be altered somewhat to establish the initial margin required by the relevant futures exchange.

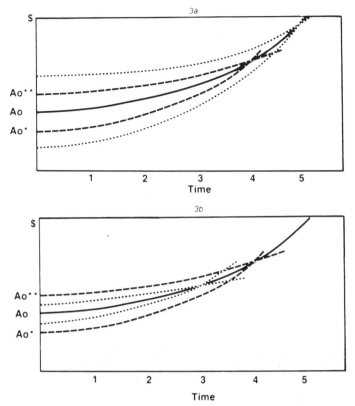

Figure 3-3. Growth paths of cash portfolios versus cash and futures portfolios.

In both graphs, the solid line represents the total portfolio growth path for a portfolio of A_0 dollars invested in cash and futures securities. This growth path occurs when rates do not change unexpectedly.

In both graphs, the lower dashed line represents the cash portion of the total portfolio growth path given that rates rise unexpectedly. This rate increase is assumed to occur just after the portfolio is acquired. The difference between A_0 and A_0^* gives the immediate decline in cash value due to the rate increase. The upper line similarly reports the cash portion of the total portfolio growth path given that rates fall unexpectedly. The difference between A_0 and A_0^{**} gives the immediate increase in cash securities value from the rate decline.

The dotted lines in the upper graph show how long futures positions exacerbate the immediate effects of rate increases and declines on cash security values. The dotted lines in the lower graph show how short futures positions mitigate the immediate effects of rate increases and declines on cash security values.

10%. If rates never change, then as time passes the cash portfolio grows along the solid line from an initial investment of A_0 dollars at a 10% growth rate. Since no dollar costs are incurred from a futures position until rates change unexpectedly, this growth path is also that of a combined cash and futures position.

For simplicity assume only one unexpected rate change occurs, and it does so just after the portfolio is formed. If rates rise unexpectedly, then the *cash* portion of the portfolio falls in market value from A_0 to A_0^* dollars. Reinvestment occurs at a higher rate so eventually the cash value catches up and crosses the solid line. This is depicted in Figure 3-3a by the lower dashed (not dotted) line. Conversely let rates fall. This causes an immediate increase in the market value of the cash portfolio from A_0 to A_0^{**} dollars. Subsequent reinvestment income is not as great as before and so the growth path for the cash portfolio, given by the upper dashed line, again crosses the solid line. Notice that the two dashed lines intersect the solid line at the same date. This date corresponds to the original duration length of the portfolio.

The analysis to this point merely reviews the concept of immunization, although it does so in a slightly different manner than given previously. Now consider the added influence of a long futures contract. Suppose rates rise. This causes the expected future delivery price to fall. This decline must be paid today by the holder of the futures contract. (The holder of the long contract will receive upon delivery something less valuable than previously thought. By the rules of the game this loss must be realized today.) The total portfolio value becomes smaller than A_0^* dollars today. The extent of this reduction depends upon a number of factors to be discussed shortly. As was the case for the all cash portfolio, the rate increase quickens reinvestment income relative to that experienced when rates were unchanged. The lower dotted line in Figure 3-3a is the result. Suppose rates fall. Now the long futures position generates an immediate dollar profit and total portfolio value grows along the upper dotted line in Figure 3-3a. The two dotted lines cross the solid one at the same time but at a date farther into the future than was the case for the cash portfolio. This demonstrates that the inclusion of long future contracts lengthens the duration of a cash portfolio.

Figure 3-3b illustrates how a written (short) futures contract alters the interest rate sensitivity of a cash portfolio. The solid and dashed lines are interpreted exactly as in Figure 3-3a. The lower dotted line is the growth path of a portfolio of cash and *short* futures positions when rates rise. (Rising rates generate profits to writers of futures contracts.) The upper dotted line gives the total portfolio growth path should rates fall. The conclusion: short futures contracts shorten the duration of the cash portfolio.

The amount of leverage undertaken in the futures market helps determine the extent to which duration is altered in a cash portfolio. Five other factors are influential. These are:

1. The cash flow characteristics of the deliverable security.
2. The current yield curve and its implied schedules of forward interest rates.
3. The delivery date of the futures contract.
4. The stochastic process (form of uncertainty) governing interest rate uncertainty.
5. Differential credit risks of the security and the deliverable security associated with the futures contract.

A lengthy and complex discussion is needed to reveal the full importance of each factor. This cannot be done here. Our more modest goal is to describe approximately how each factor enters the analysis. The price of a futures contract depends upon the promised cash flows of the deliverable security (factor (1)) and on forward interest rates, that is, the interest rates currently expected to prevail on the delivery rate. The relevant forward rates depend upon factors (2) and (3). Futures prices change whenever forward interest rates change. These new rates depend upon the delivery date of the contract (factor (3)), which sets the starting date for forward rate calculations, and upon the new spot interest rates as determined by the stochastic process (factor (4)). They also depend upon when the futures contract ends (factor (3)). These delivery date price changes are marked to market and cause portfolio value to be altered as shown in Figure 3–3. The final factor, one of particular importance in many situations, is hedging a portfolio that may suffer from losses in value due to a revision of credit quality of the securities. This aspect of hedging is treated in Chapter 8.

How changes in current spot rates alter forward rates and futures prices has not been properly explored in the duration literature. This work has consistently made the assumption, either explicitly or implicitly, that the stochastic process causes current spot rates to change proportionally. Under this assumption the relationship between unexpected changes in current and forward rates is simplified and factor (3) becomes unimportant. The result is the following formula for the duration of a portfolio of cash and futures:

$$D_p = D_c + D_f \frac{V_f}{V_c} \qquad (5)$$

where D_p is the total portfolio duration; D_c is the duration of the cash portfolio measured from today's date, which has a value of V_c; D_f is the duration of the deliverable security underlying the futures contract *computed from point of delivery forward* using forward rates in any discounting; and V_f is the value of the deliverable securities at the delivery date (positive for long positions and negative for short positions).[12] The duration of the deliverable security, computed from the date of delivery forward enters into equation (4) to measure the interest rate sensitivity of the delivery price to unexpected changes in forward interest rates. The ratio (V_f/V_c) indicates the amount of leverage introduced into the portfolio by the inclusion of futures contracts.[13] This leverage determines the amount of price sensitivity introduced into the total portfolio by the futures position.

Reconsider Figure 3-3a where we examined a cash portfolio with a duration of four years. The futures position changed D_c from four years to a portfolio duration (D_p) of five years. Suppose V_c were \$100 and V_f were \$400. With these numbers it

---

[12]These points about the current dates from which durations are computed is treated, ambiguously at best, in R.W. Kolb, *Interest Rates Futures: A Comprehensive Introduction* (Richmond, VA: R.F. Dame, Inc., 1982) and R.W. Kolb, and R. Chiang, "Duration, Immunization, and Hedging with Interest Rate Futures," *Financial Management* (Autumn 1981).

[13]This formula is intuitively appealing. A total of V_c dollars is currently in the portfolio. This amount includes the value of the margin account. The price weighted average duration of the two instruments in the portfolio can be viewed as it was when the duration of two coupon bonds was discussed. That is, $D_p = (V_c D_c + D_f V_f)/V_c$. V_f is not the margin account value. It is the *expected* delivery value of the futures position.

is possible to back out the duration of the deliverable contract from equation (4). It is .25 years, which is consistent with a 90-day T-bill futures contract. If V_f were $12.50 instead of $400, then the D_f is eight years. This duration might be that of the cheapest to deliver security associated with a T-bond futures contract.

Equation (4) changes in two respects when the stochastic process does not alter spot rates proportionally. First, the formulas used to compute D_c and D_f must be made consistent with the new stochastic process. This adjustment is exactly like that needed to compute correctly the duration of an all cash portfolio when the stochastic process assumption changed. Second, and this is a new result, one must also adjust D_f for the time to delivery. The form of this adjustment depends upon the stochastic process assumed. Thus the duration of a combined cash and futures position continues to depend upon the separate durations of the constituent cash and futures securities. Stochastic process risk, however, takes on new importance when the portfolio includes futures instruments. This type of risk alters the price sensitivity characteristics of the futures position to a greater extent than the cash position. This differential effect means the effective exposure of a cash and futures position to stochastic process risk exceeds that of an all cash portfolio of equal duration.

One final comment needs to be made about incorporating futures in cash portfolios. Because forward commitments can be made with little cash outlay, relatively large changes in the duration of the cash portfolio are possible when futures contracts are included. The ability to use futures to lengthen durations is particularly useful for investors with very long holding periods and for investors with 7-to 10-year holding periods in high interest rate environments. In the latter case there may not be enough or even any bonds with duration longer than seven years when interest rates are high. However, large positions in futures relative to cash greatly increase the investor's risk of default. The leverage of such a position exposes the investors to the risk that a margin call could wipe out the entire cash portfolio.

SECTION V   RISK-RETURN ANALYSIS

The previous three sections focused on methods to immunize interest rate risk. Some investors may wish to achieve a higher return than that promised by the immunized strategy and are willing to adopt interest rate risk in attempts to do so. These investors pursue "active" strategies by forecasting interest rates and then positioning their portfolios to benefit from these forecasts. One caveat is in order: Duration theory assumes that current interest rates impound the market concensus interest rate forecast; the forward rates imbedded in current spot interest rates are expected to be realized in the duration formulation. Unexpected rate changes are those that alter these forward rates rather than those that realize them. Thus an investor should use duration analysis for active management only if his forecasted rates differ from forward rates.

Investors cannot determine whether or not they should follow risky strategies until the tradeoff between expected added return and increased risk has been established. The interest rate risk-return tradeoff objectively determines the price of expected added returns earned from betting on interest rate forecasts. Investors use these prices in conjunction with their subjectively determined risk tolerances to determine the extent to which active strategies will be followed.

Holding Period Risks

The first step in determining the interest rate risk-return tradeoff is the computation of holding period returns for various investments and rate forecasts. Holding period returns depend upon how far the duration, D, of the investment(s) departs from the length of the holding period, HP. The shorter D is relative to HP, the shorter the zero coupon bond equivalence relative to the maturity of the immunizing zero coupon bond, and the larger the reinvestment exposure relative to the price exposure. The longer D is relative to HP, the longer the zero coupon bond equivalence relative to the maturity of the immunizing zero coupon bond, and the larger the price risk exposure relative to reinvestment exposure.

An appealing risk formulation that is surprisingly accurate in practice is the following:[14]

$$r_R = \frac{D}{\text{HP}} \times r_p + \frac{(\text{HP} - D)}{\text{HP}} \times r^* \qquad (6)$$

where r_R denotes the realized annual interest rate for the holding period, r_p is the initially promised or expected interest rate for HP periods, and r^* is a possible HP period interest rate forecasted by the investor.

If D equals HP, then equation (6) correctly indicates that r_R equals r_p. If D is less than HP, then the portfolio earns r_p for $D/$HP portion of the holding period and r^* for the remaining portion. For example, suppose r^* equals .12. If $D = 2$ years and HP $= 4$ years then r_R becomes .11 (11%). Alternatively, suppose D is greater than HP. The realized return will be $r_p \times (D/\text{HP})$, subject to a correction given by the second term in Equation (6). This correction occurs because of the price effect of portfolio liquidation after HP years have passed. For example, let $r_p = .10$, $r^* = .12$, $D = 6$ years, and HP $= 4$ years, then r_R becomes .09. The realized rate is less than .10 because after four years pass we sell a nonmaturing bond in an environment with higher rates than when the bond was purchased.

Equation (6) is a surprisingly accurate approximation that provides an intuitively appealing method of determining holding period returns for nonimmunized portfolios. This formula reminds us that the influence of forecasted changes in interest rates increases as D departs in either direction from HP.

If an investor expects interest rates to rise during the holding period by more than the market consensus forecast, then equation (6) indicates that holding period returns will increase the smaller D is relative to HP. Setting duration shorter than the length of the holding period allows the average dollar invested to be rolled over into higher

---

[14]Gilford Babcock devised this formula which has been recently published in "Duration as a Link Between Yield and Value," *Journal of Portfolio Management* (Fall 1984).

rates during the holding period; the quicker, the better. Conversely, if an investor expects interest rates to fall relative to the market concensus forecast, then the investor should set D greater than HP to gain extra holding period returns from portfolio price appreciation at liquidation.[15]

Risk-Return Tradeoffs

Few investors are willing to structure a portfolio based on one rate forecast. But many investors may be willing to suggest a number of interest rate possibilities and assign probabilities to their outcomes. For any D and HP selected, each rate forecast generates a holding period return. These returns, once weighted by their probabilities of occurrence and the results summed, give the expected return of the strategy. Furthermore, the variation of possible returns around the probability-weighted return can be computed as an index of risk.

Figure 3-4 presents an interest rate risk-return tradeoff. It was constructed using the holding period return approximation formula given by equation (6) and a small set of rate forecasts. In Figure 3-4 we have rates forecasted to fall short of the market expectation by 100 basis points with 80% probability and to exceed the market expectation by 100 basis points with 20% probability. The vertical axis measures the expected returns of these two possibilities. The risk (variation) is graphed on the horizontal axis. Because the figure is computed for an investor with a 5-year holding period, the riskless strategy has a duration of five years. The market promises an annual 12% return to the immunized portfolio.

The more the portfolio duration departs from five years, the more risk is undertaken. Under our assumption that the investor believes a rate decline is more likely than a rate rise, risk taking is productive (returns increase) when the duration of the portfolio exceeds five years. Short duration portfolios increase risk by creating the wrong type of interest rate sensitivity relative to the rate forecasts. These portfolios are said to be inefficient. Notice that it is the duration of the portfolio that positions the interest rate risk-return characteristics of the strategy. Duration summarizes all relevant details of coupon rates, maturities, and so on of the securities in the portfolio.

By studying portfolio outcomes as duration departs year by year from the length of the holding period, one measures the incremental risk for incremental expected return. These increments provide a means by which investors can determine the appropriate durations of their portfolios given their risk preferences. Increments in added expected return are adopted one by one until the next increment has a price measured in additional risks that the investor feels is unjustifiably high. Thus the objectively determined risk-return tradeoff suggests a price schedule of returns while the subjectively determined risk tolerances of the investor dictate how much return

---

[15]Equation (6) also reminds us that the risk exposure to *unforecasted* changes in interest rates depends upon how far D departs from *HP*. Notice that in this context bonds of various durations are inherently neither risky nor nonrisky. Riskiness can only be assessed after the holding period is determined. Long bonds are risky when the holding period is short but not when it is long.

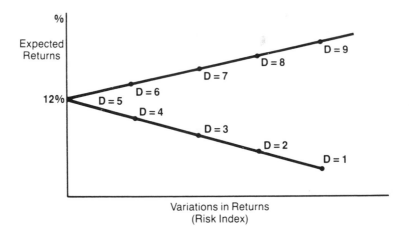

This figure is constructed using Equation (6) and the
presumption that a rate decline of 100 basis points is
expected with 80% probability, and a rate increase of 100
basis points is expected with 20% probability. Let the
probability of the rate decline increase. The upper section
of the tradeoff will rotate counterclockwise, keeping the
same anchor point or immunized return. (The lower section
rotates clockwise.)   Should this rotation occur, portfolios
with long durations improve in expected returns as risks
decline. That is, the same strategy becomes less risky when
rate forecasts become more certain.

Figure 3-4.   Interest rate risk versus expected return tradeoff from active strategies.

to buy at these prices. Some investors will pick the immunized point, others will
maximize the difference between portfolio duration and the length of the holding
period, and still others will choose durations between these extremes.

Two final points must be made. First, if probable rate increases are equal in magnitude to probable rate declines, then the risk-return tradeoff will be a horizontal line.
This indicates that when an investor has no confidence in his or her net rate forecasts,
no added return is expected from adopting active strategies. Risk, however, increases
with the departure of portfolio duration from the length of the holding period. Risk
averse investors would immunize in this situation. Second, the probability weights
assigned to the various rate forecasts may be in error, as might be the forecasts themselves. The investor may misestimate the probability distribution of possible rate outcomes and/or the sizes of interest rate changes. If misestimation occurs, the expected
risk-return tradeoff is not the true one and expected returns from active strategies
may prove illusionary. However, a particularly important idea is that the immunizing
point on the incorrect tradeoff will have the same position in the true tradeoff.

Portfolio Insurance

In Chapter 5 an expanded form of risk-return analysis, termed portfolio insurance,
is discussed. The result is an understanding that dynamic strategies, rather than the

more static ones described above, create specialized outcomes not otherwise available. These new strategies, which use much of the previous analysis, synthetically construct and then track option-like outcomes. Of particular note is the ability of dynamic strategies to create a protective put investment. In equities this strategy involves the purchase of a stock and a put option. The put prevents the total portfolio value from falling below some value (the put strike price) as long as the put has not expired. In bond portfolios relevant put options may not be available, available only in thinly traded markets, or have expiration dates shorter than the length of the holding period. Nevertheless, the outcome of a protective put, where the strike price may be better viewed as establishing a minimum rate of return, can be synthetically constructed using the theory of options and an understanding of duration.

Dynamically constructed protective put strategies form a type of portfolio insurance. They do so by altering the range of possible outcomes from an actively managed bond portfolio. In exchange for a portion of the returns when active strategies perform well, the investor acquires a guarantee that portfolio returns will not fall below a minimum rate. The full development of these ideas cannot be given here, but the basic idea can be quickly described.

Bond portfolio insurance is created synthetically by trading strategies involving a risky and a riskless portfolio. The riskless portfolio must be able to assure the minimum return selected by the investor for his or her holding period. This comes from an immunized portfolio, for no other is riskless in a holding period context. The risky portfolio must have a duration that departs from the length of the holding period to provide upside potential.

To relate portfolio insurance to the risk-return tradeoffs discussed previously, consider an investor who immunizes. This investor implicitly purchases the maximum put option protection available for the holding period. (This strategy yields the maximum value of possible minimum returns.) Such a highly protective put is expensive; all possible upside gains are "paid" to acquire the option. On the other hand, an investor who maximizes the difference between portfolio duration and the length of the holding period buys the least amount of portfolio insurance. Between these extremes, the closer duration is to the length of the holding period, the greater the option protection being purchased.

Portfolio insurance strategies are dynamic. The mix between risky and riskless portfolios, that is, portfolio duration, will be adjusted over time to replicate the protective put option. If the investor's rate forecasts prove out, then a greater percentage of the portfolio is allocated to the risky strategy. Conversely, poor performance necessitates an increase in the allocation to the riskless portfolio. Note that the trading strategy disciplines the active risk manager. More risks can be taken on only when prior successes provide the "chips" with which the risk taker places any subsequent interest rate forecast bets.

SECTION VI   UNCERTAIN HOLDING PERIODS

Fixed-income managers often do not know the exact length of their holding periods. Moreover, the effective maturity dates of some assets may be uncertain. Both possibilities create problems in the construction of immunized and active strategies. Apparently immunized financial institutions or bond portfolios become unwittingly exposed to interest rate changes. Active strategies may become more active than desired or may fail to beat the market when investors correctly forecast interest rates. The following analyses reveal that these problems can only be partially minimized.

Two forms of holding period and/or maturity uncertainty exist. The first arises because the assets acquired or the liabilities funded have interest rate dependent maturity dates. Examples include corporate bonds and fixed-rate mortgages issued with call options and consumer Certificates of Deposit issued with early redemption at par (put) options. These options have values that depend upon interest rate levels and can shorten or lengthen the associated asset or liability effective life. The second type of holding period uncertainty comes from the randomness of investment horizons. Actuarial assumptions may be proven to be incorrect in pension funds. Corporate cash pools might be liquidated early or late in the process of finding and making an acquisition, and so on.

Interest Rate Dependent Cash Flows

Securities held or issued may have associated put or call options. Some securities have both! Proper treatment of these securities in a risk controlled strategy requires that the associated put or call be studied as a security in its own right. The following analysis shows how one might approach this type of interest rate risk control in a duration framework. The asset used in this presentation is a fixed-rate mortgage with prepayment rights. The analysis is cursory but the thrust of it suggests how one might improve the approach as well as extend treatment to securities associated with other options. Chapter 7 extends this work.

A purchased mortgage is really two securities. The first is the asset consisting of an amortizing mortgage presumed to pay according to contractual terms until maturity. The second is a liability created by writing a call option to the borrower. The current market price of all *contracted* mortgage payments exceeds that of a comparable mortgage issued with no call. The difference reflects the market assessment of the value of the call. Thus, the total price of the mortgage with prepayment rights (P_T) is the price of the noncallable mortgage (P_D) which is the deliverable security should the call be exercised, less the price of the option (P_O).

If one wishes to understand the interest rate risk of the fixed-rate mortgage, the interest rate sensitivities of both securities must be determined. These sensitivities can be determined using the concept of duration. The duration of the noncallable mortgage is easily computed: assume all promised cash flows to maturity are certain and then employ the duration formula consistent with the assumed stochastic process. The duration of a call option depends upon how its value changes when interest rates change. This sensitivity can be discovered in a number of ways. For example, one might employ an options pricing model. Alternatively, one might study the sensitivity of the total mortgage price to recent interest rate changes. The option price sensitivity is what remains after the total price change is subtracted from the price change of the deliverable security. Regardless of the approach used, the resulting option value sensitivity is equated to the sensitivity of a zero coupon bond. The duration of this bond is that of the option.

The duration of a portfolio of securities is the price weighted sum of the individual security durations. Thus, the duration of a mortgage with prepayment rights is:

$$D_T = \frac{P_D \times D_D - P_O \times D_O}{P_D - P_O} \tag{7}$$

where D_D is the duration of the noncallable (deliverable) mortgage and D_O is the duration of the option. The negative signs in the equation indicate that the option security in this ''portfolio'' was sold. Rate increases cause the option to increase in value but cause the deliverable mortgage to decrease in value. One rate sensitivity offsets the other to a degree. Deep out-of-the-money options have little value and their price sensitivities for moderate rate changes are low. Thus the mortgage is likely to reach its full maturity, and therefore the mortgage duration is approximately the duration of the deliverable security. Conversely, it can be shown that deep in-the-money options have price sensitivities such that $P_O \times D_O$ nearly equals $P_D \times D_D$. In the context of equation (6) this implies that the duration of the mortgage is very close to zero. This conclusion about the value of D_T is sensible. Mortgages with high contractual interest rates are effectively short-term securities in low-rate environments.

A full treatment of the interest rate risk of options issued in conjunction with mortgage and other securities cannot be given here. Among issues ignored for the time being are (1) the leverage available in options; (2) the duration drift characteristics of options; (3) differentiating between the durations of American and European options;[16] (4) the greater sensitivity of option durations to current interest rates than other securities.[17]

Random Holding Periods

Holding period uncertainties can arise for reasons other than interest rate dependent cash flows. Because the sources of these uncertainties are less quantifiable than those of security options, less can be done with this problem. Nonetheless random holding periods can at least be partially analyzed.

The possibility of unexpectedly early portfolio liquidation normally creates more trepidation in investors than does unexpectedly late liquidation. The former may occur in rising rate environments and cause visible reported capital losses. In falling rate environments, late liquidation may cause rates of return to fall by as much as could be experienced in an early sale at higher rates. But the losses are ones of op-

---

[16]American options can be exercised prior to expiration while European options cannot. (A callable corporate bond has a European option.)

[17]The truncated return profile of options, that is, their absolute minimum return characteristics, means these securities are more curved with respect to interest rates than other fixed-income securities. As a result, the variation of duration values as the interest rate environment changes is more pronounced. This enhanced rate of duration drift due to changes in interest rates, rather than time, is studied in Chapter 7.

portunity and therefore are not as visible. This asymmetry may call for erring on the short side when the duration of the portfolio is structured.

The portfolio manager addressing these issues in a multiple liability context might begin by forming a series of probable cash needs. If probabilities can be assigned to these cash outflow patterns, then an expected outflow pattern can be derived. Examples of these patterns and their expectations are given in Table 3-4. One approach is to immunize or actively manage the expected pattern. The exposure to early liquidation losses, however, might be high using this approach. There are at least two alternatives for early liquidation loss protection. First, one can construct the quickest possible payout pattern and use it as if it were true.

This payout pattern is given by the starred numbers in the first three columns of Table 3-4. These payouts are funded to the extent possible, starting with the earliest flows. The asset duration chosen relative to the duration of the funded liabilities will structure the rate risk adopted in this context.

The investor may unduly protect against early liquidation using the quickest payout approach. This will be particularly true when the investor believes large near-term outflows occur with low probabilities. An alternative to quick payout risk control is to structure the portfolio as though the expected cash outflow pattern were certain. Once the annual expected return is computed, parts of this return can be traded for added short-term protection. This approach reveals the incremental cost of early liquidation protection.

The measurement of incremental costs caused by undertaking early liquidation protection can best be described using a single outflow scenario. Assume this single outflow might occur at the end of year four, five, or six with .30, .40, and .30 probabilities respectively. The probability weighted outflow date is five years. Suppose the investor wishes to immunize but he or she worries about early liquidation. The analysis begins by establishing the worst interest rate environment that could exist at the early liquidation date. Suppose it is a flat yield curve of 13.5% given that the current flat yield curve is 12%. The worst scenario for early liquidation is always the scenario with the largest interest rate increase. If the portfolio has a duration of five

Table 3-4. Possible Cash Outflow Patterns

	Probabilities of Occurrence			
	.25	.25	.50	Expectation
Outflow after 1 year[a]	$ 350[b]	$ 300	$ 325	$ 325
Outflow after 2 years	350	390	475[b]	423
Outflow after 3 years	400	410[b]	300	352
Totals	$1100	$1100	$1100	$1100
Durations (years)	2.05	2.10	1.98	2.02

[a]All outflows are reported in present value.
[b]These outflows constitute the quickest possible outflow pattern. The amounts fundable with a $1100 initial investment are $350 after one year, $475 after two years, and $275 out of the $410 after three years. The duration of these funded flows is 1.93 years, the shortest of all.

Table 3-5.   Early Liquidation Loss Analysis Based on Worst Case Scenarios

| Portfolio Duration | Four Year[a] | | Five Year[a] |
	Realized Rate of Return	Capital Loss	Realized Rate of Return
5.0 Years	11.63%	1.47%	12.00%
4.8	11.70%	.78%	11.92%
4.6	11.78%	.59%	11.84%
4.4	11.85%	.40%	11.77%

[a]The worst case scenario for early liquidation has rates rising from 12% to 13.5%.
[b]The worst case scenario for liquidation on the expected holding period date has rates falling from 12% to 10%.

years and liquidation occurs in five years, then the realized rate of return will be 12%. What would happen, however, should the portfolio be liquidated after four years? Equation (6) suggests that the worst-case 4-year rate of return would be approximately 11.63% and not the originally promised 12%.[18] The capital loss would be about 1.47% of the *initial* portfolio value.

Shortening portfolio duration from five years lessens these losses. A duration of 4.8 years gives a 4-year rate of return of 11.7% and a capital loss of about .78% of initial capital value. Liquidation loss has fallen by seven basis points as measured by the annualized return. The rate of return and liquidation losses for other portfolio durations are reported in the first three columns of Table 3-5.

Early liquidation loss protection is not costless. Suppose we set duration equal to 4.8 years and the portfolio is liquidated after five years. Should rates fall, opportunity losses will be incurred. Assume that the worst falling rate outcome is one whereby rates decline 200 basis points. The realized rate of return over five years will be 11.92%. Thus a seven basis point maximum reduction in early liquidation losses costs as much as eight basis points in yield over the most probable holding period length. Opportunity losses for other duration values are reported in the last column of Table 3-5. Remember that only worst-case environments have been examined. Thus only the maximum loss reductions and maximum opportunity costs will be uncovered. The analysis presented here, however, can be made considerably more sophisticated should the need arise.

SECTION VII   LIMITATIONS OF DURATION—M^2 AND CONVEXITY

As insightful as duration can be, three problems have been mentioned that limit its applicability. First, we noted that as interest rates change, duration provides a linear approximation to the true changes in the values of fixed-income securities. Second, durations of different portfolios can drift apart as time passes. Third, aberrant

[18]$1163 = (^5/_4) \times .12 + ((4-5)/4) \times .135$

changes in yield curves (also known as "stochastic process risk") reduce the accuracy of duration analysis.

Research has been devoted to buttressing the duration concept against these problems. Esoteric topics, including M^2 and interest rate "convexity," are the result. The earliest worries concerned stochastic process risk, which is introduced through assumptions of how short- and long-term interest rates change when a particular duration formula is selected. The more cash flow mismatched are the duration matched portfolios, the greater the potential for stochastic process risk.[19]

In the extreme the solution to stochastic process risk is exact cash flow matching. This approach severely restricts asset and liability choices. Hence some compromise may add value to portfolio selection. On an informal basis, stochastic process risk can be reduced by individually matching the durations of early cash flows, middle-term cash flows, and late cash flows rather than just matching the durations of all cash flows. A more formal method of reducing stochastic process risk not only matches durations but also aligns a general measure of cash flow dispersion. One measure of cash flow dispersion is[20]

$$M^2 = w_1(t_1 - D)^2 + w_2(t_2 - D)^2 + \ldots + w_T(t_T - D)^2 \tag{8}$$

where the w_is and t_is are the same ones used in equation (1), and D is the duration of the cash flows that give rise to these w's and t's. Equation (8) looks much like the statistics formula for variance. Thus matching durations and dispersion measures of two portfolios is not unlike matching the means and variances of two probability distributions.

If we match more closely the interim cash flows using the formal or informal methods described above, we will also diminish the intertemporal problem of duration drift. There is a cost to this joint solution of stochastic process risk and time drift. Our asset and/or liability choices will be more limited than when only duration matching is of concern. Thus, we limit our ability to search for the most profitable asset and/or liability mix.

A general measure of cash flow dispersion has its own limitations. Equation (8) has us believe that a dollar of present value in mismatched late cash flows introduce as much stochastic process risk as a dollar of present value in mismatched early cash flows. Yet aberrant changes in yield curves are most often found in near-term rates. Consequently, some portfolios can have better matched measures of cash flow dispersion, but have more stochastic process risk if their remaining mismatched cash-flows are more heavily weighted towards early years. If we are to reduce stochastic

---

[19]In the holding period context, the duration match is between the portfolio and the duration of a zero coupon bond maturing at the end of the desired holding period. Otherwise it is the match between the durations of the asset and liability portfolios.

[20]The more informal method of reducing stochastic process risk is discussed in G.O. Bierwag, G.G. Kaufman, and A.L. Toevs, "Bond Portfolio Immunization and Stochastic Process Risk," *Journal of Bank Research* (Winter 1983). The more formal methodology is given in H.G. Fong, and O. Vasicek, "The Hedging Between Return and Risk in Immunized Portfolios," *Financial Analysts Journal* (September/ October 1983).

process risk, yet preserve some of the flexibility of duration analysis, then it may be best to cash flow match early cash flows but duration match late cash flows.

The last problem to be addressed is that caused by the linear approximation of duration analysis. As interest rates change, the value of a fixed income security changes in a nonlinear fashion. As noted in Figure 3-2 duration will underestimate any price rise and overestimate any price fall. More technically, duration is the first term in a Taylor series approximation to the true price relationship. The higher-order terms capture the curved nature (convexity) of the price's relationship to interest rates. A second-order Taylor series approximation can be used.[21] This is the notion supporting the ''curvilinear'' duration concept discussed in Chapter 7. The second-order approximation captures much, but not all, of the curvature noted in Figure 3-2. In mathematical terms, matching second-order Taylor series approximations also matches durations and the general measure of cash flow dispersion given in equation (8). Higher-order Taylor series terms can be considered but as they are added, the requirements quickly become much like exact cash flow matching rather than cash flow matching on average.[22]

Options have interest rate sensitivities and, in the price sensitivity notion of duration, have duration values. Because options have high leverage and truncated return distributions (see Chapter 5), their durations vary in magnitude as interest rates change much more dramatically than straight debt. This means that option prices are highly ''convex'' or curved as interest rates change. Care must be taken to use more sophisticated interest rate measures. Chapter 7 shows how this is done and that duration survives as a useful interest rate measurement tool.

Notice that the three problems of duration analysis all have the same root cause— mismatched cash flows. The solution to these problems therefore is the same—control the degree of cash flow mismatching with greater care than permitted by matching average cash flow dates via duration matching. We have seen several ways of measuring the extent of relative cash flow dispersion. But *M²*, convexity, Taylor series expansions, and so on, which all amount to the same thing, are difficult concepts to grasp. Fortunately there is a more intuitive view.

Figure 3-5 shows that two portfolios with the *same* duration can have different changes in value as interest rates change. At the current level of interest rates, a small increase or decrease in rates causes these portfolios to gain or lose value equally. But as interest rates change more substantially, the two portfolios diverge. As mentioned above, the extent of this divergence depends on the extent of relative cash flow dispersion, the presence of options, and so on. And it is this divergence that lets stochastic process risk, duration drift due to the passage of time, and convexity become topics of concern. An index of all of these problems can be derived very simply— measure the quickness with which the durations of these initially duration-matched portfolios diverge as interest rates change.

[21]This strategy requires durations be matched and a second-order term be matched. This term has the following form:
$G = w_1t_1{}^2 + w_2t_2{}^2 \ldots + w_Tt_T{}^2.$
[22]Vector duration measures are presented by D.R. Chambers, *The Management of Default-Free Bond Portfolios*, Ph.D. diss., University of North Carolina, 1981.

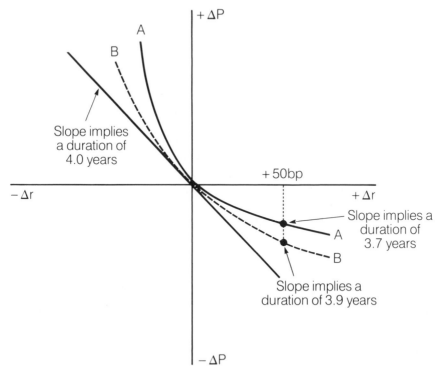

Figure 3-5.   Price behavior of duration matched portfolios with differing convexities.

Suppose both portfolios in Figure 3-5 have durations of 4.0 years at current interest rate levels. When these durations are measured with rates 50 basis points higher, suppose the duration of Portfolio A had fallen to 3.7 years while the duration of Portfolio B has fallen only to 3.9 years. This rate of duration drift due to changes in interest rates indicates the differential convexity observed visually in the figure. (Higher duration portfolios have steeper slopes, hence the relative shapes of Portfolios A and B.) It also indicates different exposures to stochastic process risk and to duration drift due to the passage of time. Drift due to changes in interest rates is a relative concept; that is, this differential rate of change in durations has to be compared to alternative portfolios to see if the duration-matched portfolios are the best available.

SECTION VIII   SUMMARY

Both theoretical research and practical experience confirm the usefulness of duration in financial analysis. Duration is valuable for a simple reason; it quickly and accurately standardizes the interest rate risk exposure of any cash flow series. The standard employed is the term to maturity of a zero coupon bond with comparable interest rate risk exposure.

Bonds or portfolios of bonds have similar changes in market values when interest rates vary from their expected course only when they have similar durations. Portfolios with high durations have more price sensitivity than portfolios with lower durations. This duration index of price sensitivity is more easily remembered than the more complicated, yet more ambiguous, traditional bond pricing rules of thumb.

Duration can also be used to construct bond portfolios that immunize or lock up returns promised on the date the securities were acquired. The rule is to set and then maintain a portfolio duration equal to the time remaining in the holding period(s). Portfolio rebalancing must be done on a periodic basis to adjust for a phenomenon known as duration drift. Properly rebalanced portfolios will yield the promised returns regardless of the number and size of interest rate changes. Portfolios must be optimized so as to achieve correctly stated promised returns, which are not properly quoted by many practitioners, for the lowest total costs.

Asset/liability models are just now becoming fully informed by duration analysis. This is particularly true in banks and thrifts. One important characteristic of duration-based analysis relative to other asset/liability techniques is that it more completely reveals the current interest rate risk exposure of the institution. As a result, management committees focus more attention on what should be their exposure and less attention on what is their exposure.

Many recent specialty applications for duration have been discovered. First, it has an important role to play in understanding the interest rate characteristics of financial futures contracts. Second, it can aid managers interested in pursuing increased expected return through deliberate adoption of interest rate risk. Duration analysis measures the price of extra returns via the added variation in returns generated by risky strategies. Third, it is possible to understand option contract interest rate characteristics by using duration. Fourth, duration analysis can be used to measure and to monitor the effects of unexpectedly early or late portfolio liquidation.

There are other known uses of duration not reported here. Even more applications will be discovered. This chapter clearly has touted duration. It does so not because duration is a perfect concept, but because the author knows no more robust framework in which to analyze the broadly divergent issues encountered in fixed-income management.

BIBLIOGRAPHY

Babcock, Gilford. "Duration as a Link Between Yield and Value." *Journal of Portfolio Management* (Fall 1984).

Bierwag, G.O., Kaufman, G.G., and Toevs, A.L. "Duration: Its Uses in Bond Portfolio Management." *Financial Analysts Journal* (July/August 1983).

Brennan and Schwartz; Nelson and Schaeffer; Bierwag, Kaufman and Toevs; Ingersoll, J.E., and Babbel in *Innovations in Bond Portfolio Management* Bierwag, G.O., Kaufman, G.G., and Toevs, A.L., editors. Greenwich, CT: JAI Press, 1983.

Kolb, R.W. *Interest Rates Futures: A Comprehensive Introduction* (Richmond, VA: R.F. Dame, 1982).

Kolb, R.W., and Chiang, R. "Duration, Immunization, and Hedging with Interest Rate Futures," *Financial Management* (Autumn 1981).

4 Hedging with Financial Futures

ALDEN L. TOEVS AND DAVID P. JACOB

INTRODUCTION

The growth in the financial futures market, both in terms of its diversity of contracts and its tremendous liquidity has been rapid by any standard of measurement. From the initial trades in 1977, the market for Treasury bond futures has grown to the point where the underlying market value of futures traded is twice the market value of actual Treasury bonds traded on a daily basis. The broad range of possible strategic uses of financial futures in portfolio management, borrowing cost hedging, and asset/liability management provides the basis for sustained growth over the forseeable future.

The focus of this chapter is on hedging positions in the fixed-income cash market with futures on fixed-income instruments. Particular emphasis is given to hedge ratio construction. The chapter begins with an overview of financial futures contracts. The basic characteristics of futures contracts such as margin, delivery features, and the gain/loss pattern of long and short positions are discussed. Understanding the relationship between prices in the cash market and the futures market is useful not only for constructing hedge ratios but also for helping one see through some of the popular misconceptions about what kinds of risk/return results can be achieved using futures. Before discussing the various approaches to hedge ratio construction, a useful classification of hedging goals is presented.

Using a particular example, various methods of hedge ratio construction are introduced, and their respective advantages and weaknesses are compared. The two basic theoretical approaches are shown to derive from the common objective of variance minimization. These approaches are then tested for their effectiveness using several sets of real data. A discussion of hedge ratio construction for alternative hedging goals follows.

The chapter concludes with a discussion on the various reasons why in practice even variance minimizing hedge ratios will have a residual risk or basis risk, and what if anything can be done to further reduce this risk.

SECTION I OVERVIEW OF FINANCIAL FUTURES CONTRACTS

A financial futures contract is a transferable, standardized agreement traded on regulated exchanges which obligates the seller to deliver and the purchaser to receive financial instruments in the future at a currently agreed upon price during a specified delivery period.

There are currently futures contracts on 3-month Eurodollar time deposits, 3-month domestic certificates of deposit, 90-day U.S. Treasury bills, U.S. Treasury notes, U.S. Treasury bonds, GNMA securities, and a contract based upon a municipal bond index.

Contracts are standardized with respect to their size, deliverable securities, and delivery period. For example, one contract on U.S. Treasury bonds traded on the Chicago Board of Trade (CBOT) represents $100,000 par value of these bonds. The purchaser of one U.S. Treasury bond contract has agreed to receive $100,000 par value of U.S. Treasury bonds during some future period. All of the fixed-income security contracts have a March, June, September, December delivery cycle; that is, there exist contracts that call for delivery in each of these months. Contracts are generally referred to by their delivery month and year, and their deliverable security. For example, the purchaser of a September 1986, U.S. Treasury bond contract has agreed to receive $100,000 par value of a U.S. Government Treasury bond sometime during September of 1986. The nearest futures contract to delivery can vary from one to approximately 90 days. The most distant delivery dates occur 18 to 30 months into the future, depending upon the type of futures contract selected.

Some contracts require the seller to deliver on a particular day in the delivery month, while others allow delivery any time during the delivery month. Contracts on 90-day Treasury bills traded on the International Monetary Market (IMM) require delivery on the first Thursday after the third weekly Treasury bill auction in the delivery month, whereas contracts on U.S. Treasury bonds permit delivery on any business day during the delivery month.

For some contracts the seller has some choice of what security to deliver to satisfy the terms of the contract. For example, a seller of a Treasury bond contract may deliver any U.S. Treasury bond with at least 15 years to maturity if not callable, or at least 15 years to call date. On the other hand, the U.S. T-bill contract specifies the delivery of a T-bill with 91 days to maturity. Some contracts such as the one on the 3-month Eurodollar time deposit do not have actual delivery, but settle based on an index. For the Eurodollar future the settlement price is the average LIBOR quote from eight major banks randomly selected by the clearing house at the termination of trading.

Futures contracts do not cost anything per se, but the buyer and the seller must deposit an initial margin whose purpose, unlike margins on securities accounts, is to assure performance of the contract rather than a partial payment for a security. This initial margin serves as a "good faith" deposit. Maintenance margin is the minimum amount of money that must be maintained in the margin account at all times. This sum is usually a bit smaller than the initial margin.

Positions in futures contracts are valued daily. When the equity in the account falls below the maintenance level a (variation) margin call will be issued requesting that enough cash be added to the account to bring the balance up to the initial (original) margin level. While the initial margin deposit may be posted using U.S. government securities, variation margin calls must be met in cash. Thus, gains and losses are settled daily in cash in the margin account. Margin requirements differ by contract. They are typically set near the maximum daily price move for a particular contract.[1] For example, the maximum daily move on a U.S. Treasury bond contract is two points on the $100,000 face value of the contract, or $2000. For hedgers the initial and maintenance margin are $1500. The initial margin and daily settlement procedure assures that adequate funds will be on deposit, which in turn helps to maintain the financial integrity of the clearing organization. With the clearing house acting as a party to every trade, futures contracts have been effectively made into contracts that can be bought or sold in secondary trading markets.

In order to understand the use of futures in hedging it is instructive to look at the gain/loss pattern of a futures contract as interest rates change. Since a futures contract represents the purchase or sale of a bond to be received or delivered in the future, the change in the price of the contract will largely reflect the change in the price of the security to be delivered. Thus if one purchases (is "long") a contract, the value of the position increases as interest rates fall and decreases as interest rates rise, as shown in Figure 4-1. Similarly, if one sells (is "short") a contract, the value of the position decreases (increases) as rates fall (rise). Notice that if the yield does not change there is no gain or loss on the futures position.

SECTION II   PRICING OF FINANCIAL FUTURES CONTRACTS

A thorough study of the price and yield relationships between futures and cash markets is essential for understanding futures market hedges. These relationships fundamentally influence the hedge outcomes for several reasons: (1) they identify hedges that promise unattainable results; (2) they help explain why a cash security might vary in price while a directly associated futures contract on the same security does not; (3) they help establish a method by which the interest sensitivities of futures contracts can be determined.

---

[1]The exchanges generally set a maximum daily price move for their contracts. If this limit is reached for several consecutive days the limit may be increased.

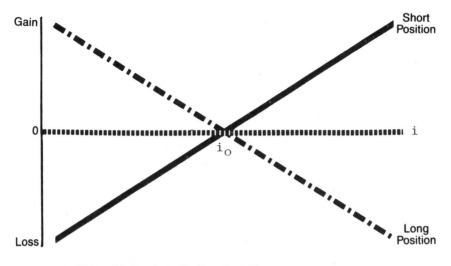

i_0: Yield on a futures contract on the date position is taken

i: Yield on a subsequent Date

Figure 4-1.   Futures contract gain/loss pattern.

Clearly the price of a futures contract on the delivery date ought to be equal to the price of the security to be delivered. Were it not so, riskless arbitrage would exist. For example, suppose that the price of the futures contract at delivery ($P_{F,t}$) were more than the *then* current price of the spot (or cash) instrument ($P_{C,t}$). One could sell the futures contract, purchase the cash instrument, and immediately cover the short futures position with the purchased security and earn $P_{F,t} - P_{C,t}$ without any risk. On the other hand if $P_{F,t}$ were less than $P_{C,t}$, one could buy futures and short sell the cash instrument and then cover the short cash position with the security received and earn $P_{C,t} - P_{F,t}$.

While the previous paragraph indicates that $P_{C,t}$ ought to be exactly equal to $P_{F,t}$ on the delivery date, it is not always so in practice. There are many reasons for this. First arbitrage works only after transaction costs, thus prices can differ by the cost of purchasing and selling the securities. For many contracts a major cause of the apparent price discrepancy is due to several uncertainties faced by the purchaser of these futures contracts. For example, the purchaser of a U.S. Treasury bond futures contract does not know exactly which security he will receive since the seller can deliver any Treasury bond with at least 15 years before its call date. Moreover, he does not know exactly when the security will be delivered since the seller may deliver the security at any time during the delivery month.[2] Thus the second part of the arbitrage argument described above is not quite perfect since the security received from the long futures position may not be the same as the cash security that was shorted.

---

[2]Some practitioners and academics have correctly recognized that these rights of the seller can be cast in an options framework and can be priced using options theory. See Richard Bookstaber, *The Complete Investment Book.*

This adds risk to the arbitrage. Nevertheless, the price for the cash and futures cannot differ by much, otherwise someone will arbitrage even if there is some degree of risk.

Consider the situation one day prior to the delivery date. The question is: How does the price of a contract that calls for delivery of this security one day hence compare with the price for the security today? Arguments similar to the one for the delivery date can be made.

Before we do this, however, it is important to review the concept of carrying costs. For real commodities such as gold, the carrying cost is nothing but the cost of financing the inventory. For bonds it is a little different since the inventory earns a return. The basic idea is that when the yield curve is positive one can presumably purchase a long maturity bond with funds borrowed at a lower rate, and so, "earn" positive carry. In practice one does not directly borrow funds to purchase U.S. Treasury bonds. Instead one enters into a repurchase agreement in which the party wishing to finance the security sells the security to another party and agrees to repurchase it at a subsequent date (usually the next day) for a slightly higher price. The price differential can be translated into a short term borrowing rate, or "repo" rate.

Bond dealers, or well-capitalized investors working through a bond dealer who want to finance long positions or earn interest on proceeds from short position on U.S. Treasury securities, usually do so through a repo transaction at the repo rate. Similarly, when the yield curve is inverted, one's financing cost exceeds the yield on the bond and there is negative carry. This is the way most of the market's participants view positive and inverted yield curve environments. Academics take issue with this view and argue (as discussed in Chapter 2) that one cannot expect to earn the carrying cost because in positive yield curve environments an expectation exists that yields will rise. Thus on an expected basis, any positive carry earned will be offset by the capital loss on the bond due to rising rates. In other words, those who argue that carry can be earned implicitly hold the view that on an expected basis the yield curve will not change. Pricing of futures contracts can be made consistent with either theory. We first demonstrate the pricing of futures using cost of carry arguments, as this argument is independent of any term structure model.

A would be investor (or an arbitrageur) has two alternatives if he is interested in owning a particular bond one day from now. He or she could purchase the bond today, or purchase a futures contract on the bond with one day to delivery. Recall that purchasing a futures contract requires no outlay of money, whereas the purchase of a bond does. To make the two alternatives comparable assume that the investor borrows the funds (or more realistically enters into a repurchase agreement) to purchase the bond.

> Alternative 1:   Borrow money and purchase the bond
>
> Alternative 2:   Purchase a futures contract on the bond

Let $P_{F,t-1}$ and $P_{c,t-1}$ equal the futures contract price for delivery tomorrow and the current bond price, respectively. Assume that interest costs for borrowing the funds to purchase the bond amounts to X and that the investor earns Y in interest on the bond. If the price of the bond on the day prior to delivery, $P_{C,t-1}$, plus the carrying cost, $Y - X$, is less than the price of the futures contract, the arbitrageur could purchase the bond with borrowed money and sell the futures contract. The bond could then be delivered the following day to satisfy the terms of the short futures contract. (This type of transaction is known as a "cash and carry" transaction.) A riskless profit of $P_{F,t-1} + (Y-X) - P_{C,t-1}$ would be earned. The reverse transaction can be made if the price of the bond plus the carrying cost is greater than the price of the futures contract. Thus for no arbitrage to exist, $P_{F,t-1} = P_{C,t-1} - (Y - X)$. A numerical example of the arbitrage argument follows.

For simplicity consider a hypothetical 30-year Treasury bond priced at par with a 12% coupon. Suppose further that one could borrow/lend funds for 90 days at 10%. Let us determine the price of a futures contract that calls for delivery of this security in 90 days. The claim is that the price of the futures contract is equal to the price of the underlying bond less the carrying cost. The carrying cost in this example is positive and equals $(.12 - .10) \times 90/360 \times \$100 = \$0.50$. Therefore, the price of the futures contract should equal $100 - .50 = 99.50$.

Case 1.   Price of the futures contract is $98. The arbitrage strategy is to short sell the bond, buy a futures contract, and close out the short position with the bond received at expiration of the contract.

Profit/Loss Statement

1.	Sell bond for $100.00	100.00
2.	Interest on proceeds of bond invested at 10% for 90 days	2.50
3.	Payment for bond under terms of futures contract including accrued interest of $3.	(101.00)
	"Riskless" profit	$ 1.50

Case 2.   Price of the futures contract is $101. The arbitrage strategy is to borrow $100 and purchase the bond, sell the futures contract and deliver the bond at the contract's expiration.

Profit/Loss Statement

1. Proceeds from delivery bond at contract expiration including accrued interest of $3.00	$ 104.00
2. Purchase bond at $100.00	(100.00)
3. Cost of borrowing $100.00 for 90 days at 10%	(2.50)
"Riskless" profit	$ 1.50

If we were to redo these calculations with a futures price of $99.50, we would find that there is no riskless profit. By an arbitrage argument we have found that the price of a futures contract is equal to the price of the underlying bond less the carrying cost. In positive yield curve environments, the cost of carry is positive and so the price of the futures contract is less than the price of the cash security; in negative yield curve environments the price of futures exceeds the price of the cash security.

Proponents of the expectations theory of the term structure argue that the price of a futures contract is merely the price of the underlying security at the forward rate on the delivery date. Under this theory forward rates are the rates expected to prevail in the future. As discussed in Chapter 2, when the yield curve is positively sloped the forward price lies below today's price. Similarly, when the yield curve is inverted the forward price lies above today's price. Below we calculate the price of a futures contract using cost of carry arguments and forward rates. For ease of exposition a futures contract on Treasury bills is priced.

On delivery date forward rates are equal to spot rates and so, using forward rates to price futures contracts, we find that on the delivery date the price of the futures contract is equal to the price of the cash instrument. We see that no matter which pricing argument one follows, the phenomenon of price convergence takes place; the price of the cash security and the futures contract are forced together, even if nothing (unexpected) happens in the financial markets. This phenomenon adds discipline to relative pricing of futures versus cash instruments prior to the delivery date.

Now consider a futures contract that calls for delivery of a 3-month Treasury bill three months from today. Assume that the 3-month and 6-month bills are priced at 97.645 and 94.491 respectively. This implies annual effective yields of 10% and 12% respectively. The cost of carry/arbitrage arguments discussed earlier showed that the price of the futures contract is equal to the current price of the deliverable security less the cost of carry. Thus the futures price can be calculated as follows:

Current market value of a 3-month bill	$97.645
Less carrying cost	$-(.875)*$
Price of the futures	$96.770

*The market value of the 6-month bill today is 94.491. In three months the 6-month bill will be a 3-month bill. This implies an increase in value of 3.154 (97.645 − 94.491). The borrowing cost is $2.279 which equals $(94.491 \times -1 + (94.491 \times -1 + 1.1^{.25})$. Thus the cost of carry is 3.154 − 2.279 = .875.

On the other hand, the forward rate is calculated to be 14.04%. This implies a forward price of $96.770. Under pure expectations theory this is the expected price of a 3-month Treasury bill in three months. Thus we see that under pure expectations the price of the futures contract is equal to the cost of carry futures price.

A similar kind of analysis can be done for futures on coupon paying instruments, though one has to be careful in calculating the forward price. To do this properly one has to work with the current spot rate curve, as discussed in Chapter 2.

SECTION III   HEDGING WITH FINANCIAL FUTURES

Many regulatory bodies have wrestled with the problem of producing an all-encompassing definition of hedging. The broadest definition would be one that includes all activities that reduce the risk of an existing or an anticipated position, where risk is defined as the variance of return. Typically hedgers are interested in minimizing (not just reducing) their risk exposure. For ease of exposition the analysis and examples that follow are written assuming that the existing or anticipated position to be hedged is an asset. Hedging liabilities or the net of assets and liabilities is similar to the asset hedge.

Any properly constructed hedge reduces risk. But frequently hedgers expect too much. The most frequent misconception is that a hedged portfolio can earn a return equal to, or nearly equal to that earned on riskier positions. For example, when yield curves are positively sloped, investors often believe that the higher yield on a long-term bond can be earned over short periods of time with little or no interest rate risk by appropriately hedging investments in this bond with interest rate futures. This cannot be true. Hedging should always be viewed as an activity that reduces total expected returns in exchange for a smaller variance in returns. Financial markets reward risk takers with the possibility of greater returns. Were it otherwise, the opposite party to the hedging transaction would be paid less to adopt the hedger's risk than what would be earned if this risk transfer were shunned.

Hedges can be constructed for currently held positions or anticipated ones. The length of time the hedge is to be in place may be known or uncertain. Hedges may be applied to assets, liabilities, or a net position of assets and liabilities. Given all these possibilities, it helps to classify the various hedges. Table 4-1 provides such taxonomy for a hedge of assets. Liability positions can be similarly classified. Asset/liability hedges are discussed in Chapter 10.

Consider the asset hedges given in Table 4-1. The inventory hedge (weak form cash hedge) is a situation where the hedge on an existing portfolio of securities will be in place over an uncertain period of time. This hedge is commonly known as a short hedge. An example might be a hedge placed on a bond dealer's inventory. The length of time the inventory will be held by the dealer is unpredictable. The dealer, therefore may wish to preserve the market value of the inventory at all times. In the majority the bid-ask spread, not portfolio returns, generates the bulk of a dealer's income. Thus the uncertainty of inventory earnings over the time held, which is a characteristic of this hedge, is of little consequence.[3]

As indicated in Table 4-1, an inventory hedge uses a short position in a near-to-delivery futures contract. When interest rates rise the cash position falls in value. A long futures contract does the same.[4] Thus a short position helps to offset the variation in the cash securities. The contract selected should be in the deliverable security with the highest covariance with the inventory. (If the securities held in inventory have varied interest rate sensitivities, then several types of futures contracts might be used to increase this covariance.) Nearness to delivery usually helps raise the degree of productive covariance with the cash position. The optimal hedge ratio, to be solved for later in this chapter, will require moderate to frequent adjustments as time

[3]Inventory hedges create from cash securities something that acts very much like overnight money. Returns on such securities are highly uncertain when held over long periods of time.

[4]A long futures position calls for the future delivery of a bond at a stated price. The value of receiving the bond at this price declines as interest rates rise.

Table 4-1. Hedge Classifications

	Time Uncertain	Time Certain
Currently Held Cash Position	**Weak Form Cash Hedge** *(Inventory Hedge)* Hedge Goal: Preserve capital on a daily basis. Hedge Strategy: Short the nearest-to-deliver futures contract.	**Strong Form Cash Hedge** *(Immunization)* Hedge Goal: Track daily the zero coupon bond due at the end of investment horizon. Hedge Strategy: Go long or short nearest-to-delivery futures contract.
Anticipated Cash Position	**Weak Form** *(Anticipatory Hedge)* Hedge Goal: Lock in currently available return or price at the uncertain cash inflow date. Hedge Strategy: Buy futures contract that expires nearest to the expected cash inflow date.	**Strong Form** *(Anticipatory Hedge)* Hedge Goal: Lock in currently available return or price at known cash inflow date. Hedge Strategy: Buy futures contract that expires nearest to the known cash inflow date.

passes. These adjustments are necessary because the maturities of the inventoried securities decline as time passes and this affects their interest rate sensitivities.

Consider the strong form cash hedge. Here the investor knows the time the portfolio will be held. The hedging goal is similar to the objectives of bond portfolio immunization. The hedge should be designed to lock in the currently expected return on the portfolio for a given investment period. Such an achievement can best be viewed as one that accomplishes two objectives. First, the hedge protects the original market value of the assets at the end of the investment period. Second, the hedge produces earnings on this market value over the investment period equal to that originally projected by the market for this period.

The hedge position may require either a purchase or a sale of interest rate futures contracts. To immunize portfolio returns, a cash and futures portfolio must be created and then maintained that has the same interest rate sensitivity as a zero coupon (pure discount) bond with an initial maturity equal to the investment period. Such a zero coupon bond, if held to maturity, guarantees the terminal return. Mirroring the zero coupon bond's initial value and its interest rate sensitivity at each point in time means following the time track of this zero coupon bond. If the interest rate sensitivity of the cash security is less than that of the zero coupon bond, futures should be *purchased* to augment the sensitivity of the cash security. Conversely, when the cash security is more interest rate sensitive than the zero coupon bond, futures should be *sold* to reduce this level of sensitivity. In either case the amount of futures needed will vary as time passes so that the zero coupon bond's interest rate sensitivity at each point in time can be matched.

An investor may think with some, but not absolute, certainty that the time horizon for holding the cash securities is known. This investor can use an immunization hedge to guarantee the total portfolio value at the expected time horizon, leaving principal value and earnings uncertain at any other date. Alternatively, an inventory hedge may be used to preserve principal value, leaving return uncertain at any date. Or some blend of these two techniques could be employed, where the allocations of these techniques depend on investor attitudes toward principal conservation and earnings stability. It is important to note that principal value and return cannot be simultaneously guaranteed for multiple dates—this is an unattainable hedging goal.

Now consider the anticipatory hedge. Table 4-1 describes two such hedges. The first is applicable when a known amount of cash will be received at a certain future date. The hedger wishes to buy cash securities at prices reflecting currently anticipated prices. Alternatively, the hedger may wish to buy securities guaranteeing a rate of return from point of acquisition to the end of a holding period. For example, suppose that the cash will be received on December 3, 1985, and that on this date the receiver intends to purchase 90-day Treasury bills. The futures price of such a bill is, say, $97.05. Based on this price, these bills have a bond equivalent yield of 12.19% from their delivery to maturity.[5] The hedging position chosen is the one that approximately locks in this market-forecasted price and yield. This hedge appears to require the acquisition of future delivery rights to as many dollars of bills as the anticipated cash inflow. Because margin calls must be financed by borrowing or using otherwise available funds, the appropriate hedge ratio will differ slightly from an exact dollar match. For this hedge to work the hedger must have sufficient liquidity to meet all margin calls on the interest rate futures contracts. Upon delivery of the bills at the expiration of the December 1985 bill contract, the investor receives approximately the originally promised yield.

The investor can use this type of strategy to lock in rates quoted for the securities deliverable on exchange traded futures contracts. However, the characteristics of the deliverables may not match those of the securities desired by the hedger upon the receipt of cash. The maturities of deliverable underlying futures contracts may not be the ones desired, and the delivery date of financial futures contracts may not be

---

[5]The price of the Treasury bill future on the International Monetary Market is based on the discount yield for a 360-day year. A "price" of 88.21 implies a discount from 100 of 11.79. This discount yield can be used to compute the corresponding price as follows: price $= 100 - (90/360) \times 11.79$. Given the price, a bond equivalent yield can be calculated.

when needed. Also, the hedger may wish to acquire security types not available in futures markets (e.g. corporate bonds). These complications limit the ability of these types of anticipatory hedges to meet the hedge goal. The more dissimilar the desired future investment vehicle is from the most closely associated futures contract, the more residual (basis) risk there is in effecting a hedge on the return of future cash receipts.

In the second type of anticipatory hedge, the goal is to lock in an acquisition price or, alternatively, a rate of interest on asset flows to be received at an unknown future date. Like the first anticipatory hedge, this hedge requires the futures contract purchased to have an interest rate sensitivity similar to that of the security to be purchased. The uncertain timing of the cash receipt complicates the formation and reduces the effectiveness of this type of anticipatory hedge. Nevertheless, this type of strategy can be used to reduce the range of possible outcomes of an unhedged position.

The 4-way hedge classification in Table 4-1 is incomplete. For example, an anticipatory hedge may be attempted when the cash to be received and the inflow date are known with certainty, but when the holding period for the investment is not. Alternatively, the cash inflow date and the holding period may be known with certainty but the amount of cash to be received may be uncertain. We do not dwell on these kinds of complications. To do so obscures the goal of developing an analytic foundation for understanding more frequently encountered hedges. The theoretical generality of the following section permits the consideration of more complicated hedges.

SECTION IV HEDGE RATIO ESTIMATION TECHNIQUES FOR WEAK FORM CASH HEDGES

For purposes of demonstration, the hedge ratio estimation techniques will be described using the following simple historical situation. On June 24, 1982 a trader had a net $10 million face value position (10,000 bonds) in the U.S. Treasury bond maturing on November 15, 2010. This bond pays a 12.75% coupon rate and was priced on June 24, 1982, at 90.125. Thus the market value of the cash position was $9.0125 million. The trader, wishing to offset the principal value risk of changing interest rates, chose as the hedging instrument the T-bond futures contract for delivery in September 1982. The futures contract traded at 59.3125 on June 24, 1982. The problem the trader faced was to determine the number of futures contracts to sell in order to create an equal and offsetting interest rate volatility to that of the cash bond held in inventory. The five methods offered in the financial literature for estimating the hedge ratio in this instance are dollar value matches, conversion factors, regression analyses using price changes, regression analyses using price levels, and the instantaneous price sensitivities (duration-based) approach.

For the remainder of this chapter, the reported hedge ratio should be taken to mean the dollars of principal value of the futures contract selected per principal dollar of the security to be hedged. This measure avoids having to explain continually the minor complications introduced by various futures contracts representing different principal commitments.[6]

Dollar Value Matches

The simplest hedge ratio is a one-for-one hedge. This hedge matches the number of dollars of principal value of the inventory to be hedged with an equal principal value in the securities underlying the futures contract. Such a naive strategy succeeds only when the instrument to be hedged has a price equal to that of the futures contract and an interest rate sensitivity like that of the futures contract. One-for-one hedges often perform so poorly that they will not be considered in subsequent discussions.

A much better although still naive, strategy computes the hedge ratio using a dollar-valued exposure in futures contracts equal to the cash inventory market value. Since the trader was long $9.0125 million in cash securities on June 24, 1982, the short position selected with this method also was priced at $9.0125 million. Given a futures price of 59.3125, this requirement translates into approximately 152 Treasury bond futures contracts.[7] The hedge ratio is 1.52. The easiest way to obtain the dollar value match hedge ratio is to divide the cash price by the futures price; that is, 1.52 equals 90.125 divided by 59.3125. This hedge ratio works well only if the interest rate characteristics of the cash bond closely match the interest rate risk characteristics of the futures market deliverable bond. In comparison to the one-for-one hedge method, the dollar value technique has a less limiting application, given that it does not require one to assume that the prices of the cash and hedging security are equal to one another.

Conversion Factor Method

The conversion factor method is fully applicable only in instances where the futures exchange allows the short future position holder to deliver several security grades in fulfillment of the contract. The conversion factor, as its name implies, corrects the invoice amount for the required par delivery of bonds for the difference between the coupon of the security being delivered, and that of the standard coupon specified by the contract. Currently, Treasury bond, Treasury note, and GNMA futures contracts allow many coupon-maturity combinations to be used as acceptable delivery grade securities. Published tables for the eligible securities can be consulted to determine these conversion factors.

---

[6]A Treasury bill futures contract on the International Monetary Market requires the delivery of $1 million in principal value, but the Chicago Board of Trade's Treasury bond futures contract requires the delivery of $100,000 of principal value.

[7]One Treasury bond futures contract priced at 59.3125 represents $59,312.50 in market value. The trader wishes to hedge $9,012,500 in inventory. The dollar value method requires $9,012,500/$59,312.50, or 152 contracts. As mentioned earlier hedge ratios as quoted in the text will ignore the complications in description brought on by the different principal value sizes of the various futures contracts. Hedge ratios report for the estimation method selected the number of par-valued dollars for the deliverable bonds per par-value dollar of the security to be hedged.

Consider the T-bond futures contract currently traded on the Chicago Board of Trade. The standard grade deliverable T-bond has a maturity of 20 years and a coupon rate of 8%. If the current interest rate is 8%, then the standard grade trades at par. The conversion factor, which is used to determine the price paid by the long position for receipt of a nonstandard grade instrument delivered by the short position, is computed as follows: determine the price of the nonstandard grade bond that causes it to yield 8%. This price relative to par gives the hedge ratio.

Our 12.75% T-bond maturing on November 15, 2010 has a conversion factor of 1.50 on June 24, 1982. This value indicates that one should sell 1.50 times the principal value in futures contract bonds as held in principal dollars in inventory. Essentially the conversion factor method presumes that if the cash bond could be delivered tomorrow (which may or may not be the case), the hedge position would have as many dollars of principal in short contracts as the cash position has in long contracts to "deliver." The accuracy of the conversion factor method increases as the delivery period is approached, and the closer the interest rate sensitivity of the cash bond is to the interest rate sensitivity of the cheapest-to-deliver bond. Hypothetical conversion factors and their implied hedge ratios can be computed for bonds that are technically not deliverable (e.g., agency bonds and corporate bonds).

The preceding elementary hedge ratio estimation techniques have convenience in application as their common strong point. None of these methods properly accounts for the differences in the price sensitivities of cash and futures contracts to changes in interest rates. Certain circumstances allow these naive approaches to be quite accurate in practice. Nevertheless, added value might be obtained by constructing hedges consistent with financial theory. The bond trader in our example wishes to assume a position in bond futures that reduces the variance of the charges in the value of his inventory. The following expression represents the change in value of a portfolio consisting of bonds and futures contracts:

$$\Delta V = \Delta P_c - (N \times \Delta P_f) \tag{1}$$

where ΔV, ΔP_c, and ΔP_f are the change in the value of the portfolio, the bond inventory, and the futures contract respectively, and N represents the number of futures contracts or the hedge ratio. The theoretically best hedge ratio minimizes the variance of changes in portfolio value. In can be shown that the optimal hedge ratio is defined by the relationship

$$N^* = \text{covariance}(\Delta P_f \text{ with } \Delta P_c)/\text{variance}(\Delta P_f) \tag{2}$$

where N^* represents the optimal number of futures contracts per cash security.

The remaining methods proposed can all be derived from the theoretical principles that give rise to equation (2). Each in its own way accounts for differential price sensitivities of cash and futures contracts to changes in interest rates. These last two assertions are proved in Toevs and Jacob (1986). In addition each method uses available information differently in estimating the covariances and variances in equation (2). Thus the relative merits of the remaining hedge ratio estimation techniques can be questioned only in the realism of their assumptions and the accuracy of their estimation techniques.

Regression Approach Relating Changes in Cash Prices to Changes in Futures Prices

This estimation methodology has its roots in the early academic literature on commodity hedging. It was the first minimum variance hedge ratio technique proposed, and despite several recently developed alternatives, continues as the most popular. The regression technique begins by using historical price data on the cash security to be hedged, and on the most closely associated futures contract, to compute individual data series on their daily, weekly, or monthly price changes. A representative series of data points for daily data is graphed in Figure 4-2. Regression analysis is applied to this scatter of points to find the best fitting straight line. The equation used in the regression is:

$$\Delta P_c = a + b\Delta P_f + \text{error} \tag{3}$$

The presumption in equation (3) is that the changes in the cash and futures prices relate to one another in a linear fashion but are subject to random errors (basis risk) that cannot be modeled. The estimated slope of the regression line, which will be

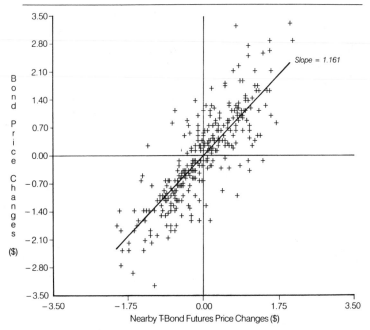

Figure 4-2.   Daily change in prices U.S. Treasury 12.75s of 2010 versus nearby T-Bond futures contract.

the statistically optimal value for b in equation (3), gives the "minimum variance hedge ratio." Since b represents the extent to which the cash price moves in the same direction as a dollar move in the futures price, the value of b represents the principal dollars of the futures contact to short per principal dollar of inventory. The value for a has little practical meaning for hedging. The values for the error term quantify basis risk. The statistical properties of regression analysis result in the value of b equaling N of equation (3), provided that ΔP_c and ΔP_f are related in a linear fashion, and that the data series used in the regression accurately reflect, as sample observations, the variance and covariance terms that comprise the true minimum variance hedge ratio. Any violation of assumptions results in larger than necessary errors and therefore augmented basis risk.

To be representative the data series has to be sufficiently long to reflect the true variance and covariance relationships that determine N. The data series included in the regression however, can, be too long. Older prices may reflect price relationships that no longer exist. Financial theory provides little guidance for determining how long the data set should be in order to obtain the best estimate of N^*.

The futures contract selected for inclusion should have, of all available contracts, the highest correlation with the cash security.[8] Several empirical problems remain besides selecting the length of the data set, the type of futures contract and the delivery date of the contract. These will be discussed when the alternative hedge ratio estimation methods are compared with one another.

Regression Approach Relating the Cash Price to the Futures Price

A variation of the regression approach statistically fits a linear relationship to historical data series on the price levels of the cash and hedging instruments. (The regression technique discussed above used price changes rather than price levels.) Figure 4-3 depicts the historical relationship between the price levels of the T-bond maturing on November 15, 2010 and those of the successive nearest-to-deliver T-bond futures contracts. (The scale of this graph is inconsistent with Figure 4-2.) These historical levels have been largely determined by prevailing interest rate levels. Low prices reflect time periods of high interest rates and vice versa.

The regression line (i.e., the statistically best fitting straight line) for these data points is also graphed in Figure 4-3. The regression equation that gives rise to this fitted line is

$$P_c = s + tP_f + \text{error} \qquad (4)$$

The values fitted by the computer for s and t are 3.13 and 1.43, respectively. The slope of the line, which is the value for t. again represents the hedge ratio. Pitts

---

[8]In practice this should be weighed against the transaction cost of this strategy. The hedge will generally be more effective if the nearest-to-delivery contract is used. This contract expires frequently, causing additional transaction costs. Also, the possibility of unexpected delivery during the delivery month could indicate use of the next nearest-to-delivery contract.

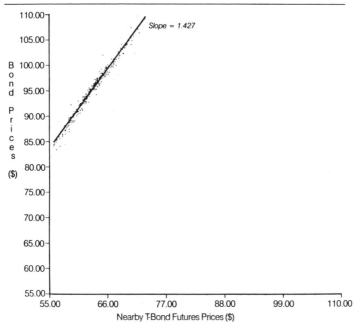

Figure 4-3.   Daily price series U.S. Treasury 12.75s of 2010 versus nearby T-Bond futures contract.

(1983) shows that this hedge ratio is mathematically equivalent to an estimate of a minimum variance hedge ratio. Note that this ratio differs in value substantially from the ratio of 1.16 found for the same bond in the regression analysis using price changes. Reasons why this might occur will be discussed in the next subsection. Intuitively what is suggested by this line is that when P_f becomes one dollar higher (lower), P_c increases (decreases) by t times this much. Thus, to obtain equal dollar valued changes in the cash security and the hedging futures position, one needs t dollars of principal value of futures per dollar of principal value of the cash security.

The more alike are the characteristics of the futures and cash securities, the more similar are their price levels for any interest rate environment. As was noted in the discussion of regression of price changes, price level regressions normally find that the futures contract having the largest covariance with the cash security price is the next deliverable security that best matches the maturity, credit, and coupon rate characteristics of the cash security. As the cash security approaches the characteristics of the deliverable security underlying the futures contract and as the time to delivery becomes very short, the price relationship approaches a situation like that depicted in Figure 4-4a.

Now, consider the price relationship that exists, over a broad spectrum of interest rate levels, between a shorter-maturity cash security and a futures contract on a similar coupon rate but longer-term bond. Less price sensitivity to changes in interest rates exists in the cash security than in the futures price on a long-term bond. More-

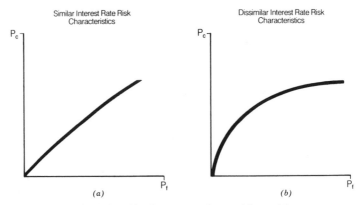

Figure 4-4. Price relationships between cash securities and futures contracts.

over, this relatively lower cash price sensitivity increases as interest rate levels decline. Figure 4-4*b* depicts the relative price movements. It should be obvious that a straight line regression fitted to Figure 4-4*a* has more accuracy than a straight line fitted to Figure 4-4*b*. Similar reasoning leads one to believe that dissimilar price sensitivities should also reduce the accuracy of linear regressions of price *changes* analyzed above.

A new variation on the above regression (that we might suggest) fits a curved line to price data. This allows more flexibility and more accuracy in hedge ratio construction. Consider, for example, the following regression equation:

$$P_c = s + tP_f + vP_f^2 + \text{error} \tag{5}$$

Equation (5) fits a curved line to the data when appropriate. The hedge ratio obtained from equation (5) no longer equals the computer fitted and fixed value for t. The ratio now becomes $t + 2vP_f$. Note that this ratio depends upon not only fixed numbers like t and v but also upon the current value for the futures price.[9] In the context of Figure 4-4*b*, this partial dependency on P_f causes the number of futures contracts sold to hedge the cash position to decrease as P_f increases.

The computer estimates for our sample bond on June 24, 1982 are 3.047 for t and -0.0128 for v. The futures price of 59.3125 on this day coupled with these estimated values gives a hedge ratio on June 24 of 1.53. This ratio is somewhat higher than the 1.43 estimated through the more standard price regression methodology.

Instantaneous Price Sensitivities Hedge Ratio Method

The price relationships depicted in Figures 4-3 and 4-4 can be exploited in a somewhat different manner. As shown by the broad, fuzzy line in Figure 4-5, a close but

---

[9]This hedge ratio comes from taking the derivative of equation (6) with respect to P_f.

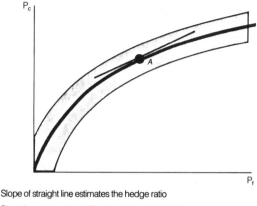

Slope of straight line estimates the hedge ratio

Slope is measured as in Equation (7) as $P_c D_c^*/P_f D_f^*$

Figure 4-5.   Instantaneous price sensitivities.

not precise price relationship exists between cash and futures prices. The fuzziness of the relationship occurs because of basis risk. (Fuzziness in the context of Figure 4-3 is depicted by the random element in the scatter of points.) Rather than fitting a straight or curved line through observed data points lying in this fuzzy band, one might establish the current price relationship in the band and ask the question: Given the current position, does financial theory indicate how this position would change if interest rates became slightly higher or slightly lower?

The rhetorical answer is yes. Consider Point A in Figure 4-5. This position was chosen to lie on the center line of the band. This midline indicates that no current basis risk is present. (In the context of the discussion on pricing, a position on the midline indicates that cash, forward, and futures prices have all been fully arbitraged.) Financial theory indicates how sensitive cash and futures prices should be to a small change in interest rates. These sensitivities may be identified in an extremely simple manner. Bond price tables give the price of the cash security at its current yield to maturity. Prices at slightly higher or lower yields can also be found. Thus the price sensitivity of the cash security to instantaneous yield changes can be computed by artificially varying the yield and observing the resulting price change. (Normally this is done for a one basis point change in yields.)

A similar process can be applied to the futures price. The following description implicitly assumes that the futures price is fully arbitraged, and therefore, acts like the deliverable bond from the futures delivery date to the deliverable's maturity date; that is, we are at a point like Point A in Figure 4-5. The futures price implies a yield to maturity *from the delivery date* to the maturity date of the delivered contract.[10] This yield is varied by one basis point, and the new futures (deliverable) price is

[10]Most contracts have a delivery month rather than a delivery date. In this case an expected delivery date must be used. A good rule of thumb is that delivery is expected to occur toward the beginning (end) of the month when the yield curve is downward (upward) sloping.

computed. Comparing the former price to the latter price gives an index of the price sensitivity of the futures contract.[11]

It is somewhat more difficult to compute the price sensitivity of a futures contract that allows for more than one delivery grade. However, the price sensitivity of the futures contract can still be estimated. Begin by identifying the security that is expected to be delivered.[12] The converted futures price (the futures price times the conversion factor) coupled with the coupon rate, delivery date, and maturity date of the estimated cheapest-to-deliver bond provide sufficient information to compute a yield to maturity on this bond upon the delivery date. Next vary this yield by one basis point and find the new price of the deliverable. Convert this price back into a *futures price* by *dividing* it by the conversion factor. The new futures price relative to the original one approximates the price sensitivity of the futures price to a one basis point change in yields.[13]

The *instantaneous price sensitivity* hedge ratio is computed by dividing the measured interest rate sensitivity of the cash security price by the measured interest rate sensitivity of the futures contract price. In its simplest form, this hedge ratio assumes that the yield on the futures contract changes in exactly the same amount as the yield change on the cash security. The instantaneous price hedge ratio measures the slope of the line tangent to Point A in Figure 4-5. As with regression techniques, this ratio represents the hedge ratio (the number of principal dollars of a futures contract used to short (long) per principal dollar of the cash security). Assuming either that price arbitrage has taken place or that existing arbitrage profits remain constant, Toevs and Jacob (1986) have shown that this hedge ratio or its duration equivalent discussed below represents a minimum variance hedge ratio as defined in equation (2). In either instance the assumption is tantamount to assuming that the futures price behaves like the idealized forward contract price of the deliverable security.

The hedge ratio constructed for instantaneous price changes can be expressed in terms of the "durations" of the cash and deliverable security. Duration is a frequently encountered statistic of bonds that measures, or indexes, the interest rate sensitivity of a series of cash flows. The standard for the duration index is the maturity of a zero coupon bond having an interest rate sensitivity equal to that of the cash flow series in question. For example, a 10-year note with an 11% coupon priced at par happens to have a duration of 6.3 years. This means that within close approximation, the coupon-paying bond currently has an interest rate sensitivity equal to

---

[11]The futures price may not be fully arbitraged. The interest rate sensitivity of this price may still be obtained under the assumption that any arbitrage premium initially present remains after the interest rate shock occurs.

[12]Take *current* market prices for all securities eligible to be delivered and compare them to the futures price converted for the security in question. (Let the cash price of an eligible deliverable be $100 and the futures be $90. If the conversion factor is 1.1, then compare $100 to $99.) The cheapest-to-delivery security—if delivery were made today—is the security with the current price less the converted future price that produces the smallest value.

[13]In practice many hedgers simply compute the price sensitivity of the standard grade deliverable. For the T-bond contract they assume a 21-year, 8% bond. When yields are high this provides an adequate but not optional estimate.

that of a 6.3 year zero coupon bond. Applications of duration in portfolio and asset/liability management are discussed in Chapters 3, 9, and 10.

A useful property of duration is that it can express the price sensitivity of a bond in a convenient and simple expression:

$$\text{change in } P \text{ per unit change in } r = -D^* \times P$$

D^* represents the duration of the bond divided by the quantity $1 + (r/2)$, where r is the yield to maturity of the bond. Many people refer to D^* as the "modified" duration. (See Chapter 3 on duration.)

The instantaneous price hedge ratio is the price sensitivity of the cash security divided by the price sensitivity of the futures contract. Thus the minimum variance hedge ratio, expressed in terms of durations rather than price sensitivities is

$$N^* = P_c \times D_c^*/P_f \times D_f^* \tag{6}$$

The subscripts refer to cash or futures prices and modified durations.

The price used for P_f when only one security is deliverable is the quoted futures price. If the contract allows the delivery of more than one grade of securities, then the theoretically best price to use for P_f is the forward price of the cheapest-to-deliver security divided by the conversion factor of this security. In practice little damage appears to be present by using the price of the futures instead of the converted forward price.[14]

The duration of a security that only promises future cash flows is interpreted somewhat differently than the duration of a cash security. The duration of a futures contract, which is itself a commodity, is conceptually very similar to that of the deliverable security. The futures contract's duration indexes the volatility of the variation margin to changes in interest rates expected on the delivery date of the associated security. A futures position does not constitute an investment. Rather it represents an instantaneous exposure of wealth, through changes in the balance of a variation margin account, to changes in market perceptions of the expected course of interest rates. Long and short futures positions constitute acquired obligations-to-wealth exposures to changes in interest rates of opposite directions. For example, wealth will be adversely affected if, when a short (long) futures position is held, interest rates fall (rise).

The duration of a futures contract is computed much like that for cash securities. In all instances, however, the durations of futures contracts are measured using the cash flows of the deliverable security, occurring after delivery of this security, and continuing to the final cash flow of the security. The calculations involving present values and time to cash inflow are computed relative to the delivery date. In essence,

---

[14]Efficient pricing in the relevant markets should drive the converted forward price of the security expected to be the cheapest to deliver towards equality with the observed futures price. Daily discrepancies between the computed forward price and the observed futures price do exist. However, sensitivity analyses show no measurable harm in taking the simpler course of using the readily available futures price.

the duration of a futures contract is the duration of the deliverable computed at the delivery date.

The simplest duration to compute is that of the T-bill futures contract. The duration of a 90-day Treasury bill at the delivery date of the contract equals .25 years. (The duration of a zero coupon bond always equals its term to maturity—in this case, the maturity date relative to the delivery date.) Note that the duration of a T-bill futures contract deliverable one month from now has a duration identical to that of a T-bill futures contract deliverable in 21 months. This does not mean that the hedge ratio computed with equation (6) would be the same if the hedging security were either of these bill contracts. First, P_f on the near and far contracts may differ. Second, modified durations (D^*s) may reflect unequal interest rates implied by the prices of these contracts. Third, relative yield volatility estimates (discussed in just a moment) suggest that the nearby T-bill futures contract tends to be more price sensitive than the more distant T-bill contract. Hence, equal durations of futures contracts need not imply equal hedge ratios.

As noted earlier, for futures contracts with multiple deliverables the price sensitivity of the futures contract best reflects that of the bond expected to be delivered. The delivery date, coupon rate, implied yield, and maturity of the cheapest-to-deliver security combine to establish the duration of the cheapest to deliver. For example, on June 24, 1982 the futures price was 59.3125. The bond expected to be cheapest to deliver (for the September 1982 contract) was the U.S. Treasury 8 3/8 of 2008. This bond had a conversion factor of 1.0375. The estimated price of this bond was, therefore, the converted price of the futures contract or 61.535. At this price the 8 3/8 of 2008 had a yield from its September delivery date of 13.88%. When this yield and price are used, the duration of the cheapest to deliver from delivery date to 2008 was 7.75 years. This information is used to compute the hedge ratio that is discussed below.

The idea of expressing instantaneous interest rate sensitivities in terms of the duration concept may appear to be cumbersome. One justification for this technique comes from the "additivity" characteristic of duration. For example, the duration of a portfolio of two securities is $(P_1 \times D_1 + P_2 \times D_2)/(P_1 + P_2)$. The duration of a portfolio of any number of cash securities can be computed using a similar price-weighted combination of the durations of the individual securities. Thus, the determination of the joint-price sensitivity of a large cash inventory requires the computation of the joint duration of all inventoried securities. Another reason justifies a duration-based hedge ratio. Many bond portfolio and asset/liability managers measure their interest rate risk by way of duration. Duration representations of futures contracts and hedge ratios allow these managers to assimilate futures contracts into their cash security analyses more directly.

The simplest duration measure to use in the construction of hedge ratios was first developed by Frederick Macaulay for other purposes. The mathematical form of this measure, which is reported in Chapter 3, correctly indexes the interest rate sensitivity of a security only when the yield curve has rates that are constant for all maturities. Furthermore, should the yield curve change unexpectedly, the Macaulay duration assumes that the yield curve will remain flat across maturities at a higher or lower rate than before. Clearly neither assumption holds in general.

In most instances the simple Macaulay duration performs surprisingly well. Modifications to the Macaulay formula, however, can add value. Some researchers have found that adjusting durations for "relative yield volatilities" has merit. Rather than assume that a one basis point change in the yield on a benchmark security implies a one basis point change in the yield on any other security, one can assume that the yield changes are related proportionally. For example, if the benchmark is a 1-year Treasury bill, then a proportionality factor of 0.9 for a 2-year Treasury note indicates that when a 10 basis point change in the bond equivalent yield occurs on the bill, the best guess is that a nine basis point change in the yield occurs on the note.

The minimum variance hedge ratio that accounts for different but proportional yield changes can be constructed by making a simple adjustment to the hedge ratio reported in equation (6). N^* becomes the value measured in equation (6) times the proportionality factor on the cash security, relative to a benchmark security divided by the proportionality factor on the futures contract relative to the same benchmark, or

$$N^* = P_c \times D_c^* \times R_c / P_f \times D_f^* \times R_f \qquad (7)$$

where R_c and R_f are the relative yield proportionality factors for the cash and futures positions respectively.

A more comprehensive modeling of both duration and relative interest rate volatilities is possible. The yield to maturity of a bond represents a complicated (geometric) average of the discount factors applicable to each cash flow associated with the fixed-income security. These individual cash flow discount factors come from the term structure of interest rates, which is also often referred to as the zero coupon bond yield curve. Duration formulas exist that use these individual discount factors. These formulas avoid having to make the assumption that yield curves are flat and change in a parallel fashion. Moreover, this approach allows each zero coupon bond equivalent interest rate to have its own relative interest rate volatility. The yield to maturity represents a specific and complicated average of these volatilities, and financial theory suggests that in general this averaged volatility measure is not strictly correct. Adjustments to equations (6) and (7) based on these considerations lie outside the set of topics that can be addressed in this introduction to hedge ratio estimation techniques.

For the U.S. Treasury 12.75 of 2010, the duration-based hedge ratio on June 24, 1982 was 1.38 uncorrected for relative yield volatilities, and 1.39 corrected for these volatilities. These hedge ratios are derived as follows: On June 24, 1982, this bond had a price of 90.125. The associated yield to maturity was 14.17%. The duration was 7.34 years, 6.85 years in modified form. The security expected to be cheapest to deliver for the September 1982 futures contract was the 8 3/8 of 2008. As noted above, this deliverable bond has a duration of 7.75 years, 7.25 years in modified terms computed as of the September 1982 delivery date. The yield volatility of the cash security relative to the futures contract is estimated to be 1.01.[15] Thus for equa-

---

[15]This was found by regressing the yield to maturity of the cash security against the yield from delivery to maturity of the cheapest-to-deliver security in prior periods.

tion (6), $N^* = (90.125 \times 6.85)/(61.535 \times 7.25)$ or 1.38, and for equation (7) $N^* = ((90.125 \times 6.85)/(61.535 \times 7.25)) \times 1.01$, or 1.39.

SECTION V THEORETICAL EVALUATION OF WEAK FORM CASH HEDGE RATIO METHODOLOGIES

Dollar matching and conversion factor hedge ratio estimation techniques are convenient but applicable only in limited circumstances. The remaining methods all can be derived from the minimum variance hedge ratio formulation. Each hedge ratio estimation method, however, is obtained in a different manner. The merits of each depend upon the consistency of their assumptions with known theory and the compromises that often must be made to conduct associated empirical analyses.

It is useful to begin a comparison among the regression and duration-based techniques with an analysis of the straight line regression of price levels. This regression was first depicted in Figure 4-3. Consider Figure 4-6, where the band represents the observed price relationships between the cash security and futures contract. If interest rates have, over recent periods exceeded the interest rates giving rise to the prices at Point A, then the data available for the regression is restricted to the lower part of the price band.[16] Suppose a straight line fit to this data gives a hedge ratio of 1.2. This ratio, if applied to our current position (Point A), overstates the interest rate sensitivity of the cash security to the deliverable security. The regression of price levels based on this best available but inappropriate data set causes the hedger to short too many futures contracts.

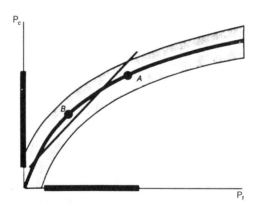

Slope of straight line estimates the hedge ratio

Hedge ratio too high

Figure 4-6.   Regression of prices historically low price experience.

---

[16]Point B will be discussed in a moment. Furthermore, it is only for expositional ease that Points A and B were chosen to fall on the midline within the band of possible prices.

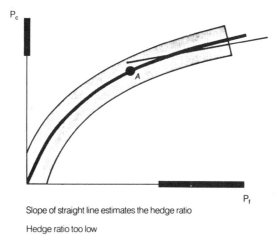

Slope of straight line estimates the hedge ratio

Hedge ratio too low

Figure 4-7.   Regression of prices historically high price experience.

The opposite conclusion holds when the available price series systematically lies above Point A because interest rates have been low, relative to the rates giving rise to current prices. A straight line fit to data points in the upper part of Figure 4-7 gives a hedge ratio of, say, 1.0. This hedge ratio understates the interest rate sensitivity of the cash security, relative to the deliverable security of the futures contract at Point A. The regression on this inappropriate data base causes the hedger to short too few futures contracts.

Only when a reasonable representation of prices exists on both sides of the current prices of the cash and hedging instrument can the hedge ratio be said to reflect fully the true minimum variance hedge ratio.[17] Such a situation is shown in Figure 4-6 by a current position of Point B. The theoretical conclusion is then: The regression of price levels produces an estimated hedge ratio that misrepresents the true ratio when interest rates have been volatile and generally low relative to the current situation, or when interest rates have been volatile and generally high relative to the current position. These situations are, unfortunately, among those when hedging adds the most value.[18]

The relationship between a cash price and a futures contract price becomes more curved as these two securities depart in their maturity characteristics. Other influences affecting the curvature include different coupon rates for similar maturities and different credit qualities, particularly those that give rise to interest rate spreads that depend on overall interest rate levels. The more curved the price relationship is, the more value is added by using regression techniques to fit a curved rather than a

[17]Another factor that can bias the regression-based hedge ratio is that the current cheapest-to-deliver security may not be the one present during the time series used for regression estimation.
[18]Another way of looking at the results pictured in Figures 4-6 and 4-7 is that representative data sets cause regression slope estimates to misrepresent the variance and covariance terms that define the minimum variance hedge ratio for the current position of cash and futures prices.

straight line to available data. See equation (5) for a simple example of such a curved line.

The hedge ratio estimation technique derived from regressions of price *changes* suffers from the same potential problems as the one involving regressions of price *levels* discussed above. An additional problem arises in this alternative regression technique. It assumes that the way prices change within the available data set also holds into the future. This added assumption in regression of price change hedge ratios introduces the troublesome problem of "path dependency." If interest rates (prices) were typically low (high) relative to today's levels, and if they moved steadily toward today's levels, then the hedge ratio derived from regressing price changes will differ from that obtained for instances when prices move less steadily toward today's levels.

The path dependency characteristic of price change regressions can be illustrated rather simply. Recall that the hedge ratio estimated for June 24, 1982 using a regression of price *levels* was 1.43 when the cash security was the 12.75 Treasury of 2010. The estimated hedge ratio found using a regression of price *changes* was 1.16. If the cash and futures-paired prices were randomly scrambled, and if the hedge ratios were reestimated, the hedge ratios would change. The regression of price levels continues to produce a hedge ratio of 1.43, as no change in data for this regression occurs, but the regression of price changes produces a hedge ratio of 1.42.

The relative instability of the regression of price changes arises from the path dependency of such regressions. For regression of price changes to provide theoretically defensible hedge ratios, prior price levels and prior average price changes must reflect today's situation. Only the former assumption need be made when using the regression of price levels.

Another problem with hedge ratios constructed using regression analysis arises out of one of the purported strengths of these techniques. Any regression-based hedge ratio methodology blends together historical experience on a number of factors influencing hedge efficacy. Among the more important are the historically observed experiences in:

1. Interest rate sensitivities of the hedged and hedging securities
2. Short-term yield movements relative to long-term yield movements
3. Cash and futures price arbitrage or lack thereof
4. Systematic changes in the basis

(Regression of price changes also considers the historical influence of the sizes of changes in prices.) The influences of the third and fourth items are ignored in the commonly used duration-based methods. The simpler the regression approach, the more melded are the averages of these separate influences. Currently the popular regression techniques meld all influences into a single number, for example t in equation (4). When this type of estimated hedge ratio is employed, the implicit assumption made by any regression-based technique is that the melded influences of average experiences on all aspects of importance to the hedge will hold in the future. One implicit assumption of note is the presumption that the yield on the hedged instrument will move in fixed proportion to the yield implied by the futures price.

Instantaneous price sensitivity or duration-based hedge ratios do not suffer from the problems of path dependency or misrepresentative samples that were just accorded to regression-based hedge ratios.[19] Duration-based hedge ratios make more explicit the assumptions on the items enumerated in the prior paragraph. First, the interest rate sensitivities of the cash and futures contracts are derived theoretically. Second, the available duration approaches assume either that cash and futures prices have been arbitraged, or that the arbitrage premium remains constant for the length of the hedge. Third, any duration formula selected assumes that interest rates change in fixed proportions to one another. These proportionality factors can be assumed by the duration formula used or estimated (e.g., estimated relative yield volatilities). Fourth, the systematic changes in the basis remain untreated by the normal duration-based hedge ratio techniques. Thus the duration approach, which one should remember is a convenient expression of the instantaneous price change hedge ratio methodology, separates the price sensitivities of arbitraged prices from changes in the basis.

Changes in the basis may be partially systematic. (This is particularly true if the assumptions made by the duration formula used are regularly misrepresentative.) Duration analysis by its prior segmentation of theoretically measured price sensitivity from residual hedge influences on hedge efficacy, presents a clear opportunity to increase hedge performance. This opportunity is not so apparent in the regression methodologies. In their simplest form duration-based hedge ratios may be as inaccurate as regression-based hedge ratios. Both techniques must make strong assumptions that may not hold in practice. Duration-based hedges, however, have the potential to become more accurate, relative to the possibilities in regression analyses. The explicit assumptions of a duration-based hedge leave observed residual hedge risks much more subject to modeling than the observed risks resulting from regression-based hedges.

A final deficiency of regression relative to duration-based hedge ratios must be mentioned here. This issue helps make the transition from theory to practice. Regressions normally ignore in practice a data problem of some importance. The data series on cash prices used in regressions usually allows the cash security to age as observations are taken. But the futures contract deliverable does not necessarily undergo the same maturation.[20] Because regression analysis has not been conducted with securities of consistent interest rate risk characteristics, differential maturation effects can distort the regression results. A theoretically precise solution is to regress a price

---

[19]Statistical errors of modest proportions enter only if the duration-based hedge ratios are augmented by estimates of relative yield volatilities.

[20]Indeed if the cheapest-to-deliver Treasury bond increases in maturity through a new or expected issue of a long bond, the maturity of the cash instrument can be shortened while that for the deliverable lengthens.

series that historically would have been associated with the coupon and maturity characteristics of the cash security to be hedged today, on the prices that would have prevailed on the currently best available futures contract. Such observations may not exist or may be difficult to find. For example, how could one perform a regression to establish the hedge ratio for a coupon rate-maturity combination bond that has just been issued? How can one artificially generate price series for a constant coupon-maturity mix bond without destroying the value thought to be added in regression methodologies that capture market imperfections in their hedge ratios?

Duration-based hedge ratios have been shown to have theoretical underpinnings that are potentially superior to those supporting regression-based hedge ratios. These ratios are also easier to compute. Regressions need not be run in order to use the simpler duration techniques. If relative yield volatilities prove to be important empirically, then regressions will be required. These regressions need not be as demanding in their data requirements, and since relative yield volatilities normally cause simpler duration hedge ratios to be adjusted only modestly, errors in these regressions do not greatly change hedging effectiveness.

Regression techniques for hedge ratio estimation are flawed theoretically. As noted above, the theoretical deficiencies associated with regressions of price changes exceed those for regressions of price levels. In application, regression-based hedge ratios can be difficult to compute. Regressions should be rerun frequently to include the latest available data. As time passes, the items in the inventory change, necessitating new regressions. Also, as noted above, existing inventoried bonds age and new regressions should be run to counter these maturation effects.

Suppose the inventory contained 20 different bonds, say a group of longer term Treasury and agency bonds. Regressions for each bond should be run to achieve maximum hedging efficacy. A particularly troublesome problem arises for the various regression techniques when the inventory includes a new bond. For example, it is unclear how helpful regression-based hedge ratios can be when the newly issued bond to be inventoried and hedged is longer in term or higher in coupon than any previously existing bonds. An often encountered suggestion that has been circularly reasoned is to substitute in the regression for the unavailable price series the price series of a comparable *duration* bond!

SECTION VI   EMPIRICAL TESTS OF INVENTORY HEDGES

The following applies hedge ratios constructed for the various methods discussed above to recent market data. The time period analyzed starts in mid-1982 and continues through all of 1983. Data for 240 trading days from the beginning of 1981 through mid-1982 is used to run the initial regressions. Regressions are updated every 20 trading days by dropping the oldest 20 days in the data set and adding the most recent 20 days. Such frequently run regressions help place regression-based hedge ratios in their most favorable light.

The "naked" position in cash securities has an observed variance in market value.

Weak form cash hedges attempt to minimize the influence of this variance by short-ing futures contracts. These short futures positions would ideally create equal and offsetting variation in market value. Perfect hedges, however, are unobtainable. The best hedge selects the number of futures that creates the greatest percentage offset to the variance of the naked position. Methods have been proposed to measure hedge effectiveness other than the percentage reduction in the variance of the cash position. One method computes the percentage reduction in the standard deviation of the na-ked position. This is a simple transformation of the percentage of variance-reduced-measure. Others pertain only to regression methodologies, making a direct compar-ison with a duration-based hedge ratio either impossible or unjustifiably complicated to explain. In this report the average percentage reduction in the variance of the un-hedged position will be used as the measure of hedge effectiveness.

Four representative examples of weak form cash hedges are reported here. The first example hedges the 12.75% Treasury due in 2010. This security possesses in-terest rate sensitivity characteristics similar to those of the cheapest-to-deliver se-curity associated with the T-bond futures contract. The second example hedges a Treasury note with the same T-bond futures contract. This example examines the maturity, but not the credit quality, cross hedge capabilities of the various hedge ratio methodologies. The third and fourth examples hedge single-and double-A rated long-term corporate bonds.

Example 1: Hedging a Bond Similar to the T-Bond Deliverable

The cash inventory to be hedged is the 12.75 Treasury of 2010. The hedging instru-ment is the nearest-to-deliver T-bond futures contract traded on the Chicago Board of Trade. During the hedging period the bond ranges in price from 90 to 120 and drops back down to 105.

Beginning with the data of June 24, 1982 hedges are constructed on a daily basis. Daily hedges suffer from large and normally random basis risk that causes hedges to reduce the inventory price variance by only about 60 to 70%. The true basis risk is worsened by two data problems. First, the data used in all examples in this chapter has not been fully synchronized in trading time; that is, the cash and futures prices have not necessarily been collected at the same time during the trading day. Second, the data set contains several days when the futures contract has a price change con-strained by the daily limit. So even if trades are synchronized, the observed prices on these days have different informational content.

The influence of these two data-related problems can be reduced by averaging the hedge result over several days. A more general reason for examining a smoothed data series is that random basis risk from all sources appears most severe when hedge performance is examined daily. All of the following examples report hedge efficacy based on 10-day and 30-day moving averages. The reported numbers in these tables give the average percent variance reduced over all experiments from June 24, 1982 to December 31, 1983.

Table 4-2 reports the percentage of the cash security's variance reduced by the

Table 4-2. Percent Variance Reduced: U.S. Treasury 12.75s of 2010

	10-Day Moving Average	30-Day Moving Average
Dollar matching	92%	96%
Conversion factor	92	96
Change in price regression	90	91
Price level regression (corrected for autocorrelation)	92	96
Duration	92	96
Duration (corrected for yield volatilities)	93	96
Curvilinear price regression	92	96

alternative hedge ratios. Take, for example, the dollar match hedge ratio results for a 10-day moving average. The reported variance reduction of 92% results from the following calculations.

1. Compute for each trading day from June 24, 1982 through December 31, 1983 the hedged and unhedged portfolio returns.
2. Average these two series using a 10-day moving average.
3. Compute the variance of these returns over the June 1982 through December 1983 period.
4. Find the percentage variance of 10-day moving averages of the unhedged position reduced by the hedged position.

As expected the hedge performances increase as one averages over more days. Because the hedge ratios for all techniques are close to one another in this example and because the cash security has such close characteristics to the deliverable security, all hedge ratio techniques produce similar and excellent hedges. The only possible exception is the change in price regression technique which performs somewhat worse than the other methods. The hedge technique labeled "curvilinear price regression" is that derived from equation (5).

Example 2: Maturity/Duration-Mismatched Hedge

Inventory positions may have maturity and duration characteristics dissimilar to those associated with the deliverable security underlying the best available futures contract. After all, only three maturities are available in the Treasury futures contracts—the 90-day T-bill, the cheapest-to-deliver T-note, and the cheapest-to-deliver T-bond. The efficacy of maturity cross hedges depends on the correlation of interest rate changes across the maturity spectrum.

A relatively severe mismatch in maturities is the context of this example. The Treasury note paying 13% due in 1990 is hedged with the nearest-to-deliver T-bond futures contract. The results are reported in Table 4-3. This example reveals the weakness of the dollar matching strategy, which ignores the different interest rate

Table 4-3.   Percent Variance Reduced: U.S. Treasury 13s of 1990

	10-Day Moving Average	30-Day Moving Average
Dollar matching	44%	68%
Conversion factor	50	72
Change in price regression	78	84
Price level regression (corrected for autocorrelation)	76	86
Duration	80	87
Duration (corrected for yield volatilities)	77	88
Curvilinear price regression	79	89

sensitivities of the hedging and hedge instruments. As expected, the hedge perform-ance for any hedge ratio method selected falls below that experienced in Example 1.

As in Example 1, the more days in the moving average, the more random basis risk is offset. All techniques other than dollar matching and conversion factor meth-ods remain tightly grouped. Note that the correction of duration hedge ratios for rel-ative yield volatilities adds little value. While this finding is somewhat surprising, variations in long-term cash market security yields are relatively close to the varia-tions in intermediate-term yields. Relative yield volatility corrections can add much more value when T-bill contracts are used. The curved line regression of prices tech-nique modestly improves the hedging efficacy of the standard regression of price levels methodology.

Examples 3 and 4: Similar Maturity, Dissimilar Credit Quality Hedges

One can attempt to hedge inventories of long-term corporate bonds with T-bond fu-tures contracts. Spread relationships in yields between corporates and Treasuries have been historically unstable, compounding the basis risk uncovered in Examples 1 and 2. The available literature and common sense support the view that the greater the credit differential, the worse the hedge performance of T-bond futures contracts. Differences in credit quality reduce the comovement in prices and substantially in-fluence hedge efficacy.[21]

Suppose the cash security is the double-A rated GMAC 8s of 2007. While this bond is callable, the high price discount of this low-coupon bond considerably re-duces the chances of a call. Effectively the duration of the bond is nearly that of a noncallable bond. Table 4-4 reports the relative performances of the various hedge ratios for the GMAC bond. Substantial portions of the variation in the naked position can be reduced by any means chosen to hedge. The convenience of dollar matching or unadjusted duration argues for their use in practice. Given the poor performance

---

[21]It is more difficult to conduct regression analysis for corporate bonds than for Treasuries. Publicly avail-able corporate bond price series have notable inaccuracies, if the prices are available at all, making regres-sion estimates for corporates much less accurate than those for Treasuries.

Table 4-4.   Percent Variance Reduced: GMAC 8s of 2007

	10-Day Moving Average	30-Day Moving Average
Dollar matching	78%	89%
Conversion factor	75	86
Change in price regression	75	80
Price level regression (corrected for autocorrelation)	75	86
Duration	78	88
Duration (corrected for yield volatilities)	78	89
Curvilinear price regression	75	86

of the naive dollar-matching strategy in other examples, however, duration-based hedge ratios appear to provide a consistently superior methodology.

The next example examines the hedge effectiveness of alternative techniques when the corporate bond has a lower credit rating than the GMAC bond. The cash security in this example is the A rated Tenneco 8 3/8 of 2002. This bond trades at a substantial price discount which makes this callable bond effectively a long-term instrument. The lower credit quality of this bond reduces the hedge effectiveness for any hedge technique chosen, relative to the GMAC bond. Proportionally, more systematic interest rate risk remains unhedged in this lower credit security than in the double-A rated bond, as shown by comparing 10-day to 30-day moving averages in Tables 4-4 and 4-5. That is the larger reduction in the unhedged variance as one averages over more days in Table 4-4 relative to Table 4-5 indicates the existence of more systematic basis risk in the lower credit bond than in the higher credit bond. (Random basis risk should average out over longer time intervals.)

The two examples just examined were for deep discount callable securities. Throughout the period they traded as though the chances of a call were small. Hedge ratio construction for callable bonds priced at a premium, or bonds fluctuating between premium and discount prices is fraught with difficulties. Consider regression-based hedge ratios. If interest rates have been falling during the recent period, the bond to be hedged may have recently been trading at a discount or near par but is now trading at a premium. At these prior prices the threat of a call is much less than current expectations. Since these expectations fundamentally influence the interest rate sensitivity of the callable bond, the regression-based hedge ratios may be severely misestimated. Duration-based hedge ratios can suffer equally if they continue to be calculated to the maturity date. But the duration of a callable bond can be adjusted for the interest rate influences of the call. This topic is treated in Chapter 7.

It should be understood that only a limited number of examples can be presented. We have selected what we believe to be representative examples that provide guidelines as to what can be expected from weak form cash hedges. Each application of the above techniques to different securities will produce a few surprises, reminding us that great care must be exercised when using interest rate futures. While perfect hedges are impossible with interest rate futures, substantial variance reductions in

Table 4-5.   Percent Variance Reduced: Tenneco 8³/₈ of 2002

	10-Day Moving Average	30-Day Moving Average
Dollar matching	64%	65%
Conversion factor	63	64
Change in price regression	64	69
Price level regression (corrected for autocorrelation)	64	69
Duration	64	69
Duration (corrected for yield volatilities)	64	70
Curvilinear price regression	64	70

inventory market volatilities are normally the rule for those hedgers knowledgeable in the proper uses of hedging techniques.

A final question can be raised about the above hedging examples: Given the theoretical inaccuracies previously described, why do regression-based hedge ratios have reasonable track records? Extreme care was exercised in the data-gathering process as well as in the hedging period to make the regression-based hedge ratios perform their best. Regressions were updated every 20 trading days. Data in cash and futures markets were synchronized as best as possible and screened for data anomalies. Probably most importantly, regressions were run on data that had sufficient price ranges to minimize some of the weaknesses noted in Figures 4-6 and 4-7; that is, the sampling period contains observations that mask many of the regression-based problems.

The assumptions made in the duration-based hedge ratio approach are often violated in practice. Yield curves are not flat, nor do they always shift in a parallel fashion. Thus the simple Macaulay duration formula is not strictly appropriate. The regression-derived relative yield volatility estimates used to enhance the hedging capability of Macaulay's duration do not materially influence hedge efficacy in practice. This finding is not overly surprising, given the cash inventories studied. Once much shorter-term securities are considered, the value of these volatility corrections becomes more apparent. More sophisticated duration formulas also add value.

Conclusions on Weak Form Cash Hedges

Several conclusions can be drawn from the analysis of alternative techniques for hedging inventory positions. First, the theoretical advantages of a duration-based hedge ratio exceed those that can be claimed by alternative minimum variance hedge ratios. Second, naive hedge strategies can work well in some but not all instances. Third, the simplest duration hedge is more conveniently constructed than any regression-based hedge. Neither historical data series nor regression analyses are required. Fourth, duration-based hedge ratios can be altered in numerous ways (e.g., estimating relative *yield* volatilities from par bond data or from zero coupon bond data, modeling the basis, accounting for the influences of call provisions on interest rate sensitivities). By segmenting the sources of interest rate risk using duration, one has the ability to model in an informed manner the residual risks of futures hedges. Fifth, cross hedges result in more basis risk than hedges of securities closely aligned with the hedging futures contract. This is true for cross-maturity and cross-credit-quality hedges. Sixth, and possibly most importantly, simple duration-based hedges work as well as any currently available techniques.

Given these specific conclusions, duration-based hedges appear to be the method to choose. The convenience and theoretical superiority of these hedges are attractive features that lower costs and increase the frequency with which one can justify new hedge ratio computations. Duration-based hedges match *price level* regression hedges empirically, and match or slightly exceed *price change* regression hedges.

SECTION VII   STRONG FORM CASH HEDGES: IMMUNIZING INTEREST RATE RISK WITH INTEREST RATE FUTURES

Unlike the weak form cash hedge, the strong form has a known investment horizon. The goal of this strategy is to maintain an originally expected return over a specified holding period despite interim changes in interest rates. Because a zero coupon bond held to maturity has a return invariant to changes in interest rates, the strong form cash hedge can be viewed as one that converts the interest rate characteristics of one bond into those associated with an interest rate risk "immunizing" zero coupon bond.

Recall that for the weak form cash hedge, the theoretically best hedge ratio minimizes the variance of changes in the value of the portfolio. For the strong form cash hedge, however, the best hedge ratio is one that minimizes the variance of the *difference* between the return on the hedged cash position and the return on the actual or hypothetical zero coupon bond that matures at the end of the investment holding period. Futures contracts are bought or sold as needed to equate the interest rate sensitivity of the cash portfolio to a level required by the strong form cash hedge. The number of futures contracts bought or sold depends upon how interest-rate sensitive the cash portfolio is relative to that needed to achieve the strong form cash hedge objective.

We begin by determining how futures positions alter the return profile of a portfolio. On the day the futures position is established, the price for delivery is set but the futures contract price does not alter the value of the portfolio. As time passes, however, interest rates may change unexpectedly, and this changes the price of the deliverable security expected to prevail on the delivery date. The difference between the old and new expected delivery prices results in a profit or loss in the margin account when first noticed by the market, not on the delivery date. Thus futures contracts influence the return profile of a portfolio through their daily changes in value that are transmitted into portfolio returns through variation margin balances.

Figure 4-8*a* illustrates how a long futures contract alters the interest rate sensitivity of an asset portfolio. For simplicity assume the yield curve is flat at 10%. If rates never change, then as time passes the cash portfolio grows along the solid line from

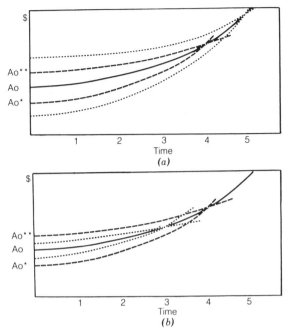

Figure 4-8.   Growth paths of cash portfolios versus cash and futures portfolios.

an initial investment of A_0 dollars at a 10% per annum growth rate. The long position in futures does not alter this growth path—no marking to market occurs until interest rates change unexpectedly. Thus the growth path from A_0 along the solid line is one of either a cash position or a cash and futures position.

Consider the influence of a single unexpected change in the interest rate on the growth path depicted by a solid line in Figure 4-8a. For simplicity assume this rate change takes place just after the cash portfolio is acquired. If rates rise unexpectedly, then the cash portfolio falls in market value from A_0 to A_0^*. But coupon reinvestment accumulates more quickly in this higher interest rate environment, so eventually the cash portfolio value grows to and then beyond the solid line. This new growth path is shown in Figure 4-8a by the lower dashed line. Conversely, let rates fall just after the portfolio is formed. The market value of the cash portfolio immediately increases to A_0^*? Because subsequent growth comes more slowly in this rate environment, the cash portfolio once again accumulates at some point to the value obtained at a 10% growth rate. Refer to the upper dashed line. Notice that the two dashed lines intersect the solid line at the same date in the future. This date corresponds to the original duration, which is measured in years, of the cash portfolio.

The analysis to this point merely reviews the concept of immunization. At the duration point the original interest rate has been earned per annum. Consider what effect a long futures contract would have if it were added to the cash portfolio. If rates rise the expected delivery price falls. This market value decline must be paid by the long position holders in futures in the form of added margin payments. Total portfolio value falls not to $A_0{}^*$ as before, but to some smaller value. The additional decline in market value depends on the number and type of futures contracts. The market value grows at the now higher interest rate and eventually overtakes the solid line as shown by the lower dotted line in Figure 4-8a. Conversely if rates fall, then the long futures position generates an immediate dollar profit causing total portfolio value to increase to a value higher than $A_0{}^{**}$, the new value of the cash position alone. This augmented market value grows more slowly at these lower interest rates, and this produces the upper dotted growth path in Figure 4-8a. The two dotted lines across the solid line at the same date, but this happens farther into the future than for the cash portfolio. This demonstrates that long futures contracts lengthen the duration (immunization period) of cash portfolios.

Figure 4-8b illustrates how short futures contracts influence the interest rate sensitivity of a cash portfolio. Short positions generate surpluses in the margin account of the futures position when rates rise, and margin calls when rates fall.

These market value influences shorten portfolio durations. The solid and dashed lines are exactly the same as those in Figure 4-8a. The dotted lines represent the growth paths of cash plus short futures positions. The upper (lower) dotted line traces the total portfolio value as rates fall (rise). Since rising (falling) rates generate gains (losses) on short futures positions the absolute change in the total portfolio value is smaller on just the cash position. Thus the dotted lines meet at an earlier point in time. Short futures positions then shorten the duration of a cash portfolio.

Hedge Ratio Estimation Techniques for Strong Form Cash Hedges

Suppose the investment holding period is H years and the cash position is one unit of a security with a price of P_c. Let the zero coupon bond due in H years have a price of P_H. What number of futures contracts, long or short, creates this zero coupon bond's price sensitivity? Unlike estimation techniques used with the weak form cash hedge, no naive or "rule of thumb" method provides reasonable answers to this question. Therefore, in the following, only methods derived from theoretical principles are discussed. Mathematically, one must find the number of futures, N, that minimizes the variance of the difference between changes in the value of the hedged portfolio and changes in the value of the zero coupon bond. This variance can be expressed as

$$\text{variance}(\Delta P_c + N \times \Delta P_f - N_H \times \Delta P_H) \tag{8}$$

where ΔP_c, ΔP_H mean the change in price of the cash instrument, futures instrument, and an H-year zero coupon bond respectively. N_H represents the number of zero coupon bonds that hypothetically can be purchased with our initial wealth of P_c dollars. This number is found by dividing P_c by P_H.

The optimal number of futures contracts for a strong form cash hedge, based upon equation (8), is given in equation (9) by N^*.

$$N^* = \frac{(P_c/P_H)\,\text{covariance}(\Delta P_f \text{ with } \Delta P_H) - \text{covariance}(\Delta P_c \text{ with } \Delta P_f)}{\text{variance}(\Delta P_f)} \tag{9}$$

When the cash position happens to be an *H*-year zero coupon bond, the obvious result holds that N^* must be zero. (The two terms in the numerator of equation (9) cancel.) Note that if the covariance of the change in the value of the cash instrument with the change in the value of the futures instrument is larger than the covariance of the change in the value of the zero coupon bond with that of the futures instrument adjusted for the ratio of prices, then N^* will be negative. A negative (positive) value for N^* indicates how many futures should be shorted (purchased) to optimize the hedge.

While equation (9) is similar in form to equation (2), some differences are noteworthy. An additional covariance term must be estimated to obtain N^*. The choice of a futures contract here is complicated by the fact that it is desirable for the contract to be highly correlated with both the cash instrument and the appropriate zero coupon bond, whereas in the weak form cash hedge only high correlation between the change in the futures price and cash price was important. Moreover, the hedge ratio now depends in part upon the ratio of the current cash price to the current price of the *H*-year zero coupon bond. In contrast, the weak form cash hedge ratio has no need for information on price levels in the hedge ratio formula. Actually, the weak form cash hedge is a special case of the strong form cash hedge. To see this, suppose the zero coupon bond we wish to track is a bond maturing today. In this instance P_H is virtually at par and experiences no interest rate induced changes in value. Thus ΔP_H equals zero and equation (9) degenerates into equation (2).

Each of the strong form cash hedge methods discussed below attempts to estimate the variance and covariance relationships of equation (9). As before, the various methods will first be described and then compared, based on their theoretical and practical merits. Issues that were discussed in the context of weak form cash hedges that also apply here will be repeated in only summary form.

Regressions of Price Changes.[22]   This method closely resembles its counterpart in the weak form cash hedge. In order to estimate the relationship between the price of the futures contract and the price of the cash instrument, equation (3) of Section II can be used. It is reproduced here for convenience:

$$\Delta P_c = a_c + b_c \Delta P_f + \text{error}$$

where b_c is the slope coefficient estimated in this regression. For the strong form cash hedge an *additional* regression must be run in order to estimate the relationship between the futures contract and the *H*-year zero coupon bond. And so:

$$\Delta P_H = a_H + b_H \Delta P_f + \text{error}$$

Provided that ΔP_c and ΔP_H and ΔP_H relate in a linear fashion, b_c estimates the covariance (ΔP_c with ΔP_f) to variance (ΔP_f) ratio. Similarly, b_H estimates the cov-

---

[22]The authors know of no other place where regression techniques are applied in the case of strong form cash hedges. We offer these as alternatives to a duration-based estimation cost involved in computing regression-based hedge ratios and to provide estimation results so that they can be compared to those derived from a duration-based approach.

ariance (ΔP_H with ΔP_f) to variance (ΔP_f) ratio. Thus N^* in equation (9) can be evaluated as

$$N^* = (P_c/P_H)b_H - b_c \qquad (10)$$

This hedge ratio can be thought of as the difference of slope coefficients adjusted by relative prices.

Suppose we wish to alter the interest rate sensitivity of the U.S. Treasury 12.75 of 2010, as priced on June 24, 1982, to that of a 5-year zero coupon bond. The futures contract, let us suppose, is the September 1982 T-bond contract. Evaluation of equation (10) begins by estimating b_c and b_H. Thus price and price change data for the T-bond cash instrument, the T-bond futures contract, and a hypothetical 5-year zero coupon Treasury note are required.[23] The regression coefficients estimated with price data from 1981 to mid-1982 are $b_c = 1.16$ and $b_H = 0.59$. These values coupled with the prices of the Treasury bond (90.125) and the 5-year zero coupon bond (49.47) give an optimal hedge ratio of -0.09. The negative sign for N^* indicates that the long bond is more price sensitive than a 5-year zero coupon bond. Selling .09 futures per cash security reduces this sensitivity to that associated with the 5-year zero coupon bond. (The long Treasury bond had a duration of 7.34 years.) This situation resembles that pictured in Figure 4-8*a*.

Regression of Price Levels.   As with the weak form cash hedge one can fit a linear relationship to historical price levels rather than to historical price changes. In order to find the hedge ratios the slope coefficient from the regression of the cash security on the futures price, and the slope coefficient from the regression of the H-year zero coupon bond price on the futures price must be found. These coefficients are employed in equation (10) in the same manner as the coefficient obtained from regressions of price changes. On June 24, 1982 the estimated slope coefficient for the cash security (b_c) is 1.43, as was found for weak form cash hedges. A value of 0.60 is obtained for the slope coefficient relating the price of H-year zero coupon bond to the futures price. Upon substitution in equation (10), a hedge ratio of -0.34 is obtained.

Instantaneous Price Sensitivities Hedge Ratio Method.   Recall that our goal is to find the number of futures contracts per unit of a cash security that causes a combined portfolio of cash and futures positions to have an interest rate sensitivity equal

---

[23]A distinct problem with this regression approach is the need to generate a data series for a 5-year zero. The stripped Treasury market now supplies such prices, but they have to be estimated for our analysis period. Two methods can be used to compute these prices. In the first, the yield to maturity of a 5-year duration bond is computed, and this yield implies a price for a 5-year zero coupon bond. This method ignores "coupon bias" effects that can result in misstating the true price. The alternative method estimates a zero coupon bond yield curve from available yields on coupon-paying bonds. The 5-year spot rate is then used to price a 5-year zero. In the following the more inaccurate but easier to compute zero coupon bond price has been used. Presumably the regression results that follow would be somewhat improved by running the price change regressions on more accurately computed prices.

to that of a specific zero coupon bond. Financial theory indicates how the price of the zero coupon bond, the cash position, and a futures position change per unit change in interest rates. In the context of the strong form cash hedge, the instantaneous hedge ratio is found by solving Equation (9) in terms of bond and futures contract durations. The duration-based solution to Equation (9) can be written as

$$N = \frac{(D_H{}^* - D_c{}^*)P_c}{D_f{}^*P_f} \tag{11}$$

where $D_H{}^*, D_c{}^*, D_f{}^*$ are the modified durations of an H-year zero coupon bond, the cash instrument, and the futures contract, respectively. The duration of an H-year zero coupon bond is H years. P_c and P_f are the respective prices of the cash instrument and futures contract. One can quickly see from equation (11) that whenever the duration of the cash instrument exceeds the duration of the H-year zero coupon bond, a short futures position will be required to reduce the duration of the portfolio to H years.

Equation (11) is nothing more than a generalized expression of what is contained in equation (6). In fact if one were to think of the weak form cash hedge as a method of adjusting the cash portfolio to act like overnight money, $D_H{}^*$ equals zero and equation (11) becomes equation (6). As with equation (6), modifications to equation (11) allow for more realistic assumptions about the various relative yield volatilities. This type of adjustment produces a hedge ratio formula of

$$N^* = \frac{(D_H{}^*R_H - D_c{}^*R_c)\,P_c}{D_f{}^*R_fP_f} \tag{12}$$

where R_c, R_H and R_f are, respectively, the estimated relative yield volatilities of the cash security, zero coupon bond, and deliverable security underlying the futures contract relative to a benchmark security. The hedge ratio derived from equation (11) is -0.46. This value is obtained by substituting the modified durations and prices of the relevant securities into the equation. For our June 24, 1982 example, $D_H{}^*$ equals 4.66 years, D_c equals 6.85 years, and the duration of the bond that is cheapest to deliver for fulfillment of the futures contract equals 7.18 years. The cash bond and futures contract prices are 90.125 and 59.3125, respectively. If relative yield volatilities are estimated and included in equation (12), then the hedge ratio becomes -0.47.

Some worthwhile insights can be gained by rewriting equation (11) in the following way.

$$D_H{}^* = D_c{}^* + \frac{N \times P_f}{P_c}D_f{}^* \tag{13}$$

In this form, the equation can be used to compute the duration of a portfolio consisting of existing positions in cash securities and futures contracts. The term ($N \times$

P_f/P_c) indicates the amount of leverage introduced into the portfolio by N futures contracts. This leverage multiplies the amount of price sensitivity (duration) introduced into the total portfolio by one unit's worth of the futures position. If the value of N is increased, then price sensitivities can be obtained that may be unattainable through ordinary cash market transactions.[24] It should be noted, however, that the risk of nonproportional changes in interest rates takes on new importance when the portfolio includes futures instruments. This type of basis risk can cause the net exposure of a cash/futures position to exceed that of an all cash portfolio of equal duration.

Theoretical Evaluation of Strong Form Cash Hedge Methodologies

The data problems typically encountered in weak form cash hedge regressions are exacerbated in the strong form case. Two regressions with not necessarily canceling errors are now the rule. As before an unrepresentative data set, as illustrated in Figures 4-6 and 4-7, cause misestimation of the hedge ratio. The path dependency argument made against regressions of price changes once again holds, now in double intensity. Furthermore, difficult to obtain prices for hypothetical zero coupon bonds are needed in these regressions. While these data related problems influence the expected or theoretical accuracy of regression-based hedges, regression analyses can incorporate systematic market influences not captured in a duration-based approach.

As time passes, the interest rate sensitivities of the cash security, the H-year zero coupon bond, and the futures contracts constantly change.[25] This requires periodic reestimation of regression coefficients, and the empirical task is arduous. These practical considerations alone argue for a duration-based approach, assuming that the duration methodology can be shown to succeed in the creation of effective strong form cash hedges.

Both the regression and duration approaches to achieving a nonzero duration portfolio by using a combination of futures and cash have an added source of basis risk that is not present in the weak form cash hedge. This added risk arises from the instability of the relationship between yields on the security underlying the futures contract and the zero coupon bond. In general how closely the hedged portfolio will mimic the zero coupon bond is a function of the basis risk, and how closely the duration and cash flow characteristics of the cash position resemble those of the zero coupon bond that is to be replicated. The more closely the cash position resembles the zero coupon bond, the smaller the necessary futures position. This observation has important implications for the outcome of an immunization program. Immuni-

---

[24]Coupon-paying securities currently have a maximum duration of no more than about 10 years. See Chapter 3 on duration for the reason. Portfolios containing cash and long futures can be made to have durations considerably in excess of 10 years.

[25]The cash security and the zero coupon will experience differential (aging) in their durations as time passes. For example in one year's time D_H becomes four not five years while D_c declines by less than one year. The phenomenon of "duration drift" is discussed in more detail in Chapter 3. In our context more and more futures contracts have to be sold as time passes to keep the portfolio on the same time track as the H-year zero coupon bond.

zation requires that the portfolio duration always equal the remaining time to the horizon. This necessitates periodic adjustment of the cash and/or futures position. In the above example, if all rebalancing is effected exclusively through the futures position, more and more futures contracts have to be shorted as time passes. All else equal, this implies that basis risk will increase with the passage of time. The additional basis risk should be weighed against the savings in transactions costs that would be realized if the adjustments were made in the futures market.

Variation margins have implications about how the hedge should be constructed. For example, consider the following two alternatives for creating a 5-year duration portfolio. One could purchase a long bond and short T-bond futures as was done above. The correct number of futures to be sold to adjust the duration was determined to be 0.46. An alternative way to create a 5-year duration portfolio is to keep all cash invested in money market instruments and to buy futures in order to increase the duration. In this case the correct number of futures to be bought would be 0.99.[26] In the long bond/short futures example, variation margin would have to be posted if rates were to fall, while in the money market/long futures example additional margin would be required if rates were to rise. The important thing to note is that for the same absolute change in rates, more than twice as much additional margin would be required in the second case as in the first. Also, the larger position in futures introduces the potential for more basis risk into the second example.

Empirical Test of Strong Form Cash Hedge

This section provides a partial test of the alternative hedge ratio methodologies for strong form cash hedges. An extremely important practical matter ignored here is whether or not an immunizer has any business attempting to immunize a cash portfolio with futures rather than altering the cash portfolio by transactions in cash markets. In any context futures hedges are complicated and introduce a large measure of residual (basis) risks into the analysis. We propose to test the effectiveness of futures contracts in strong form cash hedges by attempting to cause a cash position to mimic the interest rate risk characteristics of a bond with another duration. For example on a month-by-month basis, how closely can a long position in a Treasury bond, combined with a short position in futures create the same monthly variation in wealth as a 5-year zero coupon bond? The answer should shed some light on the value futures contracts offer to portfolio managers wishing to adjust their portfolio durations as required by an immunization program. As well the test helps determine whether or not futures contracts can be integrated with the duration concept as a useful tool in dynamic or active portfolio strategies.

The test is conducted for the period from June 1982 through December 1983. As mentioned above, the bond to be tracked is a 5-year zero coupon bond. Each month a 5-year bond is tracked for one month by the cash plus future position; that is, the artificial experiment is to begin a new 5-year immunized bond portfolio each month

---

[26]Using equation (12) on June 24, 1982, $D_H^* = 4.66$, $D_c^* = 0$, D_f, and $P_f - 59.31$. Assuming an investment of \$90.125 (P_c), the value of N that solves this equation is 0.99.

and examine its performance over only the first month of its 5-year life. This "bogey" bond has an average monthly return of 1.64% and a standard deviation of 2.33% over the trial period. Roughly speaking the standard deviation implies that in 95% of the months examined the monthly return on the bogey bond fell in a range of −3.02% to 6.30%, or two standard deviations on either side of the mean. The U.S. Treasury 12.75 of 2010 has a higher monthly mean return (1.90%) and more volatility with a standard deviation of 3.46%. The comparable range of monthly returns to that of the zero coupon bond is −5.02% to 8.82%. This higher variation in returns is expected since the duration of the long Treasury bond exceeds five years.

Using the duration and the two regression approaches discussed previously, futures positions were established at the beginning of each month to modify the duration of this long Treasury to a 5-year duration. The hedge ratios were reestimated at the start of every experiment (month). More continuous adjustments in the hedges, derived from regression-based methods would be difficult. Daily adjustment in duration-based hedges are quite possible but not employed here. If anything this less continuous hedge ratio adjustment understates the hedging performance of the duration-based method.

Table 4-6 displays the mean and standard deviation of returns for the unhedged and various hedged positions. The closer the mean and standard deviations are to those of the 5-year zero coupon bond, the more effective the strategy. The duration-based hedges outperform the regression-based approaches. Adjusting the duration for relative yield volatilities among the Treasury bond, Treasury bond futures contract, and the 5-year zero coupon bond provides additional, but modest improvement over the simpler duration approach.

Table 4-6 illustrates that hedged portfolios can be constructed to mimic closely the performance of the desired zero coupon bond. It is important, however, to analyze more closely the hedging performances of these alternative techniques. An alternative hedge effectiveness measure computes the mean and standard deviation of the *difference* between returns of the bogey and the hedged positions. The mean difference shows how well *on average* the return of the zero coupon bond was replicated. The standard deviation measures how much on a monthly basis the return on the hedged positions can deviate from the return on the bogey. A perfect hedge position would have both the mean difference and the standard deviation equal to zero.

Table 4-6. Monthly Returns

	Unhedged Treasury Bond	5-Year Zero Coupon	Duration Based		Regression Based	
			Uncorrected	Corrected[a]	Price Changes	Price Levels
Mean return	1.90%	1.63%	1.60%	1.62%	1.74%	1.67%
Standard deviation	3.46%	2.33%	2.23%	2.29%	2.55%	2.56%

[a]Based on estimated relative yield volatilities

Table 4-7.   Difference in Returns

	Unhedged Treasury Bond	Duration Based		Regression Based	
		Uncorrected	Corrected[a]	Price Changes	Price Levels
Mean difference	.27%	−.03%	−.01%	.11%	.04%
S.D. difference	1.33%	.69%	.67%	.74%	.70%

[a]Based on estimated relative yield volatilities

Thus the closer these two values are to zero, the better the tracking ability of the zero coupon bond. Table 4-7 shows the results for the example just discussed.

Obviously there is a substantial mean difference for the unhedged position. The monthly return on average for the unhedged portfolio was 27 basis points higher than the monthly return on the bogey bond. The standard deviation of 1.33% simply indicates that the returns on the unhedged position has substantially higher volatility than the 5-year zero coupon bond. This is expected since a long Treasury bond reacts much differently to changes in interest rates than a 5-year zero coupon bond. Of the available hedging techniques, the duration approach corrected for relative yield volatilities does the best job on average, mimicking the return of the zero coupon bond. The mean difference of −1 basis point indicates that on average the monthly return on the synthetically created 5-year duration portfolio differs from the return on the real 5-year zero coupon bond by 1 basis point. The standard deviation shows that even though on average the returns of the combined futures and cash position are very similar to those of the zero coupon bond, the returns are not identical in every period. A standard deviation of .67% implies that roughly 95% of the time the monthly return on the cash/futures position will fall within ±1.34% of the return on the 5-year zero coupon bond. As Table 4-7 illustrates, the regression of changes in prices hedge performs more poorly than the other approaches.

In the example above a long maturity Treasury bond (with a duration of 7.34 years) was converted into a 5-year duration bond using a short position in Treasury bond futures (with a duration of 7.75). Note that the duration of the cash instrument is relatively close to that of the futures contract. On the other hand if one were to create a 5-year duration portfolio by combining a long position in Treasury bond futures with a short-term cash position, the duration of the cash instrument would differ substantially from that of the futures instrument. This increases the basis risk and can lead to different results.

This example considered only a position in Treasury instruments. Recall that in the weak form cash hedge, we found that hedging non-Treasury instruments resulted in decreased hedge efficacy because of the unstable relationship between the yields on corporate and government securities. Similar results hold in the strong form cash hedge.

Conclusions on Strong Form Cash Hedges

First, as noted earlier there are no naive strategies for this type of hedge. Second, because regression-based approaches require data that is not easily constructed and because two regressions must always be run, these methods are not easily implemented. This reduces the value regression-based hedges offer in capturing any systematic historical influences in the hedge ratio. Third, the simplest duration approach is convenient and complements already existing immunized investment strategy methodologies. Fourth, the duration approach performs as well as or better than regression-based methodologies. Fifth, correction of relative yield volatilities offers modestly improved hedge performance. Sixth, although not noted above, modeling the basis in strong form cash hedges can be more easily incorporated in a duration-based approach than regression-based approaches.

As with the weak form cash hedge, the theoretical superiority, convenience of implementation, relatively good empirical performance, and the ease with which duration-based hedge ratios can be incorporated into portfolio management argue for their use over the regression-based approaches. While further modeling of the basis may improve the empirical results, it still becomes important to compare the results of a cash/futures immunized portfolio with one constructed entirely in the cash market. Futures contracts, properly used, normally will not produce perfect hedges.

SECTION VIII   ANTICIPATORY HEDGES

From an investor's perspective, a perfect anticipatory hedge ensures that a currently expected price or yield can be achieved upon the receipt of a future cash inflow. For this to occur the hedging instrument must generate value or yield changes between the initiation of the hedge and its termination offsetting to value or yield changes in the desired future asset. From an issuer's perspective, a perfect anticipatory hedge ensures that the currently expected issuing price or rate of a new debt instrument can be achieved on the future debt issuing date. This section discusses strong form anticipatory hedges before turning to the closely related topic of weak form anticipatory hedges. Strong form anticipatory hedges can be accomplished when the asset cash inflow date or the debt issuing date is known exactly. Weak form anticipatory hedges occur when these dates are uncertain.

Strong Form Anticipatory Hedges

Before beginning a full description and analysis of the strong form anticipatory hedge, it is useful to recall some of the material contained in the section on pricing. There it was noted that cost-of-carry arbitrage in futures, forwards, and cash markets cause hedged long-term cash securities to generate returns different from quoted yields on long-term securities. (The exception occurs in flat yield curve environments.) In other words, it is impossible to use futures to turn a 30-year security into a 1-year security without converting a 30-year yield into approximately a 1-year yield.

A similar arbitrage holds in anticipatory hedges. For example, suppose the current 1-, 2-, and 3-year spot rates are 10%, 11%, and 12% respectively. These rates imply that the 2-year rate one year from now is about 13%.[27] This yield implies a forward price of $0.78 per dollar invested for a 2-year zero coupon bond purchased one year from now. (Prices for coupon-paying 2-year securities can also be calculated from the 13% yield.) An anticipatory hedge placed for one year to protect currently expected prices and yields until cash is received and invested in 2-year securities locks in approximately a 13% 2-year yield at an acquisition price of about $0.78 per dollar of face value. It does not lock in the current 11% 2-year yield at its price of $0.81.[28] This line of reasoning suggests a useful framework for understanding anticipatory hedges. *Strong form anticipatory hedges are conceptually equivalent to hedging short forward contracts on the securities to be acquired with long futures contracts.*

The proposition that an asset anticipatory hedge is conceptually equal to a short forward contract hedged with a long futures position can be developed with the aid of a graph. (As in prior sections, the following hedge examples are described primarily from the viewpoint of a portfolio manager. A liability anticipatory hedge is conceptually the same as hedging a long forward contract with a short futures position.) In Figure 4-9 the horizontal axis measures time starting with today's date and extending to the termination date of the hedge, T. This is the date when the cash inflow is received. The value of the short forward and long futures contracts are measured on the vertical axis. When interest rates do not change unexpectedly, the net value of each of these contracts remains at zero. But since this instance is uninteresting, let us consider the value of these positions in forward and futures contracts when rates fall unexpectedly.

For expositional convenience, let the fall in interest rates occur once, just after the hedge is formed. The rate decline causes the future price of the security to be acquired to rise and, consequently, lowers the acquired yield on this future purchase. The loss is effectively realized at date T and is analogous to that experienced on a short forward contract, deliverable on date T, for the same securities. Let the loss at date T total $-\$\Delta P_{FOR}$ dollars. A fully protective hedge to the hypothetical short forward position in the futures market is a long futures position of sufficient magnitude to generate $+\$\Delta P_{FOR}$ at date T.

---

[27]The 2-year yield beginning one year from now is computed by finding the 3-year cumulative value and dividing it by the 1-year cumulative value. The result is a forward 2-year cumulative value from which the 2-year yield is easily derived. The 3-year cumulative value per dollar invested in our example is 1.12 $\times$ 1.12 $\times$ 1.12 = $1.405. The 1-year cumulative value per dollar invested is $1.10. Thus the expected 2-year cumulative value starting one year from now is $1.277. An annual yield of 13% for two years culminates in this number.

[28]The presence of liquidity premiums, transactions costs, basis risks, and other impediments means that 13% is unlikely to be realized exactly. Nevertheless, the realized return will normally be closer to the rate on the actual or idealized forward than on the current 2-year security. If the current 1-, 2-, and 3-year rates were 12%, 11%, and 10% respectively, then the hedging rate is approximately 9% not 11%.

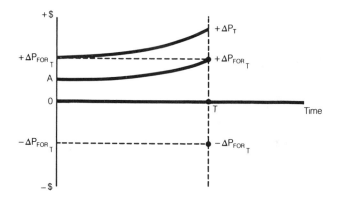

"T" indicates the date at which the cash inflow to be invested occurs.

Figure 4-9. Changes in value of futures and forward contracts.

One difficulty in obtaining an exact hedge of the short forward contract with a futures contract is that gains or losses in futures contracts are realized the day they are first noticed and not on the delivery date. Any losses must be financed and any gains earn at a rate that we assume equals the financing rate. Because gains or losses are realized in futures contracts before they are realized in forward contracts, it takes less than one futures contract to hedge the forward contract with identical delivery characteristics. If one futures contract, identical in delivery characteristics to the forward contract were purchased in our falling rate example, then the instantaneous gain on the long futures contract would be $+\$\Delta P_{FOR}$, and this figure plus interest would total $(1 + r^*)^T \times (+\$\Delta P_T)$ or $+\$\Delta P_T$ at date T. This gain exceeds the loss on the short forward contract at date T. The r term, in this expression, represents the financing/borrowing rate after the decline in interest rates. The correct number of futures contracts to buy per forward contract is $1/(1 + r^*)^T$. This generates a gain of $\$A$ today which grows to $+\$\Delta P_{FOR}$ on date T. The problem with this hedge ratio is that r^* is not known at the time the hedge is put into place, only the current financing/borrowing rate is known. The best guess hedge ratio therefore is $1/(1 + r)^T$. The inability to construct the hedge ratio based on r^* rather than on r only moderately limits hedge efficacy. It does, however, overhedge when rates increase, which results in a small net loss, and underhedges when rates decline, which results in a small net profit.

The goal of the anticipatory hedge is to lock in currently expected prices and, possibly, yields on future acquisitions. Fixing the future acquisition price of a security enables the portfolio manager to lock in the yield on this security, should the manager so choose. This is clearly the case when the acquired security is a zero coupon bond—a fixed price guarantees the yield to maturity. Less obvious is the case for coupon bonds. Hedging the acquisition price of a coupon bond keeps constant the yield to maturity are computed for the acquired bond. But, as so many introductory books on bonds show, yields to maturity are computed by implicitly assuming coupon payments are reinvested at this yield. Given an interest rate change, this reinvestment rate cannot be realized. What can be obtained, however, is the originally expected yield from the acquisition date to the date associated with the original duration date computed on the acquired security. This duration, as discussed below, is computed from the delivery date forward. The first phase in this process is fixing the acquisition price through a strong form anticipatory hedge; the second phase hedges the return on the security after it is acquired using the strong form cash hedge, as per techniques described in Section V. If the former hedge is completed without the latter, the price but not the return is hedged. Note that as in Section V, the yield to maturity on coupon bonds can never be hedged. Only the yield to the duration point can be hedged. (For zero coupon bonds the yield to maturity and yield to the duration point are equal, as are the maturity and duration dates.)

One final point must be made before we examine the alternative means of estimating hedge ratios for strong form anticipatory hedges. Anticipatory hedges can be constructed using futures with delivery characteristics that differ from those associated with the short forward contract that hypothetically represents the interest rate sensitivity of the security to be acquired. As in prior sections hedge ratios are constructed by dividing the interest rate sensitivity of the hedged position by the interest rate sensitivity of the hedging security. The more correlated these sensitivities, the better the hedge. High correlation, however, does not require that the hedging futures contract deliver the bond to be acquired, nor does the delivery date on the futures contract need to coincide with the day cash is received.

Hedge Ratio Estimation Techniques for Strong Form Anticipatory Hedges

As mentioned above, anticipatory hedges may have two phases. The first and mandatory part of the hedge attempts to offset any price change in the cash security at its acquisition date with an equally sized value change in the futures position, including margin financing costs and earnings. This hedge is similar in many but not all respects to weak form cash hedges. The second phase, trivial for zero coupon bond acquisitions, begins on the acquisition date. If chosen it transforms the hedged acquisition price into a hedged holding-period yield. Since this hedge is identical to strong form cash hedges, only the first phase of the anticipatory hedge is discussed here.

Several methods, all similar to those considered in the weak form cash hedge, have currency in financial literature. Several are quite naive and caution should be taken when these hedge ratios are employed. For purposes of demonstration the hedge ratio estimation techniques that follow are illustrated assuming that on May 24, 1982 a portfolio manager decided that the $10 million expected to be received on June 24, 1982 should be invested in U.S. Treasury 12.75s of 2010. A September delivery T-bond futures contract is used in these examples to avoid the possibility of receiving delivery on the long futures contract during the delivery month on the June 1982 futures contract. We assume in the following that the short-term rate at which the manager can borrow or lend during the month is 13.50%.

Dollar Matching.   The most naive strategy purchases a $10 million face value position in T-bond futures. This one-for-one match ignores differential interest rate sensitivities between the security to be acquired and the futures contract. It also ignores the immediate mark-to-market feature of futures contracts. A more sensible but still naive procedure is to futures contracts that have $10 million market value and then adjust this amount for the differential timing in the realization of gains and losses. The May 24, 1982 futures price for the September T-bond contract is 64.469. Thus 155 futures contracts total $10 million, a hedge ratio of 1.55. To adjust this ratio for the mark-to-market features of futures, divide the hedge ratio by $(1.1350)^{30/365}$, or 1.0105. This value represents the $(1 + r)^T$ term discussed above. (The adjustment factor is common to all hedge ratio methodologies that follow.)

Conversion Factor Method.   The conversion factor described in Section IV can be adapted for strong form anticipatory hedges. The conversion factor on the cash security to be acquired in June 1982 is 1.50. Recall that the conversion factor for a security is always computed relative to the hedging futures contract. Since the September 1982 contract used here is the same as the earlier one used, the conversion factors in these two applications are the same. The adjustment factor of 1.0105 reduces the hedge ratio from 1.50 to 1.48. Like dollar matching hedges, the conversion factor method takes into account the price *differential* of the forward and futures contracts. Since price *sensitivities* are ignored however this can only be considered a reasonable approach when the hedging instrument and the instrument to be acquired have approximately the same interest rate sensitivities. The conversion factor method has the additional advantage over the dollar matching approach in that it does not require any current market data.

Just as in Weak Form Cash Hedges, the foregoing hedges have convenience in application as their common strong point. None of these naive hedges properly constructs hedge ratios in instances when the security to be acquired differs in interest rate sensitivity from the hedging contract. The theoretically best hedge ratio minimizes the variance of future acquisition costs, net of the effect of the hedge. The objective is to select a value of N, the number of futures contracts, such that the variance $(\Delta P_{FOR_T} + N \times \Delta P_{f_T})$ is minimized. Here, ΔP_{FOR_T} represents the gain or loss in the price of the acquired security at date T, which is hypothetically equivalent to the gain or loss of a short forward contract on this security that is deliverable at date T. The change in the hedging futures contract at date T is represented by ΔP_{f_T}.

The optimal number of futures contracts to buy to minimize the changes in net acquisition costs, that is, to minimize variance $(\Delta P_{FOR_T} + N \times \Delta P_{f_T})$ is given by the formula:

$$N^* = \text{covariance}(\Delta P_{FOR_T} \text{ with } \Delta P_{f_T})/\text{variance}(\Delta P_{f_T})$$

Accounting for mark-to-market payments or receipts in the futures position, N^* becomes

$$N^* = \text{covariance}(\Delta P_{FOR_T} \text{ with } \Delta P_f)/((1 + r^*)^T \times \text{variance}(\Delta P_f)) \qquad (14)$$

The absence of T subscripts on ΔP_f indicates that the covariance is between the change in the short forward contract and the observed daily price change in futures contract price. As T approaches zero, N^* approaches the value found in Section IV. Since r^* is not known, it must be replaced with the best available estimate, which is normally the current value of r.[29]

The problem becomes one of estimating from available information the covariance and variance terms needed to find N^* of equation (14). The same basic types of regression analyses and instantaneous price sensitivity methods as were discussed in Weak Form Cash Hedges can be applied. The only change is that (ΔP_{FOR_T} replaces ΔP_c, which is the change in the inventories cash price in equation (3), and that an estimate of the financing/borrowing rate is needed in equation (14).

For short-term anticipatory hedges the difference between changes in forward prices and cash prices is quite small, and anticipatory hedges for most purposes can be viewed as cash hedges. For longer-term anticipatory hedges or for slightly more accuracy, the correct hedge ratio depends upon changes in forward prices, which must be estimated. This is most easily accomplished by discounting the cash flows of the security from its acquisition date to maturity by a forward yield.[30]

Regression of Price Changes.   This approach estimates a regression line relating ΔP_{FOR_F} to ΔP_f. The slope coefficient of this regression estimates the covariance (ΔP_{FOR_T} with ΔP_f) to variance (ΔP_f) ratio used in equation (14). This regression produced a coefficient of 1.15. Thus, the hedge ratio is 1.14. Note the close similarity to the hedge ratio found in Section IV using this methodology.

Regression of Price Levels.   This regression approach is similar to the one above. Here, P_{FOR_T} is regressed on P_f. The slope coefficient provides an alternative measure of the covariance-to-variance ratio needed in equation (14). The estimate derived for this coefficient in our example is 1.40. The hedge ratio is 1.39. Again, note the close similarity to that found in the section on the weak form cash hedge using this regression-based methodology.

Instantaneous Price Sensitivities Hedge Ratio.   The covariance-to-variance ratio used in equation (14) can be obtained by estimating DP_{FOR_T} and DP_f per basis point move in interest rates. This ratio of interest rate sensitivities divided by $(1 + r)^T$—to estimate the financing/borrowing rate on the futures contract—estimates N^*. An alternative representation of this approach uses the duration concept to estimate relative price sensitivities. The strong form anticipatory hedge ratio can be calculated as

$$N^* = -P_{FOR_T}^s \times D_{FOR_T}^{s*} / (1 + r)^T \times P_f \times D_f^* \qquad (15)$$

---

[29]Equation (14) is not strictly correct as it assumes r* is independent of $\Delta P_{FOR}T$ and ΔP_f. Nevertheless for reasonable changes in r, equation (14) suffices.

[30]More correctly, the zero coupon bond yield curve should be estimated; the forward zero coupon bond yield curve can then be derived using the security acquisition date. Individual cash flows are then discounted by these separate discount rates.

$D^{s*}_{\text{FOR}_T}$ is the modified duration of the short forward contract. It is computed using the cash flows of the security to be acquired from date T to the maturity of this security. That is, this duration is computed just as though today were date T. Since the security is sold short, its modified duration is negative in value, meaning that when rates rise the price change in the short position is positive. The discount rate used in the duration formula is computed using forward yields or, more correctly, forward zero coupon bond yields. D_f^* is the modified duration of the (cheapest-to-deliver) deliverable security associated with the futures contract. This duration is computed relative to the delivery date of the futures contract, which need not be dated.[31] For our illustrative 30-day anticipatory hedge example P_{FOR_T}, $D^{s*}_{\text{FOR}_T}$, r, P_f, and D_f^* are respectively 96.8475, -7.307, 0.1350, 64.469, and 7.432. This generates a hedge ratio of $+1.46$. These are the number of futures to buy per unit of the hypothetically shorted security to be hedged. This hedge ratio can be altered, as in prior sections, to incorporate available information on relative yield volatilities. The proper hedge ratio becomes 1.48 adjusted for relative yield volatilities.

Theoretical and Empirical Evaluation of Strong Form Anticipatory Hedges

The theoretical merits and demerits of each anticipatory hedge ratio estimation technique are exactly those discussed in the context of weak form cash hedges. The naive strategies are just that and should be avoided when sufficient information is available to compute more sophisticated hedge ratios.

The minimum variance hedge ratio requiring the least historical data analysis is the duration-based hedge ratio. This methodology assumes yield movements are proportional to one another, but so do regression-based hedges. If Macaulay's duration is employed, then the duration hedge implicitly assumes the yield curve is flat and shifts in a parallel fashion. Other duration measures make less restrictive assumptions. Regression models assume that the average of recently observed random processes governing changes in interest rates will hold in the future. But this estimated average may represent a random process that has never been observed, and therefore, may never be correct. In addition to this problem regressions combine all historical influences into one variable, the estimated slope coefficient. This summary measure may incorporate the problem of path dependency and other biases as noted in the section on weak form cash hedges. Instantaneous price sensitivity hedge ratios, which can be expressed in terms of durations, make fewer and weaker assumptions than regression-based hedge ratios. This leaves the unhedged residual from duration-based hedges more susceptible to direct modeling than the unhedged residuals of regression-based hedges.

Because all of the strong form anticipatory hedges are straightforward and slight modifications of those developed for weak form cash hedges, the relative hedge performance for the various hedge ratio methodologies found for weak form cash hedges

---

[31]The duration computed for the futures contract assumes the Treasury 9.125s of 2009 will be the cheapest to deliver in September 1982.

holds here as well. Thus we conclude that duration-based anticipatory hedges equal or slightly exceed the hedging efficacy of available alternatives.

Weak Form Anticipatory Hedges

These hedges occur when the cash inflow date is uncertain. The degree of this uncertainty governs the ultimate effectiveness of the hedge. Should the range of possible cash inflow dates be a month or less, little effective damage is done by structuring a strong form anticipatory hedge for the midpoint in this month. A probability-weighted or expected cash inflow date helps hedge efficacy by incorporation of the best available information into the hedge. As new information about the cash inflow date becomes available, the hedge ratio should be adjusted accordingly. Unless only the wildest of estimates on the cash inflow date are available, the application of anticipatory hedges should prove beneficial. A reduction in future acquisition price of modest amount has value to individuals interested in hedging.

Other characteristics govern hedge effectiveness. For example, if a fixed bond maturity or duration is to be acquired whenever the cash inflow occurs (for example the cash inflow must be used to acquire exactly a 6-month T-bill with the cash), then misestimation of the cash inflow date T causes less error than if a particular bond issue is to be acquired. The shape of the yield curve also alters hedge efficacy. Regardless of all but highly reverse yield curve shapes, however, it can be shown that the hedge ratio will be too high whenever the cash inflow occurs after the expected date and vice versa.

Weak form anticipatory hedges are not the most difficult to construct. Those we have elected to address at another time include instances when the date of the cash inflow is known but the amount to be received is not. It could be that the inflow amount and date are both uncertain. These uncertainties might be random in nature or themselves dependent on the future course of interest rates. For example, some insurance companies issue guaranteed interest contracts (GICs) with a fixed rate and a fairly long take-down period. If rates begin to fall the timing of inflows within the investment time window may shorten and the dollar amounts increase. Hedge maintenance is extremely important in this instance. Part of the function of such a hedge is to replicate dynamically the implicit call option written into these GICs. Successful hedging techniques in this case also have application to banks and thrifts making fixed-rate loan commitments.

Basis Risk

As we have seen from the examples in this chapter, even the most theoretically correct hedges are in many cases far from perfect. In this section we discuss some of the causes of this imperfection and suggest methods for further improving hedging effectiveness.

The term "basis risk" arises from the notion that if the basis—the difference between the price of the futures contract and the instrument to be hedged—is not stable then the hedge will be imperfect. This notion is not quite accurate; instability in the raw basis will not necessarily lead to a drop in hedging effectiveness. For example, consider hedging a long position in the cheapest-to-deliver Treasury bond with a short position in the Treasury bond future. We know that in a positive yield curve environment the (adjusted) futures price lies below the cash bond price. However, as time passes the process of convergence forces the (adjusted) futures and cash prices together. This would then seem to be a source of basis risk. In fact, as we noted earlier, convergence really is a realization of the positive or negative cost of carry and has little impact on the effectiveness of the hedge.[32] Another flaw in using the raw basis as a measure of risk is that it ignores the relative interest rate sensitivity of the hedging and hedged instruments. For example, if one computed the raw basis between a 10-year Treasury note and a Treasury bond future one would find that in rising (falling) rate environments the price of Treasury bond future would fall (rise) more than the Treasury note, thus altering the basis. This again leads to an erroneous conclusion about hedge effectiveness.[33] Since this aspect of the basis is changing in a predictable manner, it can be managed by properly adjusting the hedge ratio for relative interest rate sensitivity through the duration hedge. This leads to the concept of a duration or interest sensitivity adjusted basis as the appropriate measure of basis risk. That is, in examining the potential effectiveness of a hedge one should consider the stability of a duration adjusted basis rather than simply the stability of the difference in prices.

Unfortunately, basis risk remains even after adjusting the hedge for relative interest rate sensitivity. The traditional approach for dealing with the residual basis risk is to multiply the duration hedge ratio by a relative yield volatility measure is indicated in equation (7). This relative yield volatility measure is computed by regression analysis. The problem is that in many cases the measure is so unstable that there is no improvement hedge effectiveness.[34] In other words, the simple linear model that is assumed to exist between the yields on the various instruments is often inappropriate.

Minor sources of basis risk result from changes in the cheapest-to-deliver security for the T-bond contract, the option in delivery terms of the futures contract, sudden special demand for a particular security (e.g. when Treasury bonds are stripped in the market their prices can suddenly deviate from the rest of the market), daily limit moves in the futures market, and changes in short-term financing costs. For the most part the risk from these factors is small.

The two major sources of basis risk identified earlier in our examples of weak form cash hedges arise from differences in credit quality and differences in maturity between the hedging and hedged instruments.

Basis risk due to differences in maturity occur because rates at different points

[32]There is a small amount of risk induced by the variability of the financing costs implicit in the futures contract.
[33]This incorrect conclusion might have been drawn if one examined the results in Table 4-3 for the dollar matching approach where only 68% variance reduction was achieved.
[34]We observed this in our examples. See Tables 4-2, 4-3, 4-4, and 4-5.

along the yield curve change unpredictably by unequal amounts. As we have seen in Chapter 2, there is currently no accepted model of how the term structure changes. While normally all rates move up and down together there are times when short-term rates and long-term rates move in opposite directions, and when one rate moves and the other does not. Therefore, even when we adjust a hedge for differing interest rate sensitivities, risk remains because we do not have a reliable model that will predict how, for example, the 10-year rate will change when the 30-year rate moves by 10 basis points. This is why the percent variance reduced when hedging a T-note with a T-bond future was found to be approximately 87% compared with 96% when hedging a T-bond with a T-bond future. Given the current state of understanding of the yield curve, reducing this source of basis risk is more of an art than a science. This in fact is the reason why there are contracts for securities with different terms to maturity. There are contracts for T-bills, T-notes, and T-bonds. In order to increase the percent variance reduced from 87% (in the above example) one should use the T-note futures contract instead of the T-bond future hedge a cash T-note position.

Another major source of basis risk arises from differences in credit quality. In Table 4-5 we found that hedging a single-A rate long maturity corporate bond with a T-bond futures contract reduced variance by only 70%. Further studies have shown that when hedging even lower quality bonds, percent variance reduced drops off dramatically. In some cases the hedge actually increases the variance. The reason for this is that the yields of lower quality bonds are driven by other factors in addition to the general level of risk-free rates. As a result, hedging only with futures on government bonds cannot be expected to maximize the percent variance reduced. However a new technology has been developed that addresses the credit component of the basis. This technology significantly improves hedge effectiveness for lower quality credits by introducing into the hedge securities (having higher correlation with the credit components of bond price changes). This technique is described further in Chapter 8. It turns out that the duration hedge ratio described in this chapter is a subset of this new technology, so the techniques are identical for hedging high quality bonds.

SECTION IX   CONCLUSION

The concept of hedging can be traced to one of the major tenets of modern portfolio theory. Namely, interest rate risk reduction is possible only when the influence of productive covariance in price movements between hedging and hedged securities exceeds the added price variance contributed to a portfolio by the hedging security. The best hedge optimizes the size of the position taken in the hedging security that prior analysis has established as the security most correlated with the unhedged position. Nevertheless, such a hedge will rarely remove all interest rate risk.

While all hedges have as their goal the reduction of risk, different situations have different risks. Thus one of the first steps in implementing a hedging program is to state accurately and clearly the objective of the hedge. This is necessary because, as we have seen, hedge construction and management is influenced by this objective.

Weak form cash hedges have as their goal the preservation of capital, whereas strong form cash hedges attempt to fix a rate of return over an investment period. Anticipatory hedges attempt to ensure that the future purchase or sale of securities will occur at prices and/or yields "forecasted" by current market prices and yields. These classifications can each be viewed from either an asset or liability perspective, although this paper has focused on the asset side of the balance sheet.

Before implementing a hedging program using interest rate futures, it is important for the user to understand that futures do not magically produce returns (for a given level of risk) exceeding those implied by the current market. Analyzing the factors that determine the price of a futures contract enables one to distinguish what can from what cannot be hedged; this analysis determines what the hedge return will be. Market arbitrage arguments firmly establish that one cannot hedge the price risk of a long-term bond held for a short time period without altering the realized yield to be a level closely associated with short-term yields.

Many suggestions have been made on how hedge ratios for the various hedging goals should be constructed. They range from the naive to the highly sophisticated. This chapter has attempted to catagorize these hedges in terms of the quality of their theoretical heritage and in terms of their value in practical implementation. If the assumptions underlying the construction of the hedge ratio adequately reflect reality, the associated estimation methodology has merit and can generate satisfactory results. The naive or rule of thumb approaches such as one-to-one hedges, dollar value matching and the conversion factor methods are severely limited in their applicability since they assume that the interest rate risk exposure of the security to be hedged equals that of the hedging vehicle. This can lead to less than optimal results when these price sensitivities differ. Moreover, none of these simple approaches apply when the hedge goal is that of the strong form cash hedge.

With regard to the more theoretically-based approaches—those using regression and duration analyses—each can be derived from the same risk minimizing objective of modern portfolio theory. They differ in their measurement of the relative price sensitivities of the cash and futures instruments. Regression-based approaches in theory directly incorporate into their hedge ratios information on relative price sensitivities and on systematic market distortions. This blending of influences, while potentially important, limits the ultimate effectiveness of regression-based hedge ratios. Duration-based hedges, on the other hand, make fewer and more explicit assumptions. This leaves the observed unhedged risks much more subject to modeling than is the case in regression-based hedge ratios, which have been estimated from data jointly reflecting financial theory and systematic market influences. We noted as well that new data affecting the hedge ratio can be more simply and quickly integrated into a duration-based methodology. Several data-related problems occur in the regression-based approaches that can often bias the estimated hedge ratios.

In terms of hedge results obtained for the period between June 1982 and December 1983, we found for the weak form cash hedge that the simplest duration approach performs at least as well as any of the regression approaches and in many cases outperforms them. Basis risk was particularly troubling in these historical hedges. But basis risk caused by random influences should average out over time. Averaging the observed hedge performance over a number of days does improve the results for any method selected. The improvement for duration-based hedges marginally exceeded those obtained with other methods. Substantial basis risk remains, which indicates the presence of systematic influences that should be subject to modeling.

Not unexpectedly we find that the more dissimilar the hedging and hedged instruments, due to differences in credit quality, maturity, and coupon rates, the more poorly the weak form cash hedge performs. The technology described in Chapter 8 will reduce basis risk that arises when hedging lower quality instruments. Better modeling of the term structure and the introduction of other contracts (along the yield curve) will reduce basis risk due to maturity mismatch. However, it should be understood that from time to time hedge imperfections, which cannot be predicted in advance, create situations when it would have been better to have been unhedged. For example, in stable market environments the basis risk could actually increase overall variance. On average, however, it is rare to find that the variance of an unhedged portfolio is less than on a ''hedged'' portfolio. Although all of the above empirical conclusions were demonstrated in the text through examples, these conclusions are representative of conclusions derived from a study of a larger universe of bonds.

With regard to strong form cash hedges, we concluded that futures can successfully be used to alter the price sensitivity of portfolios to match particular durations. However, one must make a careful comparison with an all-cash constructed immunized portfolio, and evaluate the tradeoff between the higher transaction costs in the all-cash hedge and the higher residual (basis) risk in hedges constructed with futures.

Anticipatory hedges require slight modifications to the hedge ratios obtained in weak form cash hedges. What is crucial in anticipatory hedges is an understanding of the influence the mark-to-market feature of futures has on the hedge ratio and an understanding of what target yield is achievable from the hedge.

Overall we find hedge ratios estimated using the duration-based approach to be the method of choice. The convenience, theoretical superiority, low estimation costs, and effective empirical results obtained from this methodology relative to the known alternatives support this view.

BIBLIOGRAPHY

Black, F. ''The Pricing of Commodity Contracts.'' *Journal of Financial Economics* 3, nos. 1 and 2 (January/March 1976): 167–179.

Bookstaber, R. *The Complete Investment Book.* Glenview, IL: Scott, Foresman & Co., 1985.

Ederington, L.H. ''The Hedging Performance of the New Futures Market.'' *Journal of Finance* 34 (March 1979): 157–170.

Franckle, C.T. ''The Hedging Performance of New Futures Market: Comment.'' *Journal of Finance* 35 (December 1980): 1273–1279.

Hill, J., and Schneeweis, T. ''Risk Reduction Potential of Financial Futures for Corporate Bond Positions,'' in G.D. Gay and R.S. Kolb, eds. *Interest Rate Futures: Concepts and Issues.* Richmond, VA: Robert F. Dane, 1982.

Kane, E.J. "Market Incompleteness and Divergences between Forward and Futures Interest Rates." *Journal of Finance* 35 (May 1980) 221–232.

Kolb, R., and Chiang, R. "Improving Hedging Performance Using Interest Rate Futures." *Financial Management* 10 (1981): 72–79.

McEnally, R., and Rice, M. "Hedging Possibilities in the Flotation of Debt Securities." *Financial Management* 8, no 4. (Winter 1979): 12–18.

Morgan, G.E. "Forward and Futures Pricing of Treasury Bills." *Journal of Banking and Finance* (December 1981).

Pitts, M. "Cross Hedging, Autocorrelated Errors, and the Trade-Off Between Risk and Return," paper presented at the Financial Management Association Meetings, October 1983.

Rendleman, R., and Carabini, C. "The Efficiency of the Treasury Bill Futures Market." *Journal of Finance* 34, no. 4, (September 1979): 875–914.

Toevs, A.L., and Jacob, D.P. "Interest Rate Futures: A Comparison of Alternative Hedge Ratio Methodologies," *Journal of Portfolio Management*, (1986).

Chicago Board of Trade. "Financial Futures: The Delivery Process in Brief" (1982).

5 The Use of Options in Performance Structuring: Molding Returns to Meet Investment Objectives

RICHARD BOOKSTABER

INTRODUCTION

During the first 10 years of listed option trading, options were viewed as tactical, if not outright speculative, instruments. Investors purchased calls to gain leverage, bought puts to lock in gains or speculate on declines, and used covered writes to enhance yields on sluggish issues. The implications of options positions for the return characteristics of the overall portfolio were rarely a consideration; the concern in option trading was trade-by-trade profitability, not cumulative portfolio effects. But as option markets have matured, and as new instruments, such as index and interest rate options and futures, have been introduced to address the major sources of financial risk, the emphasis has shifted toward using options strategically in portfolio management.

This chapter addresses the role of options in portfolio management. The major purpose of the chapter is to explain the concepts behind option-related techniques for structuring portfolio returns and controlling financial risks, and to lay out both the opportunities and difficulties these techniques present. A secondary purpose is to provide a synthesis of some work we have done in originating and implementing these option techniques.

The topic of options we will address is more general than it might at first seem. Broadly speaking, options are instruments with a payoff that is contingent on the value of another, underlying security. Listed options are traded on a number of exchanges, but options can also be traded over the counter and, most important, can be created synthetically through the proper set of transactions in other securities. Listed options, while the most visible option contracts, are only a small part of the picture. When dealing with option strategies the topic of portfolio management also covers a broad area. Portfolio management can be thought of as the management of overall investment or financial risk. Besides the management of equity and bond investment portfolios, portfolio management includes balancing asset and liability risk in banks and in savings and loans, creating payment streams to match obligations in insurance companies and pension funds, and constructing securities to satisfy the financing patterns required by corporations.

Portfolio management is typically approached as a two-dimensional tradeoff between the mean and variance of returns. The only tool the manager has at his disposal in adjusting the portfolio is the mix of risky assets and cash. The mix dictates the mean-variance tradeoff the portfolio will face. Figures 5-1a and 5-1b illustrate this tradeoff. These figures depict portfolio returns with the familiar bell-shaped curve of the normal distribution. In this setting a two-dimensional mean-variance tradeoff is a natural way of looking at returns, since the normal distribution can be completely described by the mean and variance. A more conservative manager will move more funds from risky assets into cash, ending up with a return distribution as shown in Figure 5-1b with less variance and a lower expected return. A more aggressive manager will go in the opposite direction levering to achieve a higher expected return at the cost of higher variance. In either case the alterations in the structure of returns can be measured simply in terms of mean and variance.

It is unlikely this two-dimensional tradeoff, comfortable and intuitive though it is, will always result in a return distribution that meets portfolio objectives. A manager might prefer to control some other aspect of returns. For example, a manager may wish to achieve some guaranteed minimum return while retaining a portion of the upward return potential.[1] This objective would imply a nonsymmetric return distribution such as that shown in Figure 5-1c. This distribution truncates the downside risk while the right-hand tail still maintains some of the upside potential. Forming this return distribution requires more than mean-variance tradeoffs. It cannot be constructed using the conventional procedures of portfolio management. But the ability to form distributions of this type may have a value far beyond simply meeting subjective preferences . For example, the very pattern of liabilities may lead to a need for nonsymmetric, abnormal returns. The obligation of a pension fund to meet a minimum actuarial payoff would lead to a return distribution like that shown in Figure 5-1c. Other complex payoffs, such as those generated by the carefully tailored annuity products of the life insurance industry, or the variable rate liabilities of many corporations and thrift institutions, will lead to return objectives that cannot be met by simple mean-variance adjustments.

Options are the building blocks for constructing the payoffs to meet these complex return objectives. Options can be used to create the portfolio insurance depicted in

---

[1]The desirability of this type of insured portfolio is discussed in Leland, and in Brennan and Solanki. Skewness preference, i.e., a preference for a return distribution characterized by a degree of skewness as well as mean and variance, is discussed by Kraus and Litzenberger.

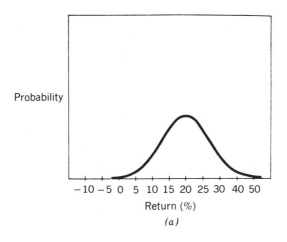

(a)

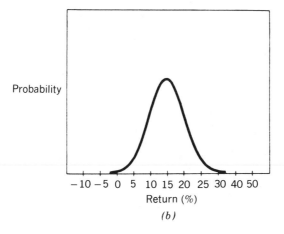

(b)

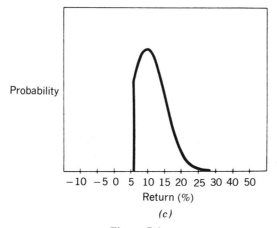

Figure 5-1.

Figure 5-1c or to mold returns to conform with virtually any other feasible distribution. This capacity for options to expand the set of contingencies has been established theoretically.[2] Here we will deal with the practical issues of how these strategies can be implemented.

Section I provides an introduction into the nature of option pricing, focusing on those features of the option contract that come into play in altering returns. Section II introduces the dynamic trading techniques that form the basis for many option-related portfolio strategies. Some of the practical difficulties with the dynamic techniques and market alternatives which help to overcome these difficulties are discussed in Section III. Section IV gives three simple yet fairly representative examples of how options can be used to alter the pattern of returns. The examples, simulations over an 11-year data set, give an indication of the actual performance that can be expected from these strategies. Section V discusses the difficulties in evaluating the performance of portfolio returns modified by option strategies. Since option strategies expand returns beyond the usual mean-variance tradeoffs, variance alone cannot be used as a meaningful measure of the risk characteristics of these strategies. Section VI concludes the chapter.

SECTION I   THE INSURANCE FEATURE OF OPTION CONTRACTS

To understand the function of options in performance structuring, it is useful to look at an option as an insurance contract. The premium for the insurance is part of the option price. The variety of payoffs from option strategies comes from taking selective positions in the insurance; buying some insurance protection over one range of security prices, selling some insurance over another.

The essential insurance feature of an option contract can be seen by constructing an option through an insurance-motivated transaction. Suppose an investor buys a security worth $1200 by investing $200 directly, and borrowing the remaining $1000. The security is retained as collateral by the lender, to be released to the investor in one year upon repayment of the $1000 loan. Further suppose the investor, wishing to have protection should the security decline in value before the loan comes due, arranges for the loan on a no-recourse basis. That is, if the investor fails to make the $1000 payment in one year, the lender will receive ownership of the security and will have no further recourse to the investor. This no-recourse feature amounts to giving the investor an insurance contract on the investment with a deductible equal to the $200 initial investment.

At the end of the year, what will be the best strategy for the investor to pursue? Obviously if the security value at the end of the year is at least as great as the $1000 necessary to gain clear ownership, the investor will pay back the loan. The investor's profit in doing so will be the security value, S^*, less the loan payment, or $S^* - 1000$. If the security is worth less than the loan payment, the investor will be better off

---

[2]See Ross, Breeden and Litzenberger, and Arditti and John.

simply to walk away from the loan and let the lender get ownership, since the $1000 payment to claim the security will net the investor a loss.

The payoff pattern from this insured loan is identical to that of a call option on the security with an exercise price of $1000. The call option gives the right to buy the security for $1000, and has a payoff that is the security price minus the exercise price, $S^* - \$1000$, or zero, whichever is greater. Using this no-recourse loan as a vehicle for analyzing a call option, we see the price of the call option can be broken up into three parts. First, there is the initial payment of $200. This payment, the difference between the security price and the $1000 exercise price, is called the *intrinsic value* of the option. Second, there is an interest carrying cost from holding the security in escrow. The investor pays the exercise price at the end of the year, but the lender has the $1000 tied up in the security over the loan period. Given an interest rate of r, this interest cost will be $(r/(1 + r))1000$. The third part of the option price is the insurance cost of the downside protection. Since the lender is absorbing the loss there will be an insurance premium, P, implicit in the price of the call option. Combining these three terms and denoting the exercise price by E we can express the call option as

$$C = (S - E) + E\,(r/(1 + r)) + P$$

This expression shows the option price consists of intrinsic value, prepaid interest, and insurance against loss.

To gain more insight into the nature of the insurance premium, P, consider the contract the lender would need in order to overcome the risk from the loan's no-recourse feature. If the security is worth more than the exercise price at the end of the year, the lender will receive the $1000 payment, and no other compensation will be necessary. If the value is less than the exercise price, the lender will have paid $1000 for a security that is now worth less than that; the lender will have lost $1000 $- S^*$. The compensating contract, then, must give a payout equal to the difference between the exercise price and security price when the security price is less than the exercise price, and give no payout when the security price is equal to or greater than the exercise price. This is exactly the payout given by a *put option*. A put option gives the right to sell the underlying security at the exercise price; its payout is the maximum of zero and the exercise price minus the security price.

Put and Call Options Redefined

The insurance premium for the no-recourse loan, P, is thus equal to a put option with one year to maturity and an exercise price of $1000. In this context we can define a call option and a put option as follows.

Call option.   A call option is a contract giving the holder the underlying security at maturity while insuring against any loss during the term of the contract beyond a deductible equal to the intrinsic value of the option.

Put option.   A put option is an insurance contract which pays off to cover fully any security price decline below the face value of the contract which is the put option's exercise price.

Some of the characteristics of option pricing are evident from viewing options in this insurance context. First, just as insurance premiums increase with an increase in riskiness, so option prices increase with an increase in the price volatility of the security. Second, call prices are an increasing function of interest rates, since higher interest rates increase the interest carrying cost. Third, just as insurance premiums decline as the amount of the deductible increases, so the insurance cost, P, drops as the intrinsic value of the call option increases. Fourth, the longer the term of the coverage, that is, the longer the time to expiration of the option, the more the option will cost.[3]

Option Strategies as Insurance Strategies: Some Examples

A variety of patterns of returns is possible by properly selecting the option coverage. We begin with a call option giving a payoff like that shown in Figure 5-2. The insurance protection kicks in as the security price drops below the exercise price of $100. The loss to the position is limited to the $5 cost of the option, while for security prices above the exercise price, the return potential is one-for-one with the security price.

It is possible to sell off the insurance value of the call option by buying the call and then selling (writing) a put option with the same exercise price. If the security is below the exercise price at expiration, the put option buyer will exercise the option by selling the security to the writer at $100 so the writer will lose $100 - S$ dollars. This strategy is commonly called a reverse conversion. The resulting payoff, shown in Figure 5-3, is a straight line with a 45 degree slope, indicating a one-for-one relationship with the underlying security price. The downside protection of the call is gone, as we would expect, so both increases and decreases in the security price are shared by this reverse conversion. Note that the payoff is shifted down from that of the security itself. The shift is $2; the call price of $5 less a $3 premium received for the put. This reflects the carrying cost of the option position. Since no funds are tied up in the security with this strategy the payoff must be less than the payoff accruing to a holder of the security.

Rather than selling off the insurance protection of the call option, an alternative strategy is to double that protection. This will lead to an increase in the payoff as the security price declines, rather than keeping the payoff constant. The investor is now overinsured, actually profiting from unfavorable price movements. Figure 5-4 shows the payoff profile for this position containing a call option and a put option. Since the call option already has put protection implicit in it, the second put leads to one-for-one gains as the security price drops below the exercise price, just as the call option allows one-for-one gains as the security price rises above the exercise price.

---

[3]These characteristics and a readable presentation of the nature of option pricing can be found in Bookstaber. A more rigorous and detailed treatment can be found in Rubinstein and Cox.

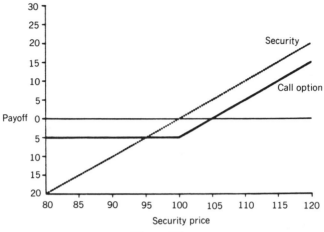

Figure 5-2.

This strategy, called a straddle, is a ''full insurance package'' that pays off no matter which way the security moves. The straddle will be attractive if the insurance implicit in the option contracts is underpriced. The total cost of insurance protection—the value of the put and call—will then be low compared to the potential for movement in the security. The minimum value of the straddle will be closer to the X-axis and the profit potential from price variations will be greater. On the other hand, if the insurance premium implicit in the options is considered to be too high because, for example, the market is overestimating the potential volatility of the security price, it is possible to profit by becoming an insurance issuer, selling the straddle by writing puts and calls.

   These payoffs are just a few of the many payoff profiles that are possible through

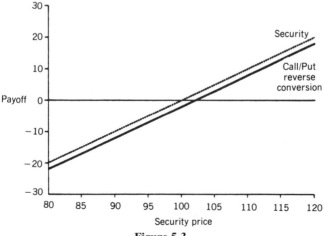

Figure 5-3.

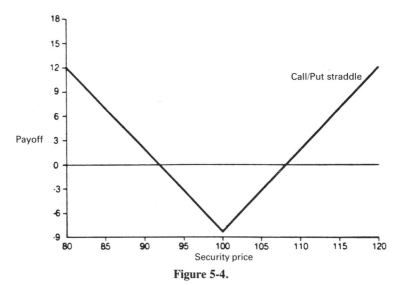

Figure 5-4.

the appropriate use of options. More complex payoffs are possible by varying the number and exercise prices of the options. For example, the return pattern of Figure 5-5 is constructed by buying two call options at an exercise price of 100, writing one call option at 110, writing another call option at 120, writing two call options at 130, and buying two options at 150. The resulting payoffs give a five-faceted approximation of a curve, depicting a particular functional relationship between the security and the investor's payoff. In theory we can get as close to a smooth curve as we want by increasing the number of adjustments made at intermediate exercise prices. And as this strategy suggests, with the proper selection of options we can create a payoff that follows any curve, that rises and falls to transform the payoff of the underlying

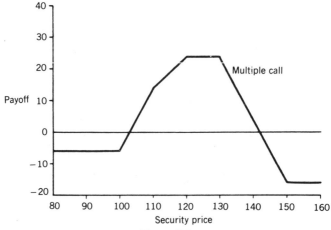

Figure 5-5.

Table 5-1.

Security Price	Value of Option with Exercise Price of $99	Value of Option with Exercise Price of $100	Value of Option with Exercise Price of $101	Total Strategy Value
-	-	-	-	-
-	-	-	-	-
-	-	-	-	-
96	0	0	0	0
97	0	0	0	0
98	0	0	0	0
99	0	0	0	0
100	1	0	0	1
101	2	−2	0	0
102	3	−4	1	0
103	4	−6	2	0
-	-	-	-	-
-	-	-	-	-
-	-	-	-	-

security into any other return structure.[4] Indeed, given options at all exercise prices and all times to expiration, we could construct the entire range of attainable return structures. To see this more concretely consider a strategy of buying one option with an exercise price of $100, writing two options each with an exercise price of $101, and buying one option with an exercise price of $102. This position, called a butterfly spread, will lead to a payoff of $1 if the underlying security is at $100 at the time of option expiration, and a payoff of zero otherwise. Such a binary payoff can be used as the basic building block from any payoff schedule. See Table 5-1.

Obviously only a small part of this set of options is actually traded on the listed exchanges. These institutional limitations would seem to be a serious constraint for turning the great theoretical potential of performance structuring into a real opportunity. However, as we will see in the next section, we are not restricted to listed options. It is possible to construct options of any exercise price and any time to expiration synthetically through the use of dynamic trading strategies.

SECTION II   THE CREATION OF OPTION POSITIONS USING DYNAMIC TRADING TECHNIQUES

The key difficulty in employing option methods is that often the appropriate option contracts do not exist in the market place. While a growing number of markets and

---

[4]While the shape of the payoff function is under the control of the investor, the height of the curve is not. It will reflect the cost of the strategy, the sum of the cost of the options purchased, and proceeds from the options written.

securities are covered by option instruments, these may not match the terms of the option contract required for the portfolio strategy. For example, the maturity of the traded options may not match the manager's time horizon, or the security underlying the option contract may not match the asset mix of the portfolio. Fortunately, even when the required option does not exist in the market, the principles of option theory can be applied to create the option contract synthetically. This is done by a dynamic reallocation of funds across sets of assets, or by a dynamic readjustment of positions in listed options and futures contracts. To develop the dynamic strategy we will concentrate on the creation of insurance provided by the protective put option. The same principles can be applied in forming other option positions and creating other return structures.

Dynamic Strategies as Multipoint Stop-Loss Strategies

The simplest and most widely known technique for achieving downside protection is the stop-loss order. An investor can assure a $100 floor on a security price by stopping out of the security at a price equal to the present value of $100, $100(1/(1 + r))^T$, and putting the funds in the risk-free asset for the remaining time period, T. Once stopped out, the funds will accrue interest at the rate r, and at the end of the time period will be worth $100. For example, if there is a year left in the holding period for the strategy, and if r is 10%, then the security would be stopped out at $91. Putting the $91 in the risk-free asset at 10% would give the desired $100 return by the end of the year. Figure 5-6 illustrates this stop-loss order. The figure overlays the security price with the percentage of the portfolio invested in the security. Note that the level of the stop approaches the floor as the end of the holding

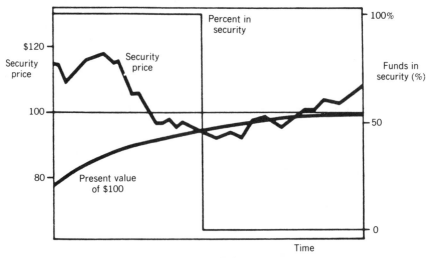

Figure 5-6.

period approaches. This is because the funds have less time to accrue interest the closer the end of the period is. Once the security price drops below the stop, all funds are taken out of the security. This insurance method is effective, but it is also costly. It fails to take into account the fact that the security may rebound from the decline, eliminating any possibility of sharing in later increases in the security price.

This deficiency can be remedied to a limited degree by allowing the stop to be reversible. Rather than pursuing this 1-point stop-loss strategy, suppose we employ a 2-point strategy where the investment is stopped out of the security when the price drops below the stop, and the security is bought when the price moves back through the stop-loss point. This will allow the required downside protection while no longer shutting the investor completely out of possible appreciation. This strategy is illustrated in Figure 5-7.

This 2-point strategy, while superior to the simple stop-loss strategy, still imposes its own costs. In addition to imposing greater transaction costs, every reversal leads to a loss equal to the distance between the selling and buying point. Setting the points close together will not eliminate these costs. The closer these two points, the smaller the cost per reversal, but the more frequently such reversals will occur. This cost will be greatest if the security vibrates around the break-even point, and will be smallest if the break-even point is never hit. Both the nonreversible 1-point stop-loss strategy and the 2-point stop-loss strategy will thus lead to a reduction in the expected return. This risk-return tradeoff is as expected since the strategies provide a reduction of downside risk. The 2-point stop-loss strategy will have the higher return, since it gives the opportunity to gain from price appreciation.

Given the results of the 2-point strategy, it is logical to consider the effects of extending the flexibility further. If we are confident the security in question will re-

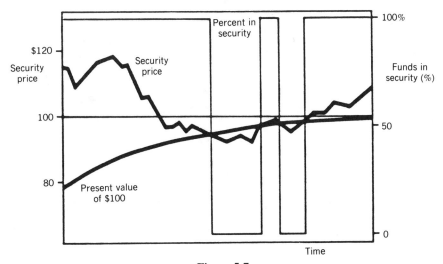

Figure 5-7.

main risky over the holding period, that is, if we believe the security will continue to be volatile, then there is no need to sell off completely when the breakeven point of $100(1/(1 + r))^T$ is reached. Instead we might move in or out of the security gradually as the security moves away from the breakeven point. This will lessen the chance of being whipsawed by repeated reversals. Given the time left in the holding period, security volatility will make periodic moves around the break-even point likely. Such moves will be more likely the longer the time left, the greater the volatility, and the closer the security price is to the break-even point. Accordingly, the proportion of the security we stop out should take all of these factors into account. Furthermore, the break-even point for the stop will change over time and with interest rates. Thus the rule we use for moving in and out of the security should be a function of the security price, the insured price, the holding period of the strategy, the interest rate, and the volatility of the security. Since these stop-loss strategies all mimic the sort of nonlinearities common to options, it is not surprising these are the same factors we discussed in Section I as determining the price of an option.

Obviously, unlimited stop-loss adjustments can be made with these factors in mind. Figure 5-8 shows the return to one particular strategy. With this alternative we hold 50% of the funds in the security and 50% in the risk-free asset when we hit the break-even point, and move completely in or out of the security only when the price has moved a significant distance away from the break-even point. We let this strategy stop out completely at a point with twice the time factor as the break-even point, $100(1/(1 + r))^{2T}$, stop out one half at the break-even point, $100(1/(1 + r))^T$, and fully invest at $100(1 + r)^T$. This 3-point stop-loss strategy continues to give the required protection. Furthermore, by both making finer adjustments and retaining a partial holding over more of the range of the security price, it will do so for the least cost of the three strategies considered so far.

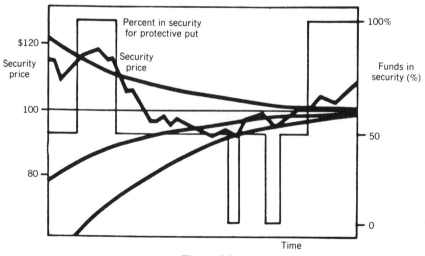

Figure 5-8.

A Put Option as the Least-Cost Insurance Strategy

A cost is imposed by the insurance protection because the dynamic adjustments gradually pull funds out of the security as it declines and only gradually put funds back into the security as it appreciates. The insured position thus cannot fully participate in the appreciation. Our objective is to find the lowest cost insurance contract. The best adjustment strategy will be that strategy which provides the downside protection while allowing the greatest sharing of security appreciation on the upside. We already know from Section I that the put option represents the ideal insurance contract for protecting against downside risk. If we could find a dynamic stop-loss strategy that replicated the behavior of a put option with a time to expiration equal to the investor's time horizon, and an exercise price of $100, we would have protection that precisely meets the insurance objectives, and, given efficient markets, that gives the protection at the lowest price.

All three stop-loss strategies considered above approximate a put option. They all give downside protection similar to that of a put option. And, like a put option, the 2-point and 3-point stop-loss strategies share in some of the upward potential of the security as well. However, they are not perfect replicas of a put option; they move in jumps as the security price changes, rather than in the smooth, continuous fashion of a put option. But they do suggest that an extension of the dynamic stop-loss strategy will get us closer to the pure put option protection desired. Option pricing theory has shown this is in fact the case; an option position can be created by pursuing a strategy that dynamically adjusts the proportion of the underlying security and the risk-free asset.[5] Since an option can be replicated by such a strategy, this further implies the option price must always equal the cost of this replicating portfolio. We can write the call option and put option equations as

$$C = a_c S - b_c B$$

and

$$P = -a_p S + b_p B$$

where S is the security price, B is the price of the risk-free bond, and where the values of a_c, a_p, b_c, and b_p, are proportionality factors that take on values between zero and one.[6]

[5]The procedure for replicating an option through a dynamically adjusted position in the underlying security and risk-free asset is implied in the original work on option pricing by Black and Scholes (1973) and Merton (1973). This procedure is discussed in simpler terms in Rubinstein and Leland, and in Chapter 4 of Bookstaber (1983). The operational considerations of these techniques are discussed in Platt and Latainer.

[6]The exact functional form these factors take on depends on the assumptions of the model being used, particularly the distributional assumptions. If stock prices are assumed to be described by a lognormal distribution, the well-known Black-Scholes model will be appropriate. The binomial model of Cox, Ross, and Rubinstein will be an approximation for this same distribution. Merton has developed a model for a jump-diffusion process, a process which allows for discrete jumps in the security price. Cox has a model that allows the volatility of the security price to vary as a function of the security price. These models differ from the Black-Scholes model in terms of the functional form for a and b.

The call option is created by borrowing money at the risk-free rate (borrowing is implied by a negative value for b_c) and using it to purchase an amount a_c of the security. The borrowing leads to the leverage that is characteristic of a call option. The put is created by shorting the security (shorting is implied by a negative value for a_p) and putting an amount equal to b_p into the risk-free asset. When the put option position is combined with a long position in the security to form an insured position, the net effect of combining the initial long position in the security with the short position required to replicate the put option is a positive, but less than full investment in the security.[7]

As was suggested by the 3-point stop-loss strategy, the proportion of stocks and bonds in the option replication varies both over time and as the security price changes. The replicating portfolio must be continuously adjusted; hence the dynamic nature of the strategy. The proportion terms a_c, a_p, b_c and b_p, are not constants; they are variables that will change with the time to the maturity of the holding period and with changes in the security price. As the 3-point strategy further suggests, these terms will also be a function of the volatility of the security and the riskless interest rate.

Figure 5-9 illustrates the proportion of investment in the security when following the dynamic stop-loss adjustment of the protective put option strategy. This strategy

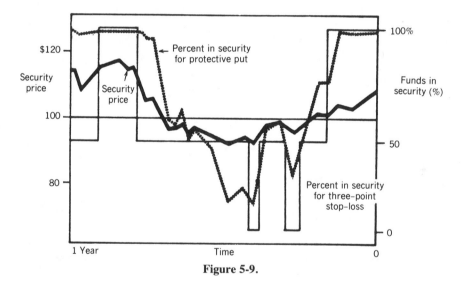

Figure 5-9.

[7]The portfolio for replicating a put option is directly related to the replicating portfolio for a call option. This relationship can be expressed by the put-call parity formula presented in Section I: $C = (S - E) + (E (r/(1 + r)) + P$ or $C = S - E(1/(1 + r)) + P$. As this formula shows, a call option can be created by holding the security, S, borrowing $E(1/(1 + r))$, (and thus repaying E at expiration), and holding a put option. This creates a protective put on a portfolio which is similar to holding a call option on the portfolio. In fact the only difference between the two is that a call option is levered through borrowing while the protective put position is not.

provides the complete downside protection at the lowest cost. The strategy is overlaid on the 3-point strategy described in Figure 5-8.

The naive 1-point stop-loss strategy has been proposed in a number of insurance settings. For example, the original construction of the contingent immunization strategy for bond portfolios involves stopping out of an interest-sensitive bond position once a critical portfolio price or interest rate level is passed.[8] It should be clear from this discussion that such strategies, while providing the desired protection, are a more costly means of securing that protection than a strategy which more closely approximates the return structure of a put option.

SECTION III   VARIATIONS ON THE DYNAMIC STRATEGY: USING LISTED FUTURES AND OPTION CONTRACTS

As with any strategy there are practical difficulties that must be considered with the dynamic strategy. These include:

1. *The need for continuous adjustment.*   Theoretically the option position requires continuous portfolio adjustments. The appropriate mix of the security and riskless asset change over time and with changes in the security price. Discrete adjustments, by failing to account for the continuous nature of the movement of the security price and of time, will lead to a margin of error in the payoff of the option, as well as in its cost.

2. *The accurate estimation of security price volatility.*   The appropriate portfolio mix will also depend on the volatility of the security. A highly volatile security will be more costly to insure since the adjustments will catch less of the price swings. If the volatility of the security is forecast incorrectly, the result may lead to a higher cost or to less than complete protection.

3. *The specification of the stochastic process driving security prices.*   The functional form of the proportionality terms in the option model depends on the nature of security price movements. The direction of the price movements has no bearing on the option model, but the way price movements tend to evolve does. For example, a security price that is typified by large periodic jumps will lead to a different model specification, and hence to a different dynamic strategy, than a security whose price never experiences discrete jumps. Accuracy in the specification of the stochastic process is as important as accuracy in the estimation of the security price volatility emerging from that process.[9]

Just how critical these factors are to the successful implementation of the dynamic option strategies is an empirical question that cannot be answered here. However,

---

[8]For example, see Liebowitz and Weinberger.

[9]In particular, if there are sudden jumps in the underlying security while the Black-Scholes model is being used, the position will be subject to unexpected losses. The strategy will be unsuccessful in replicating an option position. A more general distributional framework for option pricing methodology is introduced in Bookstaber and McDonald (1985).

some of these problems are mitigated by using listed futures and option contracts in forming the dynamic strategy. We will discuss these variations on the dynamic strategy next.

Using Futures in Dynamic Strategies

The essential feature of the dynamic strategy is that the position in the security varies as the time to maturity and the security price vary. Obviously, one way to vary the size of the position is by transacting directly in the security itself. But when there are futures on the security the position can also be varied by leaving the actual security holdings unchanged, and transacting in the futures contract instead. For example, a put option on a well-diversified stock portfolio can be replicated by using a short position in an index future. As the portfolio value declines, requiring a smaller position in the portfolio, the short position will be increased. The short position will react in a direction opposite the portfolio position, leaving a net return to market movements that is essentially the same as if a portion of the portfolio itself had been sold off and transferred to the risk-free asset. The futures act as a damper on the effective portfolio position. The futures position is an alternative for the construction of dynamic strategies for any position that is highly correlated with the movement of traded futures, be they stock, stock portfolios, bonds, foreign exchange, metals, or commodities.

Futures have a number of attractive features. First, because they combine a position in the asset with borrowing, they can lead to less costly transactions than occur with transfers between the security and cash. Second, execution is often better in the futures than in the cash market. This is particularly true when a single futures contract can be substituted for a portfolio-wide transaction, as in the case of stock or bond portfolios. And third, since futures are levered instruments, less cash is necessary to carry out the dynamic strategy.

The third point is especially important when the dynamic strategy is pursued separately from the portfolio holdings. For example, consider a pension sponsor with a number of outside managers, each managing a fraction of the fund. If the sponsor decides to pursue a dynamic strategy, the sponsor could conceivably have each manager restructure its management methods to incorporate the dynamic strategy. However, there are obvious practical and administrative difficulties in doing so. And even if it were done successfully, the end result of having options on each of the individual portfolios would be an inefficient means of attaining the desired option on the overall pension fund investment.[10] On the other hand, the alternative of having the sponsor retain enough of the fund to make the market/cash adjustments itself would greatly reduce the amount retained under the outside managers and change the character of the fund.

---

[10]This is because an option on a portfolio of securities will not behave in the same way as a portfolio of options on each of the individual securities. The portfolio of options will be more expensive than the option on the portfolio. This is discussed in Merton (1973).

The difficulties can be overcome by using futures as the vehicle for making the dynamic adjustments. The pension fund sponsor, pursuing a dynamic strategy with futures, would need only retain enough cash to meet margin requirements. The sponsor could monitor its overall fund value, and assuming its holdings are closely correlated with the overall market, use index futures to create a position that would be equivalent to selling off the necessary proportion of its holdings. It could do this without making any alteration in the managers' roles, without significant changes in the amount under management, even without the knowledge of the managers. While giving protection against poor performance, any superior management performance will still lead to relative performance gains under the dynamic strategy.

Strictly speaking, the replication of a put or call option requires a proper balancing of positions in the riskless asset as well as risky security. The position in the riskless asset serves to make the position self-financing; the position neither requires further funding nor gives out payments from the time it is initiated until the expiration of the option contract. The self-financing feature is critical to the theoretical development of option pricing. Options are, after all, self-financing instruments: once an option is purchased, no cash flow takes place until its exercise or expiration. Shifting between the risky security and the riskless asset maintains an economy in the development of the theoretical pricing argument since no other assets or transactions need to be tracked.

But when our attention moves from option pricing to hedging, and from theoretical development to practical implementation, the stringent requirements of maintaining a self-financing portfolio no longer apply. In pratice our concern is only with maintaining a position that gives a security payoff equal to that of an option. Failure to hold the proper proportion of funds in the riskless asset will not affect this essential return structure. It will only affect the *ex post* cost of the protection. For example, if the manager chooses to place funds made available from the strategy into another risky asset rather than into the riskless asset, the overall cost of the dynamic strategy may now be thought to depend on the performance of that risky asset. But clearly that facet of the strategy can easily be separated out from the insurance service the strategy is delivering.[11] It is important to recognize this role of the riskless asset when using futures contracts in constructing dynamic hedges because the most efficient use of futures may not maintain the theoretically correct position in the risk-free as-

---

[11]The role of the riskless asset in creating a synthetic option is similar to its role in creating a synthetic forward contract for foreign exchange. The textbook method for creating a synthetic forward contract involves borrowing in one currency and converting it in the spot market into a second currency where the funds are then loaned out at the risk-free rate until the maturity of the contract. The result of these transactions is an obligation to deliver the first currency (to pay off the loan) and to receive the second currency. In practice the funds need not actually be borrowed nor do they need to be loaned out as a riskless asset in the second currency. For example, the firm's own funds could be converted and the converted funds could be used for working capital needs. The end result of creating a forward contract will still be met although the contract would be entangled with other transactions, and it would be more difficult to distinguish the nature of the forward contract. However, it is clear that creating the forward contract in this fashion might be more useful to the firm.

set. Because they are levered, futures implicitly contain a short position in the risk-free asset, but this position will not necessarily equal that required for the strategy to be self-financing. The most efficient use of futures may lead to periodic payments or cash requirements. When properly treated these cause no difficulties for the construction or evaluation of the strategy. On the contrary, they may lead to important advantages over transactions in the security itself.

Using Options to Create Options

A second variation on dynamic strategies is the use of listed options. As with futures, listed options may exist on indexes and securities that are closely correlated with the security of interest. Obviously, if there is a listed option that is fairly priced and that exactly meets the time and contract specifications for hedging, then it will be preferred to constructing the option synthetically. Frequently, however, there is a listed option that only partially fits the hedging requirements. For example, the listed option may be on a slightly different underlying asset, perhaps on a treasury bond futures contract when the underlying asset is a corporate bond portfolio, or on a stock index that does not exactly match the construction of the underlying stock portfolio, or the listed option may have too short a time to maturity or be at the wrong exercise price.

The first of these problems will not be unique to the use of the listed options. It will exist for futures and may also exist when a dynamic strategy is pursued directly through the underlying asset. Dynamic adjustments of stock or bond portfolios must be done piecemeal. The subset of securities which is adjusted will not exactly match the overall portfolio. As a result it is possible the discrete adjustment of the dynamic strategy may induce more basis risk than the use of listed options which, although not perfectly correlated with the underlying asset, overcome the problems related to discrete adjustment.

The second problem of listed options, that of having a time to expiration that is shorter than the time horizon demanded for the option protection, is probably considered the greatest barrier to using listed options. Listed options often cannot be found more than three months out, while the time horizon for dynamic strategies is typically one year or more. But these short-term listed options can themselves be employed in a dynamic strategy for creating synthetic longer-term options. This strategy is similar to rolling over short-term futures contracts to create longer-term protection.

For example, suppose an investor were interested in a $100 floor for a security price for one year, and put options existed with three months to maturity. The investor might buy a 3-month put with an exercise price of $100, and upon expiration of that put, buy another 3-month put with the same exercise price. At the end of six months the position would be liquidated, a new 3-month option purchased, and the procedure would be repeated again at the end of nine months. If the option expired out of the money, there would be no proceeds from the strategy, and more funds would be necessary to roll over the strategy. If the security dropped below the floor, the put option would return the difference between the floor price and the security price, covering the loss and providing the intrinsic value for buying the next contract.[12]

The actual cost of this technique depends on the path the security price takes. To see this consider a security currently priced at $100 and a call option purchased on the security with an exercise price of $100. Suppose a 6-month option cost $10 while a 3-month option cost $6. If the security is again at $100 when the 3-month option expires, a second $6 option will need to be purchased, and the total cost of the rolling over strategy will be $12, $2 more than the cost of the 6-month option. If, on the other hand, the stock drops to $80 in three months, the price of the call option for the next three months will be far less, since the option is now $20 out of the money. The next option may cost only $1, leading the rolling-over strategy to be less costly. The same will be true if the security rises substantially to, say, $120. The first of the 3-month options will then pay off $20 at expiration and the second option, being in the money, will have a small premium above its intrinsic value, selling for, say, $21. The total cost of the rolling-over strategy will then be $7, compared to the $10 cost for the straight 6-month option. This path dependence adds uncertainty to the cost of the strategy, and this may dampen its desirability. However, it also presents an opportunity to improve return potential by the selection of the options used each time the position is rolled over. For example, the investor can choose the time to roll over to maximize gain from mispricing between options, and can choose different exercise prices to alter the strategy if past performance warrants it.[13]

The use of listed options does have a number of particularly attractive features not shared by the other dynamic methods. First, the transaction costs and the timing of the transaction are known in advance. Second, like futures, the options are already levered, requiring less of a cash commitment than the straight security/bond strategy. And third, the option contract is protected against unforeseen jumps in the security price or changes in the security price volatility.

In a perfect market setting the standard dynamic return structuring techniques using reallocations between the security and the riskless asset will replicate the desired option contract exactly. In practice, however, transactions costs, basis risk, capital constraints, and fundamental uncertainty about the return process and return volatility of the security make the proper choice of return structuring techniques more difficult. Making dynamic adjustments with the futures rather than the cash instru-

---

[12]If the exercise price of the synthetic option could not be matched by the listed options, it can still be constructed using the rolling over of listed options by following the proper hedge ratio. For example, if the hedge ratio or delta of the listed option is .5 while the hedge ratio of the desired synthetic option is .75, then .75/.5 = 1.5 of the listed option would be held for each of the synthetic options to be constructed.

[13]This problem of path dependence has occasionally been overstated. While path dependence does lead to uncertainty it need not be an overriding concern. In practice any strategy, including the straight dynamic approach, will face uncertainty because the market and security price movement will not fit the assumptions of any model precisely. The key issue is whether the risk imposed by this uncertainty and the cost of employing the strategies are large in proportion to the benefit derived from being able to form a return that comes closer to meeting the portfolio objectives. Furthermore, rolling-over positions can enhance returns if the investor has expertise in execution.

ment, or constructing the return structuring by rolling over listed options, can help to overcome some of the difficulties. Furthermore, having a number of alternative routes to achieving the desired return structuring permits the exploitation of mispricing in the various instruments. For example, if listed options are considered to be underpriced, they may be preferred to the dynamic strategy on that basis alone. These methods are not always a practical alternative, however. Since listed options and futures may not exist on the underlying security itself, the problems of basis risk may be accentuated. These aspects of return-structuring techniques should be the subject of further empirical testing and comparison.

SECTION IV   APPLICATIONS OF PERFORMANCE STRUCTURING

The flexibility of dynamic strategies allows the return distribution to be molded in a wide variety of ways. Some of our own work has extended beyond the creation of the portfolio insurance we have dealt with here to more complex and specialized applications ranging from hedging single premium deferred annuities in the life insurance industry to asset-liability management for thrift institutions. In this section we will present three examples intended to be more or less generic and to cover a range of possible strategies. These examples are based on computer simulations using historical data. They do not represent the performance of actual trades. We will first look at the protective portfolio strategies and then look at strategies for riding on the performance of the best of a set of assets. Finally, we will consider combined strategies which give the downside protection of portfolio insurance while accentuating the returns available from the better performing securities on the upside.

Cutting Losses: Protective Portfolio with Options

We have already treated the insurance implications of protective puts in some detail. This is the best known and most widely used option-type strategy, perhaps because the memory of losses from recent market downturns is still fresh. There are a number of variations on portfolio insurance designed to adapt the basic concept of the protective put to particular markets and risks. For example, protective puts can be extended beyond the bond and equity markets to insure floor prices for commodities or foreign exchange, can be set to assure returns equal to a pension plan's actuarial interest rate assumptions, or can be modified to express the floor return as a fixed differential off the Treasury bill rate or other interest rates.[14]

Table 5-2 presents the results of creating the simple dynamic put option on an equity portfolio. The objective here is to achieve a floor return of 0% from the portfolio, while maximizing the share of any increase in the equity position. The strategy used here is repeated each year with an end-of-year horizon each year. That is, a new protective put with one year to expiration is constructed each January. The perform-

[14]These are some of the applications developed by Morgan Stanley. For example, see Platt and Latainer (1983, 1984a, 1984b), Tilley and Jacob, and Tilley (1984a).

Table 5-2.   Comparison of Annual Returns for a Protective Put Strategy

Year	Equity	Dynamic Strategy			
		With Floor Exercise Price	Capture	With Variable Exercise Price	Capture
1973	-14.9%	-0.52%	Floor	-0.99%	Floor
1974	-25.2	-0.71	Floor	-0.99	Floor
1975	34.1	20.68	61%	31.20	91%
1976	23.0	14.99	65	22.42	98
1977	-7.2	-0.38	Floor	-1.02	Floor
1978	6.5	4.55	70	0.35	5
1979	18.5	16.62	90	18.48	100
1980	33.4	26.89	81	30.00	90
1981	-5.6	-0.38	Floor	-1.13	Floor
1982	20.8	11.30	54	1.96	9
1983	22.2	18.94	85	22.17	100

Cumulative Returns for 11 Years Compounded:

7.80%	9.76%		10.40%

. 52-week periods were used in stead of exact calendar years.
. EQUITY: S&P 500 Stock Index adjusted for dividends
. Capture is the dynamic strategy return as a percent of the return to the equity portfolio when the equity portfolio return exceeds the 0% floor.
. Includes transactions costs of $25 per contract round trip.
. Assets are reallocated once every week.

---

ance can thus be looked at as a series of independent trials. The table shows the annual results of this strategy for the years 1973–1983. The first column of the table gives the returns to equity (the S&P 500 Index). The next two columns relate to the performance of the synthetic option strategy. The first of these columns gives the annual return of the strategy, the second gives the capture of the strategy. The capture is the return to the synthetic option strategy as a percent of the equity portfolio. Since replicating an option position involves a gradual shift into equity as the equity increases in value, only part of the equity performance will be shared by the option position. The incomplete capture is a direct implication of option price behavior; option prices move less than one-to-one with changes in the price of the underlying asset. The incomplete capture of potential gains can be thought of as a cost of pursuing the option strategy. This serves to emphasize that option-related strategies have tradeoffs consistent with market efficiency. Changes in return structure are met with commensurate costs. The cost for the repeated 1-year protective put positions used in this example is greater than a single longer-term put option would be. The capture can be increased by taking a longer investment horizon in the performance structure.

It is evident from Table 5-2 that the portfolio performed as expected in providing the 0% floor return. In the four years that the equity market saw negative returns the return to the structured portfolio was 0%. In the years of positive return the structured portfolio shared to varying degrees in that return. In most cases the protective put returned over 75% of the return to the equity portfolio. The capture was higher in years of higher equity return and was also higher the longer the equity sustained a high rate of return. This is an attractive and natural feature of option prices. The proportion of funds in equity is the average of proportions held over the annual period. In the simulation these proportions were readjusted weekly.[15]

Going with the Winners: Strategies for Accentuating Gains

How much would it be worth to be able to receive a perfect stock-bond market timing service, a service that could always pick when holding stocks would do better than holding bonds? It is possible to create and price such a service through the simple option strategy of buying an index call option and placing the remainder of the portfolio in bonds. To see this select the call option to have an exercise price that equals the return possible through a bond investment. Then if the option pays off, it will give a return equal to the stock market return less the bond price, while if the option expires worthless, the overall portfolio return will still equal the bond return. The net effect of this strategy will be to give a return equal to the equity or the bond, whichever is greater. This is the return that would be generated by following the advice of a perfect market timer. The cost of this strategy is the cost of the call option on the market.[16]

As this perfect market timing example illustrates, options can perform a strategic as well as defensive role in portfolio management. The proper dynamic allocation between equities and bonds will replicate a call option on the market and provide a return equal to the greater of the two. Added onto an actively managed stock portfolio, such an allocation strategy can accentuate gains by increasing market participation during upswings while moving out of the market during downturns.[17] Table 5-3 shows the annual results of pursuing this strategy over the 1973–1983 period.

The gradual adjustments that constitute the dynamic technique lead the structured market timing strategy to capture only a portion of the return of the better performing asset. As we discussed in the last example, this is a result of the core feature of option returns of reacting less than one-to-one with price changes in the underlying security. In two instances, however, the option return actually is lower than either the bond or equity return. In 1976 the structured return was 16.6%, compared to 18.4% for bonds and 23% for equity, and in 1981 it was − 10.6%, compared to − 1% for bonds and − 5.6% for equity. This failure in the strategy is the result of employing only weekly adjustments in the historical simulation. While generally adjustments in the proportions of security holdings need to be made only infrequently, in the times of

---

[15]In practice it is unlikely weekly adjustments will actually be necessary. Depending on market conditions, in particular the degree of price movement, as few as four adjustments a year may be sufficient.

[16]The relationship between market timing and option valuation was first pointed out by Merton (1981). As put-call parity suggests, this relationship can also be looked at through a put option strategy. The market timing service can be created with a put option by holding the equity and buying a put option with an exercise price equal to the bond return.

[17]A variation of this strategy can be used to form a variable beta portfolio, a portfolio with a high beta, and thus high leverage in strong markets and with a low beta, and thus little reaction to the market, when the market declines. The variable beta strategy is presented in Chapter 6 of Bookstaber and Clarke (1983).

Table 5-3.   Comparison of Annual Returns for a Market Timing Strategy

Year	Bond	Equity	Dynamic Strategy	Capture
1973	0.83%	-14.86%	-5.96%	57%
1974	2.77	-25.25	-6.23	68
1975	6.96	34.15	26.34	71
1976	18.39	22.07	17.78	Floor
1977	-0.64	-7.20	-4.44	42
1978	-1.19	6.48	1.64	37
1979	-1.58	18.48	14.21	79
1980	-2.95	33.38	21.68	68
1981	-0.98	-5.58	-7.74	Floor
1982	44.99	20.79	34.93	58
1983	1.03	22.17	16.32	75

Cumulative Returns for 11 Years Compounded:

     5.41%   7.80%   8.94%

- 52-week periods were used in stead of exact calendar years.
- For purposes of this study, the asset classes are defined as follows:
  BOND: 20-year Treasury Bonds
  EQUITY: S&P 500 Stock Index adjusted for dividends
- Capture is the absolute difference of the dynamic strategy return and the lower of the bond or equity return, divided by the absolute difference of the bond and equity return.
- Includes transactions costs of $25 per contract round trip.
- Assets are reallocated once every week.

dramatic price movements adjustments may need to be made more than once a week to replicate the option position. These two years were marked by such price movements, and the inability of the simulation to make immediate allocation changes led to the inferior performance. This serves to emphasize the need for good monitoring and execution facilities in following dynamic strategies.

This market timing strategy can be adapted to other portfolio management settings. For example, it can be used to accentuate the performance of a number of managers by creating an option which will lead to a return equal to the largest of the managers' returns. The same method could be used to focus in on the best of a number of investment themes. A manager who, for example, is interested in both energy-intensive industries and recreation-related industries could create options on each area to increase the leverage of the better performing area.

Combined Strategies: Extensions to Multiple Risky Assets

Having presented examples both for cutting losses through portfolio insurance and for accentuating gains through call option positions, the next logical step is to combine the two. The resulting strategy will give the greater of the bond or equity return with a floor return equal to the short-term rate. Table 5-4 presents the result of combining the two previous strategies in this way. Over the 11-year period from 1973 to 1983, all three assets in the strategy came into use at some point. From 1973 to 1980 returns shifted between the floor of 0% and some capture of the equity rate. The capture was almost 100% in 1976 and 1979, and roughly two-thirds in 1975 and 1979. In 1982 the bond market had twice the return of equity and over three times the return of cash, and the dynamic strategy shifted toward bonds. The stock-bond option in this strategy, which represents the market timing aspect of the strategy, was sensitive enough to capture 81% of this return.

The effectiveness of this strategy is illustrated in Figure 5-10. Here the value of a portfolio of $100 million invested with the insured asset allocation strategy is compared with a portfolio invested in equity (as measured by the S&P 500 Index), and in long-term corporate bonds. The equity portfolio faltered in the first two years, and although it increased substantially in the later years, this early decline remained a costly one from a total return standpoint. As would be expected, the bond portfolio had fewer declines in value, but with the exception of 1981, also had fewer periods of major gains. In contrast, the insured asset allocation strategy avoided the periods of market decline—the insurance aspect of the strategy is evident in the figure, since the value of this portfolio never declines—while participating in some of the upward movement in equity and, in 1981, in the bond position. As a result, its value was

Table 5-4.   Comparison of Annual Returns for a Multiple Risky Asset Strategy

| | Asset Class | | Dynamic Strategy | |
Year	Bond	Equity	Floor Exercise Price	Capture
1973	0.83%	-14.86%	0.44%	53%
1974	2.77	-25.25	0.11	4
1975	6.96	34.15	16.39	48
1976	18.39	22.97	11.67	51
1977	-0.64	-7.20	0.01	Floor
1978	-1.19	6.48	3.84	59
1979	-1.58	18.48	13.20	71
1980	-2.95	33.38	16.59	50
1981	-0.98	-5.58	-0.04	Floor
1982	44.99	20.79	24.38	54
1983	1.03	22.17	13.74	62

Cumulative Returns for 11 Years Compounded:

5.41%   7.80%   8.81%

- 52-week periods were used in stead of exact calendar years.
- For purposes of this study, the asset classes are defined as follows:
  BOND: 20-year Treasury Bonds
  EQUITY: S&P 500 Stock Index adjusted for dividends
- Capture is the dynamic strategy return as a percent of the return to the equity portfolio when the equity portfolio return exceeds the 0% floor.
- Includes transactions costs of $25 per contract round trip.
- Assets are reallocated once every week.

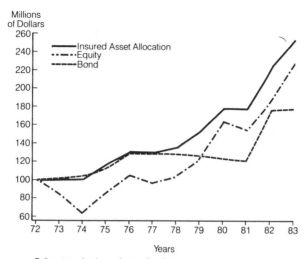

Dollar return of an insured asset allocation strategy, compared with the dollar return to equity and to bonds. Equity is measured by the S&P 500 index, bonds by the performance of long-term treasuries. The asset allocation strategy is designed to give a payoff related to the better performing of equity and bonds in each year, while insuring against loss of capital.

Figure 5-10.

greater than either the bond or equity portfolio over this 11-year period. Indeed, no static combination of equity and bonds could have outperformed the insured asset allocation strategy over this period.

This type of multiple risky asset strategy captures more fully the ability to create a performance structure for pinpointing desirable return characteristics.[18] A more extensive treatment of this strategy is given in Chapter 12. The strategy is easily extended to other risk-return considerations and to more than two risky assets. One way to look at the combined strategy is as a call option on the best performing of the risky assets with a residual position in cash. The call option gives the leverage on the upside while giving put protection on the downside. Furthermore, the call option can be selected before the fact to act like a call option only on the asset which turns out to be the best performer. If one of the areas does well, the options will pay off for that area, while if they all do poorly and the option expires out of the money, a floor return will still be guaranteed by the cash position.

The multiple risky asset strategy, like other option strategies, has a wide variety of application. As with the market timing strategy, it can be used as a global management tool for monitoring the performance of a number of portfolio managers. It is possible to generate a return that will equal the highest performing of a number of managers, while assuring some minimum floor return. The strategy can also be used to select across bond portfolios. For example, it can be used to give a return equal to the better performing of long or short maturity bonds, while guaranteeing a floor return over the holding period equal to some immunized rate.

[18]The multiple risky asset concept is presented in Tilley and Latainer (1985). A theoretical discussion of this concept is presented by Stulz (1982), and by Stapleton and Subrahamanyam (1984).

SECTION V   THE IMPLICATIONS OF PERFORMANCE STRUCTURING FOR PORTFOLIO EVALUATION

Care must be taken in evaluating portfolios with return distributions altered by option strategies. Methods of performance evaluation that depend on mean and variance measures of returns—as all of the common methods do—cannot be applied to portfolios resulting from dynamic strategies for the simple reason that those portfolios depend on more than mean and variance.[19] These strategies mold the return distributions, bringing the higher moments such as skewness and kurtosis into play. For example, the protective put leads to a truncation of the left tail of the portfolio return distribution, and a leftward shift of the distribution. The truncation reflects the protection from downside loss, and the shift reflects the cost of the insurance. Figure 5-11 shows the distribution of the underlying portfolio with the familiar normal distribution, and the distribution that results when a put option is purchased on that portfolio. In contrast to this strategy consider the distributional effect of writing a covered call option on the same underlying portfolio. The covered call has the opposite effect of the put option. It truncates the right tail of the distribution while shifting the distribution to the right. The truncation is the result of selling off the upward potential to the call buyer, and the shift reflects the premium received from that sale. Figure 5-12 compares the distribution of covered call writing with that of the underlying portfolio.

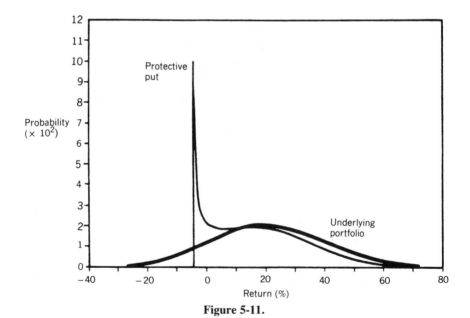

Figure 5-11.

[19]Further discussion of the problems addressed in this section is provided in Bookstaber and Clarke (1984, 1985).

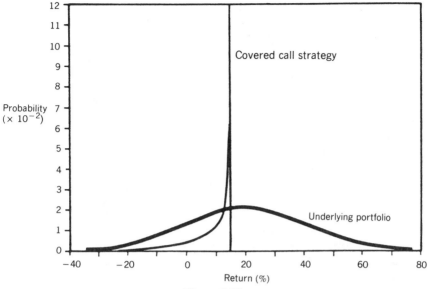

Figure 5-12.

Even a cursory reference to Figures 5-11 and 5-12 demonstrates that distributions resulting from option strategies cannot be understood by looking at the mean and variance alone. Indeed, in this particular case, an analysis based solely on expected return and variance of return will make call writing appear superior to put buying. The two strategies have much the same effect on expected return. The expected return drops from 18% for the underlying stock portfolio to 13.6% for the portfolio fully covered by a call option, and to 14.5% for the portfolio fully covered by the protective put. But the standard deviation of returns drops from 20% for the underlying portfolio to only 16.7% for the put strategy, while it is cut to 5.8% for the covered call strategy. The put strategy has a standard deviation that is nearly three times higher than for call writing. If standard deviation or variance is used as a proxy for risk, writing a covered call will be preferred to buying a protective put.[20]

However, variance is not a suitable proxy for risk, since the option strategies reduce risk *asymetrically*. The call truncates the right-hand side of the distribution, and thereby reduces the desirable upside variance. The put, on the other hand, reduces the variance on the undesirable left-hand portion of the return distribution. It is natural, then, for a reduction in variance to be compensated differently for the two strategies.

---

[20]This bias will appear for the Sharpe measure (which measures performance as the difference between the portfolio return and the risk-free rate, divided by the standard deviation of portfolio returns), the Treynor index (which measures performance as the difference between the portfolio return and the risk-free rate, divided by the portfolio beta), and the Jensen measure (which measures performance by the alpha of the security market line regression, i.e., by the vertical distance between the portfolio return and the capital market line).

This example illustrates the shortcomings of evaluation methods which rely on summary statistics such as mean and variance in dealing with option-related strategies. By trading off between the mean and the higher moments of the distribution many unusual mean-variance relationships are possible. For example, it is possible to construct a covered call strategy with both a higher expected return *and* a lower variance than the underlying portfolio. Or, by using far-out-of-the-money call options, it is possible to construct a portfolio insurance strategy that yields the same return floor as a protective put but with a higher expected return. (This strategy will give a high probability of achieving only the floor return and a small chance of receiving a very high return.) Such a strategy may not, in fact, lead to a desirable return structure. But strictly on a mean-variance basis, it certainly appears superior to the conventional insurance strategy of using a protective put.[21]

These two examples show the potential for misleading statements and inaccurate evaluations of alternative strategies. The incomplete state of performance evaluation may foster conflict between portfolio and management objectives. The strategies which lead to good measures of management success may not be those which best address the portfolio objectives. Given techniques which extend performance structuring beyond the 2-dimensional plane of mean and variance, it is natural to expect that evaluation methods for these techniques must also break out of the mean-variance framework. A new set of performance techniques must be developed for the quantitative evaluation of portfolios engaged in these strategies.

Misinterpretations are also likely in the qualitative review of the performance of dynamically structured portfolios. For example, the portfolio insurance strategy requires selling off the security as the price declines and gradually buying it back as the price rises. Viewed outside the context of dynamic management, such a pattern of trading does not lead to favorable conclusions as to the manager's trading skills. Furthermore, most managers are evaluated by rankings based on realized return performance rather than on meeting distributional objectives. In these rankings the fact that a manager successfully pursued a strategy for meeting a specified return objective may be overshadowed if a drop in realized return was a necessary cost of meeting that objective.[22] As with the misinterpretations inherent in applying the quantitative evaluation methods, the possibility of the manager pursuing a dynamic strategy may convey a mistaken impression that could keep these strategies from being correctly selected or effectively implemented.

---

[21]For this reason care must be taken in using the expected return as the sole criterion for selecting the best portfolio insurance strategy. The protective put option may be the least-cost strategy in that it provides the desired protection for the lowest drop in expected return *while preserving the features of the underlying security return distribution*. But it will not be the least-cost strategy if no constraints are placed on alteration of the security return structure above the point of protection. The same is true of other option strategies. Unless the return structure is specified over the entire range of possible outcomes there will be some strategies which fulfill the stated objectives at an apparently low cost, but do so only by making unfavorable tradeoffs in other regions of the return distribution.

[22]The potential conflict of the manager between meeting the sponsor's objectives and maximizing relative performance suggests the sponsor of the investment program might be better suited to the performance structuring role. We have discussed in Section III how futures can facilitate this.

SECTION VI   CONCLUSION

The opportunities option strategies present for molding the return distributions to meet investment objectives apply to a wide number of portfolio management and risk control problems. In their most general form option strategies allow the manager to expand the set of insurable contingencies far beyond those available with static hedging methods. The use of dynamic hedging strategies to create the desired option-type payoffs allows returns to be structured even further than is possible with listed options; risks can be defined according to the specific asset/liability mix and risk preferences of management. The tools of option theory provide the technology for expanding the dimensions of risk management to meet the specialized demands of business.

The technology of option theory may be summarized as a payoff processor which reshapes return distributions, like the payoff processor characterized in Figure 5-13. The set of return distributions for the assets enter into the processor where the dynamic hedging technology remolds them to specification. The payoffs exit the processor with distributions of the desired shape.

Naturally the benefits of dynamic return structuring are not gained without a cost. The protection of portfolio insurance is not free. Its cost, explicit in the price of a put option, is implicit in the dynamic strategy for replicating a put option, since, as

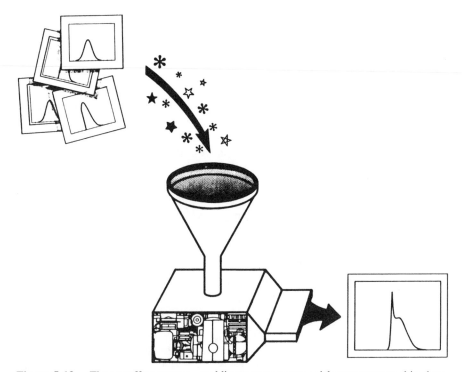

Figure 5-13.   The payoff processor—molding returns to meet risk management objectives.

we have seen, such a strategy leads to only partial participation in price increases. To state without qualification that a protective put strategy or any other dynamic strategy is superior to holding the uninsured portfolio ignores the risk-return tradeoffs which form the basis of asset pricing. While it is no doubt true that *ex post* the insured strategy will do better over some particular time period, *ex ante* the insurance will impose a cost. The same point can be made for other strategies as well. For other patterns of return structuring the strategy may initially lead to positive inflows rather than costs as does, for example, the writing of covered call options. But in this case the cost balancing of the initial inflow will be a reduction in the potential return from later price movements.

The major issue we have addressed in this Chapter is how to minimize the cost of performance structuring; how to find the dynamic strategy that best fulfills a given objective while still preserving the other features of the portfolio distribution. The least-cost dynamic strategy for meeting the objective of portfolio insurance will be the strategy which best replicates a put option. This conclusion flows over into a wide range of other portfolio objectives. In general, the least-cost means of return structuring can be represented through the appropriate set of put and call options on the underlying asset. This leads the goal of minimizing costs one step further: finding the dynamic strategy which best replicates the required set of put and call options.

We have dealt with this and with the related issue of finding the most effective strategy, the strategy that gives the greatest chance of meeting the investment objectives under all possible market scenarios. We have addressed only indirectly a second vital issue of performance structuring: finding the strategy that meets the needs and objectives of the investor. Poorly written insurance policies can be formed just as easily with dynamic strategies as with more conventional insurance techniques. A strategy must not only meet its objectives and do so at the least cost; the objectives themselves must also be intelligently conceived.

Like policies in insurance or contracts in law, creating the proper performance structure in finance can only be done once the nature of the risks and the objectives of the client are known. This requires more than an understanding of the tools of performance structuring. It requires a knowledge of the business being analyzed. The investment needs of the pension fund differ in scope and complexity from those of the insurance company, which in turn differ from those of the thrift institution.[23]

Because of the fundamentally individual nature of risks and objectives, the design of proper strategies and objectives, as opposed to the implementation of a given strategy, is probably better illuminated through case studies than through any attempt to seek out general theories or principles. We have touched on this in the various examples and applications, especially those in Section III. But even there we could only give an indication of the individualized character of return structure design. This is an area that is part art, part science, where judgment and experience are of key importance.

---

[23]Our approaches to product design take these differences into account at the outset. For example, strategies in the insurance area include hedging single premium deferred annuities and universal life policies. For savings and loans these techniques have been applied to asset-liability management and cash management. Other applications range from protecting investments in foreign currencies from adverse currency price movements to hedging the credit risk of high-yield bond portfolios.

BIBLIOGRAPHY

Arditti, F., and John, K. "Spanning the State Space with Options." *Journal of Financial and Quantitative Analysis* 15 (March 1980): 1–9.

Arditti, F., and Levy, H. "Portfolio Efficiency Analysis in Three Moments: The Multiperiod Case." *Journal of Finance* 30 (June 1975): 797–809.

Black, F., and Scholes, M. "The Pricing of Options and Corporate Liabilities." *Journal of Political Economy* 81 (May 1973): 637–654.

Bookstaber, R. *Option Pricing and Strategies in Investing.* Reading, MA: Addison-Wesley, 1981.

Bookstaber, R., and Clarke, R. "Options Can Alter Portfolio Return Distributions." *Journal of Portfolio Management* 7 (Spring 1981a): 63–70.

Bookstaber, R., and Clarke, R. "An Algorithm to Calculate the Return Distribution of Portfolios with Option Positions." *Management Science* (April 1981b).

Bookstaber, R., and Clarke, R. *Option Strategies for Institutional Investment Management.* Reading, MA: Addison-Wesley 1983.

Bookstaber, R., and Clarke, R. "Option Portfolio Strategies: Measurement and Evaluation." *Journal of Business* 57 (October 1984): 469–492.

Bookstaber, R., and Clarke, R. "Problems in Evaluating the Performance of Portfolios with Options." *Financial Analysts Journal* 41 (January/February 1985): 48–62.

Bookstaber, R., and McDonald, J. "A Generalized Option Pricing Valuation Model for the Pricing of Bond Options." *Review of Research in Futures Markets* 4 (May 1985): 60–83.

Breeden, D., and Litzenberger, R. "Prices of State-Contingent Claims Implicit in Option Prices." *Journal of Business* 52 (October 1978): 621–651.

Brennan, M., and Solanki, R. "Optimal Portfolio Insurance." *Journal of Financial and Quantitative Analysis* 16 (September 1981): 279–300.

Cox, J., and Ross, S. "The Valuation of Options for Alternative Stochastic Processes." *Journal of Financial Economics* 3 (March 1976): 145–166.

Kraus, A., and Litzenberger, R. "Skewness Preference and the Valuation of Risky Assets." *Journal of Finance* 31 (September 1976): 1085–1100.

Leland, H. "Who Should Buy Portfolio Insurance?" *Journal of Finance* 35 (May 1980): 581–594.

Liebowitz, M., and Weinberger, A. "Contingent Immunization, Part I: Risk Control Procedures." *Financial Analysts Journal* 38 (November/December 1982): 17–31.

Merton, R. "Theory of Rational Option Pricing." *Bell Journal of Economics and Management Science* 4 (Spring 1973): 141–183.

Merton, R. "Option Pricing when Underlying Stock Returns Are Discontinuous." *Journal of Financial Economics* 3 (March 1976): 125–144.

Merton, R. "On Market Timing and Investment Performance. I. An Equilibrium Theory of Value for Market Forecasts." *Journal of Business* 54 (July 1981): 363–406.

Merton, R., Scholes, M., and Gladstein, M. "The Returns and Risk of Alternative Call Option Portfolio Investment Strategies." *Journal of Business* 51 (April 1978): 183–242.

Merton, R., Scholes, M., and Gladstein, M. "The Returns and Risks of Put-Option Portfolio Investment Strategies." *Journal of Business* 55 (January 1982): 61–67.

Platt, R., and Latainer, G. "Risk-Return Tradeoffs of Contingent Insurance Strategies for Active Bond Portfolios." *Financial Analysts Journal* 40 (May/June 1984): 34–39.

Platt, R., and Latainer, G. *Replicating Option Strategies for Portfolio Risk Control.* New York: Morgan Stanley Fixed Income Research (1983a).

Platt, R., and Latainer, G. *Replicating Option Strategies—Part II: Applications of Portfolio Insurance.* New York: Morgan Stanley Fixed Income Research (1983b).

Ross, S. "Options and Efficiency." *Quarterly Journal of Economics* 90 (February 1976): 75–89.

Rubinstein, M., and Leland, H. "Replicating Options with Positions in Stock and Cash." *Financial Analysts Journal* 37 (July 1981): 63–72.

Rubinstein, M., and Cox, J. *Option Markets*. Englewood Cliffs, NJ: Prentice-Hall. 1985.

Stapleton, R.C., and Subrahamanyain, M.G. "The Valuation of Multivariate Contingent Claims in Discrete Time Models." *Journal of Finance* 39 (March 1984): 207–228.

Stultz, R.M. "Options on the Minimum or the Maximum of Two Risky Assets." *Journal of Financial Economics* 10 (July 1982): 161–185.

Tilley, J., and Jacob, D. *Asset/Liability Management for Insurance Companies* New York: Morgan Stanley Fixed Income Research (1983).

Tilley, J. *Hedging Interest Rate Risk for Interest Sensitive Products.* New York: Morgan Stanley Fixed Income Research (1984a).

Tilley, J. and Latainer, G. *A Synthetic Framework for Asset Allocation.* New York: Morgan Stanley Fixed Income Research (1985).

3 Special Analytical Techniques and Instruments

6 Mortgage-Backed Securities: An Analytical Framework

SCOTT M. PINKUS

INTRODUCTION

The unprecedented growth in the mortgage-backed securities (MBS) market over the last several years has stimulated tremendous interest in these instruments. Mortgage debt outstanding currently totals almost $2 trillion, exceeding even the U.S. Government debt market in size. Since only about $300 billion of this amount has actually been securitized, the potential for further growth of the mortgage-backed securities market is considerable.

As the ability of thrift institutions to continue as the primary source of mortgage money diminished during the late 1970s and early 1980s, the capital markets and nontraditional mortgage investors began to play a greater role in housing finance. The need to tap large sources of capital to provide funds for mortgage lending encouraged the rapid development and growth of the mortgage-backed securities market. Recognizing the attractive opportunities available in this evolving market, investors who had not before participated in the mortgage market began to look seriously at mortgage-backed securities for their fixed-income portfolios. The influx of these new and relatively more sophisticated investors has altered the traditional mortgage business and forced a closer examination of the issues related to pricing and valuing mortgage-backed securities.

This chapter explains what mortgage-backed securities are and how they work, and develops an analytical framework for pricing and valuing these securities. It discusses the various methodologies currently used in the marketplace when pricing MBSs, and gives some insights into where the market is going in this regard. Institutional and market realities will be highlighted throughout the chapter, as they are critical for developing an effective understanding of mortgage-backed securities as well as any investment or trading strategies utilizing these instruments. While this chapter focuses on the characteristics of mortgage securities and the market for these securities, any investment decision should be considered within the context of one's entire fixed-income portfolio and the overall management strategies for that portfolio.

One final note regarding the complexity of mortgage-backed securities and the confusing terminology and practices that pervade this market: a common and very reasonable question that is often asked when investors first look seriously at this market is, "Why bother?" The answer is simple—yield. Given the attractive yields on these securities relative to Treasuries, and the quality and liquidity of most mortgage-backed securities, they are an investment that must be considered for any fixed-income portfolio.

SECTION I   WHAT IS A MORTGAGE?

A mortgage defines any loan secured by some form of real property, generally real estate. The property such as a house can be claimed by the lender (the mortgagee) if the borrower (the mortgagor) fails to make payments to the lender as required by the loan obligation. The market value of the property, therefore, must be considered along with the credit of the borrower when assessing the overall credit quality of a mortgage loan.

The bulk of the securities currently outstanding in the mortgage-backed securities market are backed by residential mortgages including loans secured by single-family homes as well as those on mobile homes. Mortgages on multifamily developments, such as apartment buildings, and mortgages backed by commercial properties, however, promise to play a major role in the growth of the MBS market over the next several years.

Until recently, when a prospective homeowner thought about a mortgage, he or she was probably thinking of a 30-year obligation with a fixed contractual interest rate and a constant or level payment amount over the entire term of the loan. The dominance of this so-called *30-year, fixed rate, level pay mortgage* began when the Federal Housing Administration (FHA) succeeded in creating a standardized mortgage instrument in the 1930s. The standard FHA mortgage was and continues to be attractive to borrowers since it is a long-term obligation that is fully amortized over the term of the loan, which means that the borrower's monthly payments consist of some principal as well as all of the interest due each month. The principal balance of the loan is gradually paid off over the term of the loan. As can be seen in Figure 6-1, the constant monthly payment consists of principal and interest in varying proportions over the term of the mortgage. Whereas most of the payment in the early years consists of interest, as the loan ages more of the payment goes toward paying off the principal balance of the loan.

Over the last several years other types of mortgage instruments have gained in popularity. The *15-year, fixed rate, level pay mortgage* has appealed to many bor-

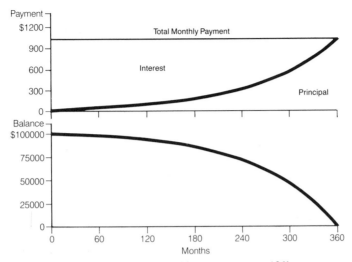

Figure 6-1. Composition of monthly payments on a 12% mortgage.

rowers who prefer a shorter term obligation. *The graduated payment mortgage* (GPM) retains the fixed-rate feature of the standard mortgage but allows a borrower to make lower monthly payments in the early years of the loan. The monthly payment amount, however, increases annually by a fixed percentage for several years (usually 5 or 10 years), before levelling off and remaining constant throughout the remaining term of the loan. The loan employs a feature known as negative amortization, which describes the capitalization of interest that accrues on the loan during the early years, but is not paid as a result of the artificially low payment schedule for those years. This interest shortfall is added to the principal balance of the loan each month. The *graduated equity mortgage* (GEM) is similar to the GPM in that scheduled payments increase over time. Since the payment amount on a GEM loan is always sufficient to pay the interest accrued each month, though, the increased payment amount each year goes toward faster reduction of the principal balance of the loan.

The alternative mortgage instrument that has had by far the greatest impact on the mortgage market is the *adjustable rate mortgage* (ARM). The ARM essentially shifts much of the interest rate risk of a long-term loan from the lender to the borrower. The borrower's contractual interest rate is pegged to some published index (such as the Federal Home Loan Bank of San Francisco Cost of Funds Index or the U.S. Treasury's 1-Year Constant Maturity Index), and will change at designated adjustment intervals as the index changes. Most ARMs have features that protect the borrower from rapid increases in their mortgage payments caused by rising interest rates. Many loans limit the amount by which the interest rate can change at each adjustment date and/or over the life of the loan. Other loans limit the amount by which payments can be increased at each adjustment. In addition, most ARMs limit negative amortization to a maximum percentage of the original loan balance, usually 125%.

ARMs accounted for over one-half of total residential mortgage originations in 1984. They have not, however, been securitized to any great degree as of this writing, largely because of the lack of standardization among the ARM loans being originated. ARMs will probably play a more significant role in the MBS market in the near future as the market moves toward greater standardization.

SECTION II   INTRODUCTION TO THE MORTGAGE-BACKED SECURITIES MARKET

Before explaining *what* a mortgage-backed security is, it is important to understand *why* they were created. While a secondary market for nonsecuritized mortgages, or whole loans, existed before MBSs were issued and continues to this day, the whole loan market is cumbersome to participate in and offers only sporadic liquidity. Trading large blocks of whole loans requires specialized and extensive underwriting and operational capabilities far beyond what most nontraditional mortgage investors are willing or able to supply. The mortgage-backed securities market was created primarily to simplify trading of mortgage-related instruments and encourage wider participation in mortgage investments.

Assessing the credit of an individual mortgage loan requires an evaluation of the borrower's ability to make future payments and the market value of the property to which a creditor can turn if the borrower defaults on his or her obligation. While the existence of FHA insurance or other private mortgage insurance on the loan reduces the potential losses from poor underwriting, it does not eliminate those potential losses and does not guarantee timely payments each month.

The mortgage-backed security structure specifically addresses this problem by adding an additional layer of insurance or guarantees at the security level, supplementing that on the individual loans. The Government National Mortgage Association (GNMA or "Ginnie Mae"), for instance, guarantees the timely payment of principal and interest each month on its securities and backs this with the full faith and credit of the U.S. Treasury. Regardless of what happens to the individual FHA or VA mortgages underlying a GNMA pool, the investor is assured of timely payments each month. Investors, therefore, no longer have to concern themselves with the credit quality of the individual mortgage loans.

Mortgage-backed securities have also substantially simplified the settlement and operational difficulties associated with mortgage investments. The MBS investor need not be concerned with the collection of monthly payments on each individual mortgage loan underlying a pool, as he or she will receive a single check for the entire pool based on his or her pro rata share. Settlement dates and procedures have also been standardized for mortgage securities through the efforts of the Public Securities Association.

While *mortgage pass-through securities* could technically be considered a subset of *mortgage-backed securities,* the terms are generally used interchangeably and will be referred to that way throughout this discussion. The term *pass-through,* however, probably provides a better description of how these securities actually work.

A GNMA pass-through security, for example, is a certificate issued against a pool of FHA insured or VA guaranteed mortgages. A portion of the cash flow from those mortgages is "passed-through" the issuer of the GNMA (assuming the issuer continues to service the mortgages) to the ultimate investor who owns the GNMA security. The scheduled cash flow of principal and interest (less servicing fees) from the underlying mortgages is received by the investor on the fifteenth day of each month. In addition to these scheduled payments, any unscheduled payments of principal are passed through as they are received by the issuer/servicer. Unscheduled payments occur when mortgage borrowers prepay some or all of the outstanding principal balance on their mortgage loans. Prepayments usually result from borrowers having moved or refinanced their mortgages at lower rates. Defaulted loans also lead to unscheduled principal payments, with the FHA or the VA ultimately picking up most of the difference between the outstanding principal balance owed and any receipts from foreclosure proceedings.

The issuer/servicer agrees to make all scheduled payments to GNMA security holders on their due dates, regardless of whether or not such payments have been received from the mortgage borrowers, or in the case of defaulted loans, from the FHA or VA. The Government National Mortgage Association (GNMA), though, provides the ultimate cash flow protection to the GNMA investor by backing up its guarantee to make timely payments of principal and interest to the investor with the full faith and credit of the United States government.

The GNMA program is the largest, oldest, and best known of the various mortgage-backed security programs currently in existence. As of December 31, 1984, the outstanding balance of all GNMAs issued totaled $181 billion. The two next largest programs come under the auspices of quasi-governmental agencies: the Federal Home Loan Mortgage Corporation (FHLMC or "Freddie Mac") and the Federal National Mortgage Association (FNMA or "Fannie Mae"). At the end of 1984, the outstanding balance of all FHLMCs amounted to $68 billion, while FNMAs outstanding totaled $36 billion.

There are several key differences between these latter MBS programs and the GNMA structure. To begin with, the FHLMC and FNMA programs are oriented more toward conventional mortgages than the FHA insured, VA guaranteed, or Farmers Housing Administration guaranteed mortgages that are the mainstay of the GNMA program. Only seasoned FHA/VA mortgages (mortgages that are one or more years old) can be included in the FHLMC or FNMA programs, while conventional mortgages can be either newly originated or seasoned to qualify.

The nature of the guarantee also varies among these three MBS programs. Neither FHLMC nor FNMA securities are backed by the full faith and credit of the U.S. Treasury. FNMA guarantees the timely payment of principal and interest each month on their MBSs, whether or not such payments are collected. FNMA is a federally chartered, privately owned corporation that has the ability to borrow up to $2.25 billion from the U.S. Treasury (at the discretion of the Secretary of the Treasury). The Federal Home Loan Mortgage Corporation, on the other hand, guarantees the timely payment of interest and the eventual payment of principal on its mortgage participation certificates (PCs). FHLMC like FNMA is not a government agency, but rather a corporate instrumentality of the United States owned by the Federal Home Loan Banks and their member thrift institutions.

There are numerous other differences between the three major MBS programs that influence their pricing and trading relationships, a few of which will be highlighted here. GNMAs issued under the original program guidelines, except in some rare instances, are relatively homogeneous. The mortgages underlying these securities are all FHA/VA loans which have the same coupon rate and were originated within one year of each other.[1] Ninety percent of the underlying mortgages must have an original maturity between 20 and 30 years. The newer GNMA II program allows the interest rate on the underlying mortgages to vary by up to 100 basis points.[2]

Under FHLMCs original PC program, "regular" or "standard" PCs were backed by mortgages from Freddie Mac's own portfolio. There were virtually no restrictions on the coupon rates or maturities of the loans that could be packaged into a PC. FHLMC's Guarantor or "Swap" program was created to encourage thrift institutions to package and sell some of the old, discounted mortgages that they held in portfolio. (These loans can be sold to FHLMC and "swapped" for a FHLMC PC backed by the loans.) While there are no limitations on the original or remaining terms on the loans that are pooled, the loans must have rates that are greater than or equal to the security coupon rate on the PC plus the servicing fee (paid to the servicer) and the guarantee fee (paid to FHLMC). In addition, the highest mortgage rate in a pool cannot be more than 200 basis points above the lowest rate in the pool.

The FNMA MBS program is very similar to the FHLMC Guarantor PC program, with the major differences being in the day of payment each month and the delay until first payment. FNMAs pay on the 25th day of the month following purchase, while Freddie Macs pay on the 15th day of the second month after purchase. GNMAs pay on the 15th day of the month following purchase.

In addition to the three large government-related MBS programs just discussed, there have been numerous other mortgage pass-throughs created by private issuers such as the Bank of America and Norwest. These programs, while similar in many respects to the GNMA, FHLMC, and FNMA programs, have a multitude of subtle and not-so-subtle differences in their structures and in their eligibility requirements for mortgage collateral. While a large number of these pass-throughs have been issued since 1977, no single private issuer has to date gained a major share of the MBS market.

Collateralized Mortgage Obligations (CMOs), which are serialized sequential-pay bonds collateralized by mortgages or mortgage pass-through securities, have begun to play a significant role in the mortgage securities market since the first such offering by FHLMC in 1983. This type of instrument is actually a hybrid between the mortgage pass-through security and the more traditional corporate sinking fund

---

[1]Exceptions to this include GNMA mobile home pass-throughs, which allow for some variation in underlying mortgage rates, and VA-Vendee mortgage loans, which are sold from the VA's portfolio and may be seasoned when they are pooled into GNMAs.

[2]For a further discussion of the GNMA II program, see Mara, Susan D., "The GNMA II Program Revisited," *Mortgage Banker* (July 1985).

bond, often resembling one more than the other. While many of the concepts discussed in the following pages are relevant to the valuation of CMOs, they are a unique instrument in many ways and must be afforded more individualized attention, which is beyond the scope of this chapter.[3]

SECTION III   PREPAYMENTS: THE NATURE OF THE PROBLEM

As one becomes more actively involved in the mortgage market and with mortgage-backed securities, one inevitably begins to focus more attention on the issue of prepayments. The actual cash flow an investor receives from a mortgage-backed security depends on the particular termination pattern (resulting from prepayments and defaults) of the many individual mortgages making up the pool. Each mortgage borrower has, through his prepayment option, what essentially amounts to an "unrestricted" call provision on the loan.[4] The variability of these prepayments, along with the variability that is implied by defaults, combine to make the cash flow that is actually received from a mortgage investment very uncertain. The actual cash flow that an MBS investor will receive from his or her interest in the underlying pool of mortgages, therefore, also is not known with certainty.

Since an MBS investor is assured of the ultimate repayment of his or her share of the principal balance of the pool, the actual termination pattern and the resulting cash flow from the pool will not affect the yield from the investment so long as he or she purchased the security at its parity price (the par value adjusted for the delay in monthly payments).[5] If the MBS was purchased at any other price (involving a discount or a premium) however, the investor's yield would vary significantly depending on the actual termination pattern and its effect on the timing of the repayment of the pool's principal balance.

The effect of price on the yield to termination relationship of a mortgage is illustrated in Figure 6-2. When a new 11% mortgage is priced at par or 100, the yield will be equal to its coupon rate of 11%, regardless of whether it prepays in the fifth, twelfth, or twentieth years, or even runs to maturity.

If, on the other hand, the mortgage is priced at a discount (such as 85%), the yield increases as the length of time a mortgage is outstanding before it terminates (the life-to-termination) is reduced. This occurs since the value of the discount from par (15%) is recouped over a shorter period of time. While the investor may have paid

---

[3]See Silpe, Stuart L. and Pinkus, Scott M., "Collateralized Mortgage Obligations: A Framework for Analysis," Merrill Lynch Capital Markets, January 1984 and Pinkus, Scott M. and Mara, Susan D. "Special Report: The PSA Standard Prepayment Model," Morgan Stanley, June 1985.

[4]While FHA insured and VA guaranteed mortgages prohibit the use of prepayment penalties, some conventional mortgages employ a penalty schedule for early prepayments, thus discouraging though not restricting prepayments.

[5]The MBS investor does not receive his payment on the first day of every month, as with a standard mortgage, but at a later date, such as the fifteenth day of each month (as in the case of a GNMA). By postponing his stream of annuity payments by 14 days, the delay acts as a penalty to the investor and lowers the yield relative to that on a regular annuity instrument (e.g., a standard mortgage).

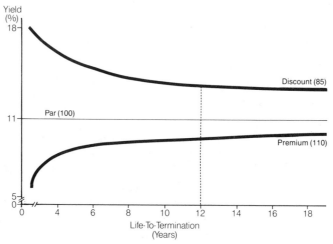

Figure 6-2.   Yield to termination on a new 11% mortgage at various secondary market prices (discount, par, premium).

only 85% of the face value or principal balance of the loan, the loan principal will be paid back to him at 100% of its face value over its life. If that life is shortened by an early prepayment, the 15% discount from par will be received by the investor sooner, and as a result of the time value of money, is worth more to him, increasing his yield. A dramatic example of this effect would be one in which an investor paid 85% of face value for a new 11% mortgage that ends up prepaying (at 100% of face) after one month, providing a huge yield of almost 225% (on an annual basis) for the 1-month investment.

Conversely, if the mortgage is priced at a premium, its yield decreases as the assumed life-to-termination is shortened. In this case the investor pays a premium over par for a relatively valuable stream of monthly coupon payments which, by ending prematurely at the time of prepayment, reduced his return on the premium paid and thus his yield on the investment.

Figure 6-3 illustrates how the *magnitude* of the discount on an MBS affects the relationship between the yield and the life-to-termination assumption. As one might have guessed from Figure 6-2, the termination assumption has a much greater impact on the yield of a new GNMA 11 when it is priced at 88, than when it is priced at 98. Clearly, the greater the discount, the greater the absolute and percentage increase in yield resulting from an early termination. The yield to a 12-year bullet prepayment, for example, on the GNMA 11 is 11.25% when it is priced at 98, and 12.95% when it is priced at 88. When the prepayment is assumed to occur in the fourth year, however, the yield of the mortgage when it is priced at 98 increases by 2.1% to 11.49%, while the yield of the mortgage when it is priced at 88 increases by almost 15% to 14.86%.

Before moving on, one point should be clarified. Whereas the *yield* on a mortgage or MBS priced near par will be insensitive to prepayments, the *total return* from such

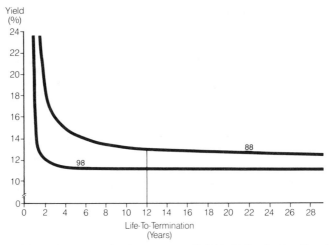

Figure 6-3.   Yield to termination on a new GNMA 11% priced at 98 and 88.

an investment may not, and probably will not, be insensitive to prepayments. Since prepayments tend to increase as interest rates fall—as there is a greater incentive to refinance high-rate mortgage loans at lower market rates or, conversely, a reduced disincentive to prepay a relatively low-rate loan—the increased cash flow on an MBS must be reinvested at lower rates. The cumulative influence of this reduced return on reinvested cash flows can have, over time, a tremendous influence on the total return of such an investment regardless of its purchase price. Conversely, when prepayments slow down in a rising rate environment a reduced cash flow is available to reinvest at higher rates, thus diminishing the total return on the investment.

SECTION IV   MODELING PREPAYMENTS

Since the actual termination pattern on the mortgages underlying a MBS can have a significant influence on the yield and total return of the investment, it is critical that this uncertainty be explicitly considered in any risk-return analysis of mortgage securities. Although mortgage terminations can be caused by either prepayments or defaults, the net effect to the pass-through investor is virtually identical—the investor receives principal payments over and above those resulting from normal amortization. Such unscheduled principal payments on the mortgage pass-through, therefore, will be referred to collectively as prepayments.

Points Estimates

The simplest approach to modeling prepayments on pass-through securities is to assume a point estimate of prepayment, or a bullet prepayment at a single point in time for all of the mortgages underlying a pass-through. The 12-year life convention was, until a few years ago, the standard prepayment assumption used in quoting yields on 30-year mortgages and pass-through securities. This convention assumes a security is backed entirely by new 30-year mortgages whose cash flows consist of interest and scheduled amortization of principal for 12 years, and full prepayment of the remaining principal at the end of the twelfth year.

The 12-year life convention was adopted during the early years of the mortgage securities market to standardize mortgage calculations. The assumptions behind this convention, however, are not realistic in today's marketplace. Since many of the securities outstanding in the market are significantly aged, the assumption that they are new is blatantly incorrect. In addition, the convention was adopted during a period of relatively stable interest rates when the range of mortgage rates outstanding was narrow. In the current volatile interest rate environment with a wide range of security coupons outstanding, the assumption of full prepayment after 12 years cannot be meaningfully applied across these varying coupons. While a point estimate other than 12 years could be used to better reflect the different prepayment expectations across varying coupons, choosing the appropriate assumption is a highly arbitrary procedure.

When looking at an individual mortgage loan, the cash flow pattern described by a point estimate of prepayment is not unrealistic—that is, a mortgage generates level payments of interest and scheduled principal until it prepays in full.[6] This pattern, however, does not describe well the cash flows generated by a portfolio or pool of mortgages where prepayments can be expected to be distributed over time. In addition, when examining a pool of mortgages, the nonlinear relationship between the yield and point estimate of prepayment on a mortgage can bias the yield estimate on a pool of loans. This nonlinearity, which was pointed out by Curley and Guttentag,[7] can be seen in Figure 6-2 by the falling and rising curves, rather than lines, representing the discount and premium respectively. For a mortgage priced at a discount or premium, prepayment has a greater influence on yield in the early years than in the later years. For a portfolio of discounted mortgages, then, the average of the yields on each of the individual mortgages if they prepaid in different years would be significantly greater than the yield based on the average life-to-termination of all of the mortgages. The use of any point estimate of the average life-to-termination of all of the mortgages in a portfolio would, therefore, bias yield estimates for the portfolio. The bias would underestimate the yields of discount portfolios and overestimate the yields of premium portfolios. To eliminate this bias in the yield estimate for a portfolio or pool of mortgages, a point estimate of the average life-to-termination must be replaced with a model utilizing a distribution of prepayments over time.

[6]This example ignores the possibility of partial prepayments.
[7]Curley, Anthony J. and Guttentag, Jack M., "The Yield on Insured Residential Mortgages," *Explorations in Economic Research* (Summer 1974) and "Value and Yield Risk on Outstanding Insured Residential Mortgages," *Journal of Finance* (May 1977).

FHA Experience

A commonly used technique for viewing prepayments as a distribution over time involves the use of "FHA experience." Prepared by the Actuarial Division of the Federal Housing Administration, FHA experience represents the average prepayment and default experience of all FHA insured, single-family, 30-year mortgages over many years. The series released in 1982 was based on the experience of mortgages originated between 1957 and 1981, while the series released in both 1984 and 1985 included the experience of only those mortgages written after 1970.

Each FHA experience series consists of 30 termination rates, one for each year of a 30-year mortgage's life. The termination rates, hereafter referred to simply as prepayment rates, represent the average percentage of FHA loans that prepaid in each year of their life relative to the total number of loans of the same age outstanding at the beginning of the period. Table 6-1 illustrates how the FHA series released in 1982 was constructed. The first prepayment rate included in the FHA series is based on the average prepayment experience of all FHA mortgages originated between 1957 and 1981 in the first year of their existence. The second rate is based on the average second year prepayment experience of mortgages written between 1957 and 1980.

While the FHA experience series provides a benchmark for viewing the prepayment experience of a group of mortgages as they age, these base rates are often adjusted to reflect higher or lower expected prepayments in the future. If one expects that prepayments on a particular MBS pool will be twice as fast as that implied by

Table 6-1.   Breakdown of FHA Experience (Released Spring 1982)

Age in Years	Origination Years	Observation Years	Number of Years Observed	Prepayment Rates
1	1957–1981	1957–1981	25	1.13
2	1957–1980	1958–1981	24	3.77
3	1957–1979	1959–1981	23	5.17
4	1957–1978	1960–1981	22	5.73
5	1957–1977	1961–1981	21	6.21
6	1957–1976	1962–1981	20	6.80
7	1957–1975	1963–1981	19	7.12
8	1957–1974	1964–1981	18	7.23
9	1957–1973	1965–1981	17	7.00
10	1957–1972	1966–1981	16	6.69
11	1957–1971	1967–1981	15	6.59
12	1957–1970	1968–1981	14	6.43
13	1957–1969	1969–1981	13	6.12
14	1957–1968	1970–1981	12	5.86
15	1957–1967	1971–1981	11	5.59
16	1957–1966	1972–1981	10	5.34
17	1957–1965	1973–1981	9	5.10
18	1957–1964	1974–1981	8	4.89
19	1957–1963	1975–1981	7	4.67
20	1957–1962	1976–1981	6	4.40
21	1957–1961	1977–1981	5	4.11
22	1957–1960	1978–1981	4	4.94
23	1957–1959	1979–1981	3	5.78
24	1957–1958	1980–1981	2	6.68
25	1957	1981	1	7.62
26–30	Forecasted Data Points		0	

the base FHA experience series, one will adjust the FHA series accordingly, and refer to his or her assumed prepayment distribution as ''200% FHA.'' Conversely, 50% FHA would be assumed if one felt that prepayments would be one-half as fast as the benchmark FHA series. Under this terminology, 0% FHA would be equivalent to no prepayments over time.

Using FHA experience as a benchmark to predict prepayments is far superior to using a point estimate because the FHA series considers the fact that prepayments are likely to occur throughout the term of a pool, rather than all at once. There are so many problems inherent in the use of this methodology, however, that it is often of little real value in providing more realistic yield and total return estimates for MBSs.

One problem with the use of FHA experience relates to the way the underlying data is aggregated. As was shown in Table 6-1, the prepayment rate for the first year of a mortgage's life is derived from the percentage of mortgages originated in the years 1957–1981 that prepaid after one year. Thus a mortgage written at the beginning of 1957 would be examined at the end of 1957 to see whether it prepaid in its first year, one written in 1958 examined at the end of 1958, and so on. Since the prepayment rates for each of the succeeding years of a mortgage's life are derived in a similar manner, the number of distinct observation years included in each sample declines from 25 for the first-year prepayment rate (from mortgages originated between 1957 and 1981) to 1 for the twenty-fifth-year prepayment rate (from mortgages originated in 1957 only). The effect of this breakdown is to create a serious bias in the aggregate FHA experience data. The prepayment rates for the early years of a mortgage's life are based on the experience of mortgages originated at the various market rates existing between 1957 and the early 1980s, while prepayment rates in the later years represent only the experience of mortgages originated in the late 1950s and early 1960s when rates were uniformly low, thus making these loans less likely to prepay in the high interest rate environment of the late 1970s and early 1980s.

While the Federal Housing Administration has historically updated the FHA experience series every one or two years by incorporating the most recent experience of both old and newly originated loans into the series, the series released in 1984 is based only on the experience of loans originated since 1970. By removing the experience of the very old FHA loans from the data, the newer FHA series better reflects more recent experience and reduces, though does not eliminate, the bias built into the earlier series. Since the newer FHA series includes only the experience of mortgages originated between 1970 and 1983, however, the average prepayment rates calculated for mortgage years 14 through 30 were not based on actual experience, but were estimated.

In addition to the bias caused by the aggregation of the FHA data and the confusion related to the periodic updating of the FHA experience series, there also exists a more obvious and fundamental problem associated with averaging. While the relationship between the actual coupon rate on a mortgage and current market rates has a significant impact on prepayments (due to refinancings and assumptions), FHA experience, through its averaging of individual mortgage data, effectively ignores this important relationship. Recognizing this limitation investors often adjust FHA experience to account for an expected shift in prepayment rates caused by various factors, the most important one being the relationship between the mortgage rate and current market rates. Choosing the ''correct'' percent FHA adjustment factor, however, is a difficult and somewhat arbitrary procedure.

One of the greatest advantages of the FHA experience methodology, though, is its consideration of the relationship between mortgage age and prepayments. The FHA series builds into the prepayment distribution the generally accepted phenomenon that, everything else being equal, the probability of a mortgage prepaying increases during its first several years and stabilizes somewhat after that. This makes intuitive sense if one considers that the circumstances which led someone to move in the first place are less likely to occur again after one year than after two years, and so on.[8]

While the influence of aging on prepayments is critical for newly originated mortgages, it is much less significant for loans that are substantially seasoned, where prepayments are far less a function of age than of other socioeconomic factors. Using a rigid prepayment model such as FHA experience also can be seriously misleading when measuring or forecasting the prepayment experience of mortgages or MBSs, priced at a premium. Prepayments on these instruments are almost entirely driven by the refinancing incentive that exists for these loans, with the age of the loan being relatively insignificant. For example, Table 6-2 illustrates the prepayment experience of two hypothetical 17% GNMA pools which were one year and two years old, respectively. Both pools were assumed to have actually prepaid at the same rate over the most recent month. Calculating the percentage of FHA experience that would have to have been assumed for each loan to match the actual prepayment rates experienced over the month, however, can lead one to an inaccurate conclusion. Pool A was shown to have prepaid at a rate equivalent to 6100% FHA over the month, while Pool B prepaid at only 1800% FHA, though in reality the prepayment rates actually experienced on both pools were identical (50% CPR) over the month.

Since FHA experience offered a more sophisticated approach to measuring and forecasting prepayment rates on mortgage pass-throughs than the 12-year life con-

Table 6-2. Measuring Historical Prepayment Experience—Using CPRs versus FHA Experience

	Age[a]	Outstanding Balance[a]	Total Principal Payment	Prepaid Principal	Actual Annualized Prepayment Rate (CPR)	Calculated % FHA Experience (1981 Series)
Pool A	1 Year	$1 Million	$56,214	$56,120	50% CPR	6100% FHA
Pool B	2 Years	$1 Million	$56,231	$56,119	50% CPR	1800% FHA

a = Beginning of Month

[8]While I will refer to the influence of mortgage age on prepayments throughout the chapter, several other time-related factors are implicitly included under that designation. For a further discussion of this, see Peters, Helen F., Pinkus, Scott M., and Askin, David J., ''Figuring the Odds: A Model of Prepayments,'' *Secondary Mortgage Markets* (May 1984), and Peters, Helen F., *Termination Distributions on FHA Insured Residential Mortgages,* Unpublished Ph.D. diss., University of Pennsylvania, 1979.

vention, its use increased dramatically during the late 1970s and early 1980s. Its popularity has declined during the last few years, however, as the level of refinancing-driven prepayments increased substantially (after 1982), and the flaws and confusion inherent in the use of the FHA experience methodology became more apparent.[9]

Conditional Prepayment Rates (CPRs)[10]

Recently the use of conditional prepayment rates (also known as constant prepayment rates or single monthly mortalities) has gained in popularity as a technique for analyzing prepayments. The conditional prepayment rate (CPR) is the percentage of principal outstanding at the beginning of a period that prepays during that period. (CPR usually refers to an annualized prepayment rate while single monthly mortality or SMM refers to the unannualized monthly rate.)[11] A conditional prepayment rate reflects the actual prepayment experience of mortgage securities and therefore does not suffer the drawback of being an arbitrary calculation such as the 12-year life convention or of being linked to an inaccurate and confusing prepayment distribution such as FHA experience. The cash flow distribution that is generated using a constant CPR, or series of varying CPRs, can be more representative of the actual distribution of prepayments on a mortgage security. More significantly, a CPR is a pure number which can be easily interpreted, understood, and monitored on a historical basis.

The greatest disadvantage in using a single CPR for estimating future prepayments on an MBS is, not surprisingly, the greatest strength of the FHA experience methodology: that a single prepayment rate estimate applied over the entire remaining term of an MBS cannot, by definition, accurately portray the influences of aging on prepayments during the early years of a mortgage's life. At a constant interest rate level, prepayments on a new mortgage pool can be expected to increase during the first several years of its life largely as a function of mortgage age, before generally levelling off. While a series of CPRs could be used to better reflect the varying influence of prepayments on mortgage cash flows over the life of a mortgage security, estimating the appropriate CPRs is a difficult and often subjective process, and may ultimately involve some of the same problems associated with the use of FHA experience. A simpler and, as a result, more commonly used approach for incorporating the age relationship into a single CPR prepayment estimate is to use a CPR

---

[9]For a further discussion of FHA experience see Pinkus, Scott M., and Firestone, Evan B., "Mortgage Securities: Predicting Prepayments," *Mortgage Banker* (December 1983), and Peters, Helen F., "Pricing a Mortgage-Backed Security—The Misuses of FHA Experience," *The Money Manager,* December 17, 1979. While the use of FHA experience to analyze mortgage pass-throughs has declined recently, the FHA methodology continues to be important in the CMO market. However, a new prepayment benchmark, known as the PSA Standard Prepayment Model, was developed by member firms of the Public Securities Association to replace FHA experience when quoting yields on CMOs. For a detailed discussion of this new prepayment model, see Pinkus and Mara, "Special Report: The PSA Standard Prepayment Model."

[10]For a more detailed discussion of the CPR methodology, see Pinkus and Firestone, "Mortgage Securities: Predicting Prepayments."

[11]A monthly SMM can be converted to an annualized *CPR* by the formula:

$$CPR = (1 - (1 - SMM/100)^{12}) \times 100$$

that approximates the time-weighted average of a series of varying CPRs over time, where a far greater weight is given to the earlier years' expected prepayment experience as a result of the time value of money and their greater impact on the price/yield relationship.

For a seasoned pool of mortgages and for pools with coupon rates above the current market level, however, the single CPR methodology is more than adequate, since mortgage age has a much less significant influence on prepayments. The relationship between the coupon rate on the pool (or more precisely, the contract rate on the underlying mortgages) and the mortgage rate currently available in the market is the dominant influence on prepayments. This will determine the degree of the *incentive* to refinance a high-rate mortgage for a new mortgage with a lower rate. For older, seasoned mortgages the current level of mortgage rates will determine how strong is a mortgagor's *disincentive* to pay off his relatively low-rate mortgage. This disincentive can lead a borrower to postpone a desired move; permit his loan to be assumed (if allowable) when he does move; or take out a second or wrap-around mortgage if he seeks greater leverage, rather than prepaying his existing loan and refinancing the total amount at current market rates.

While the disincentive to pay off a low-rate mortgage is far less sensitive to interest rates than is the positive incentive that exists to refinance a high-rate mortgage loan, the level of interest rates, nevertheless, remains the most critical factor to be considered when estimating prepayments on mortgage securities. By regularly monitoring the prepayment experience, on a CPR basis, of the pass-through securities issued under the major MBS programs, one can begin to observe the influence of interest rates on prepayments in the current environment. Segregating homogeneous securities, such as GNMA 30-year, single-family pass-throughs, by coupon rate and approximate mortgage age allows one to fine-tune this process and better isolate the differing influences of mortgage aging and changing interest rates. Where older discount pools or premium securities are involved, the difference between the mortgage rate currently available in the market and the rate on the mortgages underlying various coupon groups can be related to the actual level of prepayments experienced by each coupon group. Comparing these relationships can provide valuable insight as to how various securities might react under different interest rate environments in the future.

Econometric Models

The level of sophistication of the MBS market has increased tremendously over the past several years, particularly in the understanding of prepayment uncertainty and the evaluation of the potential risks and rewards associated with it. In order for new analytical techniques to be generally accepted in the marketplace they must be understood by the various participants in the market and prove practical for assisting in day-to-day business decisions. The use of econometric modeling techniques, on the one hand, and options pricing theory, on the other, are two approaches to modeling the prepayment uncertainty associated with mortgage securities that offer much promise for the near future, but are currently not practical for large scale day-to-day use.

An econometric model to predict mortgage prepayments can be derived from the detailed historical prepayment and default experience of any large portfolio of individual mortgage loans or mortgage securities.[12] The key factors which influence prepayment rates on a MBS, such as mortgage coupon rates, future market interest rates, and mortgage age, can be explicitly considered as variables in such a model. This avoids having to make arbitrary or subjective adjustments to a prepayment assumption, as is required with the use of point estimates of prepayment, FHA experience and, to a lesser extent, the CPR methodology.

By defining the statistical relationship between one or several independent variables and the dependent variable to be forecasted, an econometric model acts as a formal proxy for the informal evaluation techniques employed by an experienced decision maker. The sophisticated MBS investor usually bases his prepayment rate estimates on his judgment of the influence of mortgage coupon rates, future market rates, and other key factors (explanatory variables) on prepayments—derived from his experience in the mortgage and MBS markets—in conjunction with his best estimate of the future values of those key factors. An econometric model for predicting prepayment rates, on the other hand, substitutes clearly defined statistical relationships, derived from large data bases of mortgage and borrower characteristics and individual mortgage prepayment and default experiences, for an investor's informal judgment based on his relatively limited experience. Such models, while formalizing and refining the decision-making process, nevertheless leave to the user the crucial task of defining the relevant environment (the forecast of explanatory variables) within which the decision is to take place.

While econometric modeling techniques offer a systematic and statistically sound method of estimating prepayments, they require that the user explicitly estimate the future values of a number of variables which are often difficult to estimate and are generally unfamiliar to most investors (e.g., regional migration patterns, average home costs, or housing starts). In addition, an econometric model must be based on a large sample of data over a fairly long period of time to be statistically significant and to accurately represent the influence of time-period variables such as mortgage age. The statistical relationships that proved meaningful during the 1960s or even during the 1970s, however, often do not hold true in the more volatile current interest rate environment, and can even be misleading for predicting behavior today.

Options Pricing Theory

Options pricing theory is playing an increasingly greater role in almost all facets of the fixed-income securities market. The attractiveness of this approach for the evaluation of mortgage-backed securities is understandable if one envisions a MBS as a combination of a noncallable bond and a call option. While a detailed discussion of this methodology is beyond the scope of this chapter (see Chapter 7) the primary

---

[12]For a more detailed discussion of the use of econometric modeling techniques for predicting mortgage prepayment rates, see Peters, Pinkus, and Askin, "Figuring the Odds: A Model of Prepayments," Peters, "Termination Distributions on FHA Insured Residential Mortgages" and Curley and Guttentag, "The Yield on Insured Residential Mortgages."

benefit of this approach lies in its theoretically appealing specification of the financial incentive to refinance a high rate mortgage (where the call option is "in the money").

The primary weakness of the options approach lies in its inherent inability to effectively consider the nonfinancial factors that also affect prepayments. These factors usually relate to institutional or demographic aspects of the market and, therefore, tend to be less easily quantified. Options theory, for example, cannot readily account for the significantly faster prepayment experience of discount conventional mortgages relative to otherwise similar FHA insured loans, since this difference is more a function of differing borrower and institutional characteristics than of financial factors. As a result, options pricing theory offers greater potential as a tool for analyzing the relative price volatility of mortgage securities than as an approach to modeling prepayments.

A Final Note

The previous sections discussed several different approaches to modeling the prepayment and cash flow uncertainty inherent in a mortgage security. The use of each method involves certain advantages and disadvantages relative to the others, with no one approach offering "the perfect solution." It is important to recognize, though, that all of these methods are used to some degree by those involved in the MBS market.

The CPR methodology, however, will be employed throughout the remainder of this chapter, as it has become the approach most commonly used by the more sophisticated market practitioners. It is a straightforward concept which can be easily implemented in any analysis of MBSs. In addition, the CPR approach permits one to more accurately measure and monitor the actual historical prepayment experience of existing mortgage-backed securities.

SECTION V   PREPAYMENT ASSUMPTIONS: GENERIC VERSUS POOL-SPECIFIC

When valuing mortgage securities priced at a discount or premium, the magnitude and timing of future principal payments has a critical impact on the actual yield and total return performance of these securities. While the principal amortization payments will be scheduled on the basis of the coupon rate, remaining term to maturity, and current balance of each mortgage, the level of future prepayments on each loan can only be estimated.

There are two distinct approaches to handling this cash flow uncertainty when evaluating mortgage securities, differing largely as a result of the two fundamentally different ways that MBS transactions can be executed. Mortgage securities can be traded on a *generic* or *pool-specific* basis. A generic trade is one where the specific pools to be delivered are not identified at the time of the trade, and any pool with the agreed upon coupon rate can be delivered at the specified price. An MBS trade can also be done on a specified pool basis. In these instances, specified pools with predetermined original certificate balances are defined at the time of the transaction.

When evaluating a generic MBS transaction, future principal payments on the securities must be estimated based on the average characteristics of all securities with similar characteristics to those being examined. For example, when a generic transaction involving GNMA 8% 30-year, single-family securities is being contemplated, the average age and average historical prepayment experience of all similar securities should be considered when determining the amount of scheduled principal that can be expected, as well as the level of prepayments that are likely under different interest rate scenarios. Given a lack of information to the contrary, the GNMA 8% pools that will ultimately be delivered should, on average, perform like the entire population of similar securities.

When an MBS transaction is done on a pool-specific basis, the parties involved have the added advantage of knowing the specific characteristics of the individual pools being traded, as well as the historical principal paydown experience of each pool. While this additional information can be useful when evaluating a potential transaction, its value is often overestimated by many in the market.

When valuing a specific mortgage pool, the historical prepayment experience of the pool is relevant only to the extent it provides insight into how the pool will prepay in the future. Many market participants jump to the conclusion that a "fast-pay" pool, or one that historically prepaid principal at a faster rate than the average for similar pools, will continue to prepay at a faster-than-average rate, and thus is worth more than an average pool with similar characteristics (assuming one is looking at discount securities). Although many transactions are done with this assumption in mind, the assumption is usually not accurate.

The historical prepayment data on a pool must be carefully evaluated to determine how *consistently* the pool prepaid faster or slower than the average for similar securities, and over what time period. For example, a pool might have had an average prepayment rate over a 2-year period that is higher than the average for similar pools over the same period. However, if the pool's actual monthly prepayment history indicates that there were little or no prepayments in most months and only a few months with large prepayments, there is little evidence to suggest that the pool will have faster-than-average prepayments in the future. On the other hand, it is possible that a pool will have consistently prepaid faster than average as a result of the specific characteristics of the mortgages included in the pool (e.g., the geographic distribution of the loans). It is only the latter situation that warrants treating a specified discount pool as anything other than a generic or average pool when estimating the value of its future prepayments.

Table 6–3 shows the actual prepayment experience of two specific GNMA 8% pools, as well as the average experience of all GNMA 8% pools. Pool 10747 had prepayments which were consistently faster than the average for all GNMA 8% pools (the generic data shown), indicating that the pool may be somewhat more valuable than a generic or nonspecific pool. Pool 10749, on the other hand, had only one prepayment over the last nine months, and in fact, had not had another prepayment since 1979. The fact that the average prepayment rate of Pool 10749 over the last 6 or 12 months was faster than the average for all 8% GNMAs is irrelevant when one considers the pool's monthly prepayment experience.

Table 6-3.   Generic versus Pool Specific Prepayment Data

	All GNMA 8% Pools "Generic Data"	GNMA 8%-Pool 10747 "Consistently Fast"	GNMA 8%-Pool 10749 "Sporadic Prepayments"
Mar 1985	2.3% CPR	5.0% CPR	0% CPR
Feb 1985	2.4	11.0	0
Jan 1985	2.3	5.6	0
Dec 1984	2.3	0	0
Nov 1984	2.3	8.2	47.4
Oct 1984	2.0	11.5	0
Sep 1984	2.6	3.8	0
Aug 1984	3.0	0	0
Jul 1984	3.7	15.0	0
Summary Statistics:			
3-mo avg	2.3% CPR	7.2% CPR	0% CPR
6-mo avg	2.3	7.0	10.2
12-mo avg	2.8	5.2	5.3
Avg to date	3.4	7.5	7.5

SECTION VI   THE MATURITY ASSUMPTION[13]

As should be apparent by this point, any valuation of mortgage securities must incorporate a projection of future scheduled and unscheduled principal payments on the underlying mortgage loans. While most market participants currently recognize the importance of the prepayment assumption when valuing these securities, the projection of future amortization payments can also be a critical element in their evaluation.

In order to calculate accurately the scheduled principal payments for a mortgage security, it is necessary to know the mortgage rate and maturity of each of the mortgages in the pool. Because this information is rarely available, it is necessary to make assumptions about the distribution of the maturities and mortgage rates given the information that is available. The most detailed maturity information that is generally available for any mortgage security is the weighted average maturity (WAM) of the mortgages in a pool as of the pool's issue date.[14] This information is provided for all FNMA securities and for FHLMC Guarantor securities issued after June 1983. For all GNMA securities and for all FHLMC securities issued prior to July 1983, however, the only maturity information available is the final maturity date of the mortgage with the longest remaining term as of the pool's issue date.

Table 6–4 illustrates how estimates of principal amortization payments can vary when the exact distribution of the maturities on the individual mortgages in a pool is not known. In this hypothetical example, a $3 million pool has a final maturity at

[13]See Pinkus, Scott M. and Mara, Susan D., "Measuring the Maturity of a Mortgage Security: When Is a WAM Not a WAM?" *Mortgage Banker* (February 1985).
[14]The original weighted average maturity (WAM) is the average maturity of all of the loans in a pool, with each loan's maturity weighted by the amount of its principal balance outstanding when the pool is formed.

issue date of 350 months. While the pool's WAM is approximately 283 months, the actual maturities range from 200 to 350 months. If all of the mortgages in the pool are assumed to have the same maturity as the pool's final maturity, the pool's next scheduled principal payment would be calculated as $951.03. Using the WAM as a single maturity assumption for the pool, the scheduled principal payment would be calculated as $1909.74. Both of these payment amounts, however, are substantially different from the $2432.53 total of scheduled principal that would actually be paid on the underlying mortgages. The greater the dispersion of the maturities on the loans in a pool, the less useful the published maturity information will be in calculating the pool's scheduled principal payments.

If a pool's scheduled principal payments are misestimated because the actual distribution of maturities on the underlying loans is not known, the amount of prepaid principal calculated for the pool will also be incorrect. Principal prepayments are calculated as the principal paid in excess of the amount of principal scheduled to be paid. To the extent a pool's historical scheduled principal payments are *understated* by using either the pool's WAM or final maturity to calculate payments, the pool's prepayment experience will be *overstated*.

Table 6–5 illustrates a hypothetical pool's total principal payment for a given month, together with the breakdown of amortization payments and prepaid principal that would be calculated under two different maturity assumptions—the final maturity of the pool and the original weighted average maturity adjusted for seasoning. The interaction between the maturity assumption and the calculation of prepayments can be clearly seen. The longer the remaining term to maturity is assumed to be, the smaller the portion of total principal payments that is considered to be scheduled principal, and the greater the portion that is assumed to be prepaid principal. When comparing the historical prepayment experience of different pools, therefore, it is critical to consider the maturity assumption that was made when the prepayment rates were calculated. While the prepayment rate calculated for a pool using its WAM is

Table 6-4.   Impact of Maturity Distribution on Estimated Scheduled Principal Payments

Principal Balance	% of Pool's Total Balance	Maturity (Months)	Scheduled Principal Payment	% of Pool's Total Payment
	Pool Maturity Distribution (12% Mortgages)			
$1,000,000	33.3%	200	$1,583.28	65.1%
1,000,000	33.3	300	532.24	21.9
1,000,000	33.3	350	317.01	13.0
$3,000,000	100.0%	283	$2,432.53	100.0%

Estimated Scheduled Principal Payments	
Maturity Assumptions	Scheduled Principal Payment
Final Maturity (350 months)	$ 951.03
Weighted Average Maturity (283 months)	1,909.74
Actual Scheduled Principal	2,432.53

Table 6-5.   Impact of Maturity Assumption on Prepayment Estimates and Projected Yields

	FNMA 8%	
Security Principal Balance:		$1,000,000
Final Maturity:		300 Months
Adjusted WAM:		200 Months

	Final Maturity	Adjusted WAM
Total Principal Payment:	$5,000.00	$5,000.00
Assumed Amortization Principal:	968.94	2,282.88
Estimated Prepaid Principal:	$4,031.06	$2,717.12
Conditional Prepayment Rate (CPR):	4.7%	3.2%
Assumed Price:	77.25	77.25
Projected Yield: *	12.29%	12.77%

* The projected cash flow yields are based on the maturity assumptions shown and the historical CPRs calculated using those maturity assumptions.

likely to be lower than one calculated for a similar pool for which a WAM is unavailable and a final maturity was used, the total principal payments on the two pools could, in fact, be identical.

Table 6–5 also shows that when a shorter remaining term is assumed (the adjusted WAM) and a lower prepayment rate is calculated for the pool, the yield produced when that prepayment rate is projected over the same remaining term is actually the higher of the yields shown. Conversely, the lower yield results when the longer remaining term (the final maturity) and a higher prepayment rate are assumed for the future. Clearly, the faster amortization schedule that is implicitly projected when the shorter maturity is assumed more than offsets the impact of the lower prepayment rate in the yield calculation.

Since the maturity assumption can have a significant impact on the yield estimated on a mortgage-backed security trading at a discount or premium, it is critical to explicitly identify the nature of the maturity assumption used in any valuation and recognize the direction and extent of any bias it is likely to introduce. At a minimum, the remaining term used to calculate a yield should be consistent with the remaining term used when calculating historical prepayment rates.

SECTION VII   RELATIVE VALUE ANALYSIS[15]

Analyzing the relative value of a particular MBS pool or a generic MBS security involves the same fundamental process as would be employed in the analysis of any fixed-income security. Two factors, however, make evaluations within the MBS

[15]While a detailed discussion of the duration characteristics of mortgage securities is beyond the scope of this chapter, it has important implications for determining the relative value of these securities. For a detailed discussion of this topic, see Pinkus, Scott M. and Chandoha, Marie A., "The Relative Price Volatility of Mortgage Securities," Morgan Stanley, New York (January 1986).

market unique. The first relates to the uncertainty regarding the yield on a mortgage security and the critical assumptions about the level of prepayments that can be expected, which must be explicitly made by an individual investor and that is implicitly made by the market as a whole. The other factor has to do with the structure of the MBS market in terms of the various MBS programs in existence and the multitude of coupons within each program that can be compared and traded.

Determining when a security has *value* relative to other securities is, by its very nature, a subjective process that in many ways depends on what a portfolio manager is trying to accomplish with his or her portfolio. Given actual market prices, if the estimated yield on a particular MBS security, after applying what one feels is a reasonable prepayment assumption, is greater than the estimated yield on another security, the first security is in some sense more valuable as a result of its yield advantage. Other differences between the securities compared, such as credit quality, liquidity, price volatility, or prepayment risk, however, can more than offset any yield advantage when viewed within a risk-return framework.

Any yield advantage between two otherwise similar securities should also be viewed from an historical perspective. If, for instance, the yield difference or spread between two securities is currently 25 basis points (or 0.25%), but this is the narrowest that the spread has been in the last several years, the higher yielding security may actually be considered the less valuable security. If the yield spread between these securities is expected to widen toward its historical average, the higher yielding security can be expected to depreciate in market value relative to the other security, with the relative loss in market value potentially offsetting any yield advantage. Figure 6–4 illustrates an historical yield spread analysis of the GNMA 8% coupon versus the GNMA 13% coupon, assuming a 3% CPR and 5% CPR, respectively.

Fundamental to any yield evaluation of mortgage securities, however, is the prepayment assumption. Choosing the appropriate assumption to use for different securities at any point in time is probably more of an art than a science. A few points, though, should be considered during this process. The recent prepayment experience of similar securities can provide a good starting point for any estimate. The interest rate environment over the period examined, however, should be taken into consideration before drawing any conclusions from recent experience. (Consider also that there is normally a lag of from two to six months from the time interest rates change substantially to the time these changes show up through faster or slower prepayment rates.) As was discussed previously, if the securities examined are relatively new, current coupon pools, the aging influence on prepayment should be factored into any prepayment estimate. In addition, if a pool-specific transaction is being contemplated, the actual prepayment experience of the individual pool should be reviewed for consistent patterns which may warrant a change from one's generic prepayment assumptions when examining the pool. Finally, an element of conservatism should be built into any prepayment estimate, which, in practice, translates into a somewhat lower prepayment assumption for discount securities and a higher assumption for premiums.

Relative value can also be gauged by determining the prepayment rate implicit in the market price for a security and comparing it to one's own estimate of prepayments

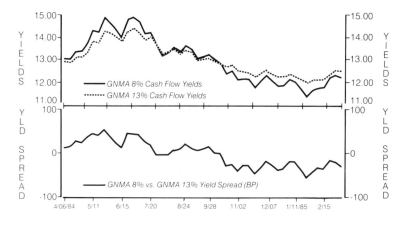

Note: Cash flow yields assume 3% CPR for GNMA 8% and 5% for CPR GNMA 13%

Figure 6-4.   Cash flow yield spread GNMA 8% versus GNMA 13%.

for that security. This implicit prepayment rate or break-even prepayment rate (BEPR) is the rate that equates the yield on a discount or premium security to the yield on the coupon priced closest to, but below, par (the benchmark security). The benchmark security is defined as such since its *yield* is relatively insensitive to prepayment rates (as it is trading very close to par), and this security tends to be among the most actively traded areas of the MBS market.

By calculating the prepayment rate that is required on a discount MBS for it to provide the same yield as the benchmark security, one can avoid having to make specific prepayment rate projections when comparing the value of a discount MBS to the current coupon security, and focus simply on whether prepayments on the discount coupon can be expected to be slower or faster than the calculated BEPR. If one feels a discount security will prepay significantly faster than its BEPR, the discount will provide a more attractive yield than the benchmark security. Conversely, the discount will be less attractive than the benchmark issue if it is expected to prepay at a slower rate than its BEPR. Premium securities act in the reverse manner, since faster prepayments reduce the yield on these securities.

The BEPR approach is most useful when a discount MBS is being compared to a current coupon issue. Its greatest weakness, however, lies in its implicit assumption that an investor would be indifferent when choosing between a discount coupon security and a current coupon issue if they offer the same yield. In reality, investors might be willing to accept a lower yield on a discount security as a result of its relatively more stable prepayment pattern and, consequently, greater cash flow certainty. In the case of a premium security, the perceived shorter effective maturity of these issues relative to current or lower coupon securities can make any comparison to the yield on the current coupon security misleading. The yields on premium coupons are often compared to the yields on shorter maturity securities which, in a normal Treasury yield curve environment, generally offer lower yields than longer term securities. The BEPR, as defined, would be a less valuable approach in either of these situations.

This discussion has so far ignored the sensitivity of prepayments to interest rates. As the dominant influence on prepayments, interest rate sensitivity must be viewed almost as a separate issue. The sensitivity of a security's yield and total return to changes in interest rates, and thus prepayment rates, must be evaluated. Since discount MBSs tend to have more stable prepayments than either current coupon or premium issues, they are fundamentally more attractive, everything else being equal, to anyone with an aversion to prepayment uncertainty. One's view of the likelihood of various interest rate scenarios actually occurring will have a substantial impact on how one evaluates the risk-return tradeoff of various securities in terms of their sensitivity to interest rates.

While the unique features of the mortgage instrument make determining the relative value of mortgage securities a difficult and imprecise task, the various MBS programs in existence (e.g., GNMA, FHLMC, and FNMA) and multitude of coupons and individual pools within each program, provide for a plethora of trading opportunities within the MBS market as well as across the Treasury and corporate bond markets.

Comparing the relative values of the various coupons within a particular MBS sector, such as GNMAs, in the manner just discussed can highlight the most attractive generic areas in which to make new investments, as well as point out trading opportunities for an existing portfolio. If one already has a preference for a particular coupon range within the MBS market, analyzing the relative value of those coupons across MBS sectors can determine which security type will provide the greatest return for an investment in that coupon range.

Analyzing the relative values of securities within the MBS market requires a solid understanding of how mortgage securities work and how the market reacts to various phenomenon such as changing interest rate expectations or prepayment trends. A systematic approach to the analysis of relative values, however, can significantly improve one's ability to find attractive investment and/or trading opportunities within the MBS market.

SECTION VIII   PORTFOLIO CONSIDERATIONS

This chapter has attempted to provide an overview of the mortgage-backed securities market and develop a basic framework for analyzing the value of these securities. After developing a basic understanding of mortgage securities and the MBS market, it is important to broaden ones perspective from the mortgage security itself to the overall fixed-income portfolio, with the mortgage security being one component of that. The risk and return objectives for the entire fixed-income portfolio must be established before one can determine what investment or trading opportunities within the MBS market will best meet those objectives.

The extent to which a particular mortgage security offers an attractive yield in the market relative to another fixed-income investment must be measured against its impact on the total risk profile of the portfolio. The yield on a portfolio can usually be increased if one is willing to reduce the credit quality of the investments or increase the interest rate risk that can be attributed to them. Such strategies, however, by increasing the overall risk exposure of the portfolio, may not improve its performance and may be inconsistent with the portfolio management objectives.

A portfolio perspective is important not only to ensure that all investment activities are working toward the same objectives, but also to improve total performance by maximizing opportunities for synergy within the portfolio. The performance characteristics of the various securities which are often included in fixed-income portfolios differ in many respects. As a result, different securities can sometimes be combined in a portfolio such that their total risk-return characteristics are more attractive than those of the individual securities.

A clear example of portfolio synergy can be found if one first views a mortgage security investment as a combination of a noncallable bond and a short position in a call option that can be exercised against the bond. If one were to purchase a call option in the market to offset the influence of the option that is implicitly included in the mortgage security, the risk and return characteristics of the combined assets may prove more attractive than those of the individual securities.

While the unique features and characteristics of the mortgage security must be carefully evaluated when participating in the MBS market, any investment or trading strategy should be viewed within a portfolio context.

BIBLIOGRAPHY

Curley, Anthony J., and Guttentag, Jack M., "The Yield on Insured Residential Mortgages," *Explorations in Economic Research* (Summer 1974).

Curley, Anthony J., and Guttentag, Jack M., "Value and Yield Risk on Outstanding Insured Residential Mortgages," *Journal of Finance* (May 1977).

Mara, Susan D., "The GNMA II Program Revisited," *Mortgage Banker* (July 1985).

Peters, Helen F., *Termination Distributions on FHA Insured Residential Mortgages,* Unpublished Ph.D. diss., University of Pennsylvania, 1979.

Peters, Helen F., "Pricing a Mortgage-Backed Security—The Misuses of FHA Experience," *The Money Manager* (December 17, 1979).

Peters, Helen F., Pinkus, Scott M., and Askin, David J., "Figuring the Odds: A Model of Prepayments," *Secondary Mortgage Markets* (May 1984).

Pinkus, Scott M., and Chandoha, Marie A., "The Relative Price Volatility of Mortgage Securities," Morgan Stanley, New York (January 1986).

Pinkus, Scott M., and Firestone, Evan B., "Mortgage Securities: Predicting Prepayments," *Mortgage Banker* (December 1983).

Pinkus, Scott M., and Mara, Susan D., "Measuring the Maturity of a Mortgage Security: When is a WAM not a WAM?" *Mortgage Banker* (February 1985).

Pinkus, Scott M. and Mara, Susan D., "Special Report: The PSA Standard Prepayment Model," Morgan Stanley, New York (June 1985).

Silpe, Stuart L., and Pinkus, Scott M., "Collateralized Mortgage Obligations: A Framework for Analysis," Merrill Lynch Capital Markets, New York (January 1984).

7 Hedging Interest Rate Risk of Fixed-Income Securities with Uncertain Lives

ALDEN L. TOEVS

INTRODUCTION

This chapter presents a method to quantify the interest rate risk of fixed-income securities with uncertain lives. These securities have indeterminate maturities because their contractual terms offer call or put options. Representative fixed-income securities with call options include callable bonds, mortgages with prepayment options, and installment loans. Purchasers write these options to the security issuers. Representative fixed-income securities with put options include putable bonds, certificates of deposit with early redemption rights, and redeemable insurance contracts. Here the issuers write options for the purchasers of these securities.

The right to call or put a security may occur at market determined prices. In this instance, the option might alter the effective maturity date of the security, but it does so without changing the interest rate sensitivity of the contractual cash flows. More common are options that require exercise at prespecified prices. Since the difference between the market and option exercise values depends in part on interest rate levels, these options alter the effective maturity dates and interest rate sensitivities of the securities to which they are attached. It is these options that are studied in this chapter.

This chapter appears in substantially the same form in the Spring 1985 issue of the Journal of Portfolio Management.

We believe fixed-income securities with option features should be studied at this time for three reasons. All major financial institutions hold and issue fixed-income securities with put and call options. Despite record interest rate volatility only a few portfolio or asset/liability managers have carefully studied the interest rate risk introduced by such options. And the limited work on this subject has yet to be made consistent with popular techniques for measuring the interest rate risk of option-free securities.

This chapter is divided into four sections. Section I discusses the valuation of fixed-income securities with option features. Section II measures the interest rate risk of these securities using duration analysis. We use this index of interest rate risk because many portfolio and asset/liability managers find duration helpful in measuring the interest rate risk of option-free securities. Section III discusses hedging securities with uncertain lives, and Section IV summarizes the chapter.

SECTION I   VALUATION OF FIXED-INCOME SECURITIES WITH UNCERTAIN LIVES

We begin by discussing fixed-income securities containing explicitly or implicitly written call options. We then turn to fixed-income securities with put options. In either case the securities considered have cash flows remaining when the option is exercised and the market value of these flows may differ from the exercise price of the option. Predetermined exercise penalties, if any, are viewed as an adjustment to the price received upon the exercise of the option.

Unlike a stock option, an option on a fixed-income security normally does not trade separately from the security that is deliverable against the option. Rather it is an integral part of the security. The purchase, sale, or exercise of an option must be accompanied by the sale, purchase, or delivery of the associated security.[1] The purchaser of a callable security, for example, is long one unit of the deliverable security and short one call option. In this taxonomy the security deliverable against the option represents the title to all remaining contractual payments of principal and interest.

Fixed-Income Securities with European Calls

Many fixed-income securities contain European call options. These securities permit the issuer to call the bond away from the holder at a specific future date for a fixed price. Many corporate bond issues have such features. The market value of these bonds can be expressed as

$$P_M = P_C + P_D - P_{EC} \qquad (1)$$

---

[1]Bonds issued with detachable warrants are becoming more common, particularly in Europe. Debt issues with detachable options are now being considered in the United States. See Bookstaber, Haney, and Noris (1984).

where P_M is the market value of this callable bond, P_C is the present value of the contractual cash flows occurring on or before the exercise date of the call, and P_D represents the present value, measured from today's date, of the contractual cash flows that occur after the call date of the bond. P_D is the present value of the cash flows deliverable in exchange for the strike price of the call option should this option be exercised. P_{EC} is the value of the European call option as derived from an appropriate option pricing model.[2]

Since the call option is written (shorted) by the purchaser to the issuer, its value enters equation (1) negatively—the value of the option is a cost to the holder of the security. Purchasers of callable bonds receive premiums for extending options to the issuer of the debt. In some instances, this premium takes the form of an upfront payment. More normally a yield higher than would be earned had no call option been written provides the option premium.[3] We view either of these premium payments as adjustments to $P_C + P_D$.

The pricing of a callable bond requires that the three terms in equation (1) be quantified. To determine the value of the contractual cash flows one needs to discount these flows by the rates applicable for noncallable securities. This discounting reveals the premium paid the holder for writing the call option to the issuer. This increment in present value must, at the transaction date, equal P_{EC}, otherwise the option would be mispriced. As time passes P_{EC} may depart from the premium received. Should the security be sold, however, the new purchaser will receive a new premium commensurate with the then new value of P_{EC}.

This leaves P_{EC} as the remaining item to be valued. The mechanics of option pricing is not the topic of direct concern in this chapter. Rather, we wish to measure the interest rate risk of securities with attached options using methods comparable to those used on option-free securities. Hence, only the items of options pricing necessary to our developments will be given here.

An option can be properly valued only by using a pricing model consistent with the characteristics of the option. These models exist in varying degrees of completeness and accuracy for put and call options of both European and American forms.[4] Values derived from these models combine the time value of the option with the intrinsic value of an American option or the present value of the exercise of a European option. The intrinsic value of the option is the easier part to value. For a European call it is the larger of zero or $P_D - P_S$, where P_S is the present value of the exercise (strike) price of the option. Since the exercise of an option requires a voluntary action on the part of the option holder, the intrinsic value is restricted to be zero or positive in value. Thus, for in-the-money European calls

$$P_{EC} = (P_D - P_S) + P_{ECT}$$

[2]Many corporate bonds have a hybrid call option. The bond is not callable for a fixed period and then it becomes callable at any date thereafter. The analysis of this bond's interest rate sensitivity becomes a blend of the material given here for American and European calls.

[3]See Boyce and Kalotay (1979).

[4]See Bookstaber and McDonald (1985), Brennan and Schwartz (1977), and Geske and Johnson (1984) for examples.

Otherwise,   (2)

$$P_{EC} = P_{ECT}$$

where P_{ECT} represents the time value of the option.

The time value of any option must be positive. It depends on the expiration date of the option, the current and exercise prices of the security, and the expected volatility of the bond price. The longer the period over which an option remains in force, the greater its time value. All other things equal, the more deeply a call option is in or out of the money, the smaller is its time value. Finally, the more volatile the factors that influence the market value of the cash flows deliverable against an option, the greater the option's time value.

Using equation (2) we can rewrite equation (1) for in-the-money European calls as[5]

$$P_M = P_C + P_S - P_{ECT}$$

For at-the-money or out-of-the-money European calls: (3)

$$P_M = P_C + P_D - P_{ECT}$$

Note that $P_C + P_D$ is the present value of the contractual cash flows to the maturity date of the callable security, while $P_C + P_S$ is the present value of the cash flows of the bond should it be called. Suppose we have a 10-year bond with an option to call the bond in five years at par. As shown in equation (3) the market price of this bond becomes either a 10-year bond less the time value of the call or a 5-year bond less the time value of the call.

Much as the value of a callable bond depends on adding up the relevant values of its parts, the sensitivity of this bond's price to a change in interest rates is the sum of the interest rate sensitivities of its parts. Thus, when the European call option is in the money

$$\Delta P_M = \Delta P_C + \Delta P_S - \Delta P_{ECT}$$

Otherwise   (4)

$$\Delta P_M = \Delta P_C + \Delta P_D - \Delta P_{ECT}$$

ΔP_M is the dollar change in the market value of the callable bond per basis point change in the "interest rate," and other variables are similarly interpreted.[6]

---

[5]We could have elected not to introduce this dichotomous treatment of fixed-income securities by keeping the intrinsic and time value of the option aggregated. Such was the methodology employed in Toevs and Wernick (1983). Neither approach is perfectly suited for the points we desire to make. The relative advantage of the approach used in equation (3) is a clearer determination of how the interest rate risk of securities with options change as these options go from deeply in to deeply out of the money.

[6]Proper discounting of cash flows should be done with a term structure of interest rates (the yield curve for zero coupon bonds). We have simplified the discussion in this chapter by assuming that the yield curve is flat and shifts in a parallel fashion. Our results are easily generalized to more sophisticated interest rate environments.

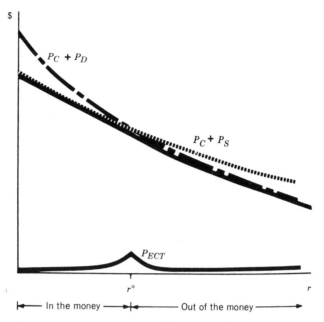

Figure 7-1.   Interest rates and European callable bond values.

Figure 7-1 uses a dashed line to depict the relationship between the present value of all contractual cash flows of a bond with a European call option and the level of interest rates, r. This value reaches a maximum when the interest (discount) rate equals zero, where it becomes the sum of all the nondiscounted contractual cash flows. As r become very high, $P_C + P_D$ tends toward but never reaches zero. These two extreme observations imply that $P_C + P_D$ and r relate to one another in the curvilinear fashion drawn in Figure 7-1. One representation of $\Delta P_C + \Delta P_D$, but by no means the best, is the slope of the $P_C + P_D$ line in Figure 7-1.

If the call is exercised, the holder receives in present value terms $P_C + P_S$ not $P_C + P_D$. The present value of cash flows assuming call will take place is not as interest rate sensitive as is the present value of the cash flows to maturity. This is shown in Figure 7-1 by the dotted line having less slope than the dashed one. The slope of this line is $\Delta P_C + \Delta P_S$.

Normally an option will be exercised only when interest rates fall below r^*, the rate that equates P_D and P_S. (Throughout this chapter r^* will denote the interest rate that causes an option to be "at the money.") When rates are in excess of r^*, it is cheaper to buy the security in the open market than exercise the option. Thus the present value of the deliverable cash flow *less* the present value of the option's intrinsic value is $P_C + P_S$ for interest rates below r^* and $P_C + P_D$ for rates in excess of r^*. This shift has been emphasized by the bold underline in Figure 7-1. To repeat, this bold line gives the value of contractual cash flows to maturity less the intrinsic value of the option.

The solid line at the bottom of Figure 7-1 graphs the time value of a European option relative to various interest rate levels. At extreme interest rate levels the time value of the option is nearly zero. Its value is maximized when the call is at the money. Note how critically the slope of P_{ECT} depends on the current level of interest rates. To find this slope, P_{ECT} is evaluated at the current interest rate and then again at a rate one basis point higher. The difference defines P_{ECT} at the initial interest rate.

While the slope of P_{ECT} is small at extreme interest rates, near r^* the slopes of both P_{ECT} and the upper solid line in Figure 7-1 are most subject to change (unstable). Technically neither is defined at r^*.[7] This means that an at-the-money European call option has an unstable interest rate sensitivity.

Figure 7-1 was constructed assuming that the maturity of the bond, the time to option expiration, the exercise price, and the assessment of interest rate volatility remain constant as interest rate levels vary.[8] Changes in any of these values cause the placement of the curves in Figure 7-1 to shift. Consequently the slopes of the lines in this figure, at any given value of r, may also change.

If the time value of the call option is subtracted from the bold underline in Figure 7-1, we obtain a graphical illustration of equation (2). This subtraction has been done in Figure 7-2. Note how the callable bond's value can differ from the pattern of a noncallable but otherwise comparable bond. We will carefully study this difference in Section III.

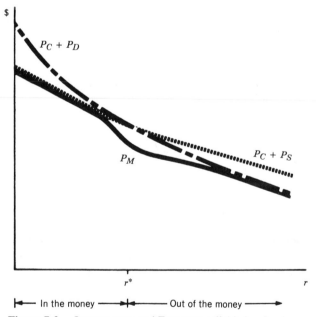

Figure 7-2.   Interest rates and European callable bond values.

[7]While the slopes of the two solid lines in Figure 7-1 are undefined when we are at r^*, substracting the "spike" in P_{ECT} from the upper solid line leaves a smooth and differentiable function, which is equation (1). We know this because $P_C + P_D$ is a smooth function, as is P_{EC}.

[8]It may seem odd that if interest rates change dramatically that our assessments of interest rate volatility would not also change. This assumption is made only for convenience and need not be incorporated in any actual analysis. Option pricing however becomes more complex when these considerations are added.

Fixed-Income Securities with American Calls

The market value of a security that has been written with a call option allowing exercise on any date can be expressed as

$$P_M = P_{D'} - P_{AC} \qquad (5)$$

P_M is the market price of the security. P_D' is the present (time discounted) value of all contractual cash flows of the security. Conceptually, P_D' is the economic value of the security that one delivers when the American call option is exercised. P_{AC} represents the current price of the American call option.

Figure 7-3 shows how a fixed-income security with an American call option is valued for various interest rates. At interest rates equal to or below r^*, the bond is priced as $P_M = S - P_{ACT}$, where S is the currently available strike price and P_{ACT} is the time value of the American call option. At any interest rate higher than r^*, P_M equals $P_D' - P_{ACT}$. Again the slope of P_M, one measure of interest rate sensitivity of the callable bond, is quite unstable near r^*.

Putable Fixed-Income Securities

A fixed-income security with a European put option confers the option to the holder rather than the issuer of the security. Thus

$$P_M = P_C + P_P + P_{EP} \qquad (6)$$

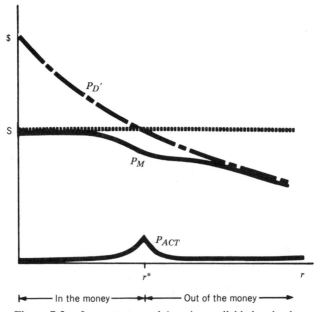

Figure 7-3. Interest rates and American callable bond values.

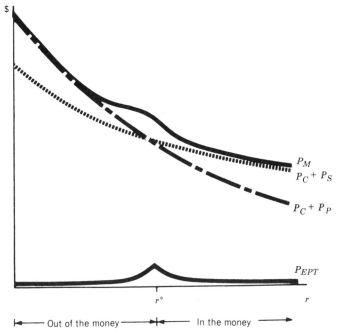

Figure 7-4.   Interest rates and European putable bond values.

P_M is the market value of a security with an American put. P_C is the present value of the contractual cash flows occurring on or before the exercise date of the put. P_P is the present value of the cash flows putable should the option be exercised. And P_{EP} is the value of the European put.

The purchaser of putable bonds must pay the issuer a premium for the option right. Discounting the cash flows including any up-front payment and reduced coupon rates relative to comparable but nonputable bonds with option-free interest rates reveals this premium. The bond will be mispriced if the premium does not equal P_{EP}.

Netting the intrinsic value component of the European put option with the contractual cash flows gives, for in-the-money European puts,[9]

$$P_M = P_C + P_S + P_{EPT}$$

Otherwise   (7)

$$P_M = P_C + P_P + P_{EPT}$$

Here P_{EPT} is the time value of the European put. Figure 7-4 shows the values for P_M and its constituent parts for various interest rate levels. Note how this solid line converges to the present value of the contractual cash flows to the put date at high interest

---

[9] P_{EP} equals $P_S - P_P + P_{EPT}$ when the put is in the money, else it equals P_{EPT}. Here P_S is the strike price at which the holder exercises the option, normally only when it exceeds the market value of the cash flows the holder surrenders upon exercise of the option.

rates, and to the present value of the contractual cash flows to maturity at low interest rates.

The analysis of the interest rate sensitivity of this fixed-income security with an uncertain life follows the same course as when callable securities were analyzed. In geometric form the dollar change in P_M per basis point change in interest rates can be obtained by evaluating the interest rate sensitivities of the separate components of equation (7). Thus for in-the-money European puts,

$$\Delta P_M = \Delta P_C + \Delta P_S + \Delta P_{EPT}$$

Otherwise   (8)

$$\Delta P_M = \Delta P_C + \Delta P_P + \Delta P_{EPT}$$

Now, $\Delta P_C + \Delta P_S$ equals the slope of the dotted line in Figure 7-4, and $\Delta P_C + \Delta P_P$ equals the slope of the dashed line in Figure 7-4. ΔP_{EPT} is the slope of the line drawn at the bottom of Figure 7-4. These effects sum to the slope of the upper solid line in this figure.

Fixed-income securities with American puts are analyzed similarly. Figure 7-5 summarizes the findings. At high interest rates, P_M converges to the immediately available strike price of the put (S). At low interest rates, P_M converges to the present value of all contractual cash flows (P_P'). As with other optioned securities, the slope of P_M is most subject to change in the vicinity of r^*.

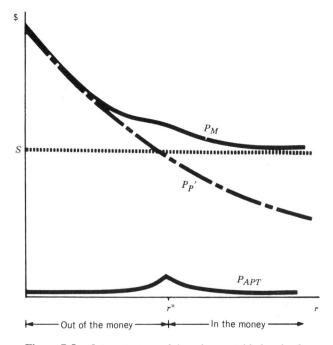

Figure 7-5.   Interest rates and American putable bond values.

Summary

This section has demonstrated two simple but fundamentally important concepts: the value of an optioned security is the sum of its parts, and its interest rate sensitivity is the sum of the interest rate sensitivities of these same parts. In the following section the graphical techniques for measuring interest rate sensitivity that were developed above are reexpressed in terms of duration.

SECTION II THE DURATIONS OF FIXED-INCOME SECURITIES WITH UNCERTAIN LIVES

Duration is a statistic that was first developed to measure the life of any series of fixed and known cash flows, such as those arising from an option-free fixed-income security. Term to maturity is an unambiguous measure of the life of a zero coupon bond. But because term to maturity ignores the amount and timing of all cash flows save the final payment, it incompletely measures the life of other securities. Duration standardizes any fixed-income security's life using a zero coupon bond equivalent term to maturity. This approach is compelling because an option-free security can be conceptually viewed as nothing more than a bundle of zero coupon bonds with various maturity (cash flow) dates.

Besides providing a means by which average live can be standardized, duration also measures the instantaneous price sensitivity of an option-free security. In its simplest representation[10]

$$\Delta P_F = -[D_F/(1 + r)] \times P_F \tag{9}$$

where ΔP_F is the dollar price change in an option-free security per unit change in interest rates, and D_F is the duration of this security (maturity of an equivalently interest rate sensitive zero coupon bond). This formula is only an approximation as it is nothing more than the slope of a straight line tangent to a bond price curve like that graphed for $P_C + P_D$ in Figure 7-1. The approximation error is small when rates change in small increments, but it grows with the size of the change in interest rates. This error can be minimized, however, by frequent recalculations of duration.

A valuable property of duration is its "additivity" characteristic. A portfolio of

---

[10]Duration was defined by Macaulay (1939) as

$$D = \sum_{t=1}^{T} w_t \times t$$

of the bond maturing at date T contributed by the cash flow occurring at date t. This formula uses the yield to maturity of the bond when discounting cash flows needed to determine the w's. Thus duration tends to shorten when interest rates rise. Macaulay's duration formula is used implicitly in this paper to ease the discussion. It is the simplest of many duration formulas and it is consistent with the earlier assumption, again made only for expositional convenience, that the yield curve is flat and shifts in a parallel fashion. Other more realistic duration formulas are given in Bierwag, Kaufman, and Toevs (1983). Also see Chapter 3 for a more extensive treatment of duration.

two or more option-free securities has a combined duration that equals a value-weighted average of the durations of the individual securities. For example, suppose we invest $100 in a 4-year duration bond and $200 in a 6-year duration bond. One-third of the portfolio by value has a 4-year duration and two-thirds by value has a 6-year duration. Thus, the portfolio duration is 5.33 years. The cash flows of this portfolio have an interest rate sensitivity equivalent to that for a 5.33 year zero coupon bond.

Duration analysis can be applied to asset/liability management as well as portfolio management problems. Indeed, a financial institution might best be viewed as a "net bond." Equity claimants own the net cash flow pattern generated by existing assets and liabilities. Understanding the interest rate risk of the market value of equity then becomes one of understanding the zero coupon bond with comparable interest rate risk.[11]

Duration of Callable Fixed-Income Securities

Recall from equation (4) that, ignoring the interest rate risk of up-front receipts of call premiums, the interest rate sensitivity of a security with a European call option is either $\Delta P_C + \Delta P_D - \Delta P_{ECT}$ or $\Delta P_C + \Delta P_S - \Delta P_{ECT}$. Now, ΔP_C, ΔP_D, and ΔP_S are the interest rate sensitivities of option-free securities. They are approximated by

$$\Delta P_X = -(P_X \times D_X)/(1 + r) \tag{10}$$

where the X subscript denotes C, D, or S depending on the cash flow stream of current concern.

The option pricing model that values the European call option can also be used to measure the duration of its time value (D_{ECT}). In this context duration can only be interpreted as a measure of the interest rate sensitivity of the option's time value. No reasonable interpretation of duration as the option's "average life" can be made. If D_{ECT} equals "90 years," which we will see to be possible in a moment, then P_{ECT} has the interest rate sensitivity of a 90-year zero coupon bond. As discussed in Section II, the option pricing model can be used to estimate both P_{ECT} and ΔP_{ECT}. The value for D_{ECT} is obtained by backing its value out of the formula.

$$\Delta P_{ECT} = -(P_{ECT} \times D_{ECT})/(1 + r) \tag{11}$$

The time value of near-the-money options are quite sensitive to changes in interest rates. That is, their durations can be large in magnitude. These durations can also be negative in value. Note that at low interest rates an increase in interest rates increases the time value of a call option. Hence P_{ECT} and ΔP_{ECT} are greater than zero, and therefore, D_{ECT} is negative. This means that the option's time value is as sensitive as a short position in the zero coupon bond of similar duration. Shortly we will provide specific examples of option durations.

---

[11]This reasoning is developed in Chapter 10.

Since there is some zero coupon bond with a similar sensitivity,

$$\Delta P_M = -(P_M \times D_M)/(1 + r) \qquad (12)$$

D_M is the duration of the callable security. At this point our representation is hypothetical; we cannot use equation (12) to determine D_M, but substituting equations (10), (11), and (12) into equation (3) and solving for D_M gives, for bonds with in-the-money European calls,

$$D_M = (P_C \times D_C + P_S \times D_S - P_{ECT} \times D_{ECT})/(P_C + P_S - P_{ECT})$$

Otherwise $\qquad\qquad\qquad\qquad\qquad\qquad\qquad\qquad\qquad\qquad\qquad\qquad (13)$

$$D_M = (P_C \times D_C + P_D \times D_D - P_{ECT} \times D_{ECT})/(P_C + P_D - P_{ECT})$$

If one understands the additive property of duration, then equation (13) has immediate intuitive appeal. A callable bond represents a portfolio of three securities: the cash flows to the option's expiration date, either the set of deliverable cash flows or the strike price, and the short position in the call option. The duration formula in equation (13) is nothing more than the price weighted average of these constituent parts. (The minus signs in the numerator and denominator of equation (13) denotes that the short position in the call option.)

Reconsider Figure 7-2. At extreme interest rate levels P_{ECT} becomes quite small. Therefore D_M approaches the duration of the contractual cash flows to the maturity date of the bond for high interest rates, and it approaches the duration of the cash flows should the call be exercised at low interest rates. For more moderate interest rates the duration of the callable bond becomes a blend between these two more extreme positions. And the duration value itself can become quite sensitive to the level of interest rates. This is a reminder that the interest rate sensitivities of near-the-money callable bonds are relatively unstable. Figure 7-6 illustrates these points with the dashed line and the two reference solid lines. This example was constructed using a 10-year bond with a face value of $100. This bond pays a coupon of 10.5% and is callable in five years at par.

Table 7-1 gives the present values and durations for the components of the bond depicted in Figure 7-6 for various interest rates. When the noncallable interest rate is 10% the bond is valued at par. Here the call option has a time value of $1.94 and the present value of its intrinsic value is $1.18. If the bond is currently issued at par the 50 basis points in added coupon yield over the noncallable yield represents the premium the original holder obtained for the option written. The minimum duration of the callable bond in Table 7-1 is 4.16 years. This is the duration of a 5-year noncallable bond paying a 10.5% coupon when rates are quite low. As rates go to high levels note how the duration of the callable bond converges to the duration of a noncallable 10-year bond.

The time value of the option behaves as expected at both low and high interest rates: P_{ECT} is low. It reaches a peak when interest rates are 10.5% at $2.41. Its du-

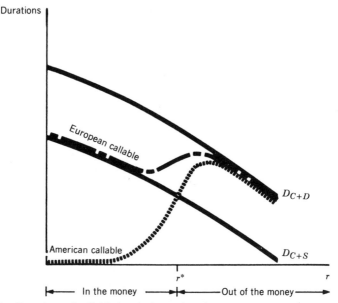

Figure 7-6. Durations of callable bonds for various interest rates. D_{C+D} is the duration of all cash flows to maturity; D_{C+S} is the duration of all cash flows received if the European put option is exercised.

ration also behaves as expected. It is first negative, indicating that ΔP_{ECT} rises with interest rates, and then it becomes positive after the call goes in the money.[12]

The interpretation of $+56.92$ for D_{ECT} when rates are at 10.5% is that for a one basis point increase in rates, the loss in value on an "investment" of $2.41 in the option's time value is comparable to that of $2.41 invested in a 57-year zero coupon bond. The duration of -43.96 when rates are at 10.4% is that for a one basis point increase in rates the gain in value on an investment of $2.31 in the option's time value is comparable to that for $2.31 shorted in a 44-year zero coupon bond.

Fixed-income securities with American calls can be similarly analyzed. The duration of such a bond becomes, for in-the-money American calls,

$$D_M = (S \times D_S - P_{ACT} \times D_{ACT})/(S - P_{ACT})$$

Otherwise

$$D_M = (P_{D'} \times D_{D'} - P_{ACT} \times D_{ACT})/(P_{D'} - P_{ACT})$$

(14)

---

[12]The reason why the duration of the time value of the option gets smaller as the option approaches its at-the-money position, while the slope of the time value in absolute magnitude, as depicted in Figure 7-1 gets larger, is that the slope of the time value is $-D_{ECT} \times P_{ECT}/(1 + r)$. That is, the relatively large time value at or near r^* makes the product of duration and price large in magnitude. The opposite holds when the time value of the option is small.

Table 7-1.   10-Year Bond with 5-Year European Call*

10.5% Coupon
4.5% Price Volatility

Rate	P_C	P_D	P_S	P_{FCT}	P_{FC}	P_M	D_C	D_D	D_S	D_{FTC}	D_M	D_{C-S}	D_{C-D}
4.00	47.16	105.98	82.03	0.02	23.97	129.18	2.67	9.15	5.00	− 122.95	4.16	4.15	7.15
5.00	45.95	96.92	78.12	0.05	18.85	124.02	2.65	9.13	5.00	− 108.24	4.17	4.13	7.04
6.00	44.78	88.69	74.41	0.13	14.42	119.06	2.63	9.11	5.00	− 94.28	4.22	4.11	6.93
7.00	43.66	81.21	70.89	0.31	10.63	114.24	2.61	9.09	5.00	− 81.16	4.32	4.09	6.82
8.00	42.58	74.41	67.56	0.64	7.49	109.50	2.59	9.07	5.00	− 68.95	4.49	4.07	6.71
9.00	41.54	68.21	64.39	1.17	5.00	104.76	2.57	9.05	5.00	− 57.76	4.74	4.05	6.59
9.10	41.44	67.63	64.09	1.24	4.78	104.28	2.57	9.04	5.00	− 56.70	4.77	4.04	6.58
9.20	41.34	67.04	63.78	1.31	4.57	103.81	2.57	9.04	5.00	− 55.65	4.79	4.04	6.57
9.30	41.24	66.47	63.48	1.38	4.37	103.33	2.56	9.04	5.00	− 54.61	4.82	4.04	6.56
9.40	41.14	65.90	63.17	1.45	4.17	102.86	2.56	9.04	5.00	− 53.59	4.85	4.04	6.55
9.50	41.04	65.33	62.87	1.53	3.98	102.38	2.56	9.04	5.00	− 52.57	4.88	4.04	6.54
9.60	40.94	64.77	62.57	1.61	3.80	101.90	2.56	9.03	5.00	− 51.57	4.91	4.03	6.53
9.70	40.84	64.21	62.28	1.69	3.62	101.43	2.56	9.03	5.00	− 50.58	4.94	4.03	6.51
9.80	40.74	63.66	61.98	1.77	3.45	100.95	2.55	9.03	5.00	− 49.60	4.97	4.03	6.50
9.90	40.64	63.12	61.68	1.85	3.28	100.47	2.55	9.03	5.00	− 48.63	5.00	4.03	6.49
10.00	40.54	62.58	61.39	1.94	3.12	99.99	2.55	9.03	5.00	− 47.67	5.03	4.03	6.48
10.10	40.44	62.04	61.10	2.03	2.97	99.51	2.55	9.02	5.00	− 46.72	5.06	4.02	6.47
10.20	40.34	61.51	60.81	2.12	2.82	99.03	2.55	9.02	5.00	− 45.79	5.09	4.02	6.46
10.30	40.25	60.99	60.52	2.21	2.68	98.55	2.54	9.02	5.00	− 44.87	5.12	4.02	6.44
10.40	40.15	60.46	60.23	2.31	2.54	98.07	2.54	9.02	5.00	− 43.96	5.14	4.02	6.43
10.50	40.05	59.95	59.95	2.41	2.41	97.59	2.54	9.01	5.00	56.92	5.17	4.01	6.42
11.00	39.57	57.44	58.54	1.82	1.82	95.20	2.53	9.00	5.00	61.17	5.31	4.00	6.36
12.00	38.64	52.76	55.84	0.98	0.98	90.42	2.51	8.98	5.00	70.22	5.55	3.98	6.25
13.00	37.74	48.49	53.27	0.48	0.48	85.75	2.49	8.96	5.00	79.86	5.71	3.96	6.13
14.00	36.87	44.59	50.83	0.22	0.22	81.24	2.47	8.94	5.00	89.95	5.79	3.94	6.01
15.00	36.04	41.03	48.52	0.09	0.09	76.97	2.45	8.92	5.00	100.34	5.78	3.92	5.89
16.00	35.23	37.77	46.32	0.03	0.03	72.97	2.44	8.89	5.00	110.94	5.73	3.89	5.78
17.00	34.45	34.80	44.23	0.01	0.01	69.23	2.42	8.87	5.00	121.64	5.64	3.87	5.66

* The price volatility is the annualized standard deviation of bond returns. This volatility estimate is considered low by current market standards and is used for illustrative purposes only.
  The interest rates in the first column are noncallable bond rates for comparable credit risks.
  D_{C-S} is the duration of the cashflows to the five-year call date of a 10.5% coupon bond.
  D_{C-P} is the duration of the cashflows for all ten years of a 10.5% coupon bond.

As interest rate levels rise well above r^* in Figure 7-3 P_{ACT} becomes quite small. The duration of the callable bond approaches D_D', which is the duration of the cash flows to contractual maturity. When interest rates fall well below r^*, P_{ACT} again approaches zero. Now, D_M approaches D_S. But the fixed and currently available strike price has no interest rate sensitivity. The call is so deeply in the money that call is imminent. The bond behaves like a very short-term instrument.

The durations of a 10-year bond with a 10.5% coupon and an American call option has been drawn with a dotted line in Figure 7-6. Note how much more volatile this duration is in the vicinity of r^* than was encountered with the European call on the same underlying bond. This occurs because the American call has more time value to be lost in the vicinity of r^* than does the European call on a comparable bond.

The Duration of Putable Fixed-Income Securities

The analysis for putable securities follows straightforwardly from that just completed for callable securities. The duration of a security with in-the-money European put is

$$D_M = P_C \times D_C + P_S \times D_S + P_{EPT} \times D_{EPT})/(P_C + P_S + P_{EPT})$$

Otherwise   (15)

$$D_M = P_C \times D_C + P_P \times D_P + P_{EPT} \times D_{EPT})/(P_C + P_P + P_{EPT})$$

When rates are much above r^*, P_{EPT} approaches zero and D_M approximates the duration of the cash flows assuming the bond will be put. When rates are much below r^*, P_{EPT} again approaches zero and D_M behaves much like that of the contractual cash flows to maturity. Figure 7-7 uses a dotted line to graph the relationship between D_M and interest rate levels.

Table 7-2 illustrates in a similar manner to Table 7-1 the prices and durations of a 10-year bond with a $100 face and a 9% coupon. It has a 5-year put with a strike price at par. This bond trades at par when rates are 9.5%. The loss of 50 basis points in coupon from what a 10-year nonputable bond pays is the premium paid for the put. Note how the duration of the putable bond approximates that of the cash flows to the put date when rates are high (D_{C+S}). Note also that the duration of the putable bond approximates the duration of the cash flows to the maturity of the bond when rates are low (D_{C+P}). The duration of the time value of this put is similar to that for

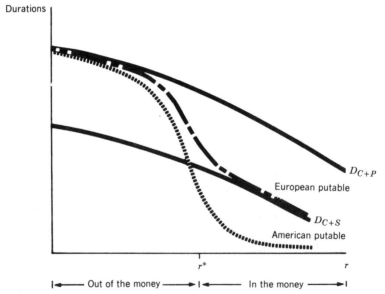

Figure 7-7. Durations of putable bonds for various interest rates. D_{C+D} is the duration of all cash flows to maturity; D_{C+S} is the duration of all cash flows received if the European put option is exercised.

Table 7-2.   10-Year Bond with 5-Year European Put*

9.0% Coupon
4.5% Price Volatility

Rate	P_C	P_P	P_S	P_{BCT}	P_{BC}	P_M	D_C	D_P	D_S	D_{BTC}	D_M	D_{C-S}	D_{C-P}
4.00	40.42	100.46	82.03	0.07	0.07	140.95	2.67	9.23	5.00	−106.47	7.28	4.23	7.35
5.00	39.38	91.79	78.12	0.20	0.20	131.37	2.65	9.21	5.00	− 92.03	7.09	4.21	7.24
6.00	38.39	83.93	74.41	0.45	0.45	122.77	2.63	9.19	5.00	− 78.50	6.82	4.19	7.13
7.00	37.42	76.79	70.89	0.90	0.90	115.11	2.61	9.17	5.00	− 66.00	6.45	4.17	7.02
8.00	36.50	70.30	67.56	1.61	1.61	108.40	2.59	9.15	5.00	− 54.63	5.99	4.15	6.91
9.00	35.61	64.39	64.39	2.58	2.58	102.58	2.57	9.13	5.00	58.46	5.50	4.13	6.80
9.10	35.52	63.83	64.09	2.44	2.69	102.05	2.57	9.13	5.00	59.36	5.45	4.13	6.79
9.20	35.43	63.28	63.78	2.31	2.81	101.52	2.57	9.13	5.00	60.27	5.40	4.13	6.77
9.30	35.35	62.73	63.48	2.18	2.92	101.00	2.56	9.13	5.00	61.18	5.36	4.13	6.76
9.40	35.26	62.18	63.17	2.05	3.04	100.48	2.56	9.13	5.00	62.10	5.31	4.13	6.75
9.50	35.17	61.64	62.87	1.93	3.16	99.98	2.56	9.12	5.00	63.03	5.26	4.12	6.74
9.60	35.09	61.11	62.57	1.82	3.28	99.48	2.56	9.12	5.00	63.97	5.22	4.12	6.73
9.70	35.00	60.58	62.28	1.71	3.40	98.99	2.56	9.12	5.00	64.92	5.17	4.12	6.72
9.80	34.92	60.06	61.98	1.61	3.53	98.50	2.55	9.12	5.00	65.88	5.12	4.12	6.70
9.90	34.83	59.54	61.68	1.51	3.66	98.02	2.55	9.12	5.00	66.84	5.08	4.12	6.69
10.00	34.75	59.02	61.39	1.41	3.78	97.55	2.55	9.11	5.00	67.82	5.04	4.11	6.68
10.10	34.66	58.51	61.10	1.32	3.91	97.09	2.55	9.11	5.00	68.80	4.99	4.11	6.67
10.20	34.58	58.01	60.81	1.24	4.04	96.63	2.55	9.11	5.00	69.78	4.95	4.11	6.66
10.30	34.50	57.51	60.52	1.16	4.17	96.18	2.54	9.11	5.00	70.78	4.91	4.11	6.65
10.40	34.41	57.01	60.23	1.08	4.31	95.73	2.54	9.11	5.00	71.78	4.87	4.11	6.64
10.50	34.33	56.52	59.95	1.01	4.44	95.29	2.54	9.10	5.00	72.79	4.83	4.10	6.62
11.00	33.92	54.13	58.54	0.71	5.12	93.17	2.53	9.09	5.00	77.93	4.65	4.09	6.57
12.00	33.12	49.67	55.84	0.32	6.49	89.28	2.51	9.07	5.00	88.63	4.38	4.07	6.45
13.00	32.35	45.61	53.27	0.13	7.79	85.75	2.49	9.05	5.00	99.76	4.20	4.05	6.33
14.00	31.61	41.91	50.83	0.05	8.97	82.49	2.47	9.03	5.00	111.18	4.09	4.03	6.21
15.00	30.89	38.53	48.52	0.02	10.01	79.42	2.45	9.01	5.00	122.79	4.03	4.01	6.09
16.00	30.20	35.44	46.32	0.00	10.88	76.52	2.44	8.99	5.00	134.47	4.00	3.99	5.97
17.00	29.53	32.62	44.23	0.00	11.61	73.76	2.42	8.97	5.00	146.17	3.97	3.97	5.85

*The price volatility is the annualized standard deviation of bond returns. This volatility estimate is considered low by current market standards and is used for illustrative purposes only.

The interest rates in the first column are noncallable bond rates for comparable credit risks.

D_{C-S} is the duration of the cashflows to the five-year put date of a 9% coupon bond.

D_{C-P} is the duration of the cashflows for all ten years of a 9% coupon bond.

the time value of the 5-year call in Table 7-1, just as the time value curves are similar in Figures 7-1 and 7-3. Figure 7-7 illustrates the findings of Table 7-2 using a dashed line for the putable bond.

The duration of a bond with an in-the-money American put is

$$D_M = (S \times D_S + P_{APT} \times D_{APT})/(S + P_{APT})$$

Otherwise

$$D_M = (P_{P'} \times D_{P'} + P_{APT} \times D_{APT})/(P_{P'} + P_{APT})$$

(16)

The dotted line in Figure 7-7 tells the now familiar story.

SECTION III   DURATION DRIFT AND CURVILINEAR DURATION

The duration concept is an extremely valuable tool because it standardizes the price sensitivity of any option-free fixed-income security using a measure with some intuitive appeal. As we have seen, it also allows the price sensitivity of a callable or putable bond to be quickly determined. Against these advantages are two costs. First, the selected duration formula must be consistent with the essential characteristics of the random process generating new interest rates. Second, duration represents only a linear approximation to the true price relationship. The former problem has been addressed at length elsewhere. This material is therefore not repeated here.[13] The second problem, one source of "duration drift," has also been studied in the academic literature.[14] But it is of particular importance when options are present, and consequently it deserves our attention.

Asset-Liability Management

With option-free bonds, matching the market value and duration of the assets with those of the liabilities minimizes interest rate risk.[15] But this policy prescription can lead to sizable errors when fixed-income securities have options associated with them. An increasing disparity in bond values is seen in the callable and putable bonds examined in Tables 7-1 and 7-2 as rates move away from the 10% level. (To compare these duration-matched bonds as rates change, one must scale up the smaller investment in the putable bond.) But the bonds in Tables 7-1 and 7-2 are both sufficiently in the money so that the disparate price changes are not at their maximums. Figure 7-8 tells a more "graphic" story. Duration matching 10-year bonds, one with an American call and the other with an American put, can be disastrous when rates change suddenly and in sufficient magnitude for the influences of the duration drift depicted in Figure 7-8 to become effective.

If interest rates are currently at r^*, then the durations of the American callable asset bond and an American putable liability bond in Figure 7-8 are matched, but they soon become mismatched when interest rates vary. When rates rise the duration of the asset grows while the duration of the liability quickly falls toward zero. The initial duration match prevents a net gain or loss from the first small change in interest rates, but subsequent rate rises will cause the sensitivity of the asset to exceed that of the liability, and as a consequence the net position loses substantial value. Alternatively, if rates decline by one basis point, there will again be an initial wash in the net position. But the duration of the asset falls while the duration of the liability does just the opposite. Subsequent interest rate declines will again result in net losses because of the duration imbalance. Fastidious repositioning of the assets and liabilities can minimize the influence of rapid "duration drift" but transaction costs and managerial time commitments will be substantial.

[13]See the development on "stochastic processes" in Bierwag, Kaufman, and Toevs (1983).
[14]Livingston (1979), Yawitz (1977), and Chambers (1981) are representative examples of this literature.
[15]For asset managers, the liability of concern in the "bogey" bond with the interest rate risk and return characteristics the asset portfolio is to mirror.

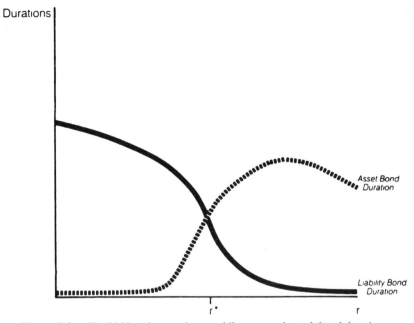

Figure 7-8.   The hidden short option straddle as seen through bond durations.

Some banks, thrifts, and insurance companies seem to specialize in acquiring American callable assets and issuing American putable liabilities. In these pairings the institution has essentially formed a portfolio of option-free assets and liabilities with whatever interest rate risk they have plus a short American "straddle." A straddle is a common option strategy, one where an American call and an American put are both sold.[16] The premiums for writing both options initially increase the income of these institutions. This strategy is ultimately profitable only if neither the call nor the put goes sufficiently in the money to wipe out the combined premiums.

In essence the hidden straddle strategy is a bet that financial markets underestimate interest rate volatility. Such a bet is ironic as the past five years have been determined to be ones when financial markets got blasted by an unexpected increase in interest rate volatility. Coupling the maturity mismatch in the assets and liabilities attached to the put and call options with the implicit straddle has added to the recent losses in financial institutions.

Curvilinear Duration

We have seen that adjusting the durations of fixed-income securities with uncertain lives for the influences of put and call options can significantly alter the measured durations of these securities. Adjusting duration estimates for option features can

[16]Strictly speaking, a straddle is formed by selling equal numbers of puts and calls of similar terms, including expiration dates. Nevertheless, the essence of the argument still applies.

substantially increase the accuracy with which interest rate risk is measured. At a minimum such adjustments should take place. Nevertheless, matching asset and liability durations, so adjusted, may not reduce interest rate risk to acceptable levels.

The duration of any coupon-paying security moves away from its original value as time passes and as interest rates change. Both sources of duration drift become exaggerated in the presence of put and call options. Of particular importance is the duration drift caused by changes in interest rates. Figure 7-8 dramatically illustrates the differential speed with which durations can drift apart when American puts and calls are contained in the asset/liability mix. The question is, what can be done about this source of drift?

Duration drift due to changes in interest rates comes from making the assumption that prices change linearly with interest rates. Such is not the case for either options, particularly at-the-money options, or option-free debt securities. A step in the right direction is to use a curved representation of "duration." This occurs when we set asset and liability durations equal to one another and we also equate the rate of asset duration drift with that for the liabilities. This increases the accuracy of interest rate risk management without completely giving up the main advantage of duration matching. The advantage is the added flexibility in the control of interest rate risk relative to a strategy of matching every asset cash flow with a liability cash flow, and matching every asset option with a similar liability option.

Setting the rate of duration drift due to changes in interest rates of the assets equal to that of the liabilities requires

$$\sum_{t=1}^{T} a_t \times t^2 + \Delta\Delta P_{TVA} = \sum_{t=1}^{T} l_t \times t^2 + \Delta\Delta P_{TVL} \qquad (17)$$

The a and t terms represent the cash flows from the assets due at time t as a proportion of total asset value. T is the date of the most distant asset or liability cash flow. (These cash flows are to the put or call date if the fixed-income security has an attached in-the-money put or call.) Note how close the first expression in equation (17) is to the duration formula. (See note 10.) The only difference is that these proportional weights multiply t^2 rather than t. The summation on the right hand side of equation (17) is similarly defined for the liabilities. $\Delta\Delta P_{TVL}$ is the rate by which ΔP_{TVA} changes, where ΔP_{TVA} is the current slope of the time value curve for all puts and calls attached to asset securities. $\Delta\Delta P_{TVL}$ is similarly defined for the liability portfolio.

Thus more careful asset/liability matching requires that the option-adjusted asset duration equals the option-adjusted liability duration, and that the equality expressed in equation (17) be met. Figure 7-8 is a circumstance where the option-adjusted durations are equal at r^*. Equation (17), however, does not hold. The left hand side of this equation is positive—as interest rates increase, so does asset duration. Conversely, the right hand side of equation (17) has a negative value. It is this equation and not option-adjusted durations that signal an important source of interest rate risk.

The calculations in equation (17) systematize what can be done in a simpler manner. As interest rates move from 10 to 10.1% in Tables 7-1 and 7-2, we observe that the duration of the callable bond increases by .03 year while the roughly equal duration of the putable bond decreases by .05 year. Both the magnitudes and directions of these rates of duration drift differ. This signals that duration matching alone may provide an insufficient hedge. The rates of drift are small in this example by comparison to what can be found in the presence of at-the-money American options. Equation (17) adds value in that computers can be programmed to search for available investment and funding alternatives that match both the durations and the rates of duration drift for the assets and liabilities.

SECTION IV   SUMMARY

This chapter has developed a reasonably detailed representation of the components of fixed-income securities with put or call options. These options make the effective lives of the attached securities uncertain and they complicate interest rate risk measurement. In Section I we disaggregated options into their intrinsic and time values. We then showed how the interest rate risk of an optioned security is the interest rate risk of the time value of the option coupled with the interest rate sensitivity of the cash flows of this security to either the exercise date of the option or the maturity date of the security.

Section II converted the interest rate sensitivity analysis in Section I into a duration framework. We noted that the ability of duration analysis to represent the interest rate risk of components of a portfolio with a single number is preserved, although in an altered form, when options are part of the asset or liability portfolio.

Section III discussed the problems that arise in asset/liability management when options are present. We demonstrated that options in this context can cause properly measured durations to drift apart as interest rates change, and they can do so with unacceptable speed. Section III closed by introducing the concept of "curvilinear duration" as a vehicle whereby the problems of "duration drift" can be addressed without having to resort to less flexible means of asset/liability management.

BIBLIOGRAPHY

Ball, C., and Torous, W. "Bond Price Dynamics and Options." *Journal of Financial and Quantitative Analysis* (December 1983).

Bierwag, G.O., Kaufman, G.G.; and Toevs, A.L. "Duration: Its Development and Use in Bond Portfolio Management." *Financial Analysts Journal* (July/August 1983).

Bookstaber, Richard; Haney, W.C., and Noris, P.D. "Are Option on Debt Issues Undervalued?" New York: Morgan Stanley (December 1984).

Bookstaber, Richard, and McDonald, J. "A Generalized Option Valuation Model for the Pricing of Bond Options," *Review of Research in Futures Markets* (March 1985).

Boyce, W.M., and Kalotay, A.J. "Tax Differentials and Callable Bonds!" *Journal of Finance* (September 1979).

Brennan, Michael, and Schwartz, E. "Convertible Bonds: Valuation and Optimal Strategies for Call and Conversion" *Journal of Finance* (December 1977).

Chambers, D.R. *The Management of Default-Free Bond Portfolios.* Ph.D. diss., University of North Carolina, Chapel Hill, North Carolina, 1981.

Geske, Robert, and Johnson, H.E. "The American Put Option Valued Analytically" *Journal of Finance* (December 1984).

Livingston, Miles. "Measuring Bond Price Volatility." *Journal of Financial and Quantitative Analysis* (June 1979).

Macaulay, F.R. "Some Theoretical Problems Suggested by the Movement of Interest Rates, Bond Yields and Stock Prices in the U.S. Since 1856." *National Bureau of Economic Research* (1938).

Toevs, A.L., and Haney, W.C. "Measuring and Managing Interest Rate Risk: A Guide to Asset/Liability Models Used in Banks and Thrifts." New York: Morgan Stanley (October 1984).

Toevs, A.L. and Wernick, J.H. "Hedging Interest Rate Risk, Inclusive of Prepayment and Credit Risk." Identification and Control of Risk in the Thrift Industry, Proceedings of the Ninth Annual Conference, Federal Home Loan Bank of San Francisco, 1983.

Yawitz, Jess. "The Relative Importance of Duration and Yield Volatility on Bond Price Volatility." *Journal of Money, Credit and Banking* (February 1977).

8 The Composite Hedge: Controlling the Credit Risk of High-Yield Bonds

RICHARD BOOKSTABER AND DAVID P. JACOB

INTRODUCTION

Bond hedges typically focus on controlling the interest rate risk associated with a bond position. While this focus may be appropriate for hedging positions in government or high-quality corporate bonds, it is insufficient for lower-quality corporate issues. Factors in addition to interest rates affect lower- quality bonds. In particular the possibility that the firm will be unable to make the payments on its debt obligations will clearly influence the price of these bonds. A successful hedge must consider more than interest rate risk; it must include a credit component, a component to control the price changes induced by changes in credit quality.

In this chapter we present the technique for creating such a hedge. We will show that by introducing other securities into the hedge position, and by adjusting the hedge position in the proper way, the credit component of high-yield bonds can be addressed. We propose a hedging strategy that takes both the credit risk and the interest rate risk into account by employing a composite hedge consisting of positions in government bonds or bond futures and in the stock of the firm. At the one extreme very high quality corporate bonds are optimally hedged with a position in government bonds since these bonds are essentially free of credit risk. At the other extreme are bonds that are close to default, bonds which we will show to be optimally hedged with positions in the stock of the firm and only a small position in government bonds. The reason for using stock can be seen by recognizing that these bondholders are likely to become owners of the assets of the firm, and therefore are affected by the

Table 8-1.   Corporate Bond Correlations

Rating	Correlation with Treasury Bonds	Correlation with Equity
Aaa-A	.86	.09
Baa-Ba	.77	.25
B-Caa	.51	.28

same considerations that affect the current equity holders. On the other hand, changes in the interest rate environment will have little bearing on these bondholders, since there is little likelihood of their receiving a promised stream of debt payments.

The drop in the effectiveness of an interest rate hedge with lower quality bonds is evident from Table 8-1. The first column in this table shows the correlation coefficient between long-term corporate bond and Treasury bond yields. For the higher-quality issues, those rated Aaa to A, the correlation coefficient is .86. However, as the rating drops to Baa-Ba and then to B-Caa, the correlation drops significantly down to .77 for bonds rated between Baa and Ba, and to .51 for bonds with a rating between B and Caa. The low correlation between Treasuries and low-quality bonds explains why the hedges derived from traditional interest rate hedging models are largely ineffective for this group.[1]

This lower correlation has led some to conclude that low-quality bonds have too great a residual basis risk to be hedgeable. This conclusion is not so much flawed as it is incomplete. While the correlation between Treasury bonds and corporate bonds drops with a drop in credit quality, this is offset by a rise in the correlation between the equity of the firm and the lower-quality bonds. The second column of Table 8-1 shows this correlation. For the high-quality corporations there is virtually no correlation between the equity and the bonds. These bonds behave very much like pure interest rate instruments; important events in the firm will have only a slight impact on bond price. But for lower- quality bonds the equity component becomes more significant. For the bonds rated Baa to Ba the correlation coefficient rises to .25, and for the lowest-rated group it rises to .28. This result suggests an increasing significance for the equity component the lower the quality of the bond being hedged.[2]

---

[1] The correlations in Table 8-1 are taken from a representative cross section of corporate bonds. These bonds include regulated firms and firms in the financial sector. Since the equity of these firms will be interest rate sensitive, we have also computed the correlation coefficients of Table 8-1 without these firms included. As expected, the correlation between equity and the bonds in the remaining industrial group is not as large as for those in the more interest sensitive sectors, but the correlations are significant nonetheless. For the industrial sector, the correlation results are:

Rating	Correlation with Treasury Bonds	Correlation with Equity
Aaa–A	.86	− .04
Baa–Ba	.74	.14
B–Caa	.62	.19

[2] This relationship is verified in a portfolio context by Ibbotson and Sinquefield (1982), who find a correlation between a common stock index and a long-term corporate bond index of .16, compared to a correlation between the stock index and long-term government bond index of only .02. Since the long-term corporate bond index did not differentiate between issue quality, it does not represent the ideal sample for verifying our results.

Section I of the chapter presents the framework for computing the appropriate positions in equity and interest rate sensitive instruments to achieve the optimal composite hedge. The resulting model is tested in Sections II and III. The results confirm the hedging capacity of the composite hedge. The composite hedge does uniformly better than a pure interest rate hedge in our test sample of 82 high-yield bonds. The average hedging performance of the composite hedge is one and one-half times better than the interest rate hedge, and in many cases, particularly for the lowest grade bonds and for bonds that moved into default, it gives a severalfold improvement in hedging performance. Section IV presents three case studies of the application of the composite hedge. The case studies focus on bonds with dramatic drops in credit quality and price: Kenai, Storage Technology, and International Harvester. The results of these case studies illustrate the most important attribute of the composite hedge: the ability of this technique to hedge when the price risk is the most critical.

SECTION I   A COMPOSITE BOND HEDGE

The value of all corporate securities is contingent on the underlying value of the firm. For example, equity has a residual claim to the earnings of the firm after all other claims are paid. If the firm cannot meet these obligations and goes into default, the equityholders receive nothing. The payoff to the equityholder is the greater of the value of the firm in excess of the debt obligations or zero.

The debtholder also has a contingent claim on the firm, although it is quite different from that of the equity. If the debt obligation is not satisfied, and the firm goes into default, the debtholders receive ownership of the firm. Since the firm will default when the value of the firm is less than the value of the debt obligation, the payoff to the debtholder is the smaller of the debt payment or the value of the firm.

To see the contingent nature of these securities more clearly, consider the following simplified corporate financing structure. A firm has one zero coupon bond outstanding and must make a payment of $100 million in one year to pay off this obligation. If the payment is not made, the ownership of the firm will revert to the debtholder. Figure 8-1 shows the payoff to equity and debt at the end of the year as a function of the value of the firm. The value of the debt equals the value of the firm so long as the firm value is below the $100 million due the bondholder, and is worth $100 million for any firm value above that point. The equity has no value until the firm reaches the $100 million mark, and then gains one-to-one with the firm value after that point. Naturally, since these are the only two claims on the firm, the sum of the two securities always equals the total value of the firm.

The payoff to equity is like that of a call option, with the underlying asset being the value of the firm and the exercise price of the call option being the payment due the debt holder. The payoff to the equity is the maximum of zero and the firm value minus $100 million. Similarly, the payoff to debt can be expressed as an option on the value of the firm, although the specifications of the option payoff are unusual. The debt is an option that pays off the minimum of $100 million or the value of the firm.

Representing equity by S, the bond payment by P, the value of the firm by V, and

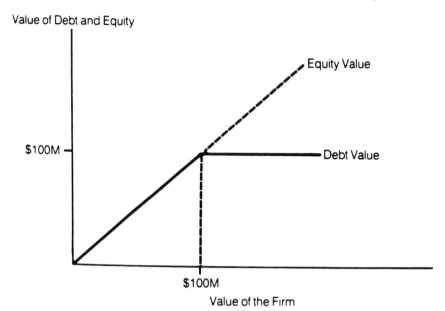

Figure 8-1. Equity and debt components of firm value.

the $100 million exercise price by E, we can represent the terminal equity and debt payoffs as

$$S = \max (0, V - E) \qquad \text{and} \qquad P = \min (V, E)$$

Since we can express the debt and equity of the firm as options, we can apply option pricing methods to price them. What is more important from the standpoint of being able to hedge the debt is that we can express their functional relationship to one another and to the value of the firm. Of course, in practice the payoff to the debtholder is more complex than the simple zero coupon bond used in this example; besides the coupon payments and call features a firm may have a number of different debt instruments outstanding, each with a competing claim on the firm. However, the same principle applies—all corporate bonds can be analyzed as contingent claims on the firm and can be analyzed as options.[3]

The key principle of option pricing theory is that any option can be constructed by taking the proper position in the asset underlying the option and in the risk-free asset. This principle forms the basis of the arbitrage pricing approach to option valuation. Since an option can be replicated by taking the proper dynamic hedging position in the underlying asset and risk-free borrowing or lending, the market price of

[3]There is a large body of theoretical literature on applying option pricing methodology to the pricing of corporate claims. Merton (1974), and Galai and Masulis (1976) are two early papers that treat the debtholder's claim to the firm in detail. A more complete treatment of the actual development of this methodology is presented in Geske (1977).

any option must equal the cost of forming this replicating portfolio. If it does not, then arbitrage opportunities will exist by taking the proper position in the mispriced option and undoing that position through the proper combination of the other assets.[4]

In particular, since a corporate bond is an option on the value of the firm, the relationship between the bond and the value of the underlying firm can be written down in the following form:

$$P = F_v V + F_f E \qquad (1)$$

In this equation, V represents the market value of the firm and E represents the "exercise price" of the debt, the amount that must be paid to the debtholders for the firm to remain solvent. The weights given to V and E represent the amount of the firm and risk-free bond that are necessary to replicate the claim of the debt. The debt of the firm is comprised of a proportion F_v of the underlying firm and a proportion F_f of a risk-free bond.

Since the value of the firm, V, is both unobservable and nontradable, we need to find a suitable proxy for the value of the firm to implement the model. The equity of the firm can be used as such a proxy. Specifying the relationship with a slightly different functional form, equation (1) then becomes

$$P = D_s S + D_f E \qquad (2)$$

where S is the market value of the equity of the firm, and where D_s is the corresponding equity weight in the creation of the bond. Since equity is itself an option on the value of the firm, D_s will have a functional relationship with V. These proportions are not constants but are variables. They are a function of a number of factors with a functional form that is quite complex, particularly for a coupon-paying bond with a call provision.[5] They will change as the value of the firm changes, as the debt comes closer to maturity, and as the capital structure and riskiness of the firm changes. However, the important properties of the weights can be explained in nontechnical terms, and can give an intuition into the composition and pricing attributes of corporate debt. The specification of the option framework for the model leads to three factors being critical in determining the composition of the bond: the debt/asset ratio of the firm, the volatility of the value of the firm, and the time to maturity of the debt.

The Debt/Asset Ratio

The larger the ratio of the present value of the debt to the asset value of the firm, the more likely the firm will fail to meet the debt payments, and the more the debt of

---

[4]This is the methodology that underlies the first major papers on option pricing, Black and Scholes (1973), and Merton (1973). A simplified exposition of this approach, and its application to portfolio strategies, is presented in Bookstaber (1981) and Bookstaber (1984).

[5]The complexity of dealing with coupon paying bonds, which must be treated as compound options, is demonstrated in Geske (1977).

the firm will take on the attributes of equity. If the debt/asset ratio becomes much greater than one, there is a high likelihood that the debtholders will become owners of the assets of the firm. The option implicit in the debt of the firm will become an in-the-money option, and the debt will behave more like the equity of the firm than it will like a pure interest rate instrument.

This behavior is readily apparent in the price behavior of very low rated debt. The price of bonds of firms near default have price volatility and sensitivity to new information like that of many equity issues. Such bonds respond modestly to interest rate movements (i.e., they have low duration), since there is little chance they will receive the scheduled flow of payments. When default is imminent, the equity of the firm becomes even more volatile, and takes on the price volatility of an option. Since the debt behaves more like equity the greater the likelihood the firm will default, the weight of the value of the equity in determining the current value of the debt will be greater the greater the debt/asset ratio.

As the firm moves closer to default, the debt will have fewer of the attributes of a pure interest rate instrument. The payoff to the debt will more likely be the firm's assets than a stream of known interest payments, so the default-free bond will have less weight in describing the makeup of the debt. Thus the proportion of default-free debt held in the replicating portfolio for the corporate debt, D_f, will be a decreasing function of the debt/asset ratio. Figure 8-2 shows how the composition of debt changes with the debt/asset ratio. The default-free component decreases as the debt/asset ratio increases; for high-quality issues, this component comprises almost all of the bond value, since it is unlikely that the bond will drop out of the money and the interest payments will not be made. The weight of the equity component increases

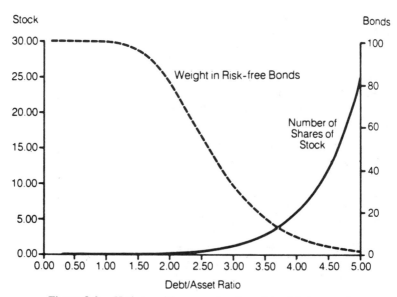

Figure 8-2.   Hedge positions as a function of the debt/asset ratio.

with the increase in the debt/asset ratio, and has increasing weight relative to the default-free bond component as the bond drops in quality.

The Volatility of the Value of the Firm

The volatility of the value of the firm will have an effect on the value of the debt and equity of the firm, since a higher volatility will increase the likelihood that an in-the-money option will move out of the money, and vice versa. We typically think of volatility as being bad for the equity of the firm. But for a firm facing imminent default, the value of the equity, like that of any out-of-the money call option, will increase with an increase in the volatility of the firm. Since the equity will end up having no value if the firm does not increase beyond the bond payment, it is in the interest of the equity holder to move the firm into high risk areas. The equity holders are in essence gambling with someone else's money. This explains the business strategy seen in some troubled companies to run after high-risk, high-return projects. For the debtholder, however, an increase in volatility is never good. Unlike the equity-holder, there is a ceiling on the return to the debt, and higher volatility can only lead to a drop in the value of the debtholder's claim.

Since the equity component of a bond increases as the debt/asset ratio increases, it is natural to expect it also to increase with the riskiness of the debt. The equity component of a bond increases with an increase in its spread off Treasuries, while the pure interest rate component decreases. This means equity will play an increasingly important role in explaining price behavior for higher-yield bonds. The higher the spread of a bond, the more it will be affected by the value of the firm, and the less it will be affected by interest rates.

This explains the results of Table 8-1, that the correlation of corporate bonds with interest rates drops with bond quality, and the correlation of bonds with the equity of the firm, a proxy for the value of the firm, increases with a drop in bond quality. It also suggests the path to take in finding a suitable method of hedging lower-quality issues. A pure interest rate hedge will be unsatisfactory because high-yield bonds are only partly interest rate instruments. The hedge must also address the equity component in the bond price.

Time to Maturity

The effect of time to maturity on the composite hedge is best considered by looking at the simplified case of a firm with one zero coupon bond as its obligation. The effect of time to maturity on the chances for default depends on the initial quality of the bond. For a high-quality bond an increase in the time to maturity increases the time for a possible deterioration in quality to occur. Like the team that is ahead in a basketball game, a longer time to the final buzzer can only turn a victory into a loss. Conversely, like the team trying to play catchup late in the game, a longer time to maturity can only improve the chances of payment for the firm that cannot now meet its obligations. For this firm a current maturity would lead the debtholders to become owners of the firm. The appropriate hedge would accordingly be all equity. However, if the payment is several years away, there is still some chance the firm will recover, so the bond position will be replicated by taking some position in interest rates as well. For a low-quality bond, a longer time to maturity means a greater chance of moving out of the default level by the time the obligation is due. Therefore, there will be less equity needed in the composite hedge the longer the time to maturity.[6]

The sensitivity of the bond price to the default-free interest rate and equity value will not be static. It will change with changes in the value of the firm, the debt/asset ratio of the firm, the volatility of the firm, and other factors as well.[7] Figure 8-3 shows the variation in the size of the equity hedge and the interest rate hedge for one of the bonds in our sample, Kenai Corporation. Figure 8-3a, presents the price history of equity, corporate debt, and government bonds. Figure 8-3b traces the size of the equity hedge, D_s, and interest rate hedge, D_f, that comes out of the composite hedging methodology. For purposes of comparison it also shows the hedge ratio based on a more conventional, duration-based hedging approach.

In the early period, from October 1979 to October 1981, the composite hedge closely matches the duration-based hedge; the equity hedge is negligible, and the bond component is high. A look at the equity price during the 2-year period shows why. The equity is still relatively high in price—between $11 and $33—and the firm is not yet an inferior credit. The bond price over this period moves closely with the government bond, so evidently the choice of a high interest rate component in the hedge is a good one. The hedging mix over these two years illustrates that for higher-quality bonds the composite hedge closely matches the conventional interest rate hedge.

After October 1981 the behavior of the bond changes dramatically. While Treasury prices rise, the bond remains fixed and the spread widens. Equity drops to below the $5 range. At this point interest rates are no longer the only factors to consider;

---

[6]The effect of time to maturity, or more specifically, time to crisis, on the probability of default is treated by Johnson (1967). His empirical study notes the same points that come out of our option-related model. He notes:

> A bond of initially high quality which later deteriorated had . . . less of a chance of reaching the default level of deterioration prior to maturity if the term-to-maturity were short.. . . Bonds of low quality could also improve, remain the same, or decline in quality. But the outcome of these events produced the opposite tendencies than it did for the high quality group . . . The longer the term-to-maturity, the . . . more time was allowed for uninterrupted interest payments and for internal generation of funds to repay the principal . . . If maturity were avoided until improvement could achieve some threshold quality, crisis-at-maturity was eliminated.

> A substantial term-to-maturity could allow improvement whereas a short maturity would have imposed a refunding crisis period to the achievement of this threshold quality.

[7]The volatility of the firm and the debt/asset ratio of the firm have long been known through empirical work to be important determinants of yield spreads. Fisher (1959) showed the risk of default to be a function of "the coefficient of variation of the firm's net income," and "the ratio of the market value of the equity in the firm to the par value of the firm's debt." These two factors are similar to the volatility in firm value and the debt/asset ratio in our model. Virtually all later literature on default risk relies on these two variables as well.

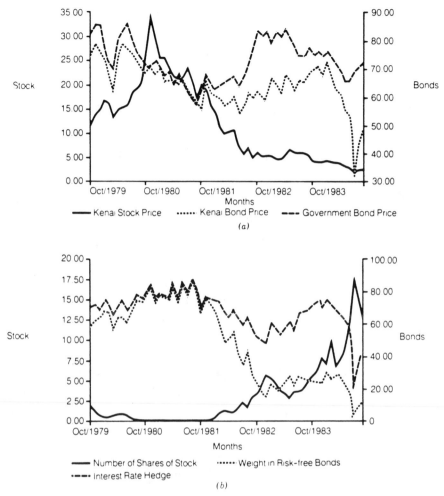

Figure 8-3.   Kenai Corporation.

credit considerations also affect the bond price. This is reflected in the composition of the hedge. The proportion of the Treasury bond held drops dramatically, from the 80% level to around 20%, while the equity position rises steeply. In contrast, the duration-based hedge remains around 60%; it does not respond to the changing character of the bond. The equity hedge is particularly sensitive to the stock price changes once the stock drops below $3. The company now approaches the point where default is a real possibility and the proportions of equity and Treasury bonds in the hedge respond accordingly.

As Figure 8-3 suggests, no static position can be effective in hedging the bonds. A dynamic hedging strategy must be developed that takes into account both of these components, and all of the factors that affect the weights of the components in bond price. The option framework presents the foundation for such a strategy. Just as dynamic hedging strategies are used to create option-like payoffs in portfolio management, here they can be applied to unbundle the complex, dynamic pricing behavior of high-yield bonds.

SECTION II THE POTENTIAL FOR HEDGING HIGH-YIELD BONDS

There are two issues to address in answering the applicability of the composite hedge model. The first obviously is whether the composite hedge is significantly better than the simpler interest rate hedge. The second is whether the model we use is a correct model for a composite hedge. It may be that while the dynamic hedging strategy we use is an improvement over the interest rate hedge, it still remains incorrectly specified, and imposes a bias in the hedging procedure. That is, it could be that while using both equity and interest rate components is a good idea, the way we employ them is wrong.

To answer these two questions we have performed two sets of tests on 82 high-yield bonds on 63 different companies. We use monthly data on each bond from 1979 to 1984, a 5-year period of historically frequent and dramatic changes in credit quality. A complete list of the bonds is presented in Appendix A, along with the summary statistics for the tests.

The Use of Interest Rate Hedges for High-Yield Bonds: A Negative Report

The most widely used form of bond hedging is the pure interest rate hedge. A relative price sensitivity between the hedging instrument and the bond is measured, and the hedge is weighted according to this sensitivity. For example, if a Treasury bond is used as the hedging instrument, and the Treasury bond is twice as sensitive to interest rate movements as is the bond to be hedged, then the hedge will have half as many dollars in the Treasury as in the bond to be hedged.

The interest rate sensitivity may be determined in an number of ways. Regression analysis may be used to determine the historical correlation between the bond and the hedging vehicle, or duration analysis can be used to compute the relative interest rate sensitivity of the two instruments.[8] In these approaches, bonds are viewed as pure interest rate instruments which differ from Treasury bonds only because of a systematic risk premium reflected in a fixed-yield spread. If the spread is constant so that no factors other than interest rates cause the price changes, then the interest rate hedge will be effective. However, as we have already shown, more than interest rates are involved in making bond prices move. For lower-quality bonds, shifts in firm value, as reflected in changes in value of equity, will have a significant impact

---

[8]The concept of duration, and its use in measuring interest rate sensitivity, is presented Toevs and Jacob (1984). That study compares the regression-based and duration-based approaches to hedging interest rate risk, and indicates that both approaches give similar results. In practice the duration-based hedge is preferable because of its computational simplicity.

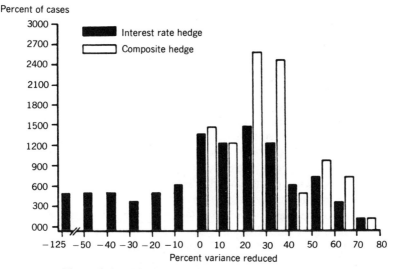

Figure 8-4.   Distribution of percent variance reduced.

on the bond price. As a result the conventional interest rate hedge may be ineffective and, as we will see, may actually increase the risk of the bond position.

Figure 8-4 shows the hedging effectiveness of a duration-based hedge. An un-hedged position in a bond has an observable variance of changes in its market price. The objective of a hedge is to reduce this variance ideally to zero. We therefore measure hedging effectiveness by the reduction in the variance of the change in the bond price. A perfect hedge will have a variance reduction of 100% while a completely ineffective hedge, having no impact on variance, will lead to a variance reduction of 0%. As Figure 8-4 shows the percent variance reduced using the interest rate hedge ranges from a high of 80% to a low of − 121%; that is, in some cases the bond price movement has so little interest rate component that the hedge only adds variance to the position. In two cases (Ames Department Stores 10% of 1995 and Welded Tube of America 10% of 1995), a concentration solely on interest rate risk more than doubles the variance of the position. This figure illustrates the problems in trying to hedge high- yield bonds with interest rate vehicles.

The Composite Hedge: A Uniform Improvement in Hedging Effectiveness

Figure 8-4 also shows the reduction in variance from using the composite hedge introduced in Section I. We use equity as a proxy for the value of the firm and Treasury bonds to reflect the interest rate component.[9] The larger the firm value component, the greater the amount of equity that is shorted against a long bond position. The greater the interest rate component, the larger the short position in Treasury instru-

---

[9]The bond used in the interest rate hedge is the U.S. Treasury bond $8^{3}/_{4}$ of 8/15/2000.

ments. The composite hedge is clearly better than the interest rate hedge in reducing the variance of the bond.

On a bond-by-bond basis, the superiority of the composite hedge is even more evident. As is shown in the appendix, in all 82 cases the composite hedge gave a variance reduction that equaled or exceeded the optimal interest rate hedge, and in a number of them was vastly superior. As would be expected, the value added by the composite hedge was higher the greater the debt/asset ratio or credit risk of the bond. For some of the higher-quality issues, such as the Teledyne 10% of 2004, the composite hedge performed nearly the same as the interest rate hedge. Both gave a percent variance reduced of approximately 80%. This is not surprising since the interest rate hedge is a special case of the composite hedge. For high quality issues the composite hedge will put little weight on the equity component, and will behave much like a pure interest rate hedge.

However, for the greater credit risk, the composite hedge often did many times better in reducing the price risk. In some cases the improvement just led from a disastrous hedge to an ineffective one. For example, Welded Tube of America, which had a variance reduction of -121% with the interest rate hedge (the worst case of interest rate hedge preformance), had an 8% variance reduced with the composite hedge. In other cases the improvement led to true hedging effectiveness. For example, Kenai, a bond whose price ranged from a high of $78.50 to a low of $31.75 over the 5-year period, had only a 7% variance reduced with the interest rate hedge. The composite hedge gave a 62% variance reduction. This is as good as the typical variance reduction gained from using a duration-adjusted interest rate hedge on an A-rated bond.

It is important to note that the hedge was most effective with the lower quality issues, and particularly with the issues that had severe credit deterioration as with Kenai and with International Harvester. The hedge is most effective where it is most critical, in protecting against catastrophic drops in value. The hedge does not do as well in protecting small variations in price. Indeed, the bulk of the variance remaining from the composite hedge is from the basis risk that remains in tracking the smaller errors. The sample we have selected is actually biased to some degree against demonstrating the full effectiveness of the hedge; in picking a 5-year period for the tests, we excluded companies in default because in many cases they did not have bond or equity price data over the 5-year period.

Some Drawbacks in the Use of Variance Reduction as a Measure of Hedging Effectiveness

Since variance is the most common measure of risk, it is also a natural measure of hedging effectiveness. However, for hedging applications the use of variance reduction as a measure of hedging effectiveness may understate the value of a hedge. All deviations from a perfect hedge increase the variance of a hedged position. A large number of minor deviations in tracking, which arise as the inevitable result of basis risk, can have as much of an effect on variance reduction as one failure to track during a significant drop in price.[10] In most hedging applications the cost of the second failure is far greater than the first. This is particularly true when dealing with hedging high-yield bonds where catastrophe protection is the overriding concern.

A more accurate representation of hedging effectiveness requires giving more weight to the protection against large price movements than to the minor relative price changes induced by basis risk. As we will see in the case studies, the composite hedge does better than the interest rate hedge in protecting against the major price changes. Most of the variance that remains in the composite hedge is due to the large degree of tracking failure and basis risk from small, uneventful vibrations in the bond and equity prices. Casual empirical study shows that on a day-by-day basis, the bond and equity of even a lower-quality firm will not correlate closely. Frequently, the bond and equity will move in opposite directions. However, during substantial movements, the two conform much more closely with the model relationship.

This section gives a demonstration of the value of the composite model in hedging high-yield bonds. The next section presents systematic statistical tests of the model (for the more technically minded reader), which provide a more rigorous confirmation of the results demonstrated above.

SECTION III   THE TEST OF THE MODEL SPECIFICATION

The objective of a bond hedging model is to match changes in the bond price one-for-one without any bias. The obvious test for the composite model then is to see if the hedging model accomplishes this, and furthermore if it does so with less tracking error than the alternative interest rate hedging model.

The composite hedging model can be restated in terms of changes in security prices as

$$dP = D_s dS + D_f dB \qquad (3)$$

where dP, dS, and dB are the change in the high-yield bond price, the change in the stock price, and the change in the risk-free bond price respectively. We can test this relationship econometrically by computing for each of the bonds in the sample, the time series regression:

$$dP_t = a + b(D_s dS_t + D_f dB_t) + e_t \qquad (4)$$

If the model specification is correct, then the regression result should not be significantly different in the statistical sense from the theoretical model expressed in equa-

---

[10]Indeed just using a smaller time interval will lead to less reduction in variance, since tracking error becomes relatively more important when it is measured on a day-to-day basis. This leads to the perverse result that empirically, variance can be reduced by using longer time intervals in the measure of hedging effectiveness, while in practice, hedging effectiveness clearly cannot be enhanced by requiring longer time periods between hedge adjustments.

tion (3). That is, verification of the model through this test requires $a = 0$ and $b = 1$.

If the model is correctly specified, it will track the bond price changes without bias, leading to a value of zero for the coefficient, and the change in the composite hedge value will equal the change in the bond price, leading to a value of one for the b coefficient.[11]

The results of this regression give strong support to the composite hedging model. Of the 82 bonds, 80 had a b coefficient that was not significantly different from one at the 95% confidence level. Furthermore, all 82 bonds had an a coefficient that was not significantly different from zero at the 95% confidence level. The outliers are themselves consistent with the model; if the model is correct, we would expect 5% of the sample to be outside the 95% confidence interval.

These results are particularly strong given the data problems that introduce error into the tests. Since many high-yield bonds are not actively traded, the price data for the bonds is subject to sampling error. Furthermore, while the stock and financial data were carefully compiled, there are difficulties in coordinating the data bases to assure consistent treatment of stock splits and other events. Also, the financial data were only adjusted yearly, leading to some inevitable timing problems.

The same methodology can be applied to test the interest rate hedging model. With this model the relationship between the change in price of the high-yield bond is hypothesized to equal the change in price of the hedging instrument, usually a Treasury bond or Treasury bond future, multiplied by the appropriate duration factor. That is,

$$dP = DdB \qquad (5)$$

where D is the ratio of the interest sensitivity of the high-yield bond to the hedging instrument. This relationship implies a test regression of the form

$$dP_t = a + bDdB_t + e_t \qquad (6)$$

where, as before, verification of the model specification requires $a = 0$ and $b = 1$.

Equation (5) makes clear the important point that the interest rate hedge is simply a special case of the more general composite hedge model. First, equity is assumed to have no impact on the change in bond price. Second, the relative durations of the bond and the hedging instrument are assumed to capture fully their relative price changes. The first of these restrictions implies $D_s = 0$. The second restriction implies $d_f = D$. Making these substitutions into equation (3) leads directly to the interest rate model shown in equation (5). The composite model is not in contradiction with

---

[11]Several weaker tests of the model can also be performed which do not put as strong a constraint on the test. One such test imposes the functional form of the D and the D_f, but allows each to enter into the regression with its own coefficient. This regression would be $dP_t = a + b_1 D_s dS_t + b_2 D_f dB_t + e_t$. This test of the model was also performed with successful results. However, since the test described in the text is the stronger one, we only report on that test in detail.

the interest rate model. It represents a special case that will be useful for high-quality bonds. However, as credit risk becomes a more important consideration, the restrictions of the interest rate model lead to increasing inaccuracies, and the more complete composite model must be used.

In contrast to the b coefficient for the composite hedging model, the b coefficient for the interest rate model was significantly different from one at the 95% level in 43 out of 82 cases tested. In some cases a good regression fit would be expected for the interest rate model, since for higher-quality issues it will give a hedge similar to the composite model.

The regressions performed above give 82 separate tests of the model. Using Zellner's seemingly unrelated regressions technique, it is possible to aggregate the bonds into a single test which condenses all of the information into one, more powerful result. The resulting regression has 4920 data points. For the composite hedge the regression gives a value for the b coefficient of .91 with a standard error of .02. The extremely tight standard of error indicates a strong relationship between the composite hedge and bond price changes. However, it indicates the composite hedge moves slightly more than one-to-one with the bond price. The a coefficient is $-.12$ with a standard error of .04, indicating a slight upward bias in the composite hedge.

In contrast, the interest rate hedge has a b coefficient of .60 with a standard error of .02, confirming that the simple interest rate hedge is a greatly misspecified model of price changes for a high-yield bond. The low value for the b coefficient in the interest rate hedge gives support to the contention that the interest rate hedge rises out of an incomplete model of high-yield bond pricing. The interest rate hedge does not include a measure of the firm value component and has an incorrect functional form; the Treasury bond position held in the interest rate hedge is essentially constant over the time period for any bond, while the proper hedge ratio is dynamic in both the interest rate and equity position.

The R-squared of .30 obtained from Zellner's method for the composite hedge is 1.5 times the R-squared of .21 obtained for interest rate hedge. There is a close relationship between the regression R-squared and the percent variance reduced in hedging effectiveness. This difference in R-squared indicates that overall the composite hedge increases hedging effectiveness by approximately 50%. The results of the tests are remarkable given the sophisticated functional specification of the composite hedging model, the potential for data inaccuracies, and the dynamic nature of the composite hedge.

Naturally the composite hedge, while giving a substantial improvement in hedging effectiveness, still leaves room for improvement. There are four sources for the remaining variance in the hedge. First, as we have already mentioned, there are the inevitable data problems in the tests. Bond prices, particularly for the less-traded high-yield issues, are often reported with error. Also, because of the large size of our data set we have only updated financial variables, such as the debt/asset ratio, annually. A change in these variables in early or midyear would not be fed back into the hedge ratio until the start of the following year. This will cause tracking errors for the hedge which would be avoidable in practice by monitoring the financial structure of the firm more carefully. Second, the model is always subject to further refinement. Third, the reality of the legal process for bankruptcy differs in unpredictable ways from what is spelled out in bond covenants. The time to the settlement of the bankruptcy claim and the resulting allocation of assets among the creditors are both uncertain, adding risk to the claims of the bondholder and to the hedging model as well. Fourth, if credit quality declines due to a leveraged buyout, the equity value may rise while the bond value declines, and the composite hedge will be inappropriate.

SECTION IV   CASE STUDIES OF HEDGING EFFECTIVENESS

Kenai Corporation

Early 1982 saw a softening in oil prices which presaged a downturn in contract drilling. Recognizing the vulnerability of their onshore drilling contracts, Kenai sought to reduce their exposure to this part of their business. However, the glut of oil rigs on the market dropped prices rapidly, and Kenai found they could not sell off their drilling operations at anything greater than fire sale prices.

Faced with a drop in revenue from the oil price decline, Kenai turned to other business areas to reduce expenditures. In mid- 1982 they cut back personnel and closed several field offices, and sold some of their oil and gas properties. In late 1982 Kenai restated a bank loan agreement with new collateral terms and deferred payments, leading to a lowering in the S&P rating of their subordinated debt to B from B + . With further deterioration in 1983 Kenai sold off more oil and gas properties, and in September 1983 announced they were getting out of the exploration and production segment of their business to concentrate on oil services: the reconditioning and manufacture of oil field equipment and tools.

By late 1983, with no recovery in sight for their drilling operations, Kenai wrote down the value of their drilling rigs and remaining oil and gas properties. This coincided with a violation of bank loan covenants and a downgrading in Moody's rating from B2 to B3. The spring of 1984 saw a severe deterioration in the fortunes of the company. Unable to sell off the oil rigs, Kenai was forced to eliminate an area of business with higher potential (exploration and production), and then in June a lawsuit threatened the area they had targeted for growth—oil services. Ironically the one area of their business that remained intact was the area they had tried to abandon two years earlier: onshore oil drilling contracts. This was the worst performing area in the oil and gas business that left them with few prospects for a return to profitability. In July 1984 Kenai completed the sale of their oil and gas properties. In August they were in default on interest payments. Their S&P rating dropped from CCC to CC, and the beginning of an unsuccessful bank restructuring followed in September, leading to a decline to a D rating the following month.

Figure 8-5 traces the effect of these events on the value of one of Kenai's subordinated debentures, the 10.50% bond due 1998. The solid line depicting the cumulative bond value shows a gradual decline in value from the benchmark value set in November 1983, with the most notable drop occurring from April 1984 (when the

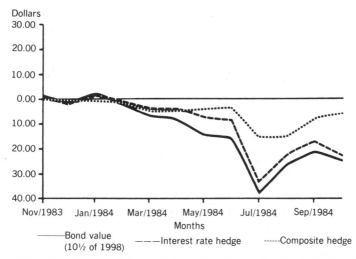

Figure 8-5.   Kenai corporation cumulative value of hedged and unhedged positions.

auditors qualified the fiscal year 1984 results, and S&P reduced their rating from B to CCC), to July, the month before default.[12] Interestingly the bond price actually improved after the default, indicating an overly pessimistic market expectation for the imminent default.

A bondholder buying this bond in October 1983 would have experienced a loss of capital of $38 by July 1984, and a loss of $25 by October 1984. Given the October 1983 bond price of $70, this means a capital loss of 54% by July and 35% by October. Figure 8-5 also shows the effect the composite hedge and the interest rate hedge would have had on this loss. The interest rate hedge, as would be expected, would have been ineffective in protecting against the decline. The value of this hedged position would have moved down virtually parallel with the bond itself. Since Kenai's difficulties had little to do with the interest rate environment this result is not surprising.

Protection from the composite is evident in this figure. Although it would not have given perfect protection, it would have limited the maximum loss to just $15 compared to the $38 for the unhedged position in July, and $6 compared to the $25 loss for the unhedged position in October. The mechanism which gives this protection, the increasing size of the short position in the hedged stock and interest rate vehicles, is shown by the top line in the figure. The total value of the hedged position is equal to the value of the bond plus the value of this hedge.

---

[12]Kenai was not the only firm in the oil industry to suffer setbacks in 1984. The entire oil industry, including oilwell equipment and service, offshore drilling, and the oil composite, experienced significant declines in equity value over this year. The S&P price index for this industry sector, which stood at 1418 in December 1983, dropped to 1209 by August 1984. In just the three months from May through July, the percentage change in equity value dropped by almost 25%. Over the same period, oil prices dropped by over 5%. While the entire industry felt the impact of oil prices in this period, the most levered firms, such as Kenai, were the most penalized.

The results shown in Figure 8-5 may understate the effectiveness of the composite hedge in at least one respect. Since monthly data was used in generating this example the hedge could only be adjusted monthly. As with any dynamic hedge, infrequent adjustments reduce effectiveness. Even better results might be expected in an actual application when the hedge can be reevaluated on a daily basis.

Storage Technology

Storage Technology grew at an annual rate of about 40% throughout the 1970s to become the nation's tenth largest computer equipment company by 1982. Storage Technology's primary market was disk drives that were compatible with large IBM mainframes. They engineered products comparable with the latest generation of IBM technology, and then would compete with IBM on the basis of price and speed of delivery. However, Storage Technology's strategy was fatally vulnerable to the increasing sophistication of disk drive technology, and to the shortening of the product life cycle for these devices. The increasing sophistication meant a lengthening lag between the introduction of a new IBM product and the development of a similar product by Storage Technology. While historically there was first a lag of about three-quarters between the emergence of a new IBM product and the production of the comparable Storage Technology device, this lag lengthened. For example, while IBM's 3380 model disk storage product was shipped starting in November 1981, the comparable Storage Technology product only started full scale production in mid-1984. The shortening of product life cycle meant a shorter time period to try to recover the fixed development and production costs. These problems were further compounded by IBM's increasingly aggressive pricing, which made competition on the basis of price far more difficult.

The risk imposed by this changing strategic environment became evident before the sudden bankruptcy of Storage Technology in November 1984.[13] In September, following a price cut by IBM, Storage Technology cut its disk drive system prices by 10%. The next month a number of signs indicated that these price cuts and the increased aggressiveness by IBM were taking their toll. The firm reported that the erosion of profit margin would lead to a $20 million loss for the third quarter. This resulted in the violation of credit covenants on its working capital requirement. To help cover these losses Storage Technology announced the layoff of 1500 workers, 10% of its work force.

This sudden run of events would give any investor cause to reevaluate a position in the bond. The critical questions are how transitory are the problems, and how likely are they to lead to default? Since as is evident from Figure 8-6, the bond had

---

[13]One credit analyst noted that "On balance, IBM's increased aggressiveness in utilizing its existing technology in the disk drive area, its price-discounting policy and its strategy of accelerating product life cycles are destabilizing the PCM (plug-compatible manufacturer) business, thereby increasing the business risk of STK." Michael J. Marocco, *Morgan Stanley Fixed Income Credit Research Report*, October 3, 1984.

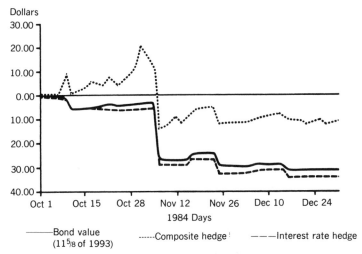

Figure 8-6.   Storage Technology.

not responded to this news, the time was ideal to institute a hedge in case the story continued to unfold for the worst.

The worst did occur. With little warning, on October 31, 1984, Storage Technology filed for Chapter 11 protection. The result came as a surprise to the market; the bond dropped $23 in one day.[14] The projected third quarter $20 million loss turned out to be closer to $65 million, and the administrative details of reorganization began.

For the unhedged bondholder, the sudden price decline would have meant a 31% drop in a bond value in one day. As Figure 8-6 shows, any attempt at an interest rate hedge would have been totally ineffective in protecting against this loss. Indeed while the loss in the unhedged bond from October 1 to November 6 would have been $26, the loss would have been $29 if the interest rate hedge had been pursued. The interest rate hedge actually led to a greater loss than the unhedged position.

What is surprising is the success of the composite hedge in protecting against this catastrophic loss. As Figure 8-6 shows, if the hedge had been initiated on October 1, 1984, the loss to the hedged position by November 6 would have been $13. This is only one-half the size of the loss that would have occurred if the position had been unhedged. By the end of the year the unhedged bond position would have dropped $31 from its October 1 level, while the properly hedged position would have dropped only $11. The hedge, although not perfect, would have provided a large measure of protection. Its effectiveness would have been limited in part by the one-day drop in

---

[14]Because the NYSE did not have a complete set of price quotes for this bond, this case is based on the Morgan Stanley bond data base. This data, while giving daily quotes, uses both actual trades and matrix pricing. Prices may differ slightly and changes in price levels may occur at different times from those quoted by the exchange. These variations have no significant effect on our results, however.

stock price on October 31, when prices dropped from a high of $4.50 to a low of $2 a share. This sudden intraday drop cannot be captured in this hedge position since in this example we have made the hedge adjustments on the basis of closing stock prices only.[15]

International Harvester

Responding to their steadily growing revenues, International Harvester began a program to expand capacity in the late 1970s. The timing for this program could not have been worse. Revenue and earnings peaked in 1979 just as the expansion began, followed by a 50% decline from 1979 through 1983. International Harvester faced losses in every year after 1979.

The downturn was considered to be a short-term aberration, and the expansion, initially financed through retained earnings, was continued with the infusion of large debt issues. In 1980, with a 6-month United Auto Workers' Union strike, writeoffs in operations due to the recession, and a 25% drop in revenues leading to a $395 million loss, International Harvester incurred $800 million in debt to finance the expansion. In late 1980 their senior debt was downgraded to BB.

Expansion continued into 1981 despite operations that were far below capacity and a worldwide recession for trucks and farm equipment. Faced with a $393 million net loss International Harvester increased their debt by another $325 million, leading to total debt of $2.5 billion. The cost of expansion, combined with the toll of the recession, led to a further downgrading of their senior debt to B in May 1981.

The need for repeated financing fueled a continuing fiscal crisis at International Harvester. In March 1981 International Harvester defaulted on their bank debt, leading to a restructuring in December 1981. In 1982 revenue was down 40%, resulting in a $1 billion loss, and in negative net worth by the end of the fiscal year. There was a second bank restructuring, a conversion of debt into equity to reduce debt by $1.3 billion, and a consolidation of operations. Still, with industry-wide overcapacity, their basic business remained in recession.

Figure 8-7 shows the effect of the deterioration of International Harvester's business. From October 1979 to April 1982 International Harvester's 8 5/8 of 1995 dropped by over 40 points, from a price of $70 to $28. In contrast to the drop in Storage Technology, which occurred in just a few days, or in Kenai, which occurred over several months, International Harvester's decline spanned more than two years. Although the length of time of International Harvester's price drop differs from the two previous case studies, the composite hedge would have been equally effective. While the bond dropped $42 from October 1979 to April 1982, the composite hedge would have led to a drop in value of only $11.

As in the other two case studies, the duration-based interest rate hedge would have been ineffective. The interest rate hedge moved down step-by-step with the bond during the period of most severe price decline, offering little protection. As we have

---

[15]Storage Technology was not included in the 82-bond sample used for the tests in Sections III and IV because of insufficient data for the time period.

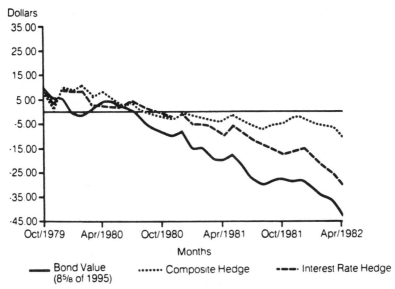

Figure 8-7.   International Harvester.

already mentioned, this is understandable, given that the drop in International Harvester was far more a function of industry and firm-related problems than it was of the interest rate environment.

SECTION V   CONCLUSION

The pure interest rate hedge is a special case of the composite hedge. The composite hedge becomes a conventional interest rate hedge for the highest quality bonds. Thus, for high quality issues, the two hedges will give identical results. However, as this study indicates, for lower-quality issues the composite hedge can give substantial improvements over the conventional interest rate hedging technology. The composite hedge offers a measure of protection for this important class of securities, a class of securities that has been considered unhedgable. And, significantly, the protection is best where it is the most needed: with the lowest-quality issues, and against the major drops in value that come with default. The comparative strength of the composite hedge increases the lower the quality of the bond being hedged. This new hedging technology opens the door for a broad range of trading strategies.

One obvious extension of the technology is to provide default insurance. A hedge is costly insurance. In protecting against loss, it cuts off potential profits as well. A more attractive strategy might be a put option to give the bondholder the right to sell the bond at a prespecified exercise price. Such an option amounts to an insurance contract that guarantees against any loss below the exercise price of the option. Since the greatest risk with high yield bonds is the catastrophic drop in prices induced by default, such protection could be given by a far out-of-the-money option. The further out of the money the option is, the less costly the insurance protection would be.[16]

An option-type payoff can be generated through the appropriate hedging strategy between the underlying instrument, in this case the high-yield bond, and the risk-free asset. Since the high-yield bond is itself an option on the value of the firm, the composite hedge technology is implemented as an intermediate step in forming the desired option payoff. Rather than following a strategy which completely counteracts the underlying bond position, the coverage from the composite hedge is adjusted to meet the dynamic hedging conditions dictated by the option to be created. The result is a compound option strategy: an option is created on an instrument that itself is treated as an option.[17]

The composite hedge can be decomposed into its interest rate and credit risk components, and a hedge can be constructed to address just one of these two risks. An investor interested in protection against only the credit risk component of bond price risk can establish a hedge based on a spread off Treasuries, rather than hedging the bond price itself. If the bond price change is due exclusively to interest rate changes, then the spread will not change appreciably, and the hedge will leave the position largely unaffected. However, if the spread changes dramatically as the result of a change in credit risk, the hedge will protect the position against the resulting change in bond value.

Option protection can be provided against the spread just as it can against the price. To illustrate such a spread option, suppose a bond currently trades 250 basis points off Treasuries. It is possible to construct a hedge which will guarantee the holder against any widening of the spread beyond, say 400 basis points. If the spread

---

[16]An intuitive understanding of default insurance comes by looking at the payoff to a high-yield bond from a slightly different perspective than that used in Section II. Rather than viewing a high-yield bond as giving the payoff presented in that section, consider a high-yield bond as giving a payoff consisting of a risk-free bond and a put option written on the value of the firm. For example, if the bond has a promised payment of $100 million in one year, then the high- yield bond can be expressed as a bond giving the $100 million payoff with no risk of devault plus a short position in a put option (a written put option) paying the maximum of zero or the difference between the value of the firm and a $100 million exercise price in one year.

It turns out this payoff is identical to that used in Section II, since $B - \max(0, B - V) = \min(V, B)$. However, expressing the payoff in terms of a put option helps us to represent the credit risk of the bond more clearly. If the bond defaults, the loss to the bondholder is equal to the loss to the put option writer: it is the difference between the firm value and the bond's promised payment. The bondholder receives a premium for writing this put option. This premium is reflected in the differential expected return above the risk-free rate that the high-yield bondholder enjoys.

The bondholder can eliminate the credit risk of the bond, then, by buying back the put option that he has implicitly written. That is, the bondholder needs to buy a put option wich will pay off the difference between the bond's promised payment and the value of the firm if this difference is positive. Naturally, if the market is pricing the bond efficiently, the cost of buying or creating this option should equal the differential return of the bond over the riskfree rate and eliminating the credit risk should lead to a yield comparable to Treasuries. However, if the high-yield bond is underpriced by the market, the result should be a positive yield differential. The investor need not fully insure the position. Buying out-of-the-money put option protection will allow a measure of protection while retaining some of the high yield.

[17]Geske (1979) presents a treatment of compound options.

widens beyond 400 basis points, the investor would have the right to swap the bond for the Treasury bond at the 400 basis point level any time before the expiration of the option.

The opportunities the composite hedge offers for altering the return distribution of high-yield bonds will undoubtedly make high-yield bond issues more attractive. Investors who have been uncomfortable with the risk characteristics of this sector of the bond market can now mold the risk-return tradeoffs to meet their investment objectives better.

Two other issues need to be addressed to complete the study of hedging opportunities for high-yield bonds. This study has addressed only the risk dimension of hedging. A decision on hedging effectiveness must consider the effect the hedge has on expected return as well. Furthermore, this study has looked only at individual bond issues. The effectiveness of hedging portfolios of high-yield bonds is an important and promising extension of the technology presented here.[18]

BIBLIOGRAPHY

Black, F., and Scholes, M. "The Pricing of Options and Corporate Liabilities." *Journal of Political Economy* 81 (1973): 637–654.

Bookstaber, R. *Option Pricing and Strategies in Investing.* Reading, MA: Addison-Wesley, 1981.

Bookstaber, R. "The Use of Options in Performance Structuring: Molding Returns to Meet Investment Objectives." *Journal of Portfolio Management 11* (1985): 36–51.

Bookstaber, R., and Jacob, D. "Risk Management for High Yield Bond Portfolios." New York: Morgan Stanley Fixed Income Research (1985).

Bookstaber, R., and Jacob, D. "Controlling the Credit Risk of High Yield Bonds." *Financial Analysts Journal* (forthcoming).

Fisher, L. "Determinants of Risk Premiums on Corporate Bonds." *Journal of Political Economy* 67 (1959): 217–237.

Galai, D., and Masulis, R. "The Option Pricing Model and the Risk Factor of Stock." *Journal of Financial Economics* 3 (1976): 54–81.

Geske, R. "The Valuation of Compound Options." *Journal of Financial Economics* 7 (1979): 63–81.

Geske, R. "The Valuation of Corporate Liabilities as Compound Options." *Journal of Financial and Quantitative Analysis* (1977): 541–552.

Ibbotson, R., and Sinquefield, R. *Stocks, Bonds, Bills and Inflation: The Past and the Future* Charlottesville, VA: Financial Analysts Research Federation, 1982.

Johnson, R. "Term Structures of Corporate Bond Yields as a Function of Risk of Default." *Journal of Finance* 22 (1967): 313–345.

Merton, R. "Theory of Rational Option Pricing." *Bell Journal of Economics and Management Science* 4 (1973): 141–183.

Merton, R. "On the Option Pricing of Corporate Debt: The Risk Structure of Interest Rates." *Journal of Finance* 29 (1974): 449–470.

Toevs, A. and Jacob, D. *Interest Rate Futures: A Comparison of Alternative Hedge Ratio Methodologies.* New York: Morgan Stanley Fixed Income Research (1984).

---

[18]These further issues are discussed in Bookstaber and Jacob (1985, forthcoming).

APPENDIX: SUMMARY STATISTICS FOR COMPOSITE AND INTEREST RATE HEDGES

	Issuer/Exchange	Coupon	Maturity	Composite Hedge					Interest Rate Hedge				
				A	Standard Error	B	Standard Error	Pct Var Red	A	Standard Error	B	Standard Error	Pct var Red
1	Api Corp/NYSE	10.75	19979801	0.04	0.40	1.15	0.20	38%	0.11	0.42	0.90	0.18	34%
2	Amerada Hess/NYSE	7.125	19960315	0.22	0.43	1.02	0.52	5	0.27	0.43	0.30	0.14	-34
3	Ames Dept Stores/NYSE	10	19950115	-0.15	0.27	0.66	0.37	6	-0.09	0.26	0.18	0.09	-111
4	Armstrong Rubber	8.625	19960815	-0.24	0.30	0.93	0.23	22	-0.17	0.31	0.38	0.10	-33
5	Buttes Gas and Oil/NYSE	10.25	19970815	-0.13	0.25	0.95	0.12	51	-0.08	0.29	0.69	0.12	30
6	Caesars World/NYSE	11.25	19971201	0.04	0.48	0.86	0.21	28	0.06	0.48	0.73	0.17	26
7	Castle and Cook/NYSE	8.5	19970515	-0.62	0.42	0.79	0.25	28	-0.56	0.42	0.47	0.15	13
8	Chris Craft/NYSE	13	19990201	-0.08	0.39	0.90	0.17	37	0.09	0.38	0.68	0.12	32
9	Chrysler Corp/NYSE	8.875	19950301	0.12	0.46	0.86	0.22	20	0.43	0.49	0.60	0.26	5
10	Chrysler Corp/NYSE	8	19981101	0.09	0.38	0.92	0.20	26	0.38	0.41	0.66	0.23	10
11	Consol Oil Gas/Amex	12	19951001	-0.09	0.36	1.03	0.23	25	-0.03	0.36	0.60	0.14	12
12	Culbro/NYSE	11.5	20050401	-0.07	0.39	0.88	0.24	22	0.08	0.39	0.53	0.13	10
13	Electro Audio Dynamics/Amex	12.875	19990201	-0.19	0.56	0.60	0.21	12	0.09	0.57	0.59	0.27	9
14	Essex Chem/NYSE	11.375	19980901	-0.10	0.33	1.01	0.13	52	0.01	0.33	0.83	0.11	49
15	Esterline Corp/NYSE	12.5	19950401	-0.27	0.36	0.86	0.21	21	-0.05	0.37	0.36	0.12	-34
16	Fairchild Ind.	9.75	19980401	-0.24	0.46	0.87	0.50	7	-0.19	0.46	0.37	0.16	-13
17	Figgie Intl	10.375	19980401	-0.11	0.33	0.85	0.16	33	-0.03	0.33	0.59	0.11	19
18	Fuqua Ind/NYSE	9.5	19980801	-0.14	0.27	1.00	0.12	57	0.09	0.27	0.86	0.10	56
19	Fuqua Ind/NYSE	9.875	19970315	-0.13	0.31	1.01	0.13	51	0.10	0.32	0.83	0.12	46
20	Global Marine/NYSE	12.375	19980801	-0.19	0.41	1.02	0.22	27	-0.14	0.41	0.60	0.14	11
21	Goodrich, B F./NYSE	7	19970815	-0.17	0.43	0.89	0.37	9	-0.11	0.43	0.42	0.17	-9
22	Gulf and Western/NYSE	7	20030701	-0.09	0.21	1.00	0.11	58	0.01	0.22	0.77	0.09	52
23	Gulf and Western/NYSE	7	20030701	-0.15	0.20	0.97	0.10	62	0.05	0.20	0.77	0.09	55
24	Gulf Resources and Chem/NYSE	10.875	19971015	-0.07	0.51	0.96	0.19	32	-0.07	0.51	0.90	0.18	31
25	Gulf Resources and Chem/NYSE	12.5	20040915	-0.11	0.45	0.95	0.18	31	-0.06	0.45	0.72	0.14	27
26	Holiday Inns	9.5	19951215	-0.17	0.37	0.84	0.20	23	-0.04	0.38	0.45	0.12	-7
27	Amer Medicorp (Humana)	11.7	19980630	0.20	0.28	0.87	0.09	67	0.20	0.28	0.87	0.09	67
28	Amer Medicorp (Humana)	9.5	19981001	-0.03	0.45	1.07	0.29	20	0.09	0.44	0.60	0.15	15
29	Ideal Basic Ind/NYSE	9.25	20000615	-0.26	0.39	0.87	0.26	16	-0.26	0.39	0.45	0.13	-10
30	Intermark/Amex	11.875	19990915	-0.14	0.36	0.93	0.17	35	-0.09	0.36	0.70	0.13	29
31	Intl Harvester/NYSE	6.25	19980301	-0.23	0.41	0.46	0.17	10	-0.41	0.42	0.20	0.21	-22
32	Intl Harvester/NYSE	8.625	19950901	0.25	0.47	0.73	0.14	30	-0.08	0.53	0.62	0.24	-2
33	Intl Harvester/NYSE	9	20040615	0.05	0.46	0.75	0.15	24	-0.25	0.49	0.69	0.21	11
34	Iroquois Brands/Amex	12	19990915	0.11	0.43	0.88	0.22	25	0.20	0.43	0.63	0.15	18
35	Kay Corp/Amex	13.5	19981201	-0.08	0.43	0.86	0.38	8	-0.07	0.43	0.29	0.14	-26
36	Kenai Corp/Amex	10.5	19980815	-0.01	0.45	0.98	0.12	62	-0.38	0.61	0.78	0.26	7
37	LTV Corp/NYSE	9.25	19970201	0.07	0.30	0.83	0.15	36	0.13	0.30	0.72	0.12	36
38	LTV Corp/NYSE	11	20070715	-0.07	0.30	1.00	0.14	50	0.02	0.30	0.77	0.11	47
39	Lear Siegler	10	20040101	-0.11	0.39	0.81	0.15	33	-0.02	0.39	0.70	0.13	30
40	Lone Star Ind/NYSE	8	19970415	-0.20	0.33	0.91	0.20	28	-0.15	0.34	0.49	0.12	6
41	Lowenstein/NYSE	8.5	19960301	-0.63	0.47	0.90	0.25	21	-0.09	0.49	0.32	0.20	-10
42	MAPCO	10.75	19990415	-0.15	0.36	0.96	0.54	3	-0.13	0.35	0.27	0.11	-71
43	Mite Corp/Amex	10	19970715	-0.17	0.31	0.82	0.25	17	-0.07	0.30	0.45	0.11	-9
44	NVF Co/Amex	10	20031115	-0.22	0.29	1.11	0.14	52	-0.04	0.32	0.86	0.14	39
45	Nortek Inc/NYSE	12.5	19990615	0.04	0.45	0.88	0.18	34	0.08	0.46	0.76	0.15	32
46	Outboard Marine	7.75	19960201	-0.38	0.29	0.91	0.32	14	-0.22	0.28	0.34	0.11	-43
47	Petro Lewis/Amex	11	19971231	-0.34	0.39	1.09	0.20	32	-0.21	0.39	0.79	0.15	28
48	Petro Lewis/Amex	12.25	19980801	-0.41	0.34	1.03	0.17	39	-0.28	0.35	0.73	0.12	30
49	Phelps Dodge/NYSE	8.1	19960615	-0.26	0.35	0.98	0.58	4	-0.24	0.36	0.01	0.13	-85
50	Savin Corp/NYSE	11.375	19981001	-0.06	0.42	1.22	0.16	47	-0.05	0.42	1.21	0.16	47
51	Singer Co/NYSE	8	19990115	0.03	0.32	0.80	0.21	23	0.10	0.32	0.50	0.13	6
52	Standard-Pacific/NYSE	12.75	19990615	-0.22	0.47	0.92	0.18	33	0.07	0.48	0.75	0.16	26
53	Sun Chemical/NYSE	11.5	19961201	-0.07	0.45	1.10	0.25	22	0.03	0.45	0.66	0.15	14
54	Sun Chemical/NYSE	11.25	19961201	-0.11	0.36	1.24	0.30	20	0.01	0.36	0.47	0.12	-12
55	Talley Indust/NYSE	8.125	19971201	-0.26	0.30	1.10	0.33	14	-0.22	0.30	0.33	0.11	-43
56	Technical Tape/Amex	10	19961231	0.06	0.35	0.73	0.53	2	0.13	0.35	0.26	0.15	-41
57	Teledyne	7	19990601	-0.31	0.30	0.91	0.18	29	-0.11	0.29	0.57	0.11	9
58	Teledyne	10	20040601	0.01	0.23	1.04	0.07	80	0.03	0.23	1.03	0.07	80
59	Telex/NYSE	9	19961101	-0.09	0.35	1.08	0.27	23	0.17	0.34	0.55	0.13	5

	Issuer/Exchange	Coupon	Maturity	Composite Hedge					Interest Rate Hedge				
				A	Standard Error	B	Standard Error	Pct Var Red	A	Standard Error	B	Standard Error	Pct Var Red
60	Telex/NYSE	11 75	19960815	-0.20	0.41	0.66	0.16	25	-0.12	0.40	0.61	0.14	24
61	Tyler	10 5	19980701	-0.31	0.43	0.89	0.19	32	-0.25	0.43	0.62	0.13	25
62	UNC Resources/NYSE	12	19981201	-0.15	0.38	0.81	0.14	37	-0.08	0.43	0.52	0.15	4
63	United Brands/NYSE	9 125	19980201	-0.14	0.34	0.90	0.16	33	0.04	0.34	0.77	0.14	29
64	United Illumin	7 75	20021001	-0.02	0.18	1.02	0.09	69	-0.04	0.18	0.82	0.07	67
65	United Illumin	8 25	20031215	-0.03	0.19	1.01	0.09	69	-0.05	0.19	0.81	0.07	66
66	United Illumin	10 25	20000615	-0.04	0.24	0.99	0.10	63	-0.06	0.24	0.80	0.08	59
67	Wainoco Oil/Amex	10 75	19981001	-0.05	0.38	1.07	0.19	31	-0.09	0.41	0.72	0.15	18
68	Jim Walter/NYSE	7 875	19970201	-0.47	0.61	0.42	1.17	0	-0.46	0.61	0.12	0.19	-38
69	Jim Walter/NYSE	8	19980801	-0.25	0.49	0.89	0.24	23	-0.15	0.49	0.70	0.20	20
70	Jim Walter/NYSE	9 5	19960201	-0.38	0.42	1.06	0.28	21	-0.28	0.45	0.35	0.16	-18
71	Warner Comm/Amex	7 625	19941201	-0.26	0.37	1.07	0.61	6	-0.17	0.37	0.25	0.14	-50
72	Warner Comm/NYSE	9 125	19961115	-0.13	0.55	0.77	0.19	22	-0.04	0.56	0.76	0.19	20
73	Welded Tube of Am/Amex	10	19951015	-0.01	0.27	0.93	0.43	8	0.01	0.26	0.08	0.11	-121
74	Western Co N Am/NYSE	10 875	19970915	-0.06	0.40	1.07	0.20	34	-0.09	0.41	0.71	0.14	26
75	Western Co N Am/NYSE	10 7	19980401	-0.03	0.34	0.97	0.14	48	-0.04	0.34	0.85	0.12	47
76	Western Pacific Ind/NYSE	10	20010701	-0.05	0.37	0.83	0.13	40	0.00	0.37	0.81	0.13	39
77	Western Union/NYSE	10 75	19970801	0.00	0.36	1.31	0.26	30	0.04	0.36	0.61	0.13	17
78	Whittaker Corp/NYSE	10	19961001	-0.08	0.36	0.94	0.19	32	-0.01	0.37	0.64	0.13	23
79	Williams Cos/NYSE	9 4	19960315	-0.26	0.40	0.72	0.18	18	-0.10	0.41	0.51	0.14	1
80	Zapata/NYSE	10 875	20010501	0.03	0.36	0.99	0.13	52	0.06	0.36	0.93	0.13	51
81	Zapata/NYSE	10 25	19970315	0.04	0.32	0.95	0.13	52	0.07	0.32	0.90	0.12	51
82	Zayre	8	19960815	-0.16	0.39	0.93	0.41	10	-0.06	0.39	0.28	0.15	-30

4 Applications of Risk Control Techniques

9 Risk Control Techniques for Life Insurance Companies

JAMES A. TILLEY

INTRODUCTION

In this chapter we apply the theory and techniques developed earlier in this text to the practical problems of managing interest rate exposure for a life insurance company operating in the United States.

The volatility of interest rates since the Federal Reserve Board's "Saturday Massacre" in October 1979 has caused life insurers to pay attention to the financial impact on their capital and surplus accounts[1] of a mismatch between the interest rate sensitivities of assets and liabilities. Few insurers have yet developed the EDP capabilities, including asset and liability data bases, necessary to examine periodically (and frequently) the interest rate exposure of their *entire* operations. However, it has become fashionable for life insurers to decompose their aggregate asset portfolios into *segments* that support various lines of business, and many insurers have developed systems to measure the interest rate exposure of some of the segments.

The primary motivation behind portfolio segmentation has been the need to tailor investment strategies appropriately to the needs of different lines of business, and within lines, to various products. At one extreme the investment strategy required to support employee benefits under group life and health insurance coverages is essentially one of optimal cash management because the average time that funds are held before claims are paid tends to be a few years at most, and often under a year. At the other extreme, the investment strategy required to support the stream of pension benefits to a closed group of employees, some of whom have already retired

[1]Insurers refer to their "net worth" as "capital and surplus."

and some of whom have not, involves very long-term fixed-income instruments because the liability stream has a long tail that can extend 50 years or longer.

The optimal asset/liability strategy for a life insurer should be determined with the needs and resources of the *entire* company in mind, although the execution of that strategy can be parceled out to various portfolio and product managers acting on behalf of specific lines of business. In this chapter we will discuss the asset/liability management problem largely along segment lines in keeping with the current thinking and abilities of most life insurers. We discuss the most useful risk measurement and control models and apply them to the asset/liability management problems for many of the "interest-sensitive" products being offered today.

Interest-sensitive products are sold primarily on the basis of their expected or promised investment performance, their deposit flexibility, and their liquidity characteristics, and not on their traditional "insurance" features involving mortality or morbidity. The asset/liability management problem for these products is very challenging because intense price competition limits insurers' strategic options considerably. Attention to the problem has heightened, though, because insurer surplus measured in true economic terms has become an increasingly scarce resource, and both insurance company management and regulators are keenly interested that it be deployed prudently and protected against loss.

Section I of this chapter describes the contractual features of several interest-sensitive products. Section II describes the types of interest rate risks posed by interest-sensitive products. Section III shows how *duration gap models*[2] can be used to measure and manage the risks for certain products, and Section IV does the same with respect to *simulation models*. Finally, applications of specialized instruments such as financial futures and options, interest rate swaps, and put bonds are covered in Section V.

SECTION I INTEREST-SENSITIVE LIFE INSURANCE AND ANNUITY PRODUCTS

Life insurers sell products to both retail and institutional clients. The former are known as *individual* products and the latter as *group* products. Customers who purchase individual products are generally referred to as *policyholders,* while those who purchase group products are generally referred to as *contractholders.*

Each policy or contract offered by an insurance company promises to pay specified benefits on the occurrence of certain contingencies. The price of the policy or contract is known as the *premium.* Sometimes the price is paid in a single amount, and sometimes it is paid in installments. The label *single premium* is generally used for the former, and *recurring premium* for the latter.

Some policies are offered on a no-load basis, while others require that a certain percentage of the premium or a fixed dollar amount be deducted as a load to help defray the selling and policy acquisition costs incurred by the insurer. All policies

---

[2]Duration gap models are described in detail in Chapter 10.

can be terminated by action of the policyholder, and in most cases, an amount known as the policy's *cash surrender value* is returned to the policyholder by the insurer. For many policies the cash surrender value is determined by applying redemption penalties, known as *surrender charges,* and specified in the policy to the policy's *account value.* The policy's account value is determined essentially the same way as the balance in a passbook account at a bank is determined. Premiums, after deducting any applicable loads, are credited to the account, charges are made against the account to provide for insurance benefits purchased by the policyholder and for administrative expenses incurred by the insurer, and interest is credited to the account as specified in the policy.

We now describe briefly the terms of several different interest-sensitive products offered by life insurers today. Examples presented in Sections III, IV, and V of this chapter are based on these products.

Universal Life Insurance

Universal life insurance is a recurring premium policy that provides benefits on the death of the insured individual to his or her surviving beneficiary. The death benefit is equal to a stated dollar amount (such as $100,000) known as the *face amount* of the policy, or a stated dollar amount plus the cash surrender value applicable at the time of the insured person's death.

Universal life policies are available on a load or no-load basis. The former often have no surrender charges while the latter always do. Surrender charges, if present, apply for a limited period, generally 10 to 15 years. The timing and amount of the recurring premiums are usually at the discretion of the policyholder, subject to certain conditions and limitations imposed by the insurer. In determining the policy's account value, monthly charges are made for the cost of the death benefit and for the insurer's administrative expenses.

The rates of interest at which the various premium payments accumulate can be the same or can differ in order to reflect the different interest rate environments in which the premiums are received. The former method of allocating the insurer's investment income to policyholders is known as the *portfolio method,* while the latter is known as the *investment generation* or *new money method.* There are also many hybrid methods in use today. In any case, the insurer generally adjusts the interest rates credited to policyholders' accounts to reflect actual investment experience.

A policyholder has access to the funds accumulated under his universal life policy either through a partial or full cash surrender or through a loan against his cash value. The insurer usually charges interest on a policy loan at a rate at least 2% higher than the interest rate credited to the borrowed amount of cash value.

Single Premium Deferred Annuity (SPDA)

The SPDA is a vehicle to accumulate funds for retirement. As for universal life insurance policies, income taxes on the interest accumulation are deferred until the policy is surrendered for cash, or until the account value is applied to purchase an income stream for the policyholder or his or her beneficiary. The "average" purchaser is generally about age 50 and deposits approximately $25,000 single premium.

SPDAs are sold today on a no-load basis with surrender charges that grade down to zero over 5 to 10 years from policy issue. A typical surrender charge scale is 7%, 6%, 5%, 4%, 3%, 2%, and 1% in years one to seven respectively. The surrender charges apply to the account value at the time the policy is "redeemed." Some of the newer style policies call for adjustment of the account value to reflect changes in market rates of interest since the policy was issued. In effect, such policies charge capital losses and pay capital gains to policyholders.

Interest credited to policyholders' accounts is generally guaranteed for at least a year and subject to change at policy anniversaries. Newer style policies provide multiyear compound interest guarantees. A traditional feature of SPDAs, becoming less common due to regulatory pressure, is the *bailout clause* that "forgives" any surrender charges when policyholders redeem their policies in a 30-day or 60-day period following insurer action dropping the credited rate of interest by more than a threshold amount, often 50 basis points, from its level at issue of the policy.

Flexible Premium Annuity

The flexible premium annuity has many of the features of the SPDA but allows policyholders to make continuing premium payments. As for universal life, the insurer credits interest to policyholder accounts by the portfolio method, the new money method, or some hybrid method.

Structured Settlement Annuity

The structured settlement annuity is a policy used to settle a court case in favor of a plaintiff who has sued for compensatory and punitive damages in a product liability suit against the corporation manufacturing the product. A typical situation might concern a defective gas tank or brakes in an automobile involved in an accident in which the occupants of the automobile are severely disabled or even killed. Instead of accepting settlement in a lump sum, the plaintiff takes a stream of monthly payments to provide income for the rest of his or her life, perhaps increasing at a fixed rate every year, and perhaps involving a schedule of deferred lump-sum payments. Some of the payments are said to be *certain,* while others are *contingent on the survival of the annuitant,* the person to whom the benefits are paid. The policy is written on a single premium form, and the liability stream typically extends for at least 20 years and potentially up to 80 years or more, depending on the age of the annuitant.

Guaranteed Interest Contract (GIC)

GICs are group annuity contracts sold primarily to pension and profit-sharing plans (including thrift and 401(k) plans). The contracts sold to pension plans are generally of the single premium form, while those sold to profit-sharing plans are generally of the recurring premium form. In the latter case the participants of the profit-sharing plan have the right to make deposits into the contract during the ''window'' or ''open'' period, usually a year. Withdrawals generally are *not* permitted from a single premium contract, except perhaps to pay benefits of the pension plan. Withdrawals for individual participants in a profit-sharing plan are generally permitted from a recurring premium GIC in the event of their death, disability, retirement, or termination of employment with the employer who has purchased the group contract in their behalf. ''In-service'' (that is, while still working for the employer) withdrawals by participants in a profit-sharing plan are usually permitted under the terms of the GIC, but these withdrawals are sometimes restricted to cases of ''hardship,'' as defined by the plan.

GICs promise that the premiums deposited with the insurer will accrue at a rate of interest guaranteed for a specified period of time, at which point the account balance will be returned to the contractholder in accordance with a payment schedule specified at issue of the contract. A common payback structure is a lump sum at the maturity date of the GIC. A single premium GIC with a lump-sum maturity payment can be treated for asset/liability matching purposes as a zero coupon bond, even though the GIC is technically an insurance contract, not a security.

Pension Plan Closeout

A corporation may decide to terminate its pension plan because it is going out of business, it is merging with or being acquired by another corporation, it can no longer ''afford'' the plan, or because the plan is overfunded and it wants to recover excess assets. In any event the corporation can liquidate its liability to retirees already drawing pension benefits and to those who have not yet retired but who have already earned deferred *vested* (nonforfeitable) benefits only by purchasing an ''insured'' contract that guarantees to fulfill all those future obligations. The single premium group annuity contract used for that purpose is often referred to as a pension plan closeout contract.

The liability stream of a pension plan closeout is very long tailed, and in many respects resembles that of a pool of structured settlement annuities. A pension plan closeout contract is more complicated in many ways, however. For example it also provides death and survivor benefits, disability benefits, and usually accommodates various options for plan participants to retire early and to select, at future points in time, different forms of payment stream.

SECTION II   INTEREST RATE RISKS POSED BY INTEREST-SENSITIVE PRODUCTS

The two sides of interest rate risk are *reinvestment risk* and *price/liquidity risk*.

Reinvestment risk arises from the possibility of having to reinvest funds when market yields are below levels guaranteed to policyholders and contractholders. The insurer may appear to be exposed to reinvestment risk whenever there is *net cash inflow*, but is actually exposed only when the duration of the assets is shorter than the duration of the liabilities.[3]

Price/liquidity risk arises from the possibility of having to liquidate assets when market yields are above levels at which the assets were purchased. The insurer may appear to be exposed to price/liquidity risk whenever there is *net cash outflow*, but is actually exposed only when the duration of the assets is longer than the duration of the liabilities.[4]

Investment antiselection by policyholders and contractholders is a source of reinvestment and price/liability risk. The antiselection is associated with *options that have been written by the life insurer to its clients. Cash inflow antiselection* arises when policyholders and contractholders have the right to deposit additional funds with the insurer under fixed-rate guarantee arrangements established at some earlier point in time; this right becomes valuable in a falling interest rate environment. *Cash outflow antiselection* arises when policyholders and contractholders have the right to withdraw funds under a fixed-rate guarantee from the insurer, subject only to modest redemption penalties not tied to market rates of interest; this right becomes valuable in a rising interest rate environment.

An insurer's bond and mortgage assets often contain *options written by the insurer to the borrower*. These are borrowers' rights to refund or call bonds it has issued or to refinance or prepay mortgages it has taken. These options cause the durations of the assets to which they are attached to shorten rather dramatically as interest rates fall, and they represent a source of reinvestment risk.

Finally, certain other risks, such as bond default and mortgage delinquency tend to increase with rising interest rates, especially if the debt service is floating rather than fixed. This "correlated" interest rate risk will not be discussed in this chapter.

SECTION III APPLICATIONS OF DURATION GAP MODELS

Duration gap models are described in detail in Chapter 10. We apply duration methodology here to the interest rate risk management problems posed by SPDAs and structured settlement annuities. In each of these situations the behavior of the liabilities as a function of interest rates is sufficiently uncomplicated that their durations can be calculated. In this section we assume that the "immunizing" condition for the insurer is to match asset and liability durations. As pointed out earlier this is appropriate when the ratio of surplus to liabilities is chosen as the "target account" (using the terminology of Chapter 10).

SPDAs

In this section we develop pricing methodology for SPDAs. The appropriate investment strategy is a byproduct of the analysis. We formulate the pricing/investment

---

[3]Duration is defined and discussed in Chapter 3. The condition stated here applies to interest rate exposure of the market value of the insurer's surplus to liability ratio. For similar conditions applying to other "accounts," see Chapter 10.

[4]See the preceding footnote.

strategy decision as a game theoretic problem. Strictly speaking there are at least three players in the game: the insurer who sells the product, the policyholder who buys it, and the agent or broker who distributes it. Although the interests of the policyholder and agent are by no means always fully aligned, we nevertheless assume that the agent will always act in the best interests of the policyholder. This allows the problem to be formulated as a two-person game.

The "rules" of the game vest the purchase and redemption decisions with the policyholder, and the choice of product features, product price, investment strategy, and adjustment options of the credited interest rate with the insurer. The insurer has the first move: designing the product and setting its price (the interest rate offered to the policyholder). The policyholder has the second move: deciding whether or not to buy the product and thus play the game. If the policy is purchased, the insurer must decide how to invest the single premium. Beyond this point the policyholder continually evaluates whether to redeem the policy, and the insurer continually evaluates whether to adjust the interest rate credited to the policyholder, and if so, by how much.

Even apart from the insurer's desire to earn a profit, it should be noted that the SPDA game, once the players have decided to play, is not "zero sum." A policyholder will evaluate whether to redeem the policy based on his or her own circumstances and objectives. This may lead to situations where it is optimal for the policyholder to exercise his or her option to redeem the SPDA even though this action does not strictly minimize the gain nor maximize the loss to the insurer. Also, the policyholder may be inefficient in the exercise of his or her redemption option due to a lack of sophistication or to preoccupation with other matters. This behavior can be summarized in a *coefficient of efficiency* that will be described in more detail later in this section. One can construct simulation models of consumer behavior (of the type described briefly in Section IV of this chapter) to estimate a range of coefficients of efficiency likely to be encountered in the real world.

In the following analysis we assume that the insurer acts to neutralize the value of the policyholder's redemption option, and to hedge the financial outcome of the SPDA game against changes in interest rates. In actuality the insurer may not be risk averse, but even in that case the strategy of optimal risk control and its cost should be understood so that strategies offering incremental gains through net exposure to interest rate risk can be evaluated intelligently.

We will continue the development by examining a specific example. The insurer has decided to offer a "traditional" SPDA having the following features:

No front-end load or administrative charges

Surrender charges of 7%, 6%, 5%, 4%, 3%, 2%, and 1% in years one to seven, respectively, and none thereafter

A bailout rate 50 basis points below the interest rate offered at issue of the policy

A "money back guarantee" that forgives the surrender charges to the extent they would otherwise invade the policyholder's original deposit, and

A noncumulative, once-per-year withdrawal of 10% of the cash surrender value free of surrender charges

The insurer has the right to reset the credited interest rate on policy anniversaries, but guarantees the rate between anniversaries.

The following expenses apply to the insurer's writing of SPDA business:

5% of the single premium as a commission to the selling agent, fully recoverable if the policy is redeemed within the first six months from issue and 50% recoverable if the policy is redeemed in the second six months

$200 to cover the costs of issuing a policy

$25 annually after the first year to maintain policy records and to prepare and mail a report to the policyholder, and

.25% of the original single premium each year as the expense of managing and accounting for the investments made by the insurer to support the SPDA liability

The insurer assumes that all recurring expenses will grow at an annual rate of 7.5%.

For simplicity in this analysis, we will ignore the value of the insurer's right to reset interest rates at policy anniversaries because the bailout provision is relatively strict in this example. The insurer's right to lower the credited rate is generally quite valuable and should be evaluated in actual situations. The example used in this section can best be interpreted in terms of an SPDA guaranteeing the initial interest rate to the investment horizon. We assume that the insurer desires to amortize the selling commission and the other acquisition costs over the 7-year period that the surrender charge scale and the bailout provision apply. For this 7-year *investment horizon* the insurer targets, in pretax terms, a present value of profits at issue equal to 2.5% of the $25,000 average single premium, independent of future redemption experience.

For this example we value the redemption option by assuming that the policyholder always makes decisions over a 3-year investment horizon. He or she will consider redeeming the SPDA policy, suffering the surrender charge, and purchasing a new SPDA policy at current rates whenever interest rates have risen high enough that he or she can break even no later than three years from the point of redemption. From the *policyholder's viewpoint* the redemption right is equivalent to an American put option on a zero coupon bond that matures three years from the date of exercise. The strike price at any time is equal to the redemption value of the SPDA and depends upon the size of the single premium, the SPDA interest rate, the surrender charge scale, the money-back guarantee, and the free withdrawal provision.

To evaluate the financial consequences *to the insurer* of having written the redemption option to the policyholder, one has to calculate the gain or loss incurred by the insurer when the policyholder exercises the option. For this purpose we assume the insurer's investment strategy involves paying out the commission and acquisition expense and deducting the present value of profits from the policyholder's premium payment, and then using the balance of the single premium to purchase:

1. Assets to fund the cash flow stream associated with all recurring expenses
2. A zero coupon bond[5] maturing at the 7-year investment horizon for a par amount

---

[5]Zero coupon bonds are discussed in Chapter 3.

equal to the policyholder's single premium accrued with interest for seven years at the SPDA interest rate

3. The particular put option that exactly neutralizes the redemption right of the policyholder

If the redemption option is exercised by the policyholder, the insurer must sell the zero coupon bond and the assets supporting the remaining stream of recurring expenses, and then pay out the redemption value of the SPDA. The insurer then recovers any "unearned" commissions throughout the chargeback provision of the agreement with the selling agent or broker.

The SPDA is properly priced when the single premium deposited by the policyholder is equal to the sum of:

The commission paid to the selling agent

The acquisition expense incurred in issuing the policy

The present value (at issue) of the recurring expenses

The market value of the zero coupon bond

The market value of the particular put required to neutralize the policyholder's redemption right

The desired present value (at issue) of profits

In practice one often prices the SPDA through an iterative algorithm that converges to the solution described by the equality given above.

On a pretax basis the amount of investable funds at issue of the SPDA is equal to the single premium less the commission and acquisition expense. The investment strategy that preserves the integrity of the pricing and executes the insurer's optimal risk-controlled game plan calls for purchasing assets to match the expense stream, purchasing a put option to neutralize the policyholder redemption right, setting aside an amount equal to the present value of profits, and purchasing a 7-year zero coupon bond with the balance of investable funds. In practice the insurer would be unable to implement the investment strategy as described. First, it is unreasonable to assume the insurer would actually "dedicate" a block of assets against the stream of recurring expenses. Second, the exact put option would not be available either as an exchange-traded or as an over-the-counter instrument, and even if it were, the insurer would be expressly prohibited from purchasing it by the insurance laws of most jurisdictions. Third, the appropriate zero coupon bonds, other than stripped U.S. Treasuries, would generally not be available in sufficient supply and would not have attractive enough yields in any event.

What type of *practical* strategy is "equivalent" to the *theoretical* strategy? The answer is to create a portfolio of fixed-income instruments that possesses the same interest sensitivity properties as the theoretical portfolio. Because the theoretical portfolio involves options it is important to pay some attention to the *convexity*[6] of the portfolio as well as to its *duration*. The practical solution to the investment strat-

---

[6]Convexity is defined and discussed in Chapter 3.

egy problem is to create the highest yield portfolio having the same duration and convexity as the theoretical portfolio.[7] Bonds, mortgages, mortgage-backed securities, options, futures, and interest rate swaps should all be considered. As with any "immunization" strategy the portfolio will have to be rebalanced as time passes and as interest rates change in order to keep the duration and convexity of the portfolio on target. Bearing in mind that accounting principles for life insurers do not reflect *immediately* the "total return" concept embodied in an immunization approach, portfolio rebalancing should be carried out through the combination of options, futures, interest rate swap positions, and cash market trading that affects the insurer's books in the desired manner. And as with most investment strategies, there are important tax considerations in the real world that we have ignored here for simplicity.

This would complete the game theoretic analysis were it not for intense competition in the marketplace due to the presence of other SPDA carriers eager to attract policyholders away from the insurer. Competitors' strategies in this *n*-person cooperative non-zero sum game prevent the insurer from pricing the full put option cost to the policyholder—to write the business the insurer must "take some risk." In our distillation of the SPDA problem to two players, the insurer and the policyholder, we can summarize the effect of the competing carriers as well as nonoptimal policyholder redemption behavior in a single *coefficient of efficiency* (defined to be that fraction of the full market value of the option reflected in the pricing of the SPDA). The insurer can gauge the competitiveness of the market at any time by calculating the maximum coefficient of efficiency that yields a competitively priced SPDA which still meets its profit objective. To determine whether the coefficient of efficiency is realistic the insurer should construct a model that simulates the redemption behavior expected from the types of policyholders with whom the insurer deals. That subject is beyond the scope of this text.

To complete the example we make the following assumptions:

The U.S. Treasury spot rate curve[8] is as shown in Table 9-1.

The insurer can invest in a portfolio of fixed-income instruments having yields, after providing for expected asset defaults, 25 basis points higher than the Treasury spot rates at the short-term end of the curve and 75 basis points at the long-term end of the curve.

Logarithmic interest rate volatility is 15% on an annualized basis.

The put option is valued using binomial lattices for interest rate movements that are converted into price lattices for the bonds needed in the valuation model.[9]

Table 9-2 shows the SPDA interest rates and the portfolio duration and convexity targets for coefficients of efficiency ranging from 0 to 1. Coefficients of efficiency

---

[7]Part of this approach amounts to creating the put option synthetically. This topic is discussed in depth in Chapter 5.

[8]Spot rates are defined and discussed in Chapter 2.

[9]Option valuation models are described in Richard Bookstaber, *Option Pricing and Strategies in Investing*.

Table 9-1.   U.S. Treasury Spot Rates

Maturity	Spot Rate[a] %	Maturity	Spot Rate[a] %
1 month	7.60	1 year	9.10
2 months	7.85	2 years	10.05
3 months	8.05	3 years	10.55
4 months	8.25	4 years	11.00
5 months	8.45	5 years	11.35
6 months	8.60	6 years	11.60
		7 years	11.80

[a]Bond-equivalent yield.

of .2 or less correspond to "competitive" SPDA rates for the assumed interest rate environment. As can be seen from Table 9-2 the effect of the put option on the pricing of the SPDA product and on the duration and convexity of the SPDA liability is dramatic. Not shown in Table 9-2 is how quickly the put option causes the SPDA liability duration to shorten as interest rates rise. Section V of this chapter illustrates how well put bonds mirror that liability behavior.

Structured Settlement Annuities

In this section we examine the investment strategy problem for structured settlement annuities. The concepts discussed here apply equally well to the management of pension plan closeout business. They also apply to GICs, especially the single premium type and the recurring premium type beyond the window period.

Figure 9-1 illustrates the cash flow profile of a typical portfolio of structured set-

Table 9-2.   SPDA Pricing/Investment Strategy Example

Coefficient of Efficiency	SPDA Interest Rate	Duration (years)	Convexity (years²)
0.0	11.18	6.9	48
0.1	10.94	6.5	55
0.2	10.68	6.0	63
0.3	10.41	5.6	69
0.4	10.11	5.2	76
0.5	9.79	4.8	80
0.6	9.45	4.3	85
0.7	9.04	3.9	89
0.8	8.60	3.5	92
0.9	8.09	3.1	94
1.0	7.42	2.5	95

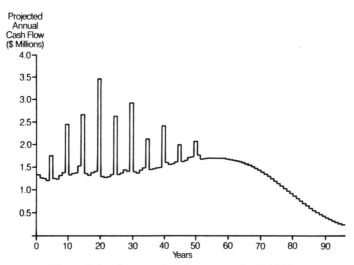

Figure 9-1. Structured settlement annuity liabilities.

tlement annuity liabilities. The cash flow runout is generally independent of the future course of interest rates (unless the benefits are inflation indexed), but depends to some extent on the mortality experience of the annuitants. For purposes of this section we will assume that the liability cash flow stream is certain.

Because there are no interest rate options buried in the liabilities, unlike the case for SPDAs, it may seem that the perfectly immunizing investment strategy is obvious: merely construct a portfolio of assets whose cash flow stream exactly matches the stream of annuity payments. (Taxes and recurring expenses will be ignored for simplicity.) Upon scrutinizing Figure 9-1 however we see that the liability stream typically extends well beyond 30 or 40 years. Because fixed-income investments maturing beyond 40 years are very rare, full cash flow matching strategies are not possible.

The need for long-term investments brings with it another difficulty. The most abundant long-maturity investments are U.S. Treasury bonds (including zeros), utility bonds, residential mortgages, and mortgage-backed securities.[10] Except for some of the Treasuries, none of these instruments is fully protected against repayment of principal earlier than scheduled.[11] In fact the period of call protection for utility bonds is usually only five years from issue and there is generally no period of prepayment protection for residential mortgages or mortgage-backed securities. The call premiums in the case of utilities are modest, often not more than one coupon, and the prepayment penalties in residential mortgages are relatively insignificant, frequently 2% or less of the outstanding principal amount.

The technique often employed by portfolio managers to control the risk of principal prepayment is to purchase discount securities with coupons significantly lower

[10]Mortgage-backed securities are described in Chapter 6.
[11]A thorough analysis of call and prepayment risk is given in Chapter 7.

than those currently available on securities trading near par. Although discount securities do not provide *contractual* protection against prepayment risk, they do provide a large measure of *economic* protection because interest rates have to drop below the level of the coupon before refinancing the debt becomes financially attractive to the borrower.

A variant of the straightforward strategy of purchasing deeply discounted securities is to purchase only mildly discounted securities and then to "trade down in coupon" as interest rates fall, in order to escape impending prepayments. The benefits of this technique are more apparent than real; significant extra yield cannot be captured while avoiding the prepayment risk. The strategy, if executed properly, really amounts to a technique for creating a synthetic call option to neutralize the options granted to the issuers of the securities held in the portfolio.[12] As such it is a hedging technique that bears a cost: the cost of the prepayment options held by the issuers. The cost arises in part from smaller capital gains as interest rates fall than would be experienced if otherwise similar noncallable or nonprepayable securities were held instead.

The trouble that life insurers have with the "discount security" solution to the problem of controlling reinvestment risk for their structured settlement annuity portfolios is that discount securities frequently carry much lower yields than those available from securities trading near par.[13] One of the reasons for this yield differential is to compensate the investor for the additional prepayment risk that higher coupon securities pose. What the portfolio manager needs is a "black box" that will give him the prepayment-risk-adjusted yield to maturity and duration for any security. Although it is not precisely correct to do so, the manager can then compare the adjusted yields among securities of like quality and duration in order to make his portfolio selections.

Faced with the impossibility of matching asset cash flows exactly to liability cash flows and with the reinvestment risks posed by most long-term securities, what risk-controlled strategy can the asset/liability manager pursue? The answer, as in the case of the SPDAs, is to create a portfolio of fixed-income instruments that possesses the same interest-sensitivity properties as the liabilities. A good start is to construct an asset portfolio whose duration matches the duration of the liabilities. Because the latter can easily be eight years or longer, the use of discounted securities or Treasury bond futures is generally necessary. An alternative strategy that provides more risk control than duration matching is to match the first 5 or 10 years of the asset and liability cash flow streams, as well as the durations of the entire streams. This approach protects the structured settlement annuity portfolio very well against changes in shape of the yield curve because the most dramatic changes in shape occur for terms to maturity up to five years.

In calculating the duration of the asset portfolio, it is important to account for

---

[12]Synthetic option strategies are described in depth in Chapter 4.

[13]We ignore any tax benefits that discount securities might offer. This issue is a difficult one due to recent, major changes in the Federal tax code applying to life insurers, and because an insurer's tax situation can change over time even if the tax code does not.

prepayment risk. The proper approach, described in Chapter 7, is to view each callable bond or prepayable mortgage as the combination of an instrument "promising" the scheduled interest and principal payments and an appropriate call option written against some or all of those payments. The duration of the composite instrument is the market-value-weighted average of the durations of the component pieces. Because the composite instrument involves a short position in the call option, the market value of the call option carries a negative sign. As interest rates drop the calls move less out of the money or more into the money and depress the market value appreciation of the composite instrument and cause its duration to shorten significantly. The process of rebalancing the portfolio to maintain the asset duration matched to the liability duration in effect "spends" premiums to "purchase" call options that offset the short positions implicit in the fixed-income instruments in the portfolio.

It is useful to examine how the matching of asset and liability cash flows for the first 5 or 10 years can be affected by prepayment risk. Figure 9-2 displays the first 10 years of the net cash flow stream (assets minus liabilities) for a hypothetical structured settlement annuity portfolio. The influence of prepayment risk is shown by "layering" the net cash flow stream according to how callable or prepayable the underlying asset flows are. If interest rates were to fall dramatically, there is the strong possibility that the uppermost layers would begin to peel away, and that the principal payment portion of those layers would compress toward the present. Viewed this way the cash flow match in the first 10 years for the hypothetical portfolio is not immune to changes in the level of interest rates.

Table 9-3 shows a sample portfolio "report card" that can be used by the asset/liability manager. It displays the financial condition of the portfolio in market value terms as well as summary statistics quantifying the net exposure to interest rate risk. Also found in the table are other statistics useful to the asset manager: average maturity and call date, average quality, average yield to maturity, and various charac-

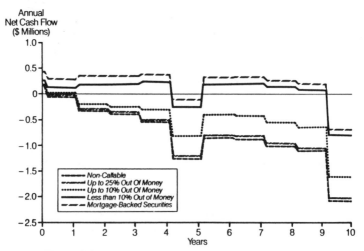

Figure 9-2.   Structured settlement annuity net cash flow.

Table 9-3.   Asset/Liability Portfolio Summary

	Assets	Liabilities	Difference
Market Value	$148.0 million	$145.2 million	$2.8 million
Average[a] Maturity	26.8 years	—	—
Average[a] Call Date	4.1 years	—	—
Average[a] Quality	A	—	—
Unadjusted[b] Duration	7.4 years	9.7 years	(2.3 years)
Adjusted[b] Duration	5.5 years	9.7 years	(4.2 years)
Average YTM Unadjusted[b]	12.41%	—	—
Average YTM Adjusted[b]	12.68%	—	—

[a]Weights are based on asset market values.
[b]For call or prepayment options contained in the assets.

teristics regarding prepayment risk. This report card should be prepared no less frequently than monthly, and more frequently when interest rates are extraordinarily volatile, so that corrective actions can be taken before a large mismatch develops and the actions potentially become very costly to implement.

Table 9-3 shows that the sample portfolio is badly mismatched, especially when adjustments are made to account for the effects of call options in the assets. The size of the duration and yield to maturity adjustments is evidence that relatively high coupon issues are present in the portfolio. An interest rate decline of only 50 basis points will cause the market value of surplus to turn negative.

Convexity should be added to the summary statistics included in the portfolio report shown in Table 9-3. The need to examine convexity derives partly from the presence of asset call options that have pronounced convexities, and partly from the very long tail of the liability stream that endows the liabilities with a larger convexity than has the typical portfolio of supporting assets. This is the opposite of the situation often encountered where the convexity of the assets exceeds the convexity of the liabilities, as for a typical GIC or pension portfolio manager striving to maximize wealth over a given horizon. In the latter situation, assuming only shape-preserving shifts in the yield curve[14] the portfolio *benefits* from any shock to interest rates, whereas in the former situation it *suffers* from any shock to interest rates.

The solution to the "convexity problem" deriving from extremely long-tailed liabilities is to increase the convexity of the assets through long zero coupon bonds or long positions in Treasury bond futures. Although this use of futures certainly qualifies as "hedging" from the standpoint of financial theory, it is unlikely to be viewed that way by state insurance regulators,[15] and zero coupon bonds may be the only practical answer.

A simplified example helps to illustrate the convexity problem for structured set-

---

[14]The definitions of duration commonly used by portfolio managers are predicated on stochastic processes involving only rigid shifts in either the yield curve or the spot rate curve.
[15]At the time of writing this text, the Insurance Department of New York would not have permitted interest rate futures to be used in this manner.

tlement annuities. Suppose the liability stream is a level *perpetuity,* consisting of payments of $100,000 per year, spread uniformly throughout each year. Suppose further that the yield curve is level at 10% on a continuously compounding basis. The present value of the liabilities is $1,000,000, and the duration and convexity are 10 years and 200 years² respectively. The most straightforward duration-matching strategy would involve purchasing a 10-year noncallable zero coupon bond. However, the convexity of that bond is only 100 years,² less than that of the liability. A 25 basis point increase in interest rates would cause the assets to depreciate by $24,690 and the liabilities by $24,390, for a net loss of $300. A 25 basis point decrease in interest rates would cause the assets to appreciate by $25,315 and the liabilities by $25,641 for a net loss of $326.

Suppose instead that the asset portfolio were invested in an equal mix of cash (overnight money) and 20-year noncallable zero coupon bonds. This more "dispersed" portfolio has a duration of 10 years and a convexity of 200 years² matching the properties of the liabilities. A 25 basis point increase in interest rates would now cause the assets to depreciate by $24,385, producing a net gain of $5. A 25 basis point decrease in interest rates would cause the assets to appreciate by $25,636, reducing the net loss to only $5.

Before leaving this section on structured settlement annuities, we will describe a special type of asset/liability mismatch strategy that may make sense to a portfolio manager whenever he believes that interest rates are at relatively high levels and that they will be down at some point within the next 5 to 10 years. The strategy involves structuring the asset portfolio so that (1) there is sufficient asset cash flow, month-to-month or quarter-to-quarter during the 5-to 10-year period, to cover the liability payments, and (2) the overall asset duration exceeds the overall liability duration. The portfolio is positioned to benefit from an interest rate drop and could then be restructured both to take out profit in the form of capital gains and to balance asset and liability durations.

To bring some discipline into the interest rate bet the portfolio manager should establish, at the *outset* of the program, target levels of interest rates at which the portfolio will be rebalanced. This avoids situations of waiting to hit a home run and then striking out. Instead of full rebalancing when interest rates drop to the indicated target level, a sequence of partial restructurings can be effected at various target levels of interest rates.

The strategic bet on falling rates begins to lose only if interest rates *never* drop to the target restructuring levels *during the period that asset cash flows equal or exceed liability cash flows.* Meeting this cash flow condition is essential to preventing realized losses from asset liquidations while interest rates are higher than the level at the time the program was initiated. In true economic terms the bet does lose if interest rates first rise because the market value of the assets will depreciate much more than the market value of the liabilities. But the loss is only *unrealized;* in fact there is more than enough asset cash flow to meet liability needs in the early periods, and the "loss" is not even apparent in the day-to-day operations of the business. The valuation actuary who must write an opinion as to the adequacy of asset/liability matching should therefore be careful to distinguish this type of carefully structured interest rate bet from those involving liabilities prone to disintermediation or those paying no attention to the state of cash flow matching in the early years.

How good is the type of interest rate bet described above? First, one has to think that it is better the higher the starting level of interest rates, for then interest rates must "surely" relax to more "historically appropriate" levels at some time over the intermediate term. Although this "reasoning" would have worked in the past, there is of course no guarantee that it will apply in the future. Second, one can expect the bet to become better the longer the initial period of asset/liability cash flow match.

Some comfort can be taken in a result from probability theory relating to the classical gambler's ruin problem.[16] Consider a commutative binomial random process in which interest rates can move only up or down at the end of specified time intervals. Choose an investment horizon and calculate the probability that interest rates will never be lower than their starting point over that period.[17] It can be shown that this probability approaches zero as the period of time approaches *infinity*, unless the probabilities of up-ticks and down-ticks are one and zero respectively.

Of course the real issue for the portfolio manager is *how fast* his "ruin probability" approaches zero. For a 10-year horizon with 50/50 chances of up and down movements at the end of each time interval, the ruin probabilities, expressed as percentages, are 1.4%, .47%, .11%, and .02% for quarterly, monthly, weekly, and daily intervals respectively. Another important issue for the portfolio manager is how to set target levels for rebalancing the portfolio. This involves computing similar probabilities for threshold levels 50 basis points, 100 basis points, 150 basis points, and so on, below the starting level of interest rates—a subject beyond the scope of this text.

SECTION IV   APPLICATIONS OF SIMULATION MODELS

After experiencing the power and simplicity of duration gap models one may wonder why anybody would want to build a simulation model to study an asset/liability management problem. There are several reasons. First, many situations are very complicated, involving too many "moving parts" to be able to write down the "equations" expressing the interest sensitivity properties of the liabilities. In those situations it is often relatively easy to construct a simulation model that accounts properly for the behavior of all the moving parts. Second, when utilizing a simulation model, the method of "discovery" involves trial and error and extensive sensitivity analysis. As a result, the asset/liability manager is able to "experience" the evolution of his business, and he or she develops a feel for the key factors that drive the financial results.

The primary weakness of simulation models relative to duration gap models is that they do not naturally offer a single or a few simple indexes of interest rate risk

---

[16]See William Feller, *An Introduction to Probability Theory and its Applications,* vol. 1, 3rd ed. New York: Wiley, 1968.

[17]For this purpose, it does not matter whether the shocks to interest rates are additive or multiplicative.

exposure from which hedging decisions involving a broad array of financial instruments can be easily made. A secondary weakness, but still important, concerns the extreme care that must be taken in developing the scenarios against which the simulations will be performed. It is vital to have a properly "unbiased" universe of economic scenarios if one is attempting to locate a "best" investment strategy using mathematical optimization procedures.

In this section we study the problem of finding good, not necessarily best, investment strategies and interest crediting rate strategies for a universal life insurance product. The application could well have been to flexible premium annuities. A simulation approach was chosen because of the desire to incorporate the receipt of recurring premiums, the writing of new business, the payment of taxes, and the use of capital directly into the analysis.

The interest rate scenarios used in financial simulations either can be constructed manually or can be created from a "black box" random number generator. An example of the former approach is found in Section V of this chapter in the discussion on interest rate swaps. The analysis in this section uses random scenarios.

The universal life simulations are based on a universe of 40 interest rate scenarios. Every scenario is a quarterly sequence of yield curves throughout the 20-year projection period. The starting yield curve is the same for every scenario and represents a current snapshot of yields available in the financial marketplace. The study of investment strategies presented here involves only bonds, and the yields are chosen to apply to A-rated industrials. Successive yield curves are generated by shocking both the short-term and long-term ends of the curve for the immediately preceding period and using a 2-piece linear interpolation for yields between the extreme ends of the curves. The short-term and long-term shocks are assumed to be jointly lognormally distributed, with a greater volatility for short-term shocks than for long-term shocks, and with positive linear correlation between the two shocks. A constraint on the maximum spread between short-term and long-term rates is imposed. Partially reflecting barriers are used to keep interest rates within "reasonable" bounds.

Interest rates in the real world certainly do *not* follow the exact process described in the preceding paragraph. Therefore, it is not appropriate to use mathematical optimization techniques to locate best investment strategies against a universe of scenarios derived from that particular random generator; the constraints imposed on interest rate movements introduce biases that the optimizer will seize upon. But using such a universe of scenarios *does* give a satisfactory comparison of risky versus risk-controlled strategies. Because 40 is *not* a large number of Monte Carlo trials, however, it is important to remember that there is considerable error in the estimates of the financial statistics that will be examined.

The simulations presented here apply to the writing of new universal life business every quarter throughout a 20-year projection period. Actuaries call this a *model office* projection, as distinguished from an *asset share* projection that applies to a single block of business written at only one point in time. In this example the first universal life policies are assumed to be written at the beginning of the projection period. It is also possible to endow the model at the start of the projection period with an existing block of business having specified characteristics.

The simulation model is able to recognize cash inflows and outflows every quarter. The elements of cash inflow are coupons and principal repayments from the asset portfolio, and initial and recurring premiums from universal life policyholders. The elements of cash outflow are death benefits, cash surrenders, policy loans, commissions, investment and insurance expenses, and federal income taxes. In addition there are cash infusions (inflow) and repayments (outflow) of *capital* required to maintain exact statutory solvency (assets equal to liabilities), quarter by quarter throughout the projection period.

Positive net cash flow each quarter, namely, inflow less outflow, is invested according to the assumed investment strategy. Negative net cash flow is borrowed according to the assumed borrowing strategy, often chosen to be the "mirror image" of the assumed investment strategy. Alternatively, the model can be run assuming asset liquidations whenever there is negative net cash flow. This is not done in the simulations presented here.

An important feature of the model is the ability to test any specified dependence of the amount and timing of cash flow elements on current and past levels of interest rates and shape of the yield curve. This is the manner in which a simulation model can be used to measure the value of interest rate options granted by the insurer to policyholders, including the effects of inefficient exercise of those options by policyholders. In this example we assume that the volume of new business, recurring premiums, cash surrenders, and policy loans all depend to some extent on interest rates.

Under a pure portfolio method of crediting interest to policyholder accounts the volume of new business can be expected to depend on the level of interest rates. Because a *single* interest rate is credited to all funds, whether new premiums or existing cash value, and because that single interest rate is generally tied to the book yield of the insurer's asset portfolio, it will tend to *lag* the time series of credited rates based directly on current market rates of interest, or, in insurance parlance, *new money credited rates*. When interest rates rise sharply the gap between new money credited rates and the insurer's portfolio credited rate will widen *unfavorably,* the insurer's product will become less competitive, and the volume of new business will contract. Conversely, when interest rates fall sharply, the gap between new money credited rates and the insurer's portfolio credited rate will widen *favorably,* the insurer's product will become more competitive, and the volume of new business will expand. For unfavorable changes in the spread one would also expect *premium suspensions* (the tendency of policyholders to cease paying recurring premiums) to increase, especially for healthy policyholders who can purchase new policies on more favorable terms.

The preceding arguments implicitly assume that the insurer will not "manage" the spread between his portfolio credited rate and the current new money credited rate, but will choose instead to let the portfolio credited rate float at a constant "margin" below the actual book yield of his investment portfolio. In adopting this approach the insurer places greater weight on maintaining profits than on writing new business. It is acceptable, and often desirable, to maintain the spread between the portfolio credited rate and the current new money credited rate within a range of up to 200 basis points in order to flatten out the peaks and valleys of sales volume, and in so doing, to induce positive and negative fluctuations in reported earnings. The latter type of strategy can be modeled effectively using simulation techniques, but is not studied here.

Neither the volume of new business nor premium suspensions should be a sensitive function of interest rates under a true new money method of crediting interest to policyholder accounts because all premiums, whether initial or recurring, get credited the new money rate prevailing at the time of their deposit.

The volume of cash surrenders consists of both a non-interest-sensitive component and an interest-sensitive component. Under both the portfolio and the new money methods, the interest-sensitive component will depend on the size of the unfavorable gap between the current new money credited rate and the composite rate credited to policyholder funds. The larger the gap the greater will be the volume of surrenders. It is reasonable to expect that interest-sensitive cash surrenders will not appear until a threshold gap is reached. The size of the threshold depends partly on policyholder inertia, a *behavioral* factor, and partly on the size of the surrender charges, if any, an *economic* factor. Moreover, it can be expected that policyholders' cash surrender behavior will exhibit memory; policyholders' tendency to surrender policies after a spike in interest rates will be greater if they were exposed to previous spikes during which they did not surrender. All these factors are incorporated into the simulation results presented here.

The volume of policy loans is a function of interest rates, but also depends on the tax benefits associated with policy loans. A detailed description of these effects is not given here. It should be noted that an increase in the volume of policy loans generally increases reported earnings because the insurer achieves on borrowed funds a greater margin between interest income and interest credited than it does on nonborrowed funds. This result stands in sharp contrast to the situation for traditional whole life insurance policies in which future cash value accumulation is unaffected by the policyholder's decision to exercise his or her option to borrow funds against his or her cash value.

The results of four universal life simulation experiments are shown in Figures 9-3, 9-4, 9-5, and 9-6. The first three figures apply to a pure portfolio credited rate method and the last to a new money credited rate method. Only naively simple investment strategies are presented because even they provide a wealth of insight. In the experiment depicted in Figure 9-3 net cash flow every quarter, whether positive or negative, is invested in 10-year par bonds. The average life of the entire bond portfolio shortens as time passes, until the portfolio reaches an approximate steady state near the end of the projection period. Figures 9-4 and 9-5 are based on 5-year and 2-year par bonds, respectively, and differ from Figure 9-3 only as to investment strategy. Figure 9-6 is based on a 5-year par bond investment strategy and a new money credited rate method and differs from Figure 9-4 only as to the method for crediting interest to policyholder accounts.

The vertical axis in each figure represents dollars of quarterly statutory earnings after federal income taxes for a block of business growing by the issue of one new average size policy at the start of every quarter. Each policy has a modest front-end load and heavy rear-end surrender charges, lasting for 15 years from policy issue.

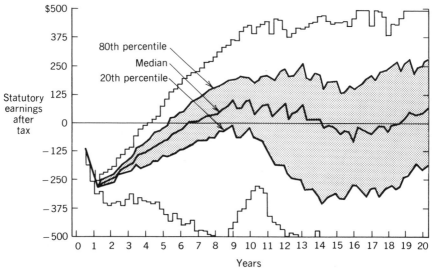

Figure 9-3. 10-Year bond investment strategy portfolio credited rate method.

The actual sales volume is more or less than one policy per quarter under the portfolio credited rate method, depending on the gap between the portfolio credited rate and the new money credited rate at time of issue. Other financial variables can be graphed the same way; an examination of policy reserves, sales, net cash flow, and interest earned less interest credited, in conjunction with statutory earnings after tax, adds to an overall understanding of the business, but has been omitted here for the sake of brevity.

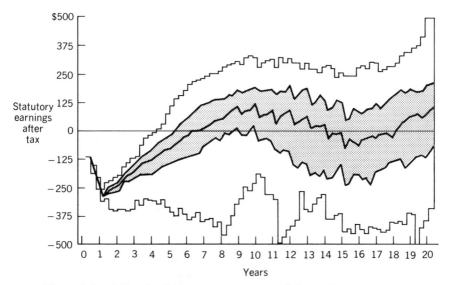

Figure 9-4. 5-Year bond investment strategy portfolio credited rate method.

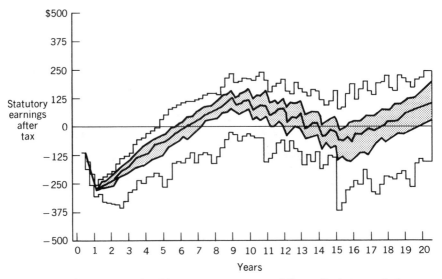

Figure 9-5.   2-Year bond investment strategy portfolio credited rate method.

Each figure displays the range of after-tax earnings across the 40 yield curve scenarios. Also shown are the median, and the 20th and the 80th precentile statistics. The line graphs of these statistics do not represent the earnings track for any one of the 40 scenarios studied, but represent for any quarter the earnings level at the appropriate point in the applicable cumulative distribution function. Thus, when viewed in terms of individual scenarios, the upper end of the range may be an *unrealistically good* result, and the lower end of the range an *unrealistically bad* result.

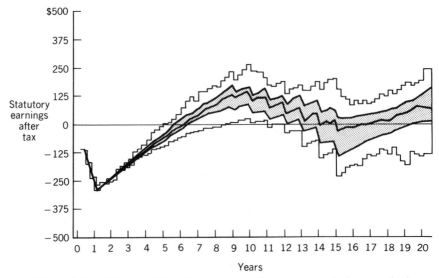

Figure 9-6.   5-Year bond investment strategy new money credited rate method.

Furthermore, as pointed out earlier in this section, there is considerable error in the estimates of these statistics especially for the upper and lower ends of the range, and conclusions should be drawn with this fact in mind.

The width of the shaded region between the 20th and 80th percentiles provides a graphic measure of the risk of pursuing a given investment/crediting rate strategy combination. The conclusions *for the example presented here* are obvious from the four figures. First, acceptable risk control is achievable for the portfolio credited rate method only if a short-term investment strategy is pursued. Second, much better risk control can be achieved if the new money credited rate method is used, even with longer investment strategies. The new money method allows the asset manager more flexibility in his asset selection decision and the ability to acquire higher-yielding investments when the yield curve is positively sloped. Although these specific conclusions stand up well to further analysis the reader is cautioned against generalizing from the results presented here.

In practice the asset/liability manager would investigate other *static* investment strategies involving *barbells,* in which investable funds are split in some fixed proportion between short-term and long-term instruments, and *ladders* in which investable funds are split in fixed proportions among instruments with maturities spread across the yield curve. He would also test various *dynamic* strategies in which either the deployment of investable funds or the rebalancing of the entire portfolio is varied as a function of both time and the level and shape of the yield curve. This "trial and error" approach is tedious and potentially costly in computer time, but if done properly will lead to the "discovery" of sound *duration-based* investment strategies to support the universal life product.

SECTION V   APPLICATIONS OF SPECIAL INSTRUMENTS

This section discusses how special instruments such as options, futures, interest rate swaps, and put bonds can be used by life insurers to help control exposure to interest rate risk. As we demonstrated through the examples in Section III and IV it is the interest rate sensitivity characteristics of fixed-income instruments that determine whether they should be used in a given risk management situation, and if so, in what proportion. What distinguishes the instruments discussed in this section from more conventional fixed-income bonds and mortgages is the special "packaging" of properties into a *single instrument.* In all cases essentially the same portfolio effects could be created *synthetically* in a more complicated fashion by establishing appropriate short and long positions in more conventional instruments.

Options and Futures

The literature on applications of options and futures to the interest rate risk management situations of financial institutions has grown and continues to grow rapidly. For the sake of brevity we do not develop specific applications in detail here, but describe only briefly certain generic types of application. This apparent deemphasis of the importance of futures and options also reflects the present regulatory situation for life insurers. As of early 1985 many states still did not permit insurers domiciled there to use interest rate options and futures. In the other states, the degree to which their use is permitted is often very limited, both on a specific basis through narrow definitions of legitimate hedging transactions, and on a general basis through the limitation to a small percentage (usually 2% or 5%) of the insurer's general account assets that can be hedged at any one time. The regulatory situation will probably improve slowly during the latter half of the 1980s.

Options and futures are highly leveraged instruments that can modify significantly, in relatively small doses, the duration and convexity properties of fixed-income portfolios toward the portfolio manager's desired targets.[18] Unfortunately, as of early 1985, the use of options and futures for this purpose by insurers domiciled in the state of New York, or domiciled elsewhere but doing business in New York, was generally not permitted. For insurers who are able to use options and futures in this manner, the applications involve calculating hedge ratios that specify what size positions in the instruments are required to effect the desired hedges.[19] Long positions in Treasury bond futures increase portfolio duration and convexity, and short positions in Treasury bond futures decrease portfolio duration and convexity. A long position in at-the-money call options acts much like a long position in futures as interest rates fall, but does not modify overall portfolio sensitivity significantly as interest rates rise. A long position in at-the-money put options acts much like a short position in futures as interest rates rise, but does not modify overall portfolio sensitivity significantly as interest rates fall.

The second generic application of options and futures, viewed somewhat more kindly by New York (and other) regulators is to redress the interest rate exposure that comes from *temporary* naked asset or liability positions. There are many applications of this type in the GIC business. An insurer who has won a bid on a GIC contract, but who will not receive funds from the contractholder until a later date, has booked a liability of known amount at a known, fixed interest rate, but has no supporting assets. This mismatch can be removed by purchasing interest rate futures to serve as a temporary substitute for permanent assets. Or the insurer who has won a GIC bid and has received funds from the contractholder may not be able to purchase immediately the desired "permanent" bond or mortgage investments to support the GIC. Once again a long position in futures can bridge the temporary gap.

Sometimes an insurer finds an asset attractively priced in the marketplace and can draw down his liquidity pool to purchase it, but has not yet booked a GIC liability for which the asset is ideal. In this case the insurer should sell futures against the purchased asset to keep its yield current until the GIC business is placed and the GIC rate is known. At that time the hedge can be lifted. If funds from several GICs are required to replenish the insurer's liquidity pool, the hedge can be closed out incrementally as the various GICs are written.

Options also have a place in interest rate risk management for GICs. Window GICs expose the insurer to cash flow antiselection during the period the contracts are

---

[18]The properties of futures and options are described in detail in Chapters 4 and 5 respectively.
[19]These techniques are developed in Chapters 4 and 5.

open to deposits. Should interest rates fall, total deposits will likely exceed the original projections, and should interest rates rise, total deposits will likely fall short of the original projections. The cash flow antiselection arises from options that the insurer has written through the GIC to the plan participants of the employer/contractholder. In this case the insurer has written both calls (more deposits during periods of falling rates) and puts (less deposits during periods of rising rates). The insurer needs to purchase both calls and puts to offset the exposure. Unfortunately, the GIC markets are so competitive that the insurer is unable to pass on to contractholders the full cost of at-the-money options by way of deductions from the guaranteed interest rate that would otherwise be applicable. The insurer can still effect a partial hedge by going naked for small interest rate rises and declines and buying out-of-the-money options to provide "stop-loss insurance" against severe cash flow antiselection associated with large interest rate rises and declines.

A practical difficulty in implementing option hedges for window GICs is that the hedges must generally cover a period of 12 to 15 months in length, because the open period usually lasts a year and the business is often placed up to three months before the start of the open period. However, there is not much liquidity in the option markets, either for options on futures or options on physicals, for other than the contracts nearest to expiration, a period of at most three months. Thus, the hedges must be rolled over to the new nearest contracts as the original options approach expiration. Such "option roll" strategies add uncertainty to the ultimate cost of the hedging program because option prices, at the time the hedge has to be rolled, may be influenced by special market conditions, and because the time value component of an option premium is much greater when the option is at the money than when it is deeply in or out of the money, and the insurer does not know, at the time of purchase of the options, the prices at which its options will expire. These difficulties could be overcome through the purchase of specially tailored over-the-counter options if insurers were legally permitted to purchase them.

The final example concerns the takedown of a privately placed commercial mortgage. The borrower usually has to deposit a nonrefundable commitment fee with the investor, but will often "walk away" from the deal if interest rates drop sufficiently for him or her to find more attractive financing elsewhere. In these circumstances, the nonrefundable deposit is seldom adequate compensation for the loss experienced by the investor. The investor can use the commitment fee to purchase out-of-the-money call options expiring on or after the closing date of the mortgage, usually 60 to 90 days after the initial application, in order to provide protection against large losses. If this action is taken, however, it should be recognized that the yield of the mortgage, if it is eventually taken down, is effectively reduced because the borrower generally "gets credit" for the deposited fee in that situation.

Interest Rate Swaps

An interest rate swap is a contractual agreement between two parties to exchange specified payment streams. The payment streams are considered to be interest rate payments on a specified principal amount, but this principal amount is only "notional'' in that it does not change hands. Under a ''plain vanilla'' interest rate swap, one party makes fixed-rate payments and the other makes floating-rate payments. A typical arrangement is a 5-year swap on a notional principal amount of $20 million requiring fixed-rate payments at 50 basis points higher than 5-year Treasury bonds (at the time the swap is initiated) in exchange for floating-rate payments at 6-month Libor.[20]

Interest rate swaps can be used as duration management tools, and can be considered as substitutes for interest rate futures in many situations. Interest rate swaps are enjoying greater use by most insurers than are interest rate futures for several reasons:

1. Their financial structure seems to be more easily comprehended.
2. They are over-the-counter instruments, and even though there has been considerable standardization of their form recently, they can be customized to the needs of the insurer.
3. Because their ''maturities'' are longer they fit better with the hedging horizons of most insurers.
4. Their regulatory status is currently much more favorable—they are permitted in all jurisdictions and generally need to be reported only as footnotes to the balance sheet, if at all.

The futures market is much more liquid than the interest rate swap market, however, and that figures importantly in the ability to adjust hedges as time passes and interest rates change. The use of futures or interest rate swaps to hedge mortgages and corporate bonds gives rise to basis risk, a topic discussed in Chapter 4.

In this section we study an example of how interest rate swaps can be utilized to reduce the duration of an asset portfolio to bring it into balance with the duration of the corresponding liability portfolio. This type of mismatch situation can arise from duration gap ''drift'' in a GIC portfolio when private placement bonds and commercial morgages are used to fund the GIC obligations. As time passes the duration of the assets tends to age more slowly than the duration of the liabilities which often resemble zero coupon bonds more closely and thus age in ''duration time'' almost as quickly as in ''calendar time.''

Any duration gap between assets and liabilities can be redressed by selling longer assets directly in the cash markets and then purchasing shorter assets, but this may be difficult if most of the asset portfolio is relatively illiquid, or may be undesirable if interest rates have risen and selling assets would lead to realized capital losses. The insurer can overcome both of the difficulties by entering into an interest rate swap in which it makes fixed-rate payments and receives floating-rate payments. The mechanics of the swap are depicted in Figure 9-7. The *capital loss* that would have been realized by trading in the cash markets now becomes a *stream of ordinary losses* during the life of the swap. The losses are due partly to a book yield for the portfolio

---

[20]Libor stands for London Interbank Offered Rate. It is the rate paid in London on short-term dollar deposits from other banks, and is used as a base rate in international lending.

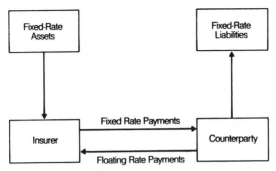

Figure 9-7.   Reducing duration via interest rate swaps.

of "retained" assets inadequate to support the fixed rate specified in the swap arrangement, and partly due to the difference between short- and intermediate-term rates. Apart from tax considerations the capital loss would equal the present value of ordinary losses if all assets were priced properly.

We now consider a specific example. Suppose an insurer's asset portfolio can be represented by $100 million par amount of an 8-year bond with a 10.50% coupon. Assume the current interest rate environment and spread relationships between U.S. Treasury bonds and interest rate swaps, and between U.S. Treasury bonds and A-rated industrial corporate bonds are as shown in Table 9-4.

The market value of the asset portfolio is approximately $91 million and its duration is 5.5 years. Suppose the liability duration target is 4.0 years, and the insurer desires to redress the duration mismatch fully. One strategy utilizing only the cash markets would involve selling $62 million par amount of the 8-year bond and purchasing $62 million of a 4-year par bond. This would cause a realized capital loss of $5.9 million, but would bring the asset and liability durations into balance.

Alternatively, suppose the insurer could enter into 3-, 5-, or 7-year interest rate

Table 9-4.   Interest Rate Levels and Spread Relationships for Interest Rate Swap Example

	U.S. Treasury Yield	Interest Rate Swaps versus Treasuries	A Industrials versus Treasuries
6 months	9.60%	+70 b.p.	+35 b.p.
1 year	10.10%	+70 b.p.	+35 b.p.
2 years	10.95%	+75 b.p.	+35 b.p.
3 years	11.15%	+75 b.p.	+35 b.p.
5 years	11.60%	+55 b.p.	+40 b.p.
7 years	11.75%	+50 b.p.	+45 b.p.
10 years	11.85%	+45 b.p.	+45 b.p.
20 years	11.90%	—	+60 b.p.

swaps as a fixed-rate payor in exchange for 6-month Libor floating-rate payments. To calculate the proper "hedge ratios" (namely, the notional principal amounts of the swaps needed to effect the desired duration rebalancing), one needs to know how to calculate the impact on portfolio duration of entering into a swap.

When interest rate swaps are initiated they can be viewed as instruments issued at *par*. Because no principal amount changes hands there is no initial outlay of funds by either party—the market value of the swap is zero. But like an interest rate future, the swap is highly levered. From the viewpoint of the insurer the swap depicted in Figure 9-7 is equivalent to a *short position* in interest rate futures, and thus can be used to *reduce* the duration of a fixed-income portfolio. More specifically, from the insurer's viewpoint a $10 million notional principal amount 5-year swap under which it pays 12.15% in exchange for 6-month Libor is equivalent to a $10 million 12.15% 5-year fixed-rate *loan* to purchase a $10 million long position in a 6-month money-market instrument, and its effect on the portfolio's overall duration can be calculated easily.

In this example, the amounts of 3-, 5-, or 7-year swaps needed to hedge away the 1.5 year asset/liability duration gap are $60 million, $35 million, and $30 million respectively. Ignoring the effect of compounding and any change in interest rates six months after the swap is initiated, the investment income "giveups" of the swap-restructured portfolios relative to the original portfolio are $.96 million, $.65 million, and $.59 million for the 3-, 5-, and 7-year swaps respectively.

Before leaving this example we will describe a risk/return framework that the insurer can use to evaluate the relative attractiveness of leaving the portfolio unhedged, restructuring via the cash markets, and restructing via the interest rate swaps of various maturities. This involves simulating total portfolio returns over the 4-year liability horizon under different yield curve scenarios. We have assumed a zero coupon structure for the liability and rebalancing of the asset portfolio every six months to hedge away any duration gap. The rebalancings are carried out by selling an appropriate portion of the original 8-year bond and investing the proceeds, together with any coupons, in a par bond maturing at the liability horizon. The interest rate swaps are left in place as long as possible and the entire portfolio is liquidated at the liability horizon.

Figure 9-8 shows the five yield curve scenarios used in the total-return horizon analysis. They include a scenario in which the yield curve is unchanged, a sharply rising scenario in which the yield curve inverts, a sharply falling scenario in which the yield curve becomes more steeply positive, and combinations of the last two to give rising/falling and falling/rising scenarios.

Figure 9-9 presents the results of the total-return[21] simulation analysis. A "band" of total returns is shown for each of the portfolio strategies. The vertical width of the band can be taken as a measure of risk[22] and some probability weighting by scenario[23] of total returns can serve as a measure of expected return.

---

[21]Total return is the annualized yield that causes the initial portfolio's market value to compound to the terminal portfolio's market value.

[22]An alternative measure would involve just the range of "downside" total returns.

[23]The assignment of these probabilities is subjective, and depends on the insurer's interest rate outlook.

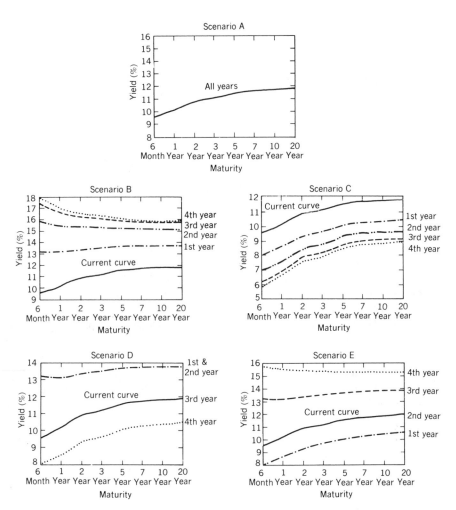

Figure 9-8.   Interest rate scenarios (U.S. Treasury yields).

The interest rate swaps control interest rate risk relative to the unhedged situation, but do so in much less spectacular fashion than the restructuring effected completely in the cash markets. The difference in risk profiles is traceable to the different convexities (and higher moments) of the two types of strategies. The interest rate swap strategies cause the portfolio to be more ''strung out'' along the yield curve than does the cash market sell/restructure strategy and are therefore more exposed to changes in the shape of the yield curve. A major part of this ''stringing out'' comes from the 6-month component of the interest rate swaps. A more appropriate type of swap for this example, and one that can be created by combining two plain vanilla swaps, is for the insurer to *pay fixed* off the 8-year point on the Treasury curve and to *receive fixed* off the 4-year point on the Treasury curve.

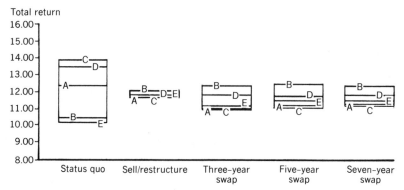

Figure 9-9. Horizon analysis for interest rate swaps.

Put Bonds

Corporate bonds that grant the investor the right, at some point in time in the future, to put the bonds back to the issuer at a specified strike price are known as *put bonds*. Several put bond issues were brought to the market in 1984, and life insurer asset/liability managers can certainly hope these bonds do not become a passing fad because they possess desirable interest rate sensitivity characteristics. This section will not dwell on risk/return considerations for put bonds, although it appears that the early issues have been undervalued and that some degree of undervaluation may persist.[24] Also, these bonds provide *indirectly* over-the-counter put options that many life insurers cannot purchase *directly* due to regulatory restrictions.

Figure 9-10 illustrates the duration and convexity[25] characteristics of several dif-

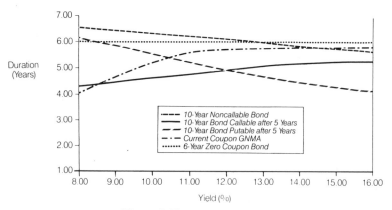

Figure 9-10. Asset durations.

---

[24]See R. Bookstaber, W. Haney, and P. Noris, "Are Options on Debt Issues Undervalued?" *Morgan Stanley Fixed Income Research* publication (December 1984).

[25]Convexity at any point on the curve of duration versus bond-equivalent interest rate is equal to the square of the duration at that point, less 100 times the slope of the curve at that point multiplied by a factor equal to one plus the interest rate divided by 200.

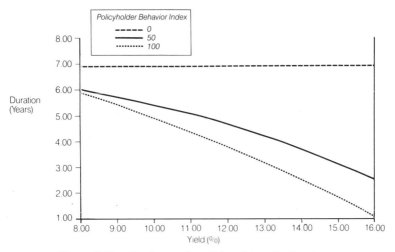

Figure 9-11.   Single premium deferred annuity durations.

ferent types of fixed-income assets. For comparison Figure 9-11 illustrates the duration and convexity characteristics of a typical SPDA for coefficients of efficiency[26]
equal to 1 (efficient exercise), .5 (partially efficient exercise), and 0 (no exercise).
As to interest rate risk control properties alone (that is, ignoring considerations of
yield) the put bond offers a much better match to the SPDA than does any of the
other assets shown in Figure 9-10. Put bonds are also appropriate to universal life
and flexible premium annuity portfolios where there is a risk of disintermediation as
interest rates rise, and in any other situations where their duration and convexity
characteristics would lead to a better match between assets and liabilities.

BIBLIOGRAPHY

Feller, William. *An Introduction to Probability Theory and its Applications,* vol. 1, 3rd ed. New York:
    Wiley, 1968.
Bookstaber, R., Haney, W., and Noris, P. "Are Options on Debt Issues Undervalued?" New York:
    Morgan Stanley Fixed Income Research, December (1984).

[26]This term is defined and described in Section III of this chapter in the discussion on SPDAs.

10 Measuring and Managing Interest Rate Risk: A Guide to Asset/Liability Models Used in Banks and Thrifts

ALDEN L. TOEVS AND WILLIAM C. HANEY

EXECUTIVE SUMMARY

The unprecedented volatility in interest rates experienced in this country over the past five years and the subsequent failure and near failure of many financial institutions has forced most bank and thrift executives to seek effective ways of hedging their own institutions from the ravages of unexpected changes in interest rates. In response to this demand, several approaches to measuring and controlling the interest rate risk exposure of banks and thrifts have been proposed. The primary objective of this chapter is to structure the context within which the resulting new techniques of risk measurement add most value. We are then able to compare the advantages and disadvantages of the different approaches to risk management. In a sense this chapter is a review of the issues that have caused many banks and thrifts to reinvent the asset/liability "wheel." We hope our report will reduce the cost and frustration so often associated with the control of interest rate risk.

We begin by distinguishing risk from uncertainty. Uncertainty arises from random events so poorly understood that exposure to them should be avoided whenever possible. The nature of the random events causing risk, on the other hand, is quantifiable. Risk-taking activities should be considered whenever the gamble has favorable odds. Many executives equate interest rate risk with interest rate uncertainty, they cannot tell if the dice are loaded. But some of the apparent uncertainties are nothing more than improperly measured risks. Thus naive or otherwise inaccurate asset/liability models have unnecessarily limited the search for profitable opportunities, and they have done so during a time period when such opportunities are more valuable because competitive pressures have made them less frequently encountered.

Properly constructed models measure both direct and correlated interest rate risks. Direct interest rate risk arises from mismatched asset and liability interest rate reset dates. These reset dates occur at maturity for fixed-rate securities or at contractually specified dates for variable-rate securities, for example, annually for adjustable rate contracts repriced annually. Correlated interest rate risks are often the culprit of mismeasured risk. They arise from sources dependent on change in interest rates, for example, interest rate induced prepayments of fixed-rate mortgages. Unfortunately, few financial institutions use asset/liability models capable of measuring correlated risks. Since these risks can be substantial, many banks and thrifts experience unanticipated volatility, hence uncertainty, in earnings and net worth. Furthermore, because these risks are not properly measured, prepayment and redemption rights, default premiums, and other sources of correlated interest rate risks cannot be appropriately priced when contracts containing these options and credit risks are written.

It is our view that product pricing is an integral part of asset/liability management. So too is the topic of transfer pricing. This "tome" however, is weighty enough so that a full treatment of these issues is best left to another time.

Most line items on the balance sheets and income statements of banks and thrifts have values that depend on the level of interest rates. Each item can be viewed as a potential target account for interest rate risk management. An asset/liability model should be capable of measuring the direct and correlated interest rate risk exposures for all of these potential target accounts. After all, the bank or thrift has a risk exposure in each of these accounts whether or not it chooses to manage them. In this chapter we examine only the following target accounts: market value of equity, the ratio of the market value of assets to the market value of equity (economic leverage), return on the market value of equity, market value of net interest income, and book value of net interest income.

Unfortunately not all of our target accounts can be controlled for risk simultaneously. Compromises therefore must be made to accomplish risk control objectives. For example, the market value of equity and the total return on the market value of equity cannot be hedged simultaneously. Some multiple hedging objectives, however, are consistent with one another; for example, any of the equity-related accounts can be hedged simultaneously with the book value of the net interest income. Jointly accomplishing several risk objectives to which the institution is most sensitive is a very important finding and one little practiced by today's risk managers.

Most banks and thrifts devote insufficient managerial attention to the formation of a consensus on the risk goals of the institution. Some fail to realize that choices among possible goals must be made; others set mutually inconsistent goals. Still others fail to manage risk because they so violently disagree on what goals should be sought. We argue that setting risk control goals for numerous target accounts, and doing so in an attainable fashion, represents the most important, yet the most difficult task of asset/liability committees.

Once the risk objectives for the various target accounts have been set, risk exposures can be measured and decisions can be made. The value of an asset/liability model depends on three basic characteristics. First, an asset/liability model should reveal the broadest range of asset and liability choices that alter the current exposure of the bank or thrift toward the desired exposure. Flexibility helps reduce the costs of risk control by maintaining the value of the firm's franchise through an accommodation of customer demands and by lowering transaction costs, tax liabilities, and so on. Second, the model must be comprehensive. All assets, liabilities, and hedging vehicles should be studied with a comparable approach. For example, the risk manager should be able to integrate the interest rate risk characteristics of interest rate futures and swaps with those of cash market securities. Third, an asset/liability model should permit risk control decisions to be made incrementally. If current risk exposures are unacceptable, but the desired positions are not immediately attainable, then the model should reveal accurate methods of changing risk exposure toward that desired.

We will study the relative abilities of three generic types of asset/liability models. The first is the Maturity Gap Approach which is currently used by most banks and thrifts. The next is the Simulation Approach, a technique with a long history and several vended models covering a wide spectrum in sophistication. The third and newest is the Duration Gap Approach. A list of attributes we feel should be included in any asset/liability model is discussed early in this chapter and used throughout our report to compare the relative strengths of each model.

Maturity gap models began with the invention of the cumulative 1-year gap model in the late 1970s. Its successor, the periodic gap model, quickly followed. These models derive their names from the "dollar gap" they were designed to measure. The dollar gap is the difference between the dollar volume of rate-sensitive assets and rate-sensitive liabilities. Rate-sensitive assets and liabilities are those that can experience contractual changes in interest rates during a selected accounting period.

The most basic gap model focuses exclusively on net interest income as the target account. If the risk manager wishes to hedge net interest income against changes in interest rates, then this model recommends setting the dollar gap equal to zero. Supposedly this causes a change in interest rates to influence interest income and interest expense equally. If interest rates are expected to rise, the dollar gap should exceed a value of zero. In this case more assets than liabilities will shift into higher earning accounts (should the rate forecast come to pass) during the accounting period. As a result, the net interest income rises above prior expectations. Similarly, if interest rates are expected to decline, the dollar gap should be set at a value less than zero.

The major problem with the basic gap model is that it computes the dollar gap as the difference between the dollar volumes of rate-sensitive assets and liabilities without due consideration of when during the accounting period the assets and liabilities are repriced. This often results in misspecified assessments of the interest rate risk exposure of a bank or thrift. While the basic gap model produces an easily interpretable index of interest rate risk, this measure is not always reliable.

The periodic gap model was developed around 1980. It measures interest rate risk by computing gaps for a number of "maturity buckets." The primary advantage of this newer model is an increase in the precision of interest rate risk measurement.

In principle it is easy to understand, and development costs are small. Despite these improvements over the basic gap model several deficiencies limit the value of periodic gap analysis. It hides some risks from bank and thrift executives. It focuses effectively on only one of many possible target accounts: net interest income. The gap patterns generated for many institutions are often difficult or impossible to interpret without the aid of computer simulation. Periodic gap models also are unable to identify all the gap patterns capable of hedging net interest income. This results in overly restrictive asset/liability alternatives for the risk manager. The periodic gap approach also limits risk managers' abilities to identify incremental hedges. There are, in fact, instances when the gap models suggest means to reduce current exposures to interest rate risk that are dead wrong.

Simulation models were developed to correct several deficiencies of the periodic gap model. This development was spurred most intensely by the inability to summarize numerous gap numbers any other way. Simulation models employ a fundamentally different analytical technique than those used in periodic gap and duration gap models. They produce their results in a dynamic or forward-looking context, whereas the alternatives produce their results statically. Dynamic modeling requires more detailed assumptions about managerial behavior, probable loan and deposit demands, and the path taken by interest rates than those needed in static models. These extra requirements arise because subjective decisions are made over a period of time rather than at one point in time.

We find the dynamic approach of carefully designed simulation models useful and appealing. Simulations help managers anticipate the timing of future events and prepare managers to neutralize the unwanted aspects of these events. Simulations also increase the value of strategic planning and profitability exercises by integrating these plans with dynamic control of interest rate risk. The outcome of any single simulation run is also easily decipherable by senior management.

Two disadvantages limit the usefulness of simulation models: they cost more to run than other types of models, and they measure *current* risk exposure clumsily. In effect the principles of finance are repeatedly rediscovered in each computer run. Risk adjustments must be made by trial and error, making simulation analysis tedious at best. Because simulations solve problems with search procedures, a thorough examination of current risks often generates volumes of computer output. Summarizing these results in a form digestible by an asset/liability committee requires great skill. This skill normally resides in an individual of such value to the bank or thrift that expecting him or her to repeatedly undertake this task may be impossible. Simulation models are often sold as black boxes and the internal structure of these models, once discovered, may fail to reflect the bank or thrift being simulated. Simulation models also rely heavily on econometric analysis and are therefore subject to the same problems that plague econometric forecasting. Finally, simulations focus on one target account, normally net interest income, and only with great limitations can be used to examine several target accounts simultaneously.

Duration is an index measure of the interest rate sensitivity of any cash flow series. The duration concept is useful primarily because it summarizes cash flow information taking into account both the magnitude and timing of these flows. It cannot hide cash flow timing mismatches as can periodic gap models within their maturity buckets. The duration gap model uses duration analysis to index, in a single number, the risk exposure for a target account. The larger the gap, the more exposure. This distillation of information helps risk managers quickly assess their risks and find the appropriate hedges.

One closes duration gaps essentially by recognizing that while interest rate risk can be minimized by matching each asset flow with a corresponding liability flow, it can also be matched by having the magnitude and timing of all asset cash flows match on average, but not exactly, the magnitude and timing of all liability cash flows. This idea is presented loosely here but the essential characteristic of duration analysis is that cash flow matching on average normally provides more net return, and certainly more flexibility, than exact cash flow matching.

Duration analysis can be performed separately on a large number of target accounts. This permits risk measurement for balance sheet items and income statement items. Duration gap models have the capacity to ask what risks are to be controlled; what compromises must be made to accomplish these objectives? A duration gap model also reveals the largest potential number of asset and liability choices capable of moving current risk exposures to more desired levels. This characteristic gives managers the opportunity to accommodate customer demands, minimize transaction costs, limit tax liabilities, and meet regulatory requirements more fully than when alternative models are used. Duration gap models, as opposed to periodic gap models, unambiguously indicate which transactions reduce the current risk exposures in target accounts when incremental hedges are put into place. Finally, analyses of correlated interest rate risk and unusual security types are more easily incorporated into the duration framework than the alternative approaches.

There are several limitations to duration analysis. It requires more management time, an expenditure that must be justified by the added flexibility in asset/liability allocations and potential for *slightly* higher returns attributable to this flexibility. Several issues of residual, presumably random risks may also temper one's appetite for duration analysis. Finally, duration analysis cannot simulate the influence of new business or adjustment in business lines as deposits or loans mature.

We recommend that duration analysis be considered for use in the measurement of current risk exposures and as an available alternative to them. It does these tasks for more target accounts with lower cost and less need for trial and error searches than do simulations. These exercises are the most important ones of risk management. Of secondary importance is the determination of the tradeoff between immediate or gradual risk adjustments, a task best performed with a simulation model. As for static maturity gap models, they should be used to fill out the reports required by regulators.

SECTION I   INTRODUCTION

Through their roles as financial intermediaries, banks and thrifts perform the socially desirable function of improving the efficiency of financial markets. These intermediation activities create profitable opportunities, but they can also introduce interest rate and credit risks into balance sheets and income statements of banks and thrifts. Those who desire long-run profitability must manage assets and liabilities so that only productive interest rate and credit risks are undertaken. These risks generate returns that on average are sufficient to compensate the bank or thrift for the possibility of losses.

The proper selection and use of an asset/liability model significantly improves bank and thrift profitability. Sophisticated and correctly used models focus managerial attention on the conceptual rather than the mechanical issues of risk control. These models also enhance managerial productivity by accurately measuring risk exposures. Finally, well constructed asset/liability models reveal a broad set of assets and liabilities from which to choose when current risk exposures are restructured toward more desirable levels. Flexible asset and liability allocations reduce transaction costs and tax payments, stabilize earnings, and more fully accommodate customer requests for specific terms on loans or deposits.

We distinguish between two sources of interest rate risk. *Direct* interest rate risk arises from mismatched asset and liability repricing dates. These repricing or reset dates occur at maturity for nonprepayable and nonrefundable fixed-rate instruments. (Amortizing instruments have many repricing dates, one for each principal payment.) Variable-rate contracts have contractually specified repricing dates that are shorter than their maturity dates. Measured differences of the asset and liability repricing dates is the task most often associated with asset/liability measurement and interest rate risk management.

There are important but less transparent sources of interest rate risk we categorize as *correlated* interest rate risk. These sources are noncontractually determined interest rate repricing. For example, loan prepayments cause the return of principal dollars for interest rate repricing at dates that are not contractually stipulated. The speed of prepayments in term is highly dependent on the current interest rate environment. This kind of correlated risk is one sided in nature. If interest rates fall from the level at which the loan was written, then prepayments quicken. Otherwise, the return of principal comes in as expected. Deposit disintermediation is another source of interest rate risk. It too is one sided in its influence. Payment shock on loans causes some borrowers to prepay loans, as often the early return of principal is a fraction of the full amount. While not all prepayments and deposit redemptions are induced by changes in interest rates, enough are induced so that these problems contribute substantially to the interest rate risk exposure of most financial institutions. Unfortunately, up to now they have been given short shrift in asset/liability models.

We find much to fault in our analyses of the competing architectures used in asset/liability models. We believe that many banks and thrifts miss profitable opportunities and incur unproductive risks by selecting asset/liability models inadequate to the task of measuring the truly complex risks faced by depository institutions. Additional losses arise because asset/liability models, whatever their levels of sophistication, are all too often used incorrectly. Consultative support can reduce the search and implementation costs associated with the selection of an adequate asset/liability model. Such support is also imperative if the bank or thrift wishes to obtain the maximum value from the selected model. Otherwise banks and thrifts will continually reinvent sound asset/liability management practices.

Our objective is to prevent some of these unnecessary losses by describing a sensible method of asset/liability management, and by criticizing the means by which available models measure interest rate risk exposures. The following detail may appear to be exhaustive, but in reality only a fraction of the important issues have been presented. These problems exist mainly because the change in monetary policy in October 1979 and subsequent deregulations of financial institutions created unexpected risk exposures to which asset/liability model inventors had to respond. Crisis management was appropriate for a time, but five consecutive years of interest rate volatility suggest that the crisis has passed as has the need for shortcuts in risk measurement. It is now time to establish a well-conceived structure for interest rate risk measurement.

We have an additional theme in this ''consumer report'' on asset/liability models. It is more subtle but also more important. Risk managers have devoted an inordinate amount of attention to asset/liability model design. Conceptual issues of risk management have, therefore, been slighted. Yet just as the drafting of blueprints precedes the cut with the saw, these issues must logically be addressed before any model can be fruitfully applied. The failure of many bank and thrift executives to recognize that an asset/liability model is a tool, not a solution, has caused these executives to do either the ''asset/liability shuffle'' or the ''asset/liability jerk.'' Dancers to the first tune are executives who arrive at the ball already tired but find their dance cards fully obligated to previously compensated vendors of clumsy soft(shoe)ware. The others, sprightly but confused, dance unpartnered amid gyrating software vendors.

Bank and thrift executives must recognize that the complex risks they face make risk management a difficult and nonroutine task. Because asset/liability models do not answer conceptual questions, the risk management process will never be automated. Indeed productive risk managers rely on asset/liability models that reveal the broadest set of asset and liability combinations capable of attaining risk management goals. These managers strive to make more decisions rather than fewer.

What might be the important conceptual issues of interest rate risk management? Data system design, admittedly a mundane issue, provides a convenient example. The precision of the data used by any asset/liability model fundamentally influences the quality of subsequent risk management decisions. Good or bad asset/liability models produce bad results when current risk exposures are misrepresented in the raw data. Unfortunately many banks and thrifts have inadequate data systems. The first issue, then, is to determine what data system enhancements are needed. Redesigning data systems entails substantial costs. Hence an important tradeoff arises between the cost of data system enhancements and the cost of mismeasured risks. Most executives find that any decision is expensive, but that attacking the problem in an informed piecemeal fashion makes more sense than total system redesign.

Risk managers worry about more than the timing and speed of data system enhancements. They must set the risk objectives of the institution. At a minimum these objectives should be made with regard to the acceptable risk exposures of capital value, capital adequacy (leverage), and net interest income. The goals for these categories have to be stated clearly and with sufficient accompanying detail to be useful in the asset/liability modeling process. Moreover, these objectives must be made to be internally consistent, which is not an easy task.

We examine three generic types of asset/liability models in this report. The first is the Maturity Gap Approach which is currently used by most banks and thrifts. We next study the Simulation Approach, a technique with a long history and several vended models covering a wide spectrum in sophistication. The third and newest is the Duration Gap Approach. The accuracy with which these models measure direct and correlated interest rate risk will also be compared.

Our comparative analyses reveal that none of the asset/liability models adequately addresses all forms of interest rate risk. The Duration Gap approach, however, contributes the most value to careful risk managers. All-or-nothing comparisons have merit only because the available asset/liability models fall distinctly into one of the three camps listed above. A pitfall we hope to avoid in our comparative analyses is a polarization of thinking on the complex issues of interest rate risk control in banks and thrifts. Our objective is not to laud a winner, but to establish a well-reasoned base from which more rapid progress in asset/liability modeling can be made. In fact we conclude that a judicious blend of duration and simulation analyses dominates exclusive reliance on any one risk measurement technique.

This chapter is outlined as follows. Section II defines direct and correlated interest rate risk in more detail. It also presents some of the issues that currently complicate interest rate risk management. This section concludes with an annotated list of the characteristics we feel should be included in an asset/liability model. Section III discusses the conceptual issues of risk management that must be resolved before any asset/liability model can be fruitfully employed. It is probably the most important section in this chapter. Section IV analyzes the Maturity Gap Approach to asset/liability management, and Section V examines the uses of simulation analyses in asset/liability management. Section VI introduces the concept of duration; this material should be read by those who do not have working knowledge of the concept. Section VII examines the Duration Gap Approach, and Section VIII summarizes and concludes the chapter.

SECTION II   ASSET/LIABILITY OVERVIEW

Before we begin to study the various approaches to asset/liability modeling, it is useful to classify the types of risks banks and thrifts face. We contend that properly constructed models ought to measure both direct and correlated interest rate risks.

Again direct interest rate risk, the normal topic in the asset/liability literature, arises from mismatched asset and liability interest rate repricing dates. Correlated interest rate risk arises in more disguised forms often through the option-like characteristics of some financial instruments. Next we distinguish risk from uncertainty. Uncertainty arises whenever random events are so poorly understood that risk managers should avoid exposure to these events whenever possible. Many bank and thrift executives currently believe that all interest rate risks are uncertainties. This is an unduly restrictive view and those taking it may significantly reduce earnings. In addition to defining the types of interest rate risks and comparing the concepts of risk and uncertainty, we discuss several issues that currently limit the management of properly measured exposures to interest rate risks. We then close this section by listing the attributes desired in asset/liability models.

Risk Intermediation

Banks and thrifts act as intermediaries primarily by engaging in denomination, default and interest rate intermediation. Denomination intermediation, which has trivial implications for this chapter, occurs whenever a number of separate deposit accounts are combined to fund a loan or vice versa. By acting as the party to every asset and liability, the bank or thrift offers ''participation'' certificates in many denominations to borrowers and depositors. Default intermediation occurs whenever the bank or thrift allows credit risks to be transferred from depositors to the intermediary. Interest rate intermediation is performed whenever the bank or thrift accommodates dissimilar demands on the timing of interest rate repricing dates by asset and liability customers.

Default intermediation transfers three types of credit risk from depositors to the intermediary. These risks arise from fraudulent, random, and interest rate induced defaults. In exchange for bearing these risks, the bank or thrift earns a fee, normally in the form of an interest rate spread, that should at least cover the expected cost of this intermediation service. Each source of loan defaults is diversifiable to a degree, and the ability of a financial institution to diversify those risks more completely than an individual depositor creates the possibility of profit. We address the default issue only tangentially in this chapter. We will integrate this subject into the asset/liability literature at a later date.

The provision of interest rate intermediation services can create, but need not, interest rate risk for banks and thrifts. Loan and deposit customers express their demands for interest rate repricing terms in numerous forms. No net interest rate risk is incurred when the interest rate repricing terms on all assets exactly equal the repricing terms on all liabilities. Hence, banks and thrifts can earn spreads from servicing a matched set of widely divergent interest rate repricing dates. But these earnings can be increased with minimal exposure to interest rate risk through the more flexible methods of offering interest rate intermediation services outlined later in this chapter. For now let us quantify the kinds of interest rate risks a bank or thrift must control to provide fully compensated interest rate intermediation services.

Some bank customers desire contracts that postpone the date on which interest rates are adjusted, while others want their interest rates to reprice frequently. Fixed-rate loans delay a single repricing date to the contract maturity date. Thus a fixed-rate customer relinquishes interim and beneficial movements in interest rates for protection against interim but costly movements. Variable-rate contracts subject the customer to costly movements in interest rates in exchange for the capture of beneficial movements during the contract period. Variable-rate contracts create interest rate risks for the borrower or lender that are two sided in nature; one side benefits the customer and the other side does the opposite.[1]

The interest rate risk borne by the bank or thrift depends on the net mismatch between asset and liability interest rate repricing dates. Net mismatches on the balance sheet leave the capital and/or income of the bank exposed to its own two-sided interest rate risk. A wise risk manager accepts this risk only under two circumstances: the manager is somehow able to estimate this risk exposure and earn a compensatory risk premium into the spread, or the manager wishes to position the firm to benefit from an interest rate forecast and the manager's predictive capacity merits this exposure.[2]

Banks and thrifts intermediate other types of two-sided and one-sided interest rate risk. Foreign currency holdings or obligations introduce exchange-rate risks into the bank or thrift. These risks are in part determined by the volatility of domestic and foreign interest rates. The interest rate component of foreign exchange-rate risk should be considered in the firm's total interest rate risk exposure. These risks are two sided in nature. Some customers willingly pay for the right to reset contractual interest rates when interest rates move in their favor. Prepayable fixed-rate mortgages exemplify such a contract. Certificates of deposit (CDs) issued with the right of redemption provide another example. The bank or thrift intermediating either of these demands takes on a one-sided interest rate risk. When interest rates rise (fall), all other things being equal, the bank or thrift experiences losses as depositors (borrowers) exercise the beneficial rights written into their contracts. One-sided interest rate risks can be borne productively, provided the bank or thrift charges a premium sufficient to generate at least compensatory returns on average.

Simultaneous intermediation of asset and liability customer demands for one-sided interest rate risk protection creates an insidious form of interest rate risk for the bank or thrift. Suppose a bank funds 5-year, fixed-rate, prepayable loans with 5-year, fixed-rate, redeemable CDs. This asset/liability mix avoids direct interest rate risk. Yet the risk exposure from two separate interest rate intermediation activities, both one-sided in nature, pinch bank profitability when rates either rise or fall; de-

---

[1]Fixed-rate deposits subject depositors to 2-sided interest rate risk on the reinvestment of interest payments and on reinvestment of principal at maturity. Contracts expected to be renewed are variable-rate contracts in disguised form.

[2]Little evidence supports the view that accepting 2-sided risk has been a major source of profits for financial institutions.

positors reset their contractual rates when rates rise, and borrowers prepay when rates fall. Such paired risks can "broadside" a bank or thrift.[3]

Interest rate induced defaults correlate or covary with any net two-sided interest rate risk on the bank's or thrift's books, as do one-sided and broadsided interest rate risks. Despite this transparent observation virtually no financial institution uses an asset/liability model capable of measuring these correlated risks. Since correlated risks can be substantial, many banks and thrifts experience unwanted volatility in earnings and net worth. Furthermore, the resulting misestimated risk exposures mean that the firm does not properly price its default risk premiums, one-sided interest rate reset options, or other intermediation service fees. While the measurement of correlated interest rate risks is admittedly an arduous task, it represents an opportunity. In the coming years the most profitable firms will be those with executives who find efficient means to deliver only productive intermediary services to their customers.

Risk versus Uncertainty

Recent economic and regulatory events have convinced many bank and thrift executives that they face interest rate uncertainty, not interest rate risk. According to theoretical economists, the important aspects of random events causing risk are quantifiable but the same cannot be said for uncertainty. Banks and thrifts therefore can determine which intermediation services generate income sufficient on average to cover possible losses due to risks. Once these services have been identified, the executive makes a choice: take on the risk in exchange for what on average will be at least a fair return, or eschew it knowing the expected cost of the action. In situations of uncertainty, so little is known about the nature of the random events that proper pricing of intermediation activities is impossible. The rational response is to avoid exposure to these random events.

Many bank and thrift executives point to post-1979 instability in earnings and capital values as evidence that they face interest rate uncertainty, not interest rate risk. Record attendance at conferences on asset/liability management also manifests this belief. It is clear that banks and thrifts currently operate in an uncertain interest rate environment. Some of this perceived uncertainty is direct and correlated interest rate risk that has been improperly measured. A sophisticated asset/liability model increases potential profits by distinguishing risk from uncertainty and by helping banks and thrifts properly measure the value customers derive from risk intermediation services.

Issues Complicating Interest Rate Risk Management

Several issues hinder interest rate risk management. (Henceforth interest rate risk management means monitoring and controlling exposure to direct and correlated in-

---

[3]A. Toevs, "Hedging the Interest Rate Risk of Fixed-Income Securities with Uncertain Lives," *Journal of Portfolio Management,* Spring 1985, likened the "broadside" risk to the writing of a "naked straddle" strategy.

terest rate risk and avoiding interest rate uncertainty whenever possible.) Although banks and thrifts operate in a much less regulated environment today than they did six years ago, substantial regulatory constraints remain limiting the flexibility of their risk management programs. The recent Continental Illinois crisis and the resulting changes in the attitudes of depository institution regulators suggest that some reregulation rather than further deregulation lies ahead.

Regulators should consider enforcing their regulations more selectively by allowing exceptions when the bank or thrift can demonstrate the exception results in a reduced exposure to uncertainty or risk. For example, some banks and thrifts wish to restructure their assets to lower interest rate exposure. They have been prevented from doing so, at least in the most logical manner, because of minimum book capital requirements. Differential accounting treatments on what are similar types of hedging transactions should also end.

Banks and thrifts have valuable franchises in their established customer base. Therefore they must be sensitive to customer requests on the terms of loans and deposits. While these requests may expose the institution to unwanted risks and uncertainty, denying them has well-defined and undesirable consequences. Recently heightened competition for bank and thrift customers has increased the value derived from servicing customer requests. Profitable banks and thrifts in volatile interest rate environments must constantly find new ways to maintain customer relationships while adopting only productive forms of interest rate risk.

Many banks and thrifts have woefully inadequate data systems that impugn the accuracy of *any* asset/liability model. Yet all too often one model is criticized relative to another because its data costs are higher. This represents illogical reasoning; if risks are to be measured properly, the data supplied to *any* asset/liability model must be accurate and comprehensive. The required information includes the cash flow profiles of all currently booked financial assets and liabilities, commitments made to customers for one-sided interest rate options, and historical data reflective of past risk exposures.[4] Decisions to use more limited data should be justified by cost-benefit studies. These analyses do not require knowledge about what asset/liability model will be used as data issues are fully independent of model choice.[5]

A final issue complicates risk management. Most banks and thrifts devote insufficient managerial attention to the formation of a consensus on the risk goals of the institution. Some fail to realize that choices among possible goals must be made. Others set mutually inconsistent goals, which invariably cause risk managers to become schizophrenic and unproductive. Still others fail to manage risk because they

---

[4]Analysis of historical data provides extremely useful insights into the current risk levels associated with correlated risks. For example this data contains information on the speed and extent of depositor response to higher yielding deposit accounts. Also credit risk analysts use past experiences when they determine the sensitivities of their variable-rate borrowers to changes in interest rates.

[5]Many models compress (aggregate) data on cash flows in an initial stage to reduce computer processing costs. This is particularly true when simulations or comparative analyses are to be performed. To preserve an accurate picture of risk exposures, compression must take place on the complete set of cash flows. Unfortunately, many models start with data that has not been derived from these cash flows. Compressing this limited data even further compounds previously committed errors.

so violently disagree on what goals should be sought. Goal setting must take place before asset/liability modeling begins. Section III presents a number of alternative goals and discusses which ones are mutually compatible.

Desirable Characteristics of Asset/Liability Models

Risk managers desire numerous characteristics in their asset/liability models. A full list is as long as a comprehensive description of the most sophisticated model. We believe, however, that the following 11 items form the core of a useful asset/liability model. Unless otherwise noted these characteristics do not appear in order of importance.

1. The most important attribute of an asset/liability model is an accurate characterization of current exposures to interest rate risk and uncertainty.

2. Next is an ability to translate these exposures into their influences on several risk control target accounts. These accounts include net interest income (margin), market value of equity, and capital adequacy. Unfortunately the book value of equity cannot be a target account. Book values blend current and past financial realities, but only the current ones are at risk.

3. The third most important characteristic is the ability to reveal all the asset and liability choices that alter the current exposure of the bank or thrift toward the desired exposure. Flexibility in risk control helps reduce the costs of risk control by maintaining the value of the firm's franchise through an accommodation of customer demands and by lowering transaction costs, tax payments, basis risk, and so on.

4. The model should be comprehensive so that all types of assets, liabilities, and hedging vehicles can be studied simultaneously and in a comparative framework. For example, the interest rate risk characteristics of interest rate futures and options must be integrated with those of cash market securities.

5. The model should measure correlated interest rate risks in addition to direct interest rate risk.

6. The model should permit risk control decisions to be made incrementally. If the current risk exposure is unacceptable, but the desired position cannot be attained immediately, then the model should reveal accurate methods of changing risk exposure toward that desired position. Flexibility in choice again is important. Most risk management is undertaken on an incremental basis. Unfortunately we will discover that some models have distinct limitations in their abilities to alter risk on an incremental basis.

7. The model should measure the risk of existing asset and liability positions and those likely to be booked in the near term. At least a limited capacity to simulate the future helps risk managers determine if their current interest rate exposures should be hedged immediately or with properly structured new business.

8. The model should allow the measurement of interest rate risk for individual balance sheet and income statement line items. This permits the application of microhedges and helps risk managers hedge macrorisk incrementally.

9. The model should be adaptable so that it can be programmed to display all major findings in a number of forms. This increases the ability of risk managers to communicate their findings to all levels of management. Nothing logically prohibits the current interest rate risk exposure measured by one comprehensive model from being formatted to look like the output derived from another model.

10. The model should require that all assumptions used in the analysis of interest rate risk be stated explicitly in a report ancillary to the output from the model. The conclusions derived from any model depend in part on the correctness of the initial assumptions. Explicit statement of assumptions hastens the process of locating error-inducing assumptions.[6]

11. The model should take into account the differences between book and market valuation. As mentioned above the book value of equity cannot be the target account for interest rate risk management. However, tax liabilities and other important considerations depend more on book (accounting) valuation than market valuation.

Useful Subsidiary Reports

Properly constructed asset/liability models use sufficiently detailed data to generate several ancillary reports. These reports may already be compiled in the bank or thrift but with less accurate data than that used by the asset/liability model. These reports should also be as consistent as possible with the structure and output of the asset/liability model. (Most banks and thrifts find it useful to review these reports during each asset/liability committee meeting.) Thus risk managers should have the option to generate these reports as the asset/liability model is run. At least six supplementary reports can be generated as subsidiary output from an asset/liability model.

1. *The market value of portfolio equity.*   This capital account is derived from netting the market valuation of currently booked financial assets and liabilities. We believe this report to be extremely important and will argue that this market value provides a leading indicator of future net interest incomes and future book values.

2. *Net cash flow forecasts for the near term.*   Managers use this report to forecast the need to purchase liquidity and plan campaigns to generate new demands for deposits or loans.

---

[6]Inadequate data systems will cause risk managers to make many assumptions. Explicit statements of these assumptions will help risk managers discover where data enhancement expenditures will produce the greatest returns. Remember, not all data problems need to be solved at the same time. Just as risks can be reduced incrementally by use of a well-designed asset/liability model, so too can data problems.

3. *Profit planning report.* Managers use this report to study the influences of business volume and other new business strategies on current profits and risk exposures. It also portrays the influences of changes in the mix of new accounts. In essence this report is generated by simulation analysis. We will argue that this report alone justifies the use of simulation analysis, but it does not mean that the asset/liability model must use simulations predominantly.

4. *Price of new accounts report.* Similar risk securities should have similar prices (interest rates). This report prices intermediation services and their associated risks on a uniform basis.

5. *Transfer prices report.* This report helps bank and thrift executives allocate available funds to the asset managers. These prices, which admittedly are often highly controversial, can lead to increased profitability, more decentralized and rational decision making, and fewer unexpected demands for liquidity. These prices should reflect the incremental cost of funds subject to adjustments for differential competition in asset markets.

6. *Incremental cost of funds report.* This report is the most important of the list given here. If profit maximization subject to risk control objectives is the goal of the bank or thrift, all valuation reports and strategic plans should be based on the incremental cost of funds.

Summary

In this section we distinguished risk from uncertainty and argued that uncertainty should be avoided whenever possible. On the other hand, risk can be both measured and controlled. Banks and thrifts must learn to adopt only productive risks so as to profitably satisfy an ever increasingly diverse set of customer demands for risk intermediation services. The primary role an asset/liability model plays in risk management is the provision of an accurate measure of current interest rate risk exposure. In addition, a properly used asset/liability model increases potential profits by helping risk managers accurately measure the value customers derive from risk intermediation services. An asset/liability model must also offer the institution flexibility in providing risk intermediation services by identifying *all* asset/liability combinations which meet risk management objectives.

SECTION III   OBJECTIVES OF ASSET/LIABILITY MANAGEMENT

This section begins with a summary of what many people call ''Modern Portfolio Theory.'' We have designed this presentation to draw two analogies. First, proper management of the interest rate exposures of banks and thrifts is not unlike proper management of bond portfolios. Second, recent advances in bond portfolio management techniques have direct applications in banks and thrifts. Of particular value are the insights of Modern Portfolio Theory in setting a rational agenda for asset/ liability managers. Our discussions with many asset/liability committee members have revealed a serious lack of understanding of the process by which logical decisions must be made to establish the desired level of interest rate risk exposure for any one target account. Moreover, we have found that many risk managers fail to realize all they should about the simultaneous management of many target accounts and the nature of the compromises in these accounts that must regularly be made.

Modern Portfolio Theory and Asset/Liability Management

According to Modern Portfolio Theory, the total rate of return on a security or portfolio of securities is the single most important number in bond portfolio analysis. (For pedagogical purposes we present this theory first in the context of a bond portfolio and then in the context of banks and thrifts.) This rate of return is computed by dividing the initial investment into the total return obtained over the investment period specified by the investor, and then expressing the result as an annualized interest rate. Total return sums the interest payments, reinvestment earnings on these cash inflows to the end of the investment period, and the change in market value of the bond portfolio over the investment period. The capital gain or loss on the portfolio includes amortization of bonds acquired at discounts or premiums.

In an uncertain interest rate environment, many bonds have uncertain total rates of return for the investment period selected. Financial theorists recognize the inability of investors to forecast rates of return with certainty and suggest that investors respond by assigning probabilities to possible interest rate outcomes. From these probability-weighted scenarios, rates of return on average (expected returns) and variations in return around this average can be calculated. The former estimates the rewards expected from the investment strategy and the latter estimates the risks.

Financial theorists assert that investors purchase bond portfolios with high variations in return only when they expect returns in excess of those associated with more certain investments. Free lunches in this setting do not exist. To increase expected returns one must lower exposures to unproductive risks or increase exposures to productive risks. The simple intuition in these observations suggests the first three tasks of risk management using Modern Portfolio Theory. One must first articulate the problem to be managed. Here, the risk manager states the time period during which risk is to be managed and his or her views on interest rates. As we will see, a perfectly acceptable interest rate outlook is "I haven't a clue." One next estimates the expected return and risk of all available securities and portfolios of securities. The risk manager then uses this information to determine which portfolios have the highest expected return for any given level of risk. These portfolios are referred to as "efficient." Note that the first task is subjective in form; there is no universally correct investment period or forecast on interest rates. The next two tasks are objective in form as anyone with the same risk control objective finds the same set of efficient portfolios.

Figure 10-1 depicts the stylized risk-return tradeoff normally associated with Modern Portfolio Theory. We have assumed in the construction of this figure that the investor has a 2-year investment period. (Remember, risks can be controlled only relative to an initial statement of the problem.) Point A demarks the expected return

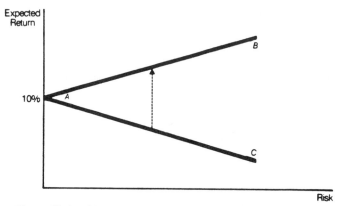

Figure 10-1.   Risk return tradeoff (two-year investment period).

and risk of the least risky portfolio. This portfolio has an annualized rate of return of 10% over the 2-year investment horizon no matter what course interest rates travel.[7]

The portion of the risk-return tradeoff between Points A and C represents the risk-return tradeoffs for inefficient bond portfolios. Each such portfolio has an expected return that can be increased without altering the risk level by converting unproductive risks to more productive ones. For example, an investment in long-term bonds is risk inefficient for a 2-year investment period when the risk manager believes that rising interest rate scenarios predominate. As the maturities on these bonds are shortened, unproductive risks decline and expected return increases. This moves the portfolio toward Point A, along the line connecting Points A and C. Aggressive shortening of the portfolio moves the original portfolio up to Point A and then out along the line connecting Points A and B. The dashed arrow in Figure 10-1 shows how inefficient portfolios behave in relation to efficient ones. Because portfolios that lie on the line connecting Points A and B have the highest return for each given level of risk, these portfolios are efficient. (Points above the line connecting A and B cannot be attained under current market conditions and forecasts.)

The tradeoffs in Figure 10-1 reflect the cash flows of the bonds considered in the analysis, the set of possible interest rates and the probabilities with which the risk manager thinks these forecasts might occur.[8] This figure correctly represents the current risk-return tradeoff only when the assumed changes in interest rates and their assigned probabilities closely resemble the characteristics of random events governing unexpected movements in interest rates. If the risk manager makes uninformed rate forecasts, then the expected tradeoffs, with one exception, will mislead the man-

[7]An example of such a security is a 2-year T-bill that yields 10%. This zero coupon bond has a total return exactly equal to the discount from date of purchase to maturity, two years hence.

[8]A detailed presentation of the creation of risk-return tradeoffs for bond portfolios can be found in G. O. Bierwag, G.G. Kaufman and A. L. Toevs, "Duration: Its Development and Use in Bond Portfolio Management," *Financial Analysts Journal* July/August 1983.

ager. For the investment period of concern the least risky portfolio on the misspecified risk-return tradeoff (Point A) continues to be the riskless portfolio in the correct tradeoff. The least risky portfolio does not depend upon the forecasting accuracy of the risk manager.

After the efficient bond portfolios have been identified, the portfolio manager has sufficient information to make an informed purchase of securities. Because no efficient portfolio unambiguously dominates another, this step introduces another subjective element into the risk control procedure. Investors should acquire portfolios with higher returns as long as the associated price, expressed in terms of more variability in returns, does not exceed a level determined by personal attitudes about variability (risk). Conservative investors eschew risky portfolios in order to obtain a more certain but lower return, while more aggressive investors reveal preferences for higher yet more variable returns.[9]

Figure 10-2 illustrates what happens when one assigns different probabilities to the same interest rate scenarios used to construct Figure 10-1. Figure 10-2 uses reversed lettering relative to Figure 10-1 to indicate symbolically that these probabilities differ so radically from earlier ones that the efficient portfolios in Figure 10-1 have become inefficient. Should the risk manager express doubts about which figure better reflects economic realities, the manager implicitly reveals that few details are known about the random events generating changes in interest rates. Risk has given way to uncertainty and the portfolio associated with Point A in both graphs becomes the only reasonable investment.

The steps required by the application of Modern Portfolio Theory to bond portfolio management have relevance in asset/liability management. Figure 10-3 summarizes these steps. Notice that the agenda begins and ends with subjective choices.

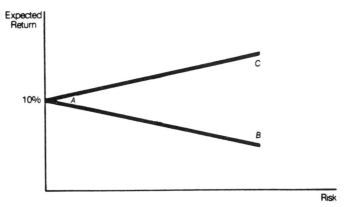

Figure 10-2.   Risk return tradeoff (two-year investment period).

[9]In terms of the stylized risk-return graphs, the subjective process ends when the investor chooses a position on the line connecting A and B in Figure 10-1 and the bond portfolio associated with this risk and return is purchased. Points near A, which should be chosen by conservative risk managers, are no more justifiable than points near B.

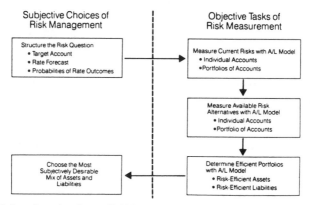

Figure 10-3. Agenda of asset liability management using modern portfolio theory.

Sandwiched between these choices lies risk measurement, where an asset/liability model becomes useful. Risk managers cannot use an asset/liability model to set the context within which risk is to be measured nor can they run the model to select the "best" risk exposure from among the efficient asset/liability mixes. The manager must make all the subjective decisions, the model can only supply objective information. While these statements may appear to be obvious, we find that many banks and thrifts operate as though the model answers both subjective and objective questions. This makes asset/liability committee meetings and reviews of asset/liability models unnecessarily trying and confusing.

Extensions of Modern Portfolio Theory

Many people have criticized the version of Modern Portfolio Theory described above for improperly measuring risk. They note that this approach considers random events that cause returns to exceed expectations to be as grievous as the opposite occurrence. If the securities selected for portfolios have symmetric exposures to random events, then no harm is done by equating risk with variations in return.

However, correlated interest rate risks are normally one-sided in nature. These risks therefore are not symmetric in form, and much of the following analysis is particularly relevant. As demonstrated in Figure 10-4 a bond has roughly symmetric exposure to interest rate increases or decreases. Hence, equating the variation of returns around an expected return with interest rate risk does little harm in traditional bond (fixed-income) security analysis. Some securities have asymmetric interest rate risks and measuring these risks by computing the variance of possible outcomes around an expected value misrepresents important aspects of the interest rate risk.

A call option on a bond provides an example of a security with asymmetric exposure to random events. Suppose this call option is at the money with an exercise price of $100 and can be purchased for a premium of $10.[10] The *purchase* of this option guarantees a minimum return of $-$10. This occurs when interest rates do

[10]The term *at the money* means that the current price of the bond equals the price obtained by exercising the call option.

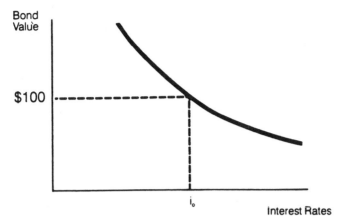

Figure 10-4.   Bond value and interest rates.

not fall from their current levels and the option subsequently expires worthless. (See the heavier line in Figure 10-5.) When interest rates fall, the return on the option equals the appreciation on the associated bond less the $10 premium paid for the option. The sale of this option, rather than its purchase, limits the option's upside to $10 when interest rates do not fall during the life of the option. Losses occur when rates fall that are equal to the gain on the associated bond less the $10 premium received for selling the option.

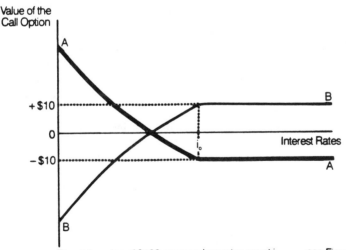

The strike price of $100 occurs when rates are at i_o —   see Figure 4.

The line demarked by As relates the values of a purchased call option to the interest rate level.

The line demarked by Bs relates the values of a written call option to the interest rate level.

Figure 10-5.   Call option value and interest rates (strike price $100).

Clearly options change in value in a somewhat one-sided manner when interest rates rise and fall. Equating variation around the probability-weighted expected return for such a contract inappropriately mixes downside risk "apples" with upside potential "oranges." Financial theorists who have wrestled with this problem suggest that we characterize portfolio returns using three summary measures: expected return, potential for upside variations in returns, and potential for downside variations in returns.[11] Efficient portfolios are now ones that cannot be improved upon in terms of expected return *or* upside potential without an accompanying increase in downside risk.

Because banks and thrifts issue many assets and liabilities with implicit options, a more sophisticated treatment of risk adds value in asset/liability management. For example, loan prepayment rights are essentially call options written into loan contracts for borrowers, and CD redemption rights are put options written for depositors. Loan defaults can be viewed as a form of loan prepayment. For these and other reasons, multidimensional risk measurement should be incorporated into asset/liability models. This topic however, is a chapter in itself. Since the general techniques of risk management in the multidimensional risk expressions of Modern Portfolio Theory follow the general outline contained in Figure 10-3, the delay in a full treatment of this subject does not seriously alter the conclusions of this chapter.[12]

Target Accounts for Interest Rate Risk Management

Most line items on the balance sheets and income statements of banks and thrifts have values that depend on the level of interest rates. The direct and/or correlated interest rate risk of any of these accounts can be studied using the framework presented above. We will examine the market value of equity, the ratio of the market value of assets to the market value of equity (economic leverage), the return on the market value of equity, market value of net interest income, and the book value of net interest income. The first three target accounts relate to balance sheet items and the last two relate to income statement items. This list, while incomplete, allows us to portray the essential ingredients of flexible and comprehensive asset/liability management.

The omission of the book value of equity from the target accounts is noteworthy. Once market and book values diverge, rate risk management of the latter account becomes impossible. The risks of current and to-be-acquired positions in assets and liabilities can be monitored and controlled. But even when past outcomes have yet to be recorded by the accountants, these events cannot be erased through the use of current risk controls. Only current and future economic realities are at risk.[13]

---

[11]A purchased call option has substantial potential on the upside with limited downside risk. A written call has just the opposite.

[12]For further exposition of modern portfolio theory in a multidimensional risk framework applied to bond portfolios, see Richard Bookstaber, *"The Use of Options in Performance Structuring: Molding Returns to Meet Investment Objectives,"* New York: Morgan Stanley (September 1984).

[13]The reason book value of net interest income can be controlled for interest rate risk but not book value of equity will become clear in Section VI. Essentially, the book value of net interest income is a forward looking concept, while the book value of equity is not.

Market Value of Equity.   Three hypothetical components sum to the total market value of a financial institution. They are the market values of portfolio equity, operation equity, and franchise equity. This total also equals the value of the bank or thrift as measured by the stock market.[14] Each of these hypothetical equity accounts has a market value that is sensitive to changes in interest rates.

We define portfolio equity as the market value of currently booked assets less the market value of currently booked liabilities. Portfolio equity can also be considered to be the value of prior contributions by stockholders to acquire the currently booked assets (this represents the principal value of equity's claim) plus the present (time discounted) value of the current and future net interest incomes generated by currently booked values and liabilities. Such a view makes portfolio equity conceptually equal to a "net" bond, one with a series of positive and negative cash flows rather than one with regular and positive cash flows. Operation equity is the present value of net future operating and fee income. The contribution of this component to total equity has grown dramatically in recent years as banks and thrifts have cut operating expenses and increased fee income. Franchise equity is the present value of claims to business not yet booked by the bank or thrift (the economically determined value for goodwill).

A proper asset/liability model should consider all forms of equity in the measurement of risk exposures. If one manages the interest rate sensitivity of the market value of portfolio equity without regard to the interest rate sensitivities of operation and franchise equity, then the interest rate risk of the stock value of the bank or thrift may be inadvertently altered to an undesirable level; the risks in one equity account may offset those in the other two equity accounts. Moreover, a healthy spread in the portfolio may come from extraordinary operating expense, perhaps because of an extensive branch network. The stable access to passbook savings that may result from such a strategy has to be tempered against the sustained payments, which will be interest rate sensitive in their own right, of the supporting operating expense items. Nevertheless, most asset/liability models have concentrated on the interest rate risk of portfolio equity. For expositional convenience we continue this emphasis in this chapter, but do not recommend this approach in practice.

The market value of portfolio equity, an expositional proxy for the total market value of equity, represents an excellent target account for interest rate risk management. Stockholders worry about the value of their investment and its sensitivity to changes in interest rates. In addition, the market value of portfolio equity is a leading indicator of the future book value of an institution. As premium or discounted items mature, book and market values converge. The market value of portfolio equity also includes the present value of all future net interest incomes from assets and liabilities currently on the books. If risk managers reduce the interest rate sensitivity of the market value of portfolio equity, then they reduce the sensitivities of book value and the future stream of net interest income. A final reason may eventually justify the consideration of this target account; regulators have become increasingly concerned

---

[14]For depository institutions operated in the form of a mutual, the total market value of equity equals the stock value expected should the institution convert to a stock charter.

with the capital adequacy of a bank or thrift as measured with mark-to-market accounting.

Structuring the interest rate risk problem for the market value of portfolio equity in the context of Modern Portfolio Theory is quite straightforward. Consider the problem of preserving market value in a simple bond portfolio context. The bond that best preserves market value in a fluctuating interest rate environment has a very short maturity.[15] Longer-term bonds experience increases in their market value when interest rates decline unexpectedly. Conversely, bond portfolios with sufficient short sales to dominate the sensitivities of any long positions decline in value when rates behave in this fashion.

The market value of portfolio equity can be viewed as the present value of the net bond of cash inflows and outflows. Conceptually, the inflows (outflows) arise out of long (short) bond holdings. Only net bonds with interest rate sensitivities similar to an investment in overnight deposits have an asset/liability mix that protects the market value of portfolio equity against changes in interest rates. Thus there is much in common between the interest rate risk measurement of the market value of portfolio equity and that of bond portfolios.

Secondary considerations arise immediately from the analogy of protecting portfolio equity by making its interest rate sensitivity that of a very short-term security. Short-term bonds preserve principal value but introduce the potential for earnings variability into the portfolio. If a bond portfolio manager values earnings stability in addition to principal preservation, then some variability in market value may have to be accepted in order to create tolerable interest rate risks and rewards in another target account. Asset/liability managers have more flexibility than bond portfolio managers, at least those who cannot short bonds, when earnings stability is considered jointly with market value preservation. In essence, liabilities can be managed to shorten the positions taken on the asset side of the balance sheet. Two examples clarify this last statement.

Consider the balance sheet in Table 10-1. The numbers used in this and the subsequent two tables are market values. To simplify the analysis we assume that assets and liabilities pay interest only at maturity and that the one percentage point spread in these interest rates remains constant even though the level of interest rates may change. Later these simple examples will be made more realistic. Table 10-1 pertains to a bank with assets and liabilities that mature tomorrow. As a result, the stockholders essentially own a $10 overnight (net bond) deposit.

Funding of overnight assets by rolling overnight deposits for a year protects the market value of the net bond throughout the year, but this strategy exposes earnings on equity to substantial interest rate risk. For example, suppose interest rates on assets and liabilities fall tomorrow by one percentage point and then remain at these lower levels for the remainder of the year. The resulting net interest income falls from $1.90 to approximately $1.80. The figure in Table 10-1 shows how equity val-

---

[15]Long-term bonds with very frequent interest rate reset dates also provide market value protection against changes in interest rates. We study the interest rate risks of variable-rate contracts more fully later in this report.

Table 10-1.   Balance Sheet Example 1

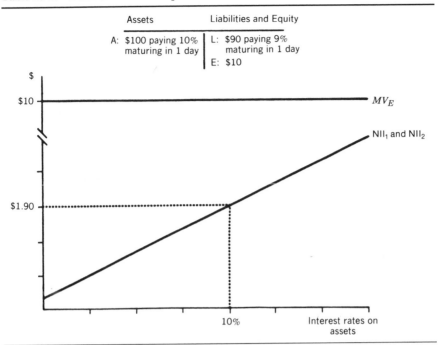

ues and net interest income react to changes in interest rates. The horizontal scale measures the interest rate on new assets. (The rate on new liabilities, by assumption, is that of the assets less one point.) The vertical axis measures net interest income and market value of equity in dollar terms. Note that the rollover strategy produces net interest income next year equal to that for this year when interest rates change once and for all on day one.[16]

Table 10-2 provides an alternative balance sheet that approximately preserves the market value of equity in rising and falling interest rate environments. Here the asset matures in one year and the liability matures in 1.1 years.[17] A single interest rate shock of any magnitude does not alter this year's net interest income. Next year's net interest income is somewhat at risk to this single shock—the asset is repriced 36 days (0.1 years) earlier than the liability in that year. These characteristics are dis-

---

[16]We do not contend that interest rates change in this fashion. If the risks associated with such a simple example can be quantified, however, then the analysis of multiple interest rate shocks is simplified.

[17]These maturity dates cause the interest rate sensitivity of the market value of the $100 asset to equal to close approximation the interest rate sensitivity of the market value of the $90 liability. In Section VI we discuss why the 1.1-year maturity of the liability equates total market value sensitivities of assets and liabilities. In essence we have chosen a longer maturity for the liability to make each dollar's worth of market value more sensitive than a dollar's worth of the asset. This increased liability volatility offsets the fewer number of liability dollars.

Table 10-2.   Balance Sheet Example 2

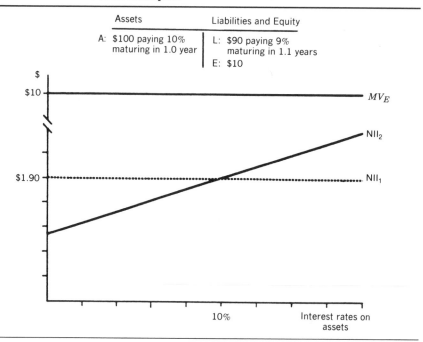

played in the figure drawn in Table 10-2. Also shown is the fact that a sudden change in interest rates does not alter the market value of portfolio equity.

These two simple examples illustrate that it is sometimes possible to achieve multiple risk objectives through proper asset/liability mixes and that risk objectives must be structured as a fundamentally important part of asset/liability management. It is relatively easy to state the interest rate risk goal for one target account, but stating objectives for multiple target accounts disproportionately increases the complexity of risk management. It is just this ability to state multiple and mutually attainable objectives that most dramatically increases the value of the risk manager and his or her asset/liability model.

Economic Leverage (Market value of asset to portfolio equity ratio).   One need not manage the risk of the market value of portfolio equity. Instead, one could choose to manage the economic leverage of the firm. We define economic leverage as the ratio of assets to portfolio equity, both measured in market terms. This ratio also measures the capital adequacy of the bank or thrift in an economic sense.[18]

The interest rate sensitivity of economic leverage depends on the *relative* market value sensitivities of assets and portfolio equity. When the market value of assets

---

[18]The leverage of the firm should be the ratio of assets to total equity. Again for expositional convenience, we have equated total equity with portfolio equity.

and the market value of portfolio equity change in a proportional manner, then interest rates do not affect the current economic leverage of the bank or thrift; that is, if the market value of assets changes by $X\%$ and so does the market value of equity, then the ratio of these two new values equals the original ratio. In the simplified bank example where all accounts mature overnight (Table 10-1), assets and equity have equal (no) interest rate sensitivities. Leverage is preserved when interest rates rise or fall. Alternatively, consider the balance sheet in Table 10-3, where the net bond is a $10 1-year investment. This bond can only fluctuate in value proportionally to the bank's assets, and therefore, economic leverage is preserved. Relative to Table 10-1, this asset/liability mix protects this year's net interest income against changes in interest rates. The market value of equity however is now somewhat more at risk than in either Table 10-1 or 10-2. Figure 10-6 graphs the interest rate sensitivity of economic leverage for examples 1, 2, and 3. In general, when the maturity of the asset equals that of the liability, economic leverage is immune from changes in interest rates. Economic leverage will increase when interest rates rise if the bank or thrift has an asset with a more distant maturity date (more price sensitivity) than the liability. This statement will be explained and generalized in Section VII[19] The mar-

Table 10-3.   Balance Sheet Example 3

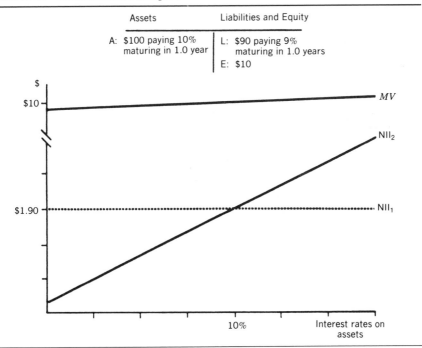

	Assets	Liabilities and Equity
	A: $100 paying 10% maturing in 1.0 year	L: $90 paying 9% maturing in 1.0 years
		E: $10

[19]We have been implicitly equating maturity to interest rate sensitivity in this section. Later we introduce the concept of duration, which more accurately represents the interest rate sensitivity of a security than does its maturity.

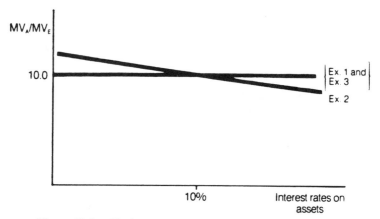

Figure 10-6.   The interest rate sensitivity of economic leverage.

ket value of portfolio equity and economic leverage cannot be hedged simultaneously.[20] We have seen in Table 10-2 that the price volatility of the liability must
exceed the price volatility of the asset to minimize the interest rate risk of the market
value of portfolio equity. We have also seen in Table 10-3 that the price volatility
of the asset must equal the price volatility of portfolio equity to immunize economic
leverage against changes in interest rates. This condition indirectly requires equal
price volatilities—equal maturity dates in our simple example—for the asset and the
liability. Thus it is impossible to immunize simultaneously equity and economic leverage.

Total Return on Equity.   The total return on the market value of portfolio equity
earned over a specific "investment period" is the final equity value target account
considered here. The net bond that is portfolio equity can be managed in much the
same way as any other bond. Banks and thrifts have very long lives, so the notion
of specifying an investment period may be a somewhat foreign concept. In the context of asset/liability management, the risk manager states an investment period not
because he or she expects the firm to cash out at the end of the period, but because
the yields and spreads earned to this point appear to be attractive.

Suppose the yield curve the manager faces looks something like the shape of the
U.S. Treasury curve of July 2, 1984. This is drawn in Figure 10-7. The manager
may believe that 3-year rates (spreads must also be considered) are attractive relative
to longer or shorter interest rates. To the extent possible the manager may decide to
lock in returns available for this period for the owners of the firm. Implicitly, the
risk manager is betting that this rate will be attractive over the period selected. As
time passes this decision will be inspired if rates decline or unfortunate if rates rise
more than expected.

---

[20]The one exception to this statement occurs when all accounts mature overnight. Since no bank or thrift
is in this situation, this exception is trivial.

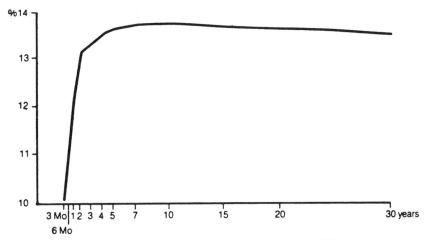

Figure 10-7.   U.S. Treasury yield curve July 2, 1984.

Net Interest Income.   The two remaining possible target accounts relate to earnings over a limited time horizon (for example, the current quarter or year). The first is the book value of net interest income and the second is the market value of net interest income.[21] The book value of net interest income is the contractual interest inflows reinvested to the end of the chosen accounting period at currently *expected* rates less the contractual interest expenses also renewed to the end of the accounting period at currently expected rates. Reinvestment earnings and expenses are adjusted for accrued interest and amortization of premiums or discounts at the end of the period but not for changes in market values. The market value of net interest income adjusts the book value of net interest income for changes in market values of interest-earning or paying accounts. The total return on the net bond that is portfolio equity for the accounting period is nothing more than the market value of net interest income.

We will see that the book value of net interest income can often be risk controlled simultaneously with equity accounts. Indeed, Tables 10-1 and 10-2 began these comparisons. The same cannot be said for the market value of net interest income. Risk control for this account requires that the market value of equity has a specific sensitivity to interest rates that often will be at odds with a different requirement for the control of interest rate risk for target accounts such as market value of equity, economic leverage, or total return on equity for an investment period different from the accounting period over which the market value of net interest income is managed.

Summary

This section has been filled with analogies of banks and thrifts to net bonds. It has suggested that banks may be managed for an investment period. Market values of

---

[21]Extensions to net interest margins are straightforward.

equity prominently figure in the discussion. Admittedly, these concepts have not been used frequently in the past. We have also asserted rather than described how the interest rate risks of these various accounts are controlled.

We hope to have piqued the interest of the reader at this point and nothing more. The analogies to bond portfolio management help establish that the path-breaking work on bond portfolio theory conducted during the last decade has relevance to asset/liability management. We contend that the introduction of issues without the provision of all relevant details at this point is logical. Asset/liability managers must state their goals and target accounts before the risk measurement process begins. Asset/liability models ought to be compared on their abilities to measure the risks of a number of separate target accounts. Any asset/liability structure chosen by a risk manager implicitly has risk exposures for all the capital and income accounts considered in this section. We argue only that these implicit risks be made explicit and be jointly risk controlled. As we will see in Section VII, however, simultaneous control of interest rate risk requires some degree of compromise in practice. The analyses of asset/liability models in the material that follows attempt to determine which model currently permits risk managers to measure risk exposures in the greatest variety of potential target accounts.

SECTION IV   THE MATURITY GAP MODEL

As an introduction to the reader, we first describe the basic maturity gap model. This model was developed in the late 1970s. After this background material has been presented, largely to introduce the jargon of gap models, a "state of the art" maturity gap model will be presented along with its underlying assumptions. The maturity gap model is then critically examined for its ability to measure interest rate risk.[22]

The Basic Maturity Gap Model

The gap model derives its name from the dollar gap (Gap$) that is the difference between the dollar amounts of rate-sensitive assets and rate-sensitive liabilities.

$$Gap\$ = RSA\$ - RSL\$ \qquad (1)$$

To use the model, a bank or thrift must supply four pieces of information. First, the risk manager must select the length of time over which net interest income is to be managed.[23] One year is usually chosen for this "gapping period." Second, the

[22]This section is an extension of research completed during the summer of 1982 when Toevs was a visiting scholar at the Federal Reserve Bank of San Francisco. The result of this preliminary research was published in "Gap Management: Managing Interest Rate Risk in Banks and Thrifts," *Economic Review* (Spring 1983).

[23]Most of the gap literature focuses on managing net interest margin rather than net interest income. Net interest margin is obtained by dividing the book value of earning assets into net interest income. Since very few maturity gap models consider growth in earning assets and because it eases mathematical developments throughout the paper, net interest income rather than net interest margin will be the income account studied. (If one understands the model in terms of net interest income, one also understands it with respect to net interest margin.)

risk manager must decide whether to preserve the currently expected net interest income for the gapping period or to attempt to better it. For the former, the maturity gap model is used to hedge net interest income against changes in interest rates; for the latter, an active (speculative) strategy is adopted. Third, if the risk manager adopts an active strategy, he or she needs to specify an interest rate forecast or a set of probability-weighted forecasts for the gapping period. Finally, the risk manager must determine the dollar amounts of the rate-sensitive assets and the rate-sensitive liabilities.

Rate-sensitive assets are those that can experience contractual changes in interest rates during the gapping period. All financial assets that mature within the gapping period are rate-sensitive. Variable rate assets "repriced" during the gapping period are also rate-sensitive regardless of their maturity dates. Interest income and the periodic return of principal, as on a mortgage, are also rate-sensitive if these flows are invested in new instruments during the period. Rate-sensitive liabilities are similarly defined.[24] CDs maturing during the gapping period, Fed Funds borrowed, Super-NOW, and money market accounts are all rate-sensitive. Because Regulation Q ceiling interest rates are currently binding, regular checking and time deposits are not considered to be rate-sensitive in many maturity gap models.[25]

If the risk manager wishes to hedge net interest income against changes in interest rates, then the basic maturity gap model recommends setting the Gap$ equal to zero. It is argued that this causes a change in interest rates to influence interest income and interest expense equally.

Those banks or thrifts wishing to be more aggressive may actively place net interest income at risk. As one Citibank official noted, "If we don't gap we can't make enough money."[26] An active gap strategy requires the formation of a mismatch between the dollar volumes of rate-sensitive assets and liabilities. The direction of this desired mismatch depends on the interest rate forecast. If rates are expected to rise, the Gap$ should exceed a value of zero. In this case more assets than liabilities will shift into higher earning accounts (should the rate forecast come to pass) during the gapping period. As a result, the net interest income realized exceeds the net interest income that would have been earned had either rates not increased or Gap$ been set at zero. These recommendations, and similar ones for when rates decline, are consistent with the formula

$$E(\Delta \text{NII}) = \text{RSA\$} \times E(\Delta i) - \text{RSL\$} \times E(\Delta i) \qquad (2)$$
$$= \text{Gap\$} \times E(\Delta i)$$

---

[24]One can compute the dollar amount of the rate-sensitive assets and the dollar amount of the rate-sensitive liabilities using either book values at the beginning of the year or the dollar values as of the repricing dates. Both have been used in the literature. On both expositional and theoretical grounds, the second method is preferable and will be used here. The qualitative conclusions, however, do not depend on which of these methods of valuation is used.

[25]Many secondary issues arise on rate sensitivity even in this simple model. Contracts tied to administered rates—like prime loans—are possibly quasi-sensitive. Time and demand deposits may be interest rate sensitive if they are maintained through advertising budgets or provision of free services that increase with the level of interest rates and the threat of deposit disintermediation. For the moment we avoid these issues to build a base on which these important issues can be considered.

[26]See Sanford Rose, "Dark Days Ahead for Banks," *Fortune* (June 30, 1980): 90.

where Δ means "change in," $E(\Delta\text{NII})$ is the expected change in net interest income and $E(\Delta i)$ is the expected change in interest rates. To obtain an expected net interest income greater than the hedged net interest income, that is, a positive expected change in net interest income, one constructs a positive Gap\$ when $E(\Delta r)$ is positive and a negative Gap\$ when $E(\Delta i)$ is negative. To hedge expected net interest income, equation (2) has us close the dollar gap.

One issue remains to be addressed. How are assets and liabilities that are automatically repriced a number of times in the gapping period, such as monthly variable rate loans, treated in measuring Gap\$? A liability or asset is said to be repriced when its contractual interest rates change, as when a maturing account is rolled over into a new account or when rates change contractually, as in a variable rate account. Each such account should be included in the values of either rate-sensitive assets or rate-sensitive liabilities one time, corresponding to the first repricing date provided this date is within the gapping period. This treatment is logically consistent with that given to maturing rate-sensitive accounts. Moreover it is consistent with an important but not often discussed assumption made in *all* gap models: each interest rate change is treated separately and in sequence.

An example helps illustrate the point that logical treatment of interest rate risk causes risk managers to worry about multiple changes in interest rates in a sequential fashion. Suppose the goal is to hedge net interest income. The Gap\$ initially constructed may hedge net interest income only against the first interest rate change. As time passes in the gapping period and the first repricing date on the asset and/or liability is reached, the funds must be redeployed to make the Gap\$, now for the *remainder* of the gapping period once again equal to zero. This procedure positions the bank or thrift to earn the net interest income expected at the beginning of the year, regardless of the direction and magnitude of the first, second, third, and so on, change in interest rates. We need, then, to explicitly consider only one rate change per gapping period to illustrate *any* gap model. We simplify the exposition even further by having the rate change occur before the first asset or liability repricing date in the gapping period.

The logic of this sequential treatment of interest rate changes is maintained throughout the remainder of this chapter. Asset/liability management must address rate changes sequentially. Simulation models often allow risk managers to study the risk exposures of sequences of changes in interest rates. The resulting simulations are informative, but risks cannot be controlled once and for all for bundles of rate changes. The target account is always exposed to the next change in interest rates. Hedging the second change in rates but not the first leaves the target account at risk. Conversely, hedging the exposure of the target account for the first change in rates does not deny the possibility of hedging the second change.

The major problem with the basic gap model is that it computes Gap\$ as the difference between the dollar values of rate-sensitive assets and liabilities regardless of when the assets and liabilities are repriced within the gapping period. All that counts in measuring Gap\$ is that repricing occurs during the gapping period; it does not matter when during the period the repricing occurs or when it occurs first, as in the case of a variable-rate instrument. In the extreme, suppose all the rate-sensitive assets are repriced on day one while all the rate-sensitive liabilities are repriced on the last day of the year. Should the volume of asset repricing equal that for liabilities, the basic maturity gap model would falsely indicate that net interest income is protected from rate changes. For this reason alone the basic maturity gap and equation (2) cannot be relied on for accurate risk measurement.

State-of-the-Art Maturity Gap Model

The newer literature attempts to solve this intraperiod problem by using periodic gap calculations. This is sometimes referred to as the "maturity bucket" approach. This asset/liability model calls for the dollar gap to be measured for each of several sequential time periods (maturity buckets) during the gapping period. Most authors recommend that Gap$ be measured for each 30- to 90-day time increment during the gapping period. We refer to these dollar gaps as the periodic Gap$s. These Gap$s sum to the total of cumulative Gap$ measured by the basic maturity gap model. Take, for example, a bank with a cumulative Gap$ of $12 for the year. This total could arise from any number of different periodic (intrayear) gaps. Several of these periodic gap patterns are depicted in Figures 10-8 and 10-9. The vertical axes in these graphs measure the net asset repricing for the associated month, a month being the assumed maturity bucket.

Suppose that an interest rate shock occurs before any repricing takes place, pattern (a) in Figure 10-8 would have a net interest income realized at year-end that differs from the originally expected net interest income by more than that for pattern (b). Similarly, pattern (b) places net interest income more at risk than pattern (c). The net interest income risk exposure of gap patterns like those in Figure 10-9 are more difficult to assess—an issue we will address in a moment. It should now be clear than any cumulative Gap$ can arise from a large number of different periodic gap patterns. Therefore many different levels of net interest income risk can be associated with one measured cumulative Gap$. Despite the convenience of a single number indexing the risk exposure of net interest income, the basic maturity gap model provides such an ambiguous risk measure that the model proves to be ineffectual.

As time passes within the gapping period, periodic gap$ change in ways that depend upon the characteristics of the rate- sensitive accounts. This becomes important when there are multiple rate changes. For example, pattern (a) in Figure 10-8 could arise either because there is a $12 asset maturing in one month or because there is a 1-year loan with an interest rate reset monthly. If it is the maturing asset, then the bank in month two is as susceptible to rate changes in month two as in the variable-rate loan case only if the maturing asset is rolled over into a 30-day loan. Should the maturing asset be rolled over into a 1-year fixed rate loan, the exposure of this year's net interest income to additional rate changes this year will be zero, unlike the continued exposure under the variable-rate loan scenario. This observation, however, does not alter the fact that each rate change must be addressed separately.

The literature advocating the periodic gap model recommends net interest income be hedged by setting each periodic Gap$ equal to zero. If rates are expected to rise, positive gaps should be put into place; the opposite holds for expected rate declines.

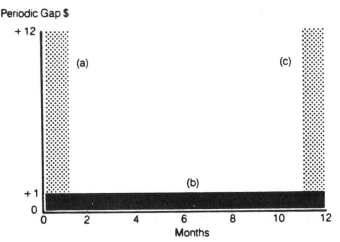

Figure 10-8.   Alternative periodic gap patterns.

The use of periodic Gap$ rather than the cumulative Gap$ increases the probability that net interest income will turn out to be as expected.

There are, however, two common but unnecessary errors made in the measurement of periodic Gap$ that can distort the purported accuracy of this maturity gap model. First, periodic Gap$s are normally measured in such a way that cash flows of interest are ignored and amortizing principal payments are attributed to the maturity bucket that includes the maturity *date* of the instrument. These omissions and false attributions misstate the true repricing date of the assets and liabilities. They arise most frequently from an expedient treatment of the data problems that make more cash flow data costly to obtain.

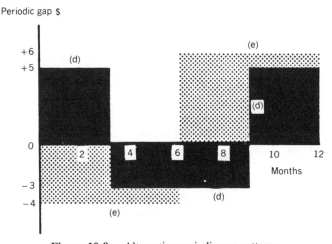

Figure 10-9.   Alternative periodic gap patterns.

The second commonly encountered measurement error in computing periodic Gap$s results from the use of large maturity buckets. Just as with the cumulative Gap$s, each periodic Gap$ will fail to reveal perverse intraperiod repricing. For example, suppose each 90-day periodic Gap$ is zero. Within these quarterly maturity buckets a risk exposure equivalent to 25% of the annual net interest income can be hidden.[27] If 30-day Gap$s are used, as much as one-twelfth of the annual net interest income can be exposed. Continuing along these lines, examples can be constructed wherein each bucket has a positive periodic Gap$ but contrary to our expectations, when interest rates rise we find net interest income decreases.

Binder and Linguist describe a gap model based on daily periodic gap measurements.[28] In exchange for the reduction in the hidden rate risk of bigger maturity buckets, they are forced to use extensive computer simulations to summarize the information content of the numerous periodic gaps into digestible form. Even the chunky and fairly simple gap patterns in Figure 10-9 are difficult to interpret without computer simulations. Thus the more sophisticated maturity gap models often become computer simulation models similar to those we will discuss in Section V.

A major criticism of the basic maturity gap model, in addition to the use of a single maturity bucket, is that it assumes interest rates change with the same magnitude for assets and liabilities of all maturities. (See equation (2).) An overwhelming body of evidence suggests that interest rates on various assets and liabilities change in different magnitudes. The periodic gap literature has handled this issue by assuming that the volatility of the rates in question is in constant proportion to the volatility of some standard interest rate. Empirical studies show this assumption to be reasonably accurate.[29] The next paragraph sketches out the required procedure.

Historical data on the interest rate volatilities of various rate-sensitive accounts are used to estimate proportionality factors that reflect differing average rate changes for the accounts studied. The standard account against which proportionality factors are standardized can be anything, but interest rate futures contracts make convenient benchmarks. Suppose a 90-day T-bill futures contract is selected as the standard. Furthermore, assume that the estimated proportionality factors for 90-day commercial paper and 90-day certificates of deposit are .95 and 1.05 respectively. These numbers indicate that, on average, the commercial paper rate has been 95% as volatile as the rate on the deliverable contract underlying the futures contract while the CD rate has been 105% as volatile. If the bank has a $100 obligation in a 90-day CD and $500 lent in the 90-day commercial paper market, then the apparent 90-day Gap$ is + $400. But taking into account the relative volatilities, the standardized Gap$ is

[27]Suppose the bank has only a $100 loan maturing on day one and an equal amount in a 90-day deposit. The 90-day incremental Gap$ is zero yet net interest income is at risk for one quarter of a year. Note that the risk would be even higher if these accounts roll over and there were multiple changes in rates.

[28]See Barret Binder and Thomas Linquist, *Asset/Liability and Funds Management at U.S. Commercial Banks,* Bank Administration Institute, 1982.

[29]This procedure has been advocated by James Baker, *Asset/Liability Management,* American Bankers Association, 1981 and Kurt Dew, "The Effective Gap: A More Accurate Measure of Interest Rate Risk," *American Banker,* (June 10, 1981, September 19, 1981, and December 9, 1981).

$370.[30] The bank can hedge its current asset sensitivity by purchasing $370 in T-bill futures.

The remaining substantive criticism of the basic maturity gap model, that it pays too little attention to the evolution of net interest income risk exposure as time passes, has also been corrected in more current maturity gap literature. As assets and liabilities mature, they can be reissued in denominations, maturities, and repricing intervals to alter periodic Gap$s that remain in the gapping period; that is, the periodic gap pattern can be dynamically reshaped during the gapping period either towards a more hedged position or a more active one. Suppose the bank has to start the gapping period with a +$1000 Gap$ on day 270. If all other daily Gap$s equal zero and the bank wishes to hedge, it should attempt to reissue maturing rate-sensitive liabilities to remature on day 270 and maturing assets to remature after year-end. If the Gap$$_{270}$ is completely eliminated before rates change, then the net interest income computed at the beginning of the year will have to be hedged. If rates change before the Gap$$_{270}$ is completely eliminated, then net interest income will not have been fully hedged but the risk will have been reduced. Similar treatment can be accorded to expected deposit inflows and the like. The dynamic maturity gap models rely heavily on simulation analysis. As such, they share many of the strengths and weaknesses of more formal simulation models. These simulation models are discussed in Section V.

In summary, the state-of-the-art maturity gap model computes periodic Gap$s over finely demarked time buckets. The outcomes of various interest rate forecasts, given specific periodic gap patterns, are simulated using computers. These periodic Gap$s may have been standardized to reflect differences in the interest rate volatilities of various rate-sensitive accounts. The dynamic evolution of the gap pattern is considered by allowing banks to interrupt computer simulations during the gapping period to restructure rate risk with maturing and new accounts. As such, the model is more complete and theoretically pleasing than the basic gap model.

Advantages and Disadvantages of the Periodic Gap Model

The primary advantage of a periodic gap model is the increased precision with which interest rate risk can be measured relative to the basic gap model. In addition, the periodic gap model is easy to understand and development costs are small. We believe, however, these advantages to be small by comparison to alternative asset/liability models.

The many remaining deficiencies can be grouped into four general categories. First, most versions of the periodic gap model have been developed based on inaccurate or misinformed assumptions. Second, they often lead to the pursuit of too restrictive asset/liability choices in the control of interest rate risk. Third, these

---

[30]The $500 in commercial paper is equivalent to the volatility of .95 × $500 = $475 in 90-day futures. The $100 CD is equivalent to the volatility of $105 in 90-day futures. This method of standardization can be extended to measure the effective periodic gaps at dates other than the maturity length associated with the standard contract. The articles by Kurt Dew cited in footnote 29 hint at how this procedure might work.

models do not provide a single index number quantifying the risk exposure of a target account. Finally, they hinder a risk manager's progress in managing simultaneously the interest rate risks of several target accounts.

Remaining Inaccuracies.   Many vended models inappropriately place net interest receipts and amortizing principal payments in maturity buckets other than those in which these payments are received. Sizable rate risk can also remain hidden in maturity buckets as small as one month. Periodic gap models cannot adequately measure interest rate risk inclusive of correlated risks. Predictable withdrawals of deposits and loan prepayments, for example, seasonal reductions in deposits, can easily be incorporated into gap models. Difficulties arise when the amount and timing of withdrawals and prepayments depend upon the spread between their contractual rates and current market rates. Unexpected changes of this sort can substantially affect realized net interest income, yet the maturity gap literature is silent on the appropriate treatment. Options that have values sensitive to interest rates, which are important in many bank and thrift contracts, receive little or no attention in the gap literature. Some of these problems can be countered by proper programming and data collection, but the result is often such a complex set of data that little information content in summary form is made available.

In addition to data and programming errors, many vendors and users improperly regard net interest income to be protected against unexpected changes in interest rates only when each periodic Gap$ equals zero. As we will show by an example, this hedging condition is unnecessarily strong, many patterns of nonzero periodic Gap$s hedge net interest income. Moreover, these patterns can be found by systematic means rather than by trial and error. Any increase in the number of hedging gap patterns affords more flexibility in risk management.

An example at this point helps to illustrate that some nonzero periodic gap patterns hedge net interest income. Suppose, simply, that all assets and liabilities currently earn or pay interest at 10% per annum. In this example, if the rate-sensitive assets repriced on each day of the year (360 days) equal the rate-sensitive liabilities repriced on the same day, then net interest income would be zero whether or not rates change. Consider now daily Gap$s that equal zero on every day but three: $\text{Gap\$}_{30} = +\$1000$; $\text{Gap\$}_{90} = -\$2000$; and $\text{Gap\$}_{152} = +\$1000$. The cumulative Gap$ for the year is zero. The basic gap model would have us believe we are hedged but the more detailed periodic gap model would seem to suggest otherwise. In this instance however it is the periodic gap model that misleads. Suppose that on day one, just after this periodic gap pattern has been acquired, interest rates generally rise on all accounts from 10% to 12%. Net interest income will change on net only from the influences of the nonzero Gap$s on days 30, 90, and 152. The first such gap causes net interest income by year end to rise by $18.17.[31] The second and third nonzero Gap$s cause net interest income to fall by $29.23 and to rise by $11.05 respec-

---

[31]Given that $1000 more assets than liabilities are repriced on day 30, this bank earns on net for the remainder of the year $100 \times (1.12)^{330/360}$ rather than $100 \times (1.10)^{330/360}$.

tively.[32] These three influences cancel. Moreover, the individual influences of the three nonzero Gap$s will cancel for changes in interest rates occuring in other sizes or direction.

An infinite number of other nonzero gap patterns also hedge net interest income. Like the example above, some have nonzero periodic Gap$s but a cumulative Gap$ of zero. This does not mean that the basic gap model is superior to the periodic gap model. Others patterns of gaps, perhaps like those in Figure 10-9, have nonzero values for both periodic and cumulative Gap$s. The following provides an example where neither of these maturity gap models would indicate the presence of a net interest income hedge when in fact such a hedge exists. Let $Gap\$_{90} = +\$1000$ and $Gap\$_{180} = -\$1536$. The cumulative Gap$ of $-\$536$ indicates, according to the basic gap model, that net interest income rises when rates fall. Let rates fall from 10% to 8%. The influence of the rate change on $Gap\$_{90}$ on net interest income is approximately $-\$14.70$ and the magnitude of $Gap\$_{180}$ is approximately $+\$14.70$.[33] Thus the original level of net interest income remains unaffected in the changing rate environment.

Restrictive Choices in Risk and Incremental Hedging.   The fixation of many users of gap models on closing their positions is troubling. We have just seen that it is unnecessary for all gaps to be set equal to zero to remove current risk exposure. Insisting on such closures by risk-averse managers means otherwise profitable business will be turned away, because it exacerbates current gap problems, with attendant damage to the bank or thrift franchise value and/or superfluous hedging costs. Furthermore, what we learn about flexibile hedging also applies to flexible but active interest rate risk management.

A good asset/liability model should allow interest rate risk to be adjusted incrementally. Risk managers cannot always restructure risk exposures to the most desired levels at an instant in time. In these circumstances the asset/liability model should reveal which incremental adjustments move the current risk exposures towards that desired. The periodic gap model, however, can suggest some transactions that supposedly incrementally alter risk exposures toward more desirable levels but in fact do just the opposite.

Consider Figure 10-10a. This gap pattern has $-\$3$, $+\$2$, $+\$3$, and $-\$2$ Gap$s in the first four quarters. For convenience these numbers are to be interpreted as the values today (present values) of maturing amounts. Also for convenience suppose interest rates for assets and liabilities of any term are 10%. With these assumptions, net interest income for Figure 10-10a in a stable interest rate environment is zero. If interest rates rise to 11% just before the first liability has to be refunded, (we assume all assets and liabilities come due on the first day of the quarter with which they are

---

[32]Equidistant timing of the equal asset (positive) cash flows around the outflow date is not what is required. The inflow of $+\$1000$ on day 152 rather than day 150 is governed by the timing and magnitude of prior cash flows.

[33]We have $-\$14.68 = +\$1000 \times (1.08^{270/360} - 1.10^{270/360})$ and $+\$14.70 = -\$1536 \times (1.08^{180/360} - 1.10^{180/360})$. Note that these two value changes are only approximately equal. The reason for this small discrepancy is well understood but outside of the main topic of this paper.

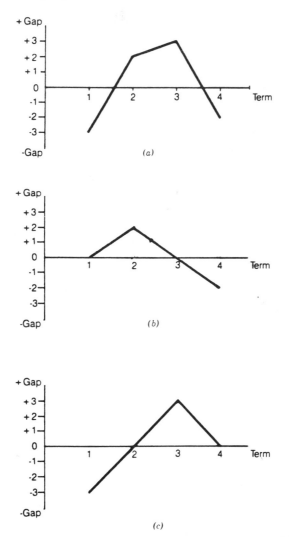

Figure 10-10.   Incremental hedges using maturity gap model.

associated), net interest income falls to $-\$0.005$. This thrift or bank is moderately net-liability sensitive.

The policy prescription of gap management would have us attempt to reduce this interest rate exposure by changing the maturity structure of our assets and liabilities to "plug" the nonzero gaps. Suppose we were able to push the maturity date of the liability maturing in the first quarter into the third quarter. We now have the gap pattern in Figure 10-10b. This gap pattern still has $5.00 in rate-sensitive assets; $2.00 in the second quarter, and $3.00 in the third quarter. There are still $5.00 in liabilities; $3 mature in the third quarter, plugging the third quarter gap and $2.00 mature in the fourth quarter.

The net interest income associated with Figure 10-10b in our 10% world will again total to zero by year end, but what happens if rates rise to 11% just after this asset/liability structure has been put in place? Net interest income will then total + $0.01. Note that by partial gap plugging we have created an asset-sensitive institution out of what was originally a liability-sensitive one.

Consider a different gap plugging strategy. Suppose we move the second quarter's asset of Figure 10-10a to the fourth quarter. We now have the gap pattern in Figure 10-10c. In a 10% world this gap pattern generates zero net interest income, but in an 10% world the result is − $0.015. This increment in gap plugging has tripled the original interest rate risk exposure of the institution.

Risk managers normally look at gap reports with the goal of using current business to offset previously booked risk whenever practical. The three examples were designed to show that offsetting gaps in this fashion need not always produce the desired movements in interest rate risk. This is one of many reasons why maturity gap models may undo as much as they do. Shortly we will reexamine these gap reports using the ''mysterious'' concept of duration to see exactly what happened to cause these perplexing results.

These three examples illustrate an important but simple point: attempts to hedge interest rate risk via gap plugging on an incremental basis will often prove ineffective or worse. Surely, if the quarterly gaps for the year are all positive or all negative, incremental gap plugging will reduce the interest rate risk of this year's net interest income. The risks of such gap patterns are so transparent that even journalists can determine the consequences. Most banks and thrifts are now striving to have more balanced gap patterns, ones that complicate the predictions of interest rate risk exposure. These gap patterns make incremental risk restructuring suggestions derived from maturity gap models ambiguous at best.

The intuitive reason why incremental gap plugging may increase risk rather than reduce it is that the timing of a gap as well as its magnitude influence total risk exposure. The inability of gap models to measure the aggregate exposure in an index form requires the use of computer simulation in instances where risk managers seek accurate incremental adjustments in risk exposure. Thus maturity gap models are weak analytical tools. Without computer simulations little of value can be derived from them.

The Absence of a Single-Index Measure of Risk.   When many maturity buckets are used the periodic gap model does not generate a single number index of the interest rate risk of the bank. The *basic* gap model provides one in the cumulative Gap$, but we have shown that this measure tells us very little. The periodic gap model would be more appealing if such index numbers existed. For one reason, incremental hedging would become less fraught with the potential for error. For another, many asset/liability committee meetings bog down when similarly minded members look at the gap report and come to different conclusions on the risk implied by these gaps. A means to summarize risk exposure into a single number is also required if risk-return tradeoffs such as those discussed in Section III are to be used. These tradeoffs provide clear cut menus of risk exposures helpful for active risk management. Because the gap model does not generate a single number for risk exposure, it cannot easily be used to determine the number of futures contracts that would hedge the overall rate risk of a bank, a calculation of current interest to many risk managers. In its current form the gap model incorporates financial futures in one of three ways, none of which is particularly appealing. One can buy (sell) sufficient futures contracts to "plug" each positive (negative) gap separately. The accuracy of this approach is less than perfect, as the maturity buckets may not correspond with delivery dates on futures contracts. The transaction cost and basis risk are increased by what amounts to be a clumsy hedge, one that does not appropriately net out off-setting hedge transactions. Alternatively, one can use interest rate futures to hedge specific instruments. The individually hedged assets and liabilities are then ignored when periodic gaps are computed. Finally, one can simulate the effect of a futures contract on net interest income in the same way or at the same time the periodic gap pattern's influence is simulated. By trial and error the appropriate aggregate hedge can be discovered. Again, notice how simulations become part of the measurement process.

Other Target Accounts.   Stockholders could quarrel with the dominant concern most periodic gap models devote to net interest income. Stockholders are interested in share values, an important determinant of which is the market value of currently booked assets and liabilities. They wish to position the interest rate risk of their equity based upon their attitudes toward risk and expected return. The maturity gap literature tends to focus on the risk exposures of current earnings more than the risk exposures of the capital of the firm. Periodic Gap$ models often use maturity buckets that begin beyond the first year, and these gaps help measure the interest rate risk exposure of equity accounts. But too often these more distant gaps are gross aggregates. A typical maturity bucket encountered in gap models for distant maturities extends from year two to year five!

Furthermore, gap models do not have the ability to study the risk exposures of economic leverage or total return on equity. We must conclude that gap models do not help risk managers attain multiple risk control objectives.

Term Structures versus Yield Curves

A final issue is logically addressed here, even though the problem does not lie with the gap model per se. Rather it arises because proponents of the model normally suggest risk management take place without information readily available in the term structure of interest rates (the yield curve of zero coupon bonds). These term-specific or spot rates, as opposed to yields to maturity, provide important, but by no means completely accurate information on the course of future interest rates.[34] The implied forecasts derived from this term structure represent the current market forecast formed by consensus in market trading. Since these forecasts are by definition al-

---

[34]The term structure may contain a liquidity premium. This can conceptually be treated as an issue separate from using the current term structure to predict future rate changes. If such a liquidity premium exists and is positive, one would wish to be somewhat shorter in the times to liability repricing than otherwise would be the case. Nevertheless, conditional on the current value of the liquidity premium, the bank's asset and liability position is still one that depends on a difference between the bank's interest rate forecast and the market's.

ready embedded in security prices, a strategy of actively managing net interest income will produce no added value relative to a hedging strategy when interest rates evolve as implied by market prices. To be successful in actively managing net interest income or any other target account, the risk manager must have a better interest rate forecast than the implicit market forecast, not just an idea about which way rates are headed.

The following example illustrates the point made in the last paragraph. Suppose the market "expects" CD interest rates, expressed on an annualized basis, to be 10% for the first quarter, 11% for the second, 12% for the third, and 13% for the fourth. This interest rate pattern gives a 1-year rate of 11.49%.[35] A risk manager looking at these rates might incorrectly infer that this year's net interest income will profit from a gap constructed, say, by booking a 1-year loan of $1000 at 11.49% and issuing a series of 90-day CDs that will roll over with interest every quarter to fund this asset.

Should rates rise as the market expects, net interest income earned for the year will be zero. Given our assumption of the same rate structure for assets and liabilities, this is the net interest income obtained by hedging. (The initial positive carry switches midyear to a negative carry, and it does so in such a way that there is no time-value benefit to the positive spread earned for the first two quarters.) Only if rates are forecasted by the risk manager to fall or to rise by less than the market forecast would this periodic gap pattern yield a net interest income in excess of that originally promised. Active management with any model requires the ability to out-forecast the implied market forecast, not just to forecast the future course of interest rates.

Summary

We have spent considerable time in this section discussing both the basic maturity gap model and its successor, the periodic gap model. While the basic maturity gap model produces an easily interpretable index of the interest rate risk exposure of net interest income, we have shown that this measure is not always reliable. The periodic gap model, which was developed to overcome this problem, does provide more accurate asset/liability repricing information, but the ensuing gap patterns it generates are often difficult or impossible to interpret without the aid of computer simulation. Both models suffer from their inability to identify the more complicated gap patterns that provide hedges of net interest income, resulting in overly restrictive asset/liability alternatives in risk management. Finally, the ability to hedge incrementally using the periodic gap approach is limited as there are instances where the gap model suggests that risks are reduced when in fact the opposite occurs.

SECTION V   SIMULATION BASED ASSET/LIABILITY MODELS

Simulation models are more difficult to describe than maturity gap and duration gap models. All simulation models have been developed for proprietary sale. As a consequence, not nearly as much academic literature exists on the theoretical constructs

---

[35]The one year interest rate of 11.49% is found by evaluating $1.10^{.25} \times 1.11^{.25} \times 1.12^{.25} \times 1.13^{.25} - 1$.

needed in a quality simulation model as exists for other types of asset/liability models. Because simulations take place interactively, additional complications arise. Descriptions of simulation models outside an interactive context create greater expositional injustices than those committed in writing about maturity gap and duration gap models. Finally, simulation models differ radically in quality among themselves, making it difficult to describe a fully representative simulation model.

We have chosen to critique a simulation model that we believe represents the theoretical ideal. Some vendors of simulation models have recently made advances in their software that meet or come close to these expectations. This high- road approach is consistent with that used in Sections IV and VII. Remember that we wish to determine the asset/liability modeling architecture, or the combination of architectures, that offers the greatest *potential* to achieve accurate, convenient, and cost effective interest rate risk measurement.

Description of Simulation Models

Four items govern the accuracy of *any* asset/liability model: the quality of the data, the correctness of the assumptions made by the users of the model, the theoretical correctness of the model design, and the quality of the summary measures of risk exposure derived from the model. Just as in any other asset/liability model, simulations require data on the cash flows of the currently booked assets and liabilities. The more accurate the representation of these cash flows, the more informative the simulations. Remember that unlike the other three items, the quality of the data stands as an issue independent of model selection. We stress this point throughout because some software vendors have found clever and convincing methods of implying that their models require less start up costs than their competitors because their models require less data—normally data on cash flows.

Simulation models employ a fundamentally different analytical technique than that used in maturity gap and duration gap models. Simulations produce their results in a dynamic or forward-looking context, whereas the alternatives produce their results statically. We will comment at length about this difference, but for now it is important to note that dynamic modeling requires assumptions about managerial behavior, probable loan and deposit demands, and the path taken by interest rates that are more detailed than those used by static models. In effect simulation models require this detail because subjective decisions are made over a period of time rather than at one point in time.

Risk managers often rely on information derived from historical studies when they make the assumptions needed by their simulation models. Creators of asset/liability models also use historical studies to form the internal structure of simulation models. Unlike data on currently contracted cash inflows and outflows, which are objective inputs that are processed by the model, historical analyses form part of the model's objective working structure and help risk managers make subjective choices in assumptions that influence simulation outcomes. Figure 10-11 shows how historical analyses become part of a simulation model. The solid arrow shows how historical studies become part of the objective structure of the model, while the dashed arrow shows the course of subjective influences.

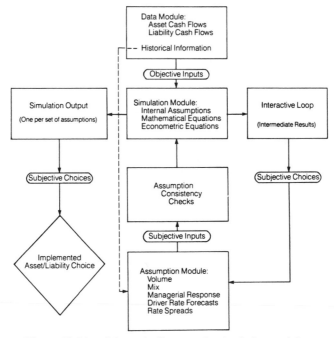

Figure 10-11.   Schematic diagram of a simulation model.

Historical studies contain information risk managers find useful when they make the five key assumptions pictured in Figure 10-11 that distinguish one simulation run from another. The past provides clues on what the volume of business and asset and liability mixes are likely to be during the simulation. For example, the past seasonal variations in demand for loans and deposits normally hold with great accuracy into the future. More difficult decisions face the risk manager wishing to simulate the influences of deposit disintermediation, loan defaults, and loan prepayments. Each of these issues arises in part for reasons independent of interest rates. Historical studies provide valuable information on these events. Deposit disintermediation and the like also occur because of changes in interest rates. No bank simulation model to our knowledge allows such correlated interest rate risks to be modeled properly or directly. Successes and failures of the past also inform risk managers as they adapt to events generated by each simulation. These assumed managerial responses can be programmed into the simulation at the outset or made at stopping points during the simulation process in reaction to the intermediate results of the simulation. (See the interactive loop in Figure 10-11 where the results occuring before the ending date of the simulation are made available to the risk manager so that the current strategy can be tempered during the simulation.) History provides only a clue to what the future might bring. Thus the historical evidence is often used most intensively when the base case, defined below, is simulated. Other case studies use assumptions that the risk manager thinks to be possible but not as reflective of the past.

Risk managers often use historical information to determine the volatility of interest rates. The greater the volatility estimate, the greater the range of interest rate forecasts used in simulations. Experienced risk managers simulate the influences of interest rate forecasts that bracket the possible, not necessarily the probable, range in interest rates. These forecasts should be made for a number of terms to maturity on a particular class of securities. The rates that comprise the U.S. Treasury bond yield curve are often used as the set of ''driver'' interest rates in simulations. This yield curve may be changed by either random or prespecified amounts every 30 to 90 days during each simulation. Historical analyses also help risk managers estimate interest rate spread relationships. By assumption, these estimates convert the changes in driver rates into changes in other interest rates.

The use of historical analyses must be undertaken cautiously. Bank or thrift histories reflect the *combined* influences of past demands for intermediation services and the managerial reaction to them. Past managerial responses should be statistically disassociated from the customer demands bringing forth these responses. Otherwise, the internal structure of the model reflects managerial responses different from those the risk manager wishes to simulate. In addition, assumptions made on the volume and mix of new business that are based on historical studies may misrepresent reality when the interactions between historical demands and managerial decisions have been intermingled.

The volume, mix, managerial response, and interest rate forecast assumptions used in any one simulation must be internally consistent. A module to check for the consistency of assumptions can add significant value to a simulation model. Volume of new loan production should be smaller than average when interest rates are assumed to be prohibitively high and vice versa. As another example, the mix between fixed-rate and variable-rate loan production should reflect the current phase of the simulated interest rate cycle. A final and most important function of this module is to let loan prepayments and deposit redemptions occur at a pace consistent with current and past interest rate levels.

Risk managers who cull out inconsistent assumptions reduce the number of simulations and increase the quality of information made available through simulation. Therefore, cost savings and accuracy justify the inclusion of a module that rejects inconsistent assumptions. The more sophisticated the simulation model, the more assumptions must be made, and therefore the more important the assumption checking module. Unfortunately, we have not seen a vended simulation model effectively screen sets of assumptions for internal consistency.

The simulation module is the heart of the model and is positioned as such in Figure 10-11. The fixed relationships programmed into this module first transform the raw cash flow data into a form consistent with the data on the structure of the institution and the assumptions made about the current simulation. Next, this body of input is transformed into final results using such things as investment pricing equations, tax rate parameters, calculations of net interest income, and the like. The primary output of simulation models used by banks and thrifts is quarter-by-quarter variations in net interest income (margin). Currently available simulation models, even more so than maturity gap models, pay scant attention to the equity value of the firm. When capital issues are addressed at all, simulations of future book values, rather than current market values or economic leverage, are the norm.

Each time one or more of the initial assumptions is changed, a new simulation must be run. Normally the base cases are simulated first. To some risk managers these simulations determine the interest rate sensitivity of the *existing* assets and liabilities. This exercise brackets the risk inherent in the "old" bank. Other risk managers simulate a momentum strategy in their base cases. The momentum strategy combines the old bank with the expected new bank based on the recently experienced volume and mix characteristics to be booked during the course of the simulation. In either approach simulations are run separately for at least high, low, and unchanged interest rate forecasts. No managerial responses are permitted to occur during these simulations. This process establishes the interest rate risk exposure of the bank or thrift when it is managed by inertia.

Base case simulations are often found closeted in maturity gap models. These simulations, usually conducted for the old bank, summarize the interest rate risk exposure associated with the periodic Gap$s. This type of simulation adds value to gap analysis whenever the pattern of periodic Gap$s varies in magnitude and sign. These variations often make it difficult to determine the interest rate risk exposure of the bank or thrift by eyeballing the gap pattern. Momentum strategy simulations are called "dynamic" gap models in the maturity gap literature. In effect, gap analysis quickly becomes simulation analysis. This observation is witnessed in the developmental history of simulation models: many evolved from an earlier incarnation as a gap model.

The next set of simulations studies the possible managerial responses to risks discovered in base case simulations. Risk managers decide whether these risks should be managed through an immediate restructuring of currently held assets and liability positions or through asset and liability allocations made possible through future growth (retrenchment). Simulations designed to study current restructuring choices resimulate the base case in every respect except to alter the cash flow profiles of assets and liabilities to reflect currently executed asset/liability restructuring transactions. Mortgage sales with reinvestment of proceeds, security swaps in the investment portfolio, interest rate swaps, new positions in interest rate futures, and debt issuance are examples of restructuring transactions. Before these new simulations are conducted it is impossible to tell whether the current asset/liability mix is risk-efficient or risk-inefficient, as defined in Section II. Without this knowledge only the most risk-averse manager has sufficient information from base case simulations to manage the institution. Filling out a risk-return tradeoff menu requires many simulations, particularly when one considers that the same level of interest rate risk can be constructed with varying levels of transaction costs, tax liabilities, managerial time, and so forth.

Rather than create the desired risk exposures immediately, managers may choose to accomplish their objectives over time. Simulations designed to study this course of action add a dynamic capability to risk management. These simulations presume that managers can influence the way maturing accounts roll over and the conditions under which new accounts are booked. Clearly the institution remains exposed to unwanted risks during an interim period. The potential cost of this interim exposure may be compensated by lower transaction costs, tax liabilities, and so on. (Regulatory constraints on capital adequacy may also force the bank or thrift into this type of risk control. Book hits from current restructuring may cause capital values to fall short of that required by law.) Again a number of simulations must be used to determine the available intertemporal risk-return tradeoffs.

The next simulations determine what influence unusual violations of the assumptions would have on the interest rate risk of the bank or thrift. This sensitivity analysis tests the reliability of all the previously conducted simulations; that is, have the results of the prior simulations been constructed from a false set of assumptions? A refined set of risk-efficient asset/liability structures has little value if modest changes in the assumptions used in prior simulations produce much different results.

Eventually simulations must end. The next step is to form a set of tidy conclusions on the available asset/liability choices. These choices represent current opportunities to restructure interest rate risk. We suggest that the conclusions be limited initially to a report of the returns on the target account(s) over rising, falling, and constant interest rate scenarios. Thus three possible outcomes are displayed for each asset/liability structure.

From the choices available the asset/liability committee should be encouraged to select a strategy using only the information on the target account's possible returns. Once this task is completed, committee members should study the required asset/liability structure and the details of its implementation. The assumption made in the analysis and the sensitivity tests should also be discussed. This procedure focuses the attention of decision makers on goal setting, streamlines the decision process, and limits the debate to only the most relevant assumptions and implementation procedures.

Decision makers often recoil when the assumptions, sensitivity analysis, and implementation schedule are revealed for the selected course of action. This process of goal definition, followed by reactions to the underlying analysis, properly elevates in importance the goal-setting exercise. It also sharpens the focus of the committee such that the obligatory second round of simulations is limited and final decisions quickly follow.

Advantages of Simulation Models

Simulations confer their primary benefits through their dynamic or forward looking capacity. Management should strive to anticipate future events so that any unwanted risks can be quickly neutralized in advance of or upon their occurrence. Dynamic risk control lessens the role crisis management has played for too long in asset/liability management. While anticipating future events is quite important, future risk exposures are not as important as current ones. After all, a careful driver thinks about what lies beyond the next curve, but not to the exclusion of the process needed to get there.

Simulations increase the value of strategic planning and profitability exercises. They create estimates of quarterly net interest income and currently have an unused capacity to measure capital values on a quarterly basis. Coupled with cash run-off schedules, simulations help managers determine the most cost effective means by which to keep maturing, "hot" dollars in the firm. The timing in this exercise is as important as the methods used (advertising, interest rate changes, etc). These share-of-market simulations can be easily integrated into the interest rate risk control procedure by attempting to roll maturing accounts into new loans and deposits that create more desirable risk exposures than those currently booked. Simulation models also allow inexperienced risk managers to try their strategies, without actual implementation, in a somewhat realistic context.

Simulation models end each simulation with a decipherable output. This contrasts to the output of maturity gap models, which we have intimated often rely on simulations to interpret what the gaps mean. We will see that the output of a duration gap model does not suffer from the ambiguity that pervades the output of a maturity gap model. But both gap models show only a snapshot of current risk exposure. These models give information like that supplied to a driver through the windshield, but neither gap model has the radar detection equipment in the simulation sedan.

Properly constructed base case simulations can measure the static interest rate risk of existing assets and liabilities more accurately than maturity gap models. We will argue later that simulation models *at best* match the accuracy with which static risk exposures are measured in duration gap models. The superiority of simulation over the maturity gap comes from two sources. Simulations of the old bank base case produce unambiguous statements such as, "When interest rates rise by 50 basis points, net interest income increases (decreases) by Y." Maturity gaps cannot so succinctly bundle the interest rate risks of individual maturity buckets.[36] Good simulation models use full detail on cash flows and therefore more accurately capture the influences of the timing of cash flows than maturity gap models, which tend to lump cash flows into artificial time buckets that destroy some of the available information on the timing of these cash flows.

Disadvantages of Simulation Models

In the past, simulation models have been unpopular because of their extensive use of computer time and hardware. Simulations depend on assumptions and data analyses that place strenuous demands on the person who structures these simulations. Erroneous assumptions, inconsistencies in the assumptions, and inappropriate interactive management decisions disguise risks and bias results.[37] The person running the model must be punctilious yet have an accurate and comprehensive perspective of the firm. Otherwise the simulation model is in the hands of the wrong person and the conclusions become highly suspect. These models, more than any other, reflect

---

[36]As Kurt Dew puts it, "the volatility of income in each 'time bucket' is treated as though it was independent of variations in income in every other time bucket." "Which Asset-Liability Management Model?" *American Banker* (February 14, 1984): 30.

[37]The module in Figure 10-11 that checks the assumptions in even the best simulation models will only catch flagrant inconsistencies.

in their results the quality of the operator. Unfortunately, the mundane operating details of simulation models often frustrate the very staff members capable of managing the simulations, and the skills needed are highly valuable in other parts of the bank or thrift.

Simulation models are black boxes. While some vendors disclose the equations used in the simulation module, few allow users to modify this structure. This approach is understandable as it protects the integrity of the product, but it prevents users from altering any assumptions they discover to be inappropriate for their management regime.

All simulation models rein in computer costs and inexperienced risk managers by making a number of decisions for them. These internally programmed and often undisclosed assumptions may differ from those relevant to a particular user. In these instances an unmodified model simulates the risks of an unknown bank or thrift. To minimize this risk a bank that acts like a thrift should purchase a simulation model developed by companies specializing in thrift problems, and vice versa. Simulation models that attempt to satisfy the needs of any institution may produce results that reflect none.

Just as with macroeconomic models, the integrity of asset/liability simulation models depends on the reasonableness of the individual equations *and* the cohesion of these equations. All simulation models have the potential to look reasonable upon examination of individual components, but give uncharacteristic results in practice due to an inconsistent fusion of these components in the simulation module. This penchant for looking reasonable but behaving otherwise is troubling. Even the thoroughly researched macroeconomic simulation models are openly admitted to be potentially unstable.

Simulations generate an enormous body of output. Something of value can be learned from any simulation run. But the current risk exposure of a bank or thrift becomes nearly as difficult to synthesize out of an extensive set of simulations as it is out of too few simulations. One might say that the person capable of running the right number of simulations and pasting the results together into the concise form needed in asset/liability committee meetings is a person who has prior and complete information about these risks. Anyone without this omniscience must wade through piles of computer output searching for a set of representative but partial truths.

The problem of digesting enormous amounts of output does not end when current risk exposures have been established. Asset/liability choices must be analyzed. Suppose the base case simulations reveal an undesirable asset sensitivity. Current choices to reduce this sensitivity include a long futures position, a floating for fixed asset-based interest rate swap, a swap of short-term for long-term investments, and issuance of CDs with the proceeds invested over a longer term than these liabilities. The implications of each risk-altering strategy must be simulated to determine the most cost effective means of altering current risk exposures. More than one simulation is needed per risk control technique to determine how extensive the asset/liability restructuring must be to alter the current risk exposure to the desired level. On net, simulations solve problems by trial and error. The better the risk manager, the fewer simulations needed to converge on the most desirable course of action.

Incremental hedging is possible through simulation analysis, but again the process is clumsy and computer intensive.

As time passes, the internal structure of simulation models frequently becomes inconsistent with economic reality. More so than alternative models, simulation models become dated. We mentioned earlier that simulation models extensively use econometric (statistical) analyses on historical data to obtain forecasting equations that become part of a simulation module. Given the nature of their derivation, these forecasting equations are most accurate when history repeats itself—when we have a nonextreme situation in a familiar environment. Now many people concede that financial markets changed radically after October 1979, yet many simulation models use forecast equations that have been estimated with data from before and after October 1979. The simulations from these models reflect an inappropriate blend of old and new realities. Thus the simulation models can become most suspect when risk assessments become most valuable, times when the bank or thrift faces new circumstances within new environments.

Current simulation models concentrate their attention on net interest income or net interest margin to the exclusion of other important target accounts. Earlier we gave reasons why a risk manager should be concerned about the market value of equity, economic leverage, and the total return on equity. None of these target accounts is simulated properly in currently available models. Some will simulate the time path of the book value of equity. If base case simulations from these models are run until all assets and liabilities currently with book values different from market values mature, then some information becomes available about the interest rate risk of capital accounts. This method is extremely tedious in comparison to duration gap models, and suspect because the accuracy of simulations deteriorates as they extend in time.

We have one final warning. Base case simulations are often run with interest rate forecasts that change several times during the time period simulated. If multiple changes occur during a period over which an interim output is computed (e.g. yearly net interest income when rates are allowed to change monthly), then multiple shocks for some asset/liability structures may reveal no risk where risk is present. It is just hidden by coincidence in the particular pattern of interest rate shocks and cash flows.

Table 10-4 illustrates this point with a simple example. The bank earns 10% on assets and pays 10% on liabilities. The old bank consists of two liabilities with face values of $542 and $656 maturing on days 1 and 181, respectively, that will be renewed for illustrative purposes as 2-year CDs. The two assets are also zero coupon bonds that will be renewed as 2-year notes. They mature on days 91 and 271. If the forecast used to simulate net interest income for the first year calls for no change in interest rates, the bank earns no net interest income. Now suppose interest rates are forecasted to rise 50 basis points per quarter and the simulation model makes these rate adjustments on the first day of each quarter. The particular asset and liability structure in our example, coupled with this rising rate forecast again results in a zero net interest income. This signals that no interest rate risk is present. The same thing happens if the forecast is for rates rising at 20 basis points per quarter. Indeed net interest income remains at zero if rates are forecasted to fall by 50 basis points per

Table 10-4. Base Case Simulations for Net Interest Income

	Quarter 1	Quarter 2	Quarter 3	Quarter 4	NII
Cash flows	− $542	+ $1050	− $656	+ $152	N.A.
Forecast 1	10%	10%	10%	10%	$0.000
Forecast 2	10–10.5%	10.5–11%	11–11.5%	11.5–12%	$0.000
Forecast 3	10–10.2%	10.2–10.4%	10.4–10.6%	10.6–10.8%	$0.000
Forecast 4	10–10.5%	10.5%	10.5%	10.5%	− $0.251

[a]The discrepancy between Forecast 4 and the other forecasts is small. We have not searched deliberately for large errors, only simple ones that can be easily replicated by the reader. The danger of simulation models, improperly used to compute base case risk, is present in unknown quantities. To avoid measurement risks of this kind, one should simulate risk exposures to a single change in rates.

quarter. But one cannot unambiguously draw the conclusion from these simulations that net interest income has been effectively hedged against interest rate risk. The only proper way to measure risk is to determine the sensitivity of the target account to a single interest rate change. The risk is then measured unambiguously. Let rates rise on day one, but only then, by 50 basis points. We now discover that the bank is asset sensitive. This is the appropriate risk exposure; any other characterization is a function of the forecasts chosen and the peculiar cash flow pattern of the bank or thrift.

What has happened is that an asset and liability structure has been put into place that hedges two very specific sets of interest rate changes (Forecasts 2 and 3). The probability of an economist predicting with confidence the direction, let alone the magnitude of four quarters' worth of interest rate changes, is slight. No one really wants to install the structure that hedges this exact pattern. But it is our experience that nine out of 10 users of simulation models fall into the trap of simulating and then hedging complex and improbable interest rate scenarios.

Summary

We find the dynamic approach of simulations useful and appealing. Simulations help managers anticipate the timing of future events (e.g. seasonal deposit disintermediation), and prepare managers to neutralize unwanted aspects of these events. Simulations increase the value of strategic planning and profitability exercises. As a training tool, simulation models are unparalleled. The outcome of any single simulation run is also easily decipherable by senior management. Indeed, maturity gap models often resort to simulations to quantify the interest rate risk contained in the current pattern of periodic gaps. Finally, it is possible to construct incremental hedges with less chance of error than in maturity gap models.

Several disadvantages limit the usefulness of simulation models. They cost more to run than maturity gap and duration gap models. They measure *current* risk exposures clumsily and with conclusions that make risk adjustments a trial and error exercise by comparison to the duration gap model to be described in Section VI. As simulations solve problems by trial and error, often a thorough examination of current risks generates enough paper to equal the weight of the computer operator. Synthesizing these outcomes into a form digestible by an asset/liability committee requires great skill. The staff of the asset/liability committee must be more able than the staffs in banks and thrifts that use alternative asset/liability models.

Simulation models are black boxes. The internal structure of these models often fails to reflect the bank or thrift being simulated. Of particular importance in this regard is the penchant of many model developers to embed assumptions in the model to reduce computer costs and the number of errors committed by inexperienced users. Purchasers of simulation models should ask to see the internal structure of the model and the set of assumptions directly incorporated by the model. Vendors should be questioned to determine if they are willing to alter these assumptions to reflect more closely the characteristics of the buying institutions.

Sophisticated simulation models rely heavily on econometric analyses. These statistical procedures estimate parameters of forecasting equations that comprise part of the simulation module, and are used by risk managers when they make the assumptions that distinguish one simulation run from another. The reliability of these parameters declines when the current structure of financial markets remains the same but events within this regime are extreme. They also decline when the structures of financial markets change, as they did in October of 1979. Thus the results of simulations become suspect when they are most needed. Other asset/liability models do not use extensive econometric analyses and have fewer problems in this regard.

Simulations focus on net interest income (margin) to the exclusion of capital accounts. This limits the ability to manage the interest rate risks of a series of important target accounts such as the market value of equity and economic leverage. At least rudimentary analyses of these risks should be demanded as an output by users of simulation models.

SECTION VI   THE DURATION CONCEPT

We have included this section and its accompanying appendix to introduce and define the duration concept. Readers familiar with the basics of duration can proceed to Section VII where an asset/liability model using duration is developed. Those readers who are less familiar with duration may find the following discussion helpful. We define duration in a somewhat more intuitively appealing manner than that found so often in academic journals and the trade press. Our approach does not supplant these alternative and more sophisticated definitions. Rather it supplements them by helping readers understand the simple idea behind this often mysterious concept. In this Chapter we have refrained from providing the complicating details needed to derive the full advantages of duration analysis.

Appendix I gives the simplest mathematical formula for duration and explains the logic of its form. This material is reprinted from the main text of a recent Morgan

Stanley publication on the general uses of duration.[38] We avoid dwelling on the mechanical details of duration calculations in this and the following section. Our intent is to determine whether or not these details are ultimately worth knowing. We feel the answer can be provided without much time spent handling a calculator.

We first illustrate the duration concept in the simplest of situations, a zero coupon bond. Next we discuss the meaning of the duration of a coupon bond. This discussion then is generalized to cover portfolios of bonds. Problems caused by differential aging of bond maturities and durations, referred to as duration drift, close this section. These basics allow the concept of duration to be applied to bank and thrift target accounts in Section VII, where the duration gap model is studied in detail.

The Duration of a Zero Coupon Bond

The simplest fixed-income security is a zero coupon bond.[39] Once an oddity, corporations are issuing these pure discount instruments in growing numbers, investment banks have created popular zeros by unbundling U.S. Treasury bond cash flows for sale in the stripped coupon market, and the U.S. government has recently caught on to all this activity and has issued its own zeros, sort of, in its STRIPS program.

Figure 10-12 depicts the obvious cash flow profile generated by a 4-year zero coupon bond. If this bond is held to maturity, the investment period is immunized against all changes in interest rates during the period. The bond does not throw off cash before maturity, which would require coupon reinvestment at uncertain future interest rates, nor does it have remaining life at the 4-year point. The former means the bond has no reinvestment risk and the latter means the bond has no price risk over a 4-year period. This bond is interest rate risk free when held to maturity. If the bond should be sold before maturity, however, the investor becomes subject to price risk. If the bond is held beyond four years, through reinvestment of the face value received in four years, the investor becomes subject to reinvestment risk. The shorter the investment period, the greater the price risk. Beyond four years, the longer the investment period, the greater the reinvestment risk. The date when price and reinvestment risks balance, by both being zero, is four years. This date is marked as the duration point in Figure 10-12. We will see that every security has a duration point, that is, a point in time when these two sources of risk offset each other.

Equation (3) gives an interesting relationship for the *instantaneous* price risk of a zero coupon bond:

$$\text{percentage change in market value} \approx -[M/(1 + i)] \times \Delta i \times 100 \qquad (3)$$

This equation says that the percentage price risk of a zero coupon bond maturing in M years equals, to close approximation, the term to maturity of the bond divided

---

[38]See "Uses of Duration Analysis for the Control of Interest Rate Risk," (New York: Morgan Stanley, January 1984).

[39]Duration analysis is most frequently used in portfolios of fixed income securities. Stocks, leases, and other securities also have durations that can be combined with those for bonds, mortgages, etc.

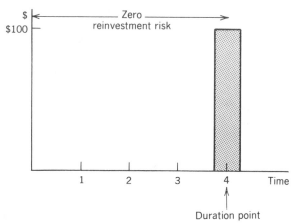

Figure 10-12. 4-year zero coupon bond.

by one plus the interest rate i times the change in interest rates.[40] Suppose our 4-year zero coupon bond has a current price of $68.30. This price implies a 4-year yield of 10% per annum.[41] If interest rates fall to 9% just after the bond is purchased, equation (3) has us believe that the bond instantly rises in value by $+3.6\%$, which means a price rise from $68.30 to $70.78. The actual price rise needed for the bond to yield 9% over four years is from $68.30 to $70.84. The difference of $.06 is in part explained by rounding and in part by the approximation inherent in equation (3). The reader should not be too troubled by this error, for it is small, and as we will see, it can be minimized further.

Equation (3) can be expressed in dollar terms rather than percentages. If both sides of equation (3) are multiplied by the current market value of the zero coupon bond, the equation becomes

$$\Delta \text{market value} \approx \frac{\text{market value} \times (-M)}{1 + i} \times \Delta i \qquad (4)$$

where Δmarket value means the dollar price change in the market value. Equation (4) is often more useful than equation (3). To illustrate its use suppose the interest rate falls from 10% to 9%. The 4-year zero coupon bond experiences a price rise of about $68.30 \times (-4/1.1) \times (-0.01)$, or $+$2.48$.

The Duration of a Coupon Bond

A coupon bond is not as conceptually clean as a zero coupon bond. A 4-year bond with a 10% annual coupon and a market value equal to par has the cash flow profile

---

[40]The interest rate, i, used in equation 3 is expressed in decimal terms so multiplying by 100 in equation 3 is needed to convert the expression to a percentage.
[41]This means that $68.30 \times 1.1 \times 1.1 \times 1.1 \times 1.1 = 100.

given in Figure 10-13. One view is that this bond is a bundle of four zero coupon bonds. If held to maturity, this bond subjects the investor to reinvestment risk from the uncertain reinvestment of the early cash flows (zero coupon bond maturities). The bond's 4-year investment period return improves when interest rates rise but declines when interest rates fall. In this sense the coupon bond acts in total like a zero coupon bond with a term slightly *shorter* than four years. If the investment period is shorter than four years the reinvestment risk of the 4-year coupon bond has an offset. The bond will have remaining life at the end of the investment period. Should rates rise (fall), the unexpected gain (loss) from coupon reinvestment is offset to a degree by the capital loss (gain) from selling the remaining life of the bond.

For any bond, the shorter the investment period, the smaller the reinvestment risk and the greater the price risk. At some date short of the bond's maturity date, one risk exactly cancels the other. Therefore, the interest rate risk characteristics of the zero coupon bond that matures on this magical date has been fabricated with a coupon paying bond. Figure 10-13 indicates that 3.49 years must pass before the reinvestment risk of a single interest rate change is sufficiently large enough to offset the price risk for the remaining life of the 4-year coupon bond. If the investment period corresponds to the 3.49 year duration point, then the 4-year coupon bond "immunizes" the return on original investment over this period against a change in interest rates.

The interest rate protection afforded by matching duration with the amount of time in the investment period is transitory for coupon bonds, but the protection available from a 3.49 year zero coupon bond lasts the full 3.49 years. This important difference in protection can be minimized by periodically rebalancing the coupon bond portfolio to maintain the offset between price and reinvestment risks. Before we begin discussing portfolio rebalancing techniques needed to protect the return on a portfolio against multiple changes in interest rates, we will study another bond example to draw some general conclusions on coupon bonds and their zero coupon bond equivalents.

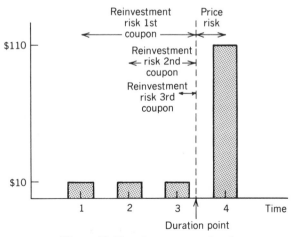

Figure 10-13.   4-year coupon bond.

Just as the 4-year coupon bond has net price and reinvestment risk equivalent to a 3.49-year zero coupon bond, a 5-year coupon bond with a 10% coupon and a market price at par has a 4.17-year zero coupon bond equivalent. That is if purchased and held for 4.17-years, an initial surprise in interest rates will have a cumulative reinvestment income gain or loss sufficient to offset the loss or gain on the sale of the remaining 1-year life of the bond. See Figure 10-14.

One interpretation of duration should be growing clear: it is the amount of time that must pass before the reinvestment effects of a sudden change in interest rates offsets the price risk of selling the remaining life of the bond. Duration is measured in increments of time (months or years) and represents the maturity of the zero coupon bond with equal interest rate risk for the investment period of concern.[42] That is, if the 4-year coupon bond discussed above was purchased by an investor with a 4-year investment period, the investment period return is as subject to a sudden change in interest rates as if a 3.49-year zero coupon bond had been purchased. This investment strategy is more risky than either the 4-year zero coupon bond, which has no interest rate risk, or the 5-year coupon bond, one with a duration closer to four years than the 4-year coupon bond.

Instantaneous Price Sensitivities of Coupon Bonds

Recall that equations (3) and (4) provide indexes of the instantaneous price response of a zero coupon bond to a change in interest rates. Since we argued above that each coupon bond has a zero coupon bond equivalent, would not equations (3) and (4) hold for coupon bonds? They do apply to close approximation for coupon bonds

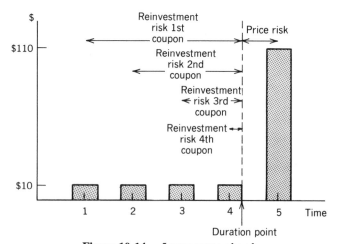

Figure 10-14.   5-year coupon bond.

---

[42]By definition a zero coupon bond has a duration equal to its term to maturity. The maturity date of a zero coupon bond is the point in time when reinvestment risk completely offsets price risk.

provided the duration of the bond is substituted for M in these equations and the interest rate used in these equations for coupon bonds is their yield to maturity. That is

$$\text{percentage change in market value} \approx -[D/(1 + i)] \times \Delta i \times 100 \qquad (3a)$$

$$\Delta \text{market value} \approx \frac{\text{market value} \times (-D)}{1 + i} \times \Delta i \qquad (4a)$$

where Δmarket value means the dollar price change in the market value. Suppose we invest \$67.20 in par valued 5-year bonds paying 10% annual coupons.[43] If interest rates fall from 10% to 9%, equation (3a) suggests the immediate price gain amounts to 3.79%; equation (4a) expresses the same result in dollar terms—a price increase of \$2.55. These results are the same as those obtained for the 4.17-year zero coupon bond. Using actual bond pricing formulas the true price change is 3.88%, or a price increase from \$67.20 to \$69.81. Notice that the price change for the 5-year coupon bond is more closely aligned with the 4-year zero coupon bond, which experiences a 3.64% price change, than with a 5-year zero coupon bond, which has a price gain of about 4.5% under these circumstances. Duration standardizes the instantaneous price sensitivity of any cash flow stream into the maturity of a zero coupon bond with comparable interest rate sensitivity. In this regard it is a more accurate method of standardization than one based on the maturity dates of bonds.

Figure 10-15 pictures our prior analyses in a slightly different way from that used in Figures 10-12, 10-13, and 10-14, which depict reinvestment risk and price risk relative to the duration date. This represents the first use of duration, a measure of interest rate risk over an investment period. Figures 10-12, 10-13, and 10-14 cannot illustrate the instantaneous price risk of these bonds, which is also measured by the duration concept.

Figure 10-15 illustrates the instantaneous price risk and the effect of reinvestment, but not the price risk experienced at the duration date, for our two coupon bonds. The solid line represents the growth in value of an initial \$67.20 investment in any security yielding 10%. Suppose rates rise by one percentage point just after \$67.20 of our 4-year coupon bond is purchased. The price falls, according to equation (4a), to about \$65.07, a loss of \$2.13. This loss is comparable to that experienced on an investment in a 3.49-year zero coupon bond. Offsetting the loss in value on the 4-year coupon bond is a quickening reinvestment of coupons in the higher interest rate environment, and in a mark-to-market setting, the amortization of the new \$2.13 discount. The quickening of asset growth causes the initial loss to be recouped by 3.49 years, the duration date. (See the lower dotted line in Figure 10-15.) Now suppose rates fall by one percentage point just after the bond is purchased. The price of our 4-year coupon bond instantly rises to about \$69.33. Subsequent reinvestment income and amortization of the new \$2.13 premium cause our \$69.33 investment to

[43]We use a \$67.20 investment to make price sensitivity analyses comparable to a 4.17 year zero coupon bond yielding 10% with a face value of \$100.

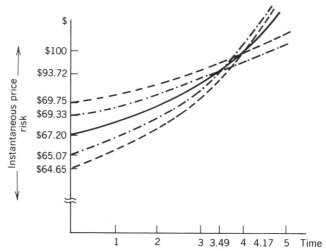

Figure 10-15.   Time profile of investment returns to a single interest rate change. A $67.20 investment compounded for 3.49 years totals $93.72. A $67.20 investment compounded for 4.17 years totals $100.00. The dashed lines indicate the investment growth profiles of a 3.49 year duration bond when interest rates rise or fall by one percentage point just after the investment of $67.20 is made. The dotted lines indicate the investment growth profiles of a 4.17 year duration bond when interest rates rise or fall by one percentage point just after the investment of $67.20 is made.

grow less quickly than before. The original growth path is once again attained at the 3.49-year duration point, now along the upper dotted line in the figure.

The growth paths for the 5-year coupon bond (4.17-year duration bond) are also traced in Figure 10-15 using dashed lines. The 5-year coupon bond growth paths are roughly equal to what would be obtained from a 4.17-year zero coupon bond.

The Additivity of Durations

Appendix I develops the mechanics of calculating the duration for a coupon bond. It is shown that the duration formula implicitly treats each of the cash flows from such a bond as an individual zero coupon bond. The resulting formula amounts to little more than an average life calculation for the individual zero coupon bond maturities, where this average is computed using the prices of these hypothetical zero coupon bonds. Since these hypothetical prices are present (time discounted) values of the cash flows, duration is an average maturity calculation that preserves information on the timing of the cash flows in both its maturity and value calculations.

This view of duration as a weighted average indirectly illustrates the "additivity" property of duration. The duration of two or more bonds can be found the long way by writing down the combined cash flows from the portfolio and applying the duration formula in Appendix I to these cash flows. A short- cut method of computing portfolio duration takes the price weighted average of the durations of the individual bonds, be they zero coupon bonds or coupon bonds. Equation (5) gives the appropriate formula:

$$D_i = \frac{(P_1 \times D_1) + (P_2 \times D_2) + (P_3 \times D_3) + \ldots + (P_n \times D_n)}{W} \qquad (5)$$

Here, the prices, durations, and total portfolio value are represented by P, D, and W respectively, and P_i and D_i represent the prices and durations of the bonds in the total portfolio. Suppose we invest \$100 in our 4-year coupon bond and \$200 in our 5-year coupon bond. The duration of this portfolio is (\$100/\$300) $\times$ 3.49 years + (\$200/\$300) $\times$ 4.17 years = 3.94 years.[44] This bond portfolio has an instantaneous price sensitivity much like that of \$300 invested in a 3.94-year zero coupon bond. To illustrate this fact, compare the instantaneous price effect of a one percentage point fall in interest rates on this portfolio to the price effect experience on a 3.94-year zero coupon bond. According to equation (3a), one-third of the portfolio experiences an instantaneous 3.17% gain in value and the other two-thirds experience an instantaneous 3.79% gain in value. The average gain therefore is 3.58%. This equals the price gain expected on a 3.94-year zero coupon bond using equation 3. If the portfolio is held for 3.94 years, then we also know that an initial change in interest rates leaves the cumulative total return unaffected after 3.94 years have passed.

Duration Drift

We mentioned in earlier sections that interest rate risk cannot be controlled in general unless the exposure to the very next rate change can be controlled. The analysis above shows how the duration concept helps risk managers measure the instantaneous price risk, and the risk exposure of investment period returns for this type of interest rate movement. We are now ready to examine how the investment period return can be controlled for multiple changes in interest rates.

The risk of several changes in interest rates must be controlled sequentially. The use of duration analysis becomes somewhat complicated because of the problem of duration drift. This problem is most easily illustrated by the influence a single interest rate change has on an initially duration-matched portfolio when this change occurs late in the investment period. Suppose a 4.17-year investment period was initially immunized by the purchase of a 5-year coupon bond with a 4.17-year duration. If interest rates do not change until just before the end of this investment period, an investment strategy of reinvesting all coupon flows back into the same bond will not protect the investment period return. The rise in interest rates causes a price decline on the now 0.83-year bond, but the rate change occurs so late in the investment period that reinvestment earnings provide no offset.

A bond that initially mimics one zero coupon bond eventually acts like a different zero coupon bond because the duration of a coupon bond changes over time in a

---

[44]Add \$300 in 6-year coupon bonds with a duration of 4.79 years to this portfolio and the total portfolio duration becomes (\$100/\$600) $\times$ 3.49 + (\$200/\$600) $\times$ 4.17 + (\$300/\$600) $\times$ 4.79 = 4.37 years.

nonlinear fashion. It drifts away from the duration of the original zero coupon bond. If interest rates do not change, an original 5-year coupon bond with a 4.17-year duration becomes in one year a 4-year coupon bond. However, the duration of this bond is not 3.17 years. This is unfortunate because the 4.17-year zero surely becomes a 3.17-year zero coupon bond, and this bond has a 3.17-year duration. As we saw earlier, a 4-year par bond with a 10% coupon has a 3.49-year duration. Thus our specific example, which has a 1-year shorting of maturity on the coupon bond, causes a reduction of only 0.68 years in duration. At the end of the next year, the now 3-year coupon bond has a 2.74-year duration: maturity shortens again by a year but duration declines by only 0.75 year. These differences accumulate so that in 4.17 years the original 5-year coupon bond has a duration not of zero, but of 0.83 years.

Portfolio managers must periodically rebalance their investments to fabricate or track the desired zero coupon bond investment as time passes. The rate of duration drift depends upon the maturity and coupon rate of the bond in question. It is highest for long-maturity, high-coupon bonds. Zero coupon bonds experience no drift; their durations, which always equal their terms to maturity, decline in lock step with maturity. Appendix I contains a graph illustrating the duration drift caused by the passage of time for bonds of various coupon rates and maturities. The rate of drift is also influenced by interim changes in interest rates. (This effect becomes particularly noticeable and troublesome for callable (prepayable) securities.)

Table 10-3 in Section III (above) illustrates duration drift, allowing interest rates to change several times as the investment period passes.[45] This table shows that with proper management, initially by reinvesting early coupon flows in short-term securities and later by rebalancing transactions, duration drift can be minimized so that the portfolio ages in its interest rate characteristics much as the initially equivalent zero coupon bond. Surely there is more management time and effort involved with using coupon paying bonds to do what zero coupon bonds are better at. This expenditure is made, therefore, only when secondary considerations are present. For example, the yield derived from using coupon bonds in a duration-matched strategy may be higher than available from a more ideally matched zero coupon bond. The enhanced yield must be sufficient to cover the extra effort involved with coupon bonds and the slight residual interest rate risk that remains with this strategy.

Summary

This section has introduced the concept of duration in what we hope readers have found to be an intuitively appealing manner. We have shown that any series of cash flows has a duration. We have also shown that duration has two distinct interpretations. First, it is the amount of time that must pass for the influence of a sudden change in interest rates on cash flow reinvestment to offset the price effect of this change in interest rates on the *remaining* cash flows. Second, duration indexes the *instantaneous* change in the market value of a cash flow series due to a change in

---

[45]"Uses of Duration Analysis for the Control of Interest Rate Risk," (New York: Morgan Stanley, January 1984): 10-13.

interest rates, to the term to maturity of a zero coupon bond with comparable instantaneous price sensitivity.

We have also briefly discussed in this section the problem of duration drift. As time passes the initial equality of durations of two separate cash flow series tends to drift apart. This holds particularly for a cash flow stream that initially matches the duration of a single cash flow. Thus tracking over time the interest rate sensitivity of a particular zero coupon bond with a stream of cash flows requires more than just once setting the duration of this stream of cash flows equal to the duration (maturity) of the zero coupon bond.

SECTION VII   THE DURATION GAP MODEL

We minimize the mechanical details in the following discussion of the duration gap model by using several simplifying assumptions. First, the bank or thrift is presumed to have one coupon bond as an asset. Second, the purchase of this asset is assumed to be financed by the sale of another coupon bond and by an equity contribution. Third, both the asset and the liability pay 10% coupons and both securities have market values equal to par.

After we develop the duration gaps for several target accounts, we discuss the possibility of simultaneously obtaining desired levels of risk exposure in these target accounts.[46] We limit the discussion of target accounts to the market value of equity, economic leverage, total return on equity, market value of net interest income, and book value of net interest income. Next come extensions of duration analysis to assets and liabilities with difficult-to-project cash flows, for example, demand deposits. This is followed by a comparison of the advantages and disadvantages of the duration gap model.

The Duration Gap of Equity

Suppose the asset owned by the bank or thrift is a $100 investment in a 5-year coupon bond which has a duration of 4.17 years, and the liability is a $90 issue of a 4-year coupon bond which has a duration of 3.49 years. The equity holders of the bank or thrift have a claim to the net cash flows from these two bonds. The discounted value of these net cash flows is, as we should expect, $10—the market value of portfolio equity. Using equation (5), which defines the additivity of durations and which ap-

[46]Prior applications of duration to asset/liability management can be found in G. O. Bierwag; G. G. Kaufman, and Alden Toevs "Management Strategies for Savings and Loan Associations to Reduce Interest Rate Risk," in *New Sources of Capital for the Savings and Loan Industry,* Fifth Annual Conference, Federal Home Loan Bank of San Francisco, 1979; G. O. Bierwag and Alden Toevs, "Immunization of Interest Rate Risk in Commercial Banks and Savings and Loan Associations," *Bank Structure and Competition,* Federal Reserve Bank of Chicago, 1982; and Alden Toevs, "Gap Management: Managing Interest Rate Risk in Banks and Thrifts," *Economic Review,* Federal Reserve Bank of San Francisco, Spring 1983. Sanford Rose has popularized the duration concept in a series of articles appearing in *American Banker.* See in particular his columns of October 9, 1983 and February 14, 1984.

plies to positive and negative cash flows, we obtain a *net* portfolio duration for equity of ($100/$10) × 4.17 years + (− $90/$10) × 3.49 years = 10.29 years.

The duration of equity is quite long, longer in fact than the duration of the asset or the liability. Its length indicates that the net bond that is equity is a highly levered purchase of an asset with a high-price volatility funded with a less-price volatile liability. More specifically the 10.29-year duration of equity indicates that the market value of equity has about as much sensitivity to a change in interest rates as a 10.29-year zero coupon bond. To confirm this analogy suppose interest rates rise from 10% to 11%. The value change in the bank's asset, according to equation (4a), is about − $3.79. Similarly, the liability has a market change of about − $2.86. Since a drop in the market value of the liability works in favor of the owners of the bank or thrift, the net change in equity value is − $0.93. This instantaneous change in the value of equity equals what we would have obtained by using equation (4a) for a $10 investment with a duration of 10.29 years. Remember that equation (4a) gives an approximate price change so that in reality equity will fall by a somewhat different amount than − $0.93. The exact change in equity derived by using an exact bond pricing formula is − $0.90.

Suppose we switch the asset security with the liability security. Now the additivity characteristics of duration give an equity duration of − 2.63 years.[47] This negative valued duration has a straightforward interpretation. The net bond that is portfolio equity has higher-price sensitivity on the liability side than on the asset side. An increase in interest rates reduces the amount the bank owes its creditors more than the amount owed the bank by its borrowers. Thus unlike the normal relationship between bond prices and interest rates, the net bond that is equity *increases* in market value when rates rise. Let the interest rate rise from 10% to 11%. The asset falls by about $3.17 while the liability falls by about $3.41; consequently the value of equity *rises* by $0.24. This rise in value is consistent with that obtained using equation (4a) using an equity value of $10 and a duration of − 2.63 years.

Some institutions have negative net market value. The same duration analysis applies. For example, suppose we have $90 in assets and $100 in liabilities. If the asset is our 4-year coupon bond and our liability is our 5-year coupon bond, the owners of the institution are short (owe) a net bond with a duration of + 10.3 years. When rates rise the market value of a positive duration bond falls; but since we are short this net bond, equity value rises from − $10 toward zero. If we switch the characteristics of our asset and liability bonds, the short net bond has a duration of − 2.63 years. This situation is the most odd of all—a negative value for both duration and equity. Because the duration is negative in value, the net bond rises in value when interest rates rise, but because our equity position is a short sale this change in interest rates results in an added loss to the bank's market value of equity.

These examples for positive and negative net worth institutions illustrate that the institution's net portfolio can have a duration of almost any value. This net bond duration indexes the interest rate sensitivity of the portfolio claim on the bank by equity holders. The greater the magnitude of the duration, either in a positive or neg-

[47]This duration is found by computing ($100/$10) × 3.49 + (− $90/$10) × 4.17.

ative direction, the greater the interest rate exposure. A short positive or negative duration does not mean the institution will expire in the near future. It merely indicates that the equity of this institution has little current market value exposure to changes in interest rates. A negative duration also does not indicate a failing institution, only an institution that will gain market value when rates rise.

The duration gap of portfolio equity measures the departure of the measured duration from a value of zero. It is defined as $DG_E = D_E$. Other target accounts have other duration gap measures, none as simple. The consequences of a duration gap can be calculated as follows by using equation (4a):

$$\Delta MV_E \approx MV_E \times [-D_E/(1 + i)] \times \Delta i = MV_E \times [-DG_E/(1 + i)] \times \Delta i \quad (6)$$

Here ΔMV_E means the dollar change in the market value of equity, D_E is the duration of equity and Δ_i is the change in interest rates. This is an extremely powerful equation. In a simple index form it quantifies the interest rate risk of the target account. The larger the duration gap, the greater the risk. If a bank has a duration gap of $+2$ and a thrift with equal net worth has a gap of $+4$, then the thrift is twice as exposed to changes in interest rates as the bank.

There is another way of expressing equation (6) that has some value:[48]

$$\Delta MV_E \approx [MV_L \times D_L/(1 + i) - MV_A \times D_A/(1 + i)] \times \Delta i \quad (7)$$

This more complicated expression is useful because it expresses the duration gap as a difference between the value-weighted durations of the assets and liabilities. When risk managers attempt to alter their current risk exposures, knowing how much the duration of either the assets or the liabilities must change to close the duration gap of equity can be useful. For example, suppose we have $100 in assets with a duration of 4.17 years, and $90 in liabilities with a duration of 3.49 years. We know from equation (7) that equity will be made interest rate insensitive if $MV_A \times D_A = MV_L \times D_L$. We also know that the former multiplication equals 417 and the latter equals 314. If we solve for the duration of assets that makes $MV_A - D_A = MV_L \times D_L$, we find it to be a duration of 3.14 years. Similarly, a change of the duration of liabilities from 3.49 years to 4.63 years would also close the duration gap.

Equation (7) helps risk managers hedge incrementally. In our simple example, we know that the asset duration currently exceeds the 3.14-year duration needed to make equity insensitive to changes in interest rates. Any transaction that moves the asset duration closer to 3.14 years reduces the risk exposure of equity. Unlike the problems encountered when attempting to hedge incrementally with the periodic gap model of Section IV, the duration gap method correctly reveals whether or not a transaction helps the manager reduce risk incrementally. This difference in abilities, which later we illustrate with a specific example, is attributable to the ability of duration to preserve information about the timing of cash flows.

---

[48]This equation implies that $D_E = (MV_A D_A - MV_L D_L)/MV_E$ which is fully consistent with the equation that expresses the additivity of duration—equation 5.

Equations (6) and (7) can be used to generate risk-return frontiers for the target account. First, the risk manager forecasts several changes in interest rates for each equity duration gap considered. Next, equation (6) or (7) is used to find the dollar gain or loss in the equity position. These outcomes are then probability-weighted and summarized in a form much like Figure 10-16. Note that the position on the risk-return frontier is determined by the duration gap of equity. The riskless position has a duration gap of zero. Equity positions with positive duration gaps are the efficient choices in this graph. Positive duration gaps will be efficient (for positive net worth institutions) only when the probability assignments on interest rate forecasts favor falling interest rates. The larger the duration gap, the more aggresively positioned is the net bond to benefit from declining interest rates. If the probability assignments predominantly favor rising interest rates, then the efficient net bond portfolios have negative durations.

Thus far our analysis has concentrated on the market value of portfolio equity to the exclusion of operations equity and franchise equity. These two hypothetical equity accounts equal the present values of net operating income, which could be negative, and income to be derived from assets and liabilities not yet booked due to the goodwill and strategic advantages of the firm. These additional equity values combine with the market value of portfolio equity to total the stock value of the bank or thrift. The cash flows that comprise operations equity and franchise equity have durations, and the interest rate sensitivity of stock values depends upon the combined interest rate sensitivities of all three equity accounts. Normally the duration of franchise equity is quite long, much like a consol bond's duration.

Operation equity may also have a high duration. To make the interest rate sensitivity of bank stock small, the combined durations of all sources of equity must be short. A negative duration for the market value of portfolio equity may be the only means to accomplish this end.

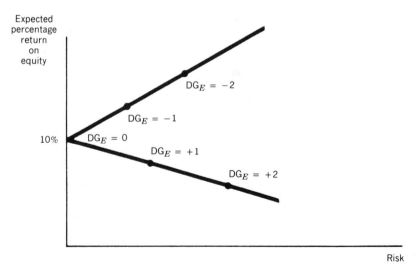

Figure 10-16.   Risk-return tradeoffs for the market value of equity.

The Pseudoprecision of Duration

It is hard to forecast cash flows associated with operation and franchise equity. Other extensions discussed below also call upon the ingenuity of risk managers. Throughout this section we attempt to show how extensions of the most basic interest rate risk problem can be handled straightforwardly in the duration framework. Unlike the alternative asset/liability architectures, duration can mechanize within a consistent framework many of the difficult interest rate measurement problems faced by banks and thrifts. This does not mean that the risk manager must take the route suggested by a duration model in every instance, for he or she may have insights that cannot be directly incorporated into any approach to asset/liability management. The pseudoprecision of a duration gap model, or any other asset/liability model, should not be allowed to limit the artful skills of a good asset/liability manager. Rather it should help the risk manager state the objectives to be obtained and summarize the information that is quantifiable. From these results the risk manager can add more value from his or her insights into the more qualitative aspects of risk control.

In the discussions to follow on risk measurement of economic leverage, net interest income and other target accounts, we continue to use simple asset and liability structures to illustrate risk measurement procedures. Only option and default-free securities with known maturity dates are used in these examples. This focuses attention on the duration concept but ignores important secondary issues, which include the application of duration to:

1. Securities not traded on secondary markets
2. Securities that have ambiguous maturities, for example, demand deposits and prepayable loans
3. Interest rate futures, interest rate swaps, and other popular vehicles designed specifically for altering current exposures to interest rates, and
4. Instances when the yield curve is not flat or does not shift in a parallel fashion, both of which have thus far been implicitly assumed in our simple balance sheet examples

The duration gap approach to these secondary issues is to make the best informed assumptions about the influences these issues have on the cash flows of the bank or thrift. These adjusted cash flows are then included as useful, but not necessarily perfect, pieces of information in the model. Proponents of this approach argue that ignoring a particular problem manages the problem through implicit assumptions that may be more erroneous than those explicitly stated. In addition, they argue the learning curve of management by inactivity falls below the alternative.

Duration Gap of Economic Leverage[49]

The issue of capital adequacy is currently very much in the news. Regulators express growing concern about the insufficient capital bases of many banks and thrifts. While

[49]This target account was first proposed by G. G. Kaufman, "Measuring and Managing Interest Rate Risk: A Primer," *Economic Perspectives* (January/February 1984).

minimum capital requirements are currently set in terms of book values, regulators have recently expressed interest in market-valued ratios. These ratios can be target accounts within the duration gap framework. In the following discussion we examine the issue of capital adequacy in terms of economic leverage, the ratio of the market value of assets to the market value of portfolio equity. Converting this analysis to the capital-to-asset ratio, measured in market value terms, is straightforward. (For reasons similar to why the book value of capital cannot be hedged, financial ratios computed with book values cannot be hedged.)

Asset-to-equity ratios remain unchanged only when both elements in them either remain unchanged or change proportionally. That is, when interest rates cause the market value of assets to increase by 1%, the market value of portfolio equity must also increase by 1% for the asset-to-equity ratio to remain unchanged.

Recall from equation (3a) that the percentage change in the market value of any security depends upon the duration of this security. Thus the duration of equity must equal the duration of the assets to immunize economic leverage against changes in interest rates. The duration gap for economic leverage is the duration of equity less that of the assets. That is, $DG_L = D_E - D_A$. This gap helps determine what percentage change in economic leverage will occur when interest rates change:

$$\text{percentage change in } (A/E) \approx \frac{(D_E - D_A)}{1 + i} \times \Delta i \times 100 = \frac{DG_L}{1 + i} \times \Delta i \times 100 \quad (8)$$

As the magnitude of DG_L increases so does the interest rate risk of economic leverage. In absolute terms the change in economic leverage is [50]

$$\Delta(A/E) \approx (A/E) \times \frac{D_E - D_A}{1 + i} \times \Delta i = (A/E) \times \frac{DG_L}{1 + i} \times \Delta i \quad (9)$$

Consider the implication of these two equations for a bank with $100 in a 4.17-year duration asset and $90 in a 3.49-year duration liability. This bank, which we examined earlier, has a duration of equity equal to 10.29 years. Thus the value for DG_L is 6.12 years. Suppose interest rates rise by one percentage point. The mismatched durations of the asset and equity result in equity experiencing a percentage decline in market value in excess of that experienced on the asset. We saw earlier that the asset loses about 3.79% ($3.79) and equity loses about 9.3% ($0.93) in response to a 1% rise in rates. Equation (8) indicates that the percentage change in economic leverage is about 5.6% when rates rise by 1%, and equation (9) indicates that the leverage increases from 10.00 to about 10.56.

Equations (8) and (9) can be reexpressed in terms of asset and liability durations. These new formulas help risk managers determine how much asset and/or liability restructuring must be accomplished to alter current risk exposures toward the desired level. Incremental hedges, which follow unambiguously from the duration gap for economic leverage, are more easily studied with the alternatives to equations (8) and

---

[50]The derivations of equations (8) and (9) are given in Appendix II.

(9). These expressions have mathematical forms that are more difficult to interpret intuitively than equations (8) and (9). Therefore, they have been relegated to Appendix II.

Equation (9) can be used to form risk-return tradeoffs for economic leverage. An example of such a tradeoff for our simple bank is given in Figure 10-17. This figure was derived assuming that rate increases are more likely than declines. Our current position is at Point A. The greater likelihood of a rate rise than a rate decline causes our bank to be more likely to increase in leverage than decrease in leverage. This positions us on the upper leg of the risk-return tradeoff. (Had our probability assessments favored rate declines, we would find ourselves on the lower leg.) The "inefficient" portion of this type of risk-return tradeoff depends on the objective of the institution. The upper leg of Figure 10-17 is efficient if the bank or thrift ultimately wishes to become more levered. More likely, however, is the case that losing on an interest rate bet is not the desired way to increase leverage. This argues for the lower leg being viewed as risk-efficient. If the duration of assets is lowered to 3.49 years, the duration of equity also becomes 3.49 years and DG_L equals zero. Alternatively, if the duration of the liabilities is lengthened to 4.17 years, the duration of equity falls to 4.17 years, and again DG_L equals zero. Economic leverage in either case becomes protected from changes in interest rates.

Comparing the duration gap for the market value of equity ($DG_E = D_E$) and the duration gap for economic leverage ($DG_L = D_E - D_A$), it is easy to see that interest rate risk cannot be simultaneously hedged for both target accounts except in the unlikely event that the duration of assets, liabilities, and equity all are zero. Otherwise the duration of equity cannot simultaneously equal zero and the duration of the assets. Unfortunately for risk-averse executives, interest rate risk in one target account must be endured to attain a hedge in the other. This realization does not witness a fault in the duration gap approach to risk measurement. No model permits simultaneous hedging in these target accounts. The duration gap model, however, indicates this fact more clearly than alternative models.

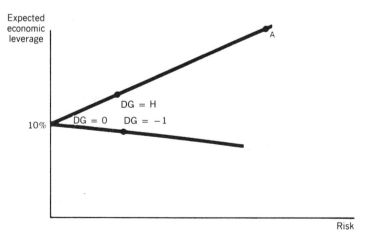

Figure 10-17.   Risk-return tradeoffs for economic leverage.

Tradeoffs must be made. Each institution will be sensitive to interest rate risk, more so in one target account than another. Suppose, for whatever subjective reasons, the institution wishes to hedge leverage. Therefore, the equity account is exposed to interest rate risk. A prudent manager would wish to leave this account exposed in a way that benefits from the most probable move in interest rates. Like it or not, risk managers who concern themselves with multiple target accounts must take some interest rate bets. All risk managers need continual access to high-quality interest rate forecasts.

Total Return on Equity

The total return on any bond over an investment period can be immunized against changes in interest rates provided that the duration of this bond initially equals the term of the investment period and is periodically adjusted to counteract duration drift. This hedging regime also applies to the net bond that is portfolio equity.

Consider our simple bank with $100 in a 4.17-year duration asset and $90 in a 3.49-year duration liability. Suppose we wish to lock in the currently available 1-year total return on equity. This return is $1.00; at the end of the year the asset produces $10 in earnings and remains at par and the liability requires $9 in payments and also remains at par. If rates rise from 10% to 11% on day one, the 1-year total return falls significantly below $1.00. The rate increase causes about a $3.79 loss on the asset. The remaining $96.21 can be thought of as being reinvested in a bond paying 11% so that at the end of one year the total return for the asset is $6.79.[51] Similarly, the liability loses $2.86 in value and in essence becomes invested in an account paying 11% after this loss. The total 1-year return on the liability is $6.73. Thus equity's total return is $+$0.06. This gain results even after the instantaneous loss of $0.94 on the market value of equity (found from applying equation (4a) to the equity position, which has a duration of 10.29 years) because the remaining $9.06 in market value of equity earns at an 11% rate.

Clearly a 1-year total return of $+$0.06 falls much below our initial expectation of $1.00. This difference arises because interest rates increased when the duration of equity was much too long to protect the expected 1-year total return. Suppose the asset chosen had a 3.24-year rather than a 4.17-year duration. The duration of equity becomes one year. The change in interest rates causes an instantaneous loss on the asset of only $2.95. The liability still loses $2.86 in value. Hence the market value of equity falls to $9.91 rather than $9.06. This new equity value earns 11%, not 10%, and by year end grows to $11.00, a total return of $1.00 on a base investment of $10.00.

The duration gap for immunizing total returns on the market value of equity is $DG_{TR} = D_E - H$ where H is the holding or investment period over which the risk

---

[51]This total return presumes only one interest rate change takes place during the course of a year. If we can manage one rate change, however, we can manage many. Also we need not ''reinvest'' the $96.21 in remaining asset values. The new asset price implies a yield on a mark-to-market basis of 11% per annum. The total asset return after one year is found by taking $96.21 \times (1.11) - $100 = $6.79.

manager wishes to lock up the currently available return. When one year is selected as the length of the investment period, the risk manager's target account is net interest income measured in market terms. Whatever the length of the investment period, when DG_{TR} equals zero, the duration of equity equals the time in the investment period and the total (market-valued) return on equity over the investment period is immunized. If this duration gap is positive, interest rate increases cause the total realized return to fall below what could have been immunized, and vice versa.

The duration of equity needed to hedge the total return on equity differs from the duration needed to hedge the market value of equity, and it often differs from the duration needed to hedge economic leverage. The risk-averse manager must therefore make compromises in meeting his or her hedging objectives on these target accounts. Active risk managers also cannot attain desired risk exposures on all these target accounts. Risk-return tradeoffs can be constructed for any target account, including the total return on equity, using the relevant duration gaps. These risk-return tradeoffs become particularly valuable when risk managers have to make compromises in their target account risk objectives. At a minimum the collective set of target account objectives becomes one of ensuring that no target account has inefficient exposures to interest rate risk.

Net Interest Income

Included in the discussion on the total return on equity was the duration gap needed to measure the interest rate risk of the market value of net interest income. The hedging condition was shown to be an equality between the duration of equity and the length of time in the accounting period over which net interest income is measured. The remaining target account to be considered in this section is the book value of net interest income. By this we mean the amount earned from currently booked assets plus reinvestment of these earnings to the end of the accounting period, minus the interest expense—booked plus refinanced to the end of the accounting period. The values at the end of the accounting period, however, remain unadjusted for changes in market values.[52] This account is the one most frequently followed by risk managers, bank stock analysts, and so on.

Appendix III contains the mathematical developments that give rise to the duration gap of net interest income. (Henceforth net interest income should be taken to mean the book value of net interest income, and one year should be taken to be the accounting period over which income is to be measured.) We begin the development by stating what net interest income would be if interest rates do not change unexpectedly within the year. We next restate net interest income in general terms for

[52]The book value of net interest income, but not the book value of equity, can be hedged. The latter is a static concept and hides any prior losses or gains in equity's true economic value. The book value of net interest income is the amount expected at the end of an accounting period. Losses on this target account occur only during the coming accounting period, by definition none are already realized but not yet booked by the accountant. This difference, which is the normal one between balance sheet and income statement items, helps explain the apparent paradox between abilities to hedge book value related accounts.

cases when rates change unexpectedly. The final step determines the overall combination of assets and liabilities that balance changes in interest income with those of interest expense. This combination immunizes net interest income from unexpected changes in interest rates.

The asset and liability structure needed to protect the book value of net interest income requires that the weighted sum of the market values of all rate-sensitive assets equals the weighted sum of all rate-sensitive liabilities.[53] The weights equal the time from cash receipt to the end of the year. A bank with three rate-sensitive asset cash flows occuring on days 30, 180, and 270 all with a market value of $50, and rate-sensitive liability cash flows currently valued at $90 and $60, which occur on days 147 and 180 respectively, has equal rate-sensitive asset and rate-sensitive liability weighted sums:

$$\$50(330/360) + \$50(180/360) + \$50(90/360)$$
$$= \$90(213/360) + \$60(180/360)$$

If these weighted sums were unequal, net interest income would be exposed to changes in interest rates. The level of risk grows with the divergence of these weighted sums. While the weighted sums use the market values of rate-sensitive cash flows, this does not mean the associated target account is the market value of net interest income. Rather the mathematical developments in Appendix III give rise to this requirement for hedging the book value of net interest income.

The duration gap for the book value of net interest income (DG_{NII} is the difference between the weighted sums of the rate-sensitive assets and the rate-sensitive liabilities. Appendix III shows that these weighted sums can be expressed as the total market value of the rate-sensitive assets multiplied by the amount of time in the accounting period (one year) less the duration of the rate-sensitive liabilities. That is,

$$DG_{NII} = MV_{RSA} \times (1 - D_{RSA}) - MV_{RSL} \times (1 - D_{RSL}) \qquad (11)$$

The intuition behind this duration gap can best be described using the following equation, which is also developed in Appendix III.

$$\Delta NII = DG_{NII} \times \Delta i \qquad (12)$$

This equation indicates that the dollar change in net interest income approximately equals the duration gap for net interest income multiplied by the change in interest rates. If the duration gap is positive, then an increase in interest rates improves net interest income. In maturity gap terminology the bank or thrift is net asset sensitive.

---

[53]Rate-sensitive refers to the cash flows occurring during the year. This includes the principal value of variable-rate accounts, which can be thought of as being returned to be repriced. Only the first repricing date is included for variable-rate contracts. We are hedging the next change in interest rates, not multiple changes, in keeping with our (theoretically correct) sequential approach to interest rate risk control.

A negative duration gap for net interest income indicates a net liability sensitive bank or thrift. Equation (12) also indicates that the exposure of net interest income grows proportionally with the duration gap.

For the duration gap of net interest income to equal zero it is sufficient, but not necessary, that the market value of rate-sensitive assets equals the market value of rate-sensitive liabilities and the duration of the rate-sensitive assets equals that of the liabilities. The equality of market values is not unlike having the cumulative dollar gap of the basic maturity gap model equal to zero. The equality of durations reminds us that equating volumes of repricings is not enough; timing is also important. The earlier in the accounting period the assets are repriced, the more influence a dollar's worth of rate-sensitive assets has on the interest rate exposure of the target account.

If the rate-sensitive asset and liability cash flows match exactly, then the duration gap for net interest income equals zero. But the duration gap measure indicates that such a strict fulfillment of the hedge condition is unnecessary. Net interest income is also hedged when the market value of rate-sensitive assets equals the market value of rate-sensitive liabilities, and the *average* repricing date (duration) for the assets equals the *average* repricing date (duration) for the liabilities. Equal durations and market values indicate that the rate-sensitive assets act as though they are all invested in an account maturing at the duration date of these assets, and a similar amount of liabilities also act as though they all mature on this date.

Another Intuitive View of Duration.   Imagine being the manager of a professional basketball team. Currently the best team in the league has a most unusual characteristic: each player scores 20 points in every game. One winning strategy would be to find players who each score 25 points in every game, but such a strategy may not be best. The search costs for this unique set of players would be high, as would the salary structure.

An alternative strategy, one with a lower search cost and salary structure, would be to find players who each score 25 points a game on average over the course of the season. The first team strategy guarantees the league championship. The second gives a very good chance, but no guarantee. The benefits of certainty must be weighed against what could be high costs.

The analogy between team management and asset/liability management is straightforward. Risk managers attempt to find the assets that match the liabilities (or vice versa). These assets can exactly match the cash flow obligations or they can do so on average through duration-matching techniques. Matching on average will take extra time but added returns are available.

Think again about the role of a manager of a quirky basketball team. The true value of a manager comes from determining how long to play those having scoring slumps, when to rest players on a roll, and so on. Good managers justify high salaries by making informed decisions on these matters.

The enhanced yield derived from duration matching comes from the ability to accomplish the interest rate risk goals of the firm by selecting from a broader set of assets than those capable of cash flow matching the liabilities. Duration matching is not a free lunch. More management time is required and residual interest rate risk, the sources of which will be discussed in a moment, are present. Thus in some instances duration matching pays and in other instances it does not.

In extreme applications duration matches can be created with grossly mismatched cash flows. Managers in this instance are akin to basketball managers who have teams that score 10 points per player in every game in the first half of the season but reach a 25-point player performance for the season by exhorting players to 40 points per game efforts in the second half. All too often such managers see the second half of the season from the bleachers, not courtside.

Examples of Duration Gaps for Net Interest Income.   Several examples that were first described in Section IV illustrate the duration gap for net interest income. The details are contained in Table 10-5. Example A was used in Section IV to show that contrary to popular belief, not all periodic gaps must equal zero for net interest income to be hedged. In this example the rate-sensitive market values and durations equal one another: the $1953 in market valued rate-sensitive assets act as though they are all repriced in 90 days and the single liability of equal market value surely has the same repricing date. Thus the duration gap equals zero even though rate-sensitive assets do not cash flow match the rate-sensitive liabilities.

Example B also has a duration gap of zero. Unlike Example A this one does not have a zero-valued cumulative maturity gap. It also differs from Example A because the duration gap equals zero even though the volume of rate-sensitive assets does not equal the volume of rate-sensitive liabilities, nor do their average repricing dates (durations) equal.

Example C has the periodic gap pattern graphed in Figure 10-10a. These cash flows have a duration gap of −0.5 years. According to equation (12), should interest rates rise by one percentage point, net interest income of this tiny bank would fall by $0.005. The bank or thrift is net liability sensitive. In market value terms, the $5.00 of rate-sensitive assets act as though they reprice in 0.4 year. The $4.86 in rate-sensitive liabilities act as though they reprice in 0.30 year.

Example D studies the periodic gap of Figure 10-10b, one obtained by plugging the first quarter's gap in Figure 10-10a with the third quarter's gap. Relative to Example C this attempt at *incremental* hedging causes the duration of the rate-sensitive liabilities to change so dramatically that the duration gap changes to a positive sign. Incremental hedging has transformed the bank in Example C from liability sensitive to asset sensitive. We have taken too far a step in the direction of the interest rate risk-free position.

Example E again examines incremental gap plugging of the gap pattern in Example C. Here we plug the second and fourth quarter gaps. The net result is a worsening of the liability-sensitive situation found in Example C.

The last three examples in Table 10-5 were created in Section IV to show the inadequacies of gap plugging exercises. These examples are realistic in the sense that most risk control has to be done incrementally and on the fly. Static gap reports are worthless, even dangerous, when the measured risks are deemed to be unacceptable and only part (an increment) of the undesired risk can be removed today. Duration

Table 10-5. Duration Gap Calculations for Net Interest Income

Example A

Assumptions: (a) Each daily Gap\$ equals zero except Gap\$$_{30}$ = +\$1000, Gap\$$_{90}$ = −\$2000, and Gap\$$_{152}$ = +\$1000. These Gap\$s are expressed in future value terms.

(b) The negative Gap\$ is treated as the only rate-sensitive liabilitie and the two positive Gap\$s as the two rate-sensitive assets.

(c) The interest rate for all accounts has been 10% from when these accounts were booked to the present time.

Outcomes: (a) The market value of the rate-sensitive liability is \$1953. This equals the total market value of the rate-sensitive assets. Thus $MV_{RSA} = MV_{RSL}$.

(b) The duration of the rate-sensitive liability is 0.25 years. This equals the durations of the rate-sensitive assets—use equation (3) to verify this statement.

(c) The duration gap as defined by equation (11) equals zero. Net interest income is zero if rates stay at 10%. Calculating the net interest income for a sudden one percentage point increase in interest rates leaves net interest income unchanged, as predicted by equation (12).

Example B

Assumptions: (a) Each daily Gap\$ equals zero except Gap\$$_{90}$ = +\$1000 and Gap\$$_{180}$ = −\$1536. These Gap\$s are expressed in future value terms.

(b) The positive gap represents the only rate-sensitive asset and the negative gap represents the only rate-sensitive liability.

(c) The interest rate for all accounts has been 10% from when these accounts were booked to the present time.

Outcomes: (a) MV_{RSA} equals \$976 and MV_{RSL} equals \$1465.

(b) D_{RSA} equals 0.25 years and D_{RSL} equals 0.5 years.

(c) DG_{NII} equals zero. NII equals −\$48.90 if rates remain unchanged. A sudden increase in rates to 11% causes net interest income to become −\$48.90. This confirms that no current risk exposure is present.

Example C (See Figure 10-10a)

Assumptions: (a) Each daily Gap\$ equals zero, in present value terms, except Gap\$$_1$ = −\$3; Gap\$$_{91}$ = +2; Gap\$$_{181}$ = +\$3 and Gap\$$_{271}$ = −\$2.

(b) The negative Gap\$s are rate-sensitive liabilities and the positive Gap\$s are rate-sensitive assets.

(c) The interest rate for all accounts has been 10% from the time when these accounts were booked.

Outcomes: (a) MV_{RSA} equals \$5 and MV_{RSL} equals \$5 because the nonzero gaps are expressed in present value terms.

(b) D_{RSA} equals 0.4 years and D_{RSL} equals 0.3 years.

(c) DG_{NII} equals $5(1 − .4) − 5(1 − .3) = −.5$. This duration gap indicates net liability sensitivity. Equation (12) predicts that net interest income will fall by \$0.005 if rates rise by one percentage point. As discussed in Section IV, net interest income is zero in a 10% interest rate environment but will change to −\$0.00503.

Table 10-5.   (Continued)

Example D (See Figure 10-10b)

Assumptions: (a)   Each daily Gap\$ equals zero, in present value terms, except Gap\$$_{91}$ = +\$2; Gap\$$_{181}$ = +\$3; Gap\$$_{181}$ = −\$3 and Gap\$$_{271}$ = −\$2. This is the gap pattern in Example C after the maturity of the first liability is extended 180 days for gap ''plugging'' purposes.

(b)   The negative Gap\$s are rate-sensitive liabilities and the positive Gap\$s are rate-sensitive assets.

(c)   The interest rate for all accounts has been 10% from the time when these accounts were booked.

Outcomes: (a) MV_{RSA} equals \$5 and MV_{RSL} equals \$5 because the nonzero gaps are expressed in present value terms.

(b) D_{RSA} equals 0.4 years and D_{RSL} equals 0.6 years.

(c) DG_{NII} equals $5(1 − .4) − 5(1 − .6) = 1.0$. This duration gap indicates net asset sensitivity. Equation (12) predicts net interest income will rise by \$0.01 if rates rise by one percentage point. This prediction is exactly right.

Example E (See Figure 10-10c)

Assumptions: (a)   Each daily Gap\$ equals zero, in present value terms, except Gap\$$_1$ = \$3; Gap\$$_{181}$ = +\$ − 3; Gap\$$_{271}$ = −\$2 and Gap\$$_{271}$ = +\$2. This is the gap pattern in Example C after the maturity of the first asset is extended 180 days to plug the fourth quarter gap.

(b)   The negative Gap\$s are rate-sensitive liabilities and the positive Gap\$s are rate-sensitive assets.

(c)   The interest rate for all accounts has been 10% from the time when these accounts were booked.

Outcomes: (a) MV_{RSA} equals \$5, as does MV_{RSL}.

(b) D_{RSA} equals 0.6 year and D_{RSL} equals 0.3 year.

(c) DG_{NII} equals $5(1 − .6) − 5(1 − .3) = −1.5$. This duration gap indicates net liability sensitivity in excess of that found in Example C. Equation (12) predicts net interest income will fall by \$0.015 if rates rise by one percentage point. The exact decline is \$0.01503.

---

analysis, however, uses the same information available from accurate static gap reports to summarize in a useful and nearly intuitive manner interest rate risk exposure.

The duration gap of net interest income yields a single-valued risk index that is both intuitively appealing and reasonably accurate. Notice how similar equation (12) is to equation (2), which was developed in Section IV for measuring the interest rate risk of net interest income and is reproduced here for convenience:

$$\Delta NII = \text{cumulative Gap\$} \times \Delta i \tag{2}$$

We indicated earlier that equation (2) provided an intuitively appealing index of the exposure of net interest income but could, unfortunately, seriously misstate this exposure. The same criticism does not apply to equation (12). Unlike the cumulative maturity gap, the duration gap of net interest income incorporates precise information about the magnitude *and timing* of cash flows.

In a sense we have come full circle. The duration gap revitalizes the very concept that started the current interest in asset/liability models. Admittedly the duration gap for net interest income is not quite as intuitively obvious as its basic gap counterpart. The transition from maturity gap measurement to duration gap measurement, however, need not be unduly traumatic as there are many appealing comparisons between these two approaches.

The duration gap of net interest income, like all the previous target account duration gaps, indicates unambiguously whether or not an incremental change in the asset/liability structure reduces current risk exposures. So long as the relevant duration gap moves toward zero, the relevant target account becomes less exposed. Also, like the other target account duration gaps, the passage of time requires rebalancing transactions to counter the presence of duration drift. Rebalancing costs to meet the following mathematical conditions, however, are small since drift is trivial for short-term (rate-sensitive) securities.

As time passes during the accounting period over which the book value of net interest income accumulates, there will be changes in market values and durations of the rate-sensitive assets and liabilities. There will also arise the need to restructure the balance sheet as maturing accounts are rebooked. Thus we must periodically rebalance the rate-sensitive assets and liabilities to reestablish the desired duration gap for net interest income. Suppose we wish to hedge net interest income. At the end of the first month into the assumed 1-year accounting period, the condition needed to set the duration gap equal to zero becomes

$$MV'_{RSA}(11/12 - D'_{RSA}) = MV'_{RSL}(11/12 - D'_{RSL})$$

The primes indicate that the market values and durations are measured at month end. Rate sensitivity now means accounts are subject to repricing during the *remainder* of the year.[54]

The duration gap for net interest income has value for managers who wish to manage actively their book values of net interest income. These managers can use equation (12) to position their exposures such that they benefit from forecasted changes in interest rates. They can also study their risk exposures from this positioning by using equation (12) with probability-weighted interest rate forecasts to derive risk-return tradeoffs for the book value of net interest income.

In one respect the duration gap for net interest income differs from the duration gaps for other target accounts. This duration gap uses the values and durations of only the rate-sensitive cash flows unlike all the other duration gaps which use the market values and durations of all cash flows. Since the rate-sensitive cash flows are

---

[54]The condition needed after two months pass becomes $MV''_{RSA} (10/12 - D''_{RSL}) = MV''_{RSL} (10/12 - DR_{SL})$, and so on. Provided there are these types of adjustments in the duration gap of net interest income, any number of unexpected interest rate changes can occur and yet the realized book value of net interest income will equal the amount originally expected.

a subset of all the cash flows, it is possible to set the duration gap for net interest income at a level independently of, or simultaneously with, the duration gap level selected for any of the balance sheet related target accounts.[55]

The currently booked assets and liabilities give rise to an expected book value of net interest income for the next accounting period, the one after that, and so forth. Thus each accounting period has a currently measurable duration gap for net interest income and these sequential duration gaps can be managed independently from one another and/or in concert with balance-sheet related target accounts. This concern over the net interest incomes for multiple accounting periods makes sense. Proper risk control cannot entail a completely myopic concern for this year's net interest income up until the last day of the year when next year's income becomes the entire focal point of risk measurement and control.

Assumptions of Duration Gap Analysis

The duration formula given in Appendix I is referred to as Macaulay's duration. The mathematical form of this duration measure, which was the first invented and remains the simplest to compute, implicitly relies on two assumptions: the yield curve is flat, and random events cause this yield curve to shift upward or downward in a parallel fashion. Rarely in history has either assumption held. The offsetting advantage of Macaulay's duration is the relative ease of computation.

Applications of Macaulay's duration in instances where yield curves are not flat or are flat but shift in a nonparallel fashion cause the duration gap for any target account to be misestimated. The magnitude of the error depends on the extent of the violations of the assumptions. Yet in instances where each cash inflow matches a cash outflow, the duration of the assets is misestimated by exactly as much as the duration of the liabilities. Not net error arises from the use of an inappropriate duration formula. Hence the measurement error also increases for duration-matched situations with the size of the divergence from exact cash flow matching. For example, a portfolio with $50 in 1-year and $50 in 7-year zero coupon CDs that fund a $100 4-year zero coupon loan has more potential for risk mismeasurement than a 4-year zero coupon CD that funds a 5-year coupon bond with a 4-year duration. Both asset/liability mixes have matched 4-year durations but the first case has less closely matched cash flows.

Many institutions with matched or closely matched durations have assets and liabilities with reasonably closely matched cash flows. For these institutions the issue of which duration formula most closely associates in its assumptions with economic reality has relatively minor importance. Instances can occur, however, when duration-matched institutions find themselves substantially cash flow mismatched. Sanford Rose in his column in the *American Banker* of October 9, 1983 suggests making fixed-rate mortgages funded by duration-matched 5-year zero coupon CDs. These

---

[55]Money center banks may have only rate-sensitive accounts if net interest income is managed for a 1-year accounting period. In this case, independently managing the duration gap of net interest income from the equity-related duration gaps becomes impossible. Duration gaps for shorter accounting periods, say a quarter, may allow for independent risk management of the book value of net interest income.

substantially cash flow mismatched securities introduce the potential for sizable mis-estimation of risk exposures using Macaulay's duration. Much more realistic dura-tion measures must be employed when taking on these contrasting security types.[56] Hedging the bank or thrift with interest rate futures also leads to duration-matched but substantially cash flow mismatched situations.

When neither durations nor cash flows match, measurement errors from the use of inappropriate duration formulas become more of a problem. But in such instances these errors may be of relatively small concern to some risk managers. The mises-timated duration gaps still reflect the direction of the rate sensitivity and roughly quantify the exposure; that is, when the bank or thrift is substantially exposed to interest rate risk in any of its target accounts, any duration measure will signal this exposure. For institutions wishing to limit their interest rate risks to small amounts, using the misestimated duration gap to restructure asset and liability positions will move the institution to a more closely matched situation, one where cash flows and durations are more closely matched. The resulting smaller duration gaps once again have relatively small measurement errors when the assumptions behind the duration formula are violated.

The use of inappropriate duration formulas has the most serious consequences for aggressive risk managers. These managers forecast rates and adopt nontrivial interest rate exposures based on these forecasts. Misestimated duration gaps lead these man-agers to believe they are at one position in a risk-return tradeoff when they may be at a quite different position, presumably less desirable, given their revealed prefer-ences. They may even find the entire set of risk-return tradeoffs to be much different from what they supposed.

Value can be added by employing more realistic duration formulas than Macau-lay's duration. The alternatives distinguish themselves by making more realistic as-sumptions about the shape of the current yield curve and about how random events influence it. Second generation duration formulas use the term structure of interest rates, which can be thought of as the yield curve for zero coupon bonds, to discount individual cash flows rather than the yield to maturity used to discount all cash flows in Macaulay's formula. The assumed random processes of these duration measures remain relatively simplistic. Some formulas assume that random events shift the term structure, which can take on any shape, as can the associated yield curve, in ways that preserve its current shape. Others assume short-term rates are more volatile than long-term rates when the term structure is inverted, but less volatile otherwise. Still others require short-term rate volatility to be some fixed multiple of long-term rate volatility.[57] Third generation duration measures use term structures rather than yield curves and assume the historically average volatilities of the term structure rates hold

---

[56]These two securities also have substantially different rates of duration drift which complicates risk con-trol by requiring extensive rebalancing transactions to keep asset and liability durations, however mea-sured, in line with one another as time passes.

[57]The details of second generation duration formulas are given in "Duration: Its Uses in Bond Portfolio Management," *Financial Analysts Journal* (July/August 1983). Second generation duration formulas dif-fer from Macaulay's formula first by the use of the term structure for cash flow discounting. They also weight the discounted cash flows by a function of the time to receipt of this cash rather than just the length of time to the receipt of cash, as used in Macaulay's formula.

with certainty in the future. Fourth generation measures of interest rate sensitivity allow short-term rates to be influenced by different random events than longer-term rates. Fourth generation measures are the only ones that have a chance of providing full protection against changes in interest rates that cause short-term rates to move in the opposite direction of long-term rates.

Duration gap models should use at least second generation duration formulas, preferably third generation ones. The academic work on fourth generation measures of interest rate sensitivity (multifactor duration measures) has yet to establish their superiority in practice. Successful multifactor risk models may be derived; for now the relevant risk factors remain to be discovered. Appendix III shows how the duration gap for net interest income changes as discounting by term structure rates is substituted for discounting by yields and then when historical average volatilities are assumed to hold into the future. Remember, though, that the value of making duration formulas more esoteric diminishes quickly for institutions that desire to minimize their interest rate risk.

The Risk Characteristics of Unusual Security Types

We have discussed the duration approach to asset/liability modeling in some detail using simple bond examples to illustrate the concept and the intuition behind what on first reading is the most complicated method of risk measurement. We now tackle the more difficult issue of determining the risks associated with more "exotic" financial instruments. For example, can interest rate swaps, interest rate futures contracts, demand deposits, and mortgages be incorporated into duration gap measures?

Not surprisingly we find that the duration concept has some difficulties in measuring the interest rate risk characteristic of the more unusual securities. The problems caused by these securities however, are, not unique to duration analysis. Assumptions have to be made about the cash flow implications of any unusual security. Once they have been made, various models can be compared by the value created through their analyses of the cash flows. The following four subsections do not cover all the securities with cash flows that are difficult to determine. Rather we study these only to demonstrate that the duration concept has some adaptibility.

Interest Rate Swaps

An interest rate swap is a bilateral arrangement between two parties who agree to transfer streams of interest payments. The normal agreement calls for one party to pay to the other party interest on a floating-rate basis in exchange for interest receipts on a fixed-rate basis. The principal amount upon which the payments are based is "notional" in that this amount is not exchanged by the parties at the maturity date of the swap. The floating-rate side usually has its payments indexed to the LIBOR, T-bill, prime, CD, or commercial paper interest rate.

The swap literature distinguishes between asset-based swaps and liability-based swaps. The former pertains to an institution motivated to enter a swap to change the interest rate reset dates on an investment. If an institution currently receives fixed-rate payments but wishes floating-rate payments, then the institution agrees to swap away these fixed-rate payments in exchange for floating-rate payments. Institutions motivated to enter into liability-based swaps wish to convert the interest rate reset terms on existing debts. To rid the institution of the current form of payments, the institution passes this obligation on to the swap partner in exchange for the opportunity to make the alternative form of payment.

The notion of asset-based and liability-based swaps is often useful, but in asset/liability management it can hinder the analysis. The swap is best thought of in an asset/liability restructuring context as "buying" an asset with a liability. We place this word in quotes because interest rate swaps have no immediate influence on the balance sheet of the institution and footnote disclosures are required only when they are material in nature. The initial market value of the hypothetical asset is the present value of all cash inflows expected from the swap including a hypothetical payment of notional principal. (A newly created swap normally has an implied market value equal to the notional principal.) Similar statements apply to the valuation of the hypothetical liability.

The cash flows and market values of both sides of a swap have implied sensitivities to changes in interest rates and therefore implied durations. These durations are calculated in the usual way. For example, a 5-year fixed-rate set of payments, based on a 10% coupon rate in a 10% interest rate world, has a duration of about four years. A 5-year floating-rate set of payments indexed to a 6-month interest rate has a duration of six months.

The additivity characteristic of duration extends to include the hypothetical market values and durations of both sides of the swap. Suppose a bank has $100 in assets with a duration of three years and $90 in liabilities with a duration of one year. The implied duration of equity is 21 years, as is the duration gap for the market value of equity. This duration substantially exposes the market value of equity to changes in interest rates. Entering into a $50 notional principal swap paying 10% for four years and receiving floating rate payments is equivalent in the duration context to booking a liability with a 3.49-year duration (provided interest rates are 10%) worth $50 and booking a 0.5-year duration asset of similar value. The total asset duration is shortened to 2.17 years, the total liability duration is lengthened to 1.89 years, and the duration of equity (duration gap for equity) becomes a positive +6.09 years, which is a substantial improvement over the magnitude of the prior risk exposure.[58]

Interest Rate Futures

Interest rate futures treat cash securities as storable commodities that can be delivered for currently agreed upon prices at a future date in time. Currently various exchanges trade interest rate futures contracts on U.S. Treasury bills, notes, and bonds; bank

---

[58]The new asset duration is $(100 \times 3.0 + 50 \times 0.5)/150 = 1.63$ years; the new liability duration is $(90 \times 1.0 + 50 \times 3.49)/140 = 1.89$ years; and the new equity duration is $(150 \times 1.63 - 140 \times 1.89)/10 = -2.01$ years.

CDs; commercial paper; Eurobonds; and GNMA certificates. In the near future a futures contract on a municipal bond index will begin trading.

The delivery price of the underlying cash security is stated contractually upon origination of the futures contract.[59] The price established in the contract is the price of the deliverable expected to prevail on the delivery date. As time passes, however interest rates may change unexpectedly. This alters the price of the deliverable security that is expected to prevail on the delivery date. The difference between the prior expected delivery price and the new one results in a profit or loss on the day the unexpected rate change occurs, not on the delivery date.[60] This daily marking-to-market effectively causes futures positions to have daily changes in market value. Thus futures positions introduce a highly levered means of injecting instantaneous price sensitivity into either the asset side (a long position) or the liability side (a short position) of the portfolio equity of an institution.

Since a futures contract experiences instantaneous price changes when interest rates move unexpectedly, it must have a well-defined duration associated with it. The duration of a futures contract can be interpreted as the term to maturity of a zero coupon bond which experiences the same instantaneous price change for a given change in interest rates, and is very closely related to the duration of the underlying cash security, calculated from the delivery date to the maturity date of the cash deliverable.

The net effect of a futures position on the duration gap of equity is given by the following equation:[61]

$$DG_E = DG_E^0 + D_F \times \frac{V_F}{MV_E} \qquad (13)$$

where DG_E is the duration gap of equity before the futures position was put in place; D_F is the duration of the deliverable security underlying the futures contract computed from point of delivery forward using forward interest rates in any discounting;

---

[59]While the delivery price of the contract is established upon origination, its price is not paid or received until delivery. However to maintain the financial integrity of their respective clearing organizations, futures exchanges require that buyers and sellers post initial margin deposits.

[60]Each trading day the exchange may require the holders of losing long or short positions to post additional margin deposits in the form of "variation" margin payments. These payments are made whenever a long or short futures position holder has a total margin balance less than the minimum required by the exchange. Accountants may be able to defer the revelation of this change in the margin account, but financially the payment or receipt does occur and the financing cost or earnings on the changed account balance have a financial reality that cannot be ignored.

[61]A futures position designed to remove the interest rate sensitivity of the net bond represented by portfolio equity essentially acts like a hedge designed to remove the interest rate sensitivity of an inventory of cash market securities. In a recent Morgan Stanley publication, this type of futures hedge was discussed using the description "Weak Form Cash Hedges." See Section VI in "Interest Rate Futures: A Comparison of Alternative Hedge Ratio Methodologies, Alden Toevs and David Jacob, New York: Morgan Stanley (June 1984).

and V_F is the value of the deliverable security at the delivery date (positive for long positions and negative for short positions).[62]

A long futures position adds price sensitivity to the existing assets' current price sensitivity with no change in the volatility of the liabilities. A short position in futures augments the sensitivity of the liabilities. Thus if the duration gap of equity is positive, indicating net sensitive assets, a short position in futures reduces the duration gap. In a sense the duration of the liabilities has been lengthened by the short position. This conclusion is supported by equation (13). Conversely, a negative duration gap for equity can be reduced by adding a long position in futures lengthening the duration of the assets by the long position. This conclusion is again supported by equation (13).[63]

Hedging economic leverage calls for a nonzero duration of equity. This requires a different amount of long or short futures contracts—long positions increase equity duration and short positions do the opposite. As Section V in our previous work on futures suggests, the number of contracts can be found in a duration framework. Hedging a total return on equity is similar in its duration of equity requirements.

Net interest income requires a balanced amount of rate-sensitive assets and liabilities, at least after the timing aspects of these near-term cash flows have been taken into account. Hedging either the book or market values of net interest income requires hedges using futures contracts much like hedging the market value of equity.[64]

Against the advantages of using futures contracts to hedge asset/liability mismatches stands the potential for large basis risk exposure. This risk grows to unnecessary amounts if the price volatilities of cash and futures contracts are misunderstood.[65] Duration analyses in futures-to-cash hedges works as well or better than alternative hedge ratio estimation techniques. Factoring in hedge ratio estimation costs makes duration a clear winner. Nevertheless, when hedge ratios are correctly measured, futures contracts trade differently enough to introduce troublingly large but random basis risks into the balance sheets and income statements of banks and thrifts.

---

[62]The equation

$$DG_E = \frac{(DG^\circ \times MV_E) + (D_F \times V_F)}{MV_E}$$

which is fully consistent with equation 5, which expresses the additivity property of duration. The term V_F does not appear in the denominator of this expression because the acquisition cost of a futures position is virtually nil since initial margins can be placed in interest bearing securities, and hence, the value of portfolio equity, MV_E will be unaffected on the day the futures position is put in place.

[63]One way of viewing futures contracts is as an acquisition of the expected price volatility of the deliverable cash security as of the delivery date but marked to market today. The price volatility of the deliverable is indexed by its duration, the implied duration of the futures contract.

[64]Exact methods of hedging target accounts with futures contracts are contained in (June 1984). *Interest Rate Futures: A Comparison of Alternative Hedge Ratio Methodologies* New York: Morgan Stanley (June 1984). Of particular relevance are Sections IV and V. Futures contracts have value as hedging instruments in that they are so highly levered that the bank's asset, liability and equity durations can be altered significantly at low cost.

[65]It was just such misunderstanding that prompted our previous analysis of the alternative hedge ratio methodologies cited in footnote 64.

Mortgages

Fixed-rate mortgages are probably the most complicated securities on the books of a financial institution.[66] They are difficult to value and difficult to hedge. Conceptually a fixed-rate mortgage has three parts. The simplest one to understand is the scheduled monthly payments of principal and interest to the maturity date of the mortgage. The second part covers the cash flows that occur earlier than expected, but not because the borrower has taken advantage of favorable interest rates to refinance the loans. They occur because of labor migration, switching houses as family size grows, and so forth. The final and most difficult part of the mortgage is the option to prepay a loan by refinancing at a lower interest rate.

The value of a mortgage is the present value of the cash flows after the contractually expected payments have been adjusted for demographic prepayments. The trick here is to predict demographically induced prepayments. Econometric studies on prepayment histories have discovered several variables that have stable relationships to prepayments. These include the age of the loan, the age of the borrower, geographical location of the house, and so on.[67] This value must be further adjusted to include the borrower's right to refinance the mortgage when rates fall. This refinancing right, which is essentially a call option written by the lender to the borrower, has a value that can be theoretically determined using option pricing formulas.

The effective value of the refinancing option lies below the theoretical value. When interest rates fall to levels making mortgages attractive to refinance, not all borrowers choose to do so. How else can the existence of GNMA certificates bearing a 17% coupon rate be explained? The percentage of borrowers with a given mortgage rate who choose to refinance may be constant, which is unlikely, or may depend in part on how much the borrower gains by refinancing, the degree of competition in loan markets, the education level of borrower, and possibly the age of the borrower.

Clearly a number of important studies must be completed on the behavior of mortgage borrowers before mortgage valuation becomes a more precise art. Useful preliminary work is only now beginning to appear. The heightened interest in mortgage-backed securities, however, should increase the speed with which useful information on demographic prepayments and interest rate induced prepayments is produced. The following indicates how this information, once available, becomes useful in estimating the interest rate sensitivity of a mortgage in the duration context.

The value of a mortgage (P_M) can be symbolically represented in two parts:

$$P_M = P_C - V_O \tag{14}$$

P_C represents the present value of the contractual cash flows as adjusted for demographically induced prepayments. V_O represents the value of the prepayment option.

---

[66]Recent advances in the bells and whistles attached to variable-rate mortgages may soon crown these securities most complicated to understand.

[67]See Helen F. Peters, Scott M. Pinkus, and David J. Askin, "Figuring the Odds: A Model of Prepayments," *Secondary Mortgage Markets* (May 1984).

Since loan refinancings take place when the market value of the remaining cash flows exceeds the outstanding principal balance, these financially induced prepayments are costs to the lender. (Hence the minus sign in equation (14).) V_O reflects this current potential for a loss to the lender plus the potential for even greater losses if prepayments occur later at even more favorable rates.

As interest rates change, the present value from the estimated cash flows associated with P_C changes as well. P_C changes in value not because prepayments quicken or slow—these mortgage cash flows are fixed—but because the discounting rate for the expected cash flow has changed. This change in value is like that experienced on any set of cash flows, and therefore, the price sensitivity of P_C can be indexed with the duration of these cash flows. As interest rates change the value of the option changes. When rates fall the amount of refinancings increase to the detriment of the lender.

What is the sensitivity of the value of the prepayment option to changes in interest rates? The price sensitivity of V_O can be obtained from the option pricing formulas applicable to mortgages. Briefly we use an option pricing formula to value V_O at current interest rates and then again at rates slightly higher or lower than the current ones. This price sensitivity is then converted to the duration index by finding the maturity of the zero coupon bond with a comparable interest rate sensitivity.

We have too little space to develop this line of reasoning in greater detail within this report. All we wish to show is that the duration concept readily allows both demographically and financially induced prepayments to be modeled from other information on the cash flows. The accuracy with which this occurs depends not on the duration concept but on our abilities to estimate the value of prepayment rights and the likelihood that a borrower exercises these rights.[68]

Demand Deposits

The non-interest rate dependent prepayments and the interest rate dependent cash flows of mortgages have direct counterparts in determining the interest rate sensitivity of demand deposits. Many banks can identify a core level of demand. These deposits remain in the bank despite seasonal disintermediation and interest rate dependent disintermediation. The duration of these core accounts, therefore, is quite long.[69] Seasonal patterns of demand deposit withdrawals are usually quite predictable. These reductions give the cash flows from which to calculate the durations of these non-interest rate dependent cash flows. The one remaining component needed to estimate the interest rate sensitivity of demand deposits is the interest rate sensitivity of demand deposit accounts that tend to disintermediate when interest rates

[68]More information on these issues can be found in "Hedging Interest Rate Risk of Fixed-Income Securities with Uncertain Lives," *Journal of Portfolio Management* (Spring 1985). Also see Alden Toevs, "Hedging the Interest Rate Risk of Fixed-Rate Mortgages with Prepayment Rights," *Handbook of Mortgage Backed Securities,* edited by Frank Fabozzi Probus Publishing.

[69]If these accounts are maintained by offering "free" services, the level of which increases with interest rates (threat of disintermediation), core accounts become a disguised form of variable-rate (short duration) contracts.

rise. Provided the bank can identify with reasonable accuracy the sensitivity of checking account balances to changes in interest rates, the duration of these outflows can also be computed. Historical studies and statistical analyses help in this regard. The point once again is that if cash flows can be identified the duration concept applies. Should these flows be so random that no predictions can be made, no asset/liability model can successfully handle the problem. The removal of Regulation Q ceilings on interest rates in 1986 complicates this analysis. Each institution must weigh the likelihood that interest rate free checking will survive in the calculation of the duration of demand deposits. For the moment most would agree, no matter what model is favored, that the interest rate sensitivity of demand deposits is unclear.

The Advantages of Duration Gap Models

The use of duration does not create information where none existed before. It only summarizes available information on cash flows in ways we believe to be useful. It cannot hide cash flow timing mismatches as can gap models in their maturity buckets. Duration gaps also appeal to risk managers by their ability to summarize in a single number—the duration gap for the target account—the information contained in a complicated periodic gap report or a number of simulations. This helps risk managers quickly assess their risk exposures and find aggregate hedges capable of reducing these measured exposures. Many of those who become comfortable with the duration concept find themselves capable of calculating the impact of hedging transactions on the backs of envelopes rather than with extended and costly computer runs.

Duration analysis can be performed on a number of target accounts. This permits risk measurement for balance sheet items and income statement items. Financial theory tells us that the risk exposures of many target accounts cannot always be controlled simultaneously, but they can be measured simultaneously. Duration analysis reveals this financial reality, shows which account objectives can be managed simultaneously, and shows how goal objectives for one target account can be slightly compromised to increase the control over less important target accounts. Duration gap models have the capacity to ask, "What risks are to be controlled, what compromises must be made to accomplish other objectives?"

A duration gap model reveals the largest potential number of asset and liability choices capable of moving current risk exposures to more desired levels. It does so by reminding us that one pocket of risk can offset another (not every gap must be hedged individually for all gaps to be hedged) so long as we recognize the importance of both the timing and the magnitude of cash flows. The ability of duration gap models to reveal extensive lists of risk altering transactions gives managers the opportunity to accommodate customer demands, minimize transaction costs, limit tax liabilities, and meet regulatory requirements more fully than when alternative models are used.

It is a rare financial institution that can accomplish realistic risk control objectives the instant these risks become known. Most hedges have to be applied incrementally. Duration gap models indicate unambiguously which transactions reduce the current risk exposures in target accounts. Earlier we showed simple examples of how maturity gap models can suggest risk-reducing transactions that in fact increase risk. Simulation models can be used to hedge incrementally as well, but in a more trial-and-error fashion.

Duration gap models are adaptable. This gives them an important advantage over other models when interest rate risk hidden in prepayment rights, redemption rights on deposits, and interest rate related defaults become important. The option-like characteristics of prepayments and deposit disintermediation have price sensitivities that make duration analysis particularly appropriate. Simulations and maturity gap models have difficulties treating in a unified framework the option-like features of so many financial institution assets and liabilities.

While we believe futures contracts are not a panacea, their liquidity, low transaction costs, and leverage recommend them as important hedging instruments. Whether these advantages offset the disadvantages caused by potentially sizable basis risks and limiting accounting treatments remains to be seen. Should a bank or thrift choose to use futures markets, the construction of an appropriate hedge ratio becomes important. Comparing the duration of the position to be hedged with the duration of the futures contract provides the most accurate and least costly means of determining the hedge ratio. Thus interest rate futures contracts can be directly incorporated into duration gap models. Other asset/liability models have much more difficulty measuring the combined interest rate risk of portfolios containing cash and futures instruments.

Disadvantages of Duration Gap Models

As the space devoted to the description of the various asset/liability models indicates, the duration gap approach is harder to describe than the alternatives. Critics have stressed this point and there is merit to their arguments. The criticism however, can be taken too far. We believe duration gaps add more value than the alternatives, and on a net cost basis we feel the argument swings the other way. Moreover, duration analysis can be made intuitively appealing. As a start one can display the results of a duration gap model in a form comparable to the results of a maturity gap model.

The accuracy of risk assessments using duration analysis relies on the fulfillment of certain assumptions. The simplest duration formula assumes the ridiculous: yield curves are flat and shift in a parallel fashion. More realistic duration formulas require other assumptions. When cash flows are grossly mismatched but duration matched, the potential error caused by a violation of the assumptions made in the selected duration formula exceeds that obtained when cash flows and durations are more closely matched. Care needs to be taken to employ a duration formula with reasonable underlying assumptions about interest rates and their movements.

Matching asset and liability risks using durations but not cash flows requires that the risk manager make frequent adjustment of asset and liability positions to minimize the problem of the asset duration drifting away, as time passes, from the liability duration. These rebalancings can be tedious and cause unwanted tax and accounting problems. Presumably the reason why a bank or thrift might be interested in creating these duration matched by cash flow mismatched asset and liability positions is that a particular demand by a customer can be met or an unusually favorable interest rate spread can be obtained.

Duration gap analysis, like maturity gap analysis, measures the current risk exposure of the bank or thrift. It gives a snapshot of the risk at one point in time. This snapshot should be the most interesting picture to the risk manager, but other pictures have value. The moving pictures created by simulations permit risk managers to be more forward looking. For example, simulations help reveal ways of accomplishing risk objectives over time. They give managers time to put into effect campaigns and strategic plans to reduce risk exposures by rebooking maturing accounts in ways that lower risk control costs over time. Simulating the balance sheet forward under differing assumptions on the disposition of maturing money must be part of a good asset/liability model. (As this glimpse of the future is obtained, some find it useful to compute the duration gaps of various target accounts.)

Summary

Duration gap models should appeal to risk managers. They economically measure the direct and correlated interest rate risks of the currently booked assets and liabilities. For each target account the duration gap indexes these risks with a single and appealing number. Devotees of duration gaps study them to determine which of their target accounts can be separately risk controlled. They also use duration gaps to form risk-return tradeoffs that are particularly valuable for active risk management, and instances when risks in several target accounts must be controlled jointly.

Duration gap models provide more flexibility in risk control than do the alternative models. The maturity gap approach focuses on hedges that match specific cash flows rather than match cash flows on average. Simulations bog down managers in oceans of detail when flexibility in risk control is sought. Incremental hedges are also dispatched more accurately and economically in duration gap models.

Against these primary advantages stand two disadvantages. Duration analysis, like any other risk measurement technique, makes assumptions that may prove unrealistic. The simplest duration formula assumes yield curves are flat and shift in a parallel fashion. More appropriate formulas are available but these too make assumptions that may prove false. The violation of the assumptions underlying the selected duration formula, however, has an offset. Errors made because the duration formula selected is incorrect in measuring asset's duration cancel with errors made on the liability side. In addition, duration analysis measures current risks (certainly the most important), but does not readily permit risk managers to study the evolution of risks over time.

SECTION VIII   CONCLUSIONS

Banks and thrifts face every imaginable type of risk. They acquire assets with credit qualities ranging from the highest to the lowest possible. They issue assets and liabilities with extremely complicated interest rate options. And they fund their assets with liabilities raised in fickle and highly competitive markets. The natural lines of business of most banks and thrifts create substantial interest rate risk, even disregarding the problems caused by the interest rate options issued as part of their assets and liabilities. Some banks and thrifts are failing, and in their death throes take on wildly aggressive risks that raise the competitive expectations of asset and liability customers for the better managed institutions.

Of particular concern is the quality of asset/liability management that has evolved in this environment. Banks and thrifts managed all the above mentioned risks with competence until October 1979, when risk management suddenly became a different and more difficult task. Crisis management for a period of time was appropriate. But we will not soon return to a stable interest rate environment. New competitive pressures have permanently eroded large interest rate spreads that once hid income variations due to moderate interest rate changes. Under these circumstances risk managers must increase the time and financial resources devoted to improving their interest rate risk measurement and management techniques.

The proper structure of risk management starts with subjective decisions on what target accounts are most important, progresses through objective exercises in risk measurement, and terminates with a subjectively determined choice from among the available risk-efficient asset/liability structures. Section III dwelt extensively on this important but often slighted topic. It is only human to focus attention more on objective tasks, which can be quantified and easily accomplished, than subjective ones. But this attention to the easily accomplished tasks limits the time spent determining the set of target accounts to be risk controlled; the outcomes desired for these target accounts; the compromises necessary in attaining one account objective to accommodate the partial or full attainment of another objective; and over what period of time the asset/liability structure will be altered to meet these interrelated objectives.

The absence of sensible risk measurement models has complicated the entire risk management process. In 1978 only a few asset/liability models existed, ones that are now considered to be grossly inadequate. The evolution of asset/liability models is not yet complete, but recent progress has been substantial. In this chapter, we considered three generic approaches to interest rate risk measurement. The first was the maturity gap approach, which is currently best represented by a periodic (maturity bucket) gap model. Several deficiencies in this model, most notably the inability to summarize the risks inherent in many separate gap numbers into a single index number, were overcome with naive simulations. The implicit reliance on simulations has spurred the development of comprehensive simulation models for the measurement of interest rate risk. A more contemporary development has been the application of duration analysis to asset/liability problems.

Table 10-6 summarizes our findings on the periodic gap, simulation and duration gap asset/liability models. This table ranks the abilities of these models to accomplish the items listed in Section II as important ones for inclusion in any asset/liability model. Table 10-6 uses relative rankings; a first-place score indicates only that the winner currently has the best available performance. In all cases there is room for improvement. An X indicates that this characteristic can be included in any model, provided that care has been taken in the model's construction.

The maturity gap model ranks below the simulation and duration gap approaches.

Table 10-6. Score Card on the Asset/Liability Models

	Maturity Gap	Simulation	Duration Gap
1. Risk measurement accuracy	3	2	1
2. Risk in several target accounts	3/2	3/2	1
3. Flexible asset/liability choices	3	2	1
4. Comprehensive treatment of securities	3	2	1
5. Treatment of correlated risks	3	2	1
6. Ability to hedge incrementally	3	2	1
7. Risk of to be booked positions	3/2	1	3/2
8. Risk measurement of individual accounts	3/2	3/2	1
9. Flexible display of results	3	1	2
10. Reveal assumptions made	X	X	X
11. Distinction between book and market values	X	X	X

We believe this model wins on no important issue of interest rate risk control. Because the maturity gap model reveals some incremental hedges that increase risk rather than reduce it, this model is potentially dangerous. The periodic gaps computed in newer models have become so numerous that simulations or alternative techniques must be used to characterize the risk exposure in any meaningful way. Given this reliance on simulation analysis we believe a good simulation model adds more value than a periodic gap model. (Schedules H and J, the new gap reports banks and thrifts compile for their regulators, have already been programmed into any non-maturity gap model worth considering.)

Simulation models do more than aggregate the separate risk exposures uncovered by maturity gap models. They also permit risk managers to study the evolution of interest rate risk. For example, a manager may wish to consider adjusting current risk exposures as time passes using new business and artful redeployment of maturing accounts. Simulations help management discover the tradeoff between the higher transaction costs of altering risk levels immediately and the potential losses if interest rates take a damaging turn during the time the risk manager takes to effect the new asset/liability structure.

The value of simulation is not readily apparent when current risk exposures are measured. These models simulate what financial theory, or simple approximations of it, readily indicate. Simulation models determine a security's interest rate sensitivity by simulating the price of this security and then again assuming an interest rate rise or fall. But immutable principles of finance also tell us these sensitivities. Repetitious simulations of what can be readily stated in a single computer instruction are silly and costly. Moreover, simulations can be inadvertently structured so that they create misinformation. We saw this in Section V, Table 10-4, where a simulation of multiple changes in interest rate incorrectly indicated that no interest rate sensitivity was present. Since simulations so clumsily reveal current risk exposures, they should be limited to applications where they add the most value.

Duration analysis should form the core of the asset/liability model. It accurately and economically reveals the current exposures of the target accounts to interest rate risk. Duration analysis is based on financial principles and has been used successfully in many applications similar to asset/liability management. Despite these quantitative credentials, the duration concept has intuitive appeal. Although senior management may grumble about learning more asset/liability jargon, they can easily learn and interpret the meaning of the various duration gaps presented in Section VII. Because duration models use the principles of finance rather than continuously rediscover them, less computer time is required than equally sophisticated simulation models.

Duration models, more than any other, focus managerial attention on the subjective aspects of risk management. Duration gaps cannot be computed until the risk manager specifies the set of target accounts of primary interest. Duration gap analyses help managers expeditiously derive risk-return tradeoffs. These tradeoffs become important when the risk objectives in one target account must be compromised to accomplish a desired level of risk control in another target account. The hedging implications for the duration gaps for several target accounts reminds the risk manager that controlling the risk in one target account does not necessarily control it for another target account.

One thing duration cannot do is simulate the influence of new business or changes in business lines as deposits or loans mature. Thus we recommend duration analysis be used to measure current risk exposures and reveal currently available incremental or total hedges. It does both of these tasks for more target accounts with lower cost and less need for trial-and-error searches than do simulations. These exercises are the most important ones of risk management. Of secondary importance is the determination of the tradeoff between immediate or gradual risk adjustments, a task best performed with a simulation model.

APPENDIX I: DURATION AND ZERO COUPON BOND EQUIVALENCY

Frederick Macaulay developed the duration concept in his search for a correct measure of the life of a bond. (Throughout this paper the term ''bond'' should be taken to mean any fixed-income security.) Term to maturity is an unambiguous measure of the life of a zero coupon (pure discount) bond. But, because term to maturity ignores the amount and timing of all cash flows save the final payment, it incompletely measures the life of a coupon bond. Macaulay decided to standardize coupon bond life using a zero coupon bond equivalent term to maturity. This reasoning is compelling both because the term to maturity of a zero coupon bond unambiguously measures this bond's life and because any coupon bond might best be viewed as nothing more than a bundle of zero coupon bonds.

The trick Macaulay faced was how to average the maturities of zero coupon bond bundles. For example, a $100 coupon bond currently at par that pays $10 in interest annually for five years may be regarded as a portfolio of five zero coupon bonds:

$10 face value zeros maturing in 1, 2, 3, and 4 years and a $110 face value zero maturing in five years. One summary measure of these five maturity dates is three years, which is the simple average of the dates. This approach, however, fails to recognize the different dollar values of the constituent zero coupon bonds.

Weighted Averages of Cash Flow Dates

More reasonable summary measures of a coupon bond's life compute average term to maturity using dollar weights. Two possible dollar weighting schemes come immediately to mind. First, the dollar weights could be computed by dividing each cash inflow by total cash to be received. For our five-year coupon bond, this dollar weighted average term to maturity (WAT) would be:

$$\text{WAT} = \frac{10}{150} \times 1\,\text{year} + \frac{10}{150} \times 2\,\text{years} + \frac{10}{150} \times 3\,\text{years}$$
$$+ \frac{10}{150} \times 4\,\text{years} + \frac{110}{150} \times 5\,\text{years} = 4.33\,\text{years}$$

Second, the dollar weights could be computed using present values of future cash flows. Because the present value of any single cash flow is the price of a zero coupon bond with a face value equal to this cash flow, these dollar weights are zero coupon bond weights. For our example bond, this price weighted average would be:

$$D = \left[\frac{10/1.10}{P}\right] 1\,\text{year} + \left[\frac{10/1.10^2}{P}\right] 2\,\text{years} + \left[\frac{10/1.10^3}{P}\right] 3\,\text{years}$$
$$+ \left[\frac{10/1.10^4}{P}\right] 4\,\text{years} + \left[\frac{110/1.10^5}{P}\right] 5\,\text{years} = 4.16\,\text{years}$$

It was this formulation Macaulay derived and called duration. The weights in this average are given in brackets. The numerator of each weight is the price of the zero coupon bond (its present or discounted value). The denominator is the *total* present value of all five zeros, which is the price of the coupon bond (P). Given our coupon bond was previously assumed to be trading at par, price is $100.

The price weighted average term to maturity or duration is a superior measure to the WAT. Duration is an average that uses dollar weights computed relative to today's date (present values) and time to receipt of cash computed from today's date. On the other hand, the WAT is internally inconsistent. It computes the time to cash receipt from today's date but the dollar weights do not depend upon today's date. The importance of this internal inconsistency will become clear as the applications of duration are revealed, not one of which is shared by WAT.

The duration of any series of cash flows ending at date t_N years can be represented in general terms as:

$$D = w_1 \times t_1 + w_2 \times t_2 + w_3 \times t_3 + \ldots + w_N \times t_N \qquad \text{(AI-1)}$$

Where w_i is the price of the zero coupon bond maturing at date t_i relative to the total price of the bundle of N zero coupon bonds hypothetically comprising the coupon bond. For illustrative purposes, Table A computes the duration of another bond. Again, "bond" should be taken to mean any series of cash flows, mortgages, annuities, and so on.

As a price weighted average term to maturity, duration is measured in years. The duration of a zero coupon bond is its maturity date. (In Equation (AI-1), all weights for a zero coupon bond maturing in t_N years are zero except W_N which equals 1.0) Any series of cash flows with a terminal flow at t_N will have a duration less than t_N. The smaller are the dollar flows occurring before t_N, the smaller are these cash flow weights and the closer the duration comes to t_N years. The relationships among the coupon rate (size of intermediate cash flows), yield to maturity, maturity date and duration are depicted in Figure A.

Duration is related to years to maturity linearly for zero coupon bonds

OA gives the duration versus maturity relationship for *current coupon* bonds (bonds priced at par)

OB gives the duration versus maturity relationship for *discounted coupon* bonds

OC gives the duration versus maturity relationship for *premium coupon* bonds

All coupon bonds have an upper limit to their duration as the maturity date became very distant. This upper limit is the number resulting from computing $(1 + r)/r$.

The duration of a portfolio of coupon bonds can be computed using Equation (AI-1) considering all cash flows generated by the portfolio. Often an easier approach

Table A. Duration of a $100 Face Value Bond Paying a 7% Coupon (Bond Priced to Give a 10% Yield to Maturity)

Cash Inflow Date	Cash Inflow Amount	Cash Inflows Discounted at 10%	Price Weights	Price Weighted Maturities
0.5 years	$ 3.50	$ 3.34 [a]	.036 [c]	.018 years [d]
1.0	3.50	3.18	.034	.034
1.5	3.50	3.03	.033	.050
2.0	3.50	2.89	.031	.062
2.5	3.50	2.76	.030	.075
3.0	103.50	77.76	.836	2.508
		$92.96 [b] (Current Price)	1.000	2.747 years [e] (Duration)

[a] $3.50/(1.10)$^{-.5}

[b] Current price sums all cash inflows discounted by the yield to maturity (10%).

[c] $3.34/$92.96

[d] .036 × 0.5 years

[e] Duration is the sum of all price weighted maturities.

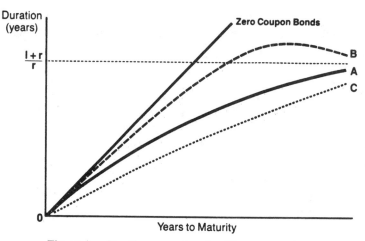

Figure A.   Duration versus length of time to maturity.

first computes the duration of each coupon bond in the portfolio separately and then makes use of the additivity characteristic of duration to find the duration of the entire portfolio. Additivity means that the duration of a portfolio is the price weighted average of the coupon bond durations. For example, a portfolio of $1000 invested in three-year duration coupon bonds and $2000 in four-year duration coupon bonds has a portfolio duration of D_P = ($1000/$3000) × 3 years + ($2000/$3000) × 4 years = 3.67 years.

APPENDIX II   DERIVATION OF THE DURATION GAP OF ECONOMIC LEVERAGE

Both the asset market value A and the equity market value E are sensitive to changes in interest rates. The derivative of A/E with respect to interest rates is

$$\delta(A/E)/\delta i = [(\delta A/\delta i) \times E - (\delta E/\delta i) \times A]/E^2 \qquad (a)$$

We know from the characteristics of duration that $\delta(A)/\delta i = A \times [-D_A/(1 + i)]$ and $\delta E/\delta i$ equals $E \times [-D_E(1 + i)]$. Thus

$$\delta(A/E)/\delta i = (A/E) \times [D_E - D_A]/(1 + i) \qquad (b)$$

This equation is mathematically equivalent to equation (9) in the main text. One can view δi as Δi. Dividing both sides of equation (b) by (A/E) produces equation (8) in the main text.

Equation (b) can be reexpressed in terms of asset and liability durations. Substitute, using the additivity characteristic of duration, $[D_A \times A) - (D_L \times L)]/E$ for D_E. The result is

$$\delta(A/E)/\delta i = \frac{(A \times L)}{E^2} \times [D_A - D_L]/(1 + i) \qquad (c)$$

APPENDIX III   DERIVATION OF THE DURATION GAP OF NET INTEREST INCOME

Assume the bank or thrift has a 1-year accounting period. Furthermore assume the yield curve is flat and shifts in a parallel fashion. Let NII_0 represent net interest income for the coming year should rates not change unexpectedly. This level of net interest income is the goal of the hedging strategy. Mathematically NII_0 can be expressed as

$$\text{NII}_0 = \sum_{j=1}^{N} A_j[(1 + r_j)^{t_j}(1 + i_j)^{1-t_j} - 1] - \sum_{k=1}^{M} L_k[(1 + r)^{t_k}(1 + i_k)^{1-t_k} - 1] \qquad (a)$$

A_j is the asset *book* value at the beginning of the year of a cash inflow that will occur at time t_j, where t_j is expressed as a *fraction* of a year. This asset has an associated contractual interest rate of r_j, expressed as an annualized rate. Upon repricing, this cash inflow is expected to earn a new rate of i_j. There are N repriced asset flows. (A long-term mortgage with monthly payments of $500, a contractual interest rate of 5% and a new interest rate of 10%—the rate on new mortgages—would have 12 flows represented in the above summation. The Xth month flow has an A_j of 500/$1.05^{x/12}$, $t_j = X/12$, $r_j = .05$ and $i_j = .10$.)

If an asset does not generate any flows during the one year gapping period, then it influences net interest income only in an accrual sense and $t_j = 1$. Similar definitions apply to L_k, one of M liability repricing flows. Consider the impact on NII of an unexpected change in all current rates by an additive amount λ, where λ can be positive or negative. For mathematical convenience, assume the interest rates change before any cash inflows occur. NII now becomes functionally dependent on λ.

$$\text{NII}(\lambda) = \sum_{j=1}^{N} A_j[(1 + r_j)^{t_j}(1 + i_j + \lambda)^{1-t_j} - 1]$$

$$- \sum_{k=1}^{M} L_k[(1 + r_k)^{t_k}(1 + i_k + \lambda)^{1-t_k} - 1] \qquad (b)$$

If $\text{NII}(\lambda)$ is to be hedged, then a set of asset and liability flows must be found that leaves $\text{NII}(\lambda)$ equal to NII_0. For this to occur, it must be true that there be no change in NII(λ) as λ departs from zero by some small amount. Mathematically, this means that the derivative of NII(λ) with respect to λ equals zero in the neighborhood of $\lambda = 0$. Now

$$\text{NII}(\lambda)/\delta\lambda = \sum_{j=1}^{N} A_j (1 + r_j)^{t_j}(1 + i_j + \lambda)^{-t_j}(1 - t_j)$$
$$- \sum_{k=1}^{M} L_k(1 + r_k)^{t_k}(1 + i_k + \lambda)^{-t_k}(1 - t_k) \tag{c}$$

If we evaluate this derivitive at $\lambda = 0$ and set the result equal to zero, we obtain

$$\sum_{j=1}^{N} A_j(1 + r_j)^{t_j}(1 + i_j)^{-t_j}(1 - t_j) = \sum_{k=1}^{M} L_k(1 + r_k)^{t_k}(1 + i_k)^{-t_k}(1 - t_k) \tag{d}$$

But $A_j (1 + r_j)^{t_j}/(1 + i_j)^{t_j}$ is the current market value MV of a contractual flow of $A_j (1 + r_j)^{t_j}$ dollars t_j periods from now. Thus the first order condition for a NII hedge is that

$$\sum_{j=1}^{N} \text{MVA}_j(1 - t_j) = \sum_{k=1}^{M} \text{MVL}_k(1 - t_k) \tag{e}$$

This last equation can be written as

$$\sum_{j=1}^{N} \text{MVA}_j - \sum_{j=1}^{N} \text{MVA}_j t_j = \sum_{k=1}^{M} \text{MVL}_k - \sum_{jk=1}^{M} \text{MVL}_k t_k \tag{f}$$

Since $\sum_{j=1}^{N} \text{MVA}_j$ is the market value of rate-sensitive assets and since $\sum_{k=1}^{M} \text{MVL}_k$ is the market value of rate- sensitive liabilities, it follows that

$$\text{MV}_{\text{RSA}}(1 - D_{\text{RSA}}) = \text{MV}_{\text{RSL}}(1 - D_{\text{RSL}}) \tag{g}$$

From equation (c) above, this means

$$\Delta\text{NII} = [\text{MV}_{\text{RSA}}(1 - D_{\text{RSA}}) - \text{MV}_{\text{RSL}}(1 - D_{\text{RSL}})] \times \Delta i \tag{h}$$

Three strong assumptions were made in developing equation (h): (1) the term structure of interest rates is flat and unexpected changes in rates keep it so, (2) the rate change on an instrument is as volatile as on any other instrument of similar maturity, and (3) deposit withdrawals and loan prepayments are not interest rate dependent. One at a time each of these assumptions is relaxed in the following to determine how the hedging condition previously expressed will change.

A.   Nonflat Term Structures That Shift in a Nonparallel Fashion

If term structures are not flat, each instrument has an annualized interest rate of $h(0,t_n)$, where $h(0,t_n)$ is an element in a term structure for the nth type of instrument with repricing at date t_n. The NII_0 for this model is the same as equation (a), except that $h(0,t_j)$ replaces i_j and $h(0,t_k)$ replaces $i_{.k}$ The stochastic process affecting interest rates must be specified. Suppose that $1 + h^*(0,t) = (1 + h(0,t))(1 + \lambda)$, where $h^*(0,t)$ is the new term structure after an unexpected interest rate shock. $NII(\lambda)$ is now

$$NII(\lambda) = \sum_{j=1}^{N} A_j[(1 + r_j)^{t_j}(1 + h(0,t_j))^{1-t_j}(1 + \lambda)^{1-t_j} - 1]$$

$$- \sum_{k=1}^{M} L_k[(1 + r_k)^{t_k}(1 + h(0,t_k))^{1-t_k}(1 + \lambda)^{1-t_k} - 1]$$

(i)

Differentiate $NII(\lambda)$ with respect to λ, evaluate at $\lambda = 0$, and set the result equal to zero. This gives

$$\Sigma A_j(1 + r_j)^{t_j}(1 + h(0,t_j))^{1-t_j}(1 - t_j) = \Sigma L_k(1 + r_k)^{t_k}(1 + h(0,t_k))^{1-t_k}(1 - t_k) \quad \text{(j)}$$

or $\qquad \Sigma MV_{A_j}(1 + h(0,t_j))(1 - t_j) = \Sigma MV_{L_k}(1 + h(0,t_k))(1 - t_k)$

A reexpression of this hedging condition using a duration measure evolves in a less direct manner than before. Nevertheless, one can rewrite this last equation as

$$MV_{RSA}T_{RSA} = MV_{RSL}T_{RSL}$$

(k)

where $T_{RSA} = \Sigma MVA_j (1 + h(0,t_j))(1 - t_j)/MV_{RSA}$, and so on. Equality of T_{RSA} with T_{RSL} is equivalent to setting a weighted average repricing date of rate-sensitive assets with that of rate-sensitive liabilities.

B.   Relative Interest Rate Changes

Return to the assumption of flat term structures that shift in a parallel fashion, but relax the assumption that the sizes of the unexpected rate changes are equal for instruments of the same maturity.

Assume instead that all unexpected rate changes are perfectly correlated but have differing magnitudes across securities. Thus $\lambda_j = p_j\lambda$ and $\lambda_k = p_k\lambda$, where p_j, and p_k are constants. These values may be found by examining historical series. $NII(\lambda)$ becomes

$$NII(\lambda) = \Sigma A_j[(1 + r_j)^{t_j}(1 + i_j + p_j\lambda)^{1-t_j} - 1$$
$$- \Sigma L_k[(1 + r_k)^{t_k}(1 + i_k + p_k\lambda)^{1-t_{jk}} - 1]$$

(l)

Differentiate this equation with respect to λ, evaluate the result for $\lambda = 0$ and set it equal to zero. This gives

$$\Sigma MVA_j(1 - t_j)p_j = \Sigma MVA_{L_k}(1 - t_k)p_k$$

(m)

Again, implicit in this equation is the possibility of hedging by equating MV_{RSA} with MV_{RSL} and a weighted average repricing date of rate-sensitive assets with that of the rate- sensitive liabilities.

C. Rate-Sensitive Withdrawals and Prepayments

The current interest rates on mortgages, consumer CD's and so on help determine the rate of loan prepayments and early deposit withdrawals. Let A_j and L_k become functionally dependent on the unexpected change in interest rates. The hedging condition becomes

$$MV_{RSA}(1 - D_{RSA}) + \Sigma \delta A_j/\delta\lambda/_{\lambda=0}(1 + i'_j) \qquad (n)$$
$$= MV_{RSL}(1 - D_{RSL}) + \Sigma \delta L_k/\delta\lambda/_{\lambda=0}(1 + i'_k)$$

where $(1 + i') = (1 + r)^t(1 + i)^{1-t}$.

BIBLIOGRAPHY

Baker, James. *Asset/Liability Management.* American Bankers Association, 1981.

Bierwag, G.O., Kaufman G.G., and Toevs, A.L. "Duration: Its Development and Use in Bond Portfolio Management." *Financial Analysts Journal* (July/August 1983).

Bierwag, G.O., Kaufman G.G., and Toevs, A.L. *New Sources of Capital for the Savings and Loan Industry,* Fifth Annual Conference, Federal Home Loan Bank of San Francisco, 1979.

Bierwag, G.O., and Toevs, A.L. "Immunization of Interest Rate Risk in Commercial Banks and Savings and Loan Associations." *Bank Structure and Competition,* Federal Reserve Bank of Chicago, 1982.

Binder, Barret, and Linquist, Thomas. *Asset/Liability and Funds Management at U.S. Commercial Banks,* Bank Administration Institute, 1982.

Bookstaber, Richard. "The Use of Options in Performance Structuring: Molding Returns to Meet Investment Objectives." New York: Morgan Stanley (September 1984).

Dew, Kurt. "The Effective Gap: A More Accurate Measure of Interest Rate Risk." *American Banker* (June 10, 1981; September 19, 1981; December 9, 1981).

Dew, Kurt. "Which Asset-Liability Management Model?" *American Banker* (February 14, 1984).

Kaufman, G.G. "Measuring and Managing Interest Rate Risk: A Primer." *Economic Perspectives*(January/February 1984).

Peters, Helen F., Pinkus, Scott M., and Askin, David J. "Figuring the Odds: A Model of Prepayments." *Secondary Mortgage Markets* (May 1984).

Rose, Sanford. "Dark Days Ahead for Banks." *Fortune* (June 30, 1980).

Rose, Sanford. "Exorcising the Prepayment Specter." *American Banker* (February 14, 1984).

Rose, Sanford. "Making Fixed-Rate Mortgages the Right Way." *American Banker* (October 9, 1983).

Toevs, Alden. "Gap Management: Managing Interest Rate Risk in Banks and Thrifts." *Economic Review* (Spring 1983).

Toevs, Alden. "Hedging the Interest Rate Risk of Fixed- Income Securities with Uncertain Lives." *Journal of Portfolio Management* (Spring 1985).

Toevs, Alden. "Uses of Duration Analysis for the Control of Interest Rate Risk." New York: Morgan Stanley (January 1984).

Toevs, Alden. "Hedging the Interest Rate Risk of Fixed-Rate Mortgages with Prepayment Rights." *Handbook of Mortgage Backed Securities.* edited by Frank Fabozzi, Probus Publishing.

Toevs, Alden, and Jacob, David. "Interest Rate Futures: A Comparison of Alternative Hedge Ratio Methodologies." New York: Morgan Stanley (June 1984).

11 A Risk Controlled Approach to Managing Corporate Cash Pools

WILLIAM C. HANEY

INTRODUCTION

Traditionally, the role of cash and marketable securities on the corporate balance sheet of nonfinancial corporations has been to finance the immediate and short-term cash needs of the company. The nature of these cash needs have required that corporate cash managers emphasize liquidity and preservation of principal in their investment choices. Most corporate cash managers have found these characteristics, and what has turned out to be excellent rates of return as well, in the short-term money markets. That part of the corporate cash pool needed to fund the day-to-day operation of the company has typically been invested in overnight government repurchase agreements or bank deposits. The remaining portion of the cash pool needed to fund ongoing working capital requirements has typically been invested in other short-term money market instruments such as banker's acceptances, term repurchase agreements, commercial paper, bank certificates of deposit, Treasury bills, or bank time deposits.

The recent economic recovery has lead to a sharp increase in corporate profitability and a coincident buildup of cash on corporate balance sheets. For many corporations these unprecedented cash levels are now well in excess of their short-term cash needs and ongoing working capital requirements. That portion of the corporate cash pool which is in excess of traditional working capital and short-term cash needs is referred to as ''strategic cash.'' Strategic cash represents investable funds likely to remain invested for an extended period of time, perhaps a year or longer, before its ultimate corporate deployment. The presence of strategic cash requires cash managers take a longer-term focus than that used for proper management of working capital balances.

Surprisingly most strategic cash balances are currently being invested by "rolling over" short-term money market instruments. Such an investment strategy of concentrating strategic and working capital investments into the same securities may be explained by the observation that, after years of investing cash to fund short-term needs, many cash managers perceive these investments to be risk free. While short-term investments have little principal risk, crucial in the management of working capital, they have sizable reinvestment risks that must not be ignored in the proper management of strategic cash.

SECTION I   RISK

The corporate cash manager faces several risks in the management of corporate cash pools:

Interest rate risk
Holding period risk
Default risk
Tax risk

Interest rate risk arises during periods of volatile interest rates. Fluctuating interest rates can noticeably affect portfolio earnings and eventual liquidation value. Holding period risk is the term used to describe the uncertainty with which a corporation forecasts its future cash needs. Holding period risk can result in a cash manager unintentionally exposing corporate cash to interest rate risk if the actual timing of corporate cash needs turns out to be different than what was originally anticipated. Default risk represents the possibility of portfolio losses due to the default of specific investments within the corporate portfolio. And tax risk denotes the after- tax return sensitivity of the corporate portfolio due to unanticipated changes in federal and/or state tax laws or the marginal tax status of the corporation.

Historically, corporations have dealt with these risks effectively. Prior to the recent economic recovery, with most corporations in a net borrowing position, all corporate cash was used for working capital purposes, to support the short-term cash needs of the company. Because the timing of corporate cash needs was very short, a short-term investment strategy was appropriate for minimizing interest rate risk. Holding period risk was not a problem because cash was not held for very long periods of time. The same reasoning applied to default and tax risks.

Most corporate investment guidelines, which normally constrain the maturities of investments to the short-term, were drafted prior to the recent economic recovery. While these guidelines were and still are appropriate in controlling the interest rate risk of working capital balances, they force cash managers to assume substantial interest rate risk when applied to strategic cash balances. A short-term investment strategy exposes strategic cash pools, which have longer-term expected lives, to substantial earnings instability in volatile interest rate environments. This can have a large impact on the ultimate value of the cash pool when it is eventually liquidated to support an alternative corporate use, even though the principal value of the portfolio is preserved throughout its life. We will show this fact by presenting alternative investment strategies which provide more stable earnings and terminal portfolio values over the investable life of a strategic cash pool. This process illustrates that an "optimal" strategy can only be identified within a framework which explicitly measures the risks and expected returns associated with each alternative strategy relative to the time period over which these portfolios are expected to remain invested.

SECTION II RISK VERSUS RETURN

The rate of return on a security or portfolio of securities is the single most important number in portfolio analysis. In an uncertain world investors do not know what the exact rate of return on their portfolios will be over their expected investable lives. However, they can formulate a distribution of probable outcomes. From such a distribution the rate of return on average (expected return) can be calculated as can the variation in possible rates of return.

Financial analysts for a long time have pointed out that investments with high-potential variation in return tend also to have high-expected return. This is what one would intuitively expect. Investors demand high rates of return in compensation for high risks. This interaction in capital markets gives rise to the notion of a risk versus return tradeoff. Free lunches in this setting do not exist; to increase returns one must adopt risks. This is not to say that risks should always be avoided, rather, financial analysts recommend that the "price of risk" be determined. Understanding this price, investors should eschew all strategies that increase risk but not expected returns. If the expected return is there, they should undertake risky strategies so long as the price does not exceed a level determined by subjective (personal) attitudes about risk.

A stylized risk versus return tradeoff is depicted in Figure 11-1. Such a tradeoff can only be constructed relative to a stated investment holding period over which

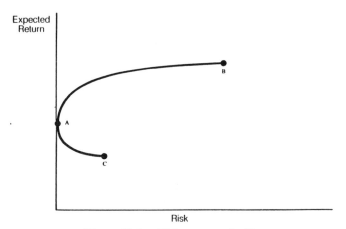

Figure 11-1.   Risk-return tradeoffs.

total rate of return can be measured. The least risky position is at Point A. The portion of the tradeoff curve between Points A and B is called "efficient"; here we have expected return increasing with risk. The portion of the tradeoff curve between Points A and C is called inefficient because risk increases as return falls. Rational investors restrict investment choices to those portfolios of securities on the efficient portion of the tradeoff curve.

Corporations face several interesting and complex risk-return tradeoffs in the management of their strategic cash pools. The four areas of risk exposure outlined in the previous section each give rise to a risk-return tradeoff. These risk-return tradeoffs will each be discussed in turn with the primary focus being directed toward interest rate risk.

SECTION III   INTEREST RATE RISK

The first area giving rise to a risk-return tradeoff is directly attributable to interest rate risk. Corporations manage pools of funds that will later be liquidated to fund alternative investments. Over the life of the portfolio, earnings and principal value may be subject to variation caused by changes in interest rates. Whether or not such exposure is present depends upon the timing of the cash inflows of principal and interest from the portfolio relative to the expected timing of cash outflows used in the asset redeployment.

If the average timing of cash inflows of the portfolio is structured to equal the average timing of cash needs, then the interest rate risk of the portfolio will be minimized. Note that it is asserted that inflows on average occur on an outflow date, not that each inflow occurs on an outflow date, for rate risk to be at a minimum. In the financial literature, matching the average cash inflow date with an outflow date is called duration matching. Matching each cash inflow date with an outflow date is called cash flow dedication. The primary advantage of duration matching relative to dedicated matching in minimizing interest rate risk is the added portfolio flexibility it affords. This flexibility translates into higher earnings on the portfolio.

The duration-matching technique has been widely and successfully used in other areas of portfolio management. But because the investment horizons of corporate cash managers have traditionally been so short, duration matching has generally been overlooked as a useful cash management tool. The computer simulations discussed below, which illustrate but do not rely on the duration concept, confirm the value of duration matching for limiting interest rate risk.

Duration is a summary measure of the interest rate risk associated with any series of cash flows, and provides a standard for comparing the interest rate characteristics of any security. This is most apparent for fixed-income securities. But one can also consider financial futures, options, and equities in a duration context. Duration is measured in years and can best be viewed as the term to maturity of a zero coupon bond with the same interest rate risk as the cash flow series in question; that is, duration synthetically constructs zero coupon bonds.[1]

---

[1] A more formal and comprehensive discussion of duration is provided in Chapter 3.

The more mismatched is the average timing of cash inflows and future cash needs, the more exposed is the investment strategy to changes in interest rates. This rate risk can be beneficial or not depending on how rates change relative to a corporate cash manager's own forecast. There is an important caveat in this reasoning. Capital markets have a "consensus" rate forecast imbedded in security prices.[2] The steep positive slope existing in the current yield curve implies a market forecast of higher future short-term interest rates. The incremental yield available on longer maturities relative to shorter maturities represents a market- determined gauge as to how high short-term rates are expected to rise. To benefit from intentional duration mismatching and anticipated rate movements, the corporate cash manager's interest rate forecast (or set of forecasts given probabilistically) must be more accurate than the market forecast. In today's economic environment this means that an investment strategy structured intentionally short relative to the expected investment horizon will outperform the riskless duration matched strategy only if short-term rates rise by more than the market anticipates. It is not enough just to correctly predict the direction of interest rates. There is ample financial research and variation in career paths of interest rate forecasters to suggest that rate forecasting is a highly inexact science. This means that risk-return tradeoffs most often rely on inaccurate interest rate forecasts. Forecasting errors causes the true risk-return tradeoff to differ from what was expected.

Refer back to Figure 11-1; in the context of interest rate risk, the least risk position at Point A represents an investment in securities with an average time to cash inflow equal to the intended holding period. That is, the risk versus return tradeoff at Point A is that of an investment in securities with a combined duration equal to the holding period. The tradeoff relationship between interest rate risk and return is constructed from a spectrum of interest rate scenarios and the probabilities of their occurrences. Each security and portfolio of securities will have its own expected return and variation around this expected outcome given the rate scenarios considered. These diverse outcomes form the points on the tradeoff curve.

The risk-return tradeoff depicted in Figure 11-1 represents the current situation only if the assumed rate changes and their assigned probabilities are reasonable. If the investor makes uninformed rate forecasts, then the expected tradeoffs will be incorrect. For the holding period of concern, however, the security that gives us Point A in the incorrect tradeoff continues to be at Point A in the correct tradeoff. This is fundamentally important. The risk versus return characteristics for all securities, except duration-matched securities, depend upon the forecast accuracy of the investor. Duration-matched securities earn an expected return that is invariant to interest rate forecasts.

The remainder of this section revolves around the derivation and analysis of the risk-return tradeoffs which characterize the current U.S. Treasury market. The discussion is lengthy and is thus divided into seven smaller subsections. The use of

---

[2]The notion of a consensus market rate forecast is developed under the discussion of pure expectations theory in Chapter 2. A brief discussion of pure expectations theory appears later in this section as well. The market forecast imbedded in the current U.S. Treasury yield curve is used extensively in the risk-return analysis and computer simulations which follow.

computer simulation in the construction of risk-return tradeoffs is discussed in the first subsection. Two distinct sets of tradeoffs are produced. Several holding periods are analyzed in each set. Risk-return tradeoffs are first derived under "pure-expectations" assumptions of the term structure of interest rates. This theory of the term structure, which is briefly described in the second subsection, identifies the consensus market interest rate forecast mentioned earlier, and enables cash managers to properly evaluate the interest rate bet implicit in duration-mismatching strategies. The computer simulations illustrate many of the conclusions stated in previous paragraphs on risk taking and risk avoiding activities. The value of duration is clearly demonstrated. In light of empirical evidence supporting the existence of liquidity premiums associated with longer term investments, a second set of risk-return tradeoffs are computed under "liquidity preference" term structure assumptions in the third subsection. The two sets of tradeoff curves are then displayed graphically, as in Figure 11-1, and jointly analyzed in the fourth subsection. Since the underlying pure-expectations and liquidity preference interest rate assumptions are of opposing theoretical extremes, the resulting risk-return curves are shown to bracket the current universe of feasible tradeoffs. The analysis results in the conclusion that short-term rollover strategies are inefficient investments over longer-term holding periods for interest rate neutral investors. In the presence of liquidity premiums, duration-matched securities are shown to be not only less risky than short-term rollover strategies, but better investments in terms of expected return as well. A brief digression is then made in the fifth subsection on the proper use of computer simulation in the measurement of interest rate risk. This is followed by a discussion in the sixth subsection of some of the theoretical and managerial aspects of duration in controlling interest rate risk. And finally, the section finishes up in the seventh subsection with the presentation of the previous risk-return tradeoffs on an after-tax basis.

Using Computer Simulations to Construct Risk versus Return Tradeoffs

Computer simulations can be used to construct the risk-return tradeoffs of a wide variety of securities. In the following example the risk-return tradeoffs which characterize the current market for investments in U.S. Treasury securities are derived and analyzed using computer simulation. A tradeoff relationship is computed for holding periods of six months, one, two, and three years. These holding periods are studied because they correspond to the expected portfolio lives of the strategic cash pools at many corporations in today's economic environment. There are four distinct steps in simulating the risk- return tradeoff for each holding period.

1. Three interest rate scenarios are examined. These scenarios are constructed to bracket a broad range of likely interest rate outcomes. Treasury yields follow the implied market forecast contained in the yield curve of January 21, 1985 in the first scenario. In the second and third scenarios Treasury rates evolve at levels 300 basis points less than and greater than the base case scenario respectively. These upward and downward shifts are assumed to occur immediately.

2. Each alternative Treasury investment is assumed to be purchased at par with a yield corresponding to the Treasury yield curve of January 21, 1985. The total return for each Treasury investment is then calculated under each of the three interest rate scenarios for holding periods of six months, one, two and three years. Total return is the sum of interest, interest on interest, and the maturity or liquidation value of the investment, including capital gain (or loss), divided by the starting value. Total returns are standardized by stating them on a bond equivalent yield basis. Thus each investment has three possible returns for each of the four individual holding periods. These total returns are reported in Table 11-1.

3. Next, probability weights are assigned to each of the three interest rate scenarios. The simulations in Table 11-1 assume the cash manager is neutral in his or her perceptions towards future movements in interest rates relative to the market forecast by making the three possible interest rate scenarios equally likely to occur. The average, or expected return for each instrument over each holding period is then calculated by weighting each possible total return outcome by its probability of occurrence and then summing. For example, Portfolio 3 in Table 11-1 for a 6-month holding period experiences returns of 8.39%, −5.81%, and 24.05% in the market forecast, +300 basis point shift, and −300 basis point shift interest rate scenarios respectively. The expected return of 8.87% is given by 8.39% multiplied by .333 plus −5.81% multiplied by .333 plus 24.05% multiplied by .333.

4. Finally, the *range,* or difference between the highest possible outcome and the lowest possible outcome, is calculated. A positive value for the range indicates that a particular investment benefits from a rise in rates relative to the market forecast, but suffers in a declining rate environment, or when rates rise by less than the market forecast. A negative value indicates just the opposite. This range represents a proxy measure of risk for each security. The larger the absolute magnitude of the range in potential return outcomes, the more risk is associated with an investment. The range of possible outcomes is one of many ways to characterize risk. Other popular measures include the statistical concept of variance, mean absolute deviation, and probability weighted ranges.

By reading down any column or by reading across any row of Table 11-1 it becomes apparent that the interest rate risk inherent in any investment depends upon the difference between duration and the length of the holding period. If duration matches the holding period, then portfolio risk is minimized. For example, a 6-month Treasury bill locks in a certain return of 8.38% over a 6-month holding period, regardless of future interest rate movements. Over longer holding periods, however, rolling over 6-month Treasury bills becomes a risky strategy. This is because 6-month Treasury bills have to be rolled over every 6-months at unknown future interest rates.

The ultimate return from a 6-month Treasury bill rollover strategy will depend on what interest rates do in the future. The longer the holding period, the greater the

Table 11-1. Risk versus Return Characteristics of the Treasury Market (Pure Expectations Interest Rate Assumptions—Total Pretax Return*)

6 MONTH HOLDING PERIOD

	DURATION (Years)	MARKET FORECAST	+300 bp SHIFT	-300 bp SHIFT	EXPECTED RETURN	RANGE IN RETURN
5 YR. NOTE	3.99	8.40%	(11.03%)	30.59%	9.32%	(4163 bp)
4 YR. NOTE	3.36	8.39%	(7.76%)	26.39%	9.01%	(3415 bp)
PORTFOLIO 3	3.00	8.39%	(5.81%)	24.05%	8.87%	(2986 bp)
3 YR. NOTE	2.66	8.39%	(3.95%)	21.80%	8.74%	(2575 bp)
PORTFOLIO 2	2.00	8.38%	(0.29%)	17.62%	8.57%	(1792 bp)
2 YR. NOTE	1.86	8.38%	0.47%	16.76%	8.54%	(1629 bp)
PORTFOLIO 1	1.00	8.38%	5.44%	11.41%	8.41%	(598 bp)
1 YR. NOTE	0.98	8.38%	5.56%	11.28%	8.41%	(573 bp)
6 MO. BILL	0.50	8.38%	8.38%	8.38%	8.38%	0 bp

1 YEAR HOLDING PERIOD

	MARKET FORECAST	+300 bp SHIFT	-300 bp SHIFT	EXPECTED RETURN	RANGE IN RETURN
5 YR. NOTE	9.00%	0.41%	18.30%	9.24%	(1789 bp)
4 YR. NOTE	9.00%	2.15%	16.30%	9.15%	(1415 bp)
PORTFOLIO 3	9.00%	3.17%	15.16%	9.11%	(1199 bp)
3 YR. NOTE	9.00%	4.15%	14.08%	9.07%	(993 bp)
PORTFOLIO 2	8.99%	6.05%	12.05%	9.03%	(600 bp)
2 YR. NOTE	8.99%	6.45%	11.63%	9.02%	(518 bp)
PORTFOLIO 1	8.99%	8.99%	8.99%	8.99%	0 bp
1 YR. NOTE	8.99%	9.06%	8.93%	8.99%	13 bp
6 MO. BILL	8.99%	10.49%	7.49%	8.99%	300 bp

2 YEAR HOLDING PERIOD

	DURATION (Years)	MARKET FORECAST	+300 bp SHIFT	-300 bp SHIFT	EXPECTED RETURN	RANGE IN RETURN
5 YR. NOTE	3.99	9.91%	7.01%	13.00%	9.97%	(599 bp)
4 YR. NOTE	3.36	9.91%	7.91%	12.01%	9.94%	(410 bp)
PORTFOLIO 3	3.00	9.91%	8.44%	11.45%	9.93%	(301 bp)
3 YR. NOTE	2.66	9.91%	8.94%	10.92%	9.92%	(197 bp)
PORTFOLIO 2	2.00	9.91%	9.91%	9.91%	9.91%	0 bp
2 YR. NOTE	1.86	9.91%	10.12%	9.70%	9.91%	42 bp
PORTFOLIO 1	1.00	9.91%	11.41%	8.39%	9.90%	302 bp
1 YR. NOTE	0.98	9.91%	11.44%	8.36%	9.90%	308 bp
6 MO. BILL	0.50	9.91%	12.17%	7.64%	9.90%	452 bp

3 YEAR HOLDING PERIOD

	MARKET FORECAST	+300 bp SHIFT	-300 bp SHIFT	EXPECTED RETURN	RANGE IN RETURN
5 YR. NOTE	10.38%	9.43%	11.42%	10.41%	(199 bp)
4 YR. NOTE	10.38%	10.04%	10.76%	10.40%	(72 bp)
PORTFOLIO 3	10.38%	10.38%	10.38%	10.38%	0 bp
3 YR. NOTE	10.38%	10.74%	10.04%	10.38%	70 bp
PORTFOLIO 2	10.38%	11.39%	9.37%	10.38%	203 bp
2 YR. NOTE	10.38%	11.53%	9.23%	10.38%	230 bp
PORTFOLIO 1	10.38%	12.40%	8.36%	10.38%	404 bp
1 YR. NOTE	10.38%	12.42%	8.34%	10.38%	408 bp
6 MO. BILL	10.38%	12.90%	7.86%	10.38%	505 bp

(*) Total Pre-Tax Return is the sum of pre-tax interest, interest on interest and the maturity or liquidation value of the investment, including capital gain (or loss), divided by the starting price and standardized to a bond equivalent basis.

NOTE:
PORTFOLIO 1 consists of .976 Dollars of the 1 YR. NOTE and .024 Dollars of the 2 YR. NOTE.
PORTFOLIO 2 consists of .828 Dollars of the 2 YR. NOTE and .172 Dollars of the 3 YR. NOTE.
PORTFOLIO 3 consists of .510 Dollars of the 3 YR. NOTE and .489 Dollars of the 4 YR. NOTE.

interest rate risk exposure of this strategy. The range in potential return outcomes for a 1-year holding period is 300 basis points, 452 basis points for a 2-year holding period, and 505 basis points for a 3-year holding period. Likewise the 2-year duration Treasury investment, referred to as Portfolio 2, is riskless over a 2-year holding period with a certain return of 9.91%. Over shorter or longer holding periods interest rate risk is present. In fact, the greater the difference between the 2-year duration of Portfolio 2 and the length of the holding period, the greater the interest rate risk exposure. The range in potential return outcomes for a 1-year holding period is 600 basis points and for a 6-month holding period 1792 basis points. For a 3-year holding period the range in potential return outcomes is 203 basis points.

Not only is the magnitude of the difference between the duration of an investment and the holding period important; the direction of the mismatch is important as well. Those investments with durations less than the holding period benefit when interest rates rise by more than the market forecast, but suffer when interest rates either decline or rise by less than the market forecast.[3] Analogously, those investments with durations greater than the holding period benefit when interest rates either decline or rise by less than the market forecast but suffer when rates rise by more.[4] This property of duration enables cash managers to properly construct riskless portfolios and to structure portfolios which are consistent with a specific interest rate forecast as well. Added risk for added return can be analyzed incrementally by "pricing" added return in terms of associated added risk. Incremental risk measurement helps cash managers determine how aggressive they should be. For example, a bullish cash manager who invests in Portfolio 2, the 2-year duration Treasury portfolio, for a 1-year holding period will pick up 306 basis points (12.05% − 8.99%) over the corresponding 1-year duration portfolio, Portfolio 1, if rates do indeed shift downwards by 300 points. However, his or her downside is − 294 basis points (6.05% − 8.99%) if exactly the opposite occurs. In this case the "price" of the incremental 306 basis points if his or her bet works is the − 294 basis points if his or her bet turns sour.

The duration-matched portfolios, Portfolio 1, 2, and 3, are constructed using individual Treasury notes with durations slightly less than and slightly greater than the overall durations of each portfolio. Portfolio 3, for instance, consists of $.510 of the 3-year note and $.489 of the 4-year note. This specific weighting results in an overall portfolio duration of three years. Likewise the specific weightings of individual notes within Portfolios 1 and 2 result in overall portfolio durations of one and two years respectively. These weightings are a direct consequence of the additivity property of duration. This property states that the overall duration of a portfolio is equal to a price weighted average of the durations of each investment comprising that portfolio. The 3-year note has a duration of 2.66 years and the 4-year note has a duration of 3.36 years. The overall duration of three years for Portfolio 3 is therefore given by .510 multiplied by 2.66 plus .489 multiplied by 3.36.[5]

[3]This is evidenced by a positive range of potential return outcomes in Table 11-1.
[4]This is evidenced by a negative range of potential return outcomes in Table 11-1.
[5]The additivity property of duration is discussed in more detail in Chapter 3.

The Market Forecast of Interest Rates: Pure Expectations Theory

The market forecast of interest rates used in the computer simulations is consistent with the "pure expectations theory" of the term structure of interest rates. This theory stipulates that intermediate and long-term interest rates are geometric averages of the current short-term rate and market expectations of future short-term rates. Investors are assumed to be risk neutral in that they will hold whatever maturity investment provides maximum expected return over their investment holding period. In equilibrium, therefore, the return on a 1-year investment must equal the expected return from rolling over two sequential 6-month investments. The return on a 2-year investment must equal both the expected return from rolling over two sequential 1-year investments and the expected return from rolling over four sequential 6-month investments. This equilibrium condition must be satisfied among all possible combinations of investments. This is the reason the returns generated from each investment under the market forecast rate scenario are identical for any individual investment holding period in Table 11-1.[6]

Analyzing investment alternatives in a pure expectations framework provides the cash manager with valuable insights. The future or forward expected interest rates predicted by this theory can be thought of as breakeven rates, since at these rates all investments of comparable credit quality provide identical returns. Portfolios with durations shorter than the investment holding period will outperform longer-term portfolios if actual interest rates in the future attain levels greater than the forward breakeven rates. Similarly, portfolios with longer durations than the investment-holding period will outperform shorter-term portfolios if future interest rates fall below the breakeven rates. The cash manager must compare his or her own interest rate forecast to the forward breakeven rates to identify which portfolio structure is optimal relative to that forecast. This is especially so if the cash manager intends to place an interest rate bet by intentionally mismatching the duration of his or her portfolio with the investment holding period. A duration-matched strategy achieves its expected return regardless of future interest rate outcomes. Additional return is possible from a duration mismatching strategy only if interest rates evolve differently than that predicted by pure expectations theory.

The market forecast for future interest rates imbedded in the Treasury yield curve of January 21, 1985 appears in Table 11-2.[7] The steep positive slope of this yield curve indicates that rates in general, especially short-term rates, are expected to rise significantly in the future. Under pure expectations theory, all Treasury investments must provide the same expected return over all investment holding periods in equilibrium. Expected short-term rates therefore must rise dramatically in order for short-term investment rollover strategies to provide the same expected return as longer-term investments in this interest rate environment. This is evident in Table 11-2. The

---

[6]See Chapter 2 for a more complete description of pure expectations theory.

[7]These rates give rise to the "market forecast" total returns in Table 11-1. The returns obtained under the +300 and −300 basis point shift columns are from interest rate scenarios which are 300 basis points greater than and less than the market forecast shown in Table 11-2.

Table 11-2.   Implied Market Interest Rate Forecast (Pure Expectations Interest Rate Assumptions)

	6 MONTH T-BILLS	1 YEAR NOTES	2 YEAR NOTES	3 YEAR NOTES	4 YEAR NOTES	5 YEAR NOTES
CURRENT YIELD CURVE(*)	8.38%	8.98%	9.85%	10.29%	10.65%	10.89%
YIELD CURVE IN 6 MONTHS	9.61	9.97	10.55	10.89	11.15	11.32
YIELD CURVE IN 1 YEAR	10.35	10.81	11.05	11.34	11.51	11.64
YIELD CURVE IN 2 YEARS	11.08	11.32	11.64	11.80	11.91	12.06
YIELD CURVE IN 3 YEARS	11.78	12.00	12.08	12.15	12.30	12.24

(*)   The CURRENT YIELD CURVE is the current coupon U.S. Treasury yield curve as of January 21,1985.

6-month Treasury bill rate rises from its current level of 8.38% to an expected level of 11.78% by the end of the 3-year simulation. This represents a 350 basis point rise. The rate on 5-year notes is expected to rise from its current level of 10.89% to 12.24% by the end of the 3-year simulation. This is a relatively modest rise of 135 basis points in comparison to the 350 basis point increase expected on 6-month Treasury bill rates. The reason for this is that 5-year notes need to make up a much smaller rate differential relative to 7-, 10-, and 20-year notes than 6-month bills need to make up relative to 3-, 4-, and 5-year notes.

Viewing these expected forward rates as breakeven rates allows the cash manager to quantify the exact magnitude of the interest rate bet implicitly made with an intentional duration-mismatching strategy. For example, consider a bearish cash manager who would like to roll over 6-month Treasury bills over a 1-year holding period in the hope of capitalizing on a general rise in interest rates. The cash manager knows that a certain return of 9.00% is possible by investing in Portfolio 1, the 1-year duration-matched Treasury investment. The current rate on 6-month Treasury bills is 8.38%. Referring to Table 11-2, the 6-month Treasury bill must be rolled over at a yield of 9.61%, a 123 basis point increase over current levels, to generate the same 9.00% return over 1-year that is available with no risk from the duration-matched strategy. Indeed our bearish cash manager would be making quite a substantial interest rate bet with the rollover strategy relative to what he can achieve with certainty via a duration-matching strategy.

Over longer holding periods the required breakeven reinvestment rates are even higher. For 2- and 3-year holding periods, riskless returns of 9.91% and 10.38% are possible with Portfolios 2 and 3, the respective duration-matching strategies. The average reinvestment rates required for the rollover strategy to match the riskless returns offered by Portfolios 2 and 3 are 10.42% and 10.78% respectively. The interest rate bet taken with the rollover strategy relative to the riskless strategies is that 6-month Treasury bill rates will on average be at least 204 basis points higher than current levels over the next two years, and 240 basis points higher than current levels over the next three years. The interest rate bet taken with even shorter-term rollover strategies currently yielding less than 6-month Treasuries is even more pronounced. Clearly the conventional view of short-term investment strategies being riskless ignores the substantial reinvestment risk this type of strategy is exposed to over longer investment holding periods.

An Alternative Interest Rate Forecast: Liquidity Preference Theory

While pure expectations theory is a useful framework from which to analyze the risk-return tradeoffs from alternative investment strategies, its use as a forecaster of future interest rates is limited. Several studies have shown that the future interest rates predicted by pure expectations theory are consistently upward biased. Theoreticians have attributed this upward bias to the presence of a liquidity premium built into the term structure of interest rates. Under this theory of the term structure, known as "liquidity preference theory," the supply of long-term debt in the market is assumed to always exceed the demand for long-term debt from investors. To induce investors to absorb the over supply of long-term debt in the market, long-term interest rates must exceed the geometric average of the expected short-term rates in the future. The difference between the actual long-term rate and the average of the expected future short-term rates is called the liquidity premium. Liquidity preference theory asserts that liquidity premiums are always positive and increasing in magnitude with the maturity of an investment. This explains why yield curves are normally positively sloped, even in some instances where the general market consensus is that interest rates are expected to fall in the future.[8]

Pure expectations theory explains the entire difference between short-term and long-term rates by investors' expectations of future short-term rates. Liquidity preference theory assigns only a portion of this difference to investors' expectations of future short-term rates, with the remainder being explained by a positive liquidity premium. Pure expectations theory can be thought of as an extreme case of liquidity preference theory, with liquidity premiums on long- term investments equal to zero. The other extreme in today's interest rate environment would be to attribute the entire difference between short-term and long-term rates to liquidity premiums. In this extreme case of liquidity preference theory, all interest rates would be expected to remain constant in the future. The risk-return tradeoffs which result from analyzing the Treasury market in this liquidity preference extreme are reported in Table 11-3.

Table 11-3 is constructed by using computer simulations to analyze the total return performance of each Treasury investment under three possible interest rate scenarios. The base case scenario assumes that all interest rates remain constant throughout the simulation. The other two scenarios assume that interest rates shift upwards (downwards) by 300 basis points immediately after the start of the simulations, and then remain constant at their new levels throughout the remainder of the simulations. The expected returns computed in the simulations are neutral towards the direction of future interest rate movements as they are obtained by equally weighting the three possible interest rate scenarios. Note that this neutrality assumption is different than that implied by the neutrality assumption in the previous pure expectations simulations. Those simulations were neutral relative to the base case market forecast, which

[8]A more rigorous treatment of liquidity preference theory is given in Chapter 2.

Table 11-3. Risk versus Return Characteristics of the Treasury Market (Liquidity Preference Interest Rate Assumptions—Total Pretax Returns*)

6 MONTH HOLDING PERIOD

	DURATION (Years)	CONSTANT RATES	300 bp RISE	300 bp DECLINE	EXPECTED RETURN	RANGE IN RETURN
5 YR. NOTE	3.99	11.73%	(7.97%)	34.21%	12.66%	(4218 bp)
4 YR. NOTE	3.36	11.68%	(4.69%)	29.93%	12.31%	(3461 bp)
PORTFOLIO 3	3.00	11.46%	(2.93%)	27.31%	11.95%	(3025 bp)
3 YR. NOTE	2.66	11.24%	(1.25%)	24.81%	11.60%	(2607 bp)
PORTFOLIO 2	2.00	11.08%	2.29%	20.44%	11.27%	(1815 bp)
2 YR. NOTE	1.86	11.04%	3.02%	19.53%	11.20%	(1651 bp)
PORTFOLIO 1	1.00	9.59%	6.62%	12.65%	9.62%	(603 bp)
1 YR. NOTE	0.98	9.56%	6.71%	12.49%	9.58%	(578 bp)
6 MO. BILL	0.50	8.38%	8.38%	8.38%	8.38%	0 bp

2 YEAR HOLDING PERIOD

	DURATION (Years)	CONSTANT RATES	300 bp RISE	300 bp DECLINE	EXPECTED RETURN	RANGE IN RETURN
5 YR. NOTE	3.99	11.58%	8.66%	14.68%	11.64%	(603 bp)
4 YR. NOTE	3.36	11.29%	9.27%	13.40%	11.32%	(413 bp)
PORTFOLIO 3	3.00	11.06%	9.57%	12.61%	11.08%	(304 bp)
3 YR. NOTE	2.66	10.84%	9.86%	11.86%	10.85%	(200 bp)
PORTFOLIO 2	2.00	9.98%	9.98%	9.98%	9.98%	0 bp
2 YR. NOTE	1.86	9.80%	10.00%	9.60%	9.80%	41 bp
PORTFOLIO 1	1.00	8.99%	10.48%	7.48%	8.98%	300 bp
1 YR. NOTE	0.98	8.97%	10.49%	7.43%	8.96%	306 bp
6 MO. BILL	0.50	8.38%	10.63%	6.13%	8.38%	450 bp

1 YEAR HOLDING PERIOD

	CONSTANT RATES	300 bp RISE	300 bp DECLINE	EXPECTED RETURN	RANGE IN RETURN
5 YR. NOTE	11.63%	2.97%	21.01%	11.87%	(1804 bp)
4 YR. NOTE	11.53%	4.62%	18.89%	11.68%	(1428 bp)
PORTFOLIO 3	11.28%	5.40%	17.50%	11.40%	(1210 bp)
3 YR. NOTE	11.05%	6.16%	16.17%	11.12%	(1001 bp)
PORTFOLIO 2	10.70%	7.73%	13.78%	10.74%	(605 bp)
2 YR. NOTE	10.63%	8.06%	13.29%	10.66%	(523 bp)
PORTFOLIO 1	9.01%	9.01%	9.01%	9.01%	0 bp
1 YR. NOTE	8.97%	9.03%	8.90%	8.97%	13 bp
6 MO. BILL	8.38%	9.88%	6.88%	8.38%	300 bp

3 YEAR HOLDING PERIOD

	CONSTANT RATES	300 bp RISE	300 bp DECLINE	EXPECTED RETURN	RANGE IN RETURN
5 YR. NOTE	11.40%	10.43%	12.45%	11.43%	(202 bp)
4 YR. NOTE	11.07%	10.71%	11.46%	11.08%	(75 bp)
PORTFOLIO 3	10.63%	10.63%	10.63%	10.63%	0 bp
3 YR. NOTE	10.21%	10.56%	9.88%	10.22%	68 bp
PORTFOLIO 2	10.10%	11.09%	9.11%	10.10%	198 bp
2 YR. NOTE	10.08%	11.20%	8.95%	10.07%	225 bp
PORTFOLIO 1	8.99%	10.99%	6.99%	8.99%	399 bp
1 YR. NOTE	8.97%	10.98%	6.94%	8.96%	404 bp
6 MO. BILL	8.38%	10.88%	5.88%	8.38%	500 bp

(*) Total Pre-Tax Return is the sum of pre-tax interest, interest on interest, interest on interest and the maturity or liquidation value of the investment, including capital gain (or loss), divided by the starting price and standardized to a bond equivalent basis.

NOTE:
PORTFOLIO 1 consists of .976 Dollars of the 1 YR. NOTE and .024 Dollars of the 2 YR. NOTE.
PORTFOLIO 2 consists of .828 Dollars of the 2 YR. NOTE and .172 Dollars of the 3 YR. NOTE.
PORTFOLIO 3 consists of .510 Dollars of the 3 YR. NOTE and .489 Dollars of the 4 YR. NOTE.

itself assumes that interest rates will rise fairly dramatically throughout the simulation. The constant-rate interest rate scenario used as a base case in the present liquidity-preference simulations eliminates this upward bias toward future rate movements.[9]

By reading down any column or by reading across any row of Table 11-3 the same conclusions as previously discussed regarding duration and interest rate risk are illustrated. The interest rate risk of any investment depends upon the mismatch between its duration and the length of the holding period. The greater the duration mismatch, the greater the interest rate risk exposure as measured by the range in possible return outcomes. Interest rate risk is minimized by matching the duration of an investment portfolio with the length of the holding period. And investments with duration less than the holding period benefit from a rise in interest rates relative to the base case scenario, while investments with duration greater than the holding period are adversely affected. Exactly the opposite occurs when rates decline relative to the base case scenario.

The Risk-Return Tradeoff Curves

The risk-return tradeoffs computed in Tables 11-1 and 11-3 are best compared in graphic form as shown in Figure 11-2 and Figure 11-3. The expected return associated with each of the Treasury investments is measured along the vertical axis, and the absolute magnitude of the range in potential return outcomes over the three simulated interest rate scenarios for each investment is measured along the horizontal axis.[10] This range is a proxy measure of the interest rate risk associated with each investment. The larger this range the more risk is associated with an investment. Because risk and return can only be measured relative to an investment horizon, a separate risk-return tradeoff chart is graphed for each holding period. Figure 11-2 shows the risk-return tradeoff curves of the Treasury market under assumptions of pure expectations theory. Figure 11-3 shows the same tradeoff curves under liquidity preference assumptions.

Under the pure expectations interest rate scenario used as a base case in the computer simulations from which the risk-return tradeoff curves in Figure 11-2 were constructed, all investments generated identical total returns over each holding period considered. Because the probability weights associated with the three scenarios used in the simulations are neutral relative to the base case, the resulting risk-return trade-

---

[9]The simple Macaulay measure of duration, as described in Chapter 3, is used in both Table 3-1 and Table 3-3. Given the underlying interest rate assumptions in the two tables, slightly more complex versions of duration should theoretically be used. A slight increase in accuracy would result with these more sophisticated measures. For the purposes of this analysis, however, the simple Macaulay measure is adequate.

[10]The expected returns in these charts differ from the expected returns referred to in the discussion of pure expectations theory and implied market rate forecasts. The expected returns used to construct the risk-return tradeoffs are probability weighted averages of the individual return outcomes from each of the three interest rate scenarios used in the respective computer simulations.

off curves are for the most part flat.[11] Flat risk-return tradeoff curves indicate that productive risk taking is not possible. Since the riskless duration-matched investment provides essentially the same expected return as investments exposed to substantial amounts of interest rate risk, it makes little sense to invest in anything but the duration-matched investment.

The risk-return tradeoff curves from the liquidity preference set of simulations in Figure 11-3 are much more steeply sloped. The positive liquidity premiums postulated by liquidity preference theory produce expected returns which increase with the duration of an investment, begetting steeply sloped tradeoff curves. With neutral probability weightings relative to the base case constant interest rate scenario, investments with durations less than the holding period appear on the previously described inefficient portion of the tradeoff curve (expected return decreasing with increasing risk), while investments with durations greater than the holding period appear on the efficient portion of the curve (expected return increasing with increasing risk).

Positively sloped risk-return tradeoff curves suggest that productive risk taking is possible, but only among those investments which form the efficient portion of the tradeoff curve. Over longer-term holding periods, interest rate neutral investors would always prefer investments with durations greater than or equal to the holding period to short-term investment strategies. Short-term investment strategies not only expose portfolios to substantial reinvestment risk, but also deprive the investor of the liquidity premium offered by less risky longer-term investments, resulting in lower expected returns for the risky short-term strategies relative to the less risky longer-term strategies.

The decision to invest in the riskless duration-matched strategy as opposed to one of the duration-mismatched strategies which appear on the efficient portion of the tradeoff curve is determined only by subjective attitudes concerning risk. Given an investor's personal appetite for risk, a risky strategy should be adopted only if the incremental return offered by that strategy is adequate compensation for the incremental risk.

The only instrument on the efficient portion of the flat risk-return tradeoff curve generated under pure expectations assumptions is the riskless duration-matched investment. Since all investments under pure expectations have identical expected returns, the optimal investment is clearly the one with the least risk. Under the liquidity preference assumptions used in the risk-return tradeoff curves of Figure 11-3, because of liquidity premiums, investments with duration greater than or equal to the length of the holding period are on the efficient portion of the tradeoff curve. In both cases short-term rollover strategies are inferior investments over longer-term holding periods for investors with unbiased future interest rate outlooks as compared to

---

[11]In the shorter holding periods the total returns of the longer duration investments experience a greater response to declines in interest rates than rises, causing a moderate upward slope in the tradeoff curve. This slight nonsymmetrical behavior is caused by the nonlinearity of the relationship between bond pricing and interest rates, sometimes referred to in the financial literature as "convexity."

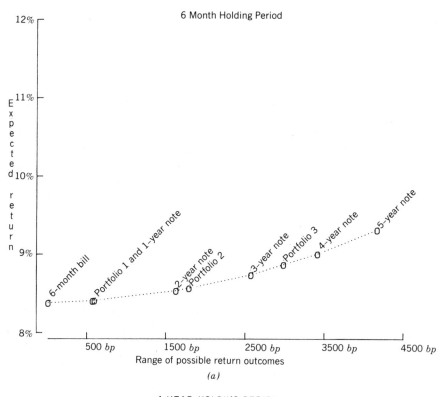

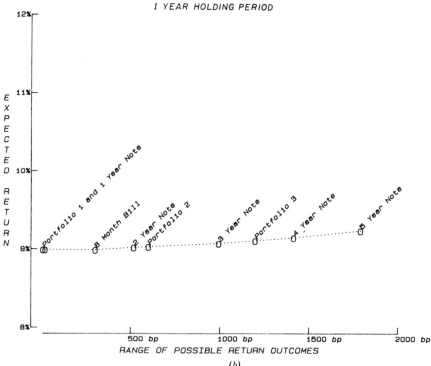

Figure 11-2. Risk versus return characteristics of the U.S. Treasury market (pure expectations interest rate assumptions).

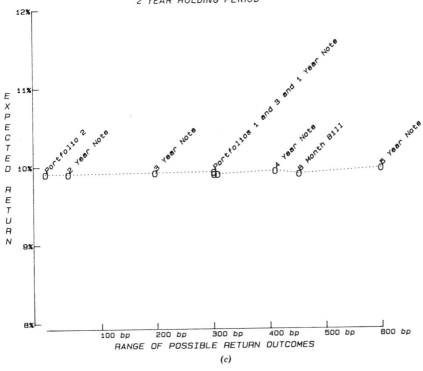

(c)

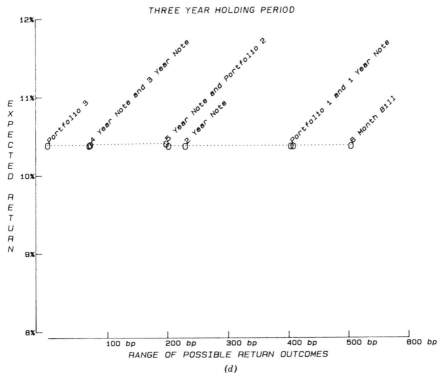

(d)

Figure 11-2. (Continued)

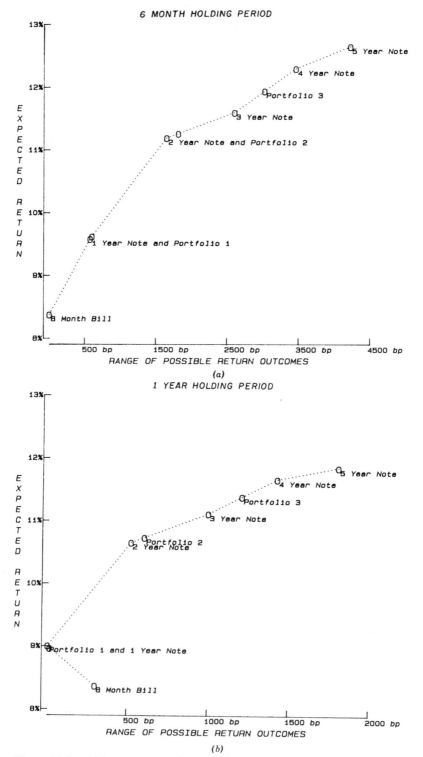

Figure 11-3. Risk versus return characteristics of the U.S. Treasury market (liquidity preference interest rate assumptions).

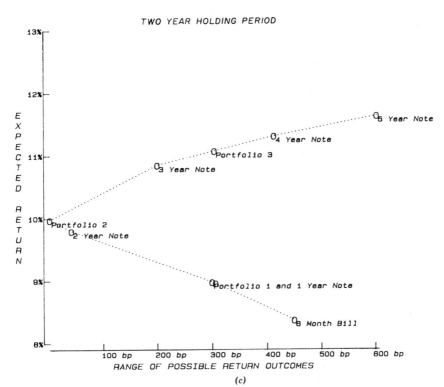

TWO YEAR HOLDING PERIOD

(c)

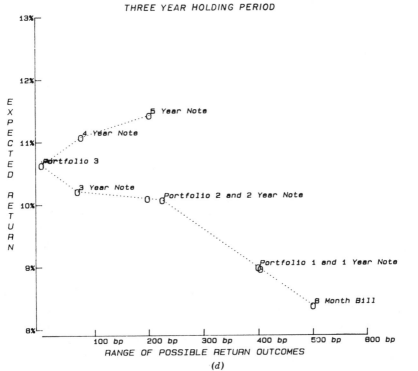

THREE YEAR HOLDING PERIOD

(d)

Figure 11-3. (Continued)

longer-term strategies which better match the investor's holding period. These same conclusions would be arrived at under most credited theories of the term structure of interest rates. Since the explanation these theories posit for the difference between short- and long-term interest rates usually involve some combination of market expectations of future short-term rates and liquidity premiums, the risk-return tradeoff curves they yield would fall somewhere between the two extremes displayed in Figures 11-2 and 11-3, and similar investment conclusions would result.[12]

The two sets of risk-return tradeoffs discussed up to this point have reflected equal probabilities of future interest rates rising or falling relative to their respective base case interest rate scenarios as defined by two competing term-structure theories. As was mentioned in the discussion of pure expectations theory and its use in breakeven analysis, if interest rates rise by more than the implied market forecast then investments with durations shorter than the holding period will outperform longer-term investments. If interest rates rise by less than the implied market forecast, or decline, then investments with durations greater than the holding period will outperform shorter-term investments. The probabilities assigned to the different interest rate scenarios used in the computer simulations determine whether the expected return of a duration-mismatched investment places it on the efficient or inefficient portion of the tradeoff curve. In the pure expectations simulations, if more probability weight was placed on the scenario where rates rise relative to the market forecast rather than fall, then the resulting tradeoff curve would show investments with durations less than or equal to the holding period on the efficient portion of the tradeoff curve and longer-term investments on the inefficient portion. Over longer-term holding periods, investors with this view of future interest rates would choose a short-term rollover strategy as opposed to the riskless duration-matched strategy only if the incremental expected return from the rollover strategy was adequate compensation (determined subjectively) for the substantial incremental risk that would be undertaken. If more probability weight was placed on the scenario where rates fall relative to the market forecast than rise, then the resulting tradeoff curve would show investments with durations greater than or equal to the holding period on the efficient portion of the tradeoff curve and shorter-term investments on the inefficient portion. The more probability weight placed on either of the rising or falling scenarios relative to the other, the more steeply sloped the subsequent tradeoff curve would be, and thus, the more productive risk-taking opportunities that would be present. In either situation the duration-matched investment would maintain its riskless position against the vertical axis. The duration-matched investment is independent of the probabilities associated with rising or falling interest rates.

The same basic conclusions concerning probability weightings hold for the liquidity preference simulations. However, since the interest rate scenarios used in the liquidity preference simulations are not symmetrically distributed around the breakeven rates given by the implied market forecast of pure expectations theory, the amount of skewness in the probability weightings required to reverse the efficient and inefficient portions of the tradeoff curve is a bit more ambiguous.

Both sets of risk-return tradeoff curves have employed interest rate scenarios with

---

[12]This of course assumes a neutral view toward future interest rates.

equal 300 basis point upward and downward shifts relative to their respective base case scenarios. If the computer simulations had used interest rate scenarios with either more or less variation than the 300 basis point shifts actually used, then the range of potential return outcomes over these scenarios would have increased or decreased for the duration-mismatched investments only, changing their relative positions along the horizontal axis. The duration-matched strategy, however, would have again retained its riskless position against the vertical axis. The duration-matched investment is independent of future interest rate volatility.

Proper Risk Measurement Using Computer Simulations

A typical exercise many portfolio managers perform at various times throughout the year is to simulate the expected total return performance of their fixed-income portfolios using the most sophisticated and comprehensive interest rate scenarios they are capable of constructing. Because of the specific interest rate scenarios chosen and the particular nature of the cash flows associated with some of the instruments within their portfolios, what usually happens is that some instruments which are in fact quite risky exhibit little risky behavior while other instruments which actually are of minimal risk exhibit quite volatile behavior. The reason for this is the financial reality that no static investment strategy, except for zero coupon bonds, experiences the same return performance under all interest rate scenarios. Riskless strategies other than zero coupon bonds are dynamic in nature; they require periodic adjustment of the investment portfolio in response to various market conditions. These strategies always work in a sequential fashion. At any given point in time these strategies define a structure for the current investment portfolio which provides a hedge against the very next unexpected shift in interest rates only. The efficacy of the strategy depends upon the proper readjustment of the current investment portfolio after each and every unexpected shift in interest rates. These adjustments must be made sequentially over the entire length of the intended holding period. No static investment strategy exists, other than zero coupon bonds, which provides a hedge against multiple unexpected shifts in interest rates. Unexpected shifts in interest rates must be hedged sequentially, one at a time. The inherent risk related to an investment cannot be ascertained from return simulations which use multiple shift interest rate scenarios. This is the motivation behind the use of single unexpected interest rate shifts in the two sets of risk-return simulations studied here.

The interest rate scenarios used in both sets of computer simulations, while seemingly simple and unrealistic, are structured as they are so as to provide correct and accurate assessments of the risk-return characteristics of the instruments being simulated. The base case scenarios used in the computer simulations are used so as to determine the target holding period returns of the alternative investments. The 300 basis point shift scenarios are intended to bracket a broad range of likely interest rate outcomes and introduce an element of interest rate volatility into the simulations. The riskless strategies are identified as those which provide indentical returns under all three scenarios.[13]

---

[13]For further discussion on computer simulation techniques see the section on simulation models in Chapter 10.

Using Duration to Control Interest Rate Risk

Because the returns promised by investments utilizing the duration-matching technique are immune from unexpected future interest rate movements, duration matching is often referred to as "bond immunization." Bond immunization is widely used among pension funds and insurance companies as a riskless funding strategy for their future liabilities.[14] The expected return from a corporate cash pool consisting solely of a zero coupon bond which matures exactly at the end of the relevant holding period for that cash pool is perfectly immunized from unexpected interest rate changes over that holding period. There are no cash flows prior to the end of the holding period which must be reinvested, nor are there any remaining cash flows at the end of the holding period which must be liquidated. All cash flow from the investment occurs at the end of the holding period when it is presumably needed to finance an alternative corporate undertaking.[15]

An immunized portfolio consisting of coupon paying bonds, however, throws off cash flow both before and after the end of the intended holding period. The cash flows that are received prior to the end of the holding period are subject to reinvestment risk, since they must be reinvested at uncertain future interest rates to the end of the holding period. The remaining cash flows must be liquidated at the end of the holding period, and hence are subject to price risk since interest rates at that time are also unknown. These risks are, fortunately, offsetting ones which work in opposite directions. An immunization strategy hedges the expected holding period portfolio return from an unexpected shift in interest rates by exactly balancing these two offsetting risks. If rates unexpectedly rise, then the cash flows which are received prior to the end of the holding period will be reinvested to the end of the holding period at higher rates than originally anticipated. This gain in reinvestment income will be exactly offset by the capital loss incurred when the remaining cash flows are liquidated at the end of the holding period, resulting in the originally expected holding period return. Conversely, if rates unexpectedly decline, the cash flows which are received prior to the end of the holding period will be reinvested at lower rates than originally anticipated. This loss in reinvestment income will be exactly offset by capital gains earnings when the remaining cash flows are liquidated at the end of the holding period, again resulting in the originally expected holding period return. This balancing property of immunized portfolios is a direct result of matching the duration of the portfolio with the length of the desired holding period. Duration measures the holding period length over which reinvestment risk and price risk exactly counterbalance if interest rates move unexpectedly.

Bond immunization is a dynamic hedging strategy. The hedging objective of this strategy is to protect the expected holding period return that is possible in the current interest rate environment from unexpected interest rate movements away from that environment. As described previously the immunization strategy must work in a sequential fashion, protecting the expected holding period return from the next unex-

---

[14]Some applications of bond immunization for insurance companies is found in Chapter 9.
[15]The issues roughly sketched in this subsection are more throughly presented in Chapter 3.

pected shift in interest rates only. This is accomplished by matching the duration of the investment portfolio to the length of the investor's desired holding period. The hedging strategy requires that the match between the duration of the investment port-folio and the remaining length of the holding period be maintained over the entire life of the strategy. Sequential adjustments to the investment portfolio in response to unexpected interest rate changes are necessary to satisfy this condition. Even in the absence of unexpected interest rate movements, periodic adjustments must be made to the investment portfolio. The mere passage of time causes the duration of the investment portfolio to depart from the remaining length of the investment hold-ing period. This tendency of the portfolio duration to age differently than the re-maining length of the holding period is called "duration drift." The periodic adjustments to the investment portfolio prompted by duration drift and unexpected interest rate movements are commonly referred to as "portfolio rebalancings." In practice no more than two to four portfolio rebalancings a year are normally required to maintain a good duration match. The amount of portfolio churning associated with each rebalancing is generally small.

An immunized investment behaves very much like a zero coupon bond which matures exactly at the end of the desired holding period. However, the actual return that an immunized investment will ultimately generate does have a small variance associated with it. The ultimate realized return depends upon the underlying process which drives the term structure of interest rates. In the two sets of simulations ana-lyzed, the immunized returns corresponding to different theories of the term structure do in fact differ slightly, by as many as 25 basis points for the 3-year holding period. Nevertheless, relative to the same 3-year holding period, the difference between the expected returns of the 5-year Treasury note in the two sets of simulations is over 100 basis points. The difference is 200 basis points for the 6-month Treasury bill rollover strategy. The sensitivity of expected immunized returns to changes in the underlying interest rate process are quite small relative to the expected return sen-sitivity of duration-mismatched investments. In addition, the duration measures used to achieve immunization in the computer simulations implicitly assume that short- and long-term interest rates make unexpected shifts in parallel. Immunized returns can be impacted if the assumptions underlying the duration measure used do not ad-equately represent the true stochastic nature of these unexpected interest rate move-ments. Other more sophisticated duration measures which take into account differential rate shifts between long-and short-term rates do exist. However, these yield curve effects tend to be reasonably small, and methods for reducing a portfo-lio's exposure to them are available.

Risk versus Return on an After-Tax Basis

The total returns reported in Tables 11-1 and 11-3 were computed ignoring the effects of taxes in the computer simulations. However, most corporations are subject to full marginal tax rates on their investment returns. The after-tax returns corresponding to the pure expectations and liquidity preference set of interest rate assumptions are reported in Table 11-4 and Table 11-5 respectively. They are generated from com-

Table 11-4. Risk versus Return Characteristics of the Treasury Market (Pure Expectations Interest Rate Assumptions—Total Pretax Returns*)

		6 MONTH HOLDING PERIOD					1 YEAR HOLDING PERIOD				
	DURATION (Years)	MARKET FORECAST	+300 bp SHIFT	-300 bp SHIFT	EXPECTED RETURN	RANGE IN RETURN	MARKET FORECAST	+300 bp SHIFT	-300 bp SHIFT	EXPECTED RETURN	RANGE IN RETURN
5 YR. NOTE	4.40	4.53%	(9.41%)	20.43%	5.18%	(2985 bp)	4.85%	(1.42%)	11.69%	5.04%	(1311 bp)
4 YR. NOTE	3.63	4.53%	(7.06%)	17.43%	4.97%	(2450 bp)	4.85%	(0.16%)	10.22%	4.97%	(1039 bp)
PORTFOLIO 3	3.00	4.53%	(4.83%)	12.22%	3.97%	(1706 bp)	4.85%	1.02%	8.68%	4.85%	(766 bp)
3 YR. NOTE	2.80	4.53%	(4.34%)	14.15%	4.78%	(1848 bp)	4.85%	1.29%	8.60%	4.91%	(731 bp)
PORTFOLIO 2	2.00	4.53%	0.09%	9.23%	4.62%	(914 bp)	4.85%	2.67%	6.78%	4.77%	(410 bp)
2 YR. NOTE	1.92	4.53%	1.16%	10.54%	5.41%	(938 bp)	4.85%	2.96%	6.81%	4.87%	(385 bp)
PORTFOLIO 1	1.00	4.53%	2.48%	6.12%	4.38%	(364 bp)	4.85%	4.85%	4.85%	4.85%	0 bp
1 YR. NOTE	0.99	4.53%	2.50%	6.61%	4.54%	(412 bp)	4.85%	4.87%	4.83%	4.85%	4 bp
6 MO. BILL	0.50	4.53%	4.53%	4.53%	4.53%	0 bp	4.86%	5.66%	4.05%	4.86%	162 bp

		2 YEAR HOLDING PERIOD					3 YEAR HOLDING PERIOD				
	DURATION (Years)	MARKET FORECAST	+300 bp SHIFT	-300 bp SHIFT	EXPECTED RETURN	RANGE IN RETURN	MARKET FORECAST	+300 bp SHIFT	-300 bp SHIFT	EXPECTED RETURN	RANGE IN RETURN
5 YR. NOTE	4.40	5.33%	3.03%	7.78%	5.38%	(476 bp)	5.59%	4.65%	6.58%	5.60%	(194 bp)
4 YR. NOTE	3.63	5.34%	3.72%	7.04%	5.36%	(332 bp)	5.59%	5.14%	6.07%	5.60%	(93 bp)
PORTFOLIO 3	3.00	5.34%	4.36%	6.27%	5.32%	(191 bp)	5.59%	5.59%	5.59%	5.59%	0 bp
3 YR. NOTE	2.80	5.34%	4.51%	6.21%	5.35%	(170 bp)	5.58%	5.69%	5.48%	5.59%	21 bp
PORTFOLIO 2	2.00	5.34%	5.34%	5.34%	5.34%	0 bp	5.58%	6.13%	5.02%	5.58%	111 bp
2 YR. NOTE	1.92	5.34%	5.40%	5.28%	5.34%	12 bp	5.58%	6.16%	4.99%	5.58%	117 bp
PORTFOLIO 1	1.00	5.35%	6.16%	4.53%	5.34%	163 bp	5.60%	6.68%	4.51%	5.60%	217 bp
1 YR. NOTE	0.99	5.35%	6.16%	4.53%	5.35%	164 bp	5.60%	6.69%	4.52%	5.60%	217 bp
6 MO. BILL	0.50	5.35%	6.56%	4.14%	5.35%	243 bp	5.61%	6.95%	4.26%	5.61%	270 bp

(*) Total After-Tax Return is the sum of after-tax interest, interest on interest and the maturity or liquidation value of the investment, including capital gain (or loss), divided by the starting price and standardized to a bond equivalent basis.

NOTE:
PORTFOLIO 1 consists of .990 Dollars of the 1 YR. NOTE and .010 Dollars of the 2 YR. NOTE.
PORTFOLIO 2 consists of .933 Dollars of the 2 YR. NOTE and .067 Dollars of the 3 YR. NOTE.
PORTFOLIO 3 consists of .817 Dollars of the 3 YR. NOTE and .183 Dollars of the 4 YR. NOTE.

Table 11-5. Risk versus Return Characteristics of the Treasury Market (Liquidity Preference Interest Rate Assumptions— Total After-Tax Returns*)

6 MONTH HOLDING PERIOD

	DURATION (Years)	CONSTANT RATES	300 bp RISE	300 bp DECLINE	EXPECTED RETURN	RANGE IN RETURN
5 YR. NOTE	4.40	6.48%	(7.70%)	22.67%	7.15%	(3037 bp)
4 YR. NOTE	3.63	6.50%	(5.29%)	19.63%	6.94%	(2492 bp)
PORTFOLIO 3	3.00	6.29%	(3.22%)	16.68%	6.58%	(1989 bp)
3 YR. NOTE	2.80	6.24%	(2.75%)	16.01%	6.50%	(1877 bp)
PORTFOLIO 2	2.00	6.18%	0.19%	12.54%	6.30%	(1235 bp)
2 YR. NOTE	1.92	6.18%	0.40%	12.29%	6.29%	(1189 bp)
PORTFOLIO 1	1.00	5.27%	3.19%	7.42%	5.29%	(424 bp)
1 YR. NOTE	0.99	5.26%	3.21%	7.37%	5.28%	(416 bp)
6 MO. BILL	0.50	4.53%	4.53%	4.53%	4.53%	0 bp

2 YEAR HOLDING PERIOD

	DURATION (years)	CONSTANT RATES	300 bp RISE	300 bp DECLINE	EXPECTED RETURN	RANGE IN RETURN
5 YR. NOTE	4.40	6.40%	4.03%	8.92%	6.45%	(488 bp)
4 YR. NOTE	3.63	6.23%	4.57%	7.98%	6.26%	(340 bp)
PORTFOLIO 3	3.00	6.02%	5.02%	7.06%	6.03%	(205 bp)
3 YR. NOTE	2.80	5.97%	5.12%	6.86%	5.98%	(174 bp)
PORTFOLIO 2	2.00	5.35%	5.35%	5.35%	5.35%	0 bp
2 YR. NOTE	1.92	5.30%	5.37%	5.24%	5.30%	12 bp
PORTFOLIO 1	1.00	4.85%	5.66%	4.04%	4.85%	162 bp
1 YR. NOTE	0.99	4.85%	5.66%	4.03%	4.85%	164 bp
6 MO. BILL	0.50	4.53%	5.74%	3.31%	4.52%	243 bp

1 YEAR HOLDING PERIOD

	CONSTANT RATES	300 bp RISE	300 bp DECLINE	EXPECTED RETURN	RANGE IN RETURN
5 YR. NOTE	6.42%	0.02%	13.41%	6.62%	(1339 bp)
4 YR. NOTE	6.39%	1.28%	11.88%	6.52%	(1060 bp)
PORTFOLIO 3	6.16%	2.26%	10.28%	6.23%	(802 bp)
3 YR. NOTE	6.11%	2.48%	9.93%	6.17%	(744 bp)
PORTFOLIO 2	5.91%	3.87%	8.02%	5.93%	(415 bp)
2 YR. NOTE	5.89%	3.97%	7.88%	5.91%	(391 bp)
PORTFOLIO 1	4.86%	4.86%	4.86%	4.86%	0 bp
1 YR. NOTE	4.85%	4.87%	4.83%	4.85%	4 bp
6 MO. BILL	4.53%	5.33%	3.71%	4.52%	162 bp

3 YEAR HOLDING PERIOD

	CONSTANT RATES	300 bp RISE	300 bp DECLINE	EXPECTED RETURN	RANGE IN RETURN
5 YR. NOTE	6.28%	5.31%	7.31%	6.30%	(200 bp)
4 YR. NOTE	6.09%	5.62%	6.58%	6.10%	(96 bp)
PORTFOLIO 3	5.64%	5.64%	5.64%	5.64%	0 bp
3 YR. NOTE	5.53%	5.64%	5.43%	5.53%	21 bp
PORTFOLIO 2	5.50%	6.04%	4.96%	5.50%	109 bp
2 YR. NOTE	5.50%	6.07%	4.92%	5.50%	115 bp
PORTFOLIO 1	4.85%	5.93%	3.77%	4.85%	216 bp
1 YR. NOTE	4.85%	5.93%	3.76%	4.84%	217 bp
6 MO. BILL	4.53%	5.87%	3.17%	4.52%	270 bp

(*) Total After-Tax Return is the sum of after-tax interest, interest on interest and the maturity or liquidation value of the investment, including capital gain (or loss), divided by the starting price and standardized to a bond equivalent basis.

NOTE:
PORTFOLIO 1 consists of .990 Dollars of the 1 YR. NOTE and .010 Dollars of the 2 YR. NOTE.
PORTFOLIO 2 consists of .933 Dollars of the 2 YR. NOTE and .067 Dollars of the 3 YR. NOTE.
PORTFOLIO 3 consists of .817 Dollars of the 3 YR. NOTE and .183 Dollars of the 4 YR. NOTE.

puter simulations of the after-tax cash flows from each of the alternative Treasury investments. Full marginal tax rates of 46% for ordinary income and 28% for capital gains are assumed.[16]

Duration defines the holding period length related to any investment over which gains or losses in expected reinvestment income are exactly offset by gains or losses in the expected liquidation value of the portfolio if interest rates change unexpectedly. Because capital gains are taxed at lower rates than ordinary income, on an after-tax basis, capital gains income is much more sensitive to unexpected changes in interest rates than reinvestment income. Therefore, the holding period length over which unexpected after-tax changes in reinvestment income are exactly balanced by unexpected after-tax capital gains or losses is longer than the corresponding holding period length on a pretax basis. In other words, after-tax duration is longer than pretax duration. Because of this difference, the weightings of the individual securities within Portfolio 1, Portfolio 2, and Portfolio 3 necessary to achieve after-tax immunization differ from the weightings which are required to achieve pretax immunization. For example, Portfolio 2 consists of $.828 of the 2-year Treasury note and $.172 of the 3-year Treasury note in the 2-year pretax immunization strategy. The weightings of Portfolio 2 become $.933 and $.067 respectively in the 2-year after-tax immunization strategy. The weightings within the pretax duration- matched portfolios were readily determined using the duration additivity relationship discussed previously. Unfortunately, this relationship does not hold on an after-tax basis because of the differential ordinary and capital gains rates at which different types of income are taxed. Subsequently, the determination of the proper weightings within the after-tax duration-matched portfolios is a bit more cumbersome. Otherwise, the same comments and conclusions concerning risk avoidance and risk taking illustrated in the pretax simulations hold equally true on an after-tax basis.

SECTION IV   HOLDING PERIOD RISK

The investment techniques described in the previous section enable corporate cash managers to deploy the cash assets of the corporation which are in excess of traditional working capital needs, into structured investment programs which eliminate the uncertainty with which known future corporate cash requirements are funded. Admittedly, the effectiveness of such programs depends crucially on the accuracy with which future cash requirements are forecasted. Depending on the nature of the business in which a corporation is engaged, some future cash requirements may be known with a reasonable degree of certainty, such as from planned capital expenditure programs, corporate expansions, or future dividend payment streams. Some corporations are able to project expected future cash requirements associated with a

---

[16]The breakeven interest rate scenario associated with pure expectations theory in the after-tax simulations assumes that the original Treasury investments are liquidated at somewhat lower yields than indicated in Table 11-2. This is to compensate for the differential rates at which ordinary income and capital gains are taxed. Otherwise, identical assumptions as were used in the earlier pretax simulations are utilized.

downturn in the business cycle or from an increase in competition within their own industry. Even in the absence of any known specific future cash requirements, many corporations are able to identify minimum investment holding periods over which no cash is foreseen to be required from the excess cash pool.

If the cash requirements of the corporation that actually come to pass differ from what was originally expected, premature portfolio liquidation or unanticipated portfolio rollovers may cause what was once thought to be a riskless investment strategy to be quite risky. Unexpectedly early cash requirements may force the cash manager to liquidate investments at substantial losses relative to shorter-term investments in a rising interest rate environment. Likewise, unexpectly late cash requirements may result in substantial losses relative to longer-term investments if the cash manager has to roll the corporation's portfolio over in a falling interest rate environment. All things being equal, most corporate cash managers would prefer this type of opportunity loss to that of the visible and reported capital losses associated with premature liquidation. This obviously leads many cash managers to structure their excess cash portfolios intentionally short relative to the expected timing of the corporation's future cash needs. However, as will be shown, the actual dollar losses in opportunity associated with unexpectedly late portfolio liquidation in falling interest rate environments tends to be at least as great as the dollar losses associated with unexpectedly early liquidation in rising interest rate environments.

Table 11-6 and Table 11-7 illustrate the unintended interest rate risk that is incurred when a corporate investment program must be liquidated either unexpectedly early or late. The premature liquidation of the immunized Treasury investments, Portfolio 1, Portfolio 2, and Portfolio 3, after only six months in a rising interest rate environment are compared to the liquidation of a 6-month Treasury bill rollover program over 1-, 2-, and 3-year holding periods in a falling interest rate environment. After-tax pure expectations interest rate assumptions are used to construct Table 11-6, and after-tax liquidity preference interest rate assumptions are used to construct Table 11-7. The interest rate scenarios which rise 300 basis points relative to their respective base case scenarios are assumed for the premature portfolio liquidations which occur after six months. The interest rate scenarios which decline 300 basis points relative to their respective base case scenarios are assumed for the liquidations of the 6-month Treasury bill rollover strategy. Both tables assume an initial investment of $100 million.

Refer to the liquidation loss analysis under pure expectations interest rate assumptions in Table 11-6; if liquidation of Portfolio 2 is required after only six months and interest rates are 300 basis points higher than expected, then the total after-tax liquidation value of Portfolio 2 is only $100,045,000. This corresponds to the 0.09% total after-tax return reported in Table 11-4 for Portfolio 2 under that interest rate scenario. The total after-tax liquidation value includes the after-tax reinvestment value of all interim interest receipts and the value of the tax deduction associated with the capital loss. The liquidation value of the 6-month Treasury bill after six months is a riskless $102,205,000. This corresponds to the 4.53% holding period return reported in Table 11-4 for that investment. Portfolio 2 loses $2,220,000 relative to the riskless holding period investment in this interest rate scenario. On a

Table 11-6. The Interest Rate Risk Imbedded in Holding Period Uncertainty (After-Tax Pure Expectations Interest Rate Assumptions; Future After-Tax Portfolio Liquidation Values (1)

	6 MONTH (2) HOLDING PERIOD	1 YEAR (3) HOLDING PERIOD	2 YEAR (3) HOLDING PERIOD	3 YEAR (3) HOLDING PERIOD
PORTFOLIO 1 6 MONTH TREASURY BILL	$101,240,000 (2.48%) $102,265,000 (4.53%)	$104,908,806 (4.85%) $104,091,006 (4.05%)	-- --	-- --
Loss Relative To Riskless Holding Period Investment (4)	($1,025,000)	$817,800		
Present Value Of Loss	($1,002,297)	$779,534		
Loss Differential (5)	($222,763)			

	6 MONTH (2) HOLDING PERIOD	1 YEAR (3) HOLDING PERIOD	2 YEAR (3) HOLDING PERIOD	3 YEAR (3) HOLDING PERIOD
PORTFOLIO 2 6 MONTH TREASURY BILL	$100,045,000 (0.09%) $102,265,000 (4.53%)	-- --	$111,115,399 (5.34%) $108,540,660 (4.14%)	-- --
Loss Relative To Riskless Holding Period Investment (4)	($2,220,000)		$2,574,738	
Present Value Of Loss	($2,170,831)		$2,317,175	
Loss Differential (5)	$146,344			

	6 MONTH (2) HOLDING PERIOD	1 YEAR (3) HOLDING PERIOD	2 YEAR (3) HOLDING PERIOD	3 YEAR (3) HOLDING PERIOD
PORTFOLIO 3 6 MONTH TREASURY BILL	$97,580,000 (-4.83%) $102,265,000 (4.53%)	-- --	-- --	$117,986,399 (5.59%) $113,480,174 (4.26%)
Loss Relative To Riskless Holding Period Investment (4)	($4,680,000)			$4,506,225
Present Value Of Loss	($4,576,346)			$3,819,275
Loss Differential (5)	($757,071)			

(1) The Future After-Tax Liquidation Value includes the reinvested value of interim after-tax interest payments. An initial investment of $100,000,000 is assumed.
(2) Premature portfolio liquidation after 6 months is assumed to occur under the interest rate scenario where rates rise by 300 basis points more than the Pure-Expectations implied market forecast. (See Table 2)
(3) Unexpectedly late portfolio liquidation after 1, 2 and 3 years is assumed to occur under the interest rate scenario where rates decline by 300 basis points relative to the Pure-Expectations implied market forecast. (See Table 2)
(4) Parenthesis indicate potential losses associated with premature liquidation. No parenthesis indicate potential reinvestment losses due to unexpectedly late portfolio liquidation.
(5) Parenthesis indicate that there are more potential losses associated with premature portfolio liquidation than unexpectedly late portfolio liquidation. No parenthesis indicate just the opposite.

Table 11-7. The Interest Rate Risk Imbedded in Holding Period Uncertainty (After-Tax Liquidity Preference Interest Rate Assumptions; Future After-Tax Portfolio Liquidation Values (1))

PORTFOLIO 1

	6 MONTH (2) HOLDING PERIOD	1 YEAR (3) HOLDING PERIOD	2 YEAR (3) HOLDING PERIOD	3 YEAR (3) HOLDING PERIOD
6 MONTH TREASURY BILL	$101,595,000 (3.19%)	$104,919,049 (4.86%)	—	—
	$102,265,000 (4.53%)	$103,744,410 (3.71%)	—	—
Loss Relative To Riskless Holding Period Investment (4)	($670,000)	$1,174,639		
Present Value Of Loss	($655,160)	$1,119,567		
Loss Differential (5)	$464,407			

PORTFOLIO 2

	6 MONTH (2) HOLDING PERIOD	1 YEAR (3) HOLDING PERIOD	2 YEAR (3) HOLDING PERIOD	3 YEAR (3) HOLDING PERIOD
6 MONTH TREASURY BILL	$100,095,000 (0.19%)	—	$111,137,045 (5.35%)	—
	$102,265,000 (4.53%)	—	$106,786,162 (3.31%)	—
Loss Relative To Riskless Holding Period Investment (4)	($2,170,000)		$4,350,883	
Present Value Of Loss	($2,121,938)		$3,914,881	
Loss Differential (5)	$1,792,943			

PORTFOLIO 3

	6 MONTH (2) HOLDING PERIOD	1 YEAR (3) HOLDING PERIOD	2 YEAR (3) HOLDING PERIOD	3 YEAR (3) HOLDING PERIOD
6 MONTH TREASURY BILL	$98,390,000 (-3.22%)	—	—	$118,158,671 (5.64%)
	$102,265,000 (4.53%)	—	—	$109,894,893 (3.17%)
Loss Relative To Riskless Holding Period Investment (4)	($3,875,000)			$8,263,778
Present Value Of Loss	($3,789,175)			$6,993,797
Loss Differential (5)	$3,204,622			

(1) The Future After-Tax Liquidation Value includes the reinvested value of interim after-tax interest payments. An initial investment of $100,000,000 is assumed.

(2) Premature portfolio liquidation after 6 months is assumed to occur under the interest rate scenario where rates rise by 300 basis points.

(3) Unexpectedly late portfolio liquidation after 1, 2 and 3 years is assumed to occur under the interest rate scenario where rates decline by 300 basis points.

(4) Parenthesis indicate potential losses associated with premature liquidation. No parenthesis indicate potential reinvestment losses due to unexpectedly late portfolio liquidation.

(5) Parenthesis indicate that there are more potential losses associated with premature portfolio liquidation than unexpectedly late portfolio liquidation. No parenthesis indicate just the opposite.

present value basis this loss measures $2,170,831. If instead portfolio liquidation occurs after two years and interest rates follow a path that is 300 basis points less than expected, then the liquidation value of the 6-month Treasury bill rollover program is only $108,540,660. The liquidation value of Portfolio 2 over this holding period is a riskless $111,115,399. The short-term rollover strategy loses $2,574,738 relative to the certain holding period return of Portfolio 2 in this interest rate scenario. In present value terms this loss is $2,317,175, roughly equal to the potential $2,170,831 loss associated with premature liquidation. In fact, the reinvestment risk exposure of 6-month Treasury bills over two years is slightly greater than the premature liquidation risk exposure of Portfolio 2, by exactly $146,344. Just the opposite occurs with the premature liquidation of Portfolio 1 and Portfolio 3 after six months. The present values of these losses relative to the 6-month Treasury bill when interest rates rise 300 basis points more than expected are $1,002,297 and $4,576,346. Again these are roughly equal to the reinvestment loss present values of $779,534 and $3,819,275 from rolling 6-month Treasury bills over 1- and 3-year holding periods when interest rates decline 300 basis points relative to market expectations. Here the premature liquidation risk exposure of Portfolio 1 and Portfolio 3 is slightly greater than the reinvestment risk exposure of 6-month Treasury bills by exactly $222,763 and $757,071 over 1- and 3-year holding periods respectively. Under pure expectations interest rate assumptions, the tradeoff in terms of dollar risk between structuring the excess cash portfolio of the corporation either too long or too short relative to the expected timing of the corporation's future cash needs is approximately symmetric.

In the presence of positive liquidity premiums built into the term structure of interest rates, the potential dollar reinvestment losses from a short-term rollover strategy far outweigh the potential dollar losses from early liquidation of longer-term strategies. Referring to Table 11-7, the present value of the reinvestment losses from rolling over 6-month Treasury bills in the 300 basis point declining interest rate scenario exceed the present value of the early liquidation losses of Portfolio 1, Portfolio 2, and Portfolio 3 in the 300 basis point rising interest rate scenario by $464,407, $1,792,943, and $3,204,622 respectively. Short-term investment strategies not only expose the corporation's excess cash portfolio to substantial reinvestment risk relative to the corporation's expected holding periods, but deny the corporation liquidity premiums it should be earning over these expected holding periods as well. On the other hand, investment strategies which better match the expected holding periods of the corporation earn liquidity premiums which partially offset premature liquidation losses over unexpectedly shortened holding periods. Clearly, in the presence of positive liquidity premiums it makes little sense in terms of dollar risk to intentionally structure the excess cash portfolio of the corporation shorter than the corporation's expected future cash needs.[17]

The determination of the target holding periods and investment objectives relative to those targets is the most important and most difficult facet of corporate cash management. Once these have been established the task of structuring an optimal in-

---

[17]This assumes that the interest rate views of the corporation are neutral.

vestment portfolio becomes a mechancial one with the aid of duration analysis. If specific future cash requirements are not known with certainty, then probabilistic assessments of the corporation's future cash needs must be relied upon to determine the appropriate target holding periods. Forecasting inaccurancies in either direction can result in substantial losses relative to currently available riskless holding period returns. As shown in Tables 11-6 and 11-7 unexpectedly long holding periods result in greater potential dollar losses than unexpectedly short holding periods because of positive liquidity premiums imbedded in the yield curve. This fact is seemingly ignored by many corporations in view of their current practice of intentionally structuring their excess cash portfolios shorter than their expected future needs for that cash. The least risk strategy in the context of uncertain holding periods matches the duration of the excess cash portfolio with the expected holding period length, or set of expected holding period lengths, derived from probabilistic assessments of the corporation's future cash needs.

SECTION V   DEFAULT RISK

The analysis of risk versus return tradeoffs discussed thus far has considered alternative portfolio structures only among default-free U.S. Treasury investments. Incremental Treasury returns in excess of the riskless holding period returns offered by duration-matched investments have been shown to be possible only if the direction or magnitude of future interest rate movements differ from market expectations. This requires that the investor not only be a better interest rate forecaster than the market, but be willing to expose portfolio returns to substantial downside interest rate risk as well. Expected incremental returns in excess of the riskless Treasury holding period returns are possible without incurring potentially unproductive interest rate risk by adopting prescribed levels of default (credit) risk. Portfolios immunized from interest rate risk can be constructed using corporate bonds, municipal bonds, preferred stock, and even mortgage-backed securities. High quality portfolios with minimal exposure to default risk, such as AAA/Aaa rated corporate bond portfolios, provide relatively modest increases in expected holding period return. Portfolios with greater exposures to default risk of course provide correspondingly higher expected incremental holding period returns. A risk versus return tradeoff among portfolios of differing credit strength therefore is defined. Investments exposed to default risk should be undertaken only if the incremental expected return from such investments provides adequate compensation, determined subjectively, for the incremental risk.

SECTION VI   TAX RISK

Municipal bonds and preferred stocks represent particularly attractive opportunities on an after-tax basis to corporate investors. The interest from municipal bonds generally is completely exempt from taxation while 85% of all intercorporate dividends qualify for a tax exclusion. The Internal Revenue Service regulates the investment activities of nonfinancial companies in the tax-exempt area. Failure to comply with IRS regulations could result in a loss of the tax exemptions normally associated with these investments. Due diligence on the part of the corporate cash manager will minimize, if not eliminate, this type of risk. In light of recently proposed federal tax legislation, these types of investments could experience adverse price behavior if the marginal tax rates of all investors were to drop significantly. This type of tax-related risk must be kept in mind when analyzing alternative investment strategies on a risk versus return basis.

SECTION VII   SUMMARY

The cash balances at many corporations are currently well in excess of traditional short-term and working capital cash requirements. Yet many of these same corporations continue to invest their entire cash balances in very short-term money market instruments, as if it is all for working capital purposes. This investment strategy was shown to expose the corporation to substantial interest rate risk.

An alternative approach to managing corporate cash pools was presented. This approach makes a distinction between pools of cash required to support working capital needs and pools of cash which are in excess of these short-term needs. The excess cash pools are referred to as strategic cash. Strategic cash is viewed as a funding source for future corporate cash requirements, and is expected to remain invested over longer holding periods than traditional working capital.

The optimal strategy for those corporations wishing to avoid making interest rate bets with their strategic cash pools was identified. This strategy requires that the duration of the strategic cash portfolio match the expected investment horizon of the corporation. In addition to reducing interest rate risk, this strategy was shown to provide superior expected returns over more traditional short-term rollover strategies.

BIBLIOGRAPHY

Bierwag, G.O., Kaufman, G.G., and Toevs, A.L. "Bond Portfolio Immunization and Stochastic Process Risk." *Journal of Bank Research* (Winter 1983).

Bierwag, G.O., Kaufman, G.G., and Toevs, A.L. "Duration: Its Uses in Bond Portfolio Management." *Financial Analysts Journal* (July/August 1983).

Brennan and Schwartz; Nelson and Schaeffer; Fisher and Leibowiz; Bierwag, Kaufman and Toevs; Ingersoll, J.E., and Babbel in *Innovations in Bond Portfolio Management* Greenwich, CT: JAI Press, 1983.

Carleton, W., and Cooper, A. "Estimation and Uses of the Term Structure of Interest Rates." *Journal of Finance* 31 (1976): 1067–1083.

Fama, E. "Forward Rates as Predictors of Future Spot Rates." *Journal of Financial Economics* (1976): 361–377.

Fong, H.G., and Vasicek, O. "The Hedging Between Return and Risk in Immunized Portfolios." *Financial Analysts Journal* (September/October 1983).

Malkiel, B. *The Term Structure of Interest Rates*. Princeton, NJ: Princeton University Press, 1966.

McCulloch, J.H. "Measuring the Term Structure of Interest Rates." *Journal of Business* 44 (1971): 19–31.

McCulloch, J.H. "An Estimate of the Liquidity Premium." *Journal of Political Economy* 83 (1975): 95–119.

12 A Synthetic Option Framework for Asset Allocation

JAMES A. TILLEY AND GARY D. LATAINER

INTRODUCTION

For many investors the asset allocation decision is the most critical decision in terms of overall investment performance. While good management within an asset class can enhance returns, it can seldom do so enough to offset the impact of incorrect asset allocation by a pension fund or balanced fund manager.

Over the last 20 years, modern portfolio theory (MPT) has been the primary influence on asset allocation. Using MPT concepts, investors can construct an efficient frontier consisting of those asset portfolios that offer the best combinations of expected return and risk. Investors then choose an asset allocation from among these many possible portfolio combinations based on their attitudes towards risk and reward.

An asset allocation theory has as a main goal being able to help investors choose favorable return distributions. In the MPT framework the risk of any distribution is quantified as the variance of expected returns, and therefore includes the possibility of gains as well as losses. However, few investors associate risk with the possibility for gains. For many investors the achievement of some guaranteed minimum return is the most important risk consideration, and for that purpose the mean-variance tradeoffs of MPT are insufficient for determining appropriate asset allocations. To secure a minimum return while retaining upside potential, option strategies must be considered.[1]

In this chapter we link option pricing theory with traditional asset allocation by

---

[1]See Chapter 5.

utilizing a special type of option: a call option that gives its holder the right to purchase a full position in the better performing of either stocks or bonds. Our solution to the asset allocation problem suggests that the investor set aside enough wealth in a riskless asset to assure a minimum return target over the holding period, and use the remaining wealth to purchase these specialized calls. Although such options are not available in the marketplace currently, their return pattern can be obtained through a trading strategy among stocks, bonds, and cash. The process of creating the call option synthetically leads to a real world dynamic asset allocation strategy among the three asset classes—stocks, bonds, and cash—that are at the center of most asset allocation decisions.

The mathematics behind both asset allocation strategies and option strategies is quite complex and this is certainly true of the synthetic option approach to asset allocation. However, an understanding of the basic concepts of the strategy can be obtained without the use of detailed mathematics, and it is the concepts that we emphasize in this chapter. Options terminology is used frequently throughout the chapter and we assume that the reader is familiar with the basic language of options.

The chapter is divided into six sections. Section I reviews the traditional mean-variance framework for asset allocation and argues why many investors may prefer instead an asset allocation strategy based on truncation of the loss tail of a return distribution. Section II shows how a call option on the better performing of two risky assets can be created. The properties of this option are discussed and the asset allocation strategy necessary to replicate the option is described. Section III applies the concepts of Section II to the management of a balanced fund and presents results of historical simulations for the 1973–1983 time period. The strategy developed for allocating funds among stocks, bonds, and cash would have been able to protect against loss each year and to achieve superior performance over the full period and many subperiods. Section IV discusses how financial futures can be incorporated into the implementation of the asset allocation strategies. Section V offers some comments on the constraints typically imposed on asset allocation, and Section VI concludes the chapter.

SECTION I   OVERVIEW OF TRADITIONAL ASSET ALLOCATION

Before considering new approaches to asset allocation, it is appropriate to review the current framework for the subject. Asset allocation involves making risk/reward tradeoffs. The concepts of modern portfolio theory have greatly enhanced portfolio managers' understanding of these tradeoffs and have provided a theoretical framework for choosing portfolios that offer ''optimal'' combinations of risk and reward.[2] An investor using the MPT approach determines asset allocations by constructing an ''efficient frontier'' consisting of those portfolios offering the highest expected return for each level of risk, and then selecting the portfolio on the efficient frontier

---

[2]A detailed treatment of modern portfolio theory can be found in E.J. Elton and M.J. Gruber, *Modern Portfolio Theory and Investment Analysis*. New York: Wiley, 1984.

that offers the best combination of risk and reward given his or her own attitudes on the matter. This selection is a subjective one and generally will differ for each investor.

To choose an optimal portfolio an investor must first specify a time horizon and then estimate each asset's expected return and risk over the time horizon. The risk and expected return estimates are based on assumed probability distributions for the asset's performance over the investor's time horizon. MPT traditionally assumes that asset return distributions are symmetric and therefore can be characterized usefully by their means and variances. In that case, although investors generally are more concerned with downside "risk" than upside "risk," the variance is an appropriate risk measure because any risk rankings based on variance will be the same as those based only on deviations below the expected return. Whether the *ex ante* returns normally analyzed by investors or the actual returns realized by investors are symmetrically distributed is not really of material importance, however. The key point is that symmetrically shaped distributions are not necessarily desired by most investors.

Consider the following two portfolios: one invested 100% in shares of common stock, and another consisting of 90% invested in T-bills yielding 11.11% and 10% in at-the-money call options on the stock.[3] Figure 12-1 illustrates their respective return distributions for the situation where the distribution of stock prices is lognormally distributed with an annual standard deviation of 20%. These two portfolios can now be plotted, along with combinations of the stock and T-bills, along an efficient frontier as in Figure 12-2.

---

[3]We define an at-the-money option as an option for which the exercise price is equal to the current price of the underlying asset, even though the expected price of the underlying asset at expiration of the option may exceed the exercise price.

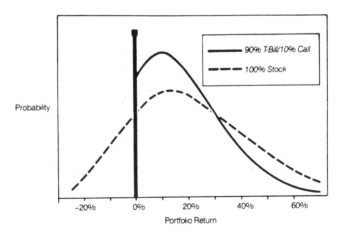

Figure 12-1.

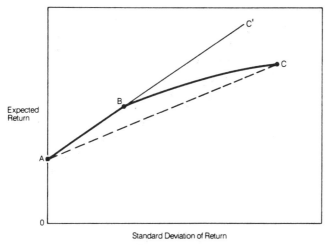

Figure 12-2.

The portfolio consisting of the call option and T-bills is not an efficient portfolio in the mean-variance sense only because there is a position in the stock combined with a position in T-bills that offers a higher expected return for the same level of risk. Many investors would prefer the T-bill plus call portfolio, however, because that portfolio has no possibility of loss over the 1-year holding period, while the stock plus T-bill portfolio of equal variance has approximately a 15% chance of loss. Suppose the investor chooses to define risk as the probability of loss. The T-bill plus at-the-money call portfolio, which has no possibility of loss, has an expected return of 11.75%. A position solely in the stock cannot be considered because it does not meet the risk requirements. For the T-bill plus stock portfolio having no possibility of loss, the expected return is 11.50%, and a look at its complete return distribution would reveal that it holds almost no upside potential.[4] To such an investor it is the T-bill plus at-the-money call portfolio that is efficient.

There are many investors for whom failure to achieve some minimum return is the relevant measure of risk. As our simple example shows, variance as a risk index cannot measure adequately the attractiveness to these investors of being able to avoid downside returns. For this reason we will adopt an approach to asset allocation in which risk is measured in terms of the extent to which the downside tail of the return distribution is truncated. Our approach to asset allocation will be grounded in option concepts because options provide the wherewithal for truncating downside risk. Furthermore, as we shall see in the next section, options already have a close connection with traditional asset allocation.

---

[4]We have suggested that a consideration of only the mean and variance of a probability distribution of returns is generally insufficient, for most investors, to choose an ''optimal'' portfolio. In this regard neither is the mean and probability of loss nor the mean and the minimum return target adequate. Investors should evaluate the shape of the possible distributions to evaluate their relative attractiveness as to the probabilities for experiencing large losses, modest losses, modest gains, and large gains.

SECTION II   CREATING OPTIONS ON THE BETTER PERFORMING OF STOCKS AND BONDS

Option pricing literature has shown that a call option on a single risky asset is equivalent to a levered position in the underlying asset in which the leverage is adjusted throughout the holding period.[5] This means that the price behavior of a call option can be replicated by holding some position in the underlying asset and financing the position through borrowing. The replicating portfolio must be rebalanced as the price of the underlying asset changes and as time passes in such a way that a larger (smaller) invested position in the risky asset and a larger (smaller) borrowed position in the riskless asset are held in the call option replicating portfolio as the risky asset price rises (falls).

This particular rebalancing of the replicating portfolio can be viewed as an allocation strategy between cash and a single risky asset. The typical asset allocation decision, of course, involves several risky assets. In this section we focus on bonds and stocks as the risky asset classes because the asset allocation decision involving stocks, bonds, and cash is appropriate for the balanced fund manager and for the major portion of pension funds and other managed portfolios. To extend option theory to the latter type of asset allocation decision, a special call option must be designed and replicated.

At the outset of any performance measurement period, a pension plan or balanced fund manager would like to be able to allocate all funds to the risky asset class (stocks or bonds) that will perform better over the period. Unfortunately, the better performing asset is not known in advance. The objective can still be (partially) achieved, however, if the manager or pension plan can buy, at the outset, a call option which grants the right to purchase at the end of the period a full position in the better performing of stocks and bonds. Then a suitable investment strategy is to invest in a riskless asset the portion of total funds sufficient to achieve the desired minimum return over the investor's performance measurement period, and to use the remaining funds to purchase the "multiple-risky-asset" call options. Since the calls will pay off if either asset performs well, and since it is not necessary to forecast which asset will be the better performer, we should expect multiple-risky-asset call options to be more valuable than single-risky-asset call options.

While the mathematics of pricing and replicating a multiple-risky-asset call option is quite complex, the various factors contributing to the option's value can be understood in nontechnical terms.[6] Intuitively the value of the option should depend on the likelihood that the two assets will perform differently over the holding period. The more likely it is that the two assets will have different returns, the greater will be the value of the option. In mathematical terms the lower the positive correlation

---

[5]See M. Rubinstein and H. Leland, "Replicating Options with Positions in Stock and Cash," *Financial Analysts Journal* (July 1981).

[6]R.M. Stulz discusses the valuation of the multiple-risky option from a slightly different perspective in "Options on the Minimum or the Maximum of Two Risky Assets," *Journal of Financial Economics* (July 1982).

or the greater the negative correlation of the returns on the two assets, the more valuable is the option. Consider two assets with perfect negative correlation. When one asset increases in value, the second asset decreases in value. In such a situation, an at-the-money option on the better performing of the two assets will always pay off and thus be very valuable.

Conversely, if two assets are highly positively correlated, there is little added value to owning the multiple-risky call compared to owning a call on either single asset because there is not likely to be any differential performance between the assets.

These concepts are illustrated in Figure 12-3. For an at-the-money option, the shaded areas of the graphs show the regions where the options will have positive value at expiration. The lower the correlation between the assets, the greater is the probability that the option will finish in the money. Figure 12-4 illustrates this effect in another way by graphing the impact of correlation on the value of the option.

Correlation is unique to the multiple-risky-asset case. However, the factors that affect the value of a single-risky-asset call also affect the value of the multiple-risky-asset call. These factors are the time to expiration, the risk-free rate of interest, the exercise price of the option, the current value of the underlying asset, and the volatilities of holding-period returns for the underlying assets. Because their effects have been described in options literature for the single-risky-asset case, we discuss them only briefly here.[7]

The effects on option value of time to expiration, the risk-free rate, and the exercise price are the same as in the single asset case; that is, the longer the time to expiration, the higher the risk-free rate, and the lower the exercise price, the higher the value of the call, and conversely. The option price also depends on the prices of the underlying risky assets. Since there are two assets, the higher the value of either, the higher the value of the call, assuming the other one is unchanged. Finally, volatility influences the call value. For a single-risky-asset option, the value increases as volatility increases, while for a multiple-risky-asset option, the effect of volatility is ambiguous.[8] Figure 12-5 illustrates the dependence of the value of the call on the ratio of standard deviations of the two risky assets. The complete pricing relationships are summarized qualitatively in Table 12-1.

The pricing formula for a multiple-risky-asset call can be written down by generalizing the usual formula for a single-risky-asset call:

$$C = \sum_{k=1}^{N} S_k^* \, \Delta_k - Xe^{-rt} \sum_{k=1}^{N} \Psi_k$$

---

[7]See C.W. Smith Jr., "Option Pricing: A Review," *Journal of Financial Economics* 3 (1976).

[8]Simultaneously increasing the volatility of each risky asset always increases the value of the option. When comparing the value of two calls for which the only difference is the volatility of one of the risky assets, increasing the volatility of the riskier asset always increases the value of the call while increasing the volatility of the less risky asset may actually decrease the value of the call, particularly if the assets are highly correlated. An intuitive explanation for this is that the closer the characteristics of the assets, the less valuable is the multiple-risky-asset call.

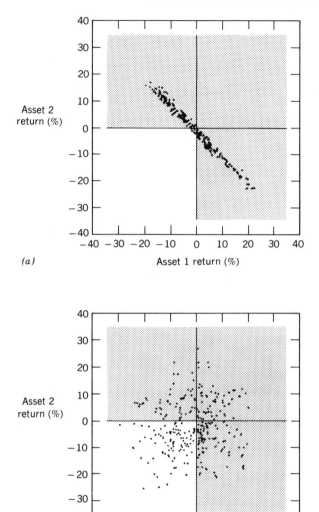

(a)

(b)

Figure 12-3.   *(a)* Highly negative correlation, *(b)* no correlation, *(c)* highly positive correlation.

where C is the value of the call, $S*k$ is the "price" of the kth risky asset, X is the strike price of the option, r is the risk-free interest rate, τ is the time remaining until expiration of the option, N is the number of risky assets (two in our case), and Δ_k, and Ψ_k are mathematical functions.

The terms Δ_k and $\Sigma\Psi_k$ are rather complicated and we do not explicitly show them here. However, they have a very useful interpretation in terms of the replicating strat-

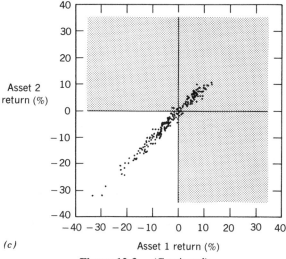

(c)

Figure 12-3.   (Continued)

egy for the multiple-risky-asset call option. To replicate the option, positions in each risky asset are held, financed by a borrowing position in the riskless asset. The significance of the terms Δ_k and $\Sigma \Psi_k$ is that they specify the size of these risky and riskless asset positions. The replicating strategy involves taking larger positions in the risky assets as they perform well, along with a larger borrowing position, and smaller positions in the risky assets as they perform poorly, along with a smaller borrowing position. The allocation of the funds invested in risky assets between stocks and bonds is such that, other things being equal, the risky asset that has per-

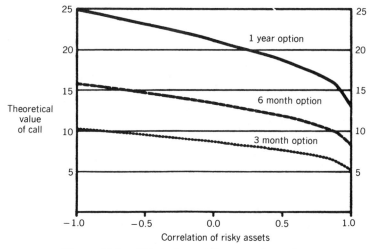

Figure 12-4.   Effect of correlation on option value.

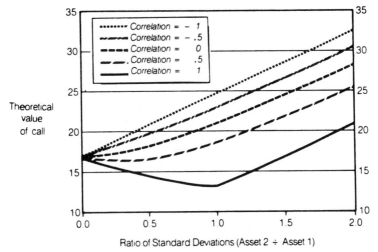

Figure 12-5.   Effect of standard deviation on option value.

formed better will receive the larger allocation, and the better that asset performs the greater the amount of funds that will be allocated to it.

At first glance the fact that a net borrowing position is required may seem to make the replication strategies impractical. However, the appropriate overall strategy is not one of solely purchasing multiple-risky-asset calls, but one of buying the calls after investing enough funds in a riskless asset to secure the desired minimum return. For the complete strategy, the borrowing position needed to replicate the option generally combines with the invested position in the riskless asset so that only net invested positions are held.[9]

Figure 12-6 highlights some of this discussion regarding the replicating portfolio. The figures assume that the investor has a 1-year time horizon. Figure 12-6a shows a hypothetical cumulative return series for stocks and bonds. Figure 12-6b shows at different points throughout the holding period the allocations among stocks, bonds, and cash, given the differential performance between stocks and bonds shown in

Table 12-1.   Determinants of Multiple-Risky Asset Call Value

Variable	Effect on Call Option Value
Correlation	Negative
Time to Expiration	Positive
Risk-Free Interest Rate	Positive
Exercise Price	Negative
Underlying Asset Value	Positive
Volatility	Ambiguous

[9]Sometimes the replication still calls for a net borrowed position. In this case the replication must be constrained so that allocations to the risky assets do not exceed 100%. Imposition of this constraint changes the strategy from one of pure option replication. It therefore causes performance to depend somewhat on the path of risky asset returns.

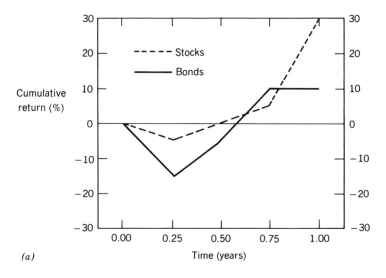

(a)

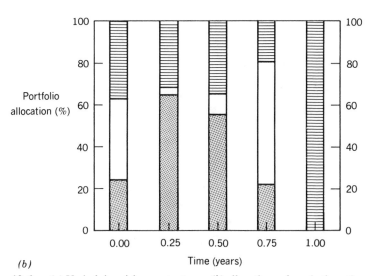

(b)

Figure 12-6.   (a) Underlying risky asset returns, (b) allocations of synthetic option strategy.

Figure 12-6a. While the return sequence is admittedly extreme it serves to illustrate the allocations called for in the replicating portfolio. The better stocks have performed relative to bonds, the greater the proportion of the portfolio held in stocks relative to bonds, and conversely. Further, the greater the total return to date the less cash that is held in the portfolio, and conversely.

To some portfolio managers these allocations may appear counterintuitive. Often investors allocate increased funds to the asset class that has underperformed to date, expecting that it then has even better return prospects. The asset allocations made in implementing a given synthetic option strategy, however, are not based on any changed expectation of future asset performance, but rather on the application of the option pricing formula to the achievement of the specific return pattern desired by the investor, and chosen by him at the outset of the holding period. Thus the worse the portfolio's total performance to date, the more chance there is of jeopardizing the minimum return requirement and the less risk that can be taken in the portfolio, requiring a larger allocation to cash. Conversely, the better the total portfolio's performance to date, the less chance there is of jeopardizing the minimum return requirement and the more risk that can be taken in the portfolio, allowing a smaller allocation to cash and a larger allocation to the risky assets. Moreover, because the investor aspires to the return on the better performing asset, a greater proportion of the funds invested in risky assets will generally be allocated to the asset that has the better performance to date.

To conclude this section we draw a few implications from the discussion above to the practical application of the synthetic option methodology. First, although the greatest amount of upside potential from a multiple-risky-asset option will be obtained when the returns on underlying risky assets are negatively correlated and highly volatile, an option on such assets will be more costly than one on underlying assets whose returns are positively correlated and less volatile. Fewer of the more expensive options can be purchased. Both the cost and upside potential of the options should be considered when deciding upon risky assets. Second, a higher level of downside protection means that a larger amount of funds must be held in the riskless asset and fewer options can be purchased. Because there is upside potential from two assets, the downside protection level normally need not be too stringent; as long as either asset does well a good return should be achieved. Evaluating the various total return profiles based on different floor returns and number of options purchased is necessary in selecting the strategy most appropriate to the investor.

SECTION III   HISTORICAL SIMULATIONS OF A SYNTHETIC OPTION STRATEGY

In this section we apply the concepts of Section II to a historical simulation. Our objective is to allocate funds among stocks, bonds, and cash in such a way that a minimum return target will be realized in any calendar year (a typical performance measurement period), and consistently good return performance will be achieved over time. Specifically, the synthetic option asset allocation strategy presented here seeks to obtain a minimum return of 0% in any calendar year. Treasury bills maturing at the end of the calendar year therefore are used as the riskless asset. The risky assets are bonds, represented by 20-year Treasury bonds, and equities, represented by the S&P 500 index. We sought a pattern of upside capture consistent with replicating deeply out-of-the-money options.

We applied the multiple-risky-asset option pricing formula on a weekly basis to determine both the initial asset allocation and the subsequent rebalancings required to execute the synthetic option strategy. In simulating the strategy, transaction costs of 1/4 point into or out of each risky asset class were assumed. Thus, a shift from bonds to equities, or vice versa, would result in total transaction costs equal to 1/2 point on the amount traded. The estimates of correlation and variance needed for the option pricing formula were based on a statistical analysis of the weekly time series of bond and equity returns. We simulated the strategy over the 1973-1983 time period, and compared the performance of the synthetic option asset allocation strategy over various measurement periods to that of the SEI Universe (formerly Becker Universe) of balanced fund managers. The time period was chosen because results of other recent work[10] covered the period 1973-1982 and because results for 1983 were available at the time of this writing.

Table 12-2, Table 12-3, and Figure 12–7 highlight the performance of the synthetic option asset allocation strategy. As can be seen from the tables the synthetic option strategy produced superior performance while achieving the desired risk control.

Table 12-2, which gives annual returns, shows that good results were usually obtained in both bull and bear markets. The strategy produced the minimum return objective in 1973, 1974, 1977, 1978, and 1981. In each of those years, except 1978, equity returns were negative and bond returns were less than 3%. During 1975, 1976,

Table 12-2.   Comparison of Annual Total Returns[1]

	Asset Class[2]			Synthetic Option Strategy	
	Cash	Bond	Equity	Return	Capture[3]
1973	5.8%	.8%	−14.9%	.0%	Floor
1974	7.4	2.8	−25.2	.0	Floor
1975	7.3	7.0	34.2	23.0	67%
1976	6.3	18.4	23.0	20.6	90%
1977	4.9	−.6	−7.2	.1	Floor
1978	7.1	−1.2	6.5	.2	Floor
1979	12.9	−1.6	18.5	17.5	95%
1980	12.2	−3.0	33.4	20.5	61%
1981	14.2	−1.0	−5.6	.0	Floor
1982	14.4	45.0	20.8	36.6	81%
1983	8.8	1.0	22.2	15.9	72%

[1] 52-week periods were used instead of exact calendar years.

[2] For purposes of this study, the asset classes have been defined as follows:

> Cash: 1-Year Treasury Bills
> Bond: 20-Year Treasury Bonds
> Equity: S&P 500 Index

[3] Synthetic option strategy return as a percent of the return for the better performing of bonds and equities when at least one has performed well.

[10]R.D. Arnott and J.N. von Germeten, "Systematic Asset Allocation," *Financial Analysts Journal* (November–December 1983).

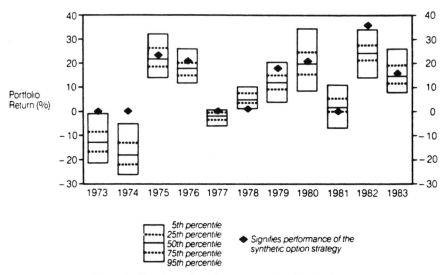

Figure 12-7. Annual performance against SEI universe.

1979, 1980, 1982, and 1983, the synthetic option asset allocation strategy captured, on average, 78% of the return on the better performing risky asset. On a relative performance basis the strategy achieved six first quartile results, as shown in Figure 12-7. The compound performance over the most recently available 3-year, 5-year, and 10-year holding periods (ending in 1983) was not only first quartile, but first decile for the 10-year period and close to first decile for the 3-year and 5-year periods.

From Table 12-3 it appears that the compound performance of the synthetic option strategy appears to be quite stable over periods longer than one year. This conclusion is also supported by results of forward-looking simulations not presented here. When selecting an interest rate assumption for valuing pension liabilities, actuaries generally attach some credibility to past investment performance and use averaging procedures to smooth out the annual fluctuations in the plan's history of total returns. Our results, particularly those in Columns 2 and 3 of Table 12-3, should give actuaries good cause to adopt long-range interest rate assumptions of at least 8% in their valuations of plans that utilize a synthetic option approach to asset allocation.

The superior performance of the strategy can be attributed partly to the volatility of risky asset returns and partly to the imposition of the ''no net borrowing'' constraint. Moreover, option strategies other than the deeply out-of-the-money one studied here would have fared somewhat worse over this particular historical period. Superior performance usually occurred when both the stock and bond markets performed poorly or when the return on one of the risky assets was good and far outpaced the return on the other. The strategy will not perform well in those years in which the better performing asset exhibits positive, but relatively mediocre returns. Also, because balanced fund managers in general exhibit a bias toward holding equities, they are better positioned to ride an ''unforeseen'' stock market rally than to

Table 12-3.   Compound Returns for Synthetic Option Strategy

Start of Period	Average Annualized Compound Return		
	Three Year Period	Five Year Period	Ten Year Period
1373	7.1%	8.2%	11.1%
1974	14.0	8.3	12.8
1975	14.1	11.8	—
1976	6.6	11.4	—
1977	5.6	7.3	—
1978	12.4	14.1	—
1979	12.3	17.5	—
1980	18.0	—	—
1981	16.5	—	—

ride an ''unforeseen'' bond market rally. Accordingly, the synthetic option strategy should perform relatively better against the SEI Universe of balanced fund managers when the returns on bonds are exceptional than when the returns on equities are exceptional.

Finally, Figure 12-8 depicts the average asset mix by quarter throughout the 11-year period. Prior to 1980 there was no significant allocation to bonds. The increased volatility of bond returns since the fourth quarter of 1979 has made it more likely that bonds can substantially outperform equities, even when equities produce good returns. This is reflected in increased allocations to bonds in the post-1979 period relative to the pre-1980 period. In 1982, the only year in which the return on bonds far exceeded a positive return on equities, a fully invested position was held in bonds throughout the fourth quarter. Figure 12-8 also shows that changes in asset allocation

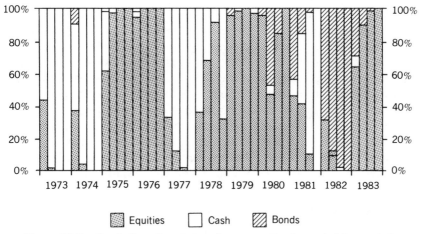

Figure 12-8.   Synthetic option strategy for consecutive 1-year holding periods.

can be sizable under a synthetic option strategy. Although not reported here, further analysis has shown that the imposition of constraints to limit changes in allocations to reasonable minimum and maximum amounts generally has little impact on portfolio returns.

SECTION IV   USING FINANCIAL FUTURES IN ASSET ALLOCATION

The mechanics of applying the synthetic option approach to asset allocation depend on the type of investment situation. Balanced fund managers, investment advisors, and in-house portfolio managers can execute the required rebalancing transactions directly in the cash markets, but there are other potential users for whom rebalancing solely by way of cash market transactions is not feasible. Many pension funds allocate assets among various outside managers. It is unreasonable to expect that these funds will shift assets among the different managers on a weekly basis. The pension fund utilizing outside managers can still execute the strategy, however, by using financial futures.

Financial futures allow investors to adjust their positions without transacting in the cash markets.[11] Investors needing to increase the cash position in their funds can sell futures against a risky asset position in lieu of actually selling part of the risky asset position. Investors needing to increase the risky asset positions in their funds can purchase futures in lieu of actually drawing down the cash position to purchase additional risky assets. Theoretically all of the dynamic allocations that can be made in the cash markets can be made in the futures markets. In practice the existence of contracts useful for this purpose is currently limited to Treasury bond and note futures and a few stock index futures.

A pension plan having an existing allocation among various outside managers can "internally" establish futures positions in order to superimpose the synthetic option strategy on the external management. The outside managers continue to manage as they have been previously doing, seeking to obtain the best performance from their particular style of management. Indeed they need not even be aware that the futures strategy is being implemented. The pension plan achieves its target allocations by buying or selling stock index and/or Treasury bond futures, as the case may be. Although in some situations there may be considerable basis risk in using futures because the outside managers may have styles that do not correlate well with the available futures, futures may be the only feasible way for pension plans utilizing outside managers to apply the synthetic option asset allocation technique. Of course if the outside managers can add incremental return relative to the index as they are expected to do, most adverse consequences of basis risk can be overcome.

Futures may also be the best way for very large investors to apply a synthetic option strategy. A manager of a $1 billion portfolio might find it difficult to shift

---

[11]For a discussion of various methods of hedging with financial futures, see A.L. Toevs and D.P. Jacob, "Interest Rate Futures: A Comparison of Alternative Hedge Ratio Methodologies" (New York: Morgan Stanley, June 1984).

10% of the portfolio from stocks to bonds in a single week without causing some disruption in the financial markets, especially since the changes would be required at a time when the markets are volatile. Furthermore, the transaction costs of executing in the futures markets are lower than in the cash markets and this can help to offset unfavorable shifts in the basis between the cash and futures markets.

SECTION V   ASSET ALLOCATION CONSTRAINTS AND THE COSTS OF RISK CONTROL

Portfolio managers often have numerous asset allocation constraints imposed upon them. Typical of such constraints are permitting no more than $X\%$ of the portfolio in equities and not allowing any bonds longer than Y years in maturity. These constraints are generally motivated by sound risk control considerations. However, they are often very costly ways to control risk because they can force a portfolio to surrender too much upside potential for a given reduction in downside risk. On the other hand, sometimes constraints of a maximum cash position or a minimum equity position are imposed. These, too, can be costly. The motivation for this type of constraint is to maintain upside potential in the portfolio, but such constraints can prevent a minimum return from being attained.

The synthetic option asset allocation strategies presented in this chapter allow an investor's desired level of protection against risk to be acquired in a cost efficient fashion. The strategies recognize that allocations are risky only when considered relative to a minimum holding period return target. If risk is associated with the possibility of loss over the investor's time horizon, a 100% allocation to equities may be very risky when the portfolio has declined 5% in value midway to the horizon, but can hardly be considered risky when the portfolio has appreciated 15% in value midway to the horizon. With the synthetic option approach, the decision maker need not be concerned with the perceived riskiness of any asset allocation since the allocation will be dynamically adjusted, if necessary, to achieve the floor return.[12]

SECTION VI   CONCLUSION

The synthetic option methodology allows investors considerable flexibility in structuring return distributions to be consistent with their objectives. There are several key decisions: the length of the holding period, the selection of the risky assets, the level of downside protection desired, and the pattern of upside capture desired. The portfolio manager often is "forced" to choose a holding period that coincides with the period over which his performance will be measured. Different investors will select different levels of downside protection. Investors selecting the same level of downside protection can still choose very different risky assets based on the pattern

---

[12]The perceived riskiness of the various asset classes however does affect how the portfolio will be dynamically adjusted.

of upside return capture they desire. Different investors will also choose different option strike prices depending on their views on correlation and volatilities of returns for the asset classes.

The investor who wants the possibility of truly superior performance in any year and is therefore willing to experience a higher probability of achieving only the floor return may choose to use small capitalization stocks and 20-year zero coupon bonds as the risky assets, and to replicate out-of-the money call options. Investors who want to participate in upside performance more frequently without the need for exceptional returns in any one year may be more conservative in their selection of risky assets and may choose to replicate at-the-money or in-the-money options. Although the actual allocation strategy does not depend on expected returns, investors should still estimate expected returns for the various risky assets in order to compare the alternative (*ex ante*) return distributions most intelligently and hence choose which assets to include in the portfolio and what option strategy to replicate.

BIBLIOGRAPHY

Arnott, R.D., and von Germeten, J.N. "Systematic Asset Allocation," *Financial Analysts Journal* (November–December 1983).

Elton, E.J., and Gruber, M.J. *Modern Portfolio Theory and Investment Analysis.* New York: Wiley, 1984.

Rubinstein, M., and Leland, H. "Replicating Options with Positions in Stock and Cash," *Financial Analysts Journal* (July 1981).

Smith Jr., C.W. "Option Pricing: A Review," *Journal of Financial Economics* 3 (1976).

Stulz, R.M. "Options on the Minimum or the Maximum of Two Risky Assets," *Journal of Financial Economics* (July 1982).

Toevs, A.L., and Jacob, D.P. "Interest Rate Futures: A Comparison of Alternative Hedge Ratio Methodologies." New York: Morgan Stanley, June 1984.

13 Contingent Insurance Strategies for Actively Managed Bond Portfolios

ROBERT B. PLATT AND GARY D. LATAINER

INTRODUCTION

A manager's decision to alter the maturity or duration of a bond portfolio is typically made within a risk-return framework that incorporates a holding period (the time over which expected returns are measured) and a benchmark, or norm, of acceptable return performance. To estimate the likely impact of maturity decisions, the manager usually performs a set of simulations over different interest rate scenarios. By evaluating the projected rates of return available under these scenarios he or she can analyze the effects of interest rate movements and determine an appropriate maturity structure. This procedure requires a set of explicit assumptions about interest rates, portfolio maturities, and quality and sector spreads. It is often cumbersome to implement and its results are difficult to interpret in terms of the return opportunities available to a portfolio manager and the risk of not achieving the benchmark return.

An alternative risk control procedure now exists. The technique, sometimes called portfolio insurance, is based on the concept of replicating option strategies through asset allocations made over time.[1] This technique offers a more precise procedure for analyzing the risk-return opportunities available to a bond manager, measuring the value enhancements to a portfolio from active management, and assuring that at least the benchmark return is achieved by the manager over the entire holding

---

[1]For a discussion of portfolio insurance, see M. Rubinstein and H.E. Leland, "Replicating Options with Positions in Stocks and Cash," *Financial Analysts Journal*(July/August 1981), and R.B. Platt and G.D. Latainer, "Replicating Option Strategies for Portfolio Risk Control" New York: (Morgan Stanley, January 21, 1983). Also see Chapter 5 of this volume.

period. This chapter illustrates how portfolio insurance can be used as an effective decision tool for such purposes.

SECTION I   CONTINGENT INSURANCE STRATEGIES

To control risk through portfolio insurance the manager must sacrifice some upside return potential in order to achieve a given level of protection on the downside. Many levels of insurance protection are available. Immunization offers the highest possible level of portfolio protection for the greatest sacrifice in upside return potential. Other insurance levels differ from immunization in both the amount of downside protection and in the potential upside return give up. The manager presumably desires a strategy that offers the greatest downside protection for the smallest potential upside loss. The optimal strategy depends on both return-risk opportunities and on the probabilities a manager assigns to being "right" or "wrong" in the interest rate bet.

Consider an active bond portfolio manager who has a 5-year holding period and a minimum annual return benchmark of 8% over that horizon. He or she expects interest rates to decline moderately over the period, so the portfolio manager structures his or her portfolio to have essentially the same duration as the Lehman Government/Corporate bond index. Over the 5-year holding period, interest rates in fact follow the path shown in Figure 13-1: a sharp downward trend with some intermittent cycles.[2]

The portfolio's wealth at any time during the holding period will equal accumulated income plus changes in the underlying securities' prices. The magnitude of the wealth will vary depending upon how successful the manager's active portfolio decisions have been. At any time the manager has the option of converting this wealth into an immunized bond portfolio for the remainder of the holding period, thus assuring some total level of return over the entire horizon. This is the method by which risk is controlled under contingent immunization.[3]

Alternatively the portfolio manager may place only a portion of the available wealth in an immunized pool, leaving the balance to be actively managed. The active bond portfolio may be considered to be the "risky" asset and the immunized portfolio the "riskless" asset. In effect the manager initiates a portfolio insurance strategy that implies some particular level of downside risk protection. The minimal insured return will be achieved if the initial allocation between the risky and riskless assets is adjusted over time according to the decision rules determined from the option strategy being replicated by the portfolio insurance procedure.[4]

---

[2]This path of interest rates was simulated by reversing the trend of bond rates over the five years prior to the major 1982 rally, and projecting this trend forward from the level of the 10-year Treasury bond rate at year end 1982.

[3]M. Liebowitz and A. Weinberg, "Contingent Immunization, Part I: Risk Control Procedures," *Financial Analysts Journal*(November/December 1982), and Liebowitz and Weinberger, "Contingent Immunization, Part II: Problem Areas," *Financial Analysts Journal* (January/February 1983).

[4]Platt and Latainer, "Replicating Option Strategies," pp. 6–11.

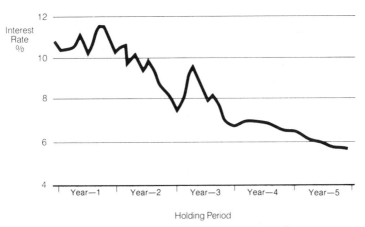

Figure 13-1.   Projected interest rate trend.

SECTION II   THE COST OF INSURANCE

Using the interest rate movements illustrated in Figure 13-1 we calculated the different levels of downside protection purchasable by allocating varying proportions of wealth to the active and immunized portfolios at different times during the 5-year holding period. Table 13-1 shows some of the results.

We assumed that the portfolio was invested 100% in the risky asset (a portfolio with the duration of the Lehman index) up to the time the calculations of the purchasable levels of insurance protection were made. Because interest rates were falling for most of the holding period, the wealth of this 100% risky portfolio increased, as the "assets available" column of the table indicates.

As the portfolio's wealth increased, the portfolio was able to buy higher levels of insurance protection, that is, to lock in a higher return over the holding period. This is evident from the remaining columns of the table. One could alternatively say that because of good active management, the manager could buy the same level of insurance protection more cheaply.

In our example the manager has a return bogey of 8% over the holding period. He or she could have assured this downside protection at the outset by establishing a portfolio insurance procedure from an initial position of 50% in the risky asset and 50% in the immunized asset. If instead the manager decided to continue to manage actively, then by the second quarter of 1987, he or she could have achieved the same downside protection by initiating an insurance procedure from a 100% risky asset position. In other words the portfolio manager could purchase the same downside protection without sacrificing any of the return that would accrue to the portfolio if rates continued to fall.

The cost of achieving a given level of insurance protection may be used as a measure of the success of active management decisions. This cost in terms of potential

Table 13-1.   Returns Available from Insurance Procedures

Beginning of Quarter	Assets Available	Implied Insured Return Over Five Years with Risky Allocation of				Return Over Five Years if Switch to Immunized
		25%	50%	75%	100%	
1/84	$1,000,000	10.12%	8.63%	6.13%	−21.09%	11.04%
2/84	1,034,293	10.46	9.43	7.71	−11.72	11.08
3/84	1,066,401	10.66	9.88	8.57	− 6.48	11.13
4/84	1,018,349	9.93	8.67	6.56	−16.86	10.70
1/85	1,128,695	10.44	9.17	7.05	−16.48	11.21
2/85	1,205,406	11.07	10.26	8.89	− 6.77	11.56
3/85	1,275,042	11.35	10.49	9.02	− 7.69	11.88
4/85	1,343,701	11.62	10.65	9.00	− 9.65	12.22
1/86	1,489,522	12.63	11.72	10.18	− 7.30	13.18
2/86	1,366,284	11.42	10.59	9.19	− 6.82	11.92
3/86	1,516,190	12.50	11.63	10.18	− 6.46	13.02
4/86	1,628,853	13.38	12.68	11.50	− 2.14	13.80
1/87	1,723,870	14.16	13.70	12.92	3.73	14.44
2/87	1,736,971	14.19	13.95	13.54	8.66	14.33
3/87	1,774,475	14.30	14.08	13.71	9.22	14.44
4/87	1,859,708	14.90	14.71	14.38	10.51	15.01
1/88	1,890,168	14.94	14.77	14.49	11.11	15.04
2/88	1,979,600	15.60	15.48	15.28	12.84	15.67
3/88	2,042,174	15.98	15.92	15.81	14.50	16.02
4/88	2,125,496	16.57	16.52	16.44	15.44	16.59
End of 5 Years	2,188,206					

*Assuming a 100 per cent risky position is taken until the insurance strategy is begun.

upside return giveup is related to the proportion of the portfolio the manager can leave in the risky asset at the initiation of an insurance procedure and still meet the benchmark minimal return. If we consider the risky asset (the actively managed portfolio) as the objective based on the manager's interest rate expectations, we can assign this portfolio a beta of one. All other insured positions would be initiated with betas between zero and one. The level of assured downside protection is thus inversely related to the beta of the insured position. This should not be too surprising: to get more insurance one has to sacrifice more upside return potential. The manager now has a well-defined risk-return tradeoff; his or her goal, as an active manager, is to increase over time the beta of the insured position necessary to achieve the benchmark return.

The data in Table 13-1 also shows the relation between contingent immunization and portfolio insurance. In the example above the manager initially took a fully active position and decided later in the holding period to initiate an insurance strategy. If under contingent immunization he or she had been forced into or chosen the immunization mode, there would have been no further upside potential; under a "contingent insurance" strategy, the manager retains upside potential because a portion of the portfolio remains in the risky asset. The option to immunize is the extreme case of insurance protection. Immunization affords the highest level of assured minimal return, but because it has a zero beta it has none of the upside potential of the risky asset should the manager's interest rate bet prove to be right over the remaining time horizon.

It is also important to note that in a good active management situation the differences between the levels of downside insurance protection offered by various beta positions decreases as time passes. For example, at the initiation of the portfolio, the downside protection available to the portfolio manager ranged from −21% (100% risky position) to +11% (100% immunized). By the first quarter of 1988 (the last year of the simulation), this range had narrowed to +11 to +15%.

The initial position in the risky asset at the time an insurance procedure is established is not a complete measure of potential upside return giveup. This is true because the asset allocation decision rule of portfolio insurance would lead the manager over time to increase his or her exposure to the risky asset if this asset continued to perform well. In other words, under the insurance procedure, the cost of insurance is related to how well the active manager is doing with the assets in the risky pool. This is an important difference between contingent immunization and portfolio insurance. If the decision to immunize is forced or taken, no assets remain in the risky pool and all the upside return potential is eliminated, hence there can be no downward adjustment in the cost of the insurance protection.

We have noted that the potential upside return give-up is related to the proportion of the portfolio in the risky asset at the initiation of the insurance procedure. In order to calculate the expected giveup from various insured positions, one needs to know the performance expectations of the portfolio manager. Assume, for example, that the portfolio manager expects to achieve a return of 20% above that available through immunizing for the remainder of the horizon. Table 13-2 shows the expected return from being 100% in the risky asset and the percentage of this return that the manager could expect to relinquish by initiating a procedure for a given level of insurance at the beginning of each year of the holding period. Table 13-3 shows the actual return give-ups at various insurance levels, given the interest rate pattern in Figure 13-1.

The percentage of potential return given up is clearly related to the initial position in the risky asset, that is, the level of insurance protection purchased. What might be somewhat surprising, however, is how small the actual percentage return give-up (Table 13-3) is for all insured positions other than the fully immunized. For example, at the beginning of the third year, the actual return give-up from immunizing for the balance of the holding period is 6.05%, whereas the actual give-up from initiating an insured position from a 25% position in the risky asset is only 1.54%. An initial 75% position in the risky asset implies a give-up of only 0.42%. The actual

Table 13-2.   Expected Return Giveup versus Fully Risky Position

Insurance Initiated Beginning of Year	Expected Risky Return Over Remaining Horizon	Immunized Return Over Remaining Horizon	Expected Give-Up From Insuring With Indicated Initial Percentage in Risky Assets*			
			0%**	25%	50%	75%
1	13.25%	11.04%	2.21%	1.66%	1.11%	0.55%
2	12.96	10.80	2.16	1.62	1.08	0.54
3	9.16	7.63	1.53	1.15	0.77	0.38
4	8.05	6.71	1.34	1.01	0.67	0.34
5	7.91	6.59	1.32	0.99	0.66	0.33

*Give-ups are over remaining horizon
**Immunized position

Table 13-3.   Actual Return Giveup versus Fully Risky Position

Insurance Initiated Beginning of Year	Actual Risky Return Over Remaining Horizon	Immunized Return Over Remaining Horizon	Actual Give-Up From Insuring With Indicated Initial Percentage in Risky Assets*			
			0%**	25%	50%	75%
1	16.96%	11.04%	5.92%	1.80%	0.84%	0.25%
2	18.00	10.80	7.20	2.25	1.10	0.35
3	13.68	7.63	6.05	1.54	0.90	0.42
4	12.67	6.71	5.96	0.80	0.18	− 0.03
5	15.77	6.59	9.18	2.02	1.00	0.38

*Give-ups are over remaining horizon
**Immunized position

return give-up is so small under all levels of insurance other than immunization because of the adaptability of the insurance procedure to the changing fortunes of the
risky asset.

SECTION III   SELECTING AN OPTIMAL INSURANCE STRATEGY

Suppose the active manager decides it is appropriate to hedge his or her interest rate
bet; what level of insurance will be optimal? To answer this question, the manager
needs to consider the potential giveups associated with being both right and wrong
in his or her interest rate expectations.

Important in this decision are the probabilities the manager assigns to these interest rate outcomes. Figure 13-2 illustrates the decision. The dashed lines are lines
of constant expected give-up. Their slopes equal the negative of the ratio of the probability of the active decision being correct to the probability of the active decision
being incorrect. These lines represent the set of desired tradeoffs. For example, with
probabilities of 75% correct and 25% incorrect, the manager is willing to give up
one basis point of expected return from being correct if he or she can insure an additional three basis points from being incorrect. The farther to the left the dashed line
is, the lower the expected give-up along the line.

The curves represent the combinations of expected give-ups possible from initiating different levels of insurance. The slope of each curve at any point determines
the tradeoff the manager is able to make in terms of additional downside insurance
provided the interest rate bet is incorrect and the expected return give-up if the interest rate bet is correct. The opportunity curve facing the manager after three years
is lower than that facing the manager after one year because of changes in the interest
rate environment over the two years.[5]

The minimum possible expected give-up is obtained when the curve is tangent to
the dashed line. At any point on the curve below this, the manager is giving up more

[5]The curves are presented as forward looking only—that is, they show the opportunities faced by the
manager over the remaining horizon. They could also be drawn based on expected giveups over the full
five-year horizon. In this case the position of the curves would reflect the manager's performance to date.
For any interest rate level, better performance by the manager to date would lead to a lower opportunity
curve. The value enhancements to a portfolio from active management can be measured in this context.

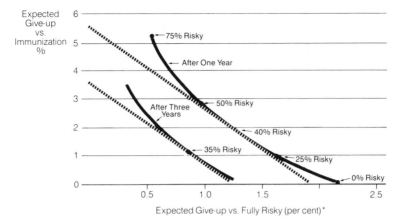

Based on expectation of fully risky return being 20 per cent greater than immunized return.

Figure 13-2.   Opportunity risk levels.

and more of the expected return from being right in order to purchase each increment of insurance against being wrong. At points on the curve above this, the manager is giving up more and more insurance in exchange for each increment of return from being right. All points not at the tangent thus involve a higher expected give-up than the tangent.

The slope of the dashed line, which is based on the ratio of probabilities, determines the desired amount of insurance. A change in the manager's estimate of the probability of being correct will thus alter the amount of insurance he or she should obtain. If the manager becomes convinced that the risky decision is correct, his or her slope will become steeper, and he or she will place a greater amount in the risky asset to begin the insurance. A manager absolutely certain of being correct will be fully invested in the risky position. On the other hand, a manager who believes the risky decision is completely incorrect will fully immunize.

Most managers are not likely to be at either of these extremes. A manager who attaches any probability to being correct in the active decision should not fully immunize. A manager who feels that there is a chance of the active decision being incorrect should not be fully invested in risky assets. Each would be better off following an insurance strategy.

INDEX

Page numbers in *italics* refer to illustrations.